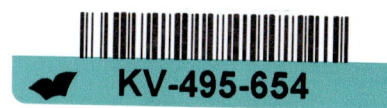

Critical Essays in Popular Musicology

Critical Essays in Popular Musicology

Edited by

Allan F. Moore

University of Surrey, UK

ASHGATE

Wherever possible, these reprints are made from a copy of the original printing, but these can themselves be of very variable quality. Whilst the publisher has made every effort to ensure the quality of the reprint, some variability may inevitably remain.

Published by
Ashgate Publishing Limited
Gower House
Croft Road
Aldershot
Hampshire GU11 3HR
England

Ashgate Publishing Company
Suite 420
101 Cherry Street
Burlington, VT 05401-4405
USA

Ashgate website: http://www.ashgate.com

British Library Cataloguing in Publication Data
Critical essays in popular musicology
1. Popular music - History and criticism
I. Moore, Allan F.
781.6'4

Library of Congress Control Number: 2007929496

ISBN 978 0 7546 2647 3

Printed in Great Britain by TJ International Ltd, Padstow, Cornwall

Contents

PART II   ADDRESSING TEXTS

Acknowledgements

The editor and publishers wish to thank the following for permission to use copyright material.

Blackwell Publishing for the essays: Dai Griffiths (1999), 'The High Analysis of Low Music', *Music Analysis*, **18**, pp. 389–435; Adam Krims (2003), 'What does it Mean to Analyse Popular Music?', *Music Analysis*, **22**, pp. 181–209.

Cambridge University Press for the essays: Philip Tagg (1989), '"Black music", "Afro-American music", and "European music"', *Popular Music*, **8**, pp. 285–98; International Advisory Editors (2005), 'Can we get rid of the "popular" in Popular Music? A Virtual Symposium with Contributions from the International Advisory Editors of *Popular Music*', *Popular Music*, **24**, pp. 133–45; Allan Moore (2002), 'Authenticity as Authentication', *Popular Music*, **21**, pp. 209–23; Allan Moore (1995), 'The so-called "flattened seventh" in Rock', *Popular Music*, **14**, pp. 185–202; Philip Tagg (1994), 'From Refrain to Rave: The Decline of Figure and the Rise of Ground', *Popular Music*, **13**, pp. 209–22; Carol Vernallis (1998), 'The Aesthetics of Music Video: An Analysis of Madonna's "Cherish"', *Popular Music*, **17**, pp. 153–85; Charles Ford (1995), '"Gently Tender": the Incredible String Band's Early Albums', *Popular Music*, **14**, pp. 175–83; Nicky Losseff (1999), 'Cathy's Homecoming and the Other World: Kate Bush's "Wuthering Heights"', *Popular Music*, **18**, pp. 227–40; Fred E. Maus (2001), 'Glamour and Evasion: the Fabulous Ambivalence of the Pet Shop Boys', *Popular Music*, **20**, pp. 379–93; Elizabeth Eva Leach (2001), 'Vicars of "Wannabe": Authenticity and the Spice Girls', *Popular Music*, **20**, pp. 143–68; Barbara Bradby (2002), 'Oh, Boy! (Oh, Boy!): Mutual Desirability and Musical Structure in the Buddy Group', *Popular Music*, **21**, pp. 63–91.

Copyright Clearance Center for the essays: Peter K. Winkler (1978), 'Toward a Theory of Popular Harmony', *In Theory Only*, **4**, pp. 3–26; Robert Walser (1995), 'Rhythm, Rhyme and Rhetoric in the Music of Public Enemy', *Ethnomusicology*, **39**, pp. 193–217; John R. Covach (1991), 'The Rutles and the Use of Specific Models in Musical Satire', *Indiana Theory Review*, **11**, pp. 119–44; Walter Everett (2004), 'Making Sense of Rock's Tonal Systems', *Music Theory Online*, **10**, [pp. 1–35].

Duke University Press for the essay: Sean McCann (1996), 'Why I'll Never Teach Rock'n'Roll Again', *Radical History Review*, **66**, pp. 191–202. Copyright © 1996 MARHO: The Radical Historians Organization, Inc. All rights reserved.

Franco Fabbri for the essay: Franco Fabbri (1999), 'Browsing Music Spaces: Categories and the Musical Mind', http://tagg.org/xpdfs/ffabbri990717.pdf. pp. 1–14.

Liverpool Universtiy Press for the essay: Serge Lacasse (2000), 'Intertextuality and Hypertextuality in Recorded Popular Music', in Michael Talbot (ed.), *The Musical Work: Reality or Invention?*, Liverpool: Liverpool University Press, pp. 35–58.

New Left Review for the essay: Andrew Chester (1970), 'Second Thoughts on a Rock Aesthetic: The Band', *New Left Review*, **62**, pp. 75–82.

Oxford University Press for the essays: Derek B. Scott (1994), 'Incongruity and Predictability in British Dance Band Music of the 1920s and 1930s', *Musical Quarterly*, **78**, pp. 290–315; Walter Everett (1986), 'Fantastic Remembrance in John Lennon's "Strawberry Fields Forever" and "Julia"', *Musical Quarterly*, **72**, pp. 360–85; Nicola Dibben (2001), 'Pulp, Pornography and Spectatorship: Subject Matter and Subject Position in Pulp's *This is Hardcore*', *Journal of the Royal Musical Association*, **126**, pp. 83–106.

Semiotica for the essay: Gino Stefani (1987), 'A Theory of Musical Competence', *Semiotica*, **66**, pp. 7–22.

Every effort has been made to trace all the copyright holders, but if any have been inadvertently overlooked the publishers will be pleased to make the necessary arrangement at the first opportunity.

Introduction

'Defining' and 'Doing' Musicology in Popular Music

As with all intellectual disciplines, musicology is permanently in flux. And, again as with all intellectual disciplines, it tends to exude a strong measure of stability on those working within it, a stability built on the efforts of generations of previous scholars. And 'generations' is apt in this case, for musicology is not a new discipline. Against this background, the dissatisfactions represented by the 'new' musicology of the 1980s resulted for some musicologists in a thorough reorientation of their view of the discipline. Indeed, some have argued that these dissatisfactions forced a reorientation of the discipline itself, although that discipline's markers – what I shall subsequently identify as being bound up with the 'text' and how to address it – have shown no likelihood of erasure, either within the academy or (equally significantly) without.

Feminist theory, post-colonial theory, cultural theory – those boxes in which the New Musicology found its ammunition – are themselves marked by concerns for the un(der)-represented. For some of the more radical scholars, the 'text' became identified less with the musical sounds to which listeners attend than with the listeners themselves who attend to musical sounds. And an inevitable consequence of this concern with the un-represented was that music hitherto deemed beyond the purview of musicology came into sight. It was in this context that 'popular musicology' originated. The term was unknown until around 1993, and it actually develops not from the new musicology, growing as it does primarily on North American soil, but from British Critical Musicology. Indeed, it does not seem to me far-fetched to construct its origination as a 'musicology of resistance', a pose developed in Dai Griffiths' trenchant essay reprinted in this collection (Chapter 5). The study of users of popular music within the fields of sociology and cultural studies in the 1970s had been strongly influenced by the notion of the use of music as a form of resistance (both by its users and by those undertaking study) to established authority or established intellectual positions[1] – it seems to me that popular musicology has a similar genesis.

This does not mean that what we might now call 'popular musicology' is less than two decades old. Some scholars had been attending to this repertoire as far back as the 1970s, but the climate was not yet such that it was able to take root. A couple of those early essays – Ronald Byrnside's on style (Chapter 12), which necessarily makes comparison with the concept's use in mainstream musicology, and Andrew Chester's use of musical praxis to energise a political debate (Chapter 6) – are reproduced in this collection. Indeed, although one of the aims of Critical Musicology was to force an encounter between musicology and critical theory (see Scott, 2000), its most prominent legacy thus far has been the legitimation of the study of popular music within the scope of musicology. And, although the term 'popular musicology'

---

1   See Hall and Jefferson (1976). The rituals of Critical Musicology were not overt, and the analogy is only partial.

is embedded in one of the discipline's journals,[2] the name is not universally welcomed. It was coined by analogy with 'medieval' or maybe 'nineteenth-century' musicology, implying a historicist outlook. Unfortunately, it does not necessarily result in output which is in itself widely used and hence popular in its own right. And the historicist pose is not dominant within the field; otherwise there would have been no need for the recent launch of the journal *Popular Music History* to address this situation (although there is frequently a necessary historical dimension to what popular musicologists produce). Nor is it the only academic discipline that claims coverage of the field – in academic departments of communication, media or cultural studies, or sociology, one finds far more reference to the field of 'popular music studies'. The publication of this volume, if nothing else, suggests the two are not identical. So, what is the difference? Well, the most obvious is that 'popular musicology' tends to be what one finds in academic departments of music or musicology. But the difference goes a little deeper. Notwithstanding the frequent observation that the field is by nature interdisciplinary,[3] popular musicologists at one level or another concern themselves with the musical text, how it operates and how it is (or has been, or could be) constructed and interpreted, whether or not they are also concerned with who it is that observes its operation, who constructs it or interprets it. The skills of musicology are fashioned to this end and popular musicology is, at root, the musicology of popular music.

Is 'text' the right, or even the best, way to identify the 'musical object' to which we attend? As both David Horn and Philip Tagg have recently demonstrated (Horn, 2000; Tagg, 2000a), we simply don't have a single term which neatly encompasses the objects that popular musicologists study. We don't even have a single ready-made term for those who compose/perform/produce it, although we could perhaps adopt the term 'originate' to cover the activity of all those who bring music into being. The term 'work' implies a level of self-reflexivity on the part of those originators, which may be unwarranted. 'Song' covers quite a large part of the area, but assumes that lyrics will be part of what listeners experience. 'Piece' is embedded in the music of the concert tradition, and so seems an inappropriate term to use. 'Track' is useful, but really only refers to recorded music, not music experienced live. And, are we even right to concentrate on 'objects'? Three decades ago, one of the godfathers of Critical Musicology, Christopher Small, urged far greater attention to processes and practices (Small, 1997), an urging which finally seems, in the CHARM project,[4] to be promising (in conventional musicology at least) a change from worrying about scores to worrying about performances. And yet, processes and practices leave their trace, whether that be a concrete object (a score, a tape), a realisable object (music stored on digital media), or a recallable object (a memory of an event). In writing, we must have reference to one or other of these and so, some notion of 'object' (something which is bounded, is distinguished from other objects) seems to me necessary to allow any sort of communicative work to take place. But we need to move to a more general level. 'Aesthetic object' (or 'musical object') would certainly be a plausible identifier were it not that it seems to imply listening with a degree of uninvolved

---

2   *Popular Musicology*, which was published by the Department of Music at the University of Salford, and subsequently became *Popular Musicology Online* - http://www.popular-musicology-online.com/.

3   Indeed, I would assert that musicology is itself interdisciplinary, in a strict understanding of the term, but that is an argument I pursue elsewhere. See Moore (forthcoming).

4   Centre for History and Analysis of Recorded Music, http://www.charm.rhul.ac.uk/.

contemplation (to something objectified, not actually made part of oneself in the process of listening) which is also foreign to the experience of what most people would label 'popular' music. It is for this reason that I shall prefer 'text', because a 'text' is always something that is 'read' or, more generally, 'interpreted'.[5] This also implies a degree of involvement with the experiencing of a musical text which, also, may not be part of the explicit experience of many listeners, but is normally part of the implicit experience – the way in which listeners construct their identity, in part, on the basis of the music they use, attests to that. The interpretation does not need to be conscious, nor does it need to be involved, but is something that we are inevitably engaged in. Now it tends to be a commonplace amongst musicians, at least, that such music is not to be understood, but merely to be experienced (listened to, danced to) and, hopefully, enjoyed. Sometimes, I am sure, this is simply a defence mechanism on musicians' part. Sometimes, it indicates what might be a preferred situation. We cannot, though, avoid the observation that as human beings we are, inevitably, always involved in the interpretation of our environment. It is part of how we function. In encountering another individual, for instance, we certainly always interpret them for ourselves – we listen to their talk, we watch their gestures and body language, we constantly judge how we want to respond to them, and how to construct ourselves for them. Interpretation of our environment, of what surrounds us, is the *sine qua non* of our existence, and the music we use is definitely a part of our environment.

So much for musicology. 'Popular music' is even less self-evident as a topic. Is it to be understood definitively, or discursively? Is it to be understood according to processes of historical change, or geographical difference? Does it only exist once it has been named? Debates over its nature have become more heated over the past few years: one of the more significant interventions recently appeared in *Popular Music* and is included in this volume. In that collection of views, the key distinction appears to be between scholars who argue that 'popular music' can be defined objectively, such that any possible exemplar can be definitively counted within that category, or excluded from it, and scholars who argue that it is a category defined by discourse, such that its characteristics are fluid, depending on who is doing the sorting, and what story they are trying to tell by means of such a sorting. Despite an early essay of Charles Hamm's, which effectively debunked the notion that popular music should be equated with rock, or pop, or youth culture generally (Hamm, 1981), the large majority of work undertaken within the field does refer dominantly to rock and pop. That is one of the reasons for the inclusion in this volume of Derek Scott's discussion of aspects of British dance band music of the inter-war years (Chapter 17). Not only is it a fine example of the linking of musical to sociocultural detail (about which more below), but it is also a reminder that popular musicology does not only concern itself with music since the rock'n'roll era. As Hamm has more recently remarked, for those working in musicology: 'popular music is a succession of individual pieces stretching back at least three centuries...' (Hamm, 2004). This wider perspective tends to be more apparent in non-Anglophone writing,[6] partly at least (I suspect) because of the geographical origins of rock. And it seems to me that this argument

---

5   Although the current vogue is to prefer the term 'reading' for the process of 'making sense of', it smuggles in an assumption that such a process is fundamentally visual (as, frankly, does the term 'text' – one must be on one's guard). For this reason, I prefer the more cumbersome 'interpreting'.

6   My thanks to Philip Tagg for recently alerting me to three good examples of such writing: Ledang (1987); Ling (1989); Kubik (2003).

still needs to be heard when the centre of scholarship, at least in popular music studies, appears to have migrated to rap and hip-hop. It is surely the case that we (English speakers) either desperately need to become fluent in other languages, or that we need to expend resources on the translation of key articles from other languages.

The guiding motive behind this collection was to bring together the most significant shorter English-language writing within the field, partly to mark the measure of maturity it has achieved, and partly to recognise that it is gaining in importance in many institutions where access to some of these papers may be quite difficult. However, determining what items to include has been surprisingly tricky. The essays which appear here both articulate and demonstrate some of the key constituents of a popular musicology. There are certain limits which I have observed, however. As far as I have been able to ascertain, none of the essays appearing here has appeared in any other key collection.[7] Thus, that early essay of Hamm, 'Some thoughts on the measurement of popularity in music', is omitted, since it appears in his own retrospective collection. Thus, too, Philip Tagg's foundational 'Analysing Popular Music: Theory, Method, and Practice', since it appears in Richard Middleton's collection *Reading Pop* (2000), as do a number of other key essays. This also means that essays originally published as part of collections[8] are omitted, as also are essays not published in English. However, even within these limits, this still leaves a great deal of writing from which to choose, my criteria being those essays of greatest importance or influence. The danger inherent here, of course, has been in taking too personal a view of which these might be. Accordingly, right at the beginning of this project, I contacted a large number of colleagues from around the world, asking each for a list of some half dozen essays which they considered should appear in such a collection, which I then intended to collate in order to produce a truly representative selection. I am, of course, much indebted to all those colleagues who offered me their suggestions and, much more importantly perhaps, to their reasons, some of which are echoed and exploited in this Introduction. Much to my surprise, not only was the list which resulted from this enquiry highly heterogeneous, but it also contained so few repetitions as to hardly help my process of selection at all. It did, of course, bring new essays to my attention, which is one of the key values of such an enterprise. However, it became clear to me that, within the community of scholars, there was no general agreement over which the most important/influential short pieces of writing were. I say 'short', because it seems to be widely felt that, in the field of popular musicology, perhaps because of its comparative newness, it is book-length pieces of writing which have had the greatest actual impact.[9] This would certainly not be the case were the exercise conducted within science disciplines, although it may be more common within the humanities, and is probably also the case within musicology as a whole. Thus, this collection cannot claim to gather together the most influential writing within the field. What I believe it does do, however, is to represent the most important thinking and present the most valuable range of ideas to stimulate further work, which anyway seems to me the most

---

7   Andrew Chester's early essay has been anthologised in Frith and Goodwin (1990) but only in part.

8   Such as the collections edited by Covach and Boone (1997) or Everett (2000). Two exceptions here: Lacasse's essay on intertextuality (the volume in which it originally appeared has not circulated widely); and Byrnside's early essay on style, unavailable for many years.

9   Volumes volunteered by my respondents most frequently included Middleton (1990); 2000; Tagg and Clarida (2003); Hamm (1983); Moore (2001; 2003); Brackett (2000); and Everett, (1999; 2001).

important role it could play. And, although each of the essays here has been recommended by at least one of my peers, it is ultimately a collection of those essays which I believe are deserving of collecting in this way. What I have explicitly chosen not to do is to make use of citation indexes to choose the most influential, such indexes necessarily failing to distinguish between essays referenced because they are so good, and essays referenced because they exemplify an unhelpful approach. What I suspect we have here, then, is a typical academic compromise, between good writing, good thinking and approaches which, at the time of writing, were innovative.

The collection is split into two parts – those essays that articulate the key questions of popular musicology, which discuss contexts for addressing texts, and those that demonstrate the discipline in practice, which actually address those texts. The first part is then subdivided into theoretical essays which indirectly, and then directly, address music. How, in a theoretical sense, do we address examples of popular music? Indeed, do we address them as examples (representing particular categories), or simply as individual things to which we listen? Theorisations most particularly of genre and, to a lesser extent, of style, suggest that we simply cannot avoid hearing particular texts as representative of (or related to) others – mentally we relate the music we encounter to other music we have already encountered, in order to incorporate it within our horizons. One of the clearest formulations of genre in popular music is Franco Fabbri's 'Browsing music spaces', included here as Chapter 4. However, the categories into which we, as listeners, sort what we hear, are just that – categories into which we sort what we hear, whether or not that corresponds to the categories used by other listeners, by the media and HMV, or by iTunes. This contradicts the view dominant until recently (and still maintained in much writing, whether explicitly or implicitly), that the 'meaning' of a piece of music is actually encoded within that music, rather than being something that develops in the act of listening. And, if we cannot assert that all listeners categorise their musical experiences in the same way, this casts some doubt on the notion of listening to music as a shared experience. Here we put an emphasis on the listener that is unusual in musicology, which despite the recent focus on performance, still considers the composer the most important individual in the process. It's easier that way, of course – you can't interrogate every listener in the same way that you can develop a biography of a composer. However, you can approach listeners theoretically, which is what Gino Stefani's exploration of musical competence (Chapter 2) did. There are issues to be had with some basic assumptions of the essays I have already discussed – first, that idiolect is a subsidiary aspect of style, for instance, and that the latter is subsidiary to genre,[10] second, the degree to which listeners are constrained to divide up the field; third, the degree to which such compartmentalisation can be ambiguous (specifically an issue in Chester)[11] – but these essays form important starting-points for thinking about the issues. Both the Stefani and Fabbri essays, however, originate in a much more widespread development, common across the humanities over the past couple of decades, and originating in gender studies, which is to oppose assumptions of essentialism. In other words, do we place something within a particular category because of essential features

---

10 I have argued against both of these conventions. See: Moore and Ibrahim (2005) and Moore (2001). Stefani does not explicitly place idiolect within style (although he implies as much in his rebuttal of Nattiez on p. 27) although Middleton (1990 p. 174), in a similar argument, does.

11 I offer a nuanced reflection on Chester's categories in Moore (1997).

(that we decide it has), features which define it, or for other reasons? The debate thus replays that between idealism (in which it is argued that we divide up the world on the basis of features we discover) and nominalism (in which it is argued that we place things in categories on the basis of distinctions we make, rather than distinctions which are deemed inherent in the objects). Because of the power relations which can be asserted on the basis of presumed essential differences, the debate has clearly come down on the side of nominalism, and it is this concern which underpins the collection's opening essay, which Philip Tagg originally published not as an essay as such, but as an 'open letter', which explains its informal and somewhat polemical tone (and which, I might suggest, is a welcome change from the dry, disengaged tone of so much academic writing, even in this field). Tagg (Chapter 1) argues that the simple use of such global terms as he addresses encourages laziness, because the terms are never adequately defined, and that their use also enables ideological positions to be smuggled into the argument once again, because the grounds for such positions are not made explicit.

'Genre' is, indeed, one of the concepts which appears again and again in popular music discourse, and which organises so much of it – it will recur in many of the essays in this collection. Adam Krims' book-length study of rap (Krims, 2000), for example, demonstrates how genre definitions can be developed, in conjunction with analysis, to argue how rap's sounds are implicated in its identity and meanings. A second such issue, one that is perhaps more common in popular music studies than in popular musicology, is that of 'subculture' or, as it is now much more commonly recast, 'music scenes'. This change, while subtle, recognises another drift away from essentialism, for in subcultures people are defined by their culture, perhaps by the music which helps constitute it,[12] whereas a scene is something one partakes in, drifts into and out of, without in any necessary way changing who one is. A third concept, though, seems to me particularly pertinent, in that it brings into focus a fundamental distinction between the ways in which scholars observe music to operate. The most concise way of identifying this concept is by asking whether scholars take up a modernist or a postmodernist stance. As soon as these words enter the discussion, of course, one's adherences immediately spring to the fore. And there is a way of understanding modernism, of course, through its validation of individual perspective, as essentialist, whereas postmodernism's emphasis on play encourages a nominalist position. Yet what I have in mind in bringing these terms to the fore is rather different, in that they intersect with questions of honesty and, dare one say it, of truth. Not that I am interested in asserting universal truths here, but in observing that modernist discourse acts as if there are such things, or at least as if they are desirable, whereas postmodernist discourse does not. In popular musicology, that distinction addresses the issue of authenticity – can we believe the self-expression of a musician, or is that expression something listeners actually construct on the basis of their own experience, with no necessarily causal relation between this construction and the musician's own subjectivity? This seems to me such a key issue that a number of these essays address it in some form. And I say this in spite of Simon Frith's assertion two decades ago that 'all distinctions between authenticity and artifice [have] broken down' (Frith, 1990, p. 125). Sampling technology made it possible to make such assertions of course, even though as Richard Middleton suggested more than a decade later: 'models built on a distinction between "art" and "trash" ... still figure strongly in

---

12   The key text here is Hebdige (1985). The 'style' referred to is not musical style. The move towards 'scenes' can be observed in Bennett and Peterson (2004).

popular discourse. But ... to rehabilitate the concept [of authenticity] would require that more attention be paid to "articulation", less to "homology"' (Middleton, 2001). This, I think, is why Sean McCann's little essay (Chapter 7) is so important, because it ably demonstrates that without that redirection of attention, authenticity is so powerful a concept as to be disabling, to totally inhibit academic work. The necessity, then, is to conceive it as an emergent, rather than an inherent, property. Some of this process has been undertaken by Timothy Taylor's dissection of the concept into three, all marked by a decontextualisation, a mobility, of the listening experience: authenticities respectively of emotionality (whereby the flexibility of listening situations – that they are not necessarily constrained by performance situations – encourages a quasi-spiritual stance of awe); of positionality (whereby a broadening of appeal is perceived as 'selling out'); and of primality (whereby some performances are felt to give access to the pure, the chthonic) (Taylor, 1997). My 'Authenticity as authentication' (Chapter 8) takes two routes towards this recasting as an emergent property. First, it reconfigures it as a property attached to individuals rather than to music (asking who a performance authenticates); second, it marks a further stage in the uncoupling of modes of authenticity from styles initially put forward by Larry Grossberg and subsequently developed by Johan Fornäs (Grossberg, 1992; Fornäs, 1995).[13] Elizabeth Leach's essay on the Spice Girls (Chapter 26) exemplifies the construction of authenticity-in-action – using clues from Richard Taruskin's reconceptualisation of the difference between (authentic) Beethoven and (inauthentic) Tchaikovsky,[14] she demonstrates that, in the wake of earlier pop acts, the Spice Girls both deconstructed conventional markers of authenticity and, in the process, re-erected them. Given time, I suspect that this debate will come to focus more closely on musicological constructions of the persona, but as yet I feel there is insufficient here to warrant inclusion in this collection.[15]

The urge to find musicians 'authentic' is, it seems to me, a modernist position, resting on the assumed authenticity and coherence of the individual listening subject. In postmodern thinking, that coherence cannot be assumed – indeed the concept of the 'decentred' subject is now commonplace. And it seems to me that the best way for musicians to avoid that 'centre', is for them to avoid as far as possible an unambiguous idiolect, by assuming a strong degree of transparency in relation to musical material – in short, by constant recourse to someone else's material. Thus, authenticity's 'other' is represented by intertextuality. This, too, is a troublesome notion, because it cannot be simply aligned with postmodernism. All music is intertextual – all music refers to other music – and as a conscious working practice the incorporation of others' musical material within one's own, or the use of others' material as a starting-point, is as old as the earliest music notations we have, and is also globally widespread. And yet the motive has perhaps changed when working with a postmodern aesthetic – there is a sense of knowingness, of parody, which many have commented on, and which has led to distinctive ways of using others' material. This is the topic of Serge Lacasse's essay (Chapter 9). Although Lacasse is concerned to translate a variety of 'intertextual' and 'hypertextual' practices from literary theory to musicology,[16] the essay's particular value is to encourage a higher degree of precision of observation, since different ways of using others'

---

13 See Wyn Jones (2005) for an essay utilising these schemas.

14 A rare example of an argument successfully being transposed from classical to popular musicology without denigrating the latter.

15 Two examples of the sort of work I have in mind: Gelbart (2003); Moore (2005a).

16 One of the most useful practical approaches to intertextuality is that of Albin Zak III, (2004).

materials have different types of outcome and derive from different initial causes, which need to be separated out. Indeed, if there is a single theme running through the essays I have chosen for this collection, it is that of precision of observation.[17] Philip Tagg's second essay included here (Chapter 10), again intended originally as a polemical intervention, argues that electronic dance music may mark a quite profound change of direction for popular music in general. However, he makes this argument not on the grounds of how it is used socially, but of how it functions musically. Without attention to the level of musical detail he makes, its significance would be totally overlooked. And there is more to his argument, of course, for in part he is responding to a strong thrust in popular music research (notably conducted outside musicology), which downplays the search for meaning in favour of the force of music on our corporality, in favour of its simple consumption (a position I have already suggested may be widely held by musicians). This refusal of meaning is perhaps the hardest to counter, ideological as it is.

However, if detail is worth attending to, then it is important to make the criteria for observing that detail relevant. In other words, it is necessary to develop a theoretical basis for accounting for the working of popular music which is self-consistent, and which is not simply borrowed from elsewhere. Two essays here represent distinct stages in the acquisition of such a theory on the part of scholars. My 'So-called flattened seventh' (Chapter 15) marks an early stage in this process, arguing as it does with respect to one particular harmonic/melodic detail why the regnant assumptions brought by some musicologists from classical music study into popular music study need to be rethought. Walter Everett's 'Making sense of rock's tonal systems' (Chapter 16) is a later exercise, developing as it does an account of a series of strategies which rock music uses tonally and, as importantly, exemplifying them through an impressive range of examples. Its size demonstrates the complexity of the issue, and also the distance that serious scholarship of popular music's melodic and harmonic behaviours has moved in the past couple of decades. Although this Everett essay is an exercise in theory, it does indicate some of the analytic richness that is possible in this field.[18] All the more surprising, on the surface, then, that few essays on popular music have appeared in the journal *Music Analysis* itself. Part of the reason for that, of course (other than that writers may not submit such essays) is ideological – the disciplinary battle between music analysis and historical musicology which saw the arrival of the new journal in the early 1980s was conducted purely within the canon, and perhaps necessarily so. However, the journal's continued distance from popular music analysis was the proximate cause behind Griffiths' intervention, reprinted here as Chapter 5. As will be clear by now, by no means all the substantial shorter writing in the field is in the form of regular journal articles. Both of Tagg's essays were originally what the journal *Popular Music* publishes as 'Middle Eight' pieces, that is shorter, opinionated writing which does not necessarily conform to the academic strictures of full-fledged articles,[19] while Griffiths' was, effectively, an extended review essay (which thus combined aspects of

---

17 'Rigour' has recently become a very important determinant of the quality of academic research, at least in the UK.

18 Again, there is a useful comparison piece: Philip Tagg's earlier harmony primer. See http://www.tagg.org/articles/xpdfs/harmonyhandout.pdf

19 The value to the academic community of such interventions is testament to the sometimes unhelpful rigidity which journals necessarily impose in order to preserve their credibility in the eyes of research managers.

both). It is by no means the only overview of the field: introductions to books are common sources,[20] while some wide-ranging collections also contain popular musicology overviews.[21] However, it differs from most of these others in attempting to relate developments in the field to developments in external culture, and indeed to the vicissitudes of the discipline and to the author's own history, a topic not usually aired in such a forum, but aired here to great effect, not least in that in so doing Griffiths makes his own preconceptions and prejudices plain, and so refuses the pose of objectivity to which so much interpretive writing is subject. Indeed, the other essay taken from *Music Analysis* also has the form of an extended review, but a slightly more orthodox one. Adam Krims (Chapter 11), though, is more directly concerned with the status of the field at a moment of change, addressing media studies, sociology, music analysis and history while the generosity of his criticism is perhaps an excellent model for how to go about this sort of task.

In the context of unconventional interventions, I should note that I had long considered including in this collection the exchange which took place in the magazine *Folk Roots* in 1987 between Leon Rosselson and Dick Gaughan, with a host of other contributors, about the nature of political songwriting (essentially whether the 'message' should be covert or overt) (Rosselson (1987a, b and c). I eventually decided not to, but the exchange does exemplify for me the difficulty of defining musicology, since it is clearly not simply 'what musicologists do': the question raised there is definitely a question which should concern musicology. Barbara Bradby's discussion of Buddy Holly and the Crickets' 'Oh Boy' (Chapter 27) pays great heed to rhythmic and vocal-textural detail in order to argue that the performance enacts contemporaneous male adolescent independence. Although she does not style herself as a musicologist, she produces exemplary musicology, and the level of detail she uses should not be beyond any active listener. The great theoretical divide between discussions of pitch structures (which usually require some musicological training in order to explicate) and rhythmic structures (which do not) is here made plain.

So, we reach that literature which is not afraid of a deep, sustained encounter with musical sounds and sound-aggregations, and which is normally explicated through a process of 'analysis'. And I think the notion of 'fear' is pertinent here, for one of the more common concerns expressed about analysis is that the attention to detail it forces can ruin the experience of music. On the face of it, of course, this is an absurd concern, for in what other field would we prefer ignorance to knowledge, in the expectation that such ignorance will improve our experience of life? (Well, that of nuclear fission, perhaps, but then that is an example of a rather different order – and 'fear' is more credible in this case.) After all, in the words of Joseph Kerman (himself not exactly a fan of analysis), 'music analysis is ... capable of more rigorous and powerful determinations in its own sphere than are available to formalistic criticism in any of the other arts ... The potential of analysis is formidable if it can only be taken out of the hothouse of theory and brought out into the real world' (Kerman, 1985). However, such fear does speak to the sense so many listeners have of music as a route to a psychic site which bypasses rational control, in other words music as a branch of magic.[22] To

---

20 Some of the more substantial are Covach and Boone (1997 pp.v–ix); Middleton (2000 pp. 1–19); Moore (2001 pp. 9–32; 2003 pp. 1–15); Tagg and Clarida, (2003 pp. 57–92).

21 Particularly Covach (1997; 1999).

22 About which I have written in the 'Introduction', Moore (2003 pp. 6–7).

therefore claim that music is rational after all is to issue a fundamental ideological challenge, and this is what the practice of analysis does. We must be careful, though, for while music may be susceptible to rational inquiry (a mode of inquiry which all scholars whose field abuts music necessarily undertake if their work is to be understood as scholarly), that is not to say that its effects are equally explicable (although they may be so to some degree) nor, most importantly, that they carry unequivocal meaning. Were this not the case, then debates over music's meaning would simply not take place, and they do. What good analysis does, it seems to me, is to show why it is that explicable musical structures can support the interpretations that we wish to put upon them. Walter Everett's discussion of John Lennon's 'Strawberry fields forever' and 'Julia' (Chapter 19) is, as far as I am aware, almost the earliest example of an authoritative piece of popular music analysis appearing in a mainstream English-language journal.[23] Re-reading it now, twenty years after its first appearance, demonstrates both the gulf which existed at the time between North American and European approaches to the popular music 'text' (a comparison of this with Tagg's 'Analysing Popular Music...' (2000b) is highly instructive, both in their respective aims and in the means through which these aims are reached), and a potential intellectual project which has since matured. To the difference first: whereas European analysis at the time was perhaps more concerned with representation and, as argued by Tagg, semiotics as the most useful methodological approach to elucidating such representation, Everett's approach is both more haphazard, in that simple analogies (Middleton's 'homologies', above) are sought between structural elements within the music and states outside it, and more closely investigative of the music, enabled by his untroubled recourse to Schenkerian analytical techniques. Much has been written about the validity of these, and I do not propose to rehearse the details of such arguments here.[24] However, their use enables him to note equivalences such as that on p. 404, where the lyric "it doesn't matter much to me" is poetically matched by a harmonic vacillation. And this is the project which, it seems to me, has become key in the last decade: to demonstrate why it is that the particular sounds, sound-complexes, sound-structures that musicians use are appropriate to the expressive circumstances they find themselves in, and therefore enable meaningful interpretations to be made of their actions in bringing about just those sounds, sound-complexes and sound-structures. In passing, we might note that Everett's essay really has nothing in common with the 'new musicology' to which I referred at the beginning of this Introduction – his concern with structure was, at the time, an 'old' musicological approach, but one which has certainly acquired a new lease of life subsequently. An alternative, sustained, approach to the same bundle of concerns can be found in Stan Hawkins' series of case studies observing how key pop texts create their effects (Hawkins, 2002). Hawkins' text is notable not only for its musicological foregrounding of identity and (since his topic is pop music per se) irony, but also because it is one of the best sustained efforts at taking on board many of the criticisms found within the New Musicology, without eschewing analysis.

---

23   His study of the Beatles' 'She's leaving home' appeared one year earlier.

24   Much of this writing has been based on misunderstanding, perhaps, and certainly on ideological difference – there is dialogue of sorts on this between both editions of my *Rock: The Primary Text* (1993; 2001), particularly p. 62 of the latter, and Walter Everett's 'Confessions from Blueberry Hill' in the first edition of *Expression in Pop-Rock music*. It should be said that even in this early article, Everett is deeply aware of the track's sound-quality, a point which is sometimes overlooked.

The potential for close reading, then, seems to me paramount, even if it is never 'fixed': as Hawkins notes elsewhere, 'textual readings are spoken by multiple voices in multiple settings through multiple listening; they are repeated over time, yet never appear quite the same...every detail that is interpretative by nature is readable as another detail' (Hawkins, 2001).[25] I want to indulge in a bit of word-play here for a moment. In many disciplines, while we may be concerned with the practice of 'reading', the distinction implied by the prefix 'close' is pertinent, is marked for special attention. 'Close' insists on the existence of its opposite – 'distanced' (otherwise there is no reason for qualifying our reading). Since we talk about 'close reading' what, then, might we mean by 'distanced' reading? If 'close' implies 'focused', then 'distanced' implies 'unfocused' – musicians often distinguish (focused, attentive) 'listening' from (unfocused, inattentive, everyday) 'hearing'. And yet 'distanced' reading implies another facet, that of a wider view, of being aware of things beyond or outside the immediate focus. In other words, the myopia risked by 'close reading' can be corrected by taking off the reading glasses/headphones, and attending to the wider field, an attention which can be ensured by insisting on a movement from the 'what' is done to the 'why' it might be done. Another way of putting this, which musicologists might recognise, is to note that 'analysis' (the dissection of an object or experience) is of questionable value without the ensuing 'synthesis' (the sewing it back together again, hiding the incisions, but now knowing the function of what was found inside).

So, let's move from 'close' to 'distanced' reading. The Everett essay makes this move in terms of seeking structural parallels between the expression and what is expressed. John Covach's discussion of the satirical use of Beatles' tracks (Chapter 20) made by the utterly 'inauthentic' (because fictional) Rutles embeds extremely close detail in Leonard Meyer's theory of style, hence attempting to bridge the gap between close reading and listener competence (and offers a different approach to the question of irony than found in Hawkins' book). Nicola Dibben's discussion (Chapter 24) of the Pulp album *This is Hardcore* starts not with the music, but with the context – here, the social context of pornographic imagery and its referencing on the album's cover. In so doing, it recognises the frequent overlap between aural and visual modes of perception in the discussion of music, an overlap which is overtly addressed in Carol Vernallis' essay (Chapter 21). This is one of few which, as yet, adequately address music in the immediate context of music video, paying full attention to all dimensions of the aesthetic experience – but even here, the analysis is in service of an argument which asks what sort of narrative, and what sorts of representations, the performance enables. This is also one of the strengths of Dibben's essay, as it moves from the album's social context to a discussion of the musical undermining of the signification of the lead guitar, a position which can only be disinterred with reference to musical detail. And it goes further still: in raising the issue of subject position (a relatively new topic in musicology), it attempts to relate this musical detail to the practice of listening, and the interpretations open to the listener, an alternative approach to completing the process (from originator, through object, to interpreter) to that instantiated by Stefani. Both of these themes – the concern for the listener, and the subject matter of the album – imply an ethical stance, a stance that may not be too commonly observed in most musicology. And yet it does raise its head surprisingly often, perhaps, in popular musicology (the discourse surrounding authenticity often has an ethical tone, even if

---

25 The best sustained defence of this lack of fixity is, to my mind, Sless (1986).

it is one which doesn't necessarily penetrate the topic too far). Ethics is a key driver in Charles Ford's analytical discussion (Chapter 22) of aspects of the music of the Incredible String Band. Indeed, it embodies a particularly eloquent demonstration of the necessity for self-interrogative analytical writing, of the never more than partial value of ethnographic studies of listeners[26] and, like the best analytic writing in all genres, offers to readers the possibility of changing their own listenings. The open-endedness of this process is beautifully managed by Ford's refusal to append to the essay the usual summary, whose function is normally to frame the experience of reading, to close it off from the rest of reality, to make it easier to undertake the reading without being fundamentally affected it. I would suggest such closure is harder than usual in the case of this essay. Fred Maus' discussion (Chapter 25) of the work of the Pet Shop Boys offers yet another exemplary study of how to address detail without losing sight of context. Here, though, the approach seems somewhat different. Rather than taking a theoretical starting-point (that of subject position) or an ethical one (that of self-interrogation), it starts from a striking musical detail and relates that to the more fundamental issue of ambivalence – both musical and contextual – as a result offering an interpretation both of the music and of its significance. Nicky Losseff's way into Kate Bush's 'Wuthering Heights' (Chapter 23) is similar in that it starts from a troublesome stretch of music – troublesome in that its harmonic waywardness calls out for explanation – but an explanation which remains firmly within the confines of the fiction the song sets out to explore, and for this sort of inquiry Losseff's essay is a valuable model. We may not understand ourselves better having read it, but we certainly make more sense of Bush's performance.

In these essays, the balance between analysis and interpretation, or between text and context, puts heavy emphasis on the text. Other successful essays, however, use musical detail less as the substance of an argument than as the detail which opens up an issue, Indeed, Robert Walser's essay (Chapter 18) goes rather further, since his argument concerns music itself – what it is, how it works – approached through understanding how hip-hop (and more specifically the music of Public Enemy) must be understood as music, and understood in a fairly sophisticated way, at that. In raising such a question, we begin to move back from matters of analysis, of details of particular tracks, to theory, to the context, or to how to understand the principles which make particular tracks work in the way they do. There is a necessary tension between these two aspects. Every interpretive move we make is based (usually implicitly) on some theoretical understanding: something operates in a particular way in a particular track because of the way it works across a large number of such tracks (theory is implicit in analytical decisions) and yet trying to articulate such theory often leads to problems because of the numerous counter-examples which can be found. Perhaps this is why discussions at the level of theory are far rarer than analytic discussions. One of the earliest essays in popular music theory, and hence one of the most often referenced (yet probably least-read), is Alf Björnberg's discussion (Chapter 14) of aeolian harmony and, more importantly, the realm of its 'affective meaning'. Again, a comparison is useful – here, I suggest, with Peter Winkler's early addressing (Chapter 13) of harmonic practice in some jazz, standards and 1950s pop, and again the differences between European and North American approaches are clear. Björnberg is uninterested in voice-leading, and much more interested in mode and

---

26   The necessity of such work has, to my mind, been rendered all but superfluous by Tagg and Clarida, 2003, as explored in my review Moore (2005b).

harmonic patterning. And, as with all good theoretical writing, it urges us to ask his questions again, at twenty years' distance, to discover to what extent things have changed. Winkler proposes a solution to the question of understanding what happens when changes of harmony don't quite coincide with key melodic pitches (a frequent feature of live performance in a number of styles), but whether to understand such passages as alternative 'readings' of a simpler structure (simultaneous elaborations of a background), or whether to understand them as cases of melody and harmony falling out of synchronisation,[27] despite being a seemingly key theoretical question, has as yet gone unresolved.

So, each of these pieces of writing either addresses, or enacts, popular musicology. And in each the critical content is clear – in none is the author simply content to accept a body of knowledge and add to it. As with all intellectual disciplines, musicology is permanently in flux and if one thing is certain, it is that any similar collection, undertaken by somebody else, or somewhere else, or at some other time, would not look the same. But it would raise the same questions.

References

Bennett, Andy and Richard Peterson (eds.) (2004), *Music Scenes*, Nashville, TN: Vanderbilt University Press.

Brackett, David (2000), *Interpreting Popular Music*, Berkeley. CA: University of California Press.

Centre for History and Analysis of Recorded Music, http://www.charm.rhul.ac.uk/.

Covach, John (1997), 'We won't get Fooled Again: Rock Music and Musical Analysis', in David Schwarz, Anahid Kassabian, Lawrence Siegel (eds), *Disciplining Music*, Charlottesville, VA: Virginia University Press, pp. 75–89.

Covach, John (1999), 'Popular Music, Unpopular Musicology', in Nicholas Cook and Mark Everist (eds), *Rethinking Music*, Oxford: Oxford University Press, pp. 452–70.

Covach, John and Graeme Boone (eds) (1997), *Understanding Rock*, Oxford: Oxford University Press.

Everett, Walter (ed.) (2000), *Expression in Pop-Rock Music*, New York: Garland.

Everett, Walter (1999/2001), *The Beatles as Musicians* (2 vols.), New York: Oxford University Press.

Fornas, Johan (1995), *Cultural Theory and Late Modernity*, London: Sage, pp. 274–79.

Frith, Simon (1990), 'Picking up the Pieces', in Frith (ed.), *Facing the music*, London: Mandarin, pp. 88–130, p. 125.

Frith, Simon and Andrew Goodwin (eds) (1990), *On Record*, London: Routledge, pp. 315–19.

Gelbart, Matthew (2003), 'Persona and Voice in the Kinks' Songs of the Late 1960s', *Journal of the Royal Musical Association*, **128**, pp. 200–41.

Grossberg, Larry (1992), *We gotta get out of this place*, London: Routledge, pp. 201–39.

Hall, Stuart and Tony Jefferson (eds.) (1976), *Resistance Through Rituals*, London: Hutchinson.

Hamm, Charles (1981), 'Some Thoughts on the Measurement of Popularity in Music', in *Putting Popular Music in its Place*, Cambridge: Cambridge University Press, pp. 116–30.

Hamm, Charles (1983), *Yesterdays*, New York: Norton.

Hamm, Charles (2004), 'Popular Music and Historiography', *Popular Music History*, **1**, pp. 9–14, pp. 11–12.

Hawkins, Stan (2001), 'Musicological Quagmires in Popular Music: Seeds of Detailed Conflict', *Popular Musicology Online* 1, http://www.popular-musicology-online.com/issues/01/hawkins.html.

Hawkins, Stan (2002), *Settling the Pop Score: Pop Texts and Identity Politics*, Aldershot: Ashgate.

---

27 As proposed in van de Merwe (1989).

Hebdige, Dick (1985), *Subculture: The Meaning of Style*, New York: Methuen.

Horn, David (2000), 'Some Thoughts on the Work in Popular Music', in Michael Talbot (ed.), *The Musical Work*, Liverpool: Liverpool University Press, pp. 14–34.

Kerman, Joseph (1985), *Musicology*, London: Fontana, pp. 12, 18.

Krims, Adam (2000), *Rap Music and the Poetics of Identity*, Cambridge: Cambridge University Press.

Kubik, Gerhard (2003), 'Présence de la musique africaine dans le jazz', in Jean-Jacques Nattiez (ed.), *Musiques du XXe siècle*; Paris: Actes Sud/Cité de la musique, pp. 1203–38.

Ledang, Ola Kai (1987), 'Europeisk barokkmusikk i koloniperspektiv', *Studia Musicologica Norvegica*, **87**, pp. 45–81.

Ling, Jan (1989), 'Musik som klassisk konst. En 1700-talsidé som blev klassisk', in *Frihetens former - en vänbok till Sven-Eric Liedman*, Lund: Arkiv, pp. 171–87.

Merwe, Peter van der (1989), *Origins of the Popular Style*, Oxford: Clarendon.

Middleton, Richard (1990), *Studying Popular Music*, Buckingham: Open University Press.

Middleton, Richard (ed.) (2000), *Reading Pop*, Oxford: Oxford University Press.

Middleton, Richard (2001), 'Pop, Rock and Interpretation' in Frith, Straw and Street (eds), *The Cambridge Companion to Pop and Rock*, Cambridge: Cambridge University Press.

Moore, Allan F. (1993; 2001), *Rock: The Primary Text*, Aldershot: Ashgate.

Moore, Allan F. (1997), 'Anachronism, Responsibility and Historical *Intension*', *Critical Musicology Journal*, http://www.leeds.ac.uk/music/info/critmus/.

Moore, Allan F. (2001), 'Categorical Conventions in music-discourse: Style and Genre', *Music and Letters*, **82**, pp. 432–42.

Moore, Allan F. (ed.) (2003), *Analysing Popular Music*, Cambridge: Cambridge University Press.

Moore, Allan F. (2005a), 'The Persona/Environment Relation in Recorded Song', *Music Theory Online* **11**, <http:www.music-theory.org/mto/issues/mto.05.11.4/

Moore, Allan F. (2005b), *Popular Music*, **24**, pp. 298–300.

Moore, Allan F. (forthcoming) 'Musicology', in Ian Inglis (ed.), *Perspectives on Popular Music*.

Moore, Allan F. and Anwar Ibrahin (2005), 'Sounds like Teen Spirit: Identifying Radiohead's Idiolect', in Joseph Tate (ed.) *Strobe-Lights and Blown Speakers: Essays on the Music and Art of Radiohead*, Aldershot: Ashgate, pp. 139–58. mto.05.11.4.moore_frames.html>.

Rosselson, Leon (1987a), 'Songs in the Dark Ages', *Folk Roots*, **47**, pp. 23–25.

Rosselson, Leon (1987b), in *Folk Roots*, **50**, pp. 59–60.

Rosselson, Leon (1987c), in *Folk Roots*, **51**, pp. 57–58.

Scott, Derek B. (2000), 'Music, Culture and Society: Changes in Perspective', in Scott (ed.), *Music, Culture, and Society, A Reader*, Oxford: Oxford University Press, pp. 1–19.

Sless, David (1986), *In Search of Semiotics*, London: Croom Helm.

Small, Christopher (1977), *Music – Society – Education*, London: John Calder.

Tagg, Philip (2000a), '"The Work": An Evaluative Charge', in Michael Talbot (ed.), *The Musical Work*, Liverpool: Liverpool University Press, pp. 153–67.

Tagg, Philip (2000b), 'Analysing Popular Music: Theory, Method and Practice', in R. Middleton (ed.), *Reading Pop*, Oxford: Oxford University Press.

Tagg, Philip and Bob Clarida (2003), *Ten Little Title Tunes*, New York, Mass Media Music Scholars' Press.

Taylor, Timothy D. (1997), *Global Pop: World Music, World Markets*, New York: Routledge, pp. 22–31.

Wyn Jones, Carys (2005), 'The Aura of Authenticity' in Joseph Tate (ed.), *Strobe Lights and Blown Speakers: Essays on The Music and Art of Radiohead*, Aldershot: Ashgate.

Zak III, Albin (2004), 'Bob Dylan and Jimi Hendrix: Juxtaposition and Transformation: "All along the Watchtower"', *Journal of the American Musicological Society*, **57**, pp. 599–644.

Part I
Contexts for Addressing Texts

Theory

[1]

'Black music', 'Afro-American music' and 'European music'[1]

PHILIP TAGG

I have recently found myself reacting with some irritation on meeting such terms as 'black music', 'white music', 'Afro-American music' and 'European music'. The aim of this letter, written mainly with white European or North American students, friends and colleagues in mind, is to question the validity of these terms, to bring some issues lurking behind their general usage out into the scribal daylight and, hopefully, to provide some ideas for a constructive debate on music, race and ideology.

Due to the sensitivity of matters cultural, ethnic and racial, I have chosen to write down what I want to say in the form of a letter. It is *not* a 'scholarly' article quoting, misquoting or otherwise attempting to attack or out-argue anyone else. The letter *is* intended as a polemical problematisation of terms like 'black music', 'white music', 'Afro-American music' or 'European music' and the reader I hope to reach is anyone interested in music who, like myself, has ever used the terms without always having a clear idea of what they actually mean.

I do *not* feel comfortable questioning such widely used terms as 'European' and 'Afro-American' or 'black music'. These very doubts initially caused the white man's burden of collective guilt to flash messages like 'Racist Thought Error' on to the monitor of my brain. However, having considered the generous contribution actually made *by* the Protestant operative system of collective guilt *to* the cause of racism, I decided to write off such error messages as ideological system failures in themselves. I also took the liberty of discarding the objection that my irritation was attributable to some sort of male menopause because I feel basically quite cheerful and secure these days. So, if I'm not an incorrigible racist nor in the throes of a personal crisis causing me to project frustrations on to everyone else, what is the point of complaining about such terms as 'black' or 'European' music? How can they be regarded as problematic, let alone insidious, when they have been in such extensive circulation for such a long time?

One basic reason is that the meaning of the terms seems to be taken for granted. We are all expected to know exactly what everybody else means and to have a clear 'common sense' notion of what is black or African about 'black music' or 'Afro-American' music and white or European about 'white' or 'European' music.

Another reason for my discontent with such terms is that I have helped spread them. I am definitely not the only white middle-class intellectual interested in forms of music outside those taught in conservatories to oppose the aesthetic dictates of élitist European bourgeois music culture with its canonisation of some musics and its deprecation of others. Many scholars champion noble and unjustly neglected cultural causes by writing with respect about the music of ethnic and social groups excluded from the European 'Art' music education tradition. A few of us study the music of the European proletariat while more study the music of African or Afro-American peoples. We see important values in these musics, values until recently ignored or declared taboo by most university music departments. We want to draw attention to these 'other' forms of musical expression and to replace the old tradition of musicology, which falsifies its own objects of study and ignores all others, with something more democratic and less restrictive.

In this process we have to define ourselves in relation to concepts created by the very tradition we seek to change. Studying 'folk', 'popular' or 'black' music from the other side of the institutional fence is *not* the same as tearing down that élitist, colonialist or racist 'fence': it just means that we have taken up a new position in the same game. If we do not wish to remain forever as interesting or troublesome exceptions to the rule of music studies, we must either become an integral part of the existing establishment, changing it from within, or, if that proves impossible, create our own structures of intellectual authority.

The existence of this journal should be proof enough that popular music studies have passed the nursery stage and that we can no longer solely rely on a position of 'opposition-ality' or 'alternativeness' (in reference to an unjust authority) to legitimate or define ourselves or our special area of study. Having established a position of authority, however small, we constantly need to review the adequacy of our old *paroles d'honneur* to discern whether they still act as clarifications of position in the 'old' game or whether they have become the same sort of authoritarian mystifications as those used by the old establishment (e.g. 'Art', 'Classical'). 'Black', 'white' and 'European' are three adjectival concepts qualifying music that popular music scholarship must refine, redefine or replace if it wants to avoid coining its own mystification phrases from new positions of authority.

'Black music' and 'white music'

Although these colourful terms appear less frequently in print, they often turn up in discussions. 'Black music' is much more common than 'white music'; just like the terms 'women's history' or 'women's music' cause fewer eyebrows to be raised than 'men's history' or 'men's music'. Such terms are relative to the hegemony of the culture of their user, so 'men's music' and 'white music' will sound stranger in a culture dominated by white males than 'women's music' or 'black music': they (blacks and women) are the exception and we (whites and men) rule. They need proof of identity, we do not. But if we are not totally satisfied with the culture we belong to – and this is shown by our use of terms denoting identities excluded from the conceptual universe of the establishment – we had perhaps better be clear about why we use the terms and what we mean by them.

Dictionary definitions

'Black' (capital 'B') is defined by my dictionary (New Collins Concise English Dictionary 1982) as:

a member of a dark-skinned race, especially a Negro (=a member of any of the dark-skinned indigenous peoples of Africa and their descendants elsewhere) or an Australian Aborigine. 'Black' can also be used as an adjective meaning 'of or relating to Blacks'.[2]

According to these definitions, 'black music' would mean music of or relating to members of a dark-skinned race, especially of one of the indigenous peoples of Africa and their descendants elsewhere, or of one of the Aborigine peoples.

'White' (capital 'W') is defined as:

a member of the Caucasoid (=denoting or belonging to the light-complexioned racial group of mankind, which includes the peoples indigenous to Europe, North Africa, South Western Asia and the Indian subcontinent or a member of this racial group) race. 'White' can also mean: 'a person of European ancestry or denoting or relating to a White or Whites'.

According to these clearly racial (not racist) dictionary definitions of 'black' and 'white', it would be necessary, if using terms like 'black music' or 'white music', to establish connections between the colour of people's skin and the sort of music they make. I will not insult readers by suggesting that they harbour hypotheses of this type but it should be clear that if we use 'black' or 'white' as adjectives qualifying 'music', and if we define 'black' and 'white' in no other way than that provided by the dictionary, we will have to establish connections between the racial (dictionary) and thereby physiological qualifiers 'black' or 'white' and the sets of cultural artefacts 'music' as produced and used by Blacks or Whites. If we have no clear *cultural* definition of black or white and if we consider music as something to be heard rather than seen – this implying that the music itself possesses neither black, white nor any other colour – then we have no logical grounds for a *cultural* definition of either black music or white music. The evidence we shall have to produce must in this case be physiological, not cultural. In short, failing to provide *cultural* working definitions of black or white when talking about black music or white music is tantamount to posing the racist hypothesis that there are physiological connections between the colour of people's skin and the sort of music people with that colour of skin produce.

Taking black music to mean the common denominators of music made by Negroes, we will find ourselves running into musicological and anthropological incongruities galore. It will mean that we must consider a vastly heterogeneous range of musics. It will mean that many musical traits frequently labelled black, such as 'blue notes' (as in the blues) and/or polyrhythm (e.g. Nilo-Sudanic traditions) and/or birhythm (e.g. *kwela*) and/or pentatonic melismas (e.g. gospel), will all have to be excluded as common structural denominators of black music because one or the other or more of these traits do not occur in certain Mauretanian, Ethiopian and South and South-East African musics. If we are still not prepared to abandon the idea of such musical traits epitomising negritude, we will just have to don our wonted imperious Eurocentric mantle and disqualify a large number of black people, both in Africa and in other parts of the world, as white or of some other hue.

'Black' as some black people and not others

It would be restricting the meaning of the term 'black music' quite severely to make it denote the music of dark-skinned people in the USA and nowhere else in the world. However, this is precisely the sort of meaning implied – seldom openly declared and even more rarely defined – on most occasions I have come across the term. This implied meaning of 'black' is not only restrictive; it is also ethnocentric.

The idea that Black=US Black reveals the same gormless sort of arrogance found in other instances of word magic in post-war American English. I am referring here to words like 'world', as in 'The World Trade Center', 'Miss World', or 'The World Bank'.[3] This 'World=USA' notion recurs frequently in US popular song too, where the 'world's' cities are enumerated as Chicago, New York, LA, New Orleans, Philadelphia and Detroit[4] or where 'USA for Africa' (the group, the effort) '*was*'[5] 'the world'.[6] Using black to denote people of African descent living in the USA and nowhere else falls into the same category of unwitting ethnocentric megalomania. It is as disrespectful to the cultural identity and integrity of all other Blacks (the majority) as the US American meaning of 'world' is to the rest of us (also a majority).[7]

Putting aside the absurdity of all these 'World=USA' fetishes for a moment and swallowing our pride as residents of the remaining 95 per cent of the world (in its real meaning), it should be clear that the meaning of 'black' as described above is almost identical to the dictionary definition of 'Afro-American'.

Afro-American music

My dictionary defines 'Afro-American' (adj.) as: 'denoting or relating to American Negroes, their history or their culture'.

It is clear that this must be narrowed down considerably, if by 'Afro-Americans' we mean black people living in the USA. We will have to exclude everyone from Tijuana and Santiago de Cuba southwards (the majority of Afro-Americans), perhaps even Canadian Afro-Americans too.[8] But even this might not be restrictive enough if we do not want to include the musical practices of middle-class US Afro-Americans in New England as part of Afro-American music. We might also take it upon ourselves to exclude The Fisk Jubilee Singers, Scott Joplin, Paul Robeson, Charlie Pride and Nat King Cole. We might even be considering banishing Prince and Lionel Richie – not to mention all the 'b-boys' of hip-hop influenced by Kraftwerk (Toop 1984), to the realms of the Euro-American or white. If this, in part or whole, is what we wanted, we would have to restrict the meaning of black and Afro-American even further, zooming in on only certain groups of people with dark skin at only certain times and only in certain places in the USA. Reading between the lines of what frequently seems to be implied by black or Afro-American, we might find ourselves concentrating on black US-Americans living in the South or on those whose ancestry can be found in that part of the USA. This may well be a bit nearer what writers seem to take for granted but it is a bit of a long shot from the dictionary definitions of 'Black' and 'Afro-American' to 'the rural or urbanised rural proletariat of African descent living in the USA, mostly with a cultural tradition from the Southern states'.

So now we have the racial concept 'black' and the ethnic concept 'Afro-American' not only directly or indirectly referring to the colour of skin of people producing the music being qualified by the adjective, but also denoting geographical, social and historical locations which, with the exception of 'African descent' are not specially 'black' (the USA, the South, 'rural', 'urban', 'proletariat', 'cultural tradition'). If this is what was meant, it would have been nice to have it clear from the outset.

Even so, the historical implications of this new definition are also problematic. At what time(s) and in which place(s) is or was the music 'truly black' or 'most genuinely Afro-American'? In Charleston, South Carolina, in 1760 when second generation slaves were sought after as jig and reel fiddlers? In 1850 at a Baptist camp meeting in Georgia? Around the turn of the century in the ragtime bars or on the streets of New Orleans? In 1920 when Bluebird were recording Atlanta street blues played on violin and banjo or in the Jug Band Music of the thirties in Memphis? Or do we find the 'truest' expressions of 'black' or 'Afro-American' music in the area around the Yazoo river in the twenties and thirties? As a black teenage fan of Lionel Richie in Minneapolis, Omaha or Seattle, does my father or his father have to have been to a club on the Chicago South Side in the fifties or have worked at Dockerey's in the forties? Does my grandad have to have been in the pen at Parchman in the twenties for my music to be considered 'black' or 'Afro-American'? As that inmate of Parchman Farm, do my great-grandparents have to be descendants of the Awuna, the Senufo, the Wolof, the Ga, the Ewe, or the Ashanti peoples for my music to warrant the qualifier 'Afro'? As a black teenager in Boston today, as a factory worker in East Saint Louis just after the war or in Atlanta in the twenties or even as a tobacco plantation slave in South Carolina in the seventeen-eighties, what is the relationship of my music, if it is not to be qualified as truly 'black' or 'Afro', to whenever and wherever 'black music' or 'real Afro-American music' are supposed to have existed? And if *all* these musics at all those times are 'black' or 'Afro-American', including Nat King Cole at Las Vegas, Prince in Portland or Lionel Richie in Bakersfield, what do they all have in common musically? And if the answer is 'not much', what is the point of using the terms?

Some musicological misconceptions

When the terms 'black music' or 'Afro-American music' are used and implicitly or explicitly opposed to 'white' or 'European music', a few typically 'black' or 'African' musical traits will occasionally get mentioned. The most popular musical characteristics to cite are: (1) 'blue notes', (2) call-and-response techniques, (3) 'syncopation' and (4) improvisation.

Blue notes

Blue notes, as used in blues and jazz, can be either slides from what the classical European tradition of music theory calls 'minor' to 'major' intervals in a scale (mostly third and seventh, in certain variants also diminished fifth to perfect fourth or augmented fourth to perfect fifth) or the placing of a tone somewhere between those intervals without a slide. Such traits can be found in the music of some West Sudanic peoples today but also occurred on a regular basis in folk music from Scandinavia and, more importantly, from Britain at the time of the main colonisation of the New World.[9] Such traits are commonly heard in old recordings of 'thoroughly White' – as opposed to the equally silly notion of 'thoroughly Black' – music from the Appalachians.[10]

Now, whether this American rural vocal tradition practised by Whites came wholesale from Britain or whether it is the result of early acculturation with West Sudanic musical elements or whether it is a bit of both is all beside the point. If groups of people with white skin in the USA have been singing between the cracks on the piano, even only over the last 150 years – a conservative estimation – it is illogical to conclude that blue notes are exclusively black/Afro or exclusively white/Euro.[11]

Call-and-response

Call-and-response techniques can be antiphonal or responsorial. They are as African as they are European as they are Indian or Jewish. Antiphonal psalm-singing and *responsoria* between priest and choir or congregation have been common over the past two thousand years in the Middle East and Europe. Quite a few people have been to church in Europe over the last nineteen hundred years. No mean number of these Europeans took their cultural luggage with them when they settled in the New World. Lining out and evangelical Hallelujahs are two such examples. This means quite simply that even though there may be lots of call-and-response in West Sudanic musics too, it cannot logically be cited as characteristic of black music or Afro-American music.[12]

Rhythm

It is with even greater confidence that syncopation is quoted as a typically black musical trait. If we were talking about the *polyrhythm* of many West and central Sudanic musics, this would be understandable, because I know of no European musics using rhythmical structures like a metric unit of, say, twenty-four sub-beats being consistently used to produce a complex of simultaneous metres like 3/8, 2/4, 3/4, 6/8, 4/4, 2/2, 3/2, 4/2 (and possible additive asymmetric subdivisions of these) on top of each other (for examples see Nketia 1974; Chernoff 1979). That would be a valid musical trait distinguishing one type of African music not only from European music in general but also from a lot of other African musics. It would unfortunately also distinguish these polyrhythmic African music traditions from most of the music made by US-Afro-Americans, including those with their cultural roots in the Southern states. So what rhythmic traits *are* being hinted at but not described when the terms like 'black music' and 'Afro-American music' are being used? Syncopation? According to the *Harvard Dictionary of Music* (ed. W. Apel, 1958),

> syncopation is . . . any deliberate upsetting of the normal pulse of meter, accent and rhythm. Our system of musical rhythm rests upon the grouping of equal beats into groups of two and three, with a regularly recurring accent on the first beat of each group. Any deviation from this scheme is felt as a disturbance or contradiction between the underlying (normal) pulse and the actual (abnormal) rhythm.

Apel then goes on to quote excerpts from typically *dance* inspired movements from works by Beethoven and Brahms. That is home ground but when he gets into examples of 'syncopation' from late fourteenth century *Ars Nova* pieces his step is not so sure, probably because he is no longer dealing with monorhythmic asymmetric metre but with manuscripts attempting to notate folk improvisation devices of the time. That is to say, the more the music diverges from the ideal monorhythmic norm of the old-style musicologist's notion of Viennese classical music, the more we move (1) in space – away from Central Europe, (2) in time – away from (a caricature of) the late eighteenth century and (3) in social status – away from aristocratic or *haut bourgeois* milieus. We move, seeing things from Adorno's perspective, towards geographical, historical and social *Randgebieten* (marginal areas or borderlands). It is obvious that there are far more references to 'popular' European traditions when Apel deals with 'abnormal' (for who?) rhythm practices than when he has to define sonata form and even clearer (in the former case) that he is treading on thin conceptual ice. For example, some of Apel's 'syncopation' citations are simplified hemiolas and expurgated rhythm patterns from galliards (very popular in sixteenth and early seventeenth century Britain).[13] The problem is that syncopation presupposes that only one rhythm and metre can be dominant at any one time (as in the Viennese classical music which forms the basis of old-style musicology). However, medieval, baroque and Tudor music performance practice, with its use of *tactus* instead of metric conducting, shows that our fixation on symmetric monorhythm – graphically represented in *later* types of notation by the omnipresent bar line – is totally foreign to the music of that time. In fact the term 'syncopation', applied to consistent hemiola shifts (as in the galliard or in Elizabethan madrigals and anthems), is highly questionable, especially in polyphonic sections where different metres occur in different voices and can be experienced simultaneously by both listener and performer.

Further evidence for the inadequacy of the term 'syncopation' and of the obvious popularity of birhythmic practices in Europe can be found *passim* in the *Fitzwilliam Virginal*

Book, compiled in the *Randgebiet* of England in the early seventeenth century. Considering the popular origin of many pieces in that collection, it would be no rash speculation to suppose that European (at least British) colonists possessed some competence in birhythmic devices when they arrived in the New World in the seventeenth and eighteenth centuries. Moreover, they brought with them the rhythmic idiosyncrasies of the English language which, in comparison with most other European languages, favours certain 'offbeat' (whose beat?) settings in music. Apart from the frequent need of triplets (as in the songs of Vaughan Williams) or of triple metre superimposed on duple or quadruple (as in madrigal settings of Byrd) it is important to mention the 'Scotch snap'[14] about which the *Harvard Dictionary of Music* remarks with inimitable ethnocentricity under the heading 'Dotted Notes III – *Inverted Dotting*':

> . . . the reverse of the ordinary dotted rhythm . . . It is a typical feature of Scottish folk tunes . . . (and) . . . of American Negro Music and of jazz . . . Inverted dotting is also very frequent in Oriental and in primitive music, where the normal dotted rhythm is rather rare . . . . This rhythm also figures prominently in the English music of the seventeenth century (John Blow, Henry Purcell), in which it is used effectively in order to bring out the short, but unaccented, first syllables which occur in so many English dissyllabics.[15]

Looking and listening through early minstrel songs,[16] there seems to be some truth in Apel's observation about the 'Scotch snap' being 'a typical feature of American Negro music'. However, that presupposes that early blackface minstrels actually did manage to copy (and caricature) the musical devices they thought warranted the burnt cork and that the sheet music (and other sources) on which modern performances of mid-nineteenth-century minstrel songs are based are reliable. Whatever the case may be, it should be clear that it is *unclear* whether 'inverted dottings' came from what Apel calls 'primitive' (in this case West African) music or from (what Apel does not call 'primitive') 'Scottish folk tunes' or from the rhythmic idiosyncrasies of English language dissyllabics. It should moreover be clear from the preceding paragraphs that it is *unclear* whether the birhythmic character of much North American popular music should be traced back to Europe or Africa.

Improvisation

Improvisation is sometimes used as a word of honour in discussions about jazz. At worst, the word seems to refer to a vaporous musical practice which Blacks are expected to do better than Whites. Taking improvisation to mean making music without *consciously* trying to perform – from memory or notation – an already existing piece or other performance, it is hard to see how anyone can say it is more typical for Blacks than Whites or people who take shoe size 9 (=42) or larger. Postulating that there is less improvising in European music traditions must stem from an uncritical acceptance of late nineteenth century bourgeois élitist concepts of European music traditions (about which more later). One guiding light in this school of thought was to canonise the individual composer's (The Artist's) score as the music's purest form of concretion. Such notions negated some of the historically most important creative practices of the European classical music tradition – Landini, Sweelinck, Buxtehude, Bach, Händel, Mozart, Beethoven, Liszt and Franck were all renown not only as composers but also as *improvisers*. The ideological aim of this notation fetish (notation being the only concrete form of musical storage and commodification at the time) was to forestall sacrilege upon the 'eternal values' of immutable Masterworks so that the cultural (and social) *status quo* of yesteryear might be preserved *in aeternam*. This strategy was so successful that it finally managed to suffocate the living tradition it claimed to hold so dear by locking up the loved one (classical music) in institutional preserving jars called 'conservatories'. One sequel to this dirty deed was that improvisation had been virtually eradicated from the classical scene by 1910.[17]

Despite the dearth of improvisation in the European art music tradition over the last seventy years, it is absurd to present this sad development as conclusive evidence supporting notions implying that improvisation is more 'black' or 'African' than 'white' or 'European'. This is not so much because 'improvisation'[18] was a central part of the European classical tradition during the most important periods of Northern European emigration to the New World (1628–1890) as because many European and most early British immigrants brought along non-classical musical traditions in which 'improvisation' – in the sense of 'making music without consciously trying to perform an already existing piece or other performance from memory or from notation' – was far from being an exceptional trait.

'African' questions

If after these objections we still want to use terms like 'black music' and 'Afro-American music' when talking about popular music in the USA, we could always try and review the African connection to become at least a little more stringent than just improvisation, blue notes, call-and-response and syncopation when it comes to *musically* determining what really is 'black' or 'African' about the music we are referring to. In order to know what differences there were between European and African traditions, and thereby establish real musicological evidence for the viability of our terms, we would have to go back to the seventeenth and early eighteenth centuries and find out *what sort of* improvisation, *what sort of* call-and-response techniques, *what sort of* rhythmic and melodic practices, etc. were common in Britain and the Savannah areas of West Africa. I am sure we could find some important differences if we could answer *these* questions.

Taking the African connection first, we would have to find out what the slaves brought with them to the New World and how this interacted with what the Europeans had brought with them. In order to know this we would have to know which African peoples were actually brought to the New World, in what numbers, where they ended up and which Europeans they had to have dealings with. Then we would need to know whether the music used in Africa today by those peoples supplying the New World with slaves in the eighteenth century is the same now as it was then or whether it has undergone any changes. We would then have to know the social conditions of newly arrived slaves, the processes of assimilation and acculturation in various parts of the South and on that basis isolate strictly African musical elements in the fast acculturating genres of the eighteenth and nineteenth centuries. Now, if that seems like a lifetime research job for a staff of over one hundred competent enthusiasts working full time, we could always opt for a more pragmatic solution, starting from the hypothesis that 'Afro-American music' is the set of the musical common denominators found in recordings labelled by the US music business as 'r&b', 'Soul', 'Blues', etc. This would be defining 'Afro-American' in the same way as the industry defines its target group (music *for* US-Afro-Americans). This might sound convenient but we would run up against exactly the same problems as mentioned earlier on, especially if using the term 'black music'. Would we include traditional jazz which has had a predominantly white audience since the war? What about Motown and its majority of white listeners since the mid-sixties? What about bebop, cool and modern jazz? Would Lester Young qualify and not Stan Getz? What do we do with Bix Beiderbecke, Django Reinhardt, Gene Krupa and Benny Goodman? If they are 'white', why is Duke Ellington 'black'? Is only Bessie Johnson's *voice* 'black' and are her black musicians all 'white'? Is ragtime 'black' music? Is Michael Jackson 'black'?

Incongruities like these make the term 'black music' as hopeless as 'white music' and I will just have to agree to differ with anyone who still wants to use either of them. However, difficulties of unestablished continental origin for the various styles feeding into the mainstream of US-American popular music raise some doubt about the validity of the term 'Afro-American music' too. One reason for such doubts is that as long as no-one really knows what musics Africans actually brought with them to the USA – a very important research priority – it is impossible to say what is specifically 'Afro' about 'Afro-American' music. Moreover, the term begs the question of what was 'American' when the slaves started being shipped into the colonies en masse. Didn't there have to be some 'African' in the music before it became 'American'? Or had English, French and Celtic traditions become so widespread and acculturated by 1720 in North America that they now had musical common denominators enabling them to be distinguished as 'American' rather than as English, French or Celtic? A rhetorical question indeed, for how could (another one) such acculturation take place so quickly in these far flung colonies on a huge continent without much by way of roads, railways, telephones, radio or television? In fact 'Afro-American' implies that people of African racial origin played no part in the creation of the 'American' part of 'Afro-American' music, just as 'Euro-American' would imply that European music styles are grafted on to an already fixed set of 'American' musics which were neither Amerindian nor, as already implied by the term 'Afro-American', African in origin. The point is: at what point in history and in which area of the USA did (US) 'American' music exist so that it could be distinguished from music of other (sub-) continents and thereby become qualifiable by the prefixes 'Afro-' or 'Euro-'? What characteristics does the main set of music called 'American' possess so that the prefixes 'Euro-' and 'Afro-' can qualify it?

'European' questions

It is important to remember that most work on the music of black US Americans is written by middle-class whites, mostly liberal or radical, and mostly European. As answering to this description, I feel it is historically understandable (though hardly excusable) if we know very little about West African history and culture: it was after all *our* forefathers, not theirs, that did the colonising and ran the slave trade.[19] It is also people of our own race who still perpetrate some of the more notorious practices of racial discrimination and neo-colonialism.

However, although we are able to deplore the oppressive deeds of our forefathers and authorities again people distinguishable from ourselves at a glance by the darker colour of their skin, we seem to remain strangely insensitive to the various types of oppression exercised within our own continent and to the fact that both forms of oppression are inextricably linked. We seem prepared to feel solidarity and sympathy for the people our race has enslaved and unwilling to exercise the same type of philanthropic understanding on oppression within Europe and ourselves. Is philanthropy insulting to us but not to them? And what does philanthropy have to do with the matter under discussion?

European music

Although 'white music' is sometimes used as an opposite pole to 'black music', the counterpart most frequently provided by white writers on 'Afro-American music' is 'European music'. The funniest thing about the use of this term – apart from being as nebulously defined as 'Afro-American music' – is that its *implied* meaning coincides with the most reactionary, élitist, bourgeois, conservative and non-dynamic view of European music imaginable. What seems to be implied is a weird caricature, not of European music, but of a small part of one out of several hundred important European music traditions. In fact it seems that many a white knight of the 'Afro-American' cause and champion of both anti-élitism and anti-authoritarianism uses the expression 'European music' in the same erratic way as his élitist and patriarchal adversaries. This 'European music' does not denote the musical practices of Viennese classicism,[20] but refers to what the untalented theory teacher in a fourth division conservatory has been told to think classical music *ought* to be. In this way the white champion of Afro-America repeats garbled descriptions of our continent's and its peoples' music: it all turns out as 'Ein-Schwein-Dry-Fear' beats to the bar, well planned *crescendi, diminuendi, rallentandi* (rarely *accelerandi* for some reason), four-square Teutonic periodicity, pompously farting woodwind, jaded brass, claustrophobic quartets, sickly grace notes, syrupy strings, bombastic or prissy pianos, ego-tripped conducting, self-controlled straight-laced audiences, no dancing (except ballet), no fun, no humour. It is all Spiritual Respect, Greatness and consequently Utter Anal-Retentive Boredom.[21]

How such a caricature of a once living and extremely popular music tradition came into being is a matter which cannot be discussed here. In *this* context the curious thing is that many of us, professing to be in opposition to such ignorant élitism, seem nevertheless, when talking of 'Afro-American music', to have opted for a mindlessly élitist view of the music of our *own* continent. It is a view which not only makes a total parody of the music it canonises (by the actual process of canonising it) but also sneers at musics in proportion to how near they are in time and place to the condition of our own proletariat.[22]

This distorted image of European music has had tragic consequences. It has meant, for example, that we know almost as little about British popular ('folk') music of the late seventeenth century as we know about West African music from the same time and that we cannot establish any clear picture of popular performance or dance practices (improvisation, birhythm, ornamentation, drone treatment, popular harmonisations of modal tunes, agogics, vocal timbre and inflection, etc.) – knowledge which would have come in handy here in trying to discover what 'Afro-American' or 'European' music might be.[23] Of course, it also means that conservatories still see fit to buy a hand-made harpsichord for the price of two recording studios and that teachers (even some students) still laugh when you propose a Jimi Hendrix memorial guitar scholarship or suggest a series of workshops on the accordion (one of Europe's most popular instruments) or try and start courses in Country and Western ensemble playing. Naturally, by putting this sort of aesthetic taboo on certain genres, the conservative music college will ultimately commit cultural harakiri.

At the same time, I am willing to bet that quite a few white European fans of 'Afro-American music' reading these lines would probably approve of the Jimi Hendrix scholarship but feel less keen on the accordion or C & W ideas. If this is true, it means that the most ironical effect of the twisted view of European music has been to perpetuate the rules of a 'holier-than-thou' game in the field of musical aesthetics, so that even those of us trying to beat the *ancien régime* actually end up by playing the same game, instead of changing the rules or moving to another sport altogether. The reason for this intellectual *débâcle* is that when we speak of the 'European tradition' and mean – without saying so of course – the reactionary caricature of European music presented to us by patriarchal bourgeois figures and institutions, we are not only misunderstanding and falsifying the historical position and role of this continent's classical music tradition, we are also, by acting 'little boy in opposition to evil authority', playing into the hands of the reactionary tradition of learning we seek to improve upon. By falling into an idealistic anti-authoritarian position, we perpetuate the ideas of the hated authorities with whom we live in unresolved Oedipal relationship of interdependence: we are disobedient sons who see no value in ourselves without the habitual presence of authoritarian fathers.[24]

In this way, instead of understanding the interrelationship of popular (folk and later) traditions with art traditions and instead of criticising the way in which the people are constantly banished to the periphery of traditional accounts of culture, we feel compelled to adopt our hated authoritarian father's definition of where the 'middle' is and of what it contains. We find ourselves reacting in the terms of Adorno or a Chinese emperor, imagining ourselves inhabiting an élitist and Eurocentric *Chung Wa*.[25] Rather than move to what we ignorantly imagine to be a deserted 'borderland' – *Randgebiet dieses Reiches der Mitte* – we project our hopes and frustrations on to a distant people the emperor enslaved. By turning our gaze elsewhere, we do not see that what were termed 'borderlands' or 'marginal areas' (*Randgebieten*) by the old régime (symbolised here by Adorno, the emperor and the fourth division music theory teacher) were in fact potential centres of power. In other words: just because we have experienced European music history teaching through books that devote three hundred pages to an inaccurate account of the Baroque and zero pages to popular music, it does not follow that we must agree with such a view, even less accept it as a valid definition of 'European music' or use it as the starting point or centre for our own discussions about European, let alone US American or African musics.

The reasons for this objection are simple. Music develops within and between people and groups of people, with their conditions of life and with their position in the productive forces of society, not according to aesthetic taboos, be they élitist old hat or élitist hip. It is therefore totally logical that what Adorno considered as two of Europe's *Randgebieten* – British folk music and central European *gesunkenes Kulturgut* – have combined so fruitfully with the even more marginal musical habits of slaves descending from West Sudanic peoples, thereby laying the foundations for the dominant global music culture of our own time.

Perhaps one of the main obstacles to this sort of reasoning has been that those of us who deplored the old 'True Genius' and 'Art' *Wertästhetik* have found new masters to serve by canonising new 'authenticities' and 'truths'. We convert the 'classical' concern for 'real art' or the 'folk' fetish for the 'genuine' into 'popular' equivalents like 'street credibility', 'intrinsic ephemerality', 'real rock', 'genuine popular expression', 'the latest', 'youth rebellion', 'anti-authoritarian', 'corporeal', 'down-home', etc. Musical 'proof' of the excellence of these often mutually contradictory concepts is rarely presented and when such attempts are made no-one is much wiser than after musical 'proof' of the superiority of Schönberg over Respighi. I think 'Black Music' and 'Afro-American music' are also terms running a severe risk of this type of aesthetic fetishisation and idealisation. This process contains other strange ingredients.

Projection and compensation: sexuality

To exemplify some of the mechanisms involved in white liberal idealisation of the 'Afro-' in 'Afro-American' (music), let us imagine that an ancestor of mine, born into family of farm-labourers in the Fens around 1700, is press-ganged in his late teens and shipped off to the American colonies. After a few years of massacring Indians he deserts and makes a fresh start in the backwoods of Virginia where he clears some woodland and starts a small plantation. He borrows extensively for the property, for equipment and building materials. He marries and has three children in quick succession. He has four mouths to feed as well as debts to pay. He works from dawn to dusk. He plans carefully: no more heavy expenses, better crop rotation and maybe a new barn would solve storage problems ? . . . If only he could get extra labour he could produce and sell more. So he buys his first slave. Production increases notably. He then invests in two more slaves, one male, one female. If they have children quickly and often , he won't have any more capital expenditure for slaves. Lack of labour is now the only thing holding his business back . . .

. . . apart from their work, they (Negroes) were required to beget more slaves; as the men laboured the women were in labour. Love played little part in this: couples mated at the orders of the plantation owner . . .

Slaves were classified below the level of cattle and when they were sold at the auction block they had to undergo the most humiliating and dehumanising examinations which were primarily designed to ascertain their strength and potential procreativity. With the stud Negro came the conception of the big buck nigger which inferred a distinctly subhuman status. Fecund mothers and fertile males were assets to the slaveholder who bred his slaves as he bred livestock. (Oliver 1960)

If profits were to increase, my fictitious ancestor would have to save, plan carefully, work hard and get his slaves to breed like rabbits, probably also making a personal contribution to the siring of his work force by taking advantage of slave girls. At the same time he probably lived in considerable awe of the church and its strict moral dogma. Contradictions between moral edicts on the one hand and business interests plus sexual urges on the other must have been hard to handle. There on your doorstep was the 'big buck nigger' who was expected to sow oats in one field after the other while you had to be a 'one woman man' and repress possible memories of pleasure spent either with your 'one man woman' (also brought up with fears and guilts about sex) or with one of the slave girls (even more sinful). No wonder our forefathers credited black males with bigger cocks as well as greater desires and sexual potency than we thought we were allowed to have. No wonder either why we projected on to black women the attributes of insatiable nymphomaniacs.

Sexual guilt among Whites and its projection[26] on to Blacks may in fact have been vital links in the chain of oppression making slavery in the New World into a going concern. My fictitious ancestor must have 'known' all too well where he stood morally in relation to his superiors (a miserable sinner) and – through his projection of guilt and longing – in relation to slaves (promiscuous animals who did and had to do all the 'naughty', 'nasty' and 'dirty' things in both work and sex).

Projection and compensation: music

It is possible that a similar sort of projection process comes into play when terms like 'Afro-American music' and 'European music' are used without proper definition. Indiscriminate use of such terms falls right in line with historical falsifications of the old European cultural patriarchy and credits Blacks with everything corporeal and spontaneous in today's popular music while attributing nothing corporeal or spontaneous to us Whites. Such an absurd stance implies that Whites have contributed nothing essential to all those 'sinful' sounds we bop around to these days and that 'European music' is what the second rate theory teacher from a fourth division conservatory has told us to believe. There is in other words the risk that by laying the trip so heavily on black people of African descent we embark on a musical equivalent to the sexual projection process described above. By disowning responsibility for our own musical corporeality we force black people into absurd court jester positions and use music we imagine to be little or none of our own doing as a corporeal panacea for own problems of subjectivity, powerlessness and alienation.

Open letter: Black music, Afro-American music and European music 295

Perhaps this is why some of us are disappointed if black artists do not live up to the stereotype behaviour we expect of them, like constant arse wiggling, pelvis grinding and jive talk.[27] Perhaps that is also why some Whites might actually consider disqualifying Paul Robeson, Charlie Pride, Nat King Cole and Milt (perhaps even Michael) Jackson as not being 'black' or 'Afro' enough. Perhaps it is also why we do not expect black musicians to write symphonies, operas or anything else in which long thematic processuality is the order of the day.[28] In cases like these, where our stereotype expectations are not fulfilled, we might feel insecure because status quos of race, culture and society are all being challenged.

Conclusion

My scepticism towards the supposed pair of opposites 'black' or 'Afro-American music' versus 'European music' has two main grounds: (1) musicological, because no satisfactory definitions of any terms are provided and (2) ideological. The latter is particularly important because not only does the implied dichotomy pre-ordain certain sets of feeling and behaviour for one race and deny them to the other, it also turns the overriding question of class into a matter of race or ethnicity.[29] So, if we do not resolve the Oedipal conflict we seem to have with Our-Father-Which-Art-In-Europe, we shall never understand how the situation and ideas of the European (rural and urban) and African (rural becoming urban) proletariats, as expressed in music, were able to acculturate so productively in eighteenth, nineteenth and twentieth century North America, thereby laying the foundations of what was to become US popular music – the dominant musical tradition of our time. Instead, ethnic or racial dichotomies will continue to be presented, showing the mirror image of the apartheid we profess to hate and concealing the system which uses racism as one of its most iniquitous mechanisms for perpetuating a class society.

Endnotes

1 The original version of this text was originally sent as a private letter to about ten colleagues in June 1987.

2 Lower case 'black' and 'white' are used in the *adjectival* meaning of 'pertaining to Blacks or Whites'. Upper case will be used in conjunction with adjectives qualifying populations only when the adjective qualifies a geographical proper noun.

3 For further examples of the 'World=USA' fetish, cf. Sky Channel's 'The World Wrestling Championships'. Such 'wrestling' may involve about two Mexicans and five Canadians but the rest are all US Americans. Moreover this US American concept of wrestling is not shared by the rest (95 per cent) of the world.

4 Martha Reeves and the Vandellas: *Dancing in the Street* (M. Stevenson, M. Gaye). Stateside SS 345.

5 The use of the verb 'to be' in US American advertising and video film trailers seems to replace the usual copula function of equivalence or identity ('he is a man', 'he is my brother'). When stressed in advertising, the verb 'to be' takes on the meaning of 'to pretend so that you might almost think him/her/it to be' ('Clint Eastwood *is* Dirty Harry', 'Diana Ross *is* Billy Holiday'). Sometimes the magic copula is not even stressed ('We Are The World', 'Coca

Cola is *it*'). What *it* is and where 'it' is 'at' cannot be discussed here.

6 The similarities between the 'USA for Africa' (*We Are The World*) event and fake UN image advertising campaigns like 'The United Colors of Benetton' are striking. Greil Marcus (1986) draws convincing parallels with a Pepsi Cola multinational singalong commercial and unveils ideological fakes behind the event in his article 'We Are The World?'.

7 Readers are at liberty to repress this objection as a case of exaggerated cultural sensitivity if it makes them feel more comfortable. Before doing so, however, they are advised to read Greil Marcus's (1986) article 'We Are The World?' (see note 6).

8 The 'World=USA' syndrome has a more particular *American* symptom. My dictionary has this to say about 'American' (note the order of the two meanings shown): '1. of or relating to the United States of America, its inhabitants, or their form of English. 2. of or relating to the American continent'. This means that if we don't accept that the USA is the world, we at least have the chance of taking a more 'moderate' option, i.e. that by saying 'America' we really only mean one of its twenty-seven constituent nations, or one quarter of its total population (the 'America=USA' syndrome).

Even stranger is the phenomenon that the English language possesses no adjective corresponding to the first definition of 'American' presented by my dictionary, i.e. there is no equivalent to the Italian adjective *statiunitense* ('il governo statiunitense'), unless we use 'US' ('the US government', 'the US army'). However, we might say 'US Blacks', 'US Whites', or even 'US popular music', and while I have tried to consistently use the noun 'US American' to denote an inhabitant of the USA (thereby avoiding ambiguity between 'America=USA' and 'America=America') it would sound strange using semantically adequate but linguistically clumsy expressions like 'Afro-US-music'. This is why I have used longer turns of phrase like 'of black US-Americans' and once or twice 'US-Afro-American'. This is a matter of respect allowing Latin Americans, Amerindians, Eskimos – and the Québécois to remain Americans. One should moreover note that the Soviet Union is never named by the continent(s) of which it is part but frequently referred to by native speakers of English, not by the name of nation state that it actually is, but by one of that nation's constituent parts ('Russia'), this diminishing its size and power in relation to the USA by means of verbal magic. Add to this the fact that the inhabitants of the USSR (nearly half of whom are not Russian) have never referred to their territory as 'Evropa', 'Azia' or 'Evrazia' and one has a fine example of the power of words.

9 Note the obvious aesthetic desirability of intervallic swooping and of bending notes when singing English folk rock, e.g. Maddy Prior in 'The Female Drummer' (Yorkshire trad. via P. Grainger, A. L. Lloyd and The Watersons) on the Steeleye Span album *Please To See The King* (United Artists UAG 29244, 1971). Such techniques may owe something to exposure to blues-based traditions but probably more to indigenous vocal traditions handed down through groups like The Watersons or to old recordings of singing from such counties as Suffolk or Dorset.

   I am also sure that I am not the only English ex-schoolboy to remember his musical socialisation into the bourgeois world in terms of having to be taught to sing and play the prescribed notes cleanly, not to 'swoop', 'slide' or 'bend' in and out of what the music teacher heard, or rather saw, to be fixed pitches in a score during singing lessons and choir practices. Where these vocal 'impurities' of ours came from is unclear. None of us Northamptonshire lads growing up in the early fifties had been extensively exposed to any-

thing much bluesier than Glenn Miller, Teresa Brewer and Humphrey Lyttelton. I even remember once being told off (musically) in choir practice for 'sliding and swooping around', not because it was like blues or jazz but because I sounded to the music teacher like a Music Hall artist.

   A far less equivocal instance of European 'blue notes', though this has very little to do with US-American popular music, can be found in the Lutheran churches of eighteenth-century Sweden, where the monochord and organ were introduced to stop the congregation from singing notes foreign to equal tempered tuning and from performing melodic ornamentation and improvisation. How the cowherds and smallholders of central Dalarna were influenced by the blues and West Sudanic music traditions in 1770 still remains a mystery.

   More serious points for musicological research should include: (1) the relationship between, on the one hand, what the central European music theory tradition ethnocentrically calls 'false relations' – be they simultaneous (mostly Tallis but also Weelkes, Tomkins and Byrd) or slightly staggered (e.g. 'English cadences') found in many a Tudor manuscript – and, on the other hand, the popular music practices of the Tudor composers' contemporaries. This should include sections on tuning and temperament, a historical account of the *tierce de Picardie* and a comparison with folk tunes using flat 7 or flat 3 as pendulum points to the main tonal (melodic and/or harmonic) centre (e.g. Farnabye's *Dream*, Dowland's *The King of Denmark's Galliard*). (2) Accompaniment and harmonisation practices for the 25 per cent of English folksong which, according to A. L. Lloyd's assessment of the Child ballads, were in Dorian or Aeolian modes. (3) The (non-) treatment or, more frequently, absence or avoidance of what Central European music theory would call 'leading notes' and how these were harmonised at later stages in the USA (cf. shape note singing and P. A. Westendorf's complaints about the unharmonisability of Irish ballads for parlour use). (4) A detailed account of early acculturation between West African and British music traditions in Virginia and other American colonies. (5) What happened when the banjo and guitar were used as accompaniment for US-American folksong of British or West African origin or in an acculturated state.

10 E.g. *The Lost Soul* as recorded by the Doc Watson Family in 1963 on Folkways FTS 31021.

11 If, as may well be the case, particular types of

Open letter: Black music, Afro-American music and European music 297

'blue note' occur more often in the music of US Afro-Americans, (e.g. slides or bends between 'major' and 'minor' intervals) it is these musical characteristics that should be stated, not general divergences from equal tempered thirds, sevenths and fifths.

12 Once again, if particular types of call-and-response technique are considered more common in the music of US Afro-Americans (e.g. short, overlapping birhythmic phrases between 'soloist' and choir/instrument(s)), then these should be cited rather than call-and-response techniques in general.

13 For important discussion of colonial (chiefly African and Latin) Afro-American influences on Southern European music (Spain, Portugal, Kingdom of Napeles) during the Baroque, cf. Ledang 1987.

14 The 'inverted dotted' rhythms of English were probably influenced by the inflections and accentuations of Celtic speech (cf. the rhythms of both Scottish and Irish Gaelic). Hungarian also contains such rhythms.

15 Please note that the norm (most musics) for dotted rhythms is 'inverted' and that 'normal' dottings are not the norm according to the norms of the *Harvard Dictionary of Music*!

16 cf. the Dan Emmett, George Christy and Cool White titles on the 'Early Blackface Minstrelsy' side of The Yankee Doodle Society's triple album *Popular Music in Jacksonian America* (dir. Joe Byrd, Musical Heritage Society MHS 834561).

17 The art of improvisation never died out among church organists in Germany, France or Britain. You have to play *until* the bride or coffin or priest deign to show up and you must round off suitably neither before nor too long after that moment. No compositions with full cut and end functions every ten seconds exist for these purposes: they would be musical absurdities! There is no other alternative but to improvise.

18 Whether we are referring to *ex tempore* composition *in toto* or to *ex tempore* ornamentation or alteration of existing melodic, rhythmic or harmonic patterns, improvisation was part and parcel of the European classical music tradition, especially at the time of the largest emigration of Northern Europeans to the New World.

19 My Ghanean friend and colleague, Klevor Abo (who speaks fluent Ewe, English, Twi, Ga, French and Spanish), successfully embarrasses me every time he quotes Chaucer, Shakespeare and the rules of cricket in perfect English, knowing full well that I only speak a handful of European languages and am totally ignorant of Ewe, Ibo, Yoruba, Hausa, Twi and Swahili epics in translation, let alone in the original.

20 See above under 'Improvisation' for further comments.

21 For a rollicking verbal showdown with conservative music education in general and untalented music theory teachers in particular, see Paul Hindemith (1952, pp. 216–21).

22 The logical consequence of this is that proletariats suffering elsewhere in place or time are legitimate objects for our philanthropy. The closer or more powerful they become, the less we welcome them into our drawing room.

23 See notes 11, 16.

24 Our father which art in New York? Washington? Harvard? Hollywood? London? Oxford? Cambridge? Vienna? Frankfurt? Wittemburg? München? Berlin? Geneva? Dunfermline? Rome? Amsterdam? Uppsala? At home? At school? In church? At university? On TV? In books on 'Afro-American music? The impotence of the disobedient son who never emancipates himself from patriarchal authority has many symptoms relevant to this argument: we abandon solidarity with peoples who gain their independence although they still need our support (e.g. Angola, Vietnam) because we are scared of responsibilities facing us when we gain our own independence as individuals in this society and are therefore unable to identify with the emancipated. By the same token it is unpopular to suggest that music from the 'suffering' 'little' people (black and white) is now the basis of the most powerful global music force, since such a statement invalidates the legitimacy of our own 'suffering' and impotence and would oblige us to take responsibility for whatever that music and its people might have become. This would be a more constructive Oedipal strategy, similar to that in *Star Wars* where Luke Starwalker decides to get rid of that four-squared, tin-helmeted dark invader, death father, Darth Vader and to create, however Nazi it might sound, a 'new and better order' himself. Besides, the *Star Wars* movies would have gone on as long as rock romanticism if there had been no resolution of the plot's central Oedipal conflict!

25 *Chung Wa* is Chinese for 'China' and means 'Centreland' or the land in the middle (i.e. the land where the middle is, or the land where it's at, or, in Coca Cola's terms, the land which is *it*). All the other places and people are out(side): we are (the) in(side), the middle, the centre, the omphalos (=navel), 'we are the world'. Everything and everybody else circles around us, not us around it or them.

26 It is also possible to put the idea of projection into Stierlin's concept of 'delegation', in the

298   *Philip Tagg*

sense of handing over to others what you cannot or do not want to do yourself. In this case we would be talking about an 'id level delegation' from the slaveholder to his 'big buck nigger'.

27 Jimi Hendrix detested the stereotype 'bad dude' behaviour that white audiences expected of him; cf. C. Welch, 1972.

28 E.g. Scott Joplin's *Treemonisha* (1911–15) failed,

not because there was anything wrong with the work, but because no (white) impresario was willing to stage an opera written by a black man; cf. Gammond, 1975, pp. 98–100.

29 This does *not* mean to say that racial and ethnic oppression are unimportant parts of US American or any other multi-ethnic class society. Please read on to the end!

References

Chernoff, J. M. 1979. *African Rhythm and Sensibility* (Chicago University Press), pp. 46–88
Gammond, P. 1975. *Scott Joplin and the Ragtime Era* (London: Sphere), pp. 98–100
Hindemith, P. 1952. *A Composer's World* (New York: Doubleday), pp. 216–21
Ledang, O. K. 1987. 'Europeisk barokkmusikk i koloniperspektiv', *Studia Musicologica Norvegica*, 13: 45–81
Marcus, G. 1986. 'We Are The World?', *Ré Records Quarterly*, 1 (4), pp. 36–9
Nketia, J. W. K. 1974. *The Music of Africa* (New York: W. W. Norton), pp. 120–74
Oliver, P. 1960. *The Meaning of the Blues* (Toronto: Macmillan), pp. 131–3
Toop, D. 1984. *The Rap Attack* (London: Pluto), pp. 128–31
Welch, C. 1972. *Hendrix* (London: Ocean Books)

[2]

A theory of musical competence

GINO STEFANI

Competence

By 'musical competence' we understand the ability to produce sense through music. In other words, the ability to realize either individual or social projects by means of music. As for 'music', we include here every social practice or individual experience concerning sounds which we are accustomed to group under this name. Our question is therefore: in what way does our culture produce sense with music?

Of course, this question is not new. Musical historiography and esthetics offer rich materials for the various eras, starting from the medieval theory of 'musica mundana, humana, intrumentalis' (which is, in fact, a model of competence). As for today, we are faced with many theoretical approaches concerning our subject: the 'intonation (*intonazia*) theory', dealing with units and strata of meaning in music, proposed by Asafiev (1976) and having a wide following in Eastern Europe; Willems's psychopedagogical idea of 'musical intelligence' (1933); Adorno's typology of hearers (1962); Blacking's anthropological approach to the question 'How musical is man?' (1973); Laske's logico-cybernetical model of a metamusic (1975); etc.

Our project implies two basic assumptions. First of all, there is some reason for thinking that musical activity, notwithstanding its variety, has some common features which enable us to view it as a unitary whole. Moreover, in connection with this, we take for granted the existence of some ability to make and/or communicate with sounds which is common to all members of a culture, although distributed and exercised in various ways and roles. Both remarks are not exclusive to music, but are also valid for other types of social expression such as gestures, painting, and so on.

As for the usefulness of this project, it is easy to see. A competence measured upon the whole of society and its sound production is an adequate frame to describe production of musical practices, the contribution of the artists, particular competences of musicologists, functions of

8   *G. Stefani*

institutions, etcetera. Such a description, moreover, might enable us to explain why and in what sense a certain practice or experience can be 'music' for some people and not for others. Finally, a model of general musical competence within a culture allows us to elaborate more clearly and firmly the aim of musical education — that is, the promotion of a certain musical competence.

Code

In the present paper, general competence in music (within our Western culture especially, but not exclusively) will be described as a complex of several *levels of codes*.

We take 'code' in a semiotic sense as the organization and/or correlation of two fields of elements viewed respectively as expression and content. In our case, we have on the one hand sound events, and on the other every reality which can be connected with them.

First, a code can be an *additional correlation* between a musical unit and a cultural content, both already constituted — for example, between a car horn and the behavior of car drivers, or between a silent film and the music which accompanied it.

Second, a code can be a *structuring correlation* between a field which is already constituted and another which is still informal and which therefore takes its structure from the first one. This is what happens when the libretto of *Trovatore* is the 'inspiration' for Verdi's music, or when Beethoven's Pastoral Symphony becomes the inspiration for Disney's famous cartoons.

Third, a code can also be a *correlating organization* of two fields which are both still informal and which therefore structure themselves simultaneously. Thus, dance codes model and correlate gesture and sounds in a corresponding manner — that is, with the same agogic, rhythmic, metric rules. In the same way, expressionist codes give form to Schoenberg's *Pierrot lunaire* as well as to a new cultural *Weltanschauung*.

As one can see, this idea of code allows us to understand the production of musical sense in two basic ways. On the one hand we find recognition, identification, and decoding — the use of codes already constituted and possessed. On the other hand there is the invention of new codes — in each of the three modes mentioned above. In this perspective, musical competence means the ability to identify and/or establish additional or structuring correlations as well as correlating organization between sound events and cultural environment.

This idea of code operates a semiotic reduction of the scheme Production-Object-Fruition which is often used for the representation of musical experience. It follows that competence, as the use or invention of codes, can be applied to musical production (musicians) as well as to fruition (hearers), so that the attribution of competence to one side or another will be of secondary importance. In this way we underline the global character of our project, which does not attach particular importance to any social role in musical experience.

The model

Musical experience is obviously ruled by a great number of codes. What criteria does our choice meet? In brief, our model has been found, by trial and error, to be the most economical one to represent simultaneously both common and specialized competence — that is, to put artistic projects into the general framework of social projects in sounds and music. This is also a good approach for the evaluation of both popular music and contemporary art music.

Our Model of Musical Competence (MMC) consists of a set of code levels articulated as follows:

General codes (GC): perceptual and mental schemes, anthropological attitudes and motivations, basic conventions through which we perceive or construct or interpret every experience (and therefore every sound experience).

Social Practices (SP): projects and modes of both material and symbolic production within a certain society; in other words, cultural institutions such as language, religion, industrial work, technology, sciences, etcetera, including musical practices (concert, ballet, opera, criticism).

Musical Techniques (MT): theories, methods, and devices which are more or less specific and exclusive to musical practices, such as instrumental techniques, scales, composition forms, etcetera.

Styles (St): historical periods, cultural movements, authors, or groups of works; that is, the particular ways in which MT, SP, and GC are concretely realized.

Opus (Op): single musical works or events in their concrete individuality.

Let us see now all these levels of musical sense in an interpretation of a popular item, the beginning of Beethoven's Fifth Symphony.

GC. In the famous theme:

10   *G. Stefani*

we hear two sets of sound impulses, of medium strength and consistency, well marked, relatively short, in a medium-low register, neither dry nor soft. These sound events can easily be interpreted as two sets of 'strokes'.

SP. From the GC, as well as from the overall form of the sequence — three short strokes followed by a longer one; then a short silence followed by a repetition of the pattern — we easily get the idea of something or somebody striking in a somewhat ritualized and conventional way, as if knocking at the door. In this we identify a signal of beginning, which creates a sense of suspense and expectation — like an announcement, or an entry in a ceremony, or the introduction of a speech.

MT. The phrase begins with the sequence G–G–G–E flat — our set of 'strokes' is 'musically' structured. These sound impulses (at least the first three of them) have a precise duration and a metrical position, a definite height on the staff, and a certain tonal function. The technical code also presents us with ambiguity, suspense, and expectation. This strange motive is not a 'melody'; its key is uncertain (C minor? E flat major?); it would be very difficult to foresee what follows these two short segments of notes.

St. However, every 'native speaker' of our main Western musical language is able to hear this beginning as a gesture of command and drama. Many of us perceive in it, more precisely, something like that 'titanic heroism' or 'heroic titanism' which traditional criticism ascribes to Beethoven's music, and we all recognize the style and content of the Fifth Symphony as a whole as Beethoven's.

Op. The beginning of this work — the motive dramatically bursting in, introducing and anticipating in a generative synthesis the whole 'history' of the first movement — was interpreted by its author as a good metaphor for 'fate knocking at the door', and it has been recognized as such everywhere, by both the public and the critics, since 1808.

Obviously we do no assert here that Beethoven's work is nothing but 'the symphony of fate'; many other interpretations would be pertinent. What we intend to do here is simply to indicate how our model can function when applied to the production of sense about a concrete piece of music.

The levels

We have looked at our model as a whole. Now let us examine its individual levels more closely.

General Codes (GC)

At the root of any production of sense upon sound and music events we find the general codes through which we perceive and interpret every experience. They are first of all the sensorial-perceptual schemes (spatial, tactile, dynamic, thermic, kinetic, etcetera) which enable us to classify a sound as high/low, near/remote, hard/soft, clear/dark, warm/cold, strong/weak, etcetera. At the same level we find the logical schemes (that is, more or less elementary processes and mental operations) by means of which we apply to everything — and therefore to sound as well — such categories as identity, similarity, continuity/discontinuity, equivalence, opposition, symmetry, transformation, etcetera.

We also include in this basic stratum of general codes those more complex categories which *homo faber, ludens, loquens* elaborates from everyday experience, both natural and cultural. We mean those common categories by which we describe an object or events as 'made this way' — for example, granular, compact, flowing, in a rounded or pointed form, like a constellation, growing slowly or by a set of explosions, in a wave form; in short, any one of the processes of which everyday life gives us countless examples. How many processes of this kind have given an explicit model for musical composition since 1950?

The competence level, which itself can be divided into many sub-levels, is the most basic and common. One might call it the 'anthropological level' of musical competence, were the term not so full of implications. We find here sound as matter or material, and the interaction between sound and sense, sound and mind. Most pedagogical projects, clinical practices, and the poetics of Cage (1961) are primarily founded upon this stratum of sense production. But the example from Beethoven has shown us that it can *never* be regarded as a parenthesis. Another important point is that everybody may exercise this stratum of codes with music.

Social Practices (SP)

Sense production in music then proceeds through codes pertaining to certain social practices. It is in this way, for instance, that the beginning of a piece of music is built and/or interpreted as a ceremonial entry or the introduction to a speech; that the articulation of a melody is described as a 'phrasing' as if it were a verbal discourse, that the curves and inflections in a melody reflect the intonations of speech, or that so many musical rhythms and meters immediately recall similar or identical features of poetry and dance, and so on. It is by this network of sense that one

12 *G. Stefani*

eventually manages to build up, more or less systematically, the relationships between music and society or, rather, between the various social practices of a culture.

As for the past, 'musical genres' give us evidence of social practices in music — think of marches, hymns, berceuses, serenades, entratas, preludes, dances, operas, and ritual forms. The practices of language, ritual, theater, and spectacle are still important codes for both producing and interpreting musical events. Since the 1950s scientific practices have also provided musical 'inspiration', for instance mathematics with combinatorial and stochastic models.

This competence level, though vast, does not have the anthropological application of the former. In fact, many social practices are limited to a certain human group, sometimes very small. Within this group, however, it is something which is codified and recognizable by every member, according to the degree of their socialization or 'general culture'.

At the bottom, this level is close to general codes; at the top, we find a set of social practices related to musical codes, and therefore called 'musical practices': singing, playing, and composing, as well as social institutions such as concerts, opera, theater, music schools, music laboratories, criticism, and musicology. As one can see, both musical and nonmusical practices contribute to sense production in music in different but equally important ways. Take for instance Ligeti's *Lux aeterna*: the meaning it gained from Kubrick's *2001: A Space Odyssey* is probably as important as that given to it by a musicological approach. Besides, many contemporary experiences (Cage and computer music, for instance), having apparently little relevance in such a musical practice as the concert, may become more relevant in a nonmusical practice such as theater or lecture.

Musical Techniques (MT)

In our culture — throughout the history of the world — there is a place for codes which are more specifically 'musical', being connected with techniques, instruments, systems, and devices specially designed or employed for music making. This is what usually is viewed as 'musical competence' with no further qualification, whereas in our model it is only one of the competence levels.

Let us recall our introductory comment about codes: they are not only supporting structures but also significant correlations. In this perspective, musical systems as codes mean musical 'languages'. Musicians and musicologists have a tendency to neglect or even to deny the semantic thickness of techniques; thus they consider music essentially as the production of objects or events. But for our society as a whole, for its general competence in music, music is always the production of signs. It is therefore particularly important here to consider ordinary people, what they think and feel about musical 'language', and what they do with it.

According to a widespread opinion, 'laymen' are ignorant about musical techniques; they do not 'understand' musical language (Karolyi 1965: Preface). As one can see, confusion reigns here between *linguistic* competence and *grammatical* competence. Speaking and understanding a language is different from studying its written grammar and theory. Now, the 'language' of our traditional music belongs to common culture; therefore the psychologist Robert Francès (1958) spoke of a 'musical mother tongue of Western people'.

We do not intend to describe this language here. We only want to recall two main features pertinent to our model: (1) its heterogeneous character, and (2) its functioning as a code in the full semiotic sense — that is, as a rule for correlating *expression* and *content*. Its heterogeneity strikes us immediately when we think of the different 'qualities' or 'parameters' constituting music: pitch, duration, dynamics, timbre, articulation, types of attack, etcetera. In fact, each of them is organized by codes which are disparate, independent, and of different strength. Even the code appearing to be the strongest one, the tonal code, is in fact a 'hypercode' which is built with the contribution of different syntactic-semantic layers, among which we may indicate: the octave pattern (expression of emphasis); the scale and individual intervals (Cooke 1958); major/minor modes with their bipolar 'ethos' still persisting in every kind of hearer; tonal syntax with its 'embodied meaning' (Meyer 1956, 1973; and Francès 1958); chordal features (consonant/dissonant); etcetera. Even more heterogeneous are the 'rhetoric' codes regulating the organization and perception of polyphonic devices, melodic structures, and musical 'forms'.

In view of this complexity it is easy to see the inadequacy of the current idea of a 'musical language' as something coherent, composed of many 'elements' hierarchically linked by a single principle — which in fact remains unstated. What advantage does our model offer, then, by describing musical language as a stratification of levels which are more or less 'coalescent', as Boulez (1963) would say? Perhaps the most prominent is the fact that, by embedding 'pre-musical' levels, our model allows us to embody not only systems of morphology, syntax, and rhetoric, but also those 'speech acts' or 'communication acts' which explain — to a certain extent — the constitution and working of these 'technical' levels.

In fact, all the various techniques and rules for intervals, dynamics, timbre, and rhetoric embodied in a Sonata, or a Fugue, or a Concerto do not provide unity themselves; unity comes rather from projects and modes of behavior which stand before or beyond techniques — that is, at GC and SP as well as St and Op levels.

Besides, depending on the technical competence of musicians, one can make music by means of any system or device: the result would automatically be a musical 'language' with as much right to be so termed as the tonal one. Actually, this idea was widespread for some decades concerning twelve-tone technique and enlarged seriality, which were considered a historically necessary evolution of the traditional musical 'language'.

The relativity of this perspective, which neglects the social aspect of language with its semantic and pragmatic implications, appears clearly in the light of our model. In this light twelve-tone technique takes on two meanings: (1) an extension of MT from inside (as in musicians' and theorists' views), and (2) an integration into the MT level of processes which originate from SP or GC levels. This integration, of course, is not at all in the nature of things, but requires motivation again to be found in previous competence levels.

It is at the MT level that one usually begins to find applicable the definition of music as 'the art of sounds', which in a narrower sense can be reformulated as 'the art of notes'. In the frame of our model this definition shows itself to be inadequate. In fact, on the one hand artistic projects with sounds can be realized outside the specific MT level (for instance, with elementary sound events); on the other, MT serve also for SP (signaling, rites, therapy, etcetera) where the artistic project is not primary or relevant.

Styles (St)

Both Corelli and Beethoven employ certain musical systems, but each in a different way and with different meanings; that is, in a different style. 'Style' is a blend of technical features, a way of forming objects or events; but it is at the same time a trace in music of agents and processes and contexts of production. Stylistic competence is, therefore, the ability to form and/or interpret both aspects.

In normal cases, the distinction between these two aspects passes unnoticed. So when speaking of baroque, romantic, Beethovenian or expressionist style we may mean, simultaneously or separately, both the musical signifier and the historical and cultural signified. Style codes are thus rooted on the one hand in MT, and on the other in SP. To MT the new competence adds an inventive way of using systems; to SP it adds the experience of precise contexts and circumstances.

According to some scholars (for example, Nattiez 1975), when dealing with music one should not speak of 'systems' or languages, but only of styles (tonal, twelve-tone, etcetera). From our point of view, this approach privileges the construction of sound objects as well as the autonomy of artistic projects, at the expense of the social functions and practices which give sense to those projects and objects. Pursuing this idea to its logical conclusion, we should here speak only of idiolects — that is, styles peculiar to single works and not susceptible to generalization into common schemes. In that case, no language could exist.

Opus (Op)

In a minimal sense, competence at opus or work level is the trivial fact of recognizing a piece; for example, 'this is Beethoven's Fifth Symphony'. Recognizing in this way is normally the lowest degree in sense production, an exercise of repetition and reproduction of identity. Only in particular cases can it become a valuable exercise requiring a considerable amount of intelligence (such as when guessing some piece which is not so very well known).

As we have said before, in our traditional highbrow culture Op level is the most pertinent to artistic projects and to the social practices which make them concrete. So in a concert, for instance, what we are directly confronted with are neither techniques nor style, but individual works. In fact, criticism — which is the most typical act of highbrow musical competence — is usually a discourse about single works. However, this has not been the only perspective in our history, nor is it today. The absolute primacy of the work as a finished product has been denied in jazz, folk song, contemporary poetics, and musical life in general because of the manifold functions we recognize in music in so many contexts, especially through mass media.

Besides, creativity displays itself in several phases: projects, models, and programs are often valuable in themselves and for their capacity to engender a great number of concrete realizations, independently of that particular realization which is called the 'opus'. After all, working with sounds does not always end in finished 'works'. Discovering and extending the processes of sense production with sounds can be as interesting musically as hearing a good piece of music.

Applications

We have presented our model in a paradigmatic form. Now we will try to apply it to various types of musical experiences. To the extent to which it

16   *G. Stefani*

proves capable of explaining (that is, putting into a coherent form) the many facets of musical experience, it will itself be verified. Moreover, several particular types of competence will take an organic place within the framework of our general model.

Continuity and hierarchy

In the foregoing semiosis of the beginning of the Fifth Symphony we may notice that single levels follow each other with continuity and according to a hierarchy. Figure 1 illustrates both relationships and clarifies some of their implications.

a.   Musical competence appears as a stratification *per genera et species*, from the 'human' to the 'social', to the specifically 'musical', becoming more and more qualified in an artistic sense.

b.   In this model, moving from the 'base' GC, every level includes all the

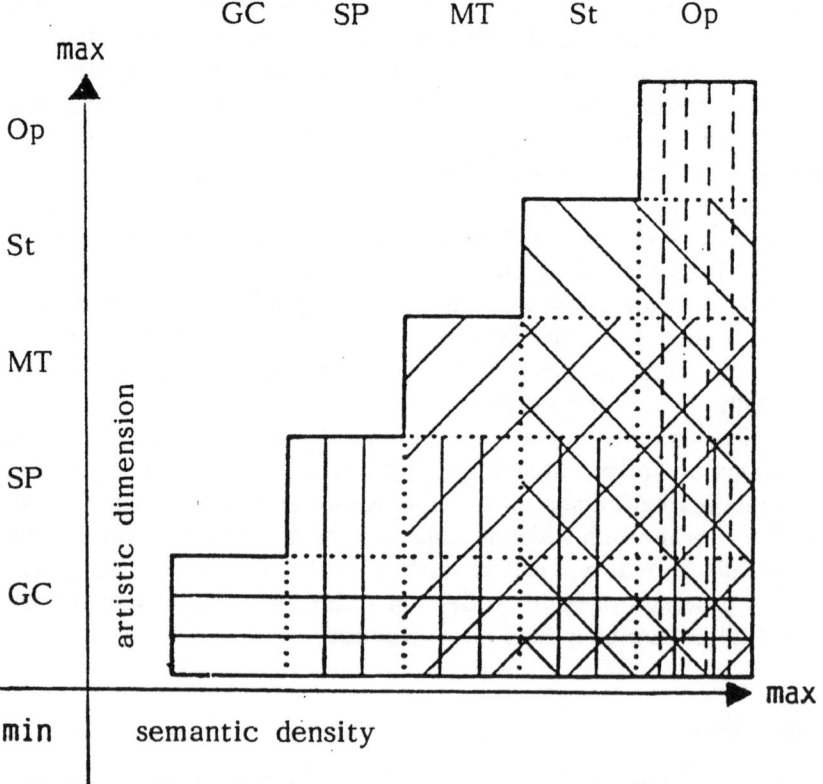

Figure 1.

preceding ones. This property of inclusion forms the basis for the following remarks.

c.   Musical competence develops across two axes or dimensions, namely the 'artistic dimension' and 'semantic density'. Taking these terms in their obvious sense, we underline the fact that the type of competence is defined by the intersection of these two axes. For example, the minimal competence is not placed at the GC level, but at the intersection GC–GC. In fact, at the intersection GC–Op we find the optimum competence, whereas at Op–Op the artistic dimension is semantically rarefied and poor. It would be easy to describe other types of competence in this way.

d.   Figure 1 illustrates the ambiguity of musical objects and discourses. For instance, the 'strokes' at the beginning of the Fifth Symphony are indeed at GC level; now, in our description they run across all intersections with other levels, including GC–Op.

Such an arrangement of the MMC might seem the most obvious, if not the only possible one. However, it does not show certain relationships between the levels, for example, the double and equal relationship which joins St with MT as well as with SP, according to our previous description. This arrangement of the MMC is therefore a partial one, and implies a choice which should already be evident, but which will be worth explaining.

High, popular, and common competence

By means of the foregoing scheme we may show, somewhat roughly and provisionally, the relationship between two different approaches to musical experience which I propose to call 'high competence' and 'popular competence'.

In brief, high (or highbrow) competence tends to approach music in a way which is specifically and autonomously artistic; it therefore considers the Op level as most pertinent and the 'lower' ones to be less pertinent the lower they are. In contrast, popular competence displays an appropriation of music which is global and heteronomous ('functional'); consequently, it exploits mostly GC and SP levels. The 'upper' ones are less pertinent the higher they are. Both types of competence are summarized in Figure 2.

The relationship between both types is further articulated in Figure 3. Within the area of general competence we also find a competence which is common to both the above-named types, as well as a space for a possible development of either one or another.

18   *G. Stefani*

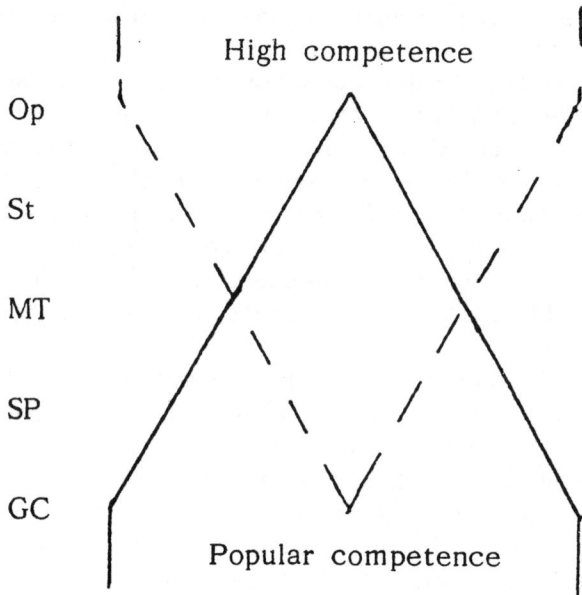

Op

St

MT

SP

GC

Figure 2.

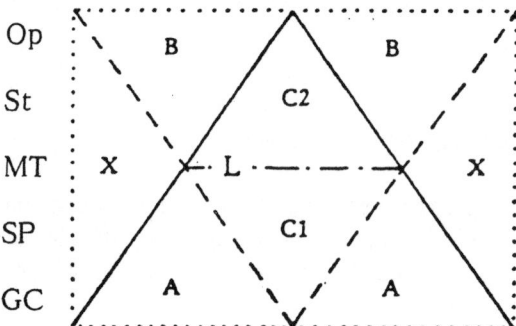

Figure 3.

A: basic zone of popular competence, not pertinent to the high;
B: basic zone of high competence, not pertinent to the popular;
L: line or limit (presumed) between the two competences;
C: common zone, subdivided into:
    C1:   a space in the general competence which is considered of no interest by high competence ('roots' either ignored or hidden);
    C2:   a space which is considered to be forbidden for popular competence and reserved for the experts;
X: potential field of sense production not yet saturated with actual competences, and open to both directions.

A theory of musical competence 19

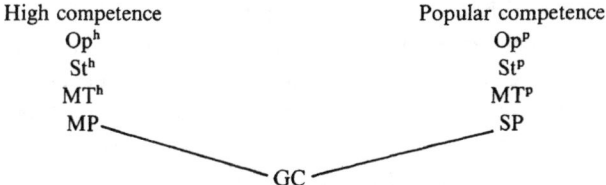

High competence   Popular competence
Op^h Op^p
St^h St^p
MT^h MT^p
MP   SP
                    GC

Figure 4.

Figure 3 is a rough and provisional scheme in that one can easily point out the divergence between competences at SP level. In fact, high competence tends to attract the whole production of sense into the range of the more specifically musical practices (for example, concert), whereas popular competence employs music and sounds mostly in other (social) contexts. Further levels would be influenced accordingly. We might therefore propose Figure 4 (where h = high, p = popular, and MP = Musical Practices).

Approaches, projects, disciplines

The scalar form of our MMC so far illustrated does not take into account every single approach to music which we find in everyday life. In fact, each social project with music involves privileging one level or another, which then naturally becomes a center of gravity for the others. We therefore need a scheme of reference wherein all levels may move freely to form all kinds of combination and hierarchy. This happens in Figure 5, where levels are equidistant (topologically equivalent) in respect to a central point (the musical object, producer, or observer).

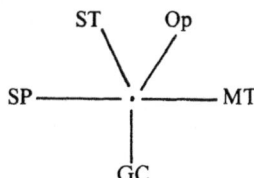

ST   Op

SP ———·——— MT

GC

Figure 5.

Let us superimpose upon this diagram some approaches and projects.
1. Adorno's ideal hearer realizes the model 'continuity and hierarchy' according to high competence (see Figure 2), thus forming a triangle St–MT–Op (vertex).

20   *G. Stefani*

2.   A 'resentful' hearer or the fan of a certain musical genre (baroque, jazz, opera, etcetera) points to St surrounded by SP and MT.

3.   An 'emotive' hearer operates a short circuit between GC and Op, bypassing all cultural codes. The same happens in music therapy centered on the hearing of musical work (Guilhot et al. 1964).

4.   Amateur practice attracts GC (customs and motivations for playing) as well as MT into a project which is based on the SP level (i.e., 'playing' without any reference to the MT quality of performance).

5.   On the contrary, professional practice is centered on MT, with reference to St quality too, and sometimes original creation (Op).

6.   As for composition, authors in the traditional sense trace the same diagram as the ideal highbrow hearer (see 1). But this is not always the case; for example, Verdi or Berio (1981) seem often to start from a platform where SP and MT are equally important; hence they aim toward Op; in their 'gestural' poetics the St level is overlooked, becoming pertinent only afterward, for critics and the highbrow public.

7.   Other compositional poetics overlook MT mediation. So it is for certain total improvization, informal ways of playing instruments, repetitive 'minimal' music, stochastic composition, etcetera. Here musical experience results from applying to sound material some principles or models drawn from GC and SP levels (psychophysiological behaviors or logical processes, mathematical or physical models, etcetera). In the most 'experimental' projects, the resulting Op may not be relevant.

8.   Our basic model can encompass even the most radical and elementary projects on music, for example, Cage's project according to which musical experience or competence is reduced to 'opening your ears', that is to sensorial-perceptive schemes at GC level; or Paynter's projects of 'composition for everybody', based upon the observation of all kinds of everyday events (at GC and SP level).

9.   Case 8 is also the basic reference for a competence exercised by musical psychology, when centered on music perception at GC levels. Various branches of this discipline then build various paths of sense between this basic level and the 'upper' ones, for example:

   GC–MT: psychological contents of musical systems (Kurth 1969; Wellek 1963; Meyer 1956; and Francès 1958);

   GC–Op: effects of works on subjects (music-therapy) and subjective meaning of works (experimental semantics);

   GC–St: style psychology.

10.   In a similar way, sense production by the sociology of music consists in correlating to a privileged SP level first of all practices and institutions, followed by St, and more rarely MT (Weber 1921; Blaukopf 1972; Lowinsky 1941; and Marothy 1974).

11.   Theory of music obviously takes MT as its point of reference and special group of codes; the more it applies the other codes to these, the more technical competence acquires cultural density. The favorite correlations are MT–St and MT–Op, which ordinarily constitute music analysis. The MT–GC and MT–Sp paths tend to coincide (although from opposite starting points) respectively with the psychology and sociology of musical systems.

12.   As for musical criticism, it favors St and Op. Reference to other levels occurs subsequently in order to characterize its special trends (psycho-sociological, formal-analytic, or 'structural' criticism).

13.   In terms of the present theory, a 'historical competence' in music appears to be the ability of the 'upper' levels (SP, MT, St, Op) to correlate and/or structure each other with reference to the whole span of Western culture or to some of its points, sometimes including a diachronic look at the levels themselves and their correlations. Describing the manifold activity which goes under the name of 'history of music' on the basis of this model would no doubt be a very interesting if very time-consuming task.

14.   Finally, semiotics of music is the discipline whose object is musical competence as we have defined it. It is, therefore, the discipline which formulated the above theory and should also criticize it.

References

Adorno, Theodor Wiesengrund (1962). *Einleitung in der Musiksoziologie*. Frankfurt: Suhrkamp.

Asafiev, Boris V. (1976). *Die musikalische Form als Prozess*. Berlin: Verlag Neue Musik.

Berio, Luciano (1981). *Intervista sulla musica*, a cura di R. Dalmonte. Bari: Laterza.

Blacking, John (1973). *How Musical is Man*. Seattle: University of Washington Press.

Blaukopf, Kurt (1972). *Musiksoziologie*. Niederteufen: Niggli.

Boulez, Pierre (1963). *Penser la musique aujourd'hui*. Paris: Gonthier.

Cage, John (1961). *Silence*. Middletown, Connecticut: Wesleyan University Press.

Cooke, Deryck (1958). *The Language of Music*. London: Oxford University Press.

Francès, Robert (1958). *La perception de la musique*. Paris: Vrin.

Guilhot, J., Guilhot, M. A., and Jost, J. (1964). *Musique psychologie et psychotérapie*. Paris: Editions Sociales Françaises.

Karolyi, Otto (1965). *Introducing Music*. Harmondsworth: Penguin.

Kurth, Ernst (1969). *Musikpsychologie*. Hildesheim: Olms.

Laske, Otto (1975). Musical semantics: A procedural point of view, in *Actes du 1er Congrès International de Sémiotique Musicale/Proceedings of the 1st International Congress on Semiotics of Music*, G. Stefani (ed.). Pesaro: Centro di Iniziativa Culturale.

Lowinsky, Edward E. (1941). The Concept of Physical and Musical Space in the Renaissance. Papers of the American Musicological Society, 57.

Maróthy, János (1974). *Music and the Bourgeois, Music and the Proletarian*. Budapest: Akadémiai Kiadó.

22   G. Stefani

Meyer, Leonard B. (1956). *Emotion and Meaning in Music*. Chicago: University of Chicago Press.
—(1973). *Explaining Music*. Berkeley: University of California Press.
Nattiez, Jean-Jacques (1975). *Fondements d'une sémiologie de la musique*. Paris: Union Générale d'Editions.
Paynter, John and Aston, Peter (1970). *Sound and Silence*. Cambridge: Cambridge University Press.
Weber, Max (1921). *Die rationalen und soziologischen Grundlagen der Musik*. München.
Wellek, Albert (1963). *Musikpsychologie und Musikaesthetik. Grundriss der Systematischen Musikwissenschaft*. Frankfurt: Akademische Verlagsgesellschaft.
Willems, Edgar (1933). *L'oreille musicale*. Genève: Droz.

Gino Stefani (b. 1929) is Professor of Semiotics of Music at the University of Bologna, Italy. His research is primarily concerned with developing a comprehensive theory of musical competence. Among his publications are *Musica barocca. Poetica e ideologia* (1974), *Introduzione alla semiotica della musica* (1976), *Insegnare la musica* (1977), and *La competenza musicale* (1982).

[3]

Can we get rid of the 'popular' in popular music? A virtual symposium with contributions from the International Advisory Editors of *Popular Music*

Recently we have been talking in the Editorial Group of the journal about the term 'popular', and wondering in particular about its epithetic role next to 'music'. Some of us have questioned what the term now means, partly because it has been used less and less in media studies and cultural sociology over the last few years. Others have pointed to the fact that it remains a vital concept, even a rallying point, in certain fields such as musicology and politics.

To follow up this issue we decided to run a virtual symposium and invite contributions from the International Advisory Editors of the journal. As you will see, the response was enthusiastic. Over a three–week period in May and June 2004, twenty-three email postings on the topic were submitted. We publish them all in full here.

Perhaps this exchange will prompt a wider debate; or perhaps we can leave the 'popular' alone for another few years. Whatever the outcome of the symposium, though, reflections on the state of our field are, as always, invited for consideration for this section.

The International Advisory Editors

1. Simon Frith, 21 May

I'm not sure whether your concern here is the use/meaning of the term 'popular' as it is used generally, or the use of the term 'popular music'. In neither case are the problems of what's meant here new: debates about the meaning of the term 'popular' have always been central to its use in cultural studies/music studies. Indeed, one could say that the meaning of 'popular' in the academy is determined by the fact that it must be argued about (it has never been easily defined against a straightforward contrasting term, 'unpopular', say).

So the question is whether the meaning of the term has become particularly problematic/redundant in the last few years. Not to my mind. For what it's worth, in the *Critical Concepts* volumes I edited for Routledge, I suggested that 'popular music' was a useful term, describing:

Music made commercially, in a particular kind of legal (copyright) and economic (market) system; music made using an ever-changing technology of sound storage; music significantly experienced as mass mediated; music primarily made for social and bodily pleasure; music which is formally hybrid.

There is a specific object of study here that must be approached differently from other kinds of music.

2. Alf Björnberg, 23 May

For a musicologist, the question of course is: What 'other kinds of music' are there? In a recent dictionary article, I have argued that (translated from the Danish original):

Technological and social developments in the course of the 20th century have resulted in several musical genres, from the point of view of production, distribution, function and use, having increasingly assumed popular-musical characteristics, for instance, the overwhelming part of historical art music or forms of non-western music previously not included in the circulation processes of the transnational music industry (cf. 'world music'). Rather than designating a particular genre or group of genres, the concept of 'popular music' could thus to an increasing extent be said to define the general conditions of music in contemporary information society.

This is arguably one of the main reasons for the current crisis within musicology, manifested in the increasingly problematic status of traditional genre categories and, particularly, the growing awareness of the irrelevance of music analysis, as it is usually done, to real-life reception situations. Both theoretically and methodologically, musicology – and its potential contribution to popular music studies – has much to gain and little to lose from a dismantling of the distinction between 'popular music' and 'music'.

3. Peter Manuel, 23 May

Although defining the 'popular' in 'popular music' is by now an old and perhaps tired topic, it hasn't gone away, and in case anyone is interested, I offer my two cents worth. The goal is clearly not to standardise a hegemonic definition *per se*, but to suggest a useful working definition that may be handy for rough taxonomies in discussion, etc. For better or worse, my thinking on the subject has not evolved at all since my 1988 *Popular Musics of the Non-Western World*. In that book I echoed some general criteria made by the editors of the journal *Popular Music*, and suggested that a primary criterion should be that the music's style can be seen to have evolved in connection with its dissemination by the mass media, as embedded in a music industry based on marketing of recordings on a mass commodity basis. There will be many ambiguities and grey areas, of course, but I still use this definition. I find Simon Frith's definition (above) insightful, as a presentation of a set of typical features of much popular music, but I think there is much music that we would be inclined to call 'popular' that has only some, rather than all, of these characteristics (e.g., is Paul McCartney's 'Blackbird' formally hybrid and made for bodily pleasure? I'm not so sure, except in the most general sense . . .)

4. Motti Regev, 23 May

'Popular music' is still a very useful term. It relates to a modern and late modern socio-cultural context, or space, of music production and consumption. We may not agree on the exact parameters of this context, but I believe the list provided by Simon Frith has the core features of such a context, or space – except maybe for the issue of function. I agree with Peter Manuel that 'music made for social or bodily pleasure' does not cover the whole range of uses and functions of popular music.

Another reason to keep using 'popular music' is the difference between this term and 'pop/rock'. We tend to conflate the difference between the two, and thus lose the cultural specificity of 'pop/rock'. In other words, 'popular music' covers wider ground than 'pop/rock'. As socio-cultural phenomena, all pop/rock styles, genres, scenes, etc., are 'popular music'. But many frameworks of 'popular music' are not pop/rock' (chanson, MPB, tango, flamenco, etc.). I think keeping in mind the difference between the two is important in order to better understand the changing relations between 'pop/rock' and other forms of popular music. I have in mind mostly what I have called the 'pop/rockisation' of popular music.

5. *Philip Tagg, 24 May*

The Messy P in PM. The 'PM' in 'IASPM' originally sought to do no more than label what was, around 1980, still in the dustbin of conventional academe, i.e. all the music ('musical practices', if you prefer) excluded from repertoires/canons then deemed fit for serious study in established institutions in the West (supply 'bang-bang' and 'Iraq' if you like, too).

What a messy label, that P in PM! The class character of the education and research establishment changes and their cannons along with them, so now that much rock (+ 'practices' again, please supply hereinafter, if you prefer), especially 'classical' rock, is about as disconnected from the social dynamic of its genesis and development as jazz was fifteen years earlier. Now delimitable as a relatively stable historical repertoire, rock can be study-packaged and recycled like Western European art music, or like the music of nomadic or rural communities which no longer exist as such and which constitute legitimate territories for ethnomusicological safaris, or like the revolutionary instrumental music of the late eighteenth- and early nineteenth-century European bourgeoisie had become by 1870, etc.

Clearly, what might have been a convenient English-language label for an educational-political agenda in 1980 had, by the 1990s, become a conceptual liability. Sorry, but in 1985 I argued that if the 'P' hadn't disappeared from 'IASPM' by 2000, we might have failed in our democratic efforts to integrate ALL types of music into the institutions of education and research where we worked (http://tagg.org/articles/montreal.html). I certainly agree with other colleagues (e.g. Peter Manuel and Alf Björnberg) that it may be useful to define the P of PM in terms of mass-mediatisation to the extent that, in 1981, I insisted that IASPM's letter-head should be bilingual (latterly suppressed) and that the French version should read *Association international pour l'étude de la musique des mass-média*. Therein lie three more problems.

Restricting the first problem to Latin languages, it is clear that 'popular music' (English) is clearly not the same as *musique populaire* or *música popular*. It is definitely not the same as *musica popolare* because the Italians, when referring to the sort of studies many IASPM-ites carry out, write and say *la popular music*, in the same way as the French sometimes refer to English-language cultural studies notions of twentieth-century French linguistic/literary/semiotic theory and philosophy as *la French theory*. 'Popular music' can, in other words, be seen as an Anglocentric term reflecting cultural, social and economic categories particular to English-speaking areas of the world, particularly those in North America and the UK.

The second problem concerns the fact that not all music still excluded from the various institutionally sanctioned cannons is mass-mediated. For example, singing 'Happy Birthday' or 'Auld Lang Syne', singing in the shower, chanting at football matches, chanting school playground rhymes, and other widespread (and popular) musical practices, don't often make it into the 'popular music' syllabus or into the pages of *Popular Music*.

The third conceptual problem concerns the changing nature of the mass media since the establishment of IASPM and of *Popular Music* (journal). Since the advent of TV (1950s) and home video (1950s), more people living in the media-saturated culture to which I belong hear more music in conjunction with moving pictures than in any other way (DVD in mid-to-late 1990s). The fact that computer games, with their more or less constant music, generate greater global sales than those of the music industry, reinforces this observation. There may, in other words, also be a problem with the term 'music' in that the audiovisual dimension of music, currently so important in the mediation of values and attitudes (games, advertising, film and TV scoring, etc., etc.), is overlooked because we are stuck in a technological time warp of the auditory as somehow distinctly separable from other senses (the visual, gestural, kinetic, tactile, etc.). How we were ever to understand what music was about without considering its synaesthetic aspects was always a mystery to me. How we are supposed to meaningfully study the social and cultural mechanisms of music in today's digital and audiovisual media by focusing so much on what can be stored and distributed on sound carriers surpasses the limits of my understanding altogether.

To summarise: 'popular' was a historically necessary label qualifying the undemocratically excluded. Those parts of the excluded now included, thanks to our efforts, will, due to the inherent inertia of the institutions in which we work (often top-heavy managerialist bureaucracies), tend to be those compatible with such inertia (e.g. socially dying or dead cultural practices). Meanwhile, 'things change', including social, cultural and economic power relations, and we are responsible for some of the good and bad our democratic efforts have resulted in. In my view, there is no point in throwing in the towel here, saying 'that's how institutions are and that's where we work, so let's just consolidate the tiny niches we've managed to carve out', because (i) that's no fun, and (ii) it doesn't help those growing up in the digital audiovisual age under quite different social, cultural and economic circumstances, with quite different socialisation (Habermas sense) strategies, etc. In my opinion, the conceptual messiness of the P in PM may in fact still be one of its most useful characteristics. Sooner or later we may have to switch labels and, if this correspondence is anything to go by, it may be sooner rather than later. Good! Let's DO something!

6. Barbara Bradby, 25 May

The irony of our claim that we don't mean 'popular-as-opposed-to-unpopular' (and that we're really talking about commodified-music-globally) is that somewhere at the core of commodified music is the 'institutional reflexivity' of the charts. This makes records peculiar commodities since the community of *consumers* reflects weekly on their (commercial) success, i.e. popularity. (One analogy is racehorses and racing results/'form' – cf. Louis Walsh's 'stable'; but in pop music, the favourite is always the winner.) A recent CD gift from Bolivia is called *Los mejores sayas*: the best ones. I bet these were the ones that sold the most records/got the most airplay. Markets have structured popularity, and we cannot rescue it at will for our definitional pleasure.

But what about non-commodified music, not in the old sense of songs sung in the home, or school bands, but in the new one of digital music circulating in 'free' (but for how long?) space on the Internet? 'Hits' on sites or 'shared files' look like a new form of popularity replacing the old market form of chart 'hits'. Alternatively, if going online is part of avoiding popularity and valuing obscurity, then are we really talking about 'popular music' any more?

7. Marcus Breen, 25 May

If this question of the popular in popular music is a dilemma, it is one that is resolved by will and commitment. By that I mean that popular is a trope, a talisman, a symbol of a particularity of production that signifies a position vis-à-vis known reality. This position is the result of choices that are made to invest particular types of cultural production with meaning. The implication is that types of music are called popular because of their resonance within a group of users. Diverse readings of popular music are made by users whose consumption is based on dynamic forms of knowledge. This knowledge is contingent, but from a structural and intellectual perspective has meaning only so far as its use may generate multiple dynamics of other as yet unknown or unanticipated uses. Replete with possibilities, the meaning of popular should include multiple meanings in an open-ended universalism. For example, John Coltrane came from North Carolina (where I currently live), and I imagine that for him in the racist south, jazz as he thought and played it was popular. I now listen to his music as representing a new set of possibilities for the popular. To remove the term popular, is to remove the range of possibilities for inventing new meaning in music's cultural production. Another way of exploring the idea of the popular is to make otherwise canon-like art and classical music popular, as indeed it increasingly is (see, for example, filmic efforts of my fellow countryman, Australian Baz Lurhman).

8. Deena Weinstein, 25 May

My take on POPULAR (I'll chicken out of the music part) is as the binary to ELITE. That dichotomy was breached a bit in the nineteenth century as composers like Tchaikovsky incorporated 'folk' (read popular) melodies into his works. But in the postmodern era (are we now in the post-postmodern era?) such either/ors were declared obsolete. Didn't you get that memo? (Bands from Deep Purple to Metallica 'working' with symphony orchestras, and much prog-rock, tried to have it both ways.)

On another tack, the distinctions between the extremes of mainstream and specialised/subcultural/cultish/etc. musics seem seriously significant – yet all of this continuum is called, unhelpfully, POPULAR.

9. Jason Toynbee, 26 May

I want to pick up on a theme developed by some of the 'popular' sceptics (Björnberg, Tagg, Bradby, Weinstein) in the debate so far. It is this. Ostensibly popular music includes:

- Classical music (Vanessae Mae, Wagner at this year's Glastonbury Festival in England)
- Non-mediated and non-commodified forms (chanting, shower singing)
- Mediated but non-commodified music (on the Internet)

138   *A virtual symposium*

- Mediated, commodified but un-popular forms (esoteric/alternative/ underground)
- Mediated, commodified music emerging from folk and classical traditions in the third world (world music)

Two questions then follow: Can the multi-aspect definition of popular music which 'popular' affirmers (Frith, Manuel, Regev, Breen) have been using cope with these exceptions? If it can, what is the nature of the music which is left outside PM?

10. *Juan Pablo Gonzalez, 26 May*

Regarding Simon Frith's reference to a 'music significantly experienced as mass mediated', I should say that normally the 'mass mediated' is understood regarding public consumption, and not musical learning, which is capital in the process of artistic/cultural transmission in popular music. The Record (physical or virtual) is the professor, the tradition, and the school in popular music (commodified or not, popular or un-popular, and even folk-rooted!).

Regarding Alf Björnberg, I agree that the popular field has influenced art music and 'world music', defining 'general conditions of music in contemporary information society'. However, are we ready for a dismantling of the distinction between 'popular music' and 'music'? I believe that it is necessary to speak not only about popular music but of Popular Musicology for a while, at least in the Latin American Academy, just to make noise.

Regarding Motti Regev's and Philip Tagg's comments, in Spanish (as Italian), popular music has been related to oral tradition and folklore, because we understand 'popular' as related to the people, even of small communities. However, regarding the general conditions of music in the contemporary information society, oral tradition is in fact 'contaminated' by mass mediation, and there is a big mess in Latin American folk studies regarding the 'pure', the 'contaminated' and the 'revival' of folklore. In the III Conference of the Latin American branch of IASPM in Bogotá (Colombia), the local institution announced IASPM-LA as . . . the study of Popular Musics (plural) of Latin America, and in fact we had many papers on folklore, that in the Conferences of Mexico (2002) and Rio de Janeiro (2004) we excluded. We are proudly contaminated, not pure.

Regarding the second question by Jason Toynbee, the nature of the music which is left outside PM, again, we should focus on the ways the performer is trained and receives his/her artistic/cultural tradition or 'capital'. This happens by the direct teaching of a Professor in classical music, and the reading of scores, ideally, an *Urtext* that is expressing faithfully the will of The Composer (this does not happen, for instance with U2 covering Cole Porter). In relation to the 'shower or birthday tradition', I do not perform (performing needs public, real or virtual), just sing. In the oral – or rather aural – folk tradition, I repeat what I see and hear directly, not in a mediated way. Maybe I have a musician to teach me (my father) and I want to be faithful to him. It is not 'my sound' which matters (as in popular music) but the sound of a community: modern values in popular music versus traditional values in folk music (also interacting).

11. *Martin Stokes, 26 May*

We habitually use the term 'popular' to indicate certain processes of musical circulation and transmission: music that is mass-mediated via specialised and complex technologies, in markets, and in the sway of certain well-defined public discourses about 'popularity' that mark both production and consumption. But there is a great deal of music which surrounds us in our everyday lives that is not 'popular' in this sense: music we have learned from family and friends, music in contexts of organised religion, sport, workplaces, educational institutions, urban soundscapes, and many other things. I agree with Barbara: I don't think we can dispense with the word 'popular' when 'popularity' is a structural property of certain kinds of musical experience that are prominent in modern life. However, I do think we need a broader field of vision, since these multiple systems of circulation, mediation and transmission (of which 'the popular' constitutes just one) inform one another and relate to one another. The question is whether this broader field of vision needs a name, and the problem that attaches to the question is that anthropologists, folklorists, ethnomusicologists and others can all, more or less plausibly, lay claim to it in terms of the kind of work that they do these days. I am more than happy to hang on to the notion of 'popular music studies', since this refers to a tradition we've built up over the last decades, committed to democratic political possibilities and engagement with everyday, material, practices and forms. It seems like a better place than most to engage intellectually and politically with *all* music, and that – for me – has always got to be the goal.

12. David Brackett, 26 May

Within the context in which I teach – a faculty of music in a large North American university – 'popular music' still serves a clear function. Here 'popular music' is defined negatively as the music (along with non-Western music) that is not taught in all the other courses offered by the faculty of music, or, for that matter, in instrumental/vocal lessons or in performing ensembles. Compared to jazz and classical music (institutionally distinct categories in this case), popular music is the new kid on the block. My main point is related to how popular music is understood in this context: despite the fact that no category of 'unpopular music' exists, 'popular music' as a category only makes sense in relation to other types of music. The instability of this relationship from moment to moment, and its inter-subjective variability according to who is doing the categorising, make 'popular music' a cloudy, albeit still useful concept.

13. Larry Witzleben, 27 May

In Asian Studies, 'popular culture' is used in a much broader sense than is common in popular music studies, and often has a historical dimension. It often overlaps with 'folk' culture, but there is also often an association with literacy, as in 'popular literature' (printed and published, but using vernacular language) or 'popular religion' (based on written scriptures, but heterodox and regionally diverse). Limiting our main focus to mass-mediated post-industrial popular music is practical in many ways, but perhaps we should keep in mind that this is also a subset of a larger – and older – category of popular music simply as music which has mass appeal and distribution.

I don't mean to take us off on a tangent, but I think it will be useful to also consider the dimensions of orality and literacy in popular music. It is true that much popular music is aurally transmitted (i.e. learning guitar licks from a recording), and its accessibility to those who do not have (written) music literacy is central to its appeal and aesthetics, but (at least in some cultures) there is also an important written component in everything from karaoke to fake books to *Rolling Stone.*

14. *Helmi Järviluoma, 27 May*

I have always liked the rigorous confusion around 'popular music' as one category of music amongst others, existing only in relation to other categories. To me it is not particularly interesting to try to find one more top-down – and as Morag Shiach has noted, often men's – definition of the 'popular' according to its contents. Rather, it is interesting to hear how, when and where it is used and needed; how its contents are being produced historically and situationally in the shifting tide waters of 'high' and 'low'. Out goes the dream of sameness. As some feminist theorists might put it, it is useful for us both to use the term ('do it') and 'trouble it' simultaneously. Perhaps 'the university rescue mission in search for the voiceless' (Visweswaran) is not as obvious within popular music studies as it used to be, but on the other hand, I do not feel that we would, in all parts of the world, have carved a too comfortable niche (cf. Tagg) for critical popular music studies. Let's go on troubling it.

15. *Jason Toynbee, 3 June*

Some recent contributors have emphasised the need to hold on to the popular for what might be described as pragmatic reasons. First, popular fits many, if not all, of the kinds of music we want to discuss. Second, it gets at a kind of cultural/musical formation which is typical of globalising modernity. Third it is a label which refers to our own tradition of scholarship; it is a banner signifying continuity and common interest.

What about the politics of the popular? Some contributors have touched on this, most recently Helmi Järviluoma. Yet the political dimension of the popular has not really been much discussed in the symposium to date. This is in contrast to the situation in the early days of popular music studies when PM was often heard as representing oppressed peoples, or else transgressing and mocking the ruling class.

In the period since, the politics of identity (ethnic, gendered, sexual) has tended to eclipse class-based criticism in the academy. Of course there has been a considerable amount of work which reflects this new kind of politics. But for me that itself raises questions about politics and the popular: In what sense are feminist, queer or black approaches to music also popular? Is there a popular aesthetics in music which extends beyond particular identities to encompass people in struggle more generally?

16. *David Hesmondhalgh, 3 June*

It's true that discussions of the problems of the popular are nothing new. Fifteen years ago, the first few pages of Richard Middleton's *Studying Popular Music* cut elegantly through the worst of the thickets surrounding the term, as applied to music, but recognised that quests for absolute definitions were folly. Nevertheless, it would be wrong to imply that the urgency surrounding the popular has remained consistently present in debates about music, and about culture. In fact, the popular as a political concept has suffered a spectacular fall from grace since its heyday of the 1980s. There are various reasons for this, but a very important one is the decline of the concept of 'the people', and this in turn is related to the complex fate of the utopian project of socialism. Stuart Hall, writing in 1981, in a collection called *People's History and Socialist Theory*, felt that the study of popular culture should always start with 'the double movement of containment and resistance'. Such talk of struggle, resistance, socialism and the people can today often feel like the language of a distant era, even to those of us who believe in greater equality and social justice. For some, the forces of conservatism are responsible for marginalising this language. But the popular and 'the people' didn't decline only because of the rise of neo-liberalism. They have also suffered because of the problems of utopianism and populism, because some have sought justifiably to question falsely universalising claims made in the name of the people.

Alongside the political defeats and disunities of the last twenty years, there have been positive developments in music studies. Particularly encouraging has been the increasing tendency to look at particular musical genres, formations, etc., as part of the whole musical field. This is apparent in studies, some of them influenced by Bourdieu, which look at questions of legitimisation and canonisation in music; in the best studies of the political economy of music; in some inspiring critical musicology and ethnomusicology; and more problematically in work on music and everyday life (this term has the same democratising and levelling intent as the popular, but while – usefully for some – it avoids the Marxian connotations of the popular, it can easily collapse into a bland pluralism). It's within the context of this important analytical move towards viewing the whole musical field that I think the notion of the popular should be retained, as a potent reminder of the utopian impulse in much musical experience, but with its problematic political legacy forefronted and questioned. In this respect, a revival of debates about the popular may have the useful benefit of making links between the study of music and the most important political question of our time: how to reconcile equality and difference.

17. Bruce Johnson, 3 June

My contribution to the discussion on 'popular music' begins by noting the usefulness of the debate, which couldn't really have been conducted without the term 'popular' itself. I am probably stating the obvious, then, when I say that, as a teacher, I use the word as a platform for such debate. Like a lot of terms by which culture is conceptualised, we discuss it 'because it is there'. I don't much care for fascism, and would like to see it off the planet; but I can't teach twentieth-century history without referring to it. 'Popular' is part of the cultural discourse and, like other 'stones in the pathway', whether you want them there or not, we, and students, can't help but stumble over them. You can't avoid them without noticing them, and for students, you have to explain why they should (or not) be avoided. I teach several university courses which incorporate in their platform such terms ('Art' and, alas, 'Postmodernism' and 'Poststructuralism' are others), and the usefulness of these courses is primarily in their progressive critique of such terms.

I think we probably agree that there are certain ways in which the term 'popular music' is widely but misleadingly used. In an age of globalised mass mediations, there is little if any music that is not potentially 'popular' in the . . . well . . . popular sense of the word. Applied simplistically as a taxonimiser of musical forms, for example, it is a cover for cultural politics. It is that kind of subterfuge which becomes the subject of my courses, and if I didn't recognise the existence of the term 'popular', I couldn't discuss in such a lucid way the operations of, for example, hegemony or ideology. A

142   *A virtual symposium*

sustained examination of the term also helps to demonstrate that cultural concepts are not positivistic, that they don't have an autonomous existence, that the way they are used depends on context, that they need to be addressed in relation to their 'neighbours' in the suburbs of music, some of whom sleep over at each other's houses. These neighbours live at addresses like 'art' music, 'folk' music, and (a term I find increasingly useful) 'vernacular' music. I define vernacularity as the character of being consumed by its producers, and that the more those two categories overlap (as, say, in a church congregation), the more vernacular is the outcome. It is precisely the problems in the protean term 'popular' that help me to talk to students about the general cultural neighbourhood, its politics, its secrets and lies.

18. Allan Moore, 4 June

I too am inclined to value the term 'vernacular', which seems to be increasingly relevant as the processes of 'production' become technologically open to more and more people. Unexpectedly (to me), the dominant line in this debate seems to be that, while (presumably) we concur with the notion that the study of popular music is an interdisciplinary matter, we don't demonstrate an interdisciplinary understanding of what it is. And it's only when a term becomes uncontested that it really loses its value.

19. Dave Laing, 6 June

Two points on the discursive status of 'popular music' (PM)

The term operates at such a high level of abstraction that it can only be usefully defined by what it excludes. This is clear from Toynbee's initial list of practices/genres that are or might be PM. It is difficult to see in what way they are the same unless it is in their common difference to or exclusion from equally abstract categories such as Classical Music, Folk Music, etc., etc.

While the initial postulation of PM as an object worthy of study was indeed heroic (rescuing music rejected by the Academy), that is no longer the case everywhere. The symposium shows that this contestatory function is still relevant in some contexts, but there is also a conservative tendency that assumes the Anglophone connotations of PM have global validity (back to the Enlightenment project!). Gonzales' comments on the Hispanic and Italian discursive fields are a reminder that the Anglophone notion of PM is not universalisable even if Jim Reeves cassettes can be found in every capital city in the world. Recent experience editing articles for the forthcoming 'Locations' volumes of the *Encyclopaedia of the Popular* (sic!) *Music of the World* has reminded me forcefully of cultural difference. I can add to Gonzales' list of 'exceptions' that *musique populaire* is much closer to the Hispanic term than to PM, and that the conceptual relationship between the classical and the modern (popular) in Arab music discourse is of a very different type to its counterpart in Anglophonia and elsewhere in Western and Northern Europe.

20. Barbara Bradby, 15 June

Tower Records' website has a great search-engine and database of recorded songs. The category I find myself searching is now called 'All music (except classical)'. I love the contradictory imperialism of this claim! 'All music' ('oh well, not quite all music'). It seems pretty similar to what we claim with 'popular'.

21. Line Grenier, 22 June

I find far less intriguing and relevant what the terms 'popular' or 'popular music' mean as abstract terms, than how they operate conjuncturally in the public discourses of specific individual, collective or institutional agents. In the conjuncture of contemporary Québec (where my research practice is situated, and one of the places from which I speak), 'popular music' and *musique populaire* (often deemed distinct yet related terms) tend to function as what Berthelot calls discursive operators: under the auspices of an assumed common taken-for-grantedness, they are used to talk simultaneously about something else (who the true creators are, what is authorship, who in the music business should receive public finding, for example). Rather than simply examining what 'popular' or 'popular music' contain as general taxonomic categories, I find it important and productive to question how they are produced, mobilised, transformed, contested, 'troubled', (cf. Helmi Järviluoma) and policed as (integral parts of) specific classificatory (hence both descriptive and normative) devices. I find especially challenging projects aimed at developing empirically based understandings of particular politics of the popular and their workings. I don't know of any better way in which to try to understand, for example, the unfading salience and usefulness of 'popular music' and *musique populaire* in Québec, and, more importantly perhaps, the effectivity of these classificatory devices and the ability of the particular cultural dispositifs which make them possible to articulate music to various 'non-musical' areas of social life.

22. Peter Wicke, 22 June

To me, the term 'popular music' is a pure discursive operator, without any fixed meaning or content, used to draw ever-shifting borders on a highly contested cultural ground. In Germany this usage of the term can be followed back till the late eighteenth century where it served, already as a heavily debated category, to distinguish 'real folk music' (Herder) as musical expression of 'the people' (the constructed subject of the bourgeois nation state) from the musics of the rabble. What this meant in musical terms depended on the authors, their views, ideology and aesthetic preferences. I can't see that much has changed since then.

To reconstruct the discursive operations mediated by this term on the musical and cultural field seems to me a much more promising academic undertaking than any attempt to fix it in a generic way. That doesn't mean that any music is popular music but it certainly means that there is not much left which couldn't become popular music given the present alliance of social and cultural forces, technological and commercial structures. The field for this discursive operation became in every respect boundless, and so the more important became this operator itself to draw these shifting and crossing lines linked today to the term 'popular music'.

23. Richard Middleton, 25 June

Despite the range of views apparent across the contributions, two overarching positions are visible, which we might term 'descriptivist' and 'discursivist', respectively. In the first, (variable) empirical features are grouped under the name; in the second, the name is positioned within a discursive field. Dave Hesmondhalgh kindly mentions the initial pages of *Studying Popular Music*, and those who have read them won't

144   *A virtual symposium*

be surprised to find me, still, in the second camp. But the key question for any neo-Gramscian approach, such as I attempted there, was always: How exactly does the 'articulation' of ideological elements get to work – or, more precisely, from where? Laclau and Mouffe's devastating critique (*Hegemony and Socialist Strategy*) of the economic essentialism surviving in Gramsci, and subsequently in Althusser (the myth of the economic 'final instance'), re-wrote 'class' as a subject whose discursive constitution can never be just 'superstructural', and opened the way to a 'post-marxist' politics of articulation. But the price was a post-structuralist conception of the subject (perpetual sliding of the signifier and all that) which comes uncomfortably close to the crudest forms of identity politics. However 'popular music' is articulated, whatever we try to make it mean, 'the people' as subject is embedded somewhere within it, and with an emotional charge that will apparently just not go away. I want to account for that investment as well as the (necessary) mutability of content. I have found the work of Slavoj Žižek helpful in thinking about (or rather, struggling with) this problem.

Following Žižek's deployment of Lacan's rather notorious aphorism, '(The) Woman does not exist', we might say that '(The) Popular music does not exist'. This doesn't mean that individual beings/objects/practices ('women'; 'songs') located under the relevant concept don't have empirical existence, but that the category as such stands for an abstract ideal which at one and the same time covers over an internal blockage (it can never fully be what it wants to be, as it were), projects its lack on to its (equally lacking) antagonistic Other, and is hence in some sense always spoken from the position of that Other, from elsewhere. (My parenthesis round the definite article – in Lacan/Žižek it's a bar through the word – marks this structure of lack.) This is why, just as (even more notoriously) 'Woman is the symptom of man', so 'popular music' is the symptom of its Other. On one level, there's a symmetry and you can try inverting the relationship (thus feminists can say, 'Man is the symptom of woman'), but such inversions don't destroy the binary structure, which, for Žižek, is in any case at bottom asymmetrical: one side (the Master) is constructed as *universal*, the other (the Slave) as that particularity which makes the Master possible. You can read this either as tough-minded realism (which would help explain, for example, why feminism hasn't yet triumphed and why most university music departments and degree courses are still given the universalistic title 'music' while 'popular music' courses have to be given their own marker) or as a problematic foreclosure of politics.

Interestingly, Žižek's position, it seems to me, is congruent with Adorno's celebrated aphorism, to the effect that 'popular' and 'serious' are 'torn halves of an integral freedom, to which however they do not add up': not as in a simplistic reading (the two sides have split apart and for historical reasons can't be stuck together again) but in the sense that they represent mutually contradictory conceptualisations *of the same field*. So is Žižek simply re-inscribing the dead end we find in negative dialectics? He says not: for him, the 'negation of the negation' doesn't freeze the dialectic but reveals negation as a sort of positivity referring back to the constitutive contradiction in the object itself (see *The Sublime Object of Ideology*, pp. 173–8). Anyway, one way or another, I suspect the answer lies, somehow, in the status of that void – Adorno's 'do not add up', that is, what 'falls out', what cannot be symbolised, when the constitutive antagonism forms – which is presented as a condition of subjectivity itself.

Žižek's position is grounded, more broadly, in an anti-descriptivist theory of naming. Names ('the people', 'music', 'popular music'), he argues, don't acquire meaning through reference to given properties but through a 'primal baptism' followed up in a 'chain of tradition'. (You can test this: Are there any properties whatsoever that would necessarily rule out a given musical experience from the category 'popular music'? I think the answer is, no.) Thus, 'popular music' is just: *that*. But the moment of the baptism is mythical: it appears with the act of naming itself, an 'always already' implied retroactively by its effects once we're in the Symbolic. The name, qua master-signifier (the Lacanian *point de capiton*, or quilting-point), is *empty*; yet it does have a sort of objective correlative, namely, the famous Lacanian *objet a* – Žižek's 'sublime object', a little bit of the Real, what is in the object more than itself, what the symbolic process must exclude if it is to function at all, the object-cause of desire. This object corresponds, on the side of the subject, with the 'belief before belief' which makes subjectivation (the articulatory play of contesting subject-positions) possible. 'Popular music' interpellates its listeners (at least it does if they turn round when it says 'Hey!'); but why should we *want* to turn – or, more precisely, *what* is it that turns? Žižek's answer is: that meaningless piece of stuff, that object in the subject, which alone ensures its consistency; it's the Real which answers.

What, for us, is this object-cause of desire but 'the people' – or rather, that meaningless and impossible site of *jouissance* underlying and supporting all social fantasies of 'the popular'?

But where does this leave politics? Lacan's answer is: traverse the fantasy; the final stage of ideological critique is to 'go through' the fantasy, achieve distance from it, and identify with its underlying mode of *jouissance* (the *Sinthome*, as Lacan neologistically calls it, to distinguish it from the ideological symptoms which it supports). The anti-utopian point that, whatever adjustments in the specific modes of social antagonism are achieved (through the work of articulation politics), the fundamental antagonism which structures subjectivity itself will remain, is one I can accept; this is a mark of the human condition itself. Still, 'pleasure' is a tough opponent (as the history of totalitarianism tells us, and the current rise of neo-fascistic and populist forces reminds us). A more radical politics of the popular – for instance, aspiring to take back the figure of 'the people' from those forces, and from the embrace of corporate capital – would seem to demand a more precise theorisation of the relationship between 'symptom' and '*Sinthome*' than Žižek has (I think) offered; to demand, perhaps, a way of conceiving that re-articulation of meaning might transform the stratum of meaninglessness on which, according to Žižek, it depends; that Symbolic work could change the Real, that (to use older, Freudian terms) consciously articulated activity might re-structure the (social and political as well as individual) unconscious, not just identify with it. Here (or rather, here especially) I'm struggling . . .

Enough: and I haven't even touched on those geo-cultural contexts where Anglophone 'popular music' is an interloper. (I suspect, actually, that a similar analysis would work, allowing for different structures in discursive and social formations; but that Anglophone imperialism will be an extra complicating factor: so that, for example, 'popular music' takes on, in part, the role of Master as well as Slave.)

Does this – at too great a length, no doubt – 'wrap up' the symposium (which is what I was asked to do)? Only, I hope, after the ironic fashion recommended by Lacan and Žižek themselves, where metalanguage claims mastery only to expose its own fraudulence; Who is this 'I' who has been speaking (in the familiar response to interpellation – even while we comply – 'that's not me!') and what is his/its mode of fantasy?

[4]

Browsing Music Spaces: Categories And The Musical Mind

Franco Fabbri – President of IASPM Italy, Milan.

1. Introduction

It seems very difficult – even impossible – to begin any activity with or about sounds without referring to categories such as 'kind', 'type', 'genre', 'style', or to metaphors like 'field', 'area', 'space'. Thinking about music, talking about music, making music: all these activities imply reference to a more or less detailed taxonomy, whose structure – not to mention its very existence – is too often taken for granted. Easy access to the world's diverse musical cultures (and so to even more 'types of music') has encouraged expanding and articulating existing taxonomies. However, some of the categories that we use date from more than two thousand years ago, and have been developed differently in different musical and/or national cultures. So, while categories like 'genre' or 'style' seem to be used mainly to 'put some order' and reduce the overall entropy in the musical universe (or, at least, in our talks and writings about music), sometimes they seem to create even more disorder and confusion.

Some questions arise: 1) why do we need musical categories? 2) How are such categories created? 3) Are historical categories like 'genre' or 'style' useful in all contexts? 4) What is the status of terms like 'field', 'area', 'space', 'boundary', and 'frontier'?

2. Categories: an overview of classical and non-classical theories.

Before we start exploring the usage and function of categories in music, it may be interesting to consider categories in general: that is, the very notion of 'category' as a term used in the philosophical and scientific discourse. I am not going to give more than an overview of the various meanings that the term has been assigned to in the history of Western philosophy: it may be enough to point out that the idea of 'category' established by Aristotle (and widely accepted for centuries)[1] is quite different from the one which was introduced by Immanuel Kant,[2] and that the modern usage of the term,

---

1. According to Aristotle, a category is the ultimate and most general predicate that can be attributed to anything. Categories have a logical and ontological function: they allow to define *entia* exactly, by relating them to their general essence. They are: substance, quality, quantity, relation, place, time, position, condition, action, passion.

mainly by cognitive psychologists, is different again. Today, if one is not a philosopher dealing with some of the historical interpretations of the term, 'category' is a class, a set of objects and events, grouped according to some criteria. Much of the discussion amongst researchers (cognitivists, semioticists, philosophers) appears to be about the criteria, about how sets are created: many seem to agree (and if they don't, they accept the common sense definition) that categories are classes of objects and events, that humans create to reduce the complexity of the empirical world. According to this view, we are able to think just as (while, or because) we are able to create categories: otherwise, we would be lost in the details of infinite multiplicity. As Umberto Eco points out (Eco 1997, p. 123) this is what in ancient philosophy was called - rather than categorizing - 'conceptualizing', that is "the problem about how our language (and our cognitive apparatus with it) leads us to speak and think by *generalia*, or, that we group individuals into sets".

Eco's remark is placed in the context of his investigation about how we recognize objects and events: like a platypus, a horse, a mouse, the skyline of a city, a bachelor, Bach's *Second Suite* for cello in a transcription for recorder: a process that Aristotle's theory of categories appears to give for granted, and Kant doesn't seem to be very interested in (Eco 1997, p. 124).

Eco suggests that semiosis be involved in this process, and locates the concept of *cognitive type* at a node in the process between perception and recognition. A cognitive type is a private set of instructions which allows us to recognize a specific perceptual experience as *an occurrence of a particular type*: Eco refuses to investigate inside the black box of this process, focusing on the proofs that recognition actually takes place (like when one asks: "bring me the red pencil on the table, please", and the result is that the red pencil is brought, and not the black ashtray). However, the instructions and descriptions which constitute the cognitive type (in a way that is invisible to anybody), can be shared publicly as a set of interpretants that form what Eco calls the *nuclear content*, described as "the way we try intersubjectively to make clear which traits make up a cognitive type" (Eco 1997, p. 116). A nuclear content (where content is used in Hjelmslevian terms, as something which is correlated to an expression) is a cultural object, that can be seen as another proof of the existence of a cognitive type - which in turn can be postulated as an individual disposition to produce a socialized nuclear content. Eco also introduces the concept of *molar content*, as 'enlarged knowledge' that includes notions which are not necessary for recognition (ibid., p. 119).

Eco maintains that what modern cognitivists call categories (and that Aristotle would have named predicables) are rather what in natural sciences are called *taxa*, nested from species to genus (or from orders to classes, or from classes to reigns). Cognitivists' basic categories are - according to Eco - cognitive types, while other categories belong to "a phase of a more complex cultural elaboration" (Eco 1977, p. 126), and "do not contribute immediately to tell us what a thing is, but rather how it is hierarchically

2. Kant's categories do not designate essential modes of reality, but the ways we know it: they are *a priori* functions of the intellect (pure concepts) that determine trascendental conditions for our experience, or the universal forms that phenomena must take to become objects of knowledge. There are twelve categories, under four general titles; every triad shows a thesis, antithesis, synthesis pattern: quantity (unity, plurality, totality), quality (reality, negation, limitation), relation (substance and inherence, causality and dependence, reciprocal action), modality (possibility and impossibility, existence and non-existence, necessity and contingency).

put into order in a system of basic, superordinate and subordinate concepts" (ibid.).

An important point is made by Eco when he examines the status of *cultural cases* (like 'cousin', 'president', bishop', the square root, or events, actions, relations like 'contract', or 'friendship') as opposed to *empirical cases* (*natural*, like 'mouse', 'cat', 'tree', or *artificial*, like 'chair, 'boat', house'). What all cultural cases have in common is that, "to be recognized as such, they need reference to a framework of cultural norms" (Eco 1997, p. 139). The existence of cognitive types must be acknowledged for cultural cases as well, says Eco; he also suggests that with cultural cases recognition proceeds from the nuclear content (that is, the publicly shared procedures which allow to recognize the object or event) to the cognitive type, rather than the opposite way (like with empirical cases), though he warns immediately that things may not be so simple (ibid., p. 150). Anyway, he comments further on that, though a cognitive type is private, when it is interpreted as nuclear content it becomes public, and a public nuclear content may provide instructions for the creation of cognitive types. So, cognitive types are continuously subject to public control, and the Community (in Eco's terms) teaches us, step by step, to adapt our cognitive types to other people's cognitive types. Education is a major agent in this process (ibid., p. 190), and another important factor is art: artists enrich our ability to perceive our environment, by suggesting alternative schemes for perception (ibid., pp. 191-192).

Sometimes Eco comes very close to a discussion of genres, specially when he makes a distinction between *generic* types and *individual* types: however, he seems more interested to demonstrate that cognitive types are involved in the recognition of individuals (like George or Robert or Louis XIV) and of *formal individuals* (like a novel or a piece of music) as well: so his only explicit reference to music in this study is about the process by which someone can recognize a specific aural experience as an occurrence of the type '*Second suite for cello* by Johann Sebastian Bach in a transcription for alto recorder as performed by Frans Brüggen' (ibid., pp. 183-188). For our purpose, which is to examine much less specific recognition processes and generic rather than individual aural experiences and music events, another part of Eco's study is more relevant: it's where he points out the difference between *dictionary-like competence* and *encyclopaedic competence*. The former is based on the ability just to place an entity in a well-defined node of a directory tree, or - according to a more traditional view - in a class of a scientific taxonomy, while the latter implies the knowledge of both the directory structure and the content of the individual directories and files, or, as it is more commonly said, of everything the Community recorded about the entity. The important point is that while linguists maintain that common linguistic competence is purely taxonomic like in a dictionary, Eco suggests that the model for linguistic competence is encyclopaedic (Eco 1997, p. 193-200);[3] he also comments that since scientific taxonomies were established only in the eighteenth century, if linguistic competence should be based on a dictionary-like model, then from the appearance of Homo Sapiens until the end of the seventeenth century nobody would have been able to use his own language properly, and Aristotle and Plato, or Descartes and Pascal, would have been talking without understanding each other. Categories that matter both for our ability to recognize things and for our linguistic competence are not like scientific taxonomies: Eco calls them *savage categories*, in that they are organized and restructured continually at the nuclear

---

3.   See also Eco 1975.

content level, grouping objects according to their utility, or to their relevance to our survival, or following formal analogies, and so on (ibid. p. 201). The savage category of 'insect' includes spiders, which, according to scientific taxonomies are not insects but arthropods (a class that includes arachnids *and* insects).

So, if we accept the term category to mean a generic set of objects or events grouped according to some criteria (which, it must be pointed out again, is not the meaning Aristotle or Kant would give to this word), then we must also admit that we deal with different concepts: a) scientific *taxa*, which allow - according to our example - to have spiders only in the class of arachnids, and not of insects; b) savage categories, which allow spiders to be insects (as possibly fastidious little animals whose bodies and legs show distinctive junctions); c) encyclopaedic entries, which (if they are really complete and include everything the Community learnt about the object) assign spiders to the correct scientific category of arachnids, while mentioning the folk usage of calling them insects (and, by just some folks and not others, of eating them).

Another rich source of warnings about categories is Lakoff 1987. Most of them are commented in Eco 1997; Eco's approach, as a philosopher and semioticist (not just as a European, if we consider his continuous reference to the work of Charles S. Peirce) is less that of a dismissal of 'old' theories about categories than in Lakoff or in the studies of other cognitivists. Many of Eco's remarks about some of the cognitivists' discoveries are acuminate: for example, when he comments the 'strange' categorizations of some Australian aboriginals, the Dyirbal, who seem to divide objects in the universe in four classes, which correspond to one of four distinct classifiers (*Bayi, Balan, Balam, Bala*) that must be used before any term included in one of the classes (Lakoff 1987, pp. 92-93). The Balan class, by the way, includes women, fire, dangerous things, as well as platypuses, echidnas, some snakes, some fishes, most birds, etc. (which explains both Lakoff's and - partly - Eco's titles for their books). Eco suggests to compare the Dyirbal's strange categories with those of two equally strange populations, living respectively in Southern and Northern Europe: the former prepends to any name one of the two words IL (with the variant LO) and LA, which apply to the following categories: IL, for men, kangaroos, bats, many snakes, many fishes, many insects, the sun, a storm, a rainbow, gold, ear, etc.; LA for woman, tiger, some snakes, some fishes, water, the moon, a star, etc.; the latter uses three different words, DER, DIE, DAS, for categories that include the moon (and men) for DER, the sun (and women, and cats) for DIE, and gold and ear for DAS. Eco's warning is clear: there is a risk to understand grammatical automatic behaviours as categorization processes (Eco 1997, p. 172-173).

Anyway, some of Lakoff's suggestions are quite stimulating, and probably deserve a more thorough comment than the one allowed in Eco's perspective. One example is basic-level categorization, as described by Roger Brown and Brent Berlin (Lakoff 1987, pp. 31-38; Brown 1965; Berlin, Breedlove, and Raven 1974). According to Brown, categorization, for a child, begins "at the level of distinctive action" and then proceeds upward to superordinate categories and downward to subordinate categories. This "first level" of categorization was seen by Brown as having the following converging properties:

- It is the level of distinctive actions.
- It is the level which is learned earliest and at which things are first named.
- It is the level at which names are shortest and used most frequently.

- It is a natural level of categorization, as opposed to a level created by "achievements of the imagination" (Lakoff 1987, p. 32).

Berlin and his students and associates go further, and examining folk classifications of plants and animals in a population living in the Chiapas region of Mexico, suggest that the basic level (or the "folk-generic level") for such classifications is that of the genus, which seems to be a psychologically basic level in the following respects:

- People name things more readily at that level.
- Languages have simpler names for things at that level.
- Categories at that level have greater cultural significance.
- Things are remembered more readily at that level.
- At that level, things are perceived holistically, as a single gestalt, while for identification at a lower level, specific details (called *distinctive features*) have to be picked out to distinguish, for example, among the kinds of oak (Lakoff 1987, p. 33).

Lakoff comments further, basing on the observations of A.J. Cain's essay "Logic and Memory in Linnaeus's System of Taxonomy" (1958), that "the heart of the Linnaean system was the genus, not the species. It is the genus that gives the *general* characteristics and the species that is defined in terms of differentiating characteristics". And "the genus, as a scientific level of classification, was set up because it was the most psychologically basic level for the purposes of the study of taxonomic biology by human beings" (Lakoff 1987, pp. 34-35). This is a quite challenging point to make, as it seems open to any kind of falsification (and actually Eco doesn't hesitate to say that "all experiments showed that our knowledge doesn't comply with this classification", Eco 1997, p. 157). Anyway, whatever the theoretical framework for basic-level categorization - including Eco's cognitive types - it is very interesting for a study of categories in music to see that *genera* appear to have a central function in the functioning of our mind, in the way we perceive the world.

Basic-level categorization was also studied by Eleanor Rosch, who was the first to provide a general perspective for all the specific cases that had already demonstrated weaknesses in the 'classical theory' of categories. Her name is mostly associated with the so-called 'prototype theory', though in the most recent phase of her studies prototypes are just seen as evidence that there is something wrong or unknown in the 'classical theory', rather than proofs of any particular 'non-classical' category structure.

A prototype, also called *cognitive reference point*, is a subcategory or category member that has a special cognitive status - that of being a 'best example' (Lakoff 1987, p. 41). If the 'classical theory' states that all category members share the same properties, then any demonstration that in a given category some members are more representative than others can be taken as a strong suggestion that the classical model is wrong. Rosch created an experimental framework for such demonstrations, based on paradigms like the following:

- *Direct rating*: Subjects are asked to rate how good an example of a category various members are.
- *Reaction time*: Subjects are asked to press a button to indicate true or false in response to a statement of the form 'An (example) is a (category name)'. Response times are shorter for representative examples.
- *Production of examples*: When asked to list or draw examples of category members, subjects were more likely to list or draw more representative examples.
- *Asymmetry in similarity ratings*: Less representative examples are often considered

to be more similar to more representative examples than the converse.

- *Asymmetry in generalization*: New information about a representative category member is more likely to be generalized to nonrepresentative members than the reverse.
- *Family resemblances*: These are perceived similarities between representative and nonrepresentative members of categories; Rosch showed a correlation between family resemblances and numerical ratings of best examples derived from the above experiments (Lakoff 1987, pp. 41-42).

Whatever their nature or structure, categories seem to play a fundamental role in our understanding of the world. It would be very strange if - while we spend most of our awake time (and Freud only knows if and how we categorize while dreaming) observing occurrences of types, processing perceptions through cognitive types, socializing nuclear contents, comparing prototypes to nonrepresentative members of categories or vice versa, locating basic categories at the level of the genus - when we listen to music or think or talk about it nothing of this kind (or type, sort, species, class, category...) happened.

3. Categorizing musics

In fact, we do use categories for music. We process our perceptions (not only aural perceptions) confronting them with cognitive types - definitely *cultural* cognitive types - that allow us to recognize what we are hearing (or seeing, or feeling, or touching) as 'music', or as 'music of a certain kind', rather than 'noise'. To this respect, Eco's model seems more appropriate than the concept of basic-level categories, if they are put into the usual framework of superordinate and subordinate categories. 'Music' is a superordinate category with respect to a basic level of 'musics of this or that kind' only in musicologists' and musicians' 'scientific' taxonomies: as a savage category, based on the elaboration of the nuclear content by the Community, it may well be at the same level of its apparently subordinate categories (music types, like genres or styles).

We perceive music events both as occurrences of music types (like when we recognize a certain event as an occurrence of the type 'classical music' or - if our cognitive types became more articulated via the collective elaboration of their nuclear content - as 'baroque music performed according to the correct Aufführung Praxis') and as occurrences of formal individuals, like Johan Sebastian Bach's *Second suite for cello*.

It may well be that basic categories for music are located at the level of the genus; to this respect, I'd like to point out that if we find out that this is the level of the categories that some people call 'genres' (and I am amongst them), it is not because of the family resemblance of the terms genus and genre, nor because of their ultimate identity in the history of Western philosophy and musicology: it is because genres (at least according to some views) have the qualities that cognitive psychologists acknowledge for basic-level categories. This may not be true for all genres and for all contexts: genres can also be seen as taxonomies superimposed to musics, usually for some 'bad' reason (by 'academics' or by the music industry, according to folk theories). But if we examine how we recognize music events, how we react to them, how we conceptualize them and organize a social response to them (including a music performance), it seems that most of our effort is concentrated around a basic set of collectively accepted norms that define types of musics, against which we confront - as occurrences - the musical events we are dealing with.

4. Genre and style

As for categories in general, there are different musical categories at work at the same time (this is probably the same as saying that there are many different musical competences, which is a much more established concept, see Stefani 1978): most of the problems with genres are probably originated at this level, where it is easy to mix genres as folk categories and genres as specialists' taxonomies - and there are also different specialist traditions). Prototype effects are common, as in all categories related to art: canons are the prototype theory's 'best examples' (or cognitive reference points), and even when taxonomies are based on detailed norms - as it happens both with genres and with styles - there is often an exemplary work or an artist that embody the norms in the most convincing way.

Despite the above mentioned folk theories, then, musical categories aren't just 'labels' applied to musics for obscure reasons related to the profit of professionals (be they musicologists, journalists, record producers, manufacturers or retailers): they seem to exist both at a private level - as cognitive types - and as socialized nuclear content, that is as socialized sets of instructions to detect occurrences of types. In a discussion of musical categories, then, it is not a matter of creating (or commenting) dictionary-like definitions according to which experts can locate an occurrence at a certain level of a directory tree. Rather, I think it is important to comment how our Community's encyclopaedia describes musical categories, accounting for existing examples and their contradictions. The following is an attempt for an encyclopaedic entry for 'genre' (which includes, in the first paragraph, a dictionary-like definition):

A genre is a kind of music, as it is acknowledged by a community for any reason or purpose or criteria, i.e., a set of musical events whose course is governed by rules (of any kind) accepted by a community.

The English term - which refers to any kind of work of art - is more specific than the French word from which it originates; in Neo-Latin languages, as well as in Latin, the equivalent for genre (Italian 'genere', Spanish 'genero', etc.) means type, kind, class, manner, race, like the ancient Greek γενος. As such, the term has been used in the philosophical debate throughout the history of Western civilization, and was very early applied to art and to music. The first clear definition of γενος was given by Aristotle: "What is predicated according to the essence of many which differ specifically"; hence the function of γενος in any definition, which implies two constituents, the γενος and the specific difference (like in "man is a rational animal", where "animal" is the γενος, and "rational" the specific difference).

Since Aristotle (*Poetics*) and his pupil Theofrastos (responsible of the first great natural taxonomy, based on the concept of γενος), the idea propagated that what can be predicated according the essence of many works of art (which differ specifically), that is, what makes them similar, worth to belong to the same γενος, is their function; it followed that the style of each work of art should be proper to its γενος (putting it clearly that genre and style are related, but are not the same concept). This is the basis of the theory of the three styles (elevated, medium, humble) which had so many followers amongst Greek and Roman philosophers, orators, poets, playwrights, artists and, as far as it is reported, musicians. The theory emerged again in the Renaissance, and formed the ground for all subsequent discussions: most aesthetic conflicts since then (in music at least since Padre Martini's critique of Pergolesi's *Stabat Mater*, accused to be written in the *opera comica* style of *La serva padrona*) have been about the decision whether the distinction amongst genres is based somehow on the human nature, or if genres are concepts defined by convention, hence subject to change.

Semioticists and cultural anthropologists in the last decades of the 20th century have set a framework of theories that allowed a wider view of the problem of genres, still in line with its philosophical origins (a matter of definition, first of all) but capable to account of the differences amongst genres - and their increasing multiplicity - in literature, theatre, dance, cinema, music. Not surprisingly, many of these modern theories focus on conventions established within communities, related to performances or their social usages (even for literature: Frye 1957).

In music, genres emerge as names to define similarities, recurrences that members of a community made pertinent to identify musical events: the process can be explicit, like in the proclamation of an aesthetic manifesto, a law, or a marketing campaign, or it can never be declared (see Lewis 1969). Rules that define a genre can be related to any of the codes involved in a musical event (i.e. also rules of behaviour, etiquettes, proxemic and kinesic codes, economic regulations, etc.), in such a way that knowing 'what kind of music' one will be listening to (or playing, or talking about, etc.) will act as a compass, helping to choose the proper codes and tools for the participant. Genres, then, can be seen as short-cuts to speed up communication within a musical community, as well as standardised codes that allow no margin for deviation, i.e. no real communication: the rise and fall of progressive rock in the late sixties-early seventies and the subsequent explosion of punk rock are a good example of a recurring process where codes are gradually elaborated, then become too strict and allow only for very predictable texts, then new codes are opposed, and so on. It must be pointed out (as punk is an excellent example for this too) that rules, codes, are made pertinent by the community: what someone sees as the most significant regularity within a certain genre may not be what the community that constituted that genre in the first place saw as its essence (in Aristotelian terms). A hierarchy of codes always defines the ideology of a genre (Eco 1975, Fabbri 1996).

And here is a similar attempt or 'style':

> A recurring arrangement of features in musical events which is typical of an individual (composer, performer), a group of musicians, a genre, a place, a period of time.

The term originates from the Latin word *stilus*, the ancient Roman writing tool, connotating 'a way of writing'. The concept migrated quite soon from literature to music, with meanings that have reflected changing attitudes to norms, rules, conventions, and to originality and individuality. So, while in the Middle Ages style implied a set of models to be adhered to, as they were imposed by tradition or authority, during the Renaissance the concept became more articulated, covering contexts for stylistic diversification as varied as personal, national, functional, hence related to emotions and affect (see Kircher 1650); later the Romantic idea of style as the representation of subjectivity and originality changed (at the end of the 19th century) into the modern concept of a set of rules, a linguistic code. According to Eco (1975) the code which governs an individual text is an *aesthetic idiolect*, while corpus idiolects or 'stream' (or historical) idiolects exist if the same set of rules is applied by the same author to many works, or by different authors when the same idiolect is accepted within a given cultural community, and/ or in a given period of time. These different levels of idiolect (style) definitions form a hierarchy of competences, an embedding of hypercodification rules: in other words, style operates at various levels, from the individual work to the genre or historical period, and the difference is a matter of focus or content, rather than quality - the same concept is at work.

As a codified way of making music, which may (or must) conform to specific social functions, style is related to genre, and is sometimes used as its synonym, more often in languages where style is a more common-sense word and genre is felt to be more technical. However, style implies an emphasis on the musical code, while genre relates to all kinds of codes that are referred to in a musical event, so the two terms clearly cover different semantic fields. In fact, though he common usage of style to indicate 'a way of' (living, behaving, dressing etc.) is a possible source of overlapping between style and genre, in this broader sense style has an even stronger aesthetic connotation, most probably an heritage of the Romantic meaning.

Much of the Romantic idea of style as personality is still at work in popular music. As a personal feature, style is supposed to be maintained across forms and genres: for example, Ennio Morricone's composing style can be recognized as such in his film music as well as in pop songs, and even in his orchestrations for songs in the singer-songwriter genre; the same can be said of many performers, though a quality that is often demanded from sessionmen and backing musicians is exactly the opposite, that is, to be able to perform in a given style, and not to impose their own. On the other hand, parody and stylistic quotation are quite common strategies in popular music, providing composers and performers with straightforward tools to create other 'selves' (and/or to hide their own): well known examples range from The Beatles' *Sgt. Pepper's Lonely Hearts Club Band* to Bob Dylan's *Nashville Skyline* to a massive part of Frank Zappa's work.

Additional material to reflect (and worry) about with reference to musical classifications was provided recently by the Internet. Whoever tries to find useful information over the World Wide Web understands immediately that classification and similarity are his best allies, and the panic we are facing when exposed to such amounts of information is a good suggestion to understand not the semioticist's but every man's and woman's anxiety to separate, define, classify. In fact, if you go for a CD on the Internet and get into the world's best known virtual record shop, CDNOW, you will be invited immediately to 'Browse Our Music Spaces', which are: Rock/Pop, Jazz/Blues, World/New Age, Urban/ Electronic, Country/Folk, Classical. You can also apply to the Album Advisor, a special database engine that will supply a list of records that you will probably enjoy, if you just indicate one that you like (investigating the rules in this database engine would throw some light on current ideas - or at least the webmaster's - about music similarities). If you look for an alternative in the largest World Wide Web bookshop, then Amazon.com will invite you to 'Browse Styles',[4] which are Alternative (including sub-categories Indie, Hardcore, New Wave, Punk...), Blues (Modern Electric, Traditional...), Country (Alternative, Bluegrass, Contemporary, Traditional...), Dance & DJ (Ambient, Electronic, Industrial, Techno-House...), Folk (Contemporary, Traditional...), International (Cajun & Zydeco, Reggae, Salsa, Tejano...), Jazz (Avant-Garde, Bebop, Fusion, Latin, Swing...), New Age (Celtic, Environmental, Meditation...), Pop (Adult Contemporary, Easy Listening, Soft Rock, Vocal...), Rap & Hip-Hop (East Coast, Gangsta, New School, West Coast...), Rock (Classic, Hard Rock, Metal, Progressive...), R&B / Soul (Contemporary, Funk, Motown, Soul...), Soundtracks (Movies, Musicals, Television...), Miscellaneous (Children's, Christian, Comedy, Spoken Word...). And beware: "Looking for Classical? Coming soon--sign up and get notified when we start selling Classical CDs! "So if we want to know how to classify the classics we have to wait for that particular commercial event.

But we might be interested just in what the Internet is mostly about, information: so why not using a search engine like Yahoo!? There we can find the following URL: http:// www.yahoo.com/Entertainment/Music/Genres,[5] which will give you a list of links to interesting genre-specific sites, such as: Alternative, Bluegrass, Blues, Cajun and Zydeco, Celtic, Children's, Classic Rock, Classical, Country and Western, Disco, Dixieland, Dub, Electronica, Flamenco, Folk, Freestyle, Funk, Gospel, Gothic, Indie, Industrial, Jazz, Lounge, March, Metal, Microtonal, Minimalism, New Age, New Wave, Noise, Novelty, Opera, Polka, Progressive Rock, Punk, Ragtime, Rap and Hip Hop, Reggae, Rock and Pop, Rockabilly, Ska, Soul and R&B, Surf Rock, Tejano, Theme Music, World Fusion.

It is worth to point out again that the listings of "music spaces", "styles" and "genres" largely overlap: webmasters seem to agree that certain kinds or types of music are broadly acknowledged, though they are probably much less interested in understanding how this knowledge is organized. This is what *we* are interested in, I believe.

Amazon.com suggestion of "style" is consistent with one of the common terms used in English, and with the importance that without any doubt is given to strictly musical elements when distinctions or similarities are made or found between or amongst musics. However, style doesn't account for other codes that may be of great importance in establishing the meaning of a musical event in a certain context: though it is a flexible and useful concept that spans from such things as "the classical style" to - say - the stylistic consistency of Richard Thompson across genres (i.e. his idiolect as a singer/songwriter and guitarist, see Moore 1998), it can't explain simple phenomena like: when you realize what music will be performed from how seats (if any) are placed on the floor, or: why does a conductor at the end of a premiere of a piece of contemporary (classical) music always look for the composer in various places in the stalls, when he knows perfectly where he is.

Rituals, etiquettes, proxemic codes, the division of labour, economic procedures and laws, common assumptions based on the music's function shared in a community, be it a rural community, an urban subculture, a group of people who have the same religious or political beliefs, or just a few bizarre intellectuals who proclaim an aesthetic

---

4.   I know this will delight my friend Allan Moore, who once said I'm using the term genre to refer to what musicologists (and other people) would call style (Moore 1993, p. 2). I read Amazon's usage of the term style, instead, as a symptom that this may sound more 'academically correct' for a bookshop. Anyway, the point here is classification per se, not according to what principles or parameters.

5.   Well, as an authority in classification, Yahoo! is definitely our time's Aristotle...

manifesto: this is the space - the hyperspace - where genres operate. Musical codes are in this space, but this doesn't mean that style be a subset of genre, or anywhere lower in a hierarchy of musical categories: or, if it is so, it's in the sense of a subordinate category compared to a basic-level category, that is at a level where *more specific* information is articulated.

There's probably more about this. Though any style is a very complex code, people who study musical styles never despair that they will be able to give the most complete description of them (just think of Charles Rosen's monumental work about *The Classical Style*); on the other hand, some regularity in the arrangement of musical elements must be found if one wants to talk about style at all. Behind the very notion of style, then, there is an assumption of whole, complete, of necessary and sufficient. We don't need *all* of that to recognize and categorize music. In our cognitive experience, we recognize types of phenomena according to partial descriptions, to truncated knowledge. Curiously, but truthfully, genre appears to be a less specific concept than style: as in Eco's example about recognizing a town after being carried there blindfolded (Eco 1997, p. 189), we know how to recognize instantly a few genres (even without listening to any music), though we would not be able to give someone else a set of instructions to carry out that recognition. We would rather point at prototypes, at 'best examples', as interpretants of our own, private cognitive type. Genres are more about beliefs and practice than about theory.

On the other hand, one can give a very detailed list of the norms involved in the definition of a genre, or of a set of genres, like I did in Fabbri 1982b for the 'System of Canzone in Italy'. But that is more an encyclopaedic definition, which tries to account both for scientific taxonomies and folk categories (or, in Eco's terms, which deals with the molar content rather than just the nuclear content). And conversely, it must be said that cognitive types for music styles do exist (styles are actually recognized), though in this case we are not at the level of detailed scientific taxonomies. In the end, the difference between genre and style remains in the wider scope of genre, which accounts for 'non-musical' properties; both genre and style can be articulated at different levels, covering just the nuclear content and basing on prototypes, 'best examples' and 'family resemblances', or expanding over the molar content; genre, at least outside the English speaking scientific community where the term is related to historically established taxonomies, is closer to common musical competence (which is less suspicious about non-musical traits), while style is closer to a more elaborated musical competence.

A meaningful effect of these discrepancies emerged during a survey on music consumption and interests (Ala, Fabbri, Fiori, Ghezzi 1985). Interviewees were presented with a list of 88 genres, with the suggestion to indicate those they liked or were interested in, and (if any) those they despised.[6] Problems arose when designing the list for classical genres, as some (it could be said in terms the authors couldn't be aware of at that time) were more basic-level categories, like 'opera' or 'electronic music', and others needed reference to subordinate, more detailed taxonomies. So - probably aiming at excessive detail - the 'Lieder' category was split into 'classical Lieder' and 'romantic Lieder'. The result was that 'classical Lieder' (a category that was intended to cover Lieder of the Classic Age, that is the not so widely known Lieder by Mozart and

---

6. Results offered a significant correlation in some cases between likers and despisers, as with disco and punk, punk and heavy metal, 'ballo liscio' and all rock-related genres.

Beethoven) received many more favourable responses than 'romantic Lieder', that is Schubert's, Schumann's etc., which is what interviewees most probably meant when they said they liked 'classical Lieder'. Common musical competence sees 'classical' as a predicate for all Western art music, while the notion of a classic age and style is elaborated at the level of the molar content, and pertains to specialists' taxonomies. This confusion of different category levels and competences is quite common, and is somehow enhanced by the easier access to information provided by electronic media and by global communication processes. Whether we enter a record megastore or a virtual shop over the Internet, we are confronted with lists that include an increasing number of music types (whatever they are called), with no apparent care about taxonomic criteria. 'World Music' doesn't seem to include Neapolitan song (which may be intended to belong to the mainstream of pop music, but no explanation is given: see *World Music. The Rough Guide.* London: Penguin Books, 1994); however, in record shops all over Europe and North America, in the World Music section, under the label Italy, you will mostly find mainstream Italian pop music.

5. Mappings and misunderstandings

CDNOW's idea of "spaces" is stimulating, and I definitely support it if it implies that musics are multidimensional cultural entities, which can be represented mentally as objects in an n-dimensional hyperspace. This is the vision suggested by Umberto Eco's Q-Model for the semantic space (1976), which most likely originates (as an extension) from the structuralist representation of semantic fields as bordering surfaces (see Ullmann 1962), like in the evergreen discussion of terms indicating trees and woods in various languages. However, if we move from this "space" concept down again to a surface model, which is one of the most common mental representations of any classification, including genres, complexity is reduced and we are immediately facing with misleading concepts like "territory", "border", "no-man's-land".

Again, we are confronted with problems at different levels: that our cognitive apparatus inclines to use interpretants that derive from our experience of space is clear (as the usage of terms like 'level' and 'inclines' in this very phrase demonstrates - see Fauconnier 1997); however, when we create a spatial mental representation of a concept, we are using a metaphor, we are moving some predicates from one domain to another, and there is no guarantee that there will be a one-to-one correspondence between properties in the two domains. For example, even if we take the most basic-level definition of a genre or style (in terms of nuclear content, that is of the description of the simplest procedures to identify that entity), we'll probably find a significant number of different properties, like in the matrix suggested by Tagg 1982 for distinguishing 'folk', 'art' and 'popular' musics. If we try to project a similar scheme onto a surface, we'll find that the spatial representation is impoverished: it doesn't account for properties that are common to all categories, not to mention all 'non-classical' effects (like prototypical effects, degrees of representation, fuzzy sets, family resemblances etc.). A complex universe becomes a map, with clear-cut borders: objects can be either on one side or on the other; to account for objects that do not fit in the representation other metaphors have to be created, like frontiers or cross-overs. This is an area (yes!) where common competence is subject to the continuous influence of a more detailed (though by no means more scientific) competence, that of music critics. It is definitely more comfortable to represent the universe of musics in terms of maps, territories, fields, etc., and to dismiss exceptions as weird objects that live across the borders, rather than account for the differences and nuances that can be found even at the most basic level of musical categories. A history of music criticism might show that such spatial metaphors are not new; however, I have the impression that the usage of terms based in the lexicons of geography and topography became more and more common in the last two decades; some suggestions from Brian Eno's album covers with maps, paralleled by discourses about 'possible musics', might locate (yes, again!) the origins of this fashion (in its current terms) between the end of the Seventies and the beginning of the following decade.[7] Fauconnier (1997, p. 9) observes that "mappings become culturally and lexically entrenched, and (...) *they actually define the category structure for the language and structure*.[8] Rather remarkably, although the vocabulary often makes the mapping transparent, we are typically not conscious of the mapping during use, and in fact are liable to be surprised and amused when it is pointed out to us. In such cases, the mapping, although cognitively active, is opaque". Fauconnier's concept of mapping is not literal and is much more articulated: however, the comment I just mentioned is in the context of mappings of 'time as space', which doesn't seem to be very different from the one I am discussing. I'd like to point out the close relation between mappings and categories: this means that if spatial metaphors become a norm in the language, then music categories will be restructured according to these metaphors. This is probably already happening.

6. Bibliography

Ala, N., Fabbri, F., Fiori, U., Ghezzi, E. 1985. *La musica che si consuma*. Milano: Unicopli.
Berlin, Brent, Dennis E. Breedlove, and Peter H. Raven. 1974. *Principles of Tzeltal Plant Classification*. New York: Academic.
Brown, Roger. 1965. *Social Psychology*. New York: Free Press.
Cain, A.J. 1958. Logic and Memory in Linnaeus's System of Taxonomy. *Proceedings of the Linnaean Society of London* 169:144-63.
Eco, Umberto. 1975. *Trattato di semiotica generale*. Milano: Bompiani.
Eco, Umberto. 1997. *Kant e l'ornitorinco*. Milano: Bompiani.
Fabbri, Franco. 1981. I generi musicali: una questione da riaprire. *Musica/Realtà* 4. Bari: De Donato.
Fabbri, Franco. 1982. What kind of music? *Popular Music* 2. Cambridge: Cambridge University Press.
Fabbri, Franco. 1982b. A Theory of Musical Genres: Two Applications. *Popular Music Perspectives*, ed. David Horn and Philip Tagg. Göteborg & Exeter: IASPM
Fabbri, Franco. 1996. *Il suono in cui viviamo*. Milano: Feltrinelli.
Fauconnier, Gilles. 1997. *Mappings In Thought And Language*. Cambridge: Cambridge University Press.
Frye, Northrop. 1957. *Anatomy of Criticism. Four Essays*. Princeton: Princeton University Press.
Kircher, Athanasius. 1650. *Musurgia universalis sive Ars Magna Consoni et Dissoni*. Roma.
Lakoff, George. 1987. *Women, Fire And Dangerous Things. What Categories Reveal about the Mind*. Chicago: The University Of Chicago Press.
Lewis, David K. 1969. *Convention - A Philosophical Study*. Cambridge: Harvard University Press.
Moore, Allan. 1993. *Rock: The Primary Text. Developing a Musicology of Rock*. Milton Keynes:

---

7.   I remember reproaching my friend Richard Middleton for his usage of terms like 'area' and 'field' (Fabbri 1982); as it is common in these cases, this is more an indication of how the usage of spatial metaphors by other, much less scrupulous critics was already disturbing me at that time.

8.   Italics are mine.

Open University Press.

Moore, Allan. 1998. *Issues of Style, Genre, and Idiolect in Rock*. Unpublished paper. Lecture at Bologna University.

Stefani, Gino. 1978. *Capire la musica*. Milano: Espresso Strumenti.

Tagg, Philip. 1982. Analysing popular music: theory, method and practice. *Popular Music* 2, Cambridge: Cambridge University Press:37-67.

Ullmann, Stephen. 1962. *Semantics: An Introduction to the Science of Meaning*. Oxford: Basil Blackwell & Mott.

[5]

THE HIGH ANALYSIS OF LOW MUSIC

DAI GRIFFITHS

> The essential difference between English and American musicians could be very crudely defined in these terms: American musicians will always ask 'How do we end?'. English musicians only ask 'How do we begin?'[1]

Greetings from the 'lower reaches of the humanities and the social sciences',[2] where pop music is always playing, loudly and intrusively, and where the musically talentless can become enormously wealthy overnight. Pop music involves music albeit, like opera, as only one element among others; and pop music has been around long enough to develop its own history. Its literature is big and growing – journalism, criticism, history – but *analysis?* Why bother? This is a far from established and far from straightforward story, and the title tries to capture what has been one of its defining features: culture clash, attitude confusion, metaphor mixture. Why blur the difference? Why cross the border? Why bother? These are the neuroses that guide what follows.[3] How do we begin?

First Opening: 'I'm a loser, baby, so why don't you kill me?'[4]

If Martin Amis's *Money*, the novel of the 1980s, enacts, among other things, the pervasiveness of ideology, so a subsequent novel, the novel of the '90s, *The Information*,[5] enacts, among other things, the dichotomy which art historian Clement Greenberg described as Avant-Garde and Kitsch.[6] Both of the latter novel's protagonists, Gwyn Barry and Richard Tull, are themselves novelists; but where the former is a ragingly successful author of fashionable best-sellers, Tull, the novel's failed hero, writes with recondite self-consciousness. Martin Amis, the middleman, is careful to make clear that the work of both authors is, in some cursorily fundamental sense, 'shit' (Tull on p. 87, Barry on pp. 112 and 155).

The two novelists find themselves dramatising familiar divergences in aesthetic theory: Barry, whose novels are instantly pleasurable to vast audiences worldwide, writes of a return to nature; while Tull, the reading of whose work comically occasions evermore-serious physical revulsion, is wedded to autonomy and objectivity. Their positions can be mapped upon elements of the four-part structure elucidated at the opening of M. H. Abrams's *The Mirror and the Lamp*.[7] Gwyn Barry appears to be returning to mimesis in his thematic concern with nature, but is firmly pragmatic in social orientation; Richard Tull, starting from a romantic perspective – including being touchingly committed as practising critic to a metropolitan Little Magazine – writes from a seethingly objective stance: 'if you had to settle on a one-word description of his stuff then you would almost certainly make do with *unreadable*' (p. 171).

What are the musical parallels to these positions? Richard Tull is easy: 'too proud and too lazy and – in a way – too clever and too nuts to write talent novels', he is 'marooned' as a modernist who 'didn't want to please the readers. He wanted to stretch them until they twanged' (pp. 170–71). Here is the Associate Editor of *Music Analysis*, Jonathan Cross, on British contemporary music's Harrison Birtwistle: 'Sir Harry has never been one for taking much notice of his audience. "I can't consider anything to do with who listens to [my music]", he told Sue Lawley on *Desert Island Discs*. So we can't say we weren't warned.'[8] And we can't say we haven't heard it all before, either: Abrams has John Keats in 1818 declaring that 'I never wrote one single Line of Poetry with the least Shadow of public thought'.[9]

But who or what is Gwyn Barry? What does he sound like? As I read the novel, I keep thinking of everything that's bad about contemporary classical music – the kind of classical music that likes to keep in with pop music, or conversely, if less heinously – misguided aspiration being more tolerable than condescension – pop music which aspires towards some reified condition of classical music. So in this pit, this hell-hole, we find: John Rutter, Andrew Lloyd Webber, Genesis, all the minimalists once they stopped being in bands and started writing operas (Philip Glass in particular),[10] modernist appropriations of jazz,[11] progressive rock, the oratorio and piano concerto needlessly resuscitated by, respectively, Paul McCartney and Keith Emerson.[12] Given his novel's pastoral bent, maybe it's the New Simplicity, or New Age ...

From the admission, played sympathetically through Tull, that the avantgarde has nothing left to offer, presumably because the modernist classics turn out to have been largely one-off explorations of artistic materiality, Amis delivers bodyblows at middlebrow taste. *The Information* sounds to me like pop music, which in turn finds itself occupying the comfortable self-sufficiency of the contemporary novel.[13] Much as Amis adapts a variety of sources – the novels of Kingsley Amis and Nabokov, and pre-eminently the big American novel, Updike, Bellow, Roth – so pop music can by now construct its own lineage from a variety of established sources. Beck, to take a recent case which received predictably genre-driven critical acclaim, assimilates Bob Dylan, Sly and the Family Stone, Dr John, blues and hip-hop. Postmodernism apart – 'speech through all the masks and voices stored up in the imaginary museum of a now global culture'[14] – these new formations, based straightforwardly upon generic association and automatically communicable meaning, contain within themselves a marked critique of the teleology of technique which so inspires Tull's lack of popular success.

The automatic objection to pop music, its rank and rancid commercialisation, now carries seemingly less weight, with an apparent easing among the Western left over the necessary evil of capitalism. Much as the Left has abandoned its hope of all-out revolutionary change – though, as we shall consider, this can seem a position devoid of historical context, with much the same true of equality of opportunity and civil rights – so modernism's alternative to the market, it turned out, was not freedom but bureaucracy and private patronage. Unlike the cardinal 'inward' modernist – artforms poetry, art, music – the novel remains, like cinema and pop music, at least in Britain, to a significant extent beyond the University: Amis's novels have to sell, and he supplements this income through journalism; market force, along with an interdisciplinary tendency or nature, may constitute part of their apparent attraction. Pop music makes its postmodern claim to attention, *both* in terms of its form or nature, *and* in some (admittedly vaguely-defined) economic or political sense. The following diagram, an adaptation by Johan Fornäs of Jürgen Habermas,[15] can serve as a summary of some of the basic issues in political economy which any artwork enters. Its bleak containment must underlie much of the following. It may be that musical analyses in future begin their careful dissections with a statement on how what they have to say fits in to this picture – unless Joyce's 'ideal reader suffering from an ideal insomnia' can still be assumed present and correct.[16] New pieces could carry with them not simply the name of their proud commissioners – mere marketing, mere advertising – but also the cost of commission, rehearsal, and performance.[17] If this makes analysis more like ethnomusicology – which is to say that establishing the claim of the object of study to attention, its nature as music, is a major part of its explication – then this may turn out to be no bad thing.[18]

The first point, then, is that pop music emerges from the 1960s and the period of postmodern uncertainty, revaluation, questioning, and change with, for better or worse, a certain claim to attention. One obvious loser is musical modernism; and the following will make little sense unless that point is first at least entertained. You've got to begin, especially around here, by at least toying with the notion that, say, Beck's 'Devil's Haircut' is in some way a truer and more rounded thing than the last BBC 'Prom' commission of Harrison Birtwistle. The point doesn't need to be conceded – far from it: the great failing has been to see the argument abandoned – but the quasi-Darwinian struggle for the space of new music of the day needs fiercely to be contested, much as Adorno aimed 'to conceive twelve-tone technique together with *Madame Butterfly* on the gramophone – this is what musical knowledge in all seriousness ought to strive towards'.[19] After all, the librarians need to know which books and records to stock.[20]

392   DAI GRIFFITHS

Table 1

Lifeworld	Exchange relations	Systems
Intimate sphere Family and friends	Labour (power)→ ← Wage money ← goods and services (money) Demand (money) →	**Market** Economy
↑ Knowledge ↓ Norms Symbols Experiences (communication)	Taxes (money)↘ ↖ Service (money) Votes (power) ↘ ↖ Political decisions (power) Demand (money) ↗ ↙ Goods and services (money)	↓ Goods and services (money) Demand (money) ↑ ↓ Taxes (money) Services (money) ↑ Political decisions↑ (power)
Cultural **Public sphere** Political	Taxes (money) → ← Service (money) ← Political decisions (power) Mass loyalty (power) →	**State** Administration

While radio is an obvious reference-point for musicians, trained to listen, if you *really* want to know what's happening, turn on the television: as the history of pop music was recounted through *Dancing in the Street,* scripted by Robert Palmer and Charles Shaar Murray – hip to contextual factors and boldly revisionist in insisting upon pop primarily as a history of black music – straight contemporary music, revised standard version, had to make do with the essays in preening self-adulation that were Simon Rattle's *Leaving Home: The History of the Music of the Twentieth-Century.*[21]

Second Opening: 'And I wanna be anarchy'[22]

The rot set in when I was about sixteen. At that time, the mid 1970s, I began listening, with tremendous earnestness and thoroughness, to BBC Radio Three, as a model recipient of the Reithian principle of using the apparatus of broadcast as a means of disseminating high culture, potentially, to the masses.[23] I started getting *The Gramophone* at the same time, too – already wedded more to records than concerts – so knew its reviewers – chaps like David Fallows, Arnold Whittall, Jeremy Noble and Iain Fenlon – like old mates. At that time, the clever money seemed to be splitting down between modernism and early music,[24] and there was a bunch of reviewers for the music in between – people like Edward Greenfield and Richard Osborne – whom I simply wanted to murder. Fortunately, too, there was a remarkable public library in nearby Llanelli, a classic case of a left-wing local council providing high culture for its masses as the gateway to liberation. Thus was I able to hear the classic modernist pieces, spiky and dissonant. The reason I was doing so was clearly a way of expressing my then-absolute loathing for the people with whom I had grown up.[25] At an age when some uncertain teenagers discover religion, I got classical and contemporary music – anything which avoided the Kitsch tunes and beats which, face it, had been my musical upbringing.[26]

In retrospect, Radio Three at that time made a lot of sense, being all of a piece. The morning's music was purposeful: each day began with records, followed by 'This Week's Composer' - positively academic in providing thorough surveys – and a live lunchtime concert; the afternoon was more relaxed: post-prandial lightness to help the lunch down (*light* music: brass bands, orchestral lollipops, military bands), eventually reaching 'Music for Pleasure' – the forerunner of today's 'drive-time' programmes – which even then gave Hans Keller cause for vituperative concern.[27] A concert in the evening, and then a variety of late things, including on Thursdays new music ('Music in Our Time'), these including pioneering concerts by the London Sinfonietta, with Arnold Whittall himself as MC. It was a fine musical education, and it meant that when I went to University I was able to hold my own with people who had received far more familial and institutional support, having been dispatched to their hideous and expensive private schools.

At University, with pop music firmly excluded from academia, and hanging out with non-musicians, I tended quickly back again towards pop music; and with punk, pop music was, irrespective of the apparent fact that we all idealise the music of our early adulthood, in a tremendous phase. The Gang of Four were a particular treat to a student, all Marxism and semiotics,[28] and there was the faint sense that some left-field pop music could, at least in theory, do the work of modernism better than modernism itself.[29]

Immediately after University, a friend got a job in the Civil Service, which involved his working at an outpost, far from Whitehall, in the heart of the City of London. Visiting him there after work, one evening for drinks, was a revelation. Radio Three suddenly made complete sense. To see the City deserted as early as 5.15 pm made clear the thinking behind 'drive-time'; the churches along the Strand and Fleet Street appeared actually to host lunchtime concerts; there was a wonderful classical record shop in Farringdon which could pretty much have displayed the sign 'Women – No!', so fleeting and noteworthy was their presence;[30] and the opera and concert halls (two opera houses and five orchestras, remember) were within easy walking distance, mimicking the radio station's peculiar practice of beginning concerts on time. The day of Radio Three was, fiercely so, the day of capital, which also explained why Whittall's tough-but-tender Sinfonietta slot was – its equivalent still is – at such guaranteed zero-audience time.[31]

Merging all of this experience with my upbringing in South Wales now also seemed difficult. Radio Three had lunchtime concerts: South Wales (along with the lower class elsewhere in the UK) doesn't even have 'lunch'. A programme called 'Man of Action' on a Saturday afternoon consisted of presentations made not, as its title suggested, by daring explorers and deep-sea divers, but retired civil servants, career diplomats, Treasury officials: they would reminisce over public school and Oxford, and explain how the combination of the music of Stanford, the sight of a choirboy, and the smell of cut grass, would give them a very English 'tingle up the spine'. Radio Three went to church often, but at something like half-past-four in the afternoon, in the middle of the week, where quite obviously chapel in Wales took place on a Sunday morning (as did services on Radio Four and on television). In summer, best of all, with positively Gallic free-thinking, Radio Three would stop broadcasting music altogether on one of its channels, and give itself over to cricket, the national sport in England alone.

Had I read *The German Ideology*, or the *Prison Notebooks*, I might have realised all along: Radio Three – Radio Home Counties might have been truer – was, behind the appearance of being an education in the higher music in truth a form of training, fine training, for the English middle-class. Confronted by this, one tactic is simply to replace transparent bourgeois ideology with another set of values, one repertory for another,[32] and such a shift occurs at the very start of what was to become Cultural Studies. Raymond Williams reads the famous list of T.S. Eliot's view of culture ('Derby Day, Henley Regatta, Cowes, the twelfth of August, a cup final, the dog races, the pin table, the dart board, Wensleydale cheese'),[33] noting its emphasis upon 'sport, food, and a little art', and allowing 'popular culture' selectively on board, later to revert to a more 'specialised' and 'exclusive sense'.[34] Behind this in turn is Eliot's scathing charge, always crucial when popular culture is entertained:

> What I try to say is this: here are what I believe to be essential conditions for the growth and for the survival of culture. If they conflict with any passionate faith of the reader – if, for instance, he finds it shocking that culture and equalitarianism should conflict, if it seems monstrous to him that anyone

should have 'advantages of birth' – I do not ask him to change his faith, I merely ask him to stop paying lip-service to culture.[35]

'Lip-service to culture': much as this passage spurred Williams himself,[36] so too the felt need to redress balance, to rehabilitate history's abandoned others, is one of the key driving forces of pop music literature. 'Marxist theory, bent on understanding the world, has always aimed at an asymptotic unity with a popular culture seeking to transform it. The trajectory of the theory has thus always been *primarily* determined by the fate of that practice'.[37] In this respect alone, it can be compared with similar efforts in the reclamation of abandoned areas of the historical past, women's music, national repertories, black music, and so on. Unlike its relation to musical modernism, where pop music is sure to appear in an oppositional or perversely critical light, in this respect its tone can be celebratory. However, the relation between pop music and those abandoned others is again anything but straightforward. Pop music continues in a certain sense as new music, albeit disparaged and debased, and is unable entirely to eradicate that critical, political aspect. Indeed, I'm going to suggest here that pop music writing, implicated in arguments about new music, is best understood as a certain literature of the left during the late twentieth-century.

Third Opening: 'And every city, the whole world round, will just be another American town'[38]

There's a track on an album of Randy Newman called 'Sigmund Freud's Impersonation of Albert Einstein in America'.[39] My guess is that the song was occasioned by Newman's working on the film music for Milos Foreman's adaptation of E.L. Doctorow's novel, *Ragtime*.[40] The idea of the song is that Freud arrives in America following Einstein's successful crossing of the Atlantic to escape Nazi persecution, but dislikes what he sees there. The opening of Newman's song is filmic-Bavarian, straight out of *Cabaret*, and reminds us of his faultless talent as orchestrator.[41] The song, when it appears, is disarmingly simple, child-like, the more to highlight in the mind a simple 'thematic process' in the piano links: (a) easily recognized in the German verse, changing into (b), a 'crossing the Atlantic' phrase, which turns out to be derived from (c), never heard as such.

During the second verse Freud carries out a psychoanalysis of the American psyche, getting it rather badly wrong; gradually but rapidly, the orchestration has subtly shifted, and the simple expedient of deleting tuba bass, cymbal, and clarinet doubling inner strings in favour of strings and brass ensemble, has lent something of the quality of American war film or American symphony. Finally, as Freud takes leave of the scene and his senses, he and the music conclude with the last line of Irving Berlin's 'White Christmas', (c) above:

Ex.1

'Sigmund Freud's Impersonation of Albert Einstein in America'. Words and Music by Randy Newman © 1985 Six Pictures Music, USA. Rondor Music (London) Ltd., London SW6 4TW. Reproduced by permission of International Music Publications Ltd.

'And may all your Christmases be white'.[42] I've always understood this to be a joke enacting Freud's contemptuous dismissal of *émigrés* to the land of commercialization.[43]

The track interestingly invites all sorts of confusions about high and low, mass culture and modernity, Europe and America, and Doctorow himself features prominently in Jameson's defining article on the postmodern.[44] It isn't particularly difficult to make a case out for the song to be of some interest, and it seems, in a rather uncontroversial sense, a great shame that someone as talented as Newman has over the years been studiously avoided by the academic journals, with seemingly little doctoral work conducted in this fecund area.[45]

On a later record, *Land of Dreams* (Warner, 1988), Newman in the title song deals with a trip which his family took from Los Angeles to New Orleans, in order to link up with family in the Southern states, at a time when his father was undertaking military service in Europe. His mother's family drive down from Jackson, Mississippi and, on the way, pretend not to be Jewish – Newman rhymes 'Jew' without mentioning the term: 'trying to do like the Gentiles do/ Christ, they wanted to be Gentiles too/Who wouldn't down there, wouldn't you?' The section ends with a grand and brassy line, 'An American Christian. God damn!', all very witty. The next song, a sparkling number called 'When New Orleans Won the War', scored again with a precise sense of imagined geography, echoes the wind band arrangements of the time. With my British ears, particularly at one point in the song where Newman on the piano accompanies a pretty clarinet solo, I think of a family coming down in the car from Jackson, linking the sound of the second track to a concert they just might have attended, some years before:

> Consider, then, the effect of the flattering occasion of being submerged in a sea
> of construals and evaluations of one's past efforts, inducing the events of one's
> compositional life to pass before one's ears, if not precisely in a flash, with a
> focused impact strategically comparable only with that moment when a small
> ten-year-old clarinet player in the Jackson (Miss.) Boys' Band realized that the

three successively highest notes (A, B, C♯) of his *dolce* clarinet solo in the *Oberon* overture, though separated by registrally lower passages occupying two and three measures respectively, were revealed – by virtue at least of their registral and instrumental placement above the 'break' – as simply a transposition of the opening three horn notes of the piece, later – but before the Byronic clarinet solo – repeated at a major second transposition. This recognition, if not a major revelation in the history of analytical theory, was yet sufficient to suggest to the clarinetist how one might do cognitive things with notes which might prove deserving of his further attention.[46]

What Milton Babbitt and Randy Newman would have heard in a wind band orchestration might stand as a little image of a tension in twentieth-century American music and, by extension, especially at the crucial time, from around 1950 to 1970, between modernism and popular music. It could have gone either way: Newman the Princeton professor, Babbitt the commercial songwriter; and it's an essential perspective here, one which I think British analysts have consistently misread, an important background for Allen Forte, student of Cole Porter, David Lewin, jazz buff, and Milton Babbitt, authority on Tin Pan Alley. To these theorists, the combination of logical positivism, as emigrated philosophical stance, parallel to developing variation, on the one hand, with, on the other, home-grown pragmatic relativism,[47] the charm of the popular song, appears not to have been such a big deal: more perhaps a matter of interest in a particular art form; less, perhaps, overlaid by the tarpaulin of aesthetic judgment. Babbitt's most famous statement, 'this bloody article',[48] the article whose title so provocatively appears to epitomise modernist elitism, does contain, after all, the following: 'There is no such thing as "serious" and "popular" music. There is only music whose title begins with the letter "X" and music whose title does not.'[49] That such a statement could never quite emanate from a British analyst has little to do with pop music, but a lot to do with all that baggage, with a certain European conception of class.

The High Analysis of Low Music: A Typology

If in these openings there were three possible paths to the point at which pop music arises as object of study – the critical relation to the failed political agenda of musical modernism, a celebratory felt need to redress balance, and the extension of a certain logical positivism – then each path engenders its own attitude in the literature. I follow with three caricatures which map out that literature, a typology is intended to an extent in the spirit of the first chapter of Adorno's *Introduction to the Sociology of Music*.[50] While Adorno's types tend to suggest too easily his appearing to be the 'distilled essence of intellectual snobbery on the Left',[51] when dealing with new, recent, 'not yet hard' phenomena like new music or pop music, so those psychological/sociological guesses or gambles which the types represent are I think a useful and not (yet) dishonest tool.

First Attitude: Earnest Onlooking

But I have made him see the light: he just wanna dance!

We should be in a relaxed setting, be rid of background sounds, and be paying careful attention. For some, it will be difficult to concentrate on that which we may have formerly treated passively; but this change is absolutely imperative if we are to succeed in musical analysis, which in turn will lead to a more complete understanding of the true nature of rock and roll.[52]

The village vicar sets up a club for disaffected local youth; sweating around the white collar, he turns a deaf ear as the rough kids mock his attempts at ping-pong. Earnest onlooking is a significant front-line activity between the consuming proletariat and the contemplating intelligentsia. Earnestness is the key trait: without it there would not be the energy to see through projects with so little immediate prospect of academic gratification.

The originary earnest onlooker for pop music as musicology was surely Wilfrid Mellers, ever ready to offer an engaged and educative trip through his record collection,[53] and the line of descent encompasses the Ealing school, Christopher Small and Allan Moore, with Charles Hamm and Richard Middleton linking to the next section. A sometimes Christian or Leavisite background leads directly to a concern with demonstration through teaching.[54] So, and notably, perhaps the earliest significant musical attentions given to popular music, which took the step of transcribing records and incorporating in footnotes identifiably musicological literature, were the series of teaching books edited by Graham Vulliamy,[55] while Mellers himself (at the University of York) was able to inform educational practice in the state schools via John Paynter.[56] The line between earnest onlooking and the next section is direct, but there's an earnest onlooker tone which never quite disappears: serious and lacking irony, morally purposeful, slightly awkward in relation to the object of study, itself the consequence of an inauthentic relation to the constituency. Pop music literature is rather haunted by the possibility of straightforward, devil-may-care, hedonistic *pleasure*. Fancy a Big Night Out with any of these lads?

I, for one, have a rather extreme dislike of being 'entertained'.

What does it mean to say that I like a song or performance, and why do other people like different ones? Clearly such questions do not have disinterested answers: neither pleasure nor value can appear except through the operation of *ideology*. Their 'natural', 'innocent', and 'obvious' qualities, far from disproving this point, are precisely the mark of its truth, for their partiality and contingency have been repressed in the interests of a false universality.

I spent a long time listening continuously to everything by all of them, which was a bad idea, in part because I wound up preferring the poppier ones for being easier to take in large doses than the straightforwardly angry, screaming ones.[58]

Perhaps a recurring feature of early reception, and important in establishing cultural capital, the earnest onlooker is also in the front-line of attempting to detach academic work from journalism,[59] perceived in its immediacy and dependence upon advertising to be a lower form, in a way which reflects the attempt to make rock the transformation of entertainment into art. Pop music journalism, however, followed 1960s pop music into self-conscious artiness, through the 'gonzo' generation – Bangs, Marcus, Cohn, Kent, giving their work far more the character of the next section.[60] Simon Frith is doubly important as a direct link between the world of rock journalism and academia, and some of the tension between journalism and earnest onlooking can be felt simply by tracking index references to Frith in Allan Moore's book. Wherever Frith appears there is some carping criticism, though in the end Moore's own programme of activity – attending to reception (or 'affordance', as Moore has it), genre, and questions of value, albeit all from a musical perspective[61] – uncomfortably describes much of Frith's entire project. In other words, an earnest onlooker can go all the way round the musical block only to find the sociologists there already, in the leathers, waiting, threateningly revving up the Harleys, ready to rock.

That said, the earnest onlookers put in the effort, and conscientiously so. Moore cannot be faulted as listener and as analyst, and his book made significant steps in reclaiming foreground singularities which both voice-leading and set-theoretic analyses had avoided in their search for common backgrounds. His sections on voice (pp. 41–7) and the relation of texture and technology in the 'soundbox' (pp. 106–10) belong in any reading-list which attempts to foster close listening, whatever the repertory. I've never quite been able to follow his harmonic system,[62] and suspect that he concedes too much of the high theoretical ground to the guitar magazine (though how often do you see genuine, ordinary talk about harmony anymore?), and any pop fan would need to be suspicious of the line that leads to progressive rock as preferred repertory on grounds of musical complexity. But this is a useful and tirelessly honest book, and I can testify to its efficacy in teaching.

Finally, bibliography and discography are two of the staple activities of earnest onlooking. Without them, the theorists have little to observe. For this to happen, the onlooker, in order to preserve seriousness of purpose, has to buy into cultural relativism, itself a key issue in the relation of high and low. So we

400   DAI GRIFFITHS

find David Brackett insisting that 'value can never inhere in an aesthetic object',[63] to which an analyst might reply, 'Never? So why choose *that* object of study over any other?' So too Allan Moore claims that 'extreme relativism... is both unavoidable and to be embraced, for it asserts that not only music's meaning, but its values too, are the preserves of listeners'.[64] Moore's point is particularly canny, since it shifts the ground onto cognition, subjectivity and critique. The people in the following section are often nuts, though, and would, in all seriousness, most probably want to reply: 'So how are such passive consumers ever going to change the world?'[65]

Second Attitude: Street Fighting Men

> That is to say, I don't understand a practice which aims to make a difference in the world, which doesn't have some points of difference or distinction, which it has to stake out, which really matter.

> I will not let postmodern scoffers deny my experience and that of many others: I am here to attest that it is possible to be steered, fairly directly, by popular music, toward fully conscious radicalization.

What can a poor boy do?[66]

Here's where pop music literature really takes off, and is the point that must be taken on board: a presentation of pop literature's past which lets this aspect go by is to my mind missing a central point, if not *the* point. A cursory example: Philip Tagg begins a book on musical semiotics not with a literature review, but with a section which makes clear his stance on the iniquities of the political system in Brazil.[67] This could happen only in pop music literature. Jim Samson by and large does not begin a book on Chopin with a few considered reflections on the foundation of Solidarity; Arnold Whittall does not cast an eye over the chances of success for the Scottish parliament before launching into another piece on Peter Maxwell Davies.

But in the pop music literature it's different, and raising the issue of political purpose is par for the course. During a review of popular music as media study, David Hesmondhalgh steps in, so to speak, in order to bring out 'very real problems for anyone trying to understand the relationship between progressive political change and political consciousness'; in Simon Frith's recent book, a cool theoretical merging of Howard Becker and Pierre Bourdieu, there's still 'enough of a Marxist' in his search for 'the *unpopular popular*'; Richard Middleton's book is called with open generosity, *Studying Popular Music*, like a come-on to the average Whitesnake obsessive, but after four pages of introduction is already mulling over some of the details of the turn to Gramsci in British cultural studies; best of all is Peter Wicke's book, which culminates, like an Eisler teaching-piece, in some stirring stuff from the hardline East European left ('an "alternative *politics* of culture"... can hardly be developed in books, but only in revolutionary praxis'; 'models of action... were missing at the critical moment').[68]

Before going further into the collision of pop music and music analysis, it is worth briefly considering, from an analytical standpoint, one possible option: bringing a liberal agenda to popular music, rather in the way in which some of the earliest sociological approaches to popular songs simply read them for their content.[69] An exemplary case here is Charles Hamm, another American who did the unthinkable for British academics by crossing from the study of Dufay and Dunstable to Tin Pan Alley. From an early stage, reflecting perhaps the impact of the 1960s, as his recent collected essays suggest,[70] Hamm wanted musicology to stretch out to sharper political purpose, and his subsequent career, his years of engagement with music in South Africa, saw this project through in a way which would put virtually anyone in musicology in the shade.

It is, however, arguable (if petty) that what he did was to take political hopes and *impose onto* a form which could not bear the weight of idealistic expectation. In, his magnificent book on Tin Pan Alley, Hamm makes the important point that, in surveying the popular songs written during the period of the great depression, one

> searches in vain for songs touching in any way on the great social and political issues of those years – the continuing desperate plight of the black American in white America; the struggle of working class citizens to combat by unionization and strikes their exploitation by management; the worsening situation of ethnic minorities in Central and Eastern Europe and the inexorable rise to power of totalitarian regimes in many of these countries.[71]

If only Charles Hamm had been alive![72] The description of social and political problems of the 1930s (beyond the hyphen) is, of course, pure Charles Hamm. An analyst might wish to suggest that the merging of tonal music, lyric (the key mediating term) and fine romance, represents a particular balance which the *form* insists upon. In fact, even 'the song most often cited as an exception to the rule that all popular songs from this era were about love',[73] Jay Gorney and Yip Harburg's 'Brother, Can You Spare a Dime?', the apparently solitary example of Tin Pan Alley demonstrating an overt social conscience, 'virtually alone in its serious treatment of poverty',[74] is of course itself a standard lyric: 'Say, don't you remember/They called me Al/It was Al all the time/ Say don't you remember? I'm your pal/Buddy, can you spare a dime?' It's ironic that Hamm was to take issue with Paul Simon over *Graceland*,[75] the hit single from which, 'You Can Call Me Al', picks up that very rhyme from Harburg's lyrics. What Hamm does is to take political change, and read it wishfully into the symbolic form of pop song. It's an expressive failing: as we will see, the idea of art forms being asked to carry directly the imitation of suffering and the conditions which require social change – that is, above and beyond their being at best escape from, or fantasy around those conditions – is a theme which returns. In this debate, music analysis would simply ask that the demands of the art *form* take precedence. Change, which was going to come, concerned not broadening the range of address, but either changing the world (the gamble which musical modernism by the 1960s too readily continued to assume), or, simply, changing the form. This latter may have happened with James Brown and with Bob Dylan in the mid-1960s. A political analysis might suggest differently, but a musical reading might wish to suppose that Simon is aware as songwriter of the limitations of pop song as form, and that this acceptance of compromise extends to his working within a limited framework with the musicians of *Graceland*.[76] Hamm writes in a positivistic tradition of popular music study, which would extend to include much of the literature of country, blues and jazz, and it is interesting to compare his approach to the politicising of popular song with Dave Laing, who has perhaps the most attenuated sense of the tension involved.[77]

Laing is a good fulcrum as the story shifts towards the heady mixture of sociology, literary and media study, and politics, which formed cultural studies itself. Here the object of study, be it a pop song, is *brought into* a framework which is politicised through and through. Laing closed his study of Marxist aesthetics with the observation that 'a theory which cannot guide practice risks a descent into academic contemplation, just as a practice proud of its spontaneity will often find itself a prisoner of the very ideology it set out to oppose'.[78] This study, published in 1978, intersects the period separating his two path-breaking books, on Buddy Holly and punk rock, from 1971 and 1985 respectively.[79] The earlier book is as analysis already perfectly methodical; the book on punk – still one of the best models available for the study of pop music – takes this methodological neatness but incorporates it into a framework which welcomes Barthes, Benjamin and Brecht.[80] The way is open for an attempted bringing-together of what a study of pop music, politicized at its inception, might look like. What is interesting at this point is to take the story of cultural studies – a relatively recent history which seems to get recounted with expressively obsessive regularity[81] – and to read it not only alongside popular music, towards which it was always unsurprisingly going to be sympathetic, but also the methodological development of music analysis itself. Distant as they may seem, they are not entirely unrelated.

Richard Johnson presents a clear account of cultural studies.[82] He, like others, makes clear that cultural studies arose from a certain *dis*satisfaction with methodology on the Marxist left, and this originary divergence can lead to the obvious charge that Street Fighting Men actually do little to effect the political change they bring to their 'readings'.[83] What followed was an attempt to move forward what was seen as something of a dead end, perhaps explaining the search for fresh rather than inherited theory, the assimilation of which (Gramsci, Althusser, Lacan) seems to have been carried through with missionary devotion at the Centre for Contemporary Cultural Studies (CCCS) in Birmingham in the 1970s. Naturally, music theory lay outside this framework, and cultural studies had little impact on music study at the time, which was turning inward to the text. Nevertheless, similar intellectual currents may have been at work. The key pull in early cultural studies, Johnson suggests, was between culturalism and structuralism. Culturalism – Williams's 'whole way of life' – was an emphasis more on socio-cultural setting, opening up discussion to real people through oral history and ethnography. The structuralist approach – Williams's famous phrase 'structures of feeling' is a delicate negotiation of the two trends – started by trying to discover common or universal features across cultures, and so saw more emphasis upon modernism and formalism.[84] It is not difficult to imagine these positions mapping onto musicology. Jean-Jacques Nattiez, to take an obvious example, veers between ethnomusicology and musical modernism, and John Shepherd and Peter Wicke's recent and elaborate concept of 'sonic saddle' pulls in elements of both tendencies. Indeed, their awkward complaint that Robert Walser writes as 'a musician, not a cultural theorist with an intimate knowledge of music's sonic, technical features', can stand as summing up the tension which the musical wing of the Street Fighting Men found themselves having to negotiate.[85]

The reason why the Street Fighting Men became involved in pop music, positively so, closely parallels the reasoning behind cultural studies itself. In Britain, the educational background was again crucial, particularly in making classroom music – as opposed to the parental ability to provide private musical lessons – a required element of the state school curriculum. Raymond Williams draws attention to the vocational nature of adult education for the generation of Williams, Hoggart and Thompson, adding that cultural studies 'was a renewal of that attempt at a majority democratic education which had been there all through the project, but which kept being sidetracked as elements of it got into institutions which then changed it'.[86]

The early days are marked by blurs and confusions: Mellers, again an expressive example, occupied a peculiar position emerging from *Scrutiny* at a time when Leavisites appear to have been determinedly opposed to commercialisation.[87] There were important differences, in a mundane contest of faculties, between musicology and sociology, and between both in turn and the literature department. For sociologists, trained in and reared upon a relatively recent and modern theory, pop music was more like common practice, and subcultural theory invested a glamorous *nostalgie de la boue* – see for instance how writers like Simon Frith, Iain Chambers and Dick Hebdige transplanted from cultural studies into constituting important areas of the pop music literature.[88] By allying themselves with the category of *youth*, curiously enough, they were reinforcing the distinction between sociology and musicology, the teaching of which is always aware of its deep historical lineage. History was on sociology's side: the merging of youth, artwork and the lifeworld appears to have been a major element of growing up through the 1960s, a background for Berio's *Sinfonia* and Bernstein's recordings of Mahler and Ives, as surely as for The Beatles or The Who. This was nothing so simple for musicians, with their proud ability to perform the classics, right here, right now, for whom canoodling with pop music involved compromising if necessary the concern for the classical tradition into which they themselves had been delivered – this all during the 1970s and 1980s when, presumably unbeknown to them, pop's claim to the condition of new music deepened simply by contrast with the seeming economic endgame of musical modernism,[89] and in turn classical music was obliged to begin learning its marketing tricks from pop. With colleagues suspicious and able to call on a handy and powerfully conservative litany of declining standards, political correctness and the culture industry, this transitional sense of betrayal of trust underlies the work of any British writer on popular music during the period. Having benefited from 'classical' music themselves, here they are seemingly denying the working-class that classical tradition, trapping them inside the disgusting products of the culture industry. Liberation or entrapment? With those kinds of gremlins liable to invade their dreams, no wonder the Earnest Onlookers needed their Gideon Bibles, the Street Fighters their *Portable Marx*.

It should be noted, however, that Marxism was not such a distant reference at the time that Street Fighting Men got involved in the politics of pop music. It's easy to reify Benjamin's piece on mechanical reproduction as the blueprint of techno-optimism while forgetting his conclusion, that what would take the place of aestheticism would be 'another practice – politics'; easy too, as I have done above, gratefully to footnote Greenberg for the terminology of Avant-garde and Kitsch while conveniently passing over the force of his peroration, that 'today we look to socialism *simply* for the preservation of whatever living culture we have right now'; even Adorno – I think it possible to downplay just how hopelessly radical an article like 'Vers une musique informelle' really is.[90]

All of the issues in this story to date, and many of those which follow, gather together in one remarkable book. Richard Middleton's *Studying Popular Music* is the most important musicological work on pop music to have appeared,[91] and finds itself balanced, precariously, as a synthesis of virtually every development described so far, overlaying them all with a centrally politicised view of the field. Stuart Hall's *cri de coeur*, 'If you lose hold of the tension, you can do extremely fine intellectual work, but you will have lost intellectual practice as a politics',[92] can stand as its guiding principle, its guiding neurosis. The same thought informs one of the book's most characteristic ideas (though Middleton's phrasing precedes Hall in this respect): 'Rather than pulling to one side, with the traditional musicologists, or the other, with the "total critics" of musicology, it will be better to *look both ways, living out the tension*' (p. 123: all italics his). My argument so far has been to suggest that reading the book as anything other than an example of a literature of the left – what Anthony Giddens describes as a worldview which takes the eradication of inequality, oppression and exploitation as its aim[93] – is akin to reading *Animal Farm* as the story of some disgruntled pigs.

That said, it also deserves to be reclaimed, here of all places, as a central text for music analysis. In such a reading the book is a sustained display of how to go around the twin towers of critique in late modernity – critical theory (Marx via Lukács via Frankfurt[94]) and cultural studies (Marx via Williams via CCCS) – and still end up believing that 'clearly, then, what is at issue for any "critical musicology" is the exact nature of the relationship between particular musical problematics and the wider cultural, social and ideological forces.' (p. 126) Middleton has an almost psycho-somatic relation to music analysis, those 'problematics': able on the one hand snarlingly to see 'autonomy like repression' (p. 40), and to describe an asphyxiation which requires 'relaxation of the analytical strangle-hold' (p. 287), while on the other hand and at the same time finding fault in a writer who 'throws away any chance of musical analysis' (p. 117), and imagining at one point an extraordinary 'universal framework' which would 'provide both ethnomusicology and popular music studies with the weapons that will dethrone traditional musicology from the centre of the *analytical* stage' (p. 192, my italic).

The section where Middleton actually 'does' music analysis is improvisatory and hardly likely to impress the Managers of the section which follows.[95] The Schenkerian reduction of a Gershwin song (p. 194), to take an obvious example, is trapped in a confusion of voice-leading and motive; but the disturbing thing about this, and to an extent the more successful, more mechanical semiotic analysis (pp. 184–9), is how it runs against the critique which the book has elsewhere mounted, by reinstating analytical method as a series of methodological bus stops, where the endless deferral which the rest of the book enacts is, even paradoxically, its biggest contribution to the activity of analysis, and these experiments and improvisations serve only to prepare the way for a fresher and more rounded methodology in the final chapter.

The cause is not helped as Middleton himself acts as a particularly critical policeman when surveying the work of other more traditional musicologists – perhaps the same is true of his approach to ethnomusicology. Alec Wilder, Charles Hamm and Wilfrid Mellers seem to be picked at from what seems at that point a perch of chirpy immunity. Hamm selects songs to discuss, and is compared, rather automatically, with the way 'historians of "classical" music used to construct their histories simply out of a selection of great works' (p. 110). Mellers is criticised in one paragraph for using notation in his Beatles book; but of the Dylan book, which avoids so doing, Middleton has it that although this 'is an important advance... it brings its own problems, for it now becomes quite difficult to talk clearly and in depth about harmony and melody and all' (p. 112).

Middleton's dismissal of available musicological practice reflects the fact that his own position was so openly interdisciplinary: the book's inclusivity is remarkable. Its bibliography assimilates two subtly distinct tendencies in the literature of cultural studies: the standard CCCS literature, Gramsci and Althusser mediated through Stuart Hall; and, particularly in its culminating analysis of repetition, the potent brew of Lacanian psychoanalysis associated at the time with the film journal, *Screen*.[96] Over the years it becomes clear just how many agendas Middleton has already pre-empted – an ability, frustrating for others in the field, he shares with Simon Frith. Allan Moore's breakthrough passages, on voice and mix, are foreshadowed at pp. 53 and 242 (the latter anticipating some of the current vogue for the analysis of performance); David Brackett's visualisations are intimated at p. 207; the description of melody, via Van der Merwe, foreshadows Allen Forte's approach to Cole Porter (p. 203). And for a music book simply to have encompassed and engaged with the following terms and their literature in one sweep during the late 1980s is impressive: erotics (pp. 257, 262), fordism (p. 287), fragment (p. 62), ecology (p. 261), bodies (pp. 258–67), parody (p. 221). Homology, the most direct sociological entry into the musical text, seems to me to be decisively challenged.[97]

Many of the most expressive moments of the book are those where Middleton as pop fan allows himself to be fascinated by the allure of what the strong socialist *ego* would clearly deny. Its tone is often embattled and brusque, and characteristic of the British left *avant Blair*. 'Struggle' appears often, three times at least in struggling italics (pp. 9, 37, 72); at p. 32 an 'ideology of riskless hedonism' is firmly middle-class, with the aristocracy and proletariat presumably exempt;[98] cultural morality at p. 139 is 'imperialist', much as gender relations arise from the 'bourgeois couple' (p. 10); narrative, goal-direction and realism all have to do with 'typical bourgeois ideological preoccupations' (p. 216), and, wonderfully, the 'vulgar self-preservation of the virtuously civilized' (p. 268). And who else would dream of ending the sentence on p. 73 – 'What has happened, in fact, is that Cutler has been forced to try to squeeze together a neo-Benjaminian theory of productive forces and a picture of productive relations which is positively Adornian' – with an exclamation-mark (!)?

Adorno, reflected in a British Marxist mirror, was sure to figure. Middleton recounts the argument (encountered earlier) that a wider sympathy on Adorno's part might have resulted in a calmer view (p. 45). But more expressive I feel are passages of 'sympathy for the devil', the sense that Adorno may well have been right in some ways – see Middleton's Adornian fascination with commercialisation at pp. 36–7, the smack at advertising on p. 50, or the comment on drugs and narcissism at p. 57. At p. 38 Middleton characteristically and rightly castigates Adorno for avoiding performance contexts, places as well as their sound, 'working-class black dance halls, bars, churches', foreshadowing a similar point made by Paul Piccone:

> Limited mostly to the manicured, homogenized middle-class enclaves of Morningdale Heights and Santa Monica, Adorno's American experience only reinforced his stereotypes of the US as what the culture industry marketed in the 1940s and 1950s as 'the American way of life'. Had he spent a little more time studying Brooklyn's and Chicago's ethnic neighbourhoods or the Mid-West rather than inventing politically-correct 'F-scales' and complaining about jazz, he may have come up with a different version of the US than one finds in, e.g. *Minima Moralia* or *Dialectic of Enlightenment*.[99]

Unlike the way in which Adorno is sometimes used merely to gaze gloomily if fashionably into the abyss, with Middleton, under the tough prose, Utopia is never too far away. The crucial passage from pp. 115–26, the manifesto of a critical musicology, has a penchant for metaphors of geography, place, topography (remap the terrain, look both ways).[100] I particularly like the moment when, scratching for examples (the *example* such a fetish for most musicology), he throws in 'whatever *you* choose' in a charming and honest self-effacement (p. 255).[101] *Studying Popular Music* stands at the cusp of where an engaged literature of the left, outward-looking and able firmly to articulate its intent, turns in to the text itself. The book's method, which is effectively to try to wrap every literature in the language of critique, endlessly deferred, seems to me its most enduring display, and right now its most important legacy and challenge. What is behind the book is a view of the world which is centrally concerned with political change: its repertory (popular music), its purpose (education as liberation), its approach (text-centred), all follow from this central fact. As pop music gradually receives more attention through its historical staying-power and where, Middleton might well ask of his italicised second-person singular, were *you* in 1972 or 1981? – various attempts to pass over the Street Fighting agenda are beginning to appear. But without the original political starting-point, it's never clear why any musician would want – really, really want – to engage with pop music. Without that perspective, 'to tell you the truth', as Stuart Hall would say, 'I don't give a damn about it'.[102]

Third Attitude: The Managers

Here they come, walking down the street. Nick Cook: 'rock theory can be said to have come of age in November 1990, when a session on rock was included at the Annual Meeting of the Society for Music Theory in Oakland, California'.[103] Against the background of the entire discussion till now, the sheer *chutzpa* of this sentence is breathtaking. So much for Richard Middleton, Philip Tagg, John Shepherd, Peter Wicke, Dave Laing, and many, many others, dismissed in Cook's previous paragraph as 'sociologically-inclined'. Look! Interesting groundwork has been carried out in some unforeseen cranny and so, now, 'why, they asked, should the *music* of rock not be accorded the same detailed scrutiny as any other widely valued repertory?' Power Analysis[TM,104] the grateful recipient of social conditions which enable Kantian activity to occur without worrying too hard over the struggle which makes those conditions possible, had up until then been concerned more to bolster the ideological categories it inherited from historical musicology. For Philip Tagg to be overlooked by the theory community will come as no surprise to him: the bibliographies of both Nattiez and Dunsby make no mention either of Britain's most determined semiotician or indeed the Italians, Franco Fabbri and Gino Stefani.[105] Note too how the great sacred cow of music analysis, the *New Grove* bibliography compiled by Ian Bent and William Drabkin,[106] amiably generous in including Charles Rosen for *Sonata Forms*, Ebenezer Prout's teaching books, some *ethno*musicology,[107] and select obscurities of the Beethoven, Wagner and Schoenberg literatures, nonetheless avoids an edition of the journal *Popular Music*, published in 1982, and explicitly entitled 'Theory and Method' – avoids it like the plague, like a teenage magazine. And *Music Analysis* itself, whose title and appearance might suggest neutrality: Middleton's *Studying Popular Music* and Allan Moore's *Rock: The Primary Text*, both with plenty to say towards the activity of music analysis, both written by British scholars (Middleton in particular an author established in the literature), both published by the Press emanating from the 1960s Labour government's finest invention[108] – both hitherto passed over for review; David Brackett, American, a relative newcomer, published by Cambridge, granted this response. The power politics involved here will be ignored only by those who believe that they stand to benefit from so doing.

Power in the phrase Power Analysis[TM] attempts to capture two things: the slippage between what it is to deal with intersubjective communication through symbolic form, on the one hand, and on the other, the world of markets and administration, the world of transnational corporation, within which all of this activity takes place (see again the Fornäs diagram above). Secondly, the slippage between the ambiguous terms of the German *die Technik*,[109] technique and technology: power analysis arises where analysis as high-technology supra-knowledge is used to contain an empirical, technical observation merely for the sake of attaining, against the background of the first slippage, power. Power Analysis appears characteristically where an observation concerning technique which is, be honest, *dead easy*, suddenly requires a load of graphs.[110]

The line from Power Analysis to pop *music* is suspiciously direct: there is one clearly established theory for tonal music, that established by Heinrich Schenker and Americanised as voice-leading theory (Salzer ever the key link).[111] Pop music is tonal music; and so there is no need *not* to apply Schenkerian models to pop music. Enter Walter Everett, who joins Janis, Jimi and Kurt in Popular Music Heaven for having broken through to the *Musical Quarterly* with an article on John Lennon.[112] The article seems in retrospect like solid, weighty musicology: pages of detailed lyrics are reproduced with little reference to words in the article, production details, close textual reading. Everett's article, really, says as much about the fate of Schenkerian/Salzerian analysis as it does about The Beatles, and the objection returns to the original one, in Babbitt's review of Salzer, that 'the analyses ... are conceived neither in the terms in which the music was composed nor in the terms by which they can be most completely comprehended'.[113]

The big point about taking Power Analysis down the roads of abandoned musics is that the analytical methods are themselves non-reflexive. No ardent Schenkerian would dream of adapting the technology to reflect the presence of, say, the things which Allan Moore has so cogently described: voice, recording or performance. This again is not unusual, and is a chicken-and-egg complaint made from the left about the relation of *langue* and *parole*: 'Although the rules of language systems determine speech acts, the everyday deployment of linguistic forms appears not to touch the language system itself'; similarly, the 'very freedom of the speaking subject is curiously inconsequential: that is, its effects on the structure in return are in normal circumstances virtually nil'.[114]

In turn, in a more general sense, the line from Saussure through structuralism to post-structuralism, the musical adaptation of which has provided *Music Analysis* with much of its most fecund material, is again difficult for the left, and may serve only to reactivate a debate reached by 1929 with Volosinov. Indeed, any appropriation of 'formalism' by music analysis ought itself to be set against this debate, a context which would include some of the century's most extreme artwork before the 1960s.[115] The turn towards structure, the 'gradual megalomania of the signifier',[116] was of little consequence in directly affecting social change, as the workings of systems came to replace any radical purpose gained in establishing the systems in the first place.

There's another way, of course, which is to pose the question: is American music theory, or British music analysis, ever intended to be a force of liberation? Even to posit the question in this way would seem to invite contradiction, not to mention hilarity, as the analytical community appeared to have taken perhaps too readily the role of the conservatism it once sought to displace. Was it ever so? Historical musicology appeared to build expensive hurdles to negotiate: access to distant libraries, language skill, standardised techniques of editing and sketch study, and, most perniciously, the thing that really needed private income, an interest in and ability to perform. Analysis, on the other hand, appeared to insist only that its student acquire a score and a recording; as much as anything, music analysis was *dead cheap*. Secondly, more or less anyone could do analysis – like the study of literature or film, all you needed was the ability to listen and musical literacy. Analysis served to show that most points about music were, once understood, *dead easy*, as indeed most of them are. And, thirdly, analysis, well, you could *make it up as you went along* – inventing structure was a case of inventing plausible *fiction*.[117]

All of this, analysis as a means of democratisation, as a means of broadening access to music's study, was always posited upon the centrality, the absolute necessity of teaching people how to understand music.[118] If so, old Nick Cook is perhaps the devil here again, as, perhaps unwittingly and curiously for the author of a primer on music analysis, he appears to have given momentum to what might be termed 'dumb-listener theory', an argument always liable to trap the study of pop music as liberating practice. Cook wanted to establish that people by and large had no conception of the precise detail of the music they heard. As a Cambridge postgraduate, he set up an experiment which involved music undergraduates listening to Webern's Symphony, Op. 21. They get a lot of the answers wrong; which is not especially surprising – were they to have listened to a hit of the day, say, Gloria Gaynor's 'I Will Survive' or Art Garfunkel's 'Bright Eyes', doubtless they would have crucified the *questions*. From this rather predictable evidence, Cook cranks up the volume and concludes that there is a Webern symphony 'for the analyst, and one for the listener'. Then, from the perspective of pop music, Simon Frith puts some weight on the exercise, and reaches in a short space the idea that 'the object the musicologist defined was not the object the pop fan heard', reinforcing his earlier explanation of 'why so much musicological analysis of popular music misses the point: its object of study, the discursive text it constructs, is not the text to which anyone else listens'.[119]

So now, for the masses, sound remains a screen: their touching dependence on this music is able to express all manner of things about the context in which it is received, but music remains a blank sheet upon which is imposed all manner of imprecise response.[120] This engenders in turn the legitimation of a kind of Beavis and Butthead outlook, represented in two recent books, by

Theodor Gracyk and Neil Nehring.[121] It's important, as ever in pop music literature, to understand the kind of music which forms the landscape, in their case a 1980s line emanating from Sonic Youth and taking in bands like Big Black and Nirvana – the loud and arty noise of the 'slacker' generation. These writers are sure of the primacy of sound as screen, sound as emotion, over any need to attend to music or words. It's especially tragic for Nehring, however, having spent 150 pages berating, with a degree of care, entire swathes of literature, that his attention to a single track, Bikini Kill's spunky 'Carnival', a track which lasts only one and a half minutes, itself lasts all of two paragraphs (pp. 165–6) – 'that's all by way of "musicology" that I intend to offer'. This nugget is preceded by sixteen splendidly ranting pages of attack on capitalist society (pp. 150–56). In this latter, however, Nehring has to accept a woeful degree of false consciousness in the artistic taste of the proletariat: it is perfectly apparent that, given the tiny morsel of capitalist 'freedom' involved in wandering the record shop, the mass of these poor oppressed people would surely not want to buy any Riot Grrrl singles, and for one very blunt reason. They sound *awful*. If you've taken a day's worth of grief from The Man, then you're not necessarily going to top it off with an evening of the unmediated imitation of that very grief emanating from the stereo. The question 'So what did you listen to last night?' is in a way the acid test; again, by never addressing the question of social change, a Schoenberg, a Webern never really prepared the *time of day* at which their music would be heard or, worse because time-consuming, understood.[122] Pop music is surely far closer to a line which can lead back from Simon Frith's insistence that 'things like shopping malls and *NME* and top 40 music and reruns of *M.A.S.H.* matter so much because people's lives are otherwise tedious and desperate and sad', through Henri Matisse's description of his painting as, 'for the businessman as well as the man of letters, a soothing, calming influence on the mind, something like a good armchair which brings relaxation from physical fatigue', to Marx's description of religion as the 'sigh of the oppressed creature, the heart of a heartless world, the spirit of spiritless conditions' and, famously, 'the *opium* of the people.'[123]

Two essential things seem to me to be getting lost, and both of them are important for eradicating the high analysis of low music, which is really to do with eradicating high and low, full stop. First, that a Noel Gallagher understands his chords without necessarily having been taught the theory around them, and that there is no violence being done to this open and liberating activity – of being in a band, which cuts down social boundaries, where working-class people get rich quick – by insisting that the observation or description of, say, 'Don't Look Back in Anger', does indeed take cognisance of that chord structure. Second, and this now is to do with analysis as what it is to write about a piece of music,[124] writing around that observation need not limit itself to that technical description – indeed the more the observation wallows in its nature as prose, the more interesting it might be. However, close listening is an integral part of its observation: there when Allan Moore accurately tots up the rhythmic cuts at the start of Elvis Costello's 'No Action', there when David Brackett brings James Brown's 'Superbad' wildly to life through a paradigmatic listing of melodic figuration; and there when Greil Marcus observes that 'those familiar "Sail Away" piano notes were back again' in Randy Newman's 'Louisiana 1927'.[125] To go from here to saying that 'one who does not hear this has yet to understand the piece totally' – a haughty observation which brings Simon Frith out in a rash of guilt over never having stuck with the piano lessons[126] – is wrong simply in the social usefulness of 'total understanding', a kind of absolute insistence which ought to be reserved for defending the National Health Service or welfare state; but to suggest, insistently if more kindly, that 'one who *does* understand these points has a deeper understanding of the musical passages they adore' seems to me not only uncontentious but an entirely good thing, and for the truth and dignity of these observations we don't need dumb-listener theory, we need the originary conception of education for everyone, the importance of musical education as mind-stretching symbolic form, and purposeful purposelessness as a social aim severed from capital.

I'd like to (teach/buy) the world (to sing/a Coke)

Those well-known usurpers of the musicological *thang*, Susan McClary and Robert Walser, are arguing here for greater attention to groove,[127] and supply a helpful list of everything you should take into account when you go about analysing pop music:

> To be sure, celebration of the beat is not the only aim of most writers on rock. The chords, melodic contours, and metric structures must be grasped analytically or else one has no way of addressing how in material terms the music manages to 'kick butt'. The reconstruction of semiotic codes is crucial, both for grounding musical procedures (including rhythmic) in terms of various discursive practices and for explaining how the music produces socially based meanings. Verbal texts, performance styles, and video imagery need to be analyzed carefully and in tandem with musical components. Modes of commercial production and distribution, the construction of star images, the history of a singer's career all have to be taken into account. And political issues (the positioning of the music with respect to class, race, gender) always must be dealt with seriously.[128]

There are two objections one might wish to raise here, one from the point of view of the purpose of low music, the other from the point of view of high analysis. One big difference between what McClary and Walser describe and the British inheritance from Williams, Hall and Middleton, is best seen in the very last element: for politics to be regarded as the last term in a carefully-considered serial progression from the minutiae of the text to the world outside would, I guess, not make sense to writers who would have seen the entire activity as political through and through, indeed its one purpose and goal. Williams doesn't get round eventually to considering the political condition of, say, *The Mill on the Floss*, or *Coronation Street*:[129] that's why he's there in the first place.

Secondly, as music analysis, it is not clear whether Walser and McClary are really saying anything specifically relevant to pop music, other than adumbrating a general musicological neatness which would not have shocked unduly the author of the average Dent Master Musician. The paragraph is a kind of paradise of equality of opportunity, of affirmative action. Action: see how busy we all are, how conscientious: 'must be grasped', 'need to be analyzed carefully', 'have to be taken into account', 'must be dealt with seriously' (the last' adverb unfortunately suggests someone who cannot be serious). And we're absolutely systematic: we're going to end up with a rounded picture of the phenomenon, and it would be churlish not to concede that both Hamm's *Yesterdays* and Walser's own *Running with the Devil* do supply just that.[130] What's more, it's not difficult to imagine that such an assiduous approach could, *should* indeed, be extended to other musics. Read the paragraph again, with, say, *Tosca* or *Erwartung* in mind, and there's little intrinsic difficulty.

Apart, that is, from an insistence upon the nature of the form itself: an analytical separation between the *music* of a piano sonata and a pop *song*. I would argue that the pop music object had little to do with music anyway, being always more importantly to do with songs, especially their inclusion first of words and latterly of supporting images in video and film. In one of his all-out death-of-civilization sections, Milton Babbitt noticed that American schoolkids had listed as their favourite composers the peculiar juke-box selection of Bob Dylan, Henry Mancini and John Lennon.[131] Babbitt's comments are instructive, and take us right to the heart of this issue, from the perspective of this journal (as opposed to the perspective of, say, *Journal of Musicology* or *Popular Music*). Babbitt has no problems with the list itself: 'that is not what interests me in the slightest. If I had been asked that when I was fifteen I'd have said DeSylva, Brown and Henderson.' First extrapolation: British analysis academics are, for class-derived reasons, incapable of saying that. But then, thinking clearly, thinking in the lineage of logical positivism, he hits it, formally, so to speak, on the head: 'it's the different cultural attitude. It's the different connotation of the word *composer*. They didn't mean *songwriter*; they meant *composer*. This is a confusion.'[132]

The really big development which underlies McClary and Walser, entirely genuinely so, is the impact of feminism. If cultural studies and music analysis both learned much from linguistics, then feminism presented an agenda which was both strongly political and strongly culturalist. Here too the contrast between British cultural studies' inheritance of a Marxist totalising view and the American attention to the various constructions of subjectivity, which arise in the progression from civil rights to affirmative action, is marked. With feminism, the totalising ambitions of the left became fractured and fragmented, as race and sexuality followed surely in gender's wake. It is against this background that Susan McClary is able to end her book with an earlier article on Madonna: it's interesting to consider how *Feminine Endings* was thus able to culminate its wide sweep through music history positively with pop music. Precedents, interestingly, stem from the *English* department, with books by Richard Poirier, Robert Pattison and Alan Durant, or pop music 'let in' as the culmination of *national* sagas.[133] The effort on behalf of women's music was nothing compared to pop music's apparent ease, and a sceptic might suggest that women's music has been easier to contain within the classical tradition than black music, where there was no question that the only places truly to reside were jazz, soul, funk and hip-hop.[134] Good news all round, you would think. But not quite: as much as anything due to their dogged avoidance of class as deep unifying essential, the various essentialisms present problems for street fighting men, be they inspired with Christian universalising or angered into Marxist totalising.[135]

Pleasure of the text became a difficult issue for the analysis of pop music, as a line from French theory – Barthes and *jouissance*, primarily, Lacan, Kristeva, Deleuze, Baudrillard – ran against a rather more earnest aspect which came through Williams, Birmingham, feminism and socialism.[136] Indeed Barthes went as far as to suggest that 'were we to succeed in refining a certain "aesthetics" of musical pleasure, then doubtless we would attach less importance to the formidable break in tonality accomplished by modernity.'[137] Being concerned about aesthetics – this despite the fact that aesthetics has provided the resting-ground for the century's finest left intellectuals, Lukács, Adorno and Sartre among them – somehow ran deeply against hardline Marxism. This may well explain too why the most fecund source for thinking through pleasure has led street fighters and others into the most immediately available theory of subjectivity: psychoanalysis. And there have been interesting and suggestive appropriations: Barthes from Lacan via Kristeva, Richard Middleton from Freud and Lacan, Shepherd and Wicke from Lacan and Kristeva.[138] It is questionable, though, whether the analytical community at large has been listening to these incorporations: the tension within the text between structuralism and phenomenology – say, Forte and Clifton, Babbitt and Adorno – has had evidently little need of going so far as psychoanalysis.[139]

It's into all of these rapids that David Brackett's *Interpreting Popular Music* dives, and does a good job of swimming through.[140] The book is a model of how clearly to select themes from cultural studies, and to play those themes through pop songs. Street-fighting theory gets channelled into an introduction that is dependent upon Middleton for theoretical ballast, while stopping well short of the wider implications which Middleton attempts to draw – Michel de Certeau seems to be the book's true guiding star.

Arranged as four case studies, the book naturally displays the strengths and weakness of such an approach. It puts great emphasis upon the object chosen, the wide 'popular music' of the title effectively amounting to a mere half-an-hour on the decks. The examples are craftily chosen though, careful in particular to include white and black, country (Hank Williams) and soul (James Brown) at the centre, and, as frames, the mainstream thirties popular song, as interpreted by Billie Holliday and Bing Crosby (remarkably, so far as I can glean, Brackett doesn't make play of the fact that the voice in one case is female and the other male), and post-punk pop with Elvis Costello. What's particularly important is that he covers song as story with country, and record as performance with soul. The discussion of Crosby and Holliday is an interesting exploration of biographical interpretation, while Costello is the ground for considering pop aesthetics.

Still, if the solution for the sociology of art is 'to engage directly with the question of aesthetic value',[141] I would want to pick up on the Costello chapter. Tediously British as it is to carp over his one non-American choice, Costello's 'Pills and Soap' I took, even in 1983, as a good indication that it was time for the Attractions to split, especially the way Steve Nieve was boringly making pop songs into dull piano music. The track now seems *unlistenable*.[142] All this would go so far, if it were not for the fact that Costello's finest period was just around the corner, with the Attractions-free *King of America* and *Blood and Chocolate*, the Attractions seethingly back together. Do these little differences matter? In the world adumbrated by McClary and Walser above, clearly not; and each of Brackett's chapters is again exemplary in progressing from a context often borrowed from cultural studies into a point inside the record. But I guess here I have that difficulty with American New Musicology: by a stance which is apparently so disengaged it can so easily end up saying relatively little. Look at this sentence, unfairly extracted from the Costello chapter (pp. 189–90):

> The equivalent line in verse 3 – 'Give us our daily bread in individual slices' – conveys a sense of alienation in its emphasis on individuality (do whole loaves, then, emphasize social collectivity?), while the following line – 'and something in the daily rag to cancel any crisis' – shows how the media pacify any sense of dissatisfaction through their interminable presentation of hystericized events: this is the 're-solution' to the sense of alienation engendered by life in the (post)modern, post-industrial age.

Now this seems bad to me, and there's an *awful* lot of this kind of thing, not with Brackett by any means, for whom this is a momentary lapse, but in writing on pop music appearing out of cultural studies, of which one has the creeping sense that a publishing dam is about to break, with *stacks* soon to follow. In that passage, Brackett causes unnecessary problems by, in a rather determined manner, progressing line-by-line through the song, thereby being forced to say too much about every small detail. Both 'convey' and especially 'show' would benefit from being preceded by 'attempts to'. But what's particularly unconvincing is the suspect authority of the comment about the media (hystericised events, yes, but who wants them? and is that all they do?), and that conceptually and typographically messy listing of posts at the end. That said, Brackett wisely doesn't allow analytical technology to lead his observations, though there are – uh oh – spectrum photos of sounds at certain points, to no great avail. Generally, there's a nice sense of musical demonstration employed only so far as the cultural point needs making. With 'Superbad', the James Brown record, this involves an array of easily-followed tables and charts which assuredly lead you back to the record and invite closer listening, better understanding. Let's hope that both music departments and media studies departments try to integrate the book into their teaching.

How do we end?

These things don't happen in the faculties alone: pop music came through after the 1960s to fill a gap as musical modernism became problematic and classical music was being sucked into playing pop's own marketing games. Even world music was pushed, as a kind of warm bath of dumb-listening deflecting the way in which in the real third world, whose incomprehensible words and happy beats suffused the living rooms of the west, transnational corporations invaded and fundamentalisms increased. 'What can a poor boy do?' is, for pop music as in a rather confused sense for modernism,[143] the big question, and whether 'music' is in any sense a home for the avant-garde anymore debatable: its critical edge is more likely found in mixed-media, film, video installation and somewhere in pop music.

Meantime, we still prepare for what Kant described, in the shorter working day which Marx looked forward to, filled with the activities of listening and composing and performing which the broadening of access to music aims for; in which a canon of specific pieces listened to again and again is important not for its content as much as the various human fragilities which give rise to those choices; in which being 'an attentive listener placed between two expensive speakers in a darkened room' is a good indication that the drugs are working.[144] We'll all be analysts of a kind, both critical and creative; but until then we have to get up and fight for that world to arrive, and in order to help achieve this, as the street fighters realised all along, pop music does the job of parading social knowledge better than most other music available.

There's a track on a recent Shawn Colvin album,[145] a cover of Bob Dylan's 'You're Gonna Make Me Lonesome When You Go' (the one with the dragon clouds, purple clover, Queen Anne's Lace, Verlaine and Rimbaud, and the rhyme of Honolulu with Ashtabula).[146] Shawn Colvin is recorded live and, like the song, this performance is a wonderful thing. First, she adapts the chord sequence in the verse, so that instead of the passing note between the first two chords (scale-steps 8–7), there's V7 of IV (or a chromatic passing note: 8–♭7: first at c. 10″). In the introduction, second time round (c. 20″), she clouds the tonic chord on her guitar with an added sixth, so confusing the space between tonic and subdominant, suffusing the sound with the softness of scale degree 6. The guitar playing is controlled but in its own way dramatic. The chord change is maintained throughout, and produces a structure different from Dylan's original:

Dylan

| I | I | IV | IV | I | I | V | V |
| I | I | IV | IV | I | V7 | I | I |

Colvin

| I | I(pn) | IV | IV | I | I | V | V |
| I | I(cpn) | IV | IV | I | V7 | I | I |

But remember this is about a *songwriter* not a *composer*, and the adaptation is like a fresh coat of paint over the wall of the original lyrics. With Dylan you're always hearing the words of the verse imposed on the simple repeated chord sequence, whereas Shawn Colvin always colours the *third* line of each verse. So, any of the verse openings, achingly familiar to anyone who knows *Blood on the Tracks*, is followed in the cover by a more directed, more cadential and somehow sadder movement through the adapted third line. The cover becomes a precarious play on the memory of the original, which even as a Dylan song was a tender and poignant thing. Melodically, throughout the song, she does beautiful things – a transcription would be needed to do justice to these little variants. Moving into the words, in their musicality, there's a wonderful attack to some of her consonants. After this, the record is all about the voice, its 'sheer physical beauty, prettiness, even',[147] its glides and swoops: there's a huge thing there about her voice's being on top and in the middle of the guitar sound, where of course Dylan is firmly under and in the middle:[148] all manner of fragility starts with this absolutely gendered feature.

Then, and after having heard the original, oooh, a thousand times since 1975 ('must be grasped', 'need to be analyzed'... *as an analyst,* I don't have *time* for Walser and McClary's apparent rigour!), and having heard the cover already about a hundred times to date, what is enduring is the difference between what it is for Dylan, as male *auteur* to sing this song, and what it is for a woman to sing it: what it was to hear a man in 1975 wallowing in imagery in 1975 so feminine – gender historicised through and through, and not the transhistorical thing we may now take too easily for granted – and what it is for a woman in the 1990s, in powerful control of the entire performance, to reclaim that imagery.[149] Queen Anne's Lace, for instance, is itself like the English language giving a flower the French language's female gender. But *Blood on the Tracks,* as ever with Dylan, always keeps its femininity carefully elsewhere, as a characteristic of the addressee,[150] while coming as close as Dylan would to masquerading that otherness.[151] So Shawn Colvin is involved in ironic reclamation, sure enough, but also, by making it her own, makes it new. The old theme – these foolish things remind me of you – but also the old question: who and where are you?

When I hear something as rounded as the Shawn Colvin cover, its calm and easy resolution of the Marxist dilemma of reconciling structure and subjectivity, I'm reminded of Derek Mahon's claim that 'a good poem is a paradigm of a good politics',[152] believing that a song can lead towards revaluing freedom, social duty and civil virtue, reminding us of the sheer *waste of time* which pop music and its analysis can truly suggest.

Johan Fornäs, whose thinking-through of the issues of cultural theory and late modernity has framed this discussion, distinguishes three temporal aspects of modernity: recent times, the evasive present moment, and the new.[153] It is the sense in which pop music contests and shifts the space of newness which seems to me essential, since new music and its description inform at all times one's view of the musical past. What the pop song view of the musical world might look like may not come as good news. Emphasising direct connotations of genre and meaning, it values rhetorical and coded musical language over development and connection. Emphasising brevity over prolixity, it forms a subversive allegiance with the aphoristic forms of the nineteenth-century, the songs and piano pieces, the trivial and the domestic. Emphasising direct intersubjective communication and critique in the purpose of social change, it has little time for subsidised art and for private patronage.

Middleton's instinct of how to '*remap the terrain*', as he would italicise, is to imagine pop music's allegiance with *simple* music of the past. Imagine rather a weird continuity with a Randy Newman, a Burt Bacharach, really, the survival and continuity of the conventions of the nineteenth-century.[154] When Schoenberg was bothered by the fact that his pieces were short and always needed the instantaneous setting of texts to get finished,[155] in the pop song view of the world, he was *doing fine*. What happened next was the issue. The mid-1970s now seems a point at which several of the issues I have discussed reached a certain nerve-point, and in some ways since then we have been sleepwalking – culture has become administration, and economic survival is not one but the only game we're playing. At that time Fredric Jameson supplied for a collection of debates from the 1930s a conclusion which ended by suggesting that modernism had led back, by a strange circularity, to questions of '... realism itself!'[156] Getting out of the mindset which is the high analysis of low music, to a place where what it is to write about music is dealing with intersubjective communication through symbolic form, we could end, or start, with something similar.

Get real.

NOTES

1. Elvis Costello, sleevenotes to reissue CD *King of America* (1986, reissue, DPAM 11, 1995), no pagination.

2. Ray Monk, review of Thomas Nagel, *The Last Word* (Oxford: Oxford University Press, 1997), in *Times Higher Education Supplement*, 26 September 1997, p. 26.

3. Thanks to Dave Hesmondhalgh and Richard Middleton for reading through; to Jonathan Stock for allowing me to see a manuscript ahead of publication; and especially to the Critical Musicology Forum. Since I submitted this piece, Richard Middleton's review of Allen Forte, *The American Popular Ballad of the Golden Era 1924–1950* (Princeton: Princeton University Press, 1995) has appeared (*Journal of the Royal Musical Association*, 122 (1997), pp. 303–20), singing from a hymnsheet similar to the one used here.

4. Beck, 'Loser', *Mellow Gold* (Geffen, 1994).

5. Martin Amis, *Money: A Suicide Note* (Harmondsworth: Penguin, 1985); *The Information* (London: Harper Collins, 1995). References in text to this edition. On *Money*, see David Hawkes, *Ideology* (London: Routledge, 1996), pp. 1–2.

6. Clement Greenberg, 'Avant-Garde and Kitsch' (1939), in Francis Frascina (ed.), *Pollock and After: The Critical Debate* (London: Harper and Row, 1985), pp. 21–33. Adorno is sure to crop up in a musical discussion of this topic; the similarity between Greenberg and Adorno is examined in a reprinted article by Thomas Crow from the same volume: see his 'Modernism and Mass Culture in the Visual Arts', pp. 233–66, especially pp. 262–5.

7. M. H. Abrams, *The Mirror and the Lamp: Romantic Theory and the Critical Tradition* (Oxford: Oxford University Press, 1953), pp. 3–29.

8. Jonathan Cross, 'Thoughts on First Hearing Sir Harrison Birtwistle's "Panic"...', *Tempo*, 195 (1996), p. 34. 'Anything' there evidently didn't quite extend to the idea of sharing this *aperçu* with the hundreds of thousands of listeners to *Desert Island Discs*.

9. *Letters of John Keats: A Selection*, ed. Robert Gittings (Oxford: Oxford University Press, 1987), p. 85; see Abrams, *Mirror and the Lamp*, p. 26.

10. See also Alexander Goehr in his fifth BBC Reith Lecture, published in *The Listener*, 17/24 December 1987, p. 35.

11. According to Cross, Birtwistle 'successfully taps into the popular symbolic codes of sax and drums without ever actually adopting the language of jazz' (See Cross, 'Thoughts', p. 35).

12. Not that it's of any great import, but I would exclude Elvis Costello's *Juliet Letters*, his collaboration with the Brodsky String Quartet (Warner, 1993). At least that piece seemed like a genuine attempt at collaborative practice, not simply a reified idea of the string quartet as high-art plinth which Capital would help surmount. For art-historical perspectives, see Kirk Varnedoe and Adam Gopnik, *High and Low: Modern Art and Popular Culture* and the accompanying *Modern Art and Popular Culture: Readings in High and Low* (New York: Museum of Modern Art, 1990); also the 'alternative manifestation' of the journal *October*, 56 (1991).

13. Fans will note Amis's references to pop music: 'So what can a poor boy do?', on p. 168 of *Money*, is from The Rolling Stones's 'Street Fighting Man' (*Beggars Banquet*, London, 1968); Aretha Franklin's 'Respect' (Atlantic, 1967) is explicitly mentioned at pp. 286 and 326 of *The Information*; on p. 132 of the same Amis's description of a novelist's life ('They get sick, they get well, they hang around the inkwell') is adapted from Bob Dylan's 'Subterranean Homesick Blues' (Columbia, 1965).

14. Fredric Jameson, *Postmodernism, or, the Cultural Logic of Late Capitalism* (London: Verso, 1991), p. 18. Also see Dick Hebdige, 'Staking out the Posts', in *Hiding in the Light: On Images and Things* (London: Routledge, 1988), pp. 181–207. Neil Nehring's *Popular Music, Gender, and Postmodernism: Anger is an Energy* (London: Sage, 1997) is a sustained diatribe where 'postmodern' becomes part of a thesaurus list which can mean, adjectivally, pretty much anything bad. More measured opposition is found, classically, in Jürgen Habermas's 'Modernity versus Postmodernity', *New German Critique*, 22 (1981), pp. 3–14; and see also Robert C. Holub, *Jürgen Habermas: Critic in the Public Sphere* (London: Routledge, 1991), pp. 133–61; from British Marxism, Alex Callincos's *Against Postmodernism: A Marxist Critique* (Cambridge: Polity, 1989); and, from a curious post-post-structuralist position, Christopher Norris's *Uncritical Theory: Postmodernism, Intellectuals and the Gulf War* (London: Lawrence and Wishart, 1992).

15. Johan Fornäs, *Cultural Theory and Late Modernity* (London: Sage, 1995), p. 81.

16. *Finnegan's Wake* (London: Faber, 1975), p. 120.

17. The 'dubious name of "commission"': Theodor W. Adorno, 'Culture and Administration', in J.M. Bernstein (ed.), *The Culture Industry: Selected Essays on Mass Culture* (London: Routledge, 1991), p. 100. 'By the way, if anyone here's in marketing or advertising: kill yourself', Bill Hicks, 'Marketing and Advertising',

Arizona Bay (Rykodisc, 1997). The elision of pop music with business study meets a market, no doubt, but if pop music can't at least enter the room of a Kantian 'purposiveness without purpose' (see the discussion at pp. 26–8 of Abrams, *The Mirror and the Lamp*), then the following discussion has little relevance: part of the argument of what follows is that abandoned otherness refuses to concede any high ground at all. All of this is simply to echo what Raymond Williams said more clearly:

> It is again being said that people must gain work experience within the forms of the economy to which they must adapt. ... And while the labour movements say of such work experience that it's merely 'cheap labour' or whatever, I say what educators must say – and this is, as a matter of fact, where I see the future of Cultural Studies. Here is a group which, if it is given only what is called 'work experience', but which is actually its introduction to the routines of the foreseen formations of this new industrial capitalism – will be without that dimension of human and social knowledge and critical possibility which again and again has been one of the elements of our project.

See Williams, 'The Future of Cultural Studies', in *The Politics of Modernism: Against the New Conformists* (London: Verso, 1989), pp. 160–61. Although the lecture may have been written within the cosy confines of Williams's post at Jesus College, Cambridge, it was nevertheless delivered to the NorthEast London Polytechnic, on 21 March 1986.

18. I owe this point to Jonathan Stock, 'Old Musicology, New Musicologies: Ethnomusicology and the Study of Western Music', *Current Musicology* (forthcoming).

19. This sentence from the *Musikblätter des Anbruch*, 11 (1929) is referred to in Thomas Y. Levin, 'For the Record: Adorno on Music', *October*, 55 (1990), p. 47.

20. See Jonathan Dunsby, 'Criteria of Correctness in Music Theory and Analysis', in Anthony Pople (ed.), *Theory, Analysis and Meaning in Music* (Cambridge: Cambridge University Press, 1994), p. 85.

21. It wasn't always this way: ahead of the next section, I remember in the 1970s a BBC *television* introduction to the Second Viennese School, with Alexander Goehr as chief talking head, which was a model of its kind.

22. The Sex Pistols, 'Anarchy in the UK' (EMI, 1976). Alright, alright, as Simon Frith and Jon Savage have it, 'there is no sadder sight than the fortysomething ex-leftist, the thirtysomething ex-punk, the twentysomething ex-stylist, burying their disappointments in their search across the surface of popular culture for pure sensation'. See their 'Pearls and Swine: Intellectuals and the Mass Media', in Steve Redhead, Derek Wynne and Justin O'Connor (eds.), *The Clubcultures Reader: Readings in Popular Cultural Studies* (Oxford: Blackwell, 1997), p. 16. For particular examples of post-punk sadness, see *The Wire*, 93 (1991); also Greil Marcus, *Lipstick Traces: A Secret History of the Twentieth Century* (London: Secker and Warburg, 1989), and *In the Fascist Bathroom: Writings on Punk 1977– 1992* (Harmondsworth: Viking, 1993).

  For readers of *Music Analysis*, the following section will seem embarrassingly personal. I fully understand; though I think that a critical-creative aspect of music-analytical writing is badly missing. For one thing it's much more commonplace in certain literatures of feminism and cultural studies. As Meaghan Morris makes the point:

> since story-telling is a popular practice that varies from culture to culture, I shall again define my terms. My impression is that American culture easily encourages people to assume that a first person anecdote is primarily oriented towards the emotive and conative functions, in Jakobson's terms, of communication.. However, I take anecdotes to be primarily referential. They are oriented futuristically towards the construction of a precise, local, and *social* discursive context, of which the anecdote then functions as a *mise en abyme*. That is to say, anecdotes for me are not expressions of personal experience, but allegorical expressions of a model of the way the world can be said to be working. So anecdotes need not be true stories, but they must be functional in a given exchange.

See Morris, 'Banality in Cultural Studies', in John Storey (ed.), *What is Cultural Studies? A Reader* (London: Arnold, 1996), pp. 149–50.

23. Simon Frith has some excellent articles on the topic, as reflected in the collection *Music for Pleasure: Essays in the Sociology of Pop* (Cambridge: Polity, 1988).

24. An alliance of hipness which peaked, perhaps, with Nicholas Kenyon (ed.), *Authenticity and Early Music* (Oxford: Oxford University Press, 1988).

25. After all, as Miles Davis has it, people 'who don't change will find themselves like folk musicians, playing in museums and local as a motherfucker.' Miles Davis (with Quincy Troupe), *The Autobiography* (London: Picador, 1990), p. 386.

26. It was nothing like the upbringing Hans Keller describes – for example on pp. 17–18 of *The Great Haydn Quartets: Their Interpretation* (London: Dent, 1986). I was presumably part of the first generation of musicologist, broadly-defined, to have been brought up with little other than pop music. Even the 'classical music' of South Wales was hymn-tunes and brass bands, a long way from the Haydn quartets.
     A lovely reflection on the mixed-up confusions of highs and lows involved here, from the point of view of another twisted British provincial also obsessed with pop music, is found in Philip Larkin's poem 'Reference Back' in *The Whitsun Weddings* (London: Faber, 1964), p. 40. Written, according to Andrew Motion (*Philip Larkin: A Writer's Life* (London: Faber, 1993), p. 264), in 1955, the poem finds Larkin listening to New Orleans jazz – King Oliver's 'Riverside Blues' – though, as he says elsewhere ('Introduction' to *All What Jazz: A Record Diary* (London: Faber, 1972), p. 15), 'whatever it happens to be, parents are suspicious of it and it has a bad reputation'.

27. The magazine supplement, *The Listener*, was an erudite, weekly printed commentary on and supplement to the programmes broadcast on radio and television.

28. At home one felt, indeed, like a tourist; filled one's head with culture, and gave oneself an ulcer. ('At Home He's a Tourist', on *Entertainment!* (EMI, 1979)). See Greil Marcus's sleeve-notes to the Gang of Four, *A Brief History of the Twentieth*

Century (EMI, 1990), and entries in *In the Fascist Bathroom*. Tom Paulin, Introduction to *The Faber Book of Political Verse* (London: Faber, 1986), p. 27, describes the conservative tradition through Ecclesiastes 1, 9: 'he that increaseth knowledge increaseth sorrow'.

29.   From the perspective of critical theory, followers of Adorno suggest that, had he bothered, he could or would have appreciated any or all of the following: Frank Zappa, John Cale, Carla Bley, Henry Cow (Max Paddison, 'The Critique Criticized: Adorno and Popular Music', *Popular Music*, 2 (1982), p. 215); The Cadillacs (Bernard Gendron, 'Adorno Meets the Cadillacs', in Tania Modelski (ed.), *Studies in Entertainment: Critical Studies in Mass Culture* (Bloomington, IN: Indiana University Press, 1986), pp. 18–36; Mary Margaret O'Hara, My Bloody Valentine, Throwing Muses (Terry Bloomfield, 'Resisting Songs: Negative Dialectics in Pop', *Popular Music*, 12 (1993), pp. 13–31; Frank Zappa (Ben Watson, *The Negative Dialectics of Poodle Play* (London: Quartet, 1994)); Ornette Coleman (Theodor A. Gracyk, 'Adorno, Jazz, and the Aesthetics of Popular Music', *Musical Quarterly*, 76 (1992), p. 533).

The best single treatment of the subject I have come across is Harry Cooper's 'On *Über* Jazz: Playing Adorno against the Grain', *October*, 75 (1996), pp. 99–133. See also the debates between John Caughie ('Adorno's Reproach: Repetition, Difference and Television Genre', *Screen*, 32 (1991), pp. 127–53) and Georgina Born ('Against Negation, for a Politics of Cultural Production: Adorno, Aesthetics and the Social', *Screen*, 34 (1993), pp. 223–42), and between T.J. Clark ('In Defense of Abstract Expressionism', *October*, 69 (1994), pp. 23–48) and Jay Bernstein ('The Death of Sensuous Particulars: Adorno and Abstract Expressionism', *Radical Philosophy*, 76 (1996), pp. 7–18). See also Robert Hullot-Kentor's idiosyncratic pieces for *Telos* ('Popular Music and Adorno's "The Aging of the New Music"', 77 (1988), pp. 79–94, and 'The Impossibility of Music: Adorno, Popular and Other Music', 87 (1991), pp. 97–117), the latter, which includes a hilarious reading of The Beatles' 'I Feel Fine', aptly described by Born as 'a classic piece of neo-Adornian cant' (Born, p. 223). Adornian views of pop music may offer lively vantage-points for critical theory but are, by and large, limited as arguments on pop music's behalf.

30.   Will Straw has written some fine articles on gender, records and shops. See '"Organized Disorder": the Changing Space of the Record Shop' in Redhead, *The Clubcultures Reader*, pp. 57–65, and 'Sizing Up Record Collections: Gender and Connoisseurship in Rock Music Culture', in Sheila Whiteley (ed.), *Sexing the Groove: Popular Music and Gender* (London: Routledge, 1997), pp. 3–16.

31.   More on radio as culture can be traced in *Radiotext(e) (Semiotext(e))*, 16 (1993).

32.   See Larkin's hopeful description of the combined effect of Kingsley Amis's anthology of light verse and his own idiosyncratic anthology of twentieth-century verse: 'We shall have stamped our taste on the age between us in the end' (Motion, *Philip Larkin*, p. 434).

33.   T.S. Eliot, *Notes Towards the Definition of Culture* (London: Faber, 1948), p. 31.

34. Raymond Williams, *Culture and Society 1780–1950* (London: Chatto, 1958), p. 230.

35. T.S. Eliot, *Notes Towards the Definition of Culture*, p. 16. The many devotees of Schoenberg, who have so graced *Music Analysis* over the years, will not wish to pass up the opportunity of noting the similarity between Eliot in 1939 and Schoenberg's letter to Prince Egon von Furstenberg of 1924:

> art, a matter for princes, is beyond the judgement of common people. And only the authority of personages, in that it permits the artist to participate in the distinctive position bestowed by a higher power, is able to demonstrate this demarcation in a sensuously tangible manner to all those who are merely educated, who have worked their way up, and to make manifest the difference between those who have become what they are and those who were born what they are.

See Arnold Schoenberg, *Letters*, trans. Eithne Wilkins and Ernst Kaiser, ed. Erwin Stein (London: Faber 1964), p. 108.

36. Williams, *Culture and Society*, p. 228. See also Alan O'Connor, *Raymond Williams: Writing, Culture, Politics* (Oxford: Blackwell, 1989), pp. 57–9; Peter Scott, 'Man of the Border Country', *Times Higher Education Supplement*, 15 March 1985, p. 13; and Tony Pinkney's introduction to Raymond Williams, *The Politics of Modernism*, pp. 1–27.

37. Perry Anderson, *In the Tracks of Historical Materialism* (London: Verso, 1983), p. 14.

38. Randy Newman, 'Political Science', on *Sail Away* (Warner, 1972).

39. *Little Criminals* (Warner, 1977).

40. Elektra, 1981. Doctorow's novel appeared in 1975.

41. Randy Newman orchestrated Leiber and Stoller's 'Is That All There Is?' (1969) for the Peggy Lee recording, an impressive merging-together of Newman's own Coplandesque mode (see 'I Think It's Going to Rain Today' (1968)) and Kurt Weill, himself such a central reference in popular music through the 1950s and into the 1960s. The soundtrack of Barry Levinson's film adaptation of Bernard Malamud's *The Natural* (Warner, 1984) is the best example I know of Randy Newman without words.

42. Judging by the comment on p. xx of Alec Wilder, *American Popular Songs: The Great Innovators 1900–1950* (Oxford: Oxford University Press, 1990), and its example-free chapter on Berlin, Newman was lucky to have got so far.

43. Following his visit there in 1909, Freud is supposed famously to have said, 'America is a mistake; a gigantic mistake, it is true, but none the less a mistake'. See Ernest Jones, *The Life and Work of Sigmund Freud*, edited and abridged by Lionel Trilling and Steven Marcus (Harmondsworth: Pelican, 1964), p. 348.

44. Jameson, *Postmodernism*, pp. 21–5. Pop music's direct engagement with modernism is a rare thing; a song by Paul Simon called 'René and Georgette Magritte with their Dog After the War' (on *Hearts and Bones* (Warner, 1983)), wonderfully confuses imagery from the world of the surrealist painter with the

names of 1950s doo-wop bands, all mediated through Simon himself. See Paul Simon in Bill Flanagan, *Written in My Soul: Candid Interviews with Rock's Great Songwriters* (London: Omnibus, 1990), pp. 321–5.

45. See, however, Peter Winkler's excellent 'Randy Newman's Americana', *Popular Music*, 7 (1988), pp. 1–26.

46. Milton Babbitt, 'Responses: A First Approximation', *Perspectives of New Music*, 14/ii and 15/i (1976), pp. 3–4.

47. John Covach is a good example here, suggesting *pragmatically* that 'theorists should pay more attention to rock music because it is interesting'; but – knowing *politically* that 'interesting' is hardly enough – is forced immediately to sharpen it to mean 'challenging disciplinary assumptions about what music is' ('We Won't Get Fooled Again: Rock Music and Musical Analysis', *In Theory Only*, 13 (1997), p. 133). It's an expressive shift: rarely can thinking about Keith Moon drumming and Roger Daltrey screaming have led to a statement which in its short space mentions the word 'discipline' and its derivatives twenty-four times.

48. Milton Babbitt, in Cole Gague and Tracy Caras (eds.), *Soundpieces: Interviews with American Composers* (New York: Methuen, 1982), p. 36.

49. Milton Babbitt, 'Who Cares if you Listen', in Gilbert Chase (ed.), *The American Composer Speaks* (Louisiana, 1966), p. 238.

50. Adorno, *Introduction to the Sociology of Music*, trans. E. B. Ashton (London: Continuum, 1989), pp. 1–20.

51. Thomas Crow, 'Modernism and Mass Culture', pp. 263–4.

52. Mott the Hoople, 'Honaloochie Boogie', on *Mott* (Columbia, 1973); Charles T. Brown, *The Art of Rock and Roll*, 2nd ed. (Englewood Cliffs, NJ: Prentice-Hall, 1987), p. 15.

53. Even the titles are earnest onlooker classics: *Twilight of the Gods: The Beatles in Retrospect* (London: Faber, 1973); *A Darker Shade of Pale: A Backdrop to Bob Dylan* (London: Faber, 1984); and *Angels of the Night: Popular Female Singers of Our Time* (Oxford: Blackwell, 1986).

54. '[Poetry] imitates only as a means to the proximate end of pleasing; and pleases, it turns out, only as a means to the ultimate end of teaching', Abrams, *The Mirror and the Lamp*, p. 14.

55. A good example is Piers Spencer's 'Reggae', in Graham Vulliamy and Ed Lee (eds.), *Pop, Rock and Ethnic Music in School* (Cambridge: Cambridge University Press, 1982), pp. 154–70. See also Lucy Green's two books, *Music on Deaf Ears* (Manchester: Manchester University Press, 1988) and *Music, Gender, Education* (Cambridge: Cambridge University Press, 1997).

56. John Paynter and Peter Aston, *Sound and Silence: Classroom Projects in Creative Music* (Cambridge: Cambridge University Press, 1970). Both Richard Middleton and John Shepherd passed under Mellers's wing.

57. A *locus classicus*: Dave Harker, 'Taking Fun Seriously', *Popular Music*, 15 (1996), pp. 108–21.

58. Allan F. Moore, *Rock: The Primary Text* (Buckingham: Open University Press, 1993), p. 27; Richard Middleton, *Studying Popular Music* (Buckingham: Open University Press, 1990), p. 247; Nehring, *Popular Music, Gender, and Postmodernism*, p. 163. Nehring's self-flagellation is characteristic – at another point (p. 168) he 'cheats' by looking at a lyric sheet. Further reference in text to these editions of Moore and Middleton.

59. Pierre Bourdieu, trans. Richard Nice, *Distinction: A Social Critique of the Judgement of Taste* (London: Routledge, 1984), pp. 84–5.

60. Several anthologies of rock journalism exist: general selections can be found both in Clinton Heylin (ed.), *The Penguin Book of Rock n Roll Writing* (London: Viking, 1992) and Evelyn McDonnell and Ann Powers (eds.), *Rock She Wrote: Women Write about Rock, Pop, and Rap* (London: Plexus, 1995). Lester Bangs, Greil Marcus, Nik Cohn, Nick Kent and Charles Shaar Murray all have 'greatest hits' anthologies.

61. Moore, *Rock: The Primary Text*, pp. 186–7.

62. On pp. 47–53 of *Rock: The Primary Text*, and separately in two articles for *Popular Music*: 'Patterns of Harmony', 11 (1992), pp. 73–106, and 'The So-Called "Flattened Seventh" in Rock', 14 (1995), pp. 185–201.

63. David Brackett, *Interpreting Popular Music* (Cambridge: Cambridge University Press, 1995), 274 pp., £35.00, ISBN 0–521–47337–3. The quotation appears on p. 201. This review-article arose initially as a response to Brackett's book, which is considered more fully later.

64. Moore, *Rock: The Primary Text*, p. 185.

65. Or, to put it another way, 'the question ... is not where might art go from here: who cares? But where might we go from this desolate place, and how on earth are we to get there?', Jay Bernstein, 'Death of Sensuous Particulars', p. 17.

66. Stuart Hall, 'Cultural Studies and its Theoretical Legacies', in Lawrence Grossberg, Cary Nelson and Paula Treichler (eds.), *Cultural Studies* (London: Routledge, 1992), p. 278; Nehring, *Popular Music, Gender, and Postmodernism*, p. xxiii; Rolling Stones, 'Street Fighting Man', *Beggars Banquet*. See also the chapter on *Beggars Banquet* by Simon Frith in Greil Marcus (ed.), *Stranded: Rock and Roll for a Desert Island*, 2nd ed. (New York: Da Capo, 1996), pp. 29–39. Tom Paulin, Introduction to *The Faber Book of Political Verse*, p. 29, describes the puritan-republican tradition through John 8, 32: 'And ye shall know the truth and the truth will make you free'.

67. Philip Tagg, *Fernando the Flute: Musical Meaning in an Abba Mega-Hit* (Liverpool: Institute of Popular Music, 1991), pp. 5–10.

68. Dave Hesmondhalgh, 'Rethinking Popular Music after Rock and Soul', in James Curran, David Morley and Valerie Walkerdine (eds.), *Cultural Studies and Communications* (London: Arnold, 1996), p. 202; Simon Frith, *Performing Rites:*

On the Value of Popular Music (Oxford: Oxford University Press, 1996), pp. 19–20; Richard Middleton, *Studying Popular Music*, p. v; Peter Wicke, *Rock Music: Culture, Aesthetics, Sociology*, trans. Rachel Fogg (Cambridge: Cambridge University Press, 1990), p. 183.

69. See Simon Frith, 'Why Do Songs Have Words?', in *Music for Pleasure*, pp. 105–128, and Simon Frith and Andrew Goodwin (eds.), *On Record: Rock, Pop and the Written Word* (London: Routledge, 1990), pp. 1–3.

70. Charles Hamm, 'Rock and the Facts of Life', in *Putting Popular Music in its Place* (Cambridge: Cambridge University Press, 1995), pp. 41–54, especially pp. 41–4.

71. Charles Hamm, *Yesterdays: Popular Song in America* (New York: Norton, 1979), p. 377. See also Hamm's sleevenotes to *Brother, Can You Spare a Dime?: American Song During the Great Depression* (New World, 1977).

72. Mel Brooks' pastiche 'Springtime for Hitler', from the film *The Producers* (1968), might give a rather uncomfortable vision of what a Tin Pan Alley version might have sounded like!

73. Philip Furia, *The Poets of Tin Pan Alley: A History of America's Great Lyricists* (Oxford: Oxford University Press, 1990), p. 203.

74. Hamm, *Yesterdays*, p. 377.

75. Hamm, '*Graceland* Revisited', in *Putting Popular Music in its Place*, pp. 336–43.

76. The *Graceland* dispute is a fine debating-point for the issues discussed here. Useful starting-points with bibliographic directions: Tony Mitchell, *Popular Music and Local Identity: Rock, Pop and Rap in Europe and Oceania* (Leicester: Leicester University Press, 1996), pp. 80–84; Steven Feld, 'Notes on "World Beat"', in Charles Keil and Steven Feld, *Music Grooves: Essays and Dialogues* (Chicago: Chicago University Press, 1994), pp. 238–46; and Stacey Luftig (ed.), *The Paul Simon Companion: Four Decades of Commentary* (London: Omnibus, 1997), pp. 149–88.

77. As well as producing the theoretical and analytical studies discussed here, Laing is also one of pop's most committed codifiers – see Phil Hardy and Dave Laing (eds.), *The Faber Companion to Twentieth-Century Popular Music* (London: Faber, 1992). Compare in this latter respect Donald Clarke, who remains wedded to journalistic positivism, and has particularly nasty things to say about the Hardy and Laing volume, refusing even to footnote it, on p. 572 of *The Rise and Fall of Popular Music* (Harmondsworth: Penguin, 1995). Despite this, Clarke's book is a fine sweep through the history of popular music.

78. Dave Laing, *The Marxist Theory of Art* (Brighton: Harvester, 1978), p. 141.

79. Dave Laing, *Buddy Holly* (London: Studio Vista, 1971), and *One Chord Wonders: Power and Meaning in Punk Rock* (Buckingham: Open University Press, 1985).

80. Laing, *One Chord Wonders*, especially pp. 53–81. Since then Laing has moved into issues around public policy and the music industry: see for instance *The*

Value of Music: A National Music Council Report into the Value of the UK Music Industry (London: National Music Council, 1996).

81. See Storey (ed.), *What is Cultural Studies?*, and Lawrence Grossberg, *Bringing it All Back Home: Essays on Cultural Studies* (Durham, NC: Duke University Press, 1997).

82. Richard Johnson, 'What is Cultural Studies Anyway', in Storey, *What is Cultural Studies?*, pp. 75–114.

83. A consistent line in the work of Russell Jacoby. See his *The Last Intellectuals: American Culture in the Age of Academe* (New York: Basic Books, 1987) and *Dogmatic Wisdom: How the Culture Wars Divert Education and Distract America* (New York: Doubleday, 1994).

84. Johnson, 'What is Cultural Studies Anyway', pp. 86–8. Raymond Williams, *Marxism and Literature* (Oxford: Oxford University Press, 1977), pp. 12–20 and 128–35. See also Martin Jay, *Adorno* (London: Fontana, 1984), p. 112.

85. Jean-Jacques Nattiez, *Music and Discourse: Toward a Semiology of Music*, trans. Carolyn Abbate (Princeton, NJ: Princeton University Press, 1990). See also the discussion on pp. 223–5 of Jonathan Stock, 'The Application of Schenkerian Analysis to Ethnomusicology: Problems and Possibilities', *Music Analysis*, 12 (1993). John Shepherd and Peter Wicke, *Music and Cultural Theory* (Cambridge: Polity, 1997), pp. 149 and 159–68. [See also Kenneth Gloag's review in this issue – Ed.] Compare too in this respect Covach's charge that Middleton writes 'not as a professional theorist, but as someone who has explored theoretical approaches to popular music', 'We Won't Get Fooled Again', p. 130.

86. Raymond Williams, 'The Future of Cultural Studies', p. 154.

87. See Simon Frith, *Sound Effects: Youth, Leisure, and the Politics of Rock 'n' Roll* (London: Constable, 1983), pp. 41–3, and Dave Laing, '*Scrutiny* to Subcultures: Notes on Literary Criticism and Popular Music', *Popular Music*, 13 (1994), pp. 179–90.

88. Anthologies of extracts are like a minor manufacturing industry in cultural studies (reflecting the subject's evidently insatiable popularity on campus), but *The Subcultures Reader*, Ken Gelder and Sarah Thornton (eds.), (London: Routledge, 1997) is especially good. The best summary introduction to pop music literature from the perspective of cultural and media study is Hesmondhalgh, 'Rethinking Popular Music'.

89. Elliott Carter: '*unless* the restricted audience for serious music, whether live or recorded, is made up mainly of wealthy people – which nowadays it certainly is not – serious music will either have to be subsidized by the government or else be allowed to shrink to a tiny level of activity', in Allen Edwards, *Flawed Words and Stubborn Sounds: A Conversation with Elliott Carter* (New York: Norton, 1971), p. 26. See also Terry Eagleton's description of modernist art being for Adorno a '"solution" parachuted in from some ontological outer space' (*Ideology: An Introduction* (London: Verso, 1991), p. 131), or Raymond Williams's coruscating attack on the 'two faces of modernism', on pp. 140–43

of *Towards 2000* (London: Chatto and Windus, 1993). Interestingly, some hope is found by Williams in stand-up comedy, soap opera, and 'the intense vitality of some kinds of popular music, always being reached for by the market and often grasped and tamed, but repeatedly renewing its impulses in new and vigorous forms' (pp. 134 and 146).

90. Walter Benjamin, 'The Work of Art in the Age of Mechanical Reproduction', *Illuminations*, trans. Hannah Arendt (London: Fontana, 1973, originally 1936), p. 226; Clement Greenberg, 'Avant-Garde and Kitsch', p. 32; Theodor W. Adorno, 'Vers une musique informelle', in *Quasi una fantasia: Essays on Modern Music*, trans. Rodney Livingstone (London: Verso, 1994), pp. 269–322.

91. Newcomers to *Studying Popular Music* would do well to keep at their side Charles Hamm's excellent summary, in his review published in the *Journal of Musicology*, 9 (1991), pp. 376–98, especially up until p. 385. Of direct relevance is Middleton's own 'Popular Music Analysis and Musicology: Bridging the Gap', *Popular Music*, 12 (1993), pp. 177–90.

92. Hall, 'Cultural Studies and its Theoretical Legacies', p. 280.

93. Anthony Giddens, *Modernity and Self-Identity: Self and Society in the Late Modern Age* (Cambridge: Polity, 1991), p. 210, by way of Fornäs, *Cultural Theory and Late Modernity*, p. 79. See also Giddens, *The Consequences of Modernity* (Cambridge: Polity, 1990), pp. 154–63.

94. Martin Jay, *Marxism and Totality: The Adventures of a Concept from Lukács to Habermas* (Berkeley: University of California Press, 1984) presents a good contextualising of this line. See also Max Paddison, *Adorno's Aesthetics of Music* (Cambridge: Cambridge University Press, 1995).

95. On the problems not so much of 'doing' as of 'music', see Philip V. Bohlman, 'Musicology as a Political Act', *Journal of Musicology*, 11 (1993), pp. 411–36, especially 422–3 and 435–6.

96. The two constituencies did not always see eye to eye. See Stuart Hall, 'Recent Developments in Theories of Language and Ideology: A Critical Note', and Dave Morley, 'Texts, Readers, Subjects', in Stuart Hall, Dorothy Hobson, Andrew Lowe and Paul Willis (eds.), *Culture, Media, Language* (London: Hutchinson, 1980), pp. 157–62, and 163–73, respectively. Pam Cook (ed.), *The Cinema Book* (London: British Film Institute, 1985) is a good introduction to the *Screen* world-view until that time.

97. Surprising, then, to find Shepherd and Wicke reheating a passage from p. 145 of Shepherd's *Music as Social Text* (Cambridge: Polity, 1991), itself reproduced from an article for *Popular Music* in 1982 (see Shepherd, 'Sociomusical Analysis of Popular Musics', 2 (1982), p. 170), in their *Music and Cultural Theory*, p. 38, without reference to pp. 155–66 of Middleton. Dick Hebdige, *Subculture: The Meaning of Style* (London: Methuen, 1979) is the only book to emerge from Middleton with (almost) unhindered praise (p. 164).

98. Cross too describes how a 'powerfully erotic aspect of much modern music', apparently 'so often' causes 'the repressed middle classes' to panic ('Thoughts on

430   DAI GRIFFITHS

First Hearing "Panic" ', p. 35). Believe me, in real life these are *nice people*, and even though their minds might be veritable Eisensteins of class war, they remain, economically at least, as middle-class as they come!

99. Paul Piccone, 'The Actuality of Traditions', *Telos*, 94 (1993–4), p. 98. See also Cooper, '*Über Jazz*'. A kinder view is contained in J. Bradford Robinson, 'The Jazz Essays of Theodor Adorno: Some Thoughts on Jazz Reception in Weimar Germany', *Popular Music*, 13 (1994), pp. 1–25.

100. These I think owe something to Stuart Hall. See Hall, 'Cultural Studies and its Theoretical Legacies': 'displacement' and 'lose hold of the tension' are both on p. 284; Hall's own Benjaminian romanticism is found in the phrase 'wrestling with the angels' on p. 280.

101. In fact, Middleton's examples were, at the time of *Studying Popular Music*, still remnants of his 'milk bar' 1960s phase – Tin Pan Alley, Carl Perkins, Little Richard, Elvis, Dylan – 'My brother's back at home with his Beatles and his Stones', as David Bowie puts it ('All the Young Dudes', 1972) – and not a million miles from his earlier PhD conversion, *Pop Music and the Blues* (London: Gollancz, 1972). Punk was clearly a shock to the system; and the Specials' 'Ghost Town' gets some attention. Once the book was out of the way, Middleton seemed to jump forward into the contemporaneity of the 1980s.

102. Stuart Hall, 'Notes on Deconstructing "the Popular"', in Raphael Samuel (ed.), *People's History and Socialist Theory* (London: Routledge and Kegan Paul, 1981), p. 239. 1972 was when Middleton published his first book on pop, *Pop Music and the Blues*, and 1981 the first appearance of the yearbook/journal, *Popular Music* from Cambridge. The yearbook appeared at the same time, and in exactly the same format, as *Early Music History*. During the 1980s my impression was that University Music Departments in the UK stocked the latter title *tout de suite* – *bonum quo antiquius, eo melius* – while studiously avoiding *Popular Music*. My attempts to bolster this observation with statistics didn't get very far, but thanks to the Journals Department at CUP for at least listening. 'Really, really want' comes from the song 'Wannabe', a 'global hit' for the Spice Girls in 1996, and the starting-point for a presentation made by Middleton at the Congress of the International Musicological Society in London, 1997.

103. Nicholas Cook, 'Music Minus One: Rock, Theory, and Performance', *New Formations*, 27 (1995–6), p. 23. I should perhaps explain, egotistically and neurotically, my presence on the same page: sent the article, naturally I raised these objections with the author. However, it appears that the article was already in press at the point I was offered it to read.

104. See also my review of Anne C. Shreffler, *Webern and the Lyric Impulse: Songs and Fragments on Poems of Georg Trakl* (Oxford: Oxford University Press, 1995), in *Music Analysis*, 16/i (1997), p. 147.

105. Contrast Nattiez's complaint that 'the neutral level is *dirty*', quoted in Jonathan Dunsby, 'Music and Semiotics: The Nattiez Phase', *Musical Quarterly*, 69 (1983), p. 31, with Stuart Hall's insistence upon the 'dirtiness of the semiotic game', in Stuart Hall, 'Cultural Studies and its Theoretical Legacies', p. 278.

106. Ian Bent and William Drabkin, *Analysis* (London: Macmillan, 1987), pp. 143–76. The bibliography had, by 1987, been 'updated, expanded and corrected' (p. viii).

107. On the difficulty of *really* engaging with ethnomusicology, see the delicious paragraph juxtaposition of Derrick Puffett's 'Editorial', *Music Analysis*, 12/ii (1993), p. 126:

> So in a curious way, the three fields come together: history, analysis, and the study of distant or neglected cultures.
> Volume 12 no. 3 of *Music Analysis* will contain articles on the three main composers of the Second Viennese School.

108. In a moving passage Raymond Williams describes the Open University as 'an extraordinary attempt in the tradition of that movement towards an open-access democratic culture of an educational kind', *The Politics of Modernism*, p. 156.

109. See Theodor W. Adorno, 'Music and Technique' (1958), trans. Wes Blomster, *Telos*, 32 (1977), pp. 79–94, and 'Opera and the Long-Playing Record' (1969), trans. Thomas Y. Levin, *October*, 55 (1990), pp. 62–6.

110. The whole issue of *level* of complexity is patently difficult with relatively young fields such as music analysis, critical theory or cultural studies: who can really tell what is being pitched at school, undergraduate or postgraduate level? This would suggest that what is currently needed is to think less in terms of 'ivory-tower' research and more in terms of what exactly is being conveyed, and how, including in the classroom.

111. Compare, for more than the fecundity of their titles, William Rothstein's 'The Americanization of Heinrich Schenker', in Hedi Siegel (ed.), *Schenker Studies* (Cambridge: Cambridge University Press, 1990), pp. 193–203, with Joel Pfister's 'The Americanization of Cultural Studies', in Storey (ed.), *What is Cultural Studies?*, pp. 287–99. See also Alan O'Connor, 'The Problem of American Cultural Studies', in the same volume, pp. 187–196.

112. 'Fantastic Remembrance in John Lennon's "Strawberry Fields Forever" and "Julia" ', *Musical Quarterly*, 72 (1986), pp. 360–85. Moore deals with the article at p. 12 of *Rock: The Primary Text*.

113. Milton Babbitt, review of Felix Salzer, *Structural Hearing* (1952), in *Journal of the American Musicological Society*, 5 (1952), p. 265. A tougher, but still germane critique is found at pp. 56 and 60–61 of Jonathan Dunsby and Arnold Whittall, *Music Analysis in Theory and Practice* (London: Faber, 1988).

114. Richard Johnson, 'What is Cultural Studies Anyway?', p. 100. Perry Anderson, 'Structure and Subject', in *In the Tracks of Historical Materialism*, p. 44. See also the excellent discussion of the term 'Structure' by John Carlos Rowe in Frank Lentricchia and Thomas McLaughlin (eds.), *Critical Terms for Literary Study* (Chicago: Chicago University Press, 1990), pp. 23–38.

115. V.N. Volosinov, *Marxism and the Philosophy of Language*, trans. Ladislav Matejka and I.R. Titunik (Harvard, MA: Harvard University Press, 1986, originally 1929); Johnson, 'What is Cultural Studies Anyway?', pp. 94–6; Carlos Rowe, 'Structure', p. 26. See also Francis Frascina, 'Realism and Ideology: An

432   DAI GRIFFITHS

Introduction to Semiotics and Cubism', in *Primitivism, Cubism, Abstraction: The Early Twentieth Century* (New Haven: Yale University Press, 1993), especially pp. 122–7 and 178–80.

116. Anderson, *In the Tracks of Historical Materialism*, p. 45.

117. The 'postulation of structure as an abstract, constructed, even *fictional* model for understanding sociohistorical phenomena is consistent in virtually every structuralist use of the term', Carlos Rowe, 'Structure', 30.

118. Anthony O'Hear's entry for 'History of the Philosophy of Education', in Ted Honderich (ed.), *The Oxford Companion to Philosophy* (Oxford: Oxford University Press, 1995), pp. 213–14, suggests a consistent historical strand of including both music and sport in the curriculum.

119. Nicholas Cook, *Music, Imagination and Culture* (Oxford: Clarendon Press, 1990), pp. 58–9; Frith, *Performing Rites*, pp. 26 and 64.

120. I take this *not* to be an argument endorsed by Peter J. Martin's *Sounds and Society: Themes in the Sociology of Music* (Manchester: Manchester University Press, 1995), a fine critique of music sociology from the point of view of sociological method. Sociology, argues Martin, ought to focus *solely* on context (p. 12); however, there is no case for concluding that music should be regarded as autonomous (p. 162) – the mistake to date has arisen from the nature of the theory brought to bear on sociological evidence.

121. Theodore Gracyk, *Rhythm and Noise: An Aesthetics of Rock* (London: I.B. Tauris, 1996), and Neil Nehring, *Popular Music, Gender, and Postmodernism*.

122. Or place. 'Rock 'n' roll was music for car radios, *that's* obvious', Chuck Eddy, *The Accidental Evolution of Rock 'n' Roll: A Misguided Tour Through Popular Music* (New York: Da Capo, 1997), p. 271. Musical modernism isn't for concert halls, *that's* obvious. So where?; and when?

123. Simon Frith, *Performing Rites*, p. 20; Henri Matisse, 'Notes of a Painter' (1908), in Charles Harrison and Paul Wood (eds.), *Art in Theory 1900–1990: An Anthology of Changing Ideas* (Oxford: Blackwell, 1992), p. 76; Karl Marx, 'Contribution to the Critique of Hegel's Philosophy of Right: Introduction' (1844), in Karl Marx and Frederick Engels, *Collected Works*, 3 (London: Lawrence and Wishart, 1975), p. 175.

124. Dai Griffiths, review of Anthony Pople (ed.), *Theory, Analysis and Meaning in Music* (Cambridge: Cambridge University Press, 1995), in *Music Analysis*, 15/iii (1996), p. 392.

125. Allan Moore, *Rock: The Primary Text*, pp. 176–7; David Brackett, *Interpreting Popular Music*, pp. 127–56; Greil Marcus, *Mystery Train: Images of America in Rock n Roll Music* (London: Omnibus 1977), p. 254. Marcus was observing the 'open-fourth' piano figuration in the verse; Winkler, 'Randy Newman's Americana', transcribes the precisely relevant points in the songs on p. 7.

126. Frith, *Performing Rites*, p. 253.

127. There is perhaps a case for suggesting that their great lacuna, 'groove', has in fact received quite assiduous attention, albeit in the jazz literature on swing. See J. A. Prögler, 'Searching for Swing: Participatory Discrepancies in the Jazz Rhythm Section', *Ethnomusicology*, 39 (1995); and Charles Keil, 'Participatory Discrepancies and the Power of Music' in Keil and Feld, *Music Grooves: Essays and Dialogues* (Chicago: Chicago University Press, 1994), pp. 96–108, and *passim*. Thanks are due to my colleague Michael Young for drawing this literature to my attention. If you're bothered by 'thang', it's high time you read Rickey Vincent, *Funk: The Music, the People, and the Rhythm of the One* (New York: St Martin's Griffin, 1996).

128. Susan McClary and Robert Walser, 'Start Making Sense! Musicology Wrestles with Rock', in Simon Frith and Andrew Goodwin (eds.), *On Record: Rock, Pop, and the Written Word* (London: Routledge, 1990), pp. 289–90.

129. As in *The Country and the City* (London: Paladin, 1975), pp. 202–20, or *Television: Technology and Cultural Form* (London: Fontana, 1974), p. 61.

130. Charles Hamm, *Yesterdays*; Robert Walser, *Running with the Devil: Power, Gender and Madness in Heavy Metal Music* (Middletown, CT: Wesleyan University Press, 1993). Hamm concludes his review of Middleton, *Studying Popular Music*, with an upbeat announcement of McClary's *Feminine Endings*, pp. 397–8.

131. I used this story in 'Talking about Licence to Kill', in Elizabeth Thomson and David Gutman, *The Dylan Companion* (London: Macmillan, 1990), pp. 260–61.

132. Milton Babbitt, *Words about Music: The Madison Lectures*, ed. Stephen Dembski and Joseph N. Straus (Madison: University of Wisconsin Press, 1987), p. 181.

133. Susan McClary, *Feminine Endings: Music, Gender, and Sexuality* (Minneapolis: Minnesota University Press, 1991); Richard Poirier, *The Performing Self: Compositions and Decompositions in the Language of Contemporary Life* (London: Chatto and Windus, 1971); Robert Pattison, *On Literacy: The Politics of the Word from Homer to the Age of Rock* (New York: Oxford University Press, 1982), and *The Triumph of Vulgarity: Rock Music in the Mirror of Romanticism* (New York: Oxford University Press, 1987); Alan Durant, *Conditions of Music* (London: Macmillan, 1984); H. Wiley Hitchcock, *Music in the United States: A Historical Introduction*, 2nd ed. (Englewood Cliffs: Prentice-Hall, 1974).

134. There is a plethora of books on women and pop music, many of them based on interviews. For historical background, see Gillian G. Gaar, *She's a Rebel: The History of Women in Rock n Roll* (London: Blandford, 1993); also Lucy O'Brien, *She Bop: The Definitive History of Women in Rock, Pop and Soul* (Harmondsworth: Penguin, 1995). Theoretical substance is more evident in Mavis Bayton, *Frock Rock: Women Performing Popular Music* (Oxford: Oxford University Press, 1998), while Simon Reynolds and Joy Press, *The Sex Revolts: Gender, Rebellion and Rock n Roll* (London: Serpent's Tail, 1995) is a daring survey. Black music has a huge literature: one starting point might be Nelson George, *The Death of Rhythm and Blues* (London: Omnibus, 1988); another is Tricia Rose, *Black Noise: Rap Music and Black Culture in Contemporary America*

(Middletown, CT: Wesleyan University Press, 1994). Paul Gilroy's chapter on music in *The Black Atlantic: Modernity and Double-Consciousness* (London: Verso, 1993), pp. 72–110, is highly suggestive; while Mark Costello and David Foster Wallace, *Signifying Rappers* (Hopewell, NJ: Ecco, 1997) is a splendid theoretical essay from 'two white Boston males' (p. 20).

135. For a sense of where this paragraph is coming from, see Frank Lentricchia, *Ariel and the Police: Michel Foucault, William James, Wallace Stevens* (Brighton: Harvester, 1988), pp. 135–95; also Terry Eagleton, *The Illusions of Postmodernism* (Oxford: Blackwell, 1996), pp. 69–92.

136. It is worth mentioning Juliet Mitchell's *Psychoanalysis and Feminism* (Harmondsworth: Penguin, 1974) which brought together psychoanalysis, socialism and feminism together in a happy synthesis; also the contributions of Jacqueline Rose, *Sexuality in the Field of Vision* (London: Verso, 1986), and Toril Moi, *Sexuality/Textuality* (London: Methuen, 1985). A fine and instructive perspective on these issues is contained in Dick Hebdige's 'The Impossible Object: Towards a Sociology of the Sublime', *New Formations*, 1 (1987), pp. 47–76.

137. Roland Barthes, 'The Grain of the Voice', *Image-Music-Text*, trans. Stephen Heath (London: Fontana, 1977), p. 189.

138. See variously Roland Barthes, 'The Grain of the Voice'; the final chapter of Richard Middleton, *Studying Popular Music*, pp. 247–94 (published originally in *Popular Music*, 3 (1983), pp. 235–70); and John Shepherd and Peter Wicke, *Music and Cultural Theory*. Mention should be made too of Georgina Born's reference to the work of Melanie Klein in *Rationalizing Culture: IRCAM, Boulez, and the Institutionalization of the Musical Avant-Garde* (Berkeley: University of California Press, 1995), and of Born's important earlier article, 'On Modern Music Culture: Shock, Pop, and Synthesis', *New Formations*, 2 (1987), pp. 51–78, a breakthrough article in containing pop music literature and musical modernism in the one context.

139. Mention should be made of this undervalued aspect of the work of Christopher Wintle, who gets there presumably via Wagner and Hans Keller. See 'Rigoletto's Bottle: Psychoanalysis and Opera', *New Formations*, 26 (1995), pp. 108–19.

140. Cambridge: Cambridge University Press, 1995. Reference in text to this edition.

141. Janet Wolff, *Aesthetics and the Sociology of Art*, 2nd ed. (London: Macmillan, 1993), p. 107.

142. On a television broadcast Costello resuscitated the song in an arrangement for the Brodsky Quartet (his partners on *The Juliet Letters*). The dreadful eighties drum machine had thankfully gone, though the quartet was of course not much other than a scored piano part.

143. John Carey, *The Intellectuals and the Masses: Pride and Prejudice among the Literary Intelligentsia 1880–1939* (London: Faber, 1992) presents a good exploration of this theme.

144. David Hesmondhalgh, review of Allan Moore, *Rock: The Primary Text*, in *Cultural Studies*, p. 362.

145. Shawn Colvin, *Cover Girl* (Columbia, 1994).

146. Bob Dylan, *Blood on the Tracks* (Columbia, 1975)

147. Charles Rosen, *The Classical Style: Haydn, Mozart, Beethoven*, rev. ed. (London: Faber, 1976), p. 325.

148. As ever, David Lewin is ahead of the game: see 'Women's Voices and the Fundamental Bass', *Journal of Musicology*, 10 (1992), pp. 464–82, especially p. 473.

149. Dylan covers are legion, both male and female, a remarkable recent case being Judy Collins, *Judy Sings Dylan: Just Like a Woman* (Geffen, 1993).

150. On this, see Michael Roos and Don O'Meara, 'Is Your Love in Vain? Dialectical Dilemmas in Bob Dylan's Recent Love-Songs', *Popular Music*, 7 (1987), pp. 36–49.

151. On the Rolling Thunder Review Dylan would appear, as Allen Ginsberg put it in the greatest of sleevenotes, 'big grey hat stuck with November leaves and flowers' (*Desire*, Columbia, 1976).

152. Derek Mahon, 'Poetry in Northern Ireland', *Twentieth-Century Studies*, 4 (1970), p. 93; by way of Edna Longley, *Poetry in the Wars* (Newcastle upon Tyne: Bloodaxe, 1986), p. 173.

153. Fornäs, *Cultural Theory and Late Modernity*, pp. 19–20.

154. Middleton, *Studying Popular Music*, pp. 122 and 117–22; Hamm, *Yesterdays*, p. 368.

155. Arnold Schoenberg, *Style and Idea: Selected Writings*, ed. Leonard Stein, trans. Leo Black (London: Faber, 1975), pp. 144 and 217.

156. Fredric Jameson, 'Reflections in Conclusion', afterword to *Aesthetics and Politics*, trans. and ed. Ronald Taylor (London: Verso, 1977), p. 211.

[6]

Second thoughts on a Rock Aesthetic: The Band

Andrew Chester

In replying to Richard Merton's comment on my first article, in NLR 59[1] I take the opportunity to clarify and correct some of my own positions, and also to attack some basic errors in Merton's conception of the aesthetic status of rock music and its relationship to politics.

I willingly concede to Merton that 'the regional autonomy of the art-object from the other instances within a social formation' should not be confused with 'an idealist "independence" from it'. I did not intend to claim such an independence, though I admit that in attacking the reductionist position I may have bent the stick too far in the other direction, particularly in my last paragraph. Nor did I intend to reject 'the ABC of Marxist criticism', i.e. the importance of studying a popular art in relation to its shifting social base, but this was not what I was concerned with in this article. What I did attempt, in the very limited framework of a book review, was to raise some of the questions which would have to be solved in order to found a canon of rock musical criticism. Merton despite some excellent critical insights, refuses to accept this problem, and this leads him into a quite different enterprise, rock *political* criticism.

Firstly, insistence on the dissociable character of artistic devices, while in itself correct, is used by Merton as a pretext for dismissing the task of studying also their inter-relation. Merton excels in discussion of rock lyrics, but disarticulation of a lyric from the complex musical totality runs the risk of involuntarily subsuming this lyric under the category of 'literature', and applying pre-existing critical canons foreign to the genre. In the absence of an analysis of the function of lyric in rock performance in general, and in the work of the group discussed in particular, there are no grounds for the sweeping judgements of artists that Merton freely dispenses on the basis of lyrics alone. Merton merely hints at this articulation when he speaks of the 'alloyed, computed

---

[1] See 'For a Rock Aesthetic', NLR 59 and 'Comment', NLR 59.

sounds of the Beach Boys', which presumably 'fit' (Brian) Wilson's lyrical celebration of the US cultural universe; when he dismisses Dylan on the basis of one or two examples of 'self-pitying verse'—conveniently disregarding the greater part of Dylan's oeuvre—one wonders whether Merton's taste for tempting literary inversions (*false poetry/poetry of the false*) is not prevailing over serious analysis.

The difference between the poetic and the musical functions of lyric, and the pitfalls of confusing the two, can be illustrated by a simple, almost trivial, example. In *Long Tall Sally* Little Richard sang: 'well long tall sally she's real sweet she's got everything that uncle john need'. Once written, this couplet is immediately banal. But in the song the fact that the vocal line is broken after 'got' and not after 'sweet' produces an aesthetic charge that depends precisely on the tension between the verbal and musical messages that a sung lyric carries. Merton claims that, although in his discussion of the Stones he 'deliberately refrains from adding a single word about the *other materials* (melody, instrumentation, vocalism) which combine with the lyric to produce the musical constructs in question', nevertheless 'there would be no difficulty in demonstrating that they would extend the line of analysis here taken'. In this instance that may be true. I am not sure that the articulation is always so simple.

Merton's second point is that, while rock music cannot claim the 'creation of a musical art of a complexity comparable to Vivaldi or Telemann', its 'true merit and significance' is that 'it is the first aesthetic form in modern history which has asymptotically started to close the gap between those who *produce* and those who *appropriate* art' (Merton's emphasis). 'It alone thereby prefigures, amidst its innumerable poverties and confusions, the structure of future art in a liberated social formation: communism.' He opposes this combined aesthetic/cultural legitimation of rock to my 'hyperbolization of the possibilities of the genre'. But what precisely is involved in closing the gap between producers and appropriators? Is this a social gap, or one of artistic appreciation? Merton's description of rock as a 'people's music' strongly implies the former. But this is very dangerous ground. Sections of the Left still echo the populist defence of 'folk', skiffle, etc as forms desirable because everyone can join in. If the *social* distance between producers and appropriators is at issue, then all forms of avant-garde and experimentation are threatened as 'anti-popular' and therefore anti-communist or counter-revolutionary. A rabid campaign on just these lines was run against this year's Camden Festival by certain left-wing groups; in fact the limited space that such festivals provide for avant-garde forms is generally the only positive feature of these otherwise turgid municipal ventures. The real gap between producers and appropriators that rock music has tended to bridge is that of musical appreciation. It is not that rock is a limited form and therefore close to the masses. Rock music, as it has grown to maturity in the last few years, has in fact cultivated an aesthetically sensitive mass base, which, even allowing for all its mystifications and illusions, is continuously sharpening its critical faculty. I would not want to quarrel with Merton on the nature of art under communism; there are no conceivable scientific grounds for such prophecies. The case is rather that the critical sophistication of the student rock audience—a stratum of non-workers, but a plebeian one—prefigures a situation in which the working masses also will have sufficient free time for the demanding tasks of artistic production and appropriation.

The meaning of the term, 'people's music' and of the 'gap between those who *produce* and those who *appropriate* art' are crucial questions. Merton's implicit answers can be seen at work in the canon he employs to appraise the Stones' development. 'For our purposes, the most important element of (*Street Fighting Man*), which situates it well beyond even, say, the Doors—is the *non-equation* of music and politics in it.' (Merton's emphasis.) Merton's whole analysis in fact reduces the Stones' development to one of ideological progress alone. The Stones have reached a high point because they recognise the *non-equation* of music and politics, and are thus able to harness their musical medium to a political message. The reason that this is also good art (of a kind) is that the message (solidarity with the oppressed) is expressed via the *devices* of derision, patronisation, etc. This sophistication is apparently sufficient to rate *Salt Of The Earth* as 'an extraordinary construct, one of the boldest yet most delicate that British rock has ever achieved'.

But the generosity of this judgement has an aura of unreality. The devices cited as translating the Stones' ideological progress into a artistic construct are entirely non-specific to the medium of rock music—or any form of sound. There is scarcely an indication why *Salt of the Earth*, or indeed the whole of *Beggars Banquet*, could not be discussed in exactly the same terms if it were not *heard* at all. True, *Factory Girl* is 'punctuated by the raucous echoes of a factory siren', and we can assume that Jagger and Richard's derisive lyrics are also sung with derision. But this is like judging the performance of a play by the writer's stage directions. Merton does not even see the integration of lyric into the musical structure as a problem, as is shown by his remark that 'a return to the heavy rhythm and blues style for which the group won its early fame may have seemed the safest option in the increasingly uncertain musical conjuncture of 1969.' The 'rhythm and blues style' is here seen as a purely contingent factor. The crisis of British rock, for which *Beggars Banquet* is the 'strong solution', is *a priori* assumed as soluble by ideological development alone.

We are here at the heart of Merton's mistake. Lyric, and the ideological themes it supports, are for him not merely a level that can be dissociated for analytical purposes; this level is implicitly taken as *dominant* in the complex musical totality. No wonder there would be 'no difficulty' in taking the 'other materials' into account. For Merton never questions that these are subordinate, mere *material* for ideological expression. At best, 'the music is coherent'; at worst, there is 'tension between the genre and the group', as on *Their Satanic Majesties Request*, but the sole source of this tension is the ability of the *other materials* to serve the (dominant) ideological theme. This in turn explains Merton's use of the term 'people's music'. The narrowing gap between producers and appropriators is not just social: it is, more precisely, ideological. The real *value* of rock music for Merton is as an index of the consciousness of its social base, to be encouraged as it discards mystifications and moves towards a revolutionary anti-capitalist consciousness. I would not want to decry this instrumentalist attitude. Rock music may provide Marxists with a sensitive political barometer, and they may quite legitimately seek to harness musical practice to political requirements. But this must be clearly distinguished from an appraisal of rock as music.

One group that will serve as a test case for Merton's conceptions is The Band, to which Merton pays tribute: 'yet out of (Dylan's) vapourings emerged groups like the Byrds and The Band'. In the process of discussing this group, I will attempt to answer some of the questions raised in my earlier article. Despite Merton's compliment, I believe The Band is singularly impervious to his critical canon. On all readings Merton should find the group aesthetically barren. The matter of their lyrics seems to echo the sentimentality of the country music industry. Elderly sailors longing for retirement, unfaithful servants (and slaves— Jawbone?), the demise of the South in the Civil War. Even the more 'realist' themes of storm, crop failure and agricultural unionism are far removed from social criticism; they are treated with resignation, and bear no relation to the life of The Band or their audience. The Band would not think of using the second-order devices that play such an important role in Merton's critical canon, nor can these be discovered as objective structures in their work.

At first sight The Band might not seem to register well on the 'pure musical' criteria that I have supported. Their music is far from experimental or avant-garde, and they are not prodigous instrumentalists. However I precisely want to attack the thesis that defines the basic musical structure of rock music as inherently restricted, on the basis of criteria by which groups like The Band would be playing a very uninteresting music indeed. Is rock music a genre which cannot compete with, for example, Western classical music as an aesthetic object, for want of formal complexity, and so needs the consolation prize of cultural significance that Merton holds out? I believe this is a capitulation to bourgeois ideology. Adequate space for formal elaboration is certainly the necessary basis of all significant aesthetic expression, but the notion of 'complexity' hides many ambiguities, and the opposition that Merton accepts between rock=simple and classical=complex, is in fact one constructed on the basis of the specific mode of complexity of classical music itself.

Western classical music is the apodigm of the *extensional* form of musical construction.[2] Theme and variations, counterpoint, tonality (as used in classical composition) are all devices that build diachronically and synchronically outwards from basic musical atoms. The complex is created by combination of the simple, which remains discrete and unchanged in the complex unity. Thus a basic premise of classical music is rigorous adherence to standard timbres, not only for the various orchestral instruments, but even for the most flexible of all instruments,

---

[2] This statement is most strictly true of classical music in the narrower sense—i.e. as opposed to 'romantic'. But post-classical 'serious' music only marginally departed from the extensional principle until the post-1945 era of electronic experimentation.

the human voice. Room for interpretation of the written notation is in fact marginal. If those critics who maintain the greater complexity of classical music specified that they had in mind this *extensional* development, they would be quite correct. The rock idiom does know forms of extensional development, it cannot compete in this sphere with a music based on this principle of construction.

Rock however follows, like many non-European musics, the path of *intensional* development. In this mode of construction the basic musical units (played/sung notes) are not combined through space and time as simple elements into complex structures. The simple entity is that constituted by the parameters of melody, harmony and beat, while the complex is built up by modulation of the basic notes, and by inflexion of the basic beat. (The language of this modulation and inflexion derives partly from conventions internal to the music, partly from the conventions of spoken language and gesture, partly from physiological factors.) All existing genres and sub-types of the Afro-American tradition show various forms of combined intensional and extensional development. The history of jazz is largely a transition from one to the other, later punctuated by a reaction against 'Europeanization' and a 'return to the roots'. The almost purely intensional form of the rural blues has only received critical attention in the past decade or so, and still largely remains a minority preserve. The 12-bar structure of the blues, which for the critic reared on extensional forms seems so confining, is viewed quite differently by the bluesman, for he builds 'inwards' from the 12-bar structure, and not 'outwards'. Complexity is multi-dimensional and by no means strictly quantifiable, and the aesthetic capacity of a musical form cannot be measured by complexity alone, but the example of the country blues shows the complete adequacy of a purely intensional mode of construction to an immensely subtle and varied project of aesthetic expression.

If jazz aimed to transform intensional into extensional, musical structures, rock sought a reverse path. The founding moment of rock music was the creation of a white analogue of blues vocalism, which was achieved in its classical form with Presley's Sun recordings of 1954–55. Taking elements from both blues and country sources, the qualitative novelty of rock, first only effected at the vocal level, was a singing style that fitted into the framework of country songs rather than 12-bar blues, and whose modulations and inflexions were determined in the first instance by the cadences of Southern white speech and gesture. The primacy of the vocal that characterizes both blues and rock is almost inevitable in an intensionally constructed music which still uses instruments designed for extensional expression, and was noted in the 'fifties, not so much by the titans of Southern rock, Presley and Lewis, for whom this development was almost intuitive, but by the more articulate of their disciples. Thus Eddie Cochran: 'In rock'n'roll the beat is only supplementary to the human voice. It's the voice, coupled with an extraordinary sense of emotion, which lends to rock'n'roll a personality not sensed in other types of music, (from an interview in *New Musical Express* 1958).

The conceptual pair of extensionality/intensionality is a step towards constructing a matrix for critical examination of the contemporary rock scene, and obtaining a purchase on the more strictly musical levels of the total product. Sixties rock derives essentially from the attempts of middle-class students in the early 'sixties to reproduce, at a more sophisticated level, the music that they had appropriated in the 'fifties, without at the time being able to work in it. After the demise of 'fifties rock, these musicians explored the roots and relatives of the rock genre, delving both into white country music (via 'urban folk'/ 'protest'), but more fruitfully into the rural and urban blues. The idiom of the blues, which took some years to learn, was the key to the production of 'sixties rock, and opened up very substantial new fields of musical development. (British rhythm and blues in the 'sixties had a similar birth, though its development was mediated by its national setting.) But the limitation of 'sixties rock has been its inability to achieve a real integration of its adopted musical materials. In general, its intensional development is derivative from the blues, and its extensional development is parasitic on the European tradition. Paradoxically, though rock is recognized by both musicians and audience as a well-defined musical category, the insterstices between rock and other genres seem far more habitable than the mainstream itself. Solutions adopted by major US groups include acceptance of a derivative musical identity (blues groups such as Canned Heat), extensional elaboration of rock/blues formal elements (Grateful Dead); reliance on theme/lyric/stance and other non-musical levels (Doors/Country Joe); backsliding into country and western (Byrds) or jazz (CTA, BS & T); 'fifties revivalism (Creedence Clearwater). Even Jefferson Airplane, perhaps the most impressive group of the 'sixties generation, whose music is least obviously parasitic on other forms, depend in the last instance on contrapuntal and harmonic structures that are firmly in the European/extensional tradition. Closely connected with the failure of 'sixties rock to achieve the new synthesis it explicitly aims at is the gross disparity between the calibre of its instrumentalists and its vocalists. Middle-class (male) white youths learnt blues guitar well enough to be accepted as equals by black musicians; their singing rarely rises above mediocrity, a fact that demands psychoanalytic explanation.

The one major group that, for all its limitations, is firmly anchored in rock as an independent genre, is The Band. They alone among important contemporary groups work at a purely intensional development which continues the enterprise begun with fifties rock. This is the reason why they manage to produce work of musical value yet without significant lyrics or theme, without experimentalism, without recourse to a merger with other genres, and without any problems of presentation: the music alone speaks.

It is no coincidence that The Band's history has run an entirely different course to that of other 'sixties groups. Their origins are working class, and all except Levon Helm are Canadian. They were formed as far back as 1959, as backing group for the Arkansas-born Canadian rock king Ronnie Hawkins, and the 'strange death of rock'n'roll' passed them by. Later their work with Dylan in his most creative phase (1964–66) widened their horizons of composition and production, and after Dylan stopped touring they retired (like Dylan, but with very different consequences) to up-state New York to work for the first time at their own music. Their intense professionalism and the rigour of their collective instrumental work have never been endangered by the demand of being cultural symbols as well as musicians (the ruin of such promising groups as Country Joe/Doors), and these qualities are absolute requirements of the ultra-sensitive capacity to turn thought instantly into sound that intensional construction demands.

An important determinant of The Band's particular style is that, unlike fifties rock (and mechanical attempts to revive this project, such as Creedence Clearwater), they do not rely on a unique vocalist. Given the role of the human voice in rock music, this absence determines both the vocal style affected by all four of The Band's singers, and its instrumental style. Lacking the vocal genius that the genre was originally designed for, The Band's vocals continuously strain against the upper limits of the male register (the region most responsive to changes of timbre), and even strain to emerge at all. Simultaneously, the backing instruments have a far more important role to play than in 'fifties rock. The simple country rhythms of guitar and acoustic bass (no drums) were sufficient against the virtuosity of a Presley. The Band has to rely predominantly on its rhythm section (a misnomer) for intensional development. Presley's vocal lines, designed to carry the whole musical message, could glide securely over a rhythmic backing that served only to underpin them. In The Band's music, the vocal constantly hesitates and hangs on a note while drums and bass build whole structures of arrival and non-arrival, anticipation and resolution, on the bridge passages between chord changes. The best example of this is the opening track on *Music From Big Pink*, the Dylan song *Tears of Rage*, where these unconscious devices condense in a superb *musical* construct. Here the verbal message of the lyrics is clearly subordinate to the music, whereas the reverse is true even on Dylan's rendering of the song accompanied by The Band on the 'basement tape'. Dylan still works at delivering a verbal message. On *Music From Big Pink* the verbal message is a residue left after the lyrics have been bent to serve as a vocal line. What comes through more strongly than the precise events described, are the connotations of the lyrics as a whole. The theme of filial ingratitude perfectly matches The Band's own performance, in which the music appears to have so painful a birth.

The Band's construction is astonishingly pure rock, whose aesthetic values are purely musical. It is not a synthesis that will propel the music on a radical forward course. This will not happen until or unless the problem of rock vocalism is solved. I am not suggesting that very different departures, such as cross-fertilization of rock with certain 'serious' forms (e.g. Velvet Underground or Soft Machine) may not be a more secure way forward, and may not be from certain perspectives more aesthetically rewarding. There is no question here of a rank order —a conception quite alien to materialist criticism. Yet the extensional constructions of the 'experimental' groups lead away from rock to realms where quite different critical canons must be applied.

To conclude, I would like to attempt some partial answers and correctives to the set of questions presented in my earlier article.

Structural Co-ordinates and Socio-cultural Base. The internal co-ordinates of a musical form are not mechanically determined by its social base. The relationship is one of compatibility. Musical practice has a relative autonomy, and to each social group correspond certain acceptable genres. Analysis of this compatibility is an important and so far almost unexplored question which will require both historical materialist and psychoanalytic explanation. The role of *lyric* in rock music has been a major theme in the present discussion; as for *dance*, it is the intensional development of rhythmic inflection that made possible the qualitative break in dance styles that took place once rock music had been appropriated by its new audiences.

Dominance of the Vocal. What I attempted to grasp with this expression is in fact the dominance of intensional over extensional modes. In rock music, the overwhelming primacy of the vocal has been reduced with the development of electronic instruments and techniques, but rock remains a genre 'dominated' by the vocal, which only tends to disappear in the 'frontier' territories.

Music and Ideology. Artistic projects will continue to be distorted by ideological mystifications until dialectical materialism is generally accepted (and appropriated) as a world outlook. By 'aesthetics is the politics of art' I meant to stress the importance of the ideological struggle against these mystifications, and of materialist analysis of artistic problems, by critics and the direct producers themselves as a requirement for the progress of all forms of art.

[7]

Why I'll Never Teach Rock 'n' Roll Again

Sean McCann

Having made the attempt at various kinds of colleges and in various ways, I have decided not to teach popular culture again—and especially not that particularly diverse and unruly monster known as pop music. This is not because I believe that the products of twentieth-century mass media are without historical interest or even of artistic merit. In fact, I feel quite strongly that the opposite is often true. The issue for me rather is an institutional one and boils down to a simple—though far-reaching—idea, whose full force it took me an unfortunately long time to grasp. Pop culture is not as such teachable, at least not within the academic classroom. Indeed, from one compelling perspective, the whole point of pop culture is to be unacademic. At the very least, there is a basic friction between the realm of the classroom and the world of popular taste. There may be teachers who are gifted enough to negotiate this tension, but I know that I am not one of them.

The point I am making here is neither especially complex nor novel. (As it pertains to pop music, it has been made most forcefully by Simon Frith.) It amounts to a variation on the by-now commonplace idea that modes of attention have a significant power to constitute their objects—a dynamic that is particularly forceful when it is backed up by institutional structures like those of the university classroom. From this perspective, pop culture is simply whatever is understood by popular audiences to be pop culture. And in our historical epoch, in which the authority of high culture as aristocratic inheritance has dwindled to the point of insignificance, that means basically nonacademic culture. The anti-scholastic attitude that runs rampant through music and movies and trash fiction (as when a dweeby character in John Woo's recent film *Broken Arrow* is made shamefacedly to acknowledge his Yale training), then, is not only trivial anti-intellectualism. Nor is it mostly class resentment. Rather it amounts to the invocation of a structuring principle that can appeal easily to audiences across economic position and social standing. Pop culture simply is anti-academic culture.

To take the products of mass media as historical texts or as artistic objects worthy of academic attention is by this definition no longer to see them as pop culture. They have become topics of study in a transition that depends on cutting across the grain of popular taste with the blade of intellectual authority. My point is not that this is a transition that is in any way illegitimate. I've built my career around the conviction that, as expressions of ideology and examples of artistic invention, the materials of pop culture frequently have a great deal to teach us. It can be extremely profitable in the classroom to use the products of mass media to teach about historical attitudes, say, or about the marketing of culture, or the dissemination of tastes, or even about conceptions of the popular itself. Similarly, one can always teach students and learn from them about the wonderful artistry of particular artifacts. I simply want to emphasize that looking for such things in a classroom setting is not something we should call teaching popular culture. As Daniel Czitrom noted recently, the first thing one learns teaching a course on the history of American popular music is how impressively little students are likely to know, and, therefore, the first task one picks up is educating them to the material. In short, pop music in this situation has become a historical topic like any other, demanding much the same pedagogical efforts and calling up the same complaints from the teacher (*the students don't know anything!*), and requiring the same kinds of work from students as in other classes.

Although it may seem like splitting hairs, there is a reason to distinguish between using pop materials for academic study and teaching popular culture. A good part of the rhetoric surrounding the expansion of canonical classroom materials in the past several decades has been explicitly anti-academic. It often has disavowed the intention to treat popular materials simply as texts for analysis and interpretation, and instead has emphasized the charge that can come from transgressing intellectual boundaries or the political usefulness of tapping into a reservoir of popular will. One might think of the title of the official history of the Popular Culture Association, *Against Academia*, a book that recounts the development of a professional society of scholars with institutional support and its own academic press. But less obvious examples, with apparently different intellectual provenance and political commitments, have been commonplace over recent years—perhaps most prominently in the sudden rise of Cultural Studies, whose leading intellectuals have never been satisfied with expanding what academics study. They want to change what academics do—to make "organic intellectuals," as is sometimes said in a Gramscian vein—and to transform the classroom as a precursor to transforming society. Popular culture isn't something to study in this mode as much as it stands for an ideal to invoke. The aim, to reverse the phrasing from above, is to cut across the blade of intellectual authority with the grain of popular taste.

The point that it took me hard experience to grasp firmly is that it's not really possible to be against academia in any meaningful way from within the academy. It may be valuable to be anti-academic—to be opposed to the rigid, hierarchical, and formulaic—and I suspect that almost anyone who teaches in scholastic institutions yearns to escape their routinized structures. But to use pop culture as a source of charismatic power toward transforming the classroom depends upon a dangerous illusion. A teacher in a classroom may be stale or inventive, pedestrian or bold, and there may be exciting or dull courses. But the basic structures of institutional education remain in place even if the texts have been changed—especially so long as grades are being given. I stress the point because I think that to some degree or other the fantasy of being against academia is often at work when pop culture is invoked.

Two examples of what I consider my own pedagogical failure can illustrate this suspicion. For several years I taught beginning writing in an urban, public university populated mainly by a diverse body of working- and lower-middle-class students, many of them recent immigrants or the children of immigrants. I often began the semester with a classroom exercise that gave students the synopsis of a typical Hollywood action-adventure movie and asked them to imagine that they were scriptwriters and casting directors. Their task was to meet in small groups and to come up with descriptions of the main characters (a protagonist, a sidekick, a love-interest) and the main lines of a plot. The exercise was invariably a classroom success and generated a level of enthusiasm among the students that unfortunately was almost never approached again during the semester. I was always impressed, too, by the sheer skill of the students at the exercise—at what might be called their popular literacy. They cited and twisted filmic conventions with impressive *savoir-faire*. And, as if to illustrate the democracy of mass culture, they managed to do so with perfect ease and mutual understanding, although their groups would usually include several races and multiple first languages. Typically, at no other point in the semester would I see my students working together so purposefully, skillfully, and harmoniously.

Equally impressive to me at the time, though, was the way in which the movies the students imagined would seem so divergent from their own lives. The aim of this exercise for me was to indicate something basic about the way narrative conventions work, and about how political and social assumptions can be built into them. To illustrate these ideas I would simply point out that the work of each group of students resembled that of their peers remarkably and that their descriptions of characters were almost standard over the hundreds of students with whom I'd worked in the past. Left unstated, although always clear in the conversation, was the fact that while the students were asian, black, latino, and white, the characters they created were invariably white models of Hollywood beauty (with some flexibility given to renditions of the sidekick character). Likewise, their protagonists were always men and their love-interests women. The lesson was simple and dramatic and the students understood it immediately. Yet not so well that I could overcome a nagging sense of dissatisfaction that I always felt when the session was completed. When the students were inventing their films, they were full of vitality and confidence. At the moment when I began to point out, as gently as I could, that the characters conformed to limited and perhaps racist and sexist conventions, their faces would fall and the classroom would devolve into spiritless quiet. It took me a while to figure out what I was doing wrong.

Of course, it's never fun to have one's creativity criticized, and it's probably especially unpleasant to have one's inventions revealed as unselfconsciously formulaic and regressive. But, in retrospect, I think my students' dissatisfaction had a simpler and more obvious explanation than distaste for their "PC" professor. It was not that the students were unaware of the conventional nature of their work or that they missed its social implications. They simply took enormous pleasure in their knowledge of pop convention, and they enjoyed profoundly the capacity to manipulate stick figures that were attractive partly because they had obviously little to do with the students' own lives. Their disappointment came when I shifted the conversation away from noting clever variations on the familiar and began to pick up broader topics of analysis because that meant the game was at an end. We had entered an earnest atmosphere that was at odds with the playfulness with which the students could treat narrative structures they knew intimately. For these students, pop culture worked as Lawrence Levine has described it—as a "folklore of industrial capitalism"—and they regarded my analysis with the grim distaste that the subjects of folklorists must experience when they encounter their chroniclers. My scholarly analysis, however slight, had turned a light and unserious game into a portentous structure.

At the other type of institution at which I've taught—a small, elite, liberal arts college whose clients tend to come from the upper echelons of the professional-managerial class—such an exercise would probably be far more successful, if it did not seem so obvious that the students deciphered it long before I got to the point. For, the way of thinking built into my exercise seems to accord far more closely with their habitual ways of regarding pop culture. I have already been told several times by students at this school that learning the tools of academic analysis has given them a great new excuse for watching TV because it allows them simultaneously to enjoy and to "critique" the products of mass culture. Yet here, too, when I attempted to take advantage of this attitude to teach pop culture, I ran into problems that came to seem to me nearly insuperable.

The difficulty in this situation was not with a particular classroom exercise, but with an entire course. Titled "Writing Rock," this class aimed to introduce students to various forms of cultural and historical analysis by drawing on their knowledge of pop music and their enthusiastic habit of talking about it critically. The syllabus was divided, therefore, into various sections intended to illustrate the major topics in the critical analysis of popular culture. One section considered various definitions of mass culture, popular culture, and the avant-garde; another focused on the relation between race and commercial music; a third on the role of sexuality and gender, etc. Yet, the course never really got beyond one basic issue—the relation between "rock" and "pop"—and classroom conversation circled obsessively around the recurrent and massively dull question of whether a piece of music was or was not "authentic."

What went wrong in this situation might be taken as a direct inversion of the problem I ran into in my earlier experience. Students at the urban, public university gloried in pop culture. They had little interest in seeing it as debased or banal, and they resented my efforts to point out its limitations. At the elite, liberal-arts college, by contrast, the students were happy to see precisely those limitations, and they had great familiarity with analyzing the ideological import of popular entertainment. They simply tended to imagine that the music they liked somehow escaped such problems because it was itself inherently critical. Rock, to their minds, was basically anti-popular and in some way noncommercial. Unlike the students

from the public university who did not mind recognizing the conventionality of the movies they liked, but who resisted the notion
that conventionality itself was bad—these students described their
music as opposing convention altogether. They began with the
assumption that formula limited artistic freedom and inscribed ideological expectations, and they admired musicians who seemed able
to escape, destroy, or mock the familiar. What they resented most
was my suggestion that these attitudes themselves might be conventions of one type of popular entertainment. Such a perspective, they
complained, threatened to reduce the artistic authenticity of their
music and to suggest that in some way it was not fundamentally
distinct from ordinary pop.

I never got much beyond this question with the students in my
class on Rock 'n' Roll, and by the time the course was finished I realized that at some level their sophistication about pop culture
depended heavily on their perception that they and the music they
liked were superior to it. Truly worthwhile music by their account
existed as a thing apart—superior to commercial entertainment and,
by the same token, impervious to academic forms of analysis.
Although the terms of evaluation differed vastly, for these students
as well as for those at the urban university, classroom conversation
only really worked when it was limited to the question of whether
some artifact was good or not. The sole meaningful discourse was
one of appreciation.

I won't teach pop music again because I believe that, at least at
the elite liberal arts school where I still teach, such attitudes are all
but unnegotiable. The students' investment in Rock as a rebellious
and authentic music seems too potent to be anything but dented
during the course of a semester. It would be wrong, though, to suggest that my two examples of pedagogical mishap should be blamed
on the prejudices of students. In both cases, I was drawn to examples of pop culture for exactly the reasons that they eventually failed
in the classroom. Like the members of the PCA, or the leaders of
Cultural Studies, I wanted to draw on the students' popular literacy
and their critical sensibilities, and to take advantage of their own
readiness to embrace something that seemed anti-academic. I
shouldn't have been surprised when they resisted converting those
attitudes to academic purposes. There is an ethical issue here as well
as an intellectual and pedagogical one that I needed my students to
point out to me. As Pierre Bourdieu has noted, when an intellectual
invokes the popular it is invariably to draw on a source of authority
that seems to emerge from a terrain outside the academy. I think

that in both my examples the students realized that in some inexplicit way this was my aim. I was attempting to call on their enthusiasm for unscholastic material while asking them to regard that material from a distanced and scholarly perspective.

It is this double aim to which I refer when I say I won't teach popular culture again. I have no difficulty in taking the products of mass media as the subjects of scholarly analysis and I plan on doing it often in the future. Once they've entered the classroom, though, such materials become academic texts, and I'll be clear in treating them as such.

Writing Rock

Sean McCann
Wesleyan University
Spring 1994

> Rock journalism is people who can't write preparing stories based on interviews with people who can't talk in order to amuse people who can't read.
> —Frank Zappa

> [B]y learning to talk about music, one also learned to talk about other things.
> —David Riesman

> Rock 'n' roll was from the start ... constituted not simply as music but also as knowledge. To be a rock fan is not just to like something but also to know something, to share a secret with one's fellow fans, to take for granted the ignorance of nonfans. This common sense of rock fandom has had a constricting effect on the development of rock theory.... In a world in which everyone is an expert—everyone knows what makes their music significant, other people's music vacuous—self-proclaimed expertise is despised. Rock critics despise rock academics, rock musicians despise rock critics, rock fans despise each other.
> —Simon Frith

Required Reading

Simon Frith, *Sound Effects: Youth, Leisure, and the Politics of Rock 'n' Roll* (New York: Pantheon Books, 1981); Simon Firth and Andrew Goodwin, eds. *The Music Video Reader.*

Dick Hebdige, *Subculture: The Meaning of Style* (London: Methuen, 1979).

Greil Marcus, *Lipstick Traces: A Secret History of the Twentieth Century* (Cambridge: Harvard University Press, 1969).

Greg Tate, *Flyboy in the Buttermilk: Essays & Tales of American Music & Culture from BeBop to Hip Hop* (New York: Simon & Schuster, 1992), plus a collection of readings from the Mail Center

Recommended Reading

Robert Palmer, *Deep Blues* (New York: Viking, 1981).

Chandra Mukerji and Michael Schudson, eds, *Rethinking*

Popular Culture: Contemporary Perspectives in Cultural Studies (Berkeley: University of California Press, 1991).

Course Objectives

The aim of this course is to get at some of the promises and problems that arise when criticism trains its sights on aspects of cultural life that traditionally have fallen beneath notice. We will be thinking about pop culture and its critics in general, but, more specifically, we will listen to rock to look at Cultural Studies—a burgeoning genre of academic inquiry that stakes large claims on taking new approaches to new matters. Pop music should be an especially effective means to investigate these claims for a handful of reasons. As an exemplary feature of postwar mass culture, contemporary pop seems to present strong evidence for a key Cultural Studies argument: that our cultural maps have been so significantly altered that romantic ideas about art deserve to be discarded. Secondly, at crucial moments and in certain forms (the Woodstock-era rock revolution, the punk rebellion, soul, reggae, and rap) postwar pop music has itself seemed like a uniquely critical kind of popular culture, challenging to some dominant beliefs and offering alternative visions of contemporary life. And, to a degree no other field of mass culture can match, it has generated intellectuals from its own ranks who strenuously advance that impression. We will consider all of these features of what Simon Frith calls pop music as "knowledge" this semester.

WHY I'LL NEVER TEACH ROCK 'N' ROLL AGAIN/199

Course Requirements

We will attempt to explore these matters in practice. Consequently, *this will be a writing course.* I will ask you to complete a 2–5 page essay every two weeks, and to review these essays weekly with a group of three fellow students. You will submit a portfolio of your writing periodically, selecting for prominence what you and your peers believe is your best work. There will be no exams and no final paper assignment.

Each student will also moderate with a fellow student one class session. On these occasions, you will indicate briefly what you think are the basic approaches and issues of the assigned readings, offering one or two comparisons with other readings and suggesting a handful of questions about the material. You will also select and bring to class one or two pieces of music that you think highlight important features of the readings.

Class attendance and reading assignments are required. More importantly, *participation in review groups is absolutely essential. More than two absences from these sessions will mean a penalty to your grade, as will failure to submit written work to them. One extension, requested in advance and for extenuating circumstances, will be granted for portfolio submissions. All other late work will be penalized.*

Schedule

January 19
Course introduction
The Pixies, "Subbacultcha"

January 24
Rock is...?
Roland Barthes, "The Grain of the Voice" (p); Morris Dickstein, "The Age of Rock," *Gates of Eden* (p); Simon Frith, "Introduction," *Sound Effects*; Stuart Hall and Paddy Whannel, "The Young Audience," *The Popular Arts* (p); Allan Moore, "Introduction," *Rock: The Primary Text* (p); Bob Dylan, "I Want You"; The Beatles, "Love Me Do; The Ramones, "Sheena is a Punk Rocker"; Michael Jackson, "Beat It"; Pet Shop Boys, "What Have I Done to Deserve This?"

Folk, Mass, Pop, Avant-Garde

January 26
T. W. Adorno, "On Popular Music" (p); Carl Belz, "Rock as Folk Art," *The Story of Rock* (p); Morag Shiach, selection, *Discourse on the Popular* (p); Raymond Williams, "Aesthetic, Art, Folk, Masses, Popular," *Keywords* (p); Chuck Berry, "Sweet Little Sixteen"; Animals, "House of the Rising Sun"; Janis Joplin, "Piece of My Heart,""Summertime"; The Beatles, *White Album*
Recommended: Mukerji and Schudson, "Introduction"; Greg Tate, "Yo! Hermeneutics!"

200/RADICAL HISTORY REVIEW

January 31
Peter Burger, "On the Problem of the Autonomy of Art in Bourgeois Society," *Theory of the Avant-Garde* (p); Andreas Huyysen, "After the Great Divide" (p); Simon Frith, "Rock and Mass Culture," "Making Music," *Sound Effects*; James Brown, "Cold Sweat"; Gang of Four, "I Love a Man in a Uniform"; Sonic Youth, "Dirty"

February 2
Greil Marcus, *Lipstick Traces*, Prologue, "The Last Sex Pistols Concert," Epilogue; Julie Burchill, "The Same Old Con," *Love it or Shove it* (p); Sex Pistols, "God Save the Queen"

February 7
Fredric Jameson, "Reification and Utopia in Mass Culture"(p); Stuart Hall, "Notes on Deconstructing 'the Popular'" (p); Lester Bangs, "Of Pop and Pies and Fun: A program for Mass Liberation in the Form of a Stooges Review, or Who's the Fool?" *Psychic Reactions and Curburetor Dung* (p); Credence Clearwater Revival, "Fortunate Son"; Sly and the Family Stone, "Everyday People,""Family Affair"; The Stooges, "Search and Destroy"; Bruce Springsteen, "Thunder Road"; Pearljam, "Jeremy"

Culture, Race, Youth Culture, Subculture

February 9
Greil Marcus, "Presliad," *Mystery*

Train (p); Raymond Williams, "Culture," *Keywords* (p); Elvis Presley, "Hound Dog" *Recommended*: Clifford Geertz, "Deep Play: Notes on the Balinese Cockfight," *Rethinking Popular Culture*

February 14
Sherley Anne Williams, "Two Words on Music: Black Community," *Black Popular Culture* (p); Greg Tate, 48–55, 95–107, 120–41; Julie Burchill, "The Rage is Beige"; The Supremes, "Baby Love"; Sade, "Smooth Operator"; Public Enemy, "Fight the Power"

February 16
Guest lecturer, Ann Marlowe, pop music journalism; Simon Frith, "Making Meaning," *Sound Effects*

February 21
Dick Hebdige, *Subculture*; Simon Frith, *Sound Effects*, chaps. 8, 9, 11; the Who, "The Kids Are Alright," "My Generation"; the Specials, "Nightclub," "Too Much, Too Young"; Black Flag, "TV Party"; Suicidal Tendencies, "Institutionalized"

February 23
Steve Perry, "Ain't No Mountain High Enough: The Politics of Crossover," *Facing the Music* (p); Kristal Brent Zook, "Reconstructions of Nationalist Thought in Black Music and Culture"; *Rocking the Boat* (p); Paul Gilroy, "Sounds Authentic" (p);

WHY I'LL NEVER TEACH ROCK 'N' ROLL AGAIN/201

Grandmaster Flash, "The Message";
Ice Cube, "Check Yourself"; Tracy
Chapman, "Fast Car"; Prince, "Little
Red Corvette"

February 28
Guest lecturer, Steve Duncombe,
subcultures and subcultural pub-
lishing
Recommended: Jürgen Habermas,
"The Public Sphere," *Rethinking
Popular Culture*

March 2
Guest lecturer, Gage Averill, ethno-
musicology and pop music
**Portfolio due, submit to English
Office**

Gender and Sexuality

March 21
Simon Frith, *Sound Effects*, chap. 10;
Frith and Angela McRobbie,"Rock
and Sexuality" (p); Sheryl Garrat,
"Teenage Dreams" (p); Rolling
Stones, "Under My Thumb,"
"Bitch"; Elvis Costello, "Alison"; Liz
Phair, *Exile in Guyville*

March 23
Gina Rumsey and Hillary Little,
"Women and Pop: A Series of Lost
Encounters," *Zoot Suits and Second-
Hand Dresses* (p); Julie Burchill,
"Idols on Parade"; "Last Days of the
Locust"; Ellen Willis, "Beginning to
See the Light" (p); Lisa A. Lewis,
"Being Discovered," *Sound & Vision*;
Aretha Franklin, "Respect"; Patti
Smith, "Gloria"; Cyndi Lauper,
"Girls Just Wanna Have Fun";

Queen Latifah, "Ladies First"; P. J.
Harvey, "Dress"; L7, "You and Me
Baby till the Wheels Fall Off"

April 6
Robert Palmer, "Church of the Sonic
Guitar" (p); Andrew Goodwin,
"Sample and Hold" (p); Tricia Rose,
"Orality and Technology: Rap
Music and Afro-American Cultural
Resistance" (p); Jimi Hendrix, "Are
You Experienced?" "Purple Haze";
KRS-One, Criminal Minded; De La
Soul, Three Feet High and Rising;
Arrested Development, "People
Everyday"

April 8
**Portfolio due, submit to English
Office**

April 11
Larry Grossberg, "The Media
Economy of Rock Culture," *Sound &
Vision*; George Lipsitz, "Against the
Wind: Dialogic Aspects of Rock and
Roll" *Time Passages*; Bruce
Springsteen, "Born in the USA,"
"Highway Patrolman"

**Music Video, Consumerism,
Postmodernism**

April 13
Simon Frith, "Rock and Leisure,"
Sound Effects; Will Straw, "Popular
Music and Postmodernism," *Sound
& Vision*
Recommended: Rosalind Williams,
"The Dream World of Mass
Consumption"; Talking Heads,
"Wild Life"; Michael Jackson,

202/RADICAL HISTORY REVIEW

"Thriller"; Peter Gabriel, "Sledgehammer"; Madonna, "Like a Virgin"

April 18
Andrew Goodwin, "Fatal Distractions," *Sound & Vision*; Leslie Savan, "Commercials Go Rock," *Sound & Vision*; the Breeders, "Cannonball"; Dr. Dre, "Dre Day"

April 20
Peter Wicke, "An Aesthetics of Synthesis" *Rock Music* (p); Greil Marcus, "Born Dead," *Ranters and Crowd Pleasers* (p)

Fandom and Stardom

April 25
David Buxton, "Rock Music, the Star System, and the Rise of Consumerism," *On Record* (p); Richard Dyer, "Stars" (p); Plastic Ono Band, "Instant Karma"

April 2
Pamela Des Barres, "Every Inch of My Love," *I'm With the Band* (p); Fred Vermorel and Judy Vermorel, "Starlust" (p); Marianne Faithful, "As Tears Go By"; Joan Jett, "I Love Rock and Roll"; David Bowie, "Ziggy Stardust"

May 2
Guest lecturer: Dewar McLeod, fandom and anti-fandom in California hardcore
Recommended, Janice Radway, "Interpretive Communities and Variable Literacies," *Rethinking Popular Culture*

May 4
Dave Marsh, "Introduction," *Fortunate Son* (p)
Portfolios due, submit to English office

[8]

Authenticity as authentication[1]

ALLAN MOORE

Abstract

This article argues for the prematurity of any dismissal of the notion of authenticity as meaningful within popular music discourse. It synthesises a range of views as to how authenticity is constructed, and offers a tri-partite typology dependent on asking who, rather than what, is being authenticated. It focuses on rock and folk genres, but also argues that the generic nature of the typology makes it applicable to any other genre wherein listeners are concerned to ask whether a musical utterance can be construed as sincere.

Preamble

'Authentic'. 'Real'. 'Honest'. 'Truthful'. 'With integrity'. 'Actual'. 'Genuine'. 'Essential'. 'Sincere'. Of all the value terms employed in music discourse, these are perhaps the most loaded. They are familiar from the writings of academic scholars, as will be made plain below. They have been present, in their various ways, in fan and journalistic writing (most notably in the pages of *Rolling Stone*). In almost all cases, it is music to which these qualifiers can be attached that such writing, and presumably thinking, has prized. Of the terms, it is the first which is most familiar from academic discourse and is, therefore, the one to which I shall reduce the others for the purposes of this article. On occasions, attachment of this term can be justified with close reference to details of sonic design, even if such a process is extremely long-winded: in a previous article, I have demonstrated the viability of just such an approach.[2] Elsewhere, such an attachment is more arbitrary. In the long run, the resultant experiences in these latter cases may be even more analytically interesting in that the influence of the musical text on these occasions may be said to be nil.[3] There are, however, various authenticities, sharing a base assumption about 'essential(ized), real, actual, essence' (Taylor 1997, p. 21): they are concisely described in Gilbert and Pearson's identification of the requirements of a 1980s 'authentic' rock, wherein

artists must speak the truth of their (and others') situations. Authenticity was guaranteed by the presence of a specific type of instrumentation . . . [the singer's] fundamental role was to *represent* the culture from which he comes. (Gilbert and Pearson 1999, pp. 164–5)

The purpose of this article is to explore just some of the ramifications of the term and to offer a globalising perspective analysing the three senses conflated in the above quotation: that artists speak the truth of their own situation; that they speak the truth of the situation of (absent) others; and that they speak the truth of their own culture, thereby representing (present) others. It will do this with primary reference to rock music and to contemporary folk music, although I believe my analysis to be applicable to other genres. Only two other writers appear to have attempted to cover this general ground, and reference will be made throughout to Taylor (1997) and to Fornäs (1995). This article is not set up in opposition to them, but rather in opposition to two key features in the discourse of authenticity.

As suggested above, discussions of the attribution of authenticity cannot always take place with explicit reference to matters of sonic design. I start, therefore, from an assumption that authenticity does not inhere in any combination of musical sounds. 'Authenticity' is a matter of interpretation which is made and fought for from within a cultural and, thus, historicised position. It is ascribed, not inscribed. As Sarah Rubidge has it: 'authenticity is ... not a property *of*, but something we ascribe *to* a performance' (Rubidge 1996, p. 219). Whether a performance is authentic, then, depends on who 'we' are. However, if this quality that we call 'authenticity' does not inhere in the music we hear, where does it lie? It is my second assumption in this article that it is a construction made on the act of listening. In part, I take this tack to accommodate my own doubts about the positing of both a unified and a fragmented subject. However, it seems to me that far from resolving such doubts before advancing positions on authenticity, theorisation of observations made on how things count as authentic will in turn inform the question of how such observers constitute their subjectivity.

Thus, rather than ask *what* (piece of music, or activity) is being authenticated, in this article I ask *who*. I also recognise that, even in my proposal of a globalising perspective, my own exploration is undertaken from within a bounded cultural position. Michael Pickering is alive to this difficulty when he argues that '"authenticity" is a relative concept which is generally used in absolutist terms' (Pickering 1986, p. 213), while Fornäs argues that a 'realist' approach to the question is far too limiting in aesthetic discourses. I trust that my own subjectivity will be understood in reference to the examples I shall employ in what follows.

The issue of what can be understood as 'authentic' is not exclusive to popular music discourse. It is, of course, pertinent to the hallowed distinctions between 'pop' and 'rock' on the one hand, and to the less hallowed (because more recent) distinctions between dance music genres on the other (for instance, the necessity of 'hardcore' in relation to commercialised raves in the late 1980s). It is pertinent to debates within the 'folk' music tradition and, indeed, this understanding has historical priority. It is even pertinent to contemporary approaches to the performance of music in the Euro-American formal music tradition (Kenyon 1988 is an authoritative text), although discussion of this aspect is well outside the scope of this article. Judging from recent critical writing, one may think it has become less pertinent. Born and Hesmondhalgh have recently pointed out that the concept 'has been consigned to the intellectual dust-heap' (Born and Hesmondhalgh 2000, p. 30) since, in a postmodern world where appropriation (of material by producers of music) is everywhere evident, it no longer carries its originary force. However, there seem to me three particular reasons why such an abandonment is premature, the first two of which I develop. The first is that to identify the authentic with the original is only one understanding which is currently made, an understanding which should not be allowed to annexe the whole. The second is that in one sense, appropriation (of sonic experiences by perceivers) remains foundational to processes of authentication. The third is that the social alienation produced under modernity, which appears to me the ideological root of such striving for the authentic, and of which we have been aware for decades, grows daily more apparent.[4]

In rock discourse, the term has frequently been used to define a *style* of writing or performing, particularly anything associated with the practices of the singer/ songwriter, where attributes of intimacy (just Joni Mitchell and her zither)[5] and immediacy (in the sense of unmediated forms of sound production) tend to connote authenticity. It is used in a socio-economic sense, to refer to the social standing of the musician. It is used to determine the supposed reasons she has for working, whether her primary felt responsibility is to herself, her art, her public, or her bank balance. It is used to bestow integrity, or its lack, on a performer, such that an 'authentic' performer exhibits realism, lack of pretence, or the like. Note that these usages do not mutually exclude one another, nor do they necessarily coincide, and that all are applied from the outside. Lawrence Grossberg (1992) has argued that the distinction between 'authentic' and its opposite ('entertainment' at some times, 'commercial' at others) underpins the history of popular music from the time of Elvis Presley onwards, and that such a history proceeds as a pendulum, swinging from one extreme to the other, frequently with much disagreement among fans and critics as to which term to apply to which music – again, such attributions are to be fought for. Roy Shuker takes this historicisation further, declaring 'that using authenticity to distinguish between rock and pop is no longer valid, though it continues to serve an important ideological function' (Shuker 1994, p. 8). In each of these accounts, there is a sense in which different understandings of authenticity are conflated in the presence of this fundamental authentic/commercial paradigm, a view supported in Shuker's later discussion (Shuker 1998). In what follows, I attempt to bypass this conflation such that these different understandings become more accessible.

First person authenticity

In terms of music, it seems that debates over authenticity can best begin from the 'folk'. In praising the institution of the English folk song revival at the beginning of the last century, the composer Hubert Parry noted that folk songs had 'no sham, no got-up glitter, and no vulgarity' (quoted in Boyes 1993, p. 26). In these terms, he opposed (authentic) folk song to (commercial) music hall, thereby making plain both his, and the revivalists', disdain for the music of the urban working-class. Parry's was a voice to be listened to. He was professor of music at Oxford and the leading composer of choral and orchestral music of his (late Victorian and Edwardian) generation, arguably the first since the seventeenth century to develop a distinctive English compositional voice capable of positive comparison with central European contemporaries (the likes of Brahms or Wagner). And, his view also finds expression throughout the pan-European folk-aestheticist movement. As we now know, of course, the 'folk' are better considered a bourgeois construction, assembled by views such as these: as Harker (1985) has pointed out, their 'material' (the traces of their culture, be that song, dance, story) are unavoidably mediated. Pickering argues that this discursive move can be understood as marking the conception of a folk aesthetic as robust as that of high culture, in that both become identified by their freedom 'from commercial imperatives and influences, and thus authentic and good' (Pickering 1986, p. 205). The opposition between 'authentic' and 'commercial' is, thus, not a new one. Nor has it vanished from this particular field. As part of the second English revival of the 1950s, leading figure Ewan McColl insisted that one should sing only in one's own native tongue, and sing songs only from one's own social or cultural setting. In some clubs, this was taken to exclude not only recent (particularly US) material, but also such recent instruments as the acoustic guitar, leading in the 1970s / early 1980s to a high degree of separation between 'traditional' ('policy') and 'contemporary' clubs (as they often styled themselves), separation which in some cases even led to separate clubs in the same venue on different nights of the week:

As late as 1984, a band which played entirely 'traditional' material encountered objections on 'policy' grounds because they used electronic instruments. Yet, unaccountably, no 'policy clubs' seem to have refused to accept a performer who sang with a concertina accompaniment. The concertina was, after all, 'authentic' – old(ish), used by the Folk (sometimes) and, most of all, unsullied by modernity. (Boyes 1993, p. 238)

This issue is developed in Redhead and Street (1989). The privileging of anachronistic modes of performance, on the grounds of their 'authenticity', derives in the UK from the 1940s Dixieland jazz revival where it had a role within the bourgeois romantic critique of industrial society. Note that 'authenticity' is here opposed by Boyes to 'modernity' whereas, in the terms introduced at the beginning, it can be opposed to 'postmodernity' (on which see also Redhead 1990 and Redhead and Street 1989). The issue is confounded by Jean-François Dutertre's insistence that 'the modernity of traditional music lies in the very heart of the [original authentic] forms and lessons that it offers us' (Dutertre 1996, p. 149): the type of relationship between the authentic and the modern cannot simply be assumed.

   For Richard Middleton, any approach to music which aims to contextualise it as cultural expression must foreground discussion of 'authenticity', since 'honesty (truth to cultural experience) becomes the validating criterion of musical value' (Middleton 1990, p. 127). In rock discourse, this validating criterion is reinterpreted as 'unmediated expression', by which is assumed the possibility of the communication of emotional content (inherent possibly in the music itself, but certainly at least in the performance) untrammelled by the difficulties attendant on the encoding of meaning in verbal discourse (Moore 2001a, pp. 73–5; 181–4). The recent singing of Paul Weller provides a rich example of this. On 'Changingman' he employs gravelly vocals connoting a voice made raw from crying or shouting.[6] The assumption here is that his listeners have personal experience of what gives rise to such crying and shouting and that, therefore, the result conjures up an active memory of the cause.[7] His voice eschews the finesse of embellishments and melismas and carries no sense of being treated as an end in itself. These features can *convey* to his audience that they are perceiving real emotion (although US audiences tend more to hear his (inauthentic) references).[8] They are *supported* by a number of other factors. There is his instrumentation – a rock line-up which recalls the early 1970s – and a particular liking for using late 1960s model guitars, recalling the sound-world of Pete Townshend. There is the line of descent of his voice from Joe Cocker's 'blue-eyed soul' of the late 1960s.[9] There is the harmonic pattern inherited from Cream's 'White Room'. There is his practice of recording 'live' in the studio, i.e. with an absolute minimum of the overdubs, multi-tracking and other devices which 'cheat' the listening ear. This latter point also is historicised, since it recalls the practices of established studios like Stax in the mid 1960s (Bowman 1997), where such recording situations were normative and highly prized. Weller is, in effect, saying to the audience he attracts, 'this is what it's like to be me'.

   A related example can be found in the case of much of the punk movement of the 1970s. In its direct opposition to the growth of disco, it was read as an authentic expression (Laing 1985, pp. 14–17; Garofalo 1987, pp. 89–90). Here, authenticity is assured by 'reflecting back' to an earlier authentic practice. Bruce Johnson, however, points to the limited adequacy of such a procedure, and perhaps to the observation that it is found much more in music intended for established circuits: 'especially in vernacular music, so often generated in the moment of performance, kinaesthetics rather than artistic logic is often the key to why music sounds the way it does' (Johnson 1997, p. 13).

The expression I am discussing here is perceived to be authentic because it is unmediated – because the distance between its (mental) origin and its (physical) manifestation is wilfully compressed to nil by those with a motive for so perceiving it. This is thus one basic form of the *authenticity as primality* argument put forward by Taylor (1997, pp. 26–8), wherein an expression is perceived to be authentic if it can be traced to an initiatory instance. This argument surfaces most clearly in academic folk discourse. For Philip Bohlman, identification of the 'authentic' requires '[the] consistent representation of the origins of a . . . style' (Bohlman 1988, p. 10), such that 'When the presence of the unauthentic [sic] exhibits imbalance with the authentic, pieces cease to be folk music, crossing the border into popular music instead' (Bohlman 1988, p. 11). Thus, for Bohlman, authenticity is identified by a *purity of practice*, whereas for Grossberg, it is more clearly identified by an *honesty to experience* – a subtle distinction perhaps, but one which remains potent. Starting from a very different point, Steven Feld develops a similar line, arguing that 'authenticity only emerges when it is counter to forces that are trying to screw it up, transform it, dominate it, mess with it . . .' (Keil and Feld 1994, p. 296), equating authenticity to a concept of genuine culture dependent on the anthropology of Edward Sapir. Bohlman's identification has found its way into rock discourse, in that proximity to origins entails unmediated contact with those origins: 'Real instruments were seen to go along with real feelings in Springsteen's rise: a certain sort of musical and artistic purity going hand in hand with a sincere message' (Redhead 1990, p. 52). The constructed nature of this interpretation is clarified by comparison with Bob Dylan – in order to achieve the same result in his early work, the 'real instruments' he had to employ had not to be amplified, *contra* Springsteen.

Walser (1993) insists that this is one of two clear types of 'authenticity' that can be observed in rock in general, wherein technological mediation (whether a reliance on signal modifiers, ever more powerful means of amplification, and even technical mastery in many spheres) is equated with artifice, reinstating as authentic/inauthentic the distinction between 'vernacular' and 'trained' or 'professional'. There is thus a relationship here with an alternative category developed by Taylor, which he terms *authenticity of positionality* (Taylor 1997, pp. 22–3). Through this, he identifies the authenticity acquired by performers who refuse to 'sell out' to commercial interests. Weller exemplifies this again, as do Taylor's examples of non-Western musicians involved in 'world music' – for such musicians, 'selling out' appears to equate to 'sounding like Western musicians', i.e. by adopting the style codes of pop/rock (which codes, in such an analysis, would be seen as inherent within the individual rather than open to appropriation: see Moore 2001b).

In its incredulity towards subjective autonomy, postmodernism may seem incompatible with authenticity. Redhead (1990) argues that constructions of 'authenticity' are no longer made by denial of commercial processes, but consciously, within them, an argument paralleled in Fox's (1992) discussion of country music. Whereas in the late 1960s, authenticity was the preserve of a politicised, selfless counter-culture, in the late 1980s there was no such counter-culture, and thus 'authenticity' became allied to constructions of 'innocence', and an unreserved embrace of the 'pop' to which it was so antithetical twenty years earlier. We may observe this in the singing of Neil Tennant. In his flat, regular delivery, especially when this is combined with his generally static posture, the refusal of emotional involvement he conveys is widely perceived as a refusal to 'cheat' the listener. For Elizabeth Leach,

the contribution to the authenticity debate made by Tennant . . . merely re-inscribes the terms of the discourse. [In conversation] Tennant simply trumps one marker of authenticity that the Pet Shop Boys don't possess (the ability to perform live), with another (the personally authentic honest address to the fans who they do not attempt to deceive). (Leach 2001, p. 147)

'So hard' exemplifies this, with its matter-of-fact tone where everything seems to be kept rigidly under control (to prevent felt emotions from escaping) in singing lyrics which purport to tell a true story.[10] The listener desiring to make such an interpretation is probably not, however, one who would listen to Paul Weller in the way discussed above. Theodore Gracyk finds the concept of rock authenticity bound up with rock's association with the project of liberalism (citing in particular U2), founded as it is on the identification of a pre-existent subjectivity (Gracyk 1996, pp. 221–3). As such, he argues against Grossberg's view that authenticity has become increasingly irrelevant in the face of postmodernism, in the process equating authenticity to self-expression (Gracyk 1996, pp. 224–5).

What unites all these understandings of authenticity is their vector, the physical direction in which they lead. They all relate to an interpretation of the perceived expression of an individual on the part of an audience. Particular acts and sonic gestures (of various kinds) made by particular artists are interpreted by an engaged audience as investing authenticity in those acts and gestures – the audience becomes engaged not with the acts and gestures themselves, but directly with the originator of those acts and gestures. This results in the first pole of my perspective: *authenticity of expression*, or what I also term 'first person authenticity', arises when an originator (composer, performer) succeeds in conveying the impression that his/her utterance is one of integrity, that it represents an attempt to communicate in an unmediated form with an audience.

The presence of this conceptualisation of authenticity is undeniable. Two problems attach themselves to it. The first is the extent to which it is itself trustworthy, or whether it is mere illusion, which I have raised in the introduction and will return to. The second is that, in tending to conceive authenticity as inherent rather than attributed, this conceptualisation tends to mask two others, equally valid, to which I now turn.

Third person authenticity

The very naivety of such a *perception*, of taking on trust the unmediated utterance, is embedded in Fornäs' generalisation of Grossberg's typology of authenticity. Grossberg argues for three genre-specific authenticities, that of rock (founded in the romanticised ideology of the community, cf. Paul Weller above), of black genres (founded on the rhythmicised and sexual body), and that of self-conscious postmodernity (showing honesty in the acceptance of cynical self-knowledge, cf. the Pet Shop Boys above). Fornäs generalises these to produce *social authenticity, subjective authenticity* and *meta-authenticity*, each of which has both conservative and progressive variants (Fornäs 1995, pp. 276–7). Thus, 'social authenticity' is ensured in an act of judgement legitimate within a particular community, while 'subjective authenticity' is validated by the individual. 'Cultural or meta-authenticity' is a more recent development, validating 'synthetic' texts through the evidenced meta-reflexivity of their authors (as discussed above by Redhead). The third of these is particularly marked as an authentication of the author, although this aspect is also strong in Fornäs' first two categories. Moreover, Fornäs argues that authenticity is not directly opposed to artificiality since authenticity is, after all, necessarily a construction we place upon what we perceive (Fornäs 1995, p. 275). Such a construction is perhaps more obvious in the blues rock movement than in those cases considered above.

The blues rock movement of the 1960s was partly founded on the employment of a style ('the blues') which, in its origins in the racist and economically deprived Mississippi delta, was felt to embody such a harsh reality that the reality became embodied in the style itself. Thus, it became a matter of ideology that to employ the 'blues' within a thoroughly different social context, by venerating its originators thereby enabled the appropriation of their very authenticity. This is exemplified by the early work of Eric Clapton. Clapton's employment of the blues began with the work of urban blues artists like B.B. King but, as he discovered that style's ancestry, he worked back to the country blues particularly of Robert Johnson, in whom Clapton found 'the most powerful cry that I think you can find in the human voice . . . it seemed to echo something that I had always felt' (Clapton 1990). In performing Johnson's 'Crossroads' with Cream,[11] not only do we interpret Clapton conveying to his audience that 'this is what it's like to be me' but, doubly vicariously, that 'this is what it was like to be Johnson', with all the pain that implies: '[The blues] comes from an emotional poverty . . . I didn't feel I had any identity, and the first time I heard blues music it was like a crying of the soul to me. I immediately identified with it' (Clapton quoted in Coleman 1994, p. 31). For Clapton, for Peter Green, and to a lesser extent for guitarists like Jeff Beck and Jimmy Page, the search for the musical soul of blues singers like Robert Johnson was propelled by a desire to appropriate the 'unmediated expression' which was thought to be the preserve of the country blues style, entailing an unquestioned assumption that African Americans in the southern USA were somehow more 'natural' beings than white, college-educated Londoners. The observation that such an appropriation is commonly considered normative is dramatically conveyed by its treatment in Brunning (1986); a hagiographic narrative is constructed whereby a host of musicians discover this blessed 'other' music, and by rendering such a move unproblematic, it becomes 'natural' (in the Adornian sense).

The importance of retaining a point of origin is also exemplified in Paul Gilroy's conceptualisation of the equation for black listeners of local ('original') expressions of culture with authenticity, and more global manifestations with cultural dilution (or lack of aesthetic value: Gilroy 1993, p. 96). This is therefore a separate manifestation of the *authenticity as primality* argument, since it is the tracing back to an original which validates the contemporary. Middleton's conception of the construction of authenticity is useful here. He argues that this conceptualisation builds a refuge of meaning within the bourgeois romantic critique of industrial society. And yet, within this manoeuvre, there do hide real processes - he focuses on what he calls 'continuity' and 'active use' (which combine as 'tradition') and

216   *Allan Moore*

which suggest that 'from the debris of "authenticity"' (Middleton 1990, p. 139), we may rescue the notion of 'appropriation'. And, as he argues following Janós Maróthy, such a move is universally available; it is not tied to any particular stylistic formulations.

By appropriating, by exhibiting trust in and making available to a broader audience, the patterns of performance exemplified by black blues artists, Clapton (whose own authority was underlined by the familiar 'Clapton is God' graffito) authenticates them. Two points are worth making here. First, it is no great distance from this 'appropriation' to the actual invention of a tradition in order to authenticate contemporary practices.[12] David Harvey notes that this is no new endeavour:

the ideological labour of inventing tradition became of great significance in the late nineteenth century precisely because this was an era when transformations in spatial and temporal practices implied a loss of identity with place and repeated radical breaks with any sense of historical continuity. (Harvey 1990, p. 272)

Second, there is an important link to first person authenticity. According to Grossberg, the authentic rock singer requires '[the] ability to articulate private but common desires, feelings and experiences into a shared public language. It demands that the performer have a real relation to his or her audience' (Grossberg 1992, p. 207) in terms of shared, or at least analogous, experiences. The music needs both to transcend that experience in some way (in order to be presented as an idealised, i.e. artistic statement, rather than through everyday conversation), but also to authenticate it by expressing it in a way particular to that singer. Grossberg argues for the construction of 'community' rather than 'tradition', but the locus is the same as that posited by Harvey: disruption of continuity through geographical and social mobility requires the fabrication of a secure ground, a conceptual (if not historical) point of origin. Taylor points to a similar problem encountered by non-Western musicians as they attempt to attract Western audiences – their music must be simultaneously timeless and new (Taylor 1997, p. 28). This argument is striking in its resemblance to Ralph Vaughan Williams' construction of musical nationalism. Vaughan Williams was heavily implicated in Parry's praise (above), and his views are worth discussing in a little detail.[13]

In his writings collected under the title *National music*, Vaughan Williams suggests that the musical life of a nation is like a pyramid:

At the apex are the great and famous; below, in rank after rank, stand the general practitioners of our art ... the musical salt of the earth ... Lastly we come to the great army of humble music makers, who, as Hubert Parry says, 'make what they like and like what they make'. (Vaughan Williams 1987, p. 239)

The common people are rescued from their obsession with the burgeoning commercial music market through the activity of composers who are to return to a child-like state of musical immediacy (the folk-singer's 'state of grace') before combining this with their technique. Vaughan Williams' theories begin from two assumptions, both denying fundamental precepts of bourgeois aesthetics. Firstly, he assumes that the artist does not create from a position of total autonomy – the process of invention necessitates an audience, and is built on the work of predecessors: 'Supreme art is not a solitary phenomenon, its great achievements are the crest of a wave; it is the crest which we delight to look on, but it is the driving force of the wave below that makes it possible' (Vaughan Williams 1987, p. 50). Secondly, he denies the universality of a musical 'language': 'It is not even true that music has an universal vocabulary, but even if it were so it is the use of the vocabulary that counts' (Vaughan Williams 1987, p. 1). What is important to him is the 'rootedness' of a music in shared practices with an observable history:

The art of music above all the other arts is the expression of the soul of the nation, and by a nation I mean . . . any community of people who are spiritually bound together by language, environment, history and common ideals, and above all, a continuity with the past. (Vaughan Williams 1987, p. 68)

Thus his aim of uniting the social function of music (folk-song, founded in the above values) with the transcendent claims of a functionless art music, in a music both timeless and new. This duality seems to me key to the identification of what I shall term a third person authenticity. Gilroy, however, is heavily critical of this sort of view:

the syncretic complexity of black expressive cultures alone supplies powerful reasons for resisting the idea that an untouched, pristine Africanity resides inside these forms, working a powerful magic of alterity in order to trigger repeatedly the perception of absolute identity. (Gilroy 1993, pp. 100–1)

A second example – a very different type of strategy for tapping in to 'original' practices – can be taken, again, with reference to 'folk' genres. Many singers of the second revival (of the 1950s) developed a particular habit when playing traditional ballads of interspersing one, or two, lines of lyric with an odd number of instrumental beats, as a way of maintaining a certain traditional metrical flexibility while accommodating material to accompaniment by guitar. Thus, to take a widely known example (strictly outside this line of development, but a song learnt from revivalist singer Martin Carthy), Simon & Garfunkel's recording of 'Scarborough Fair' (1966) alternates 3+4 and 3+2 beats (where the last, strong syllable of the lyric, appears on the first of the even-numbered beats, the '4' or the '2'). There seem no intrinsic reasons why such a song needs to be performed in this way – all that can be said is that the interpolations cushion the steady monotony of the regular rhythm of the lyric.[14] Its force can be recognised by its appearance in John Lennon's 'Working-Class Hero' (1970), where the metre remains rigidly 3+4. In this song, Lennon appears to have wanted to convey an intensity, an utter lack of pretension, and an integrity to the experience he relates, making it clear that it is his own experience. The device, however, suggests that he is building on the harsh reality of the traditional singer, in an analogous way to Clapton's employment of the blues.

     The current popularity of the 'tribute' band provides another, markedly different, example. There is no single ethos which underlies the activities of this mass of everyday musicians, but that of faithful reproduction in order to recover the reality of originary performances can be widely found. Thus, the Portsmouth-based Silver Beatles are lauded because they 'purvey a far more natural feel to their performance' – Cynthia Lennon is reported as claiming that they 'look alike, sound alike and even think alike' (Silver Beatles n.d.). The US Rolling Stones cover band Sticky Fingers draw attention to the trustworthiness of their approach, in declaring themselves 'not just a band playing covers', but a real 'tribute' to the Stones (Sticky Fingers n.d.). The leading Genesis tribute band, ReGenesis, for a February 2001 gig went as far as attempting to reconstitute the 'vintage' keyboard rig played by Genesis' Peter Banks c.1973 as a way of strengthening their ability to give people access to an experience (that of a particular live performance) otherwise denied them by Genesis' demise. They play their repertoire 'because Genesis don't play it any more . . . some of us like to hear 'Supper's Ready' or 'Return of the Giant Hogweed' live once in a while' (ReGenesis n.d.). Note that for ReGenesis (and for their fans) it is the song which has an identity, which is the key to the experience. The parallel with one tradition of European concert practice, whereby contemporary performers attempt to re-create for contemporary ears the aural experience of earlier perform-ances, via the re-creation of earlier instruments, is blatant.

Robert Walser (1993) insists that the most plausible identification of authen-ticity in heavy metal (an association which is perhaps infrequently made) is in terms of the Romantic vision of the artist as hero, an identification which is frequently overplayed, and thus, compromised, by the phenomenon of heavy metal as visual spectacle. This vision of the explorer returning with a more authentic form of expression, explored here and with reference to blues rock above, is also employed by Taylor (1997, pp. 28–30) as part of his category of the *authenticity of emotionality*, which relates to the spiritual origin of the music-making impulse (Taylor 1997, pp. 23–6). The acquisition of an authentic mode of expression from those whose possession it is gives rise to the second pole of my perspective: *authenticity of execution*, or what I also term 'third person authenticity'. This arises when a per-former succeeds in conveying the impression of accurately representing the ideas of another, embedded within a tradition of performance.

Second person authenticity

While the question of why particular (groups of) listeners give value to some musical experiences above others may depend on what music connotes or denotes, it also depends on how the musical experience is constructed around a basic distinction which may be summarised as mainstream/margin, centre/ periphery, or coopted/underground. The burning question is one of belonging and, while this has been theorised in terms of subcultural theory (from Hall and Jefferson 1976 through to Thornton 1995 and beyond), a more useful source here is Green's (1988) theorisation of how music's inherent meanings affirm or aggra-vate us, as we feel positively or negatively towards a particular style's delin-eations, and as we are not necessarily united by more than music. The basic distinction most relevant at this point is that which originated in the mid-1960s between a popular music centre ('pop') and periphery ('rock'), concerning as it did the nature of the commercial enterprise surrounding examples of each par-ticular style: the degree to which it could be perceived as 'authentic'. Dispassion-ately speaking, of course, this commercial/authentic polarity is illusory, since all mass-mediated music is subject to commercial imperatives, but what matters to listeners is whether such subjection appears to be accepted, resisted, or nego-tiated with, by those to whom they are listening. Robert Walser identifies this as the second of his two identifications of rock authenticity, one upheld by critics who have equated commercial mediation with ideological compromise, and who have thus decried the reliance on recording contracts with major record companies and the ensuing big distribution deals.

In Grossberg's analysis, the growth in the 1950s of new structures of techno-logical, economic, and social practices tended to deny many (most particularly working-class, adolescent males) access to the heady, future-oriented, post-war social enterprise. This rejection engendered an alienation which was nurtured by a spirit of optimistic liberalism which in turn repressed social and cultural differences, and which was articulated by the emergence of the lascivious hips, the narcissistic gaze, and the analgesic beat of rock'n'roll. Grossberg identifies this as a key moment: the 'authenticity' which its fans found in this music was defined not by its anchorage in the past, nor by the integrity of its performers, but by its ability to articulate for its listeners a place of belonging, an ability which distinguished it from other cultural forms, particularly those which promised 'mere entertainment' (in which they invested nothing more than cash), or those belonging to hegemonic groupings (in which they could not invest). Moore (1998a) follows Allan (1986) in defining this 'place of belonging' as a 'centredness', calling attention to the experience that this cultural product offered an affirmation, a cultural identity in the face of accelerating social change, in large part because it itself had no history apparent to its participants. This 'centredness' implies an active lifting of oneself from an unstable experiential ground and depositing oneself within an experience to be trusted, an experience which centres the listener. The opposition to a post-modern characterisation of 'de-centred' experience is here intentional.

We are moving toward a third distinct authenticity here, and again two examples are pertinent. Within the synthesizer-dominated rock scene of the 1980s, focus on the guitar was taken to signify commitment to traditional rock values and, for white urban bourgeois youth, the music of musicians nominally from the Celtic periphery (U2, Big Country, Simple Minds, The Alarm, Dan Ar Braz) or socially disadvantaged areas of the USA (Bruce Springsteen) created a space within which metaphorical escape to a pre-modern communitarian ideal became possible. This was achieved through a variety of features. Dominant among these were the very employment of the guitar (physically accessible to all) together with a certain stolid simplicity (pentatonic formations and open-ended harmonic sequences – see Moore 1998b). The Celtic bands also often employed a sound-box full of sonic potential (the connotation of wide-open spaces) and at times a pre-linguistic vocality (for both, see Moore 1998a). Middleton takes his analysis (above) further, when he argues that, as listeners, we have a variety of avenues open to us in our encounters with styles, stretching from 'appropriation' at one extreme, through the milder 'acceptance', 'toleration' and 'apathy', ultimately to 'rejection'. The music we declare to be 'authentic' is the music we 'appropriate'. This recognises that the process of authentication is one of transfer, from a situation in which the 'naïve' individual, secure in her subjecthood, authenticates her actions and experience simply by undergoing them, to a situation whereby others are allotted the same vividness of experience such that their actions ground the first individual's security. And this activity is open to listening publics too. In this case, it is what I have simplistically characterised as 'white urban bourgeois youth' which undertook such an appropriation, but however they are characterised, it is not a universal appropriation but a cultural construction which is involved.

A second example comes from a more unlikely source. In her discussion of dance culture, Sarah Thornton describes the process whereby enculturation naturalises technologies. She argues that authenticity inheres in a musical form[15] at the point at which that form is essential to a particular subculture (Thornton 1995, p. 29). Part of her argument traces the reorientation of reception from live performances to records, this latter medium acquiring its own authenticity:

the authentication of discs for dancing was dependent on the development of new kinds of event and environment, which recast recorded entertainment as something uniquely its own, rather than a poor substitute for a 'real' musical event. (Thornton 1995, p. 51)

This process of enculturation which develops authentication over a period of generations thus has material foundations, but it is nonetheless in these that its listeners authenticate themselves. The artificiality of the medium is also no bar for Fornäs: 'A seemingly artificial text may also be an authentic expression of true life experiences in an artificial society' (Fornäs 1995, p. 275). Finally, no scholars with children can have failed to observe the crucial impact on their self-authentication of that conventionally most inauthentic music, that of unashamedly 'manufactured' pop.[16] Within my own daughter's peer group it is (still) currently S Club 7's 'Bring It All Back' that most clearly performs this function and, perhaps importantly, it is in imitation of bodily gestures as much as in imitation of vocal mannerisms that this group seems to discover itself. So, here we have what I identify as 'second person' authenticity, or *authenticity of experience*, which occurs when a performance succeeds in conveying the impression to a listener that that listener's experience of life is being validated, that the music is 'telling it like it is' for them.

Conclusion

In practice, these three authenticities overlap, but maintaining their virtual separation makes for a more incisive analysis of any particular case. Within the British folk community, Dick Gaughan's authenticity goes entirely unchallenged. On the album *Sail on*, in the song 'No Cause for Alarm', the rock instrumentation, strong presence of a mixolydian VII, Gaughan's self-expressive electric guitar breaks and the palpable anger in his voice at the words 'They're trying to say our time is past – Hell, it hasn't even started' illustrate his widely known radical socialism in enabling a first person authentication. The album's following song, Hamish Henderson & James Robertson's 'The 51st (Highland) Division's Farewell to Sicily' employs a manner of (solo) acoustic guitar figuration which, when combined with the song's excessive length (nearly twelve minutes) and slowness, indubitably recalls the tradition of the piobaireachd, enabling a third person authentication. The next song, 'No Gods and Precious Few Heroes' combines a (third person) use of acoustic guitar and a (first person) rhythmic freedom in vocal delivery with a 'realistic' characterisation of contemporary Scotland which, for an English Celtophile audience enables a second person authentication. The strength of this procedure taken across this range of material is such that Gaughan can include on the same album a cover of Jagger & Richard's overt fantasy 'Ruby Tuesday', read (I think) through Melanie Safka's highly fey interpretation, without compromising his authenticity.

So, in acknowledging that authenticity is ascribed to, rather than inscribed in, a performance, it is beneficial to ask who, rather than what, is being authenticated by that performance. Three types of response are possible, according to whether it is the performer herself, the performer's audience, or an (absent) other who is being authenticated. Siting authenticity within the ascription carries the corollary that every music, and every example, can conceivably be found authentic by a particular group of perceivers and that it is the *success* with which a particular performance conveys its impression that counts, a success which depends in some part on the explicitly musical decisions performers make. Whether such perceivers are necessarily fooled by doing so is, perhaps, beside the point since we may learn as much from creative misunderstanding as from understanding. Although I believe it outside the scope of what I have attempted here to theorise either the rehabilitation of an 'authentic subject' or processes of the construction of subjectivity, it seems to me that the evidence arrayed above far more easily supports the latter position. Academic consideration of authenticity should thus, I believe, shift from consideration of the intention of various originators towards the activities of various perceivers, and should focus on the reasons they might have for finding, or failing to find, a particular performance authentic.

Endnotes

1. In various forms, this article has been presented at a Critical Musicology forum (University of Surrey, 2000), at a Comparative Music Praxes conference (University of Middlesex, 2000), and to various of my own students. My thanks also to my colleagues Andy Bennett and Dan Grimley for their comments and neat turns of phrase.
2. Moore 1998a. Some of the discussion of theories of authenticity on which I expand here appeared in that article.
3. Some of the circumstances under which this is the case are explored, from a musicological standpoint, in Kennett (forthcoming).
4. I write this (May 2001) in the midst of much media-related dismay at the high level of a(nti)pathy currently shown toward UK consensual politics in the run-up to a General Election.
5. Although gendered discourse is unavoidable here, and I prefer the feminine for reasons of balance, in this genre it happens also to be more accurate.
6. Gilbert and Pearson (1999, p. 134) go even further in claiming that *any* evidence of 'noise', as opposed to a 'cleaned up' production, is evidence of the authentic. They ally this to the lack of 'training' such a positioned voice has (p. 68).
7. Some substantive support for this position can be gleaned from the work of Paul Newham

and Melanie Harrold (see Jungr forthcoming). There is clearly a cross-cultural element involved here: flamenco *cante jondo* singers, for example, appear to employ the same technique to the same end. See Woodall (1992, p. 95ff.)
8. My thanks to Robynn Stilwell for pointing this out.
9. In Cocker's performance at Woodstock, the physical rigidity of the front of his neck as his head is thrown back in order to eject his apparent pain is manifest. Weller holds his body in a very similar way in singing this song, as evident in his performance broadcast live on BBC2, 23 February 1996.
10. As Craig Kaczorowski argues in *Tension* magazine, they 'are dedicated to crafting the perfect pop bauble ... [yet they] rarely lose sight of the fact that pop music today is supposed to be danceable yet desolate' (Kaczorowski 1998).
11. Headlam (1997) explores some of the musical differences between these performances.
12. The classic exposition of this is, perhaps, Trevor-Roper (1984).
13. My gratitude to Charlie Ford for once suggesting this line of interpretation.
14. My own favourite example of this feature is Ossian's 'I will set my ship in order'.
15. Rather than in instances of that form.
16. As Roe (1996, p. 94) points out, the almost total lack of research in this area is unsustainable.

References

Allan, G. 1986. *The Importances of the Past* (New York)
Bohlman, P.V. 1988. *The Study of Folk Music in the Modern World* (Bloomington)
Born, G., and Hesmondhalgh, D. (eds.) 2000. *Western Music and its Others* (Berkeley)
Bowman, R. 1997. *Soulsville U.S.A.: the Story of Stax Records* (New York)
Boyes, G. 1993. *The Imagined Village: Culture, Ideology and the English Folk Revival* (Manchester)
Brunning, B. 1986. *Blues: the British Connection* (Poole)
Clapton, E. 1990. Liner notes to Robert Johnson's complete recordings, CBS
Coleman, R. 1994. *Clapton: the Authorized Biography* (London)
Coyle, M., and Dolan, J. n.d. 'Modeling authenticity, authenticating commercial models', in *Reading Rock and Roll*, ed. K. Dettmar and W. Richey (New York), pp. 17–35
Dutertre, J.-F. 1996. 'Traditional music/topical music?', in *Music in Europe* (European Commission: European Music Office), pp. 145–9
Fornäs, J. 1995. *Cultural Theory and Late Modernity* (London)

222   *Allan Moore*

Fox, A.A. 1992. 'The jukebox of history: narratives of loss and desire in the discourse of country music', *Popular Music*, 11/1, pp. 53–72

Frith, S. 1989. 'Towards an aesthetic of popular music', in *Music and Society*, ed. R. Leppert and S. McClary (Cambridge)

Garofalo, R. 1987. 'How autonomous is relative: popular music, the social formation and cultural struggle', *Popular Music*, 6/1

Gilbert, J., and Pearson, E. 1999. *Discographies: Dance Music, Culture, and the Politics of Sound* (London)

Gilroy, P. 1993. *The Black Atlantic* (London)

Gracyk, T. 1996. *Rhythm and Noise* London)

Green, L. 1988. *Music on Deaf Ears* (Manchester)

Grossberg, L. 1992. *We Gotta Get Out of This Place* (London)

Hall, S., and Jefferson, T. 1976. *Resistance Through Rituals* (London)

Harker, D. 1985. *Fakesong* (Buckingham)

Harvey, D. 1990. *The Condition of Postmodernity* (Oxford)

Headlam, D. 1997. 'Blues transformations in the music of Cream', in *Understanding Rock: Essays in Musical Analysis*, ed. Covach and Boone (New York), pp. 59–92

Johnson, B. 1997. 'In the jumble, the genre jumble: the prison house of popular music discourse', unpublished paper delivered to Nordic popular music researchers, Magleås, Denmark, April

Jungr, B. forthcoming. 'Vocal expression in the blues and gospel', in *The Cambridge Companion to Blues and Gospel Music*, ed. A.F. Moore (Cambridge)

Kaczorowski, C. 1998. 'Post-Disco: the Pet Shop Boys', http://www.vsd.cape.com/~mesh5/tension/current/pet—shop1098.html

Keil, C., and Feld, S. 1994. *Music Grooves* (Chicago)

Kennett, C. forthcoming. 'Is anybody listening?', in *Analysing Popular Music*, ed. A.F. Moore (Cambridge)

Kenyon, N. (ed.) 1988. *Authenticity and Early Music: a Symposium* (Oxford)

Laing, D. 1985. *One Chord Wonders: Power and Meaning in Punk Rock* (Buckingham)

Leach, E.E. 2001. 'Vicars of "Wannabe": authenticity and the Spice Girls', *Popular Music*, 20/2, pp. 143–67

Middleton, R. 1990. *Studying Popular Music* (Buckingham)

Moore, A.F. 2001a. *Rock: the Primary Text* (Aldershot)
       1998a. 'U2 and the myth of authenticity in rock', *Popular Musicology*, 3, pp. 5–33
       1998b. 'In a big country: the portrayal of wide open spaces in the music of Big Country', in *Musica Significans: Proc. of the 3rd Int. Congr. on Musical Signification*, ed. R. Monelle (Harwood Academic), pp. 1–6
       2001b. 'Conventions in music-discourse: style and genre', *Music and Letters*, 82/3, pp. 432–42

Negus, K. 1992. *Producing Pop* (London)

Pickering, M. 1986. 'The dogma of authenticity in the experience of popular music', in *The Art of Listening*, ed. McGregor and White (Beckenham), pp. 201–20

Redhead, S. 1990. *The End-of-the-Century Party* (Manchester)

Redhead, S., and Street, J. 1989. 'Have I the right? Legitimacy, authenticity and community in folk's politics', *Popular Music*, 8/2

ReGenesis. n.d. www.users.globalnet.co.uk/~andyrh/index2.html

Roe, K. 1996. 'Music and identity among European youth', in *Music in Europe* (European Commission: European Music Office), pp. 85–97

Rubidge, S. 1996. 'Does authenticity matter? The case for and against authenticity in the performing arts', in *Analysing Performance*, ed. P. Campbell (Manchester), pp. 219–33

Shuker, R. 1994. *Understanding Popular Music* (London)

Shuker, R. 1998. 'Authenticity', in *Key Concepts in Popular Music* (London), pp. 20–1

Silver Beatles. n.d. www.silverbeatles.co.uk/main.htm

Sticky Fingers. n.d. www.StickyFingersBand.com/about.htm

Taylor, T. 1997. *Global Pop: World Musics, World Markets* (New York)

Thornton, S. 1995. *Club Cultures: Music, Media and Subcultural Capital* (Cambridge)

Trevor-Roper, H. 1984. 'The invention of tradition: the Highland tradition of Scotland', in *The Invention of Tradition*, ed. Hobsbawm and Ranger (Cambridge)

Vaughan Williams, R. 1987. *National Music and Other Essays* (Oxford, originally published between 1934 and 1955)

Walser, R. 1993. *Running with the Devil: Power, Gender, and Madness in Heavy Metal Music* (Hanover, NH)

Woodall, J. 1992. *In Search of the Firedance* (London)

Discography

Cream, 'White Room'. Polydor. 1969

Dick Gaughan, 'The 51st (Highland) Division's Farewell to Sicily', 'No Cause for Alarm', 'No Gods and Precious Few Heroes', 'Ruby Tuesday', *Sail on.* Greentrax. 1996

John Lennon, 'Working Class Hero', *John Lennon: Plastic Ono Band.* Apple. 1970

Melanie, 'Ruby Tuesday', *Candles in the Rain.* Buddah. 1970

Ossian, 'I Will Set My Ship In Order', *Best of Ossian.* Iona. 1994

Pet Shop Boys, 'So hard', *Discography.* Parlophone. 1991

S Club 7, 'Bring It All Back', *S Club.* Polydor. 1999

Simon & Garfunkel, 'Scarborough Fair', *Parsley, Sage, Rosemary & Thyme.* C.B.S. 1966

Paul Weller, 'Changingman', *Stanley Road.* Go! Discs. 1995

[9]

Intertextuality and Hypertextuality in Recorded Popular Music

Serge Lacasse

Presentation

In 1994 the late Lucien Poirier (to whom this essay is dedicated) held a postgraduate musicology seminar at Université Laval (Québec) entitled *La Musique au second degré*. The seminar's title referred to Gérard Genette's book *Palimpsestes: la littérature au second degré*.[1] In this study Genette develops a theory of 'hypertextuality', which studies and characterises particular relationships that occur between different works of literature. The goal of Poirier's seminar was, therefore, to explore the possibility of applying this theory to music.[2] The present essay is an attempt to apply the process, in part, to recorded popular music, which means that I will be considering the recording as the main object of my inquiry. By no means, however, is the process intended to be exhaustive; it aims simply to provide some new ways of looking at recorded popular songs, especially when one is

---

1. Gérard Genette, *Palimpsestes: la littérature au second degré*, Paris, Seuil, 1982. All quotations and references are taken from Gérard Genette, *Palimpsests: Literature in the Second Degree*, translated by Channa Newman and Claude Doubinsky, Lincoln and London, University of Nebraska Press, 1997.
2. Of course, since this was a 'traditional' musicology seminar, the works examined came mainly from the 'classical' repertoire. Following the seminar, an article has been published by Vincent Brauer, Serge Lacasse and Renée Villemaire: 'Analyse d'une oeuvre hypertextuelle: *Las Meninas, vingt et une variations transformelles sur les* Kinderszenen *de Robert Schumann*, de John Rea', *Les Cahiers de l'ARMuQ*, Vol. 17, May 1996, pp. 35–44. For other examples of intertextual relationships found in the classical repertoire, see Robert S. Hatten, 'The Place of Intertextuality in Music Studies', *American Journal of Semiotics*, Vol. 3 no. 4, 1985, pp. 69–82.

considering the relationships occurring between a number of them.[3]

Gérard Genette's *Palimpsests*

Genette's 'hypertextuality' should be regarded as a subcategory of what a large number of theorists, following Kristeva's definition,[4] have come to know as 'intertextuality'.[5] In his introduction Genette uses the term 'transtextuality' when referring to the ensemble of any type of relation, explicit or not, that may link a text with others – which is how most theorists seem to use and understand the term 'intertextuality'.[6] Actually, Genette considers intertextuality as a subcategory of transtextuality along with four others: paratextuality, metatextuality, architextuality and, of course, hypertextuality. 'Intertextuality' is defined by Genette in a more restrictive sense, and is used to identify 'a relationship of copresence between two texts or among several texts: that is to say, eidetically and typically as the actual presence of one text within another' (quoting, allusion and plagiarism being its most important, if not only, manifestations).[7] It is in reference to these definitions that I will be using the terms 'intertextuality' and 'transtextuality' in the pages that follow.

Again according to Genette's nomenclature, 'paratextuality' refers to the ensemble of relationships between a particular text and some of its accompanying features, such as the general title, chapter titles,

---

3. For intertextual analyses of some rock songs, see John R. Covach, 'The Rutles and the Use of Specific Models in Musical Satire', *Indiana Theory Review*, Vol. 11 (1990), pp. 119–44; also id., 'Stylistic Competencies, Musical Humor, and *This is Spinal Tap*', in *Concert Music, Rock, and Jazz since 1945: Essays and Analytical Studies*, ed. Elizabeth West Marvin and Richard Hermann, Rochester, N.Y., University of Rochester Press, 1995, pp. 172–228. Although Covach's analyses are quite enlightening, it seems to me that more attention should have been paid to technological musical parameters; indeed, the discussion focuses mainly on melody and harmony, making little reference to recording techniques.
4. Julia Kristeva, *Sèméiôtikè: recherches pour une sémanalyse*, Paris, Seuil, 1969.
5. For a quite comprehensive account of the evolution of the notion of intertextuality (especially in literature), see Donald Bruce, *De l'intertextualité à l'interdiscursivité: histoire d'une double émergence*, Toronto, Paratexte, 1995.
6. Judith Still and Michael Worton, 'Introduction', in *Intertextuality: Theories and Practices*, ed. Judith Still and Michael Worton, Manchester, Manchester University Press, 1990, p. 22.
7. Genette (1997), pp. 1–2.

foreword, illustrations and cover. Similarly, Genette defines 'metatextuality' as a commentarial relation which links one text with another, the most important examples being reviews and critiques. Another subcategory of transtextuality is named 'architextuality' by Genette and denotes a more abstract relationship between texts by virtue of their belonging to the same particular genre (novel, poem, essay, etc.).[8]

Finally, Genette considers the last type of transtextual relation, 'hypertextuality', which is the subject of the remainder of his book and is defined as 'any relationship uniting a text B [the 'hypertext'] to an earlier text A [the 'hypotext'], upon which it is grafted in a manner that is not that of commentary'.[9] In other words, a hypertext is a result of some kind of transformation or imitation of a hypotext, two practices which lie at the centre of Genette's theory. I will thus be considering relations between songs in terms of practices: first, practices that aim at including some elements of a previous text within the present text (intertextuality); second, practices which aim at producing a new text out of a previous one (hypertextuality).

II

In this section we will study some examples of intertextuality and hypertextuality in recorded popular music. As a matter of fact, we will be looking very briefly at intertextual practices, focusing mainly on hypertextuality, for which Genette has provided a much more comprehensive paradigm. The main reason why I still wish to discuss certain aspects of intertextual practices is that some of them are closely bound up with recording techniques – in particular, with sampling, which constitutes the foundation of a large number of today's recorded popular songs.

Intertextual Practices

As mentioned in the introduction, intertextuality is defined by Genette as 'the actual presence of a text within another'. Genette gives the examples of quotation and allusion as illustrations of inter-

8. Ibid., pp. 3–5.
9. Ibid., p. 5.

textuality.[10] We will thus be describing as 'intertext' the text in which one finds elements from a previous text. I would like, first, to look at some cases of quotation in recorded popular music.

Quotation

A quotation is characterised by the actual insertion of an excerpt from a given text within another. In literature, for example, it is possible to transcribe part of a given text and insert it directly into another. This inclusion is usually acknowledged by quotation marks (a form of indication that is obviously not possible in music). According to this definition of a quotation, it seems to me that there are two kinds of quotation when one is dealing with recorded music. I would like to term them 'allosonic' quotation and 'autosonic' quotation, respectively.[11]

Allosonic quotation can be illustrated by the following example. It is quite common in jazz that a musician performing a solo decides to 'quote' a snatch from another tune. Here, the melodic line he is quoting is of an abstract nature and could have been performed in any number of ways, by any musician and with any (melodic) instrument. In other words, what is shared between the original text and the intertext consists of an abstract structure. Although allosonic quotation is interesting from a general point of view, it is not especially typical of recording techniques and will therefore not be studied at length here.[12] But I wished to use this example to introduce the 'autosonic' and 'allosonic' pair of concepts, to which we will constantly return in the present essay.

Conversely, autosonic quotation is intimately linked with recording techniques. Its nature can be illustrated by a practice commonly used nowadays: sampling. When we import a sample taken directly from a recording into another (for example, a drum loop), what is common

10. Plagiarism as such will not be studied here, but we will later examine a practice involving copying.
11. I am of course partly and freely drawing from Nelson Goodman's terminology ('allographic' and 'autographic') as introduced in *Languages of Art: An Approach to a Theory of Symbols*, New York, Bobbs-Merrill, 1968. I would like to thank Lydia Goehr for pointing out to me that an unmodified use of Goodman's terminology would not have been appropriate in the context of this essay.
12. It is naturally possible to find allosonic quotations within recordings; what I mean is that we do not need recording techniques in order to produce allosonic quotations.

to both recordings is of a physical nature. What is shared is not so much a 'sameness of spelling' (to borrow an expression used by Goodman when characterising allographicity) as a 'sameness of sounding'. The technique of sampling is usually associated with autosonic quotation. Note, however, that digital sampling is not the only way of doing this, for one can still use analogue techniques (rere-cording, splicing, collage, etc.) – but, of course, digital technology is much easier to manipulate.

It is important to realise that, most of the time, autosonic quota-tions are altered in one way or another: one can speed them up or slow them down, loop them, modify their spectral content (through equalisation), add reverb, echo or flanging to them, etc. It is likewise rare to hear an autosonic quotation that has not been immersed, so to speak, within the overall sonic texture, mostly by juxtaposing other sounds with it (for example, drum loops are often mixed with other rhythmic programming, as in Peter Gabriel's *Digging in the Dirt*).[13] Both manipulations can make it difficult to identify the recording from which the quotation has been extracted (as is sometimes made evident in legal disputes concerning copyright infringement).[14] Most of the time, however, identification is fairly easy, since quotation is usually used in order to relate the intertext to some previous record-ing(s). For example, when listening to Puff Daddy's *Been Around the World*, we can hear very clearly a sample taken from David Bowie's *Let's Dance*.[15] The sample has been looped and slowed down, and some rhythmic programming added to it; nevertheless, it remains easily recognisable. Such practice is very common and typical of rap and other related musical styles.

Another song by Puff Daddy employs quotation in a quite different manner. Indeed, in the song *Come With Me* there is a very obvious quo-

---

13. Peter Gabriel, *Digging in the Dirt*, 'Us' Geffen GEFSD 24473. For an extensive analysis of this song, see Serge Lacasse, 'Une analyse des rapports texte-musique dans "Digging in the Dirt" de Peter Gabriel', M.A. dissertation, Québec, Uni-versité Laval, 1995.
14. D. M. Howard and others, 'Acoustic Techniques to Trace the Origins of a Musical Recording', *Journal of the Forensic Science Society*, Vol. 33 (1993), pp. 33–37.
15. Puff Daddy and The Family, *Been Around the World*, 'No Way Out', Bad Boy 78612-73012-2, 1997; David Bowie, *Let's Dance*, 'Let's Dance', EMI SO 517093, 1983.

tation of Led Zeppelin's *Kashmir*.[16] But what could be taken as samples from the original Led Zeppelin recording are actually not this: Jimmy Page (formerly Led Zeppelin's guitarist), and a number of musicians and arrangers, have reperformed the whole musical track for Puff Daddy's *Come With Me*. Interestingly enough, most musical elements stay very close to the original recording of *Kashmir*. For example, not only are the drums played in a very similar fashion, but the sound is also quite similar (although the sound quality is now much better). In fact, one feels as if Puff Daddy's song is **pretending** to have used sampled excerpts from Led Zeppelin's original recording —which I find quite interesting, and which may reveal some new trend.[17] It is thus possible to have allosonic quotations that mimic the autosonic. We are entering here the domain of pastiche and copy, which are examined in the next section; but just before, a word about allusion.

Allusion

Some other forms of intertextual practice may be found in recorded popular music. For example, the lyrics of The Beatles' *Glass Onion* contain many allusions to other songs of theirs, mostly by reference to their titles. The songs evoked in *Glass Onion* include *Strawberry Fields Forever*, *The Fool on the Hill*, *Lady Madonna*, *Fixing a Hole*, and *I am the Walrus*. I do not believe, however, that it is possible to have autosonic allusions, for the very fact of being autosonic would imply that a direct quotation was entailed (unless one were to consider a very much altered sampling as an autosonic allusion rather than a quotation). It is, of course, possible to find many other occurrences of allusion (and of intertextual practices in general) in recorded popular music, but I would like now to move on to the main topic for consideration: hypertextual practices in recorded popular music.

Hypertextual Practices

As we have seen earlier, hypertextuality is defined as the production of a new text (hypertext) from a previous one (hypotext). Genette is well aware of the fact that it would be possible, according to this def-

16. Puff Daddy, *Come With Me*, 'Come With Me', Epic/Sony 34K 78954, 1998; Led Zeppelin, *Kashmir*, 'Physical Graffiti', Swan Song CD 92442, 1975.
17. Of course, even a superficial comparison between the two songs suffices to confirm that Puff Daddy's song contains no direct sampling from Led Zeppelin's original recording.

inition, to relate, in some shape or form, any text to any other text. For this reason, he claims that we need to find some kind of 'agreement' linking the hypertext to its hypotext.[18] Such agreement could simply appear in the title, or in any other paratextual element (the liner notes of a recording, for example). It may also be less explicit (such as a short allusion somewhere), but it should be there in some guise or other in order to restrict the corpus. As we shall see from the following examples, it is usually quite easy to find some form of agreement either in the recordings themselves or in some paratextual declaration. I will therefore begin with cases that I find easier to describe and which are related to the idea of parody.

Parody

The first example to be considered is Weird Al Yancovick's *Smells Like Nirvana*, a parody of Nirvana's *Smells Like Teen Spirit*.[19] Already in the title we can find part of the agreement we are looking for: it is very clear from which hypotext the hypertext originates. Genette writes apropos of parody that it 'gravitates to short texts (and, it goes without saying, to texts that are sufficiently well known for the effect to be noticeable)'.[20] Indeed, when hearing Yancovick's parody, a listener familiar with Nirvana's original version (and there are many) will find it very easy to identify the hypotext.[21] But, most importantly, Genette characterises a parody as retaining the **stylistic** properties of the original text while diverting its **subject**. The example thus conforms exactly to this definition of parody: the overall song sounds very close to the hypotext (similar style), but with new lyrics (different subject). Even within the new lyrics some important structural properties are preserved, such as most of the rhyme patterns and the prevalence of the vowel 'o' in the chorus. Further, Yancovick's singing is quite similar to Cobain's, which can be regarded as another common stylistic feature. In this instance, the relation between the hypertext and its hypotext could be described as occurring in an

18. Genette (1997), pp. 8–10.
19. Weird Al Yancovick, *Smells Like Nirvana*, 'Off the Deep End', Scotti 72392 75256-2, 1992; Nirvana, *Smells Like Teen Spirit*, 'Nevermind', Geffen DGCD 24425, 1991.
20. Genette (1997), p. 31.
21. A very good discussion of listeners' competencies can be found in Covach (1990, *passim*), where the author analyses cases of intertextual practice that seem to correspond to Genette's *chimera* (pp. 47–48 in Genette's *Palimpsests*).

allosonic mode, because the elements subject to transformation are of an abstract nature (melodic line, musical style, singing style, etc.). In other words, there is no **direct** manipulation of the hypotext (viewed as a recording) in order to produce the hypertext (which distinguishes this example from some others that we shall encounter).

Travesty

I should like now to turn to another example, which could be considered very similar: Mike Flowers's version of Oasis's *Wonderwall*.[22] Again, this is a humorous version of an earlier song (at least, it should be perceived as such by a large number of rock music listeners; we will return to this point later). But, unlike the previous example, Flowers's version does not transform the subject (in this case, the lyrics) of Oasis's song so much as its musical style. Even if some lyrics are removed,[23] there is no mistaking that the whole point is to serve up a well-known song in a completely different style: the melody and lyrics are the same, but they now have a new orchestration and vocal style, which is very close to that cultivated by American crooners of the 1960s.[24]

This type of transformation looks very much like Genette's category of 'travesty', defined as the rewriting of some 'noble' text as a new text that retains the fundamental content but presents it in another style in order to 'debase' it.[25] Another example of this kind of transformation would be *A Fifth of Beethoven* (1976) by Walter Murphy and the Big Apple Band, a travesty of Beethoven's *Fifth Symphony* that turns the great master's theme into a disco tune.[26] We are

22. The Mike Flowers Pops, *Wonderwall*, 'A Groovy Place', London 828 743.2, 1996; Oasis, *Wonderwall*, '(What's the Story) Morning Glory?', Epic CEK 67351 928366T, 1995.
23. For example, Flowers sings only the first verse.
24. I would like to thank Mike Brocken at the Institute of Popular Music (University of Liverpool), who has brought to my attention a couple of recordings that could be considered as sources for Mike Flowers's style: Jack Jones, *Follow Me*, RCA 1703, 1968; Andy Williams, *The Face I Love*, CBS 2675, 1966.
25. Genette (1997), p. 58.
26. For some time now, lounge music has been exploiting travesty. One example would be the version by Zacharias of the Doors' *Light My Fire*, which can be found on 'Rock 'n' Roll Hits: On the Rocks Part One', Capitol 7243 8 65161 2 2, 1997. Although this is an instrumental, I believe it can still can be regarded as a travesty; there is no doubt that the contrast between this version and the original is more a matter of style than content. We will come later to the case of instrumental versions.

once again in the realm of the allosonic, for the same reasons given when discussing parody.

Such forms of travesty that aim to 'debase' the hypotext are described as 'burlesque' by Genette. But there is one interesting point about travesty (and any type of transformation or imitation that aims to provoke a given effect in the listener): its power to evoke humour depends largely on the listener's own point of view and socio-cultural background. A disco fan may find Murphy's version of Beethoven's piece interesting (or simply entertaining), while a classical music lover might find it funny or (most probably) outrageous.[27] Further, we can find other forms of travesty which aim (by inversion, as it were) to 'ennoble' a quite 'vulgar' song. There are plenty of examples of Beatles songs turned into 'classical' pieces. There is even a string quartet version of Jimi Hendrix's *Purple Haze* performed by the Kronos Quartet.[28] Here again, depending on the listener's personal standpoint, the new versions may be considered either 'nice' or 'ridiculous'. Of course, Genette pays more attention to the author's intentions than to the work's reception, for which reason I would prefer simply to use the single term 'travesty' without regard to the practice's intended function (debasement or ennoblement).[29]

Pastiche

As we mentioned earlier, hypertextuality comprises a set of practices implying transformation or imitation. So far, we have been dealing with typical (allosonic) transformations of hypotexts in order to produce new hypertexts. However, things become a little different with pastiche, defined by Genette as the imitation of a particular style applied to a brand new text. In other words, an author of a pastiche identifies and assimilates a particular set of stylistic features in order

27. Of course, the same thing could be said, up to a point, of parody. It is quite possible to find rock music listeners who will find Yancovick's treatment of *Smells Like Teen Spirit* really funny, whereas some Kurt Cobain fanatics will detest it.
28. Kronos Quartet, *Purple Haze*, 'Kronos Quartet', Nonesuch 79111, 1995. An interesting thing about this recording is that the entire mix has been treated with flanging, which somehow recalls Hendrix's electric guitar sound.
29. This 'omission' by Genette (his failure to confront the factor of reception) has been criticised by some theorists of intertextuality, notably by Donald Bruce, in *De l'intertextualité à l'interdiscursivité*. Genette has partly revised his position, or at least explored the point of view of reception, in his *L'Oeuvre de l'art: les relations esthétiques*, Vol. 2, Paris, Seuil, 1997.

to create an entirely new text displaying the stylistic configuration in question. This means, then, that the hypertext has no precise hypotext. There is a difference here from travesty, in that the hypertext is entirely new: that is, there is no content common to the hypertext and its presumed hypotext, only a stylistic similarity. It is possible, for example, to imagine a band that would record a new song in the style of (say) The Beatles with such success that some listeners who were not very familiar with The Beatles' *oeuvre* believed that they were actually listening to a new Beatles song. We might therefore consider that such a hypertext has not one but many hypotexts, consisting of the ensemble of texts sharing similar stylistic properties and thus belonging to a common generic corpus (for example, the whole of The Beatles' songs). It is from this ensemble of hypotexts that the author of a pastiche will 'extract' the stylistic features characterising his or her new song.

In the previous section we encountered an example of travesty by Mike Flowers. On the same album Flowers has written three original songs that are neither travesties nor parodies,[30] but which could be considered pastiches of 1960s-vintage crooners' pop songs.[31] Genette sums up this situation when he writes:

> The parodist or the travesty writer gets hold of a text and transforms it according to this or that formal constraint or semantic intention, or transposes it uniformly and as if mechanically into another style. The pastiche writer gets hold of a style [...] and this style dictates the text.[32]

Pastiche, then, can be considered only from an allosonic point of view, since its very nature relies on a purely abstract feature: style.

We will now move to a series of practices for which there are (presumably) no equivalents in literature. This forces us sometimes to depart from Genette's nomenclature and to try to find terms that are acceptable in a popular music context. Naturally, I do not claim to be 'inventing' anything, since most terms that I will be using already exist within the vocabulary of popular music. My main intention in this discussion is to interpret these 'new' expressions in terms of Genette's hypertextuality.

---

30. *A Groovy Place*, *Crusty Girl* and *Freebase*, in The Mike Flowers Pops, 'A Groovy Place'.
31. See note 22.
32. Genette (1997), p. 82.

Copy

When talking about practices of imitation (such as pastiche), Genette writes: 'It is impossible to imitate a text directly; it can be imitated only indirectly, by practicing its style in another text'.[33] This claim is certainly true for literature, since an exact imitation of a particular text (viewed allosonically) would result in a mere copy, which would obviously be of no aesthetic value. In popular music, however, copying might possibly assume an aesthetic value, as when a cover band playing in pubs tries to be as faithful as possible to the original recording of the song being covered,[34] or, as Richard Middleton points out, 'when bands focus their live performances on accurate reproduction of their own recording – or when audiences complain that they have not succeeded'.[35] An exact (autosonic) copy, though – as in a digital rerecording of a song appearing on an album – would be of no aesthetic interest, being the equivalent of a new edition (from standing type) of a given written text.

In the context of popular music, I will therefore define a copy as a performance that aims at being the closest possible imitation of a preexistent, usually recorded, performance.[36] The aesthetic value here resides in the ability of a particular artist to reperform as faithfully as possible what has been already performed. So it is possible to regard copying (in the sense of 'copying a performance') as a hypertextual practice in popular music, although such a practice applies more frequently to live performance, which lies beyond the scope of this essay.

Covering

The next hypertextual practice that I would like to examine is covering. In this essay 'covering' has a different meaning from 'copying'

33. Ibid., pp. 83–84.
34. For some years now, there has existed a new fashion for 'tribute' bands. Only last year (1997) in Québec, there have been, apart from the usual Beatles and Elvis imitations, tributes to Genesis, Deep Purple, Yes, Led Zeppelin, Pink Floyd and Red Hot Chili Peppers, to mention just a few.
35. See chapter 3, p. 77 (my emphasis).
36. For obvious reasons, it is much easier to imitate a performance by listening to a recording than by attending one or more live performances. See H. Stith Bennett, 'The Realities of Practices', in *On Records: Rock, Pop, and the Written Word*, ed. Simon Frith and Andrew Goodwin, New York, Pantheon Books, 1990, pp. 221–37.

and is associated with the idea of interpretation or reading.[37] Covering, then, should be conceived as a rendering of a previously recorded song that displays the usual stylistic configuration of the covering artist. In other words, a 'cover' is an (allosonic) hypertext consisting of a rendering of a hypotext that reveals no intention to be either a travesty or a copy.[38] I am well aware of the vagueness of such a definition, but let us look at some examples in order to clarify the concept.

A simple example would be Elvis Presley's cover of Arthur 'Big Boy' Crudup's *That's All Right*.[39] It is assumed that this cover was not intended to make fun of Crudup's song, nor to ennoble it (although some might argue so). This is therefore not a travesty as we understand the term here (the style is somewhat different but shows no clear intention to 'debase' or 'ennoble' the original version); and we are certainly not dealing with a parody (the subject is clearly the same) or a copy. It is simply a rendering of Crudup's song by Elvis, which means a performance displaying a set of stylistic features peculiar to Elvis Presley's 'sound'.

Many artists themselves cover some of their older songs. The 'unplugged versions' that are so popular nowadays are good examples of such 'auto-covers'.[40] Another interesting example would be the auto-cover of Led Zeppelin's *Kashmir* (again!) by Jimmy Page and Robert Plant, two former prominent members of Led Zeppelin.[41] Without going into detail about this version, it is worth noting, first,

37. For an interesting discussion of covering see Chapter 1, pp. 29–30.
38. There is naturally no clear demarcation between travesty, cover, copy and even parody. The point here is simply to try to outline a number of practices in conformity with Genette's theory. In any case, this point will be discussed again later.
39. Elvis Presley, *That's All Right* (1954), 'The Sun Sessions', RCA 6414-2-R, 1987; Arthur 'Big Boy' Crudup, *That's All Right* (1943), 'Arthur 'Big Boy' Crudup: Complete Recorded Works, Volume 2', Document DOCD-5202. Presley has recorded two other songs by Crudup: *My Baby Left Me* and *So Glad You're Mine*, both in 1956.
40. Just think of 'unplugged versions' by Nirvana and Eagles, to mention only the two most popular. Sting and Phil Collins, among others, made unplugged versions (probably before this expression had been coined) of a couple of their earlier hits during the 1981 Amnesty International Gala in London: *Roxanne* and *Message in the Bottle* by Sting, and *In the Air Tonight* by Collins. The recordings can be found on 'The Secret Policeman's Other Ball', Island XILP 9698, 1982.
41. Led Zeppelin, *Kashmir*, 'Physical Graffiti'; Jimmy Page and Robert Plant, *Kashmir*, 'No Quarter', Atlantic CD 82706, 1994.

that this hypertext results from a live recorded performance, and, second, that it includes new arrangements (such as the inclusion of a traditional Egyptian band, to which a whole section of the new version is devoted). Nevertheless, it is quite clear that we are still hearing the song *Kashmir*, albeit presented in a different manner. Thousands, probably millions, of covers exist; it would need very detailed stylistic analysis to provide us with a clear picture of how we arrived at a given hypertext from a given hypotext. Such a process would certainly lead us to formulate subcategories of covering, which might be useful for a consideration of certain social behaviours related to music.[42]

Translation
The translation of lyrics into another language is another hypertextual practice. But here again, there is a wide range of possible ways of doing it. For example, some translations imply remixes and even new arrangements, as is the case for the song *Fernando* by Abba, which has been recorded in English, Swedish and Spanish, each version displaying particular characteristics.[43] We thus find ourselves oscillating between the allosonic and the autosonic, depending on the amount and kind of change which is at issue.[44]

Instrumental Cover
It is quite common to find, in the popular music repertoire, instrumental versions of well-known songs (for example, a 'muzak' instrumental version of The Beatles' *Yesterday*, with the string section playing the melody in straight eight notes). An 'instrumental cover', as I understand the term here, is an instrumental (and allosonic) rendering of a previously recorded song where the main vocal line has

---

42. For example, what musical stylistic configuration is proper to Paul Anka's cover of *Tutti-Frutti* and Little Richard's original version respectively? And how, when listening to it, could we relate each version to the corresponding social group according to this stylistic analysis? Of course, such an examination would inevitably deal with racial issues, but I believe that an analysis of musical style would cast extra light on the whole problem.
43. For a detailed examination of the three versions and their relationships with each corresponding audience, see Philip Tagg, *Fernando the Flute*, Liverpool, Institute of Popular Music, 1991.
44. A possible way of circumventing the problem would be to consider lyrics and music separately.

been replaced by an instrumental melodic line (which has, of course, to follow the original melody in some way or another). It therefore has to be distinguished from a 'remix' of a song from which the voice track has simply been removed (we will come to remix in a moment). Again, there is no clear-cut boundary between a cover and an instrumental version, for it is possible to find covers in which sung lines have been partly (but incompletely) retained. Usually, however, it is possible to distinguish one from the other. I would now like to move to a quite recent practice which is peculiar to some styles of recorded popular music and has risen greatly in importance: the remix.

Remix

There are so many kinds of remix practice that it will not be possible here to describe them all. However, I would like to examine what appear to be the most important or usual ones. Remix practices range from simple edited versions to complex remixes entailing a large number of new performances. Once again, human practices resist becoming entirely conceptually distinct, remix being no exception.

Edited version

I call an 'edited version' a hypertext that is shorter or longer in length than the hypotext but otherwise shows no apparent change in the overall sound. In other words, an edited version sounds as if someone has cut out some part of the master tape (for shorter edited versions) or has inserted some additional material, again by cutting and pasting. An edited version can also entail some reordering of sonic information. It could, on that basis, be considered autosonic in relation to its hypotext, since its transformations deal directly with the hypotext. There are many edited versions of songs to be found in albums intended for air play. One example would be *While the Earth Sleeps* by Peter Gabriel and Deep Forest (written for the motion picture *Strange Days*).[45] It is worth noting that the expressions 'album version' and 'long version' are added in the respective cases to the

---

45. Deep Forest and Peter Gabriel, *While the Earth Sleeps (Album version)* and *While the Earth Sleeps (Long version)*, 'While the Earth Sleeps', Columbia COL 662821-2, 1995. Attentive listening will reveal that there are some tiny diffrences in the mixes of the two versions (for example, the dynamic level and stereophonic behaviour of some background sounds), but I believe that these differences should be viewed as negligible in the perspective of the overall sound.

common title *While the Earth Sleeps*, which would constitute our hypertextual agreement.[46]

Instrumental remix

An 'instrumental remix' is different from an 'instrumental cover' in that it consists of a remix of the original song from which the leading voice has simply been removed. Instrumental remixes are often used for TV shows in which the artist sings live over the instrumental remix.[47] Obviously, it may happen that an instrumental remix is edited as well; when one deals with remixes, all kinds of hybrid manifestation can occur.

Remix

Remixing is a practice directly related to the technology of multitrack recording. Strictly speaking, a 'mix' denotes a particular configuration (in time) of a number of parameters of previously recorded material.[48] A pure 'remix' would thus consist of a new configuration of the original prerecorded elements. But the term encompasses a much larger number of related practices. For example, it is possible to make drastic changes during a remix process simply by removing important parts (such as the leading voice). It is also possible to add new material (most of the time, through synchronised MIDI programming). Further, most remixes are edited in some way (a remix is usually much longer than its hypotext). It thus becomes difficult to give a comprehensive account of the large range of possibilities that we can obtain.

---

46. What is not so clear, however, when one considers edited versions, is which one is to be regarded as the hypotext. People will usually agree that the album version should be considered as the hypotext, even though this may not necessarily be the case.
47. This could be regarded as similar to karaoke, except that, most of the time, karaoke instrumental versions are entirely reconstructed through MIDI programming (which would make them instrumental, and allosonic, covers without the principal melodic line). At any rate, karaoke is becoming a very common practice in popular music, but it is not directly related to recorded popular music, since it is a kind of live performance. However, one specific element of karaoke, interaction between the listener and the song, will be discussed later, when I consider a couple of CD-ROMs.
48. Such parameters would include loudness, stereophonic position, spatial environment and timbral characteristics. For a very good book on the subject, see William Moylan, *The Art of Recording: The Creative Resources of Music Production and Audio*, New York, Van Nostrand Reinhold, 1992.

Actually, a whole paper (if not a book) should be devoted to the question. Therefore, we will look at just a couple of examples.

Some remixes (such as the instrumental remix mentioned earlier) are still quite easily related to their hypotext by listeners. But it is also possible to produce remixes that are very remote from their hypotexts – remote enough to be considered almost as separate pieces. For example, Peter Gabriel's *Digging in the Dirt* has been remixed by David Bottrill in such a way that the song is hardly recognisable, except for such elements as guitar riffs and short vocal lines (which are heavily processed).[49] Because of these few common (autosonic) elements, we can still relate the remix to its hypotext. An even more complex form of remixing of Miles Davis's and Bob Marley's music by Bill Laswell has been illuminatingly discussed by Richard Middleton.[50] Such a hypertext is very distant from its hypotext and could even be considered as a work in its own right (although someone conversant with Davis's or Marley's music would still be able to recognise the hypertextual filiation).

There are even forms of 'interactive' remix: that is, remixes that are intended to be performed by the listener. I have in mind the CD-ROMs *Xplora 1* and *Eve* by Peter Gabriel, which allow the 'listener' to remix (and edit) for himself or herself particular songs (in the case of *Xplora 1*, the song is our familiar *Digging in the Dirt*).[51] Of course, the CD-ROMs do not allow the listener a totally free hand. It is a matter of a limited number of 'premixed' tracks that the listener can manipulate to a certain extent.[52] Nevertheless, since the sounds evolve over time, control over even that small number of parameters can still lead to an infinite number of possible 'remixes'. This kind of interaction (of which Gabriel's attempt constitutes, I believe, just the timid beginning) undoubtedly places the question of artistic 'authorship' in a new perspective.

More usually, though, remixes aim to present a given song in a different style ('dance' versions for clubs offer one example). In such cases they could be considered, in part, as a form of 'autosonic

49. Peter Gabriel, *Digging in the Dirt* (instrumental), 'Digging in the Dirt', Geffen GEFDM 21816, 1992.

50. Chapter 3, especially pp. 62–71.

51. Peter Gabriel, *Xplora 1*, CD-ROM, Real World, 1994; *Eve: The Music and Art Adventure*, CD-ROM, Real World, 1996.

52. In the case of *Eve*, we are dealing more with editing than with remix, but manipulations still have to be carried out by the user.

travesty'. I say 'in part' because most remixes include some new material added in order to render the desired style (rhythmic programming, new bass line, etc.). The autosonic 'portion' of the remix would constitute the material that appears in both the hypotext and the hypertext (in a fairly similar guise, as in the case of autosonic quotation).[53] Indeed, if a remix exhibits no autosonic elements (or only very few, of minor importance) in relation to its hypotext, it becomes, by definition, a cover. I therefore regard remixing as an essentially autosonic practice, even if it rarely displays its autosonic aspect in its purest form.[54]

John Oswald

The Canadian composer John Oswald has developed some quite interesting practices that entail the transformation of recorded popular songs. I would like to end this incomplete exploration of hypertextual practices by examining some of his 'works'.

Plunderphonics

David Mandl writes the following about a piece by John Oswald:

> In 1989, Oswald released *Plunderphonic*, a CD containing manipulations of music by The Beatles, Dolly Parton, Public Enemy, Michael Jackson, and others ... Sources were scrupulously credited, with catalogue numbers etc. provided. One thousand copies were produced, with Oswald footing the bill himself and giving them away for free (and specifically stipulating that no copies should be bought or sold). In February 1990, the Canadian Recording Industry Association demanded that Oswald cease distribution and destroy the three hundred remain-

---

53. A good example of a typical remix would be War's *Low Rider* (Remix), remixed by Arthur Baker in 1987, the hypotext being *Low Rider* (1975). Both versions appear on War, 'The Best of War, and More', Priority CDL9467, 1991. As one can hear, the original voice is still present in Baker's remix, but has been edited so it appears in different places (in relation to the original version). Moreover, a lot of rhythmic programming has replaced the original rhythmic section. Many other alterations makes the remix both different and interesting.

54. In other words, there have to be some significant autosonic elements in the hypertext for it to be considered a remix. An example of a hypertext that is presented as a remix, but which I regard as an auto-cover, is Peter Gabriel, *Blood of Eden* (Special mix for Wim Wenders's 'Until the End of the World'), Real World PGSCD9, 1993. Indeed, even the lead vocal track is entirely new.

ing copies. Not wanting to fight a potentially costly lawsuit, Oswald complied.[55]

The reason for this strong reaction from the Canadian Recording Industry Association was that Oswald had used commercially released recordings as his basic material. On his *Plunderphonic* each track presents a well-known recorded piece with an entirely new sonic configuration. Such a practice (which is autosonic, by the way) could be viewed as a 'mega-editing' process; but I would like to draw a distinction between plunderphonics and edited versions, because the former clearly aim to denature the hypotext. Moreover, the amount of manipulation is much greater than in the case of a simple edited version. Because of its singularity, I would like to coin the expression 'plunderphonics' to denote this practice, which, incidentally, is not new. Oswald himself cites Jim Tenney's *Collage 1* (1961) as an early example of such a practice applied to popular music, in which, as Oswald explains:

> Elvis Presley's hit record 'Blue Suede Shoes' (itself borrowed from Carl Perkins) is transformed by means of multi-speed tape recorders and razor blade. In the same way that Pierre Schaeffer found musical potential in his *objet sonore*, which could be (for instance) a footstep, Tenney took an everyday music and allowed us to hear it differently. At the same time, all that was inherently Elvis radically influenced our perception of Jim's piece.[56]

From this last sentence, one can start reflecting on the impact of hypertextuality on listeners. To what extent does the knowledge of hypotexts affect our listening of hypertexts? Or, to pose the question in a better form suggested by Oswald: to what extent does our 'reading' of a given hypertext influence our perception of the corresponding revisited hypotext? I believe that such questions, which can obviously be applied to intertextuality as well, should be investigated

---

55. Note by David Mandl in John Oswald, 'Plunderphonics, or Audio Piracy as a Compositional Prerogative', Internet document, http://www.halcyon.com/robinja/mythos/Plunderphonics.

56. John Oswald, 'Plunderphonics, or Audio Piracy as a Compositional Prerogative' (see n. 55). Looking at practices commented on earlier, one can see that Oswald's practice differs from Laswell's: Oswald's basic material is not a master tape that he remixes but the final mixes themselves, which he directly manipulates. He is therefore not remixing but patching.

in some depth. We need a better understanding of the 'social' interaction of listeners with music.

Cento

In a more recent work Oswald has even merged together very short samples from about 5,000 recordings of popular songs.[57] Is this intertextuality (quotations) or hypertextuality? Since the whole thing is made up of excerpts from other recordings, I would argue that it consists of a hypertext that has an unusually large number of hypotexts. Indeed, Genette identifies a fairly similar practice in literature which he calls *cento* and defines as a blending technique 'which consists in taking from here and there a line of poetry in order to constitute a whole poem that should be as coherent as possible'.[58] To draw out lines 'here and there' sounds similar to drawing out quotations 'here and there'; since, in the case of Oswald's piece, the (very) short quotations are autosonic, I would coin the expression 'autosonic *cento*' for this final hypertextual practice.[59]

III

As I have said throughout this essay, the list of intertextual and hypertextual practices in recorded popular music could be lengthened considerably. I have tried here to identify some of them with reference to Genette's terminology. In this section, I would like to propose a preliminary categorisation of transtextual practices. The main criterion I have chosen for this suggested categorisation is the allosonic/ autosonic dichotomy. But before this preliminary categorisation is presented, we need to return to a couple of concepts encountered earlier in this essay.

Preliminary Considerations

First, I would like to discuss travesty again. I have a problem with the

57. John Oswald, *Plexure*, Japan, Avant AVAN 016, 1993.
58. Genette (1997), p. 46.
59. The corresponding allosonic practice would be the medley, I suppose. However, it might be difficult to reproduce allosonically what Oswald is doing autosonically with recording techniques, since the longest of the samples he uses for *Plexure* lasts about two seconds (most of the other samples having durations that should be measured in milliseconds).

idea of considering travesty as a 'transformational practice' as such. Indeed, travesty is more of an effect following some transformation than an actual transformational process. I would therefore like to attempt to identify its underlying procedure. A first step would be to consider travesty as a subcategory of covering (an author of a travesty produces a new rendering of the hypotext which is, presumably, humorous). I would therefore propose as a term for their common underlying procedure 'transtylisation'. This would denote the process of altering specifically the stylistic features of a given song in order to obtain a new version of it.[60] Such a version could subsequently be examined in relation to its intended effect. A travesty would then result from a transtylisation procedure that aimed to denature a given piece in some way. Conversely, a cover would presumably have no such intention, though resulting equally from a process of transtylisation (the new stylistic configuration being the covering artist's own).[61]

According to the preceding reasoning, a copy would result from a minimal transtylisation. Indeed, the cover band strives for a performance that exhibits, in as exact a form as possible, the stylistic configuration of the original recording (same sound, same instrumental playing, same voice – and often same looks!). In other words, the cover band aims at a *degré zéro* of transtylisation. I would therefore regard all the following practices as forms of allosonic transtylisation: copy, cover (including instrumental cover) and travesty.

I would prefer to classify allosonic parody as a category on its own because of its possible autosonic counterpart. Indeed, parody has been regarded as a practice characterised by the alteration of the subject of a song without changing its style. Plunderphonics, then, seems to be one possible example of autosonic parody: the style is somewhat the same, since we retain the sonic structure; however, the content is altered through a number of manipulations which, in my opinion, modify the song's 'subject'. In any case, plunderphonics appears to be more closely related to parody than to travesty. A lot has to do with the sonic content: plunderphonics still sounds like the hypotext but

---

60. Genette uses the term 'transtylisation' to denote another practice peculiar to literature, and which is not so far removed from what I am proposing here; see Genette (1997), pp. 226–28.

61. As we have seen earlier, transtylisation may present some minor changes in content (formal structure, lyrics, chord progression, etc.); but most of the fundamental elements are usually still present; if this were not the case, the hypotext would obviously not be recognisable.

displays a different linear content. In other words, travesty (along with any transtylisation practice) transforms its hypotext paradigmatically, while parody (allosonic **and** autosonic) acts syntagmatically on its hypotext.

This paradigmatic/syntagmatic dichotomy can help us to classify some other practices. Translation, for example, could be considered as related to transtylisation, since it acts paradigmatically on its hypotext (we still say the same thing but use a different system). As one can see, most of these categories (and the following ones) are not mutually exclusive. For example, it is quite easy to imagine a song that would be both a translation and a parody of a given hypotext.[62] For their part, both *cento* and medley, which are respectively autosonic and allosonic, are practices that join their hypotexts syntagmatically.

Finally, pastiche is an interesting case in that it is the ultimate paradigmatic and allosonic practice: paradigmatic because the hypertext is constructed from scratch according to a given stylistic configuration; and, of course, entirely allosonic, because the hypertext is not produced by any autosonic transformation of a given hypotext (in fact, there is no precise hypotext but merely some abstract common features belonging to a group of songs).

Summary Table of Transtextual Practices in Recorded Popular Music

I would now like to present a summary table of transtextual practices employed in the recording of popular music. As I have argued in the preceding section, the main criterion for categorisation is the allosonic/autosonic dichotomy. The table displays, however, an additional column based on a paradigmatic/syntagmatic dichotomy (the

---

62. I have two examples in mind. The first is taken from the music heard in Québec during the 1960s, when there was a fashion called *yé-yé* that consisted mostly of translated covers of hits originally sung in English. But most of the translations were so terrible that many of them were (and still are) regarded as parodies. My second example, which concerns cinema, occurred during an Academy Awards presentation that I was watching on TV. At a certain point during the show, some excerpts from a number of originally English-language movies were projected in different languages (for example, we could see and hear Humphrey Bogart saying something like 'Je t'aime, ma chérie!'). I was quite surprised when, after a short while, the audience started laughing very loudly. As a French-speaking person, I did not realise until then that even an entirely faithful translation could, in the right circumstances, become hilariously funny.

syntagmatic column displaying practices dealing mostly with subject or content, and the paradigmatic column showing practices involving transformation or imitation of a style or system). Further, I have tried to arrange the elements in the table according to an increasing order of abstraction. First, along the autosonic/allosonic axis; second, along the syntagmatic/paradigmatic axis. I have also tried to order elements contained within the cells according to the same principle wherever possible. Naturally, the table is incomplete, and I hope that others will try to add practices and – why not? – extra lines and columns.

Table 1: Summary Table of Transtextual Practices in Recorded Popular Music

	Syntagmatic (Subject/Content)	*Paradigmatic (Style/System)*
Autosonic	Autosonic Quotation Autosonic Parody *Plunderphonics* Cento Instrumental Remix	Remix
Allosonic	Allosonic Quotation Allusion Allosonic Parody	Transtylisation *Copy* *Cover* *Travesty* Translation Pastiche

As one can see, remix stands alone in its cell, which does not wholly reflect reality, since remix ought to stand somewhere in between 'autosonic' and 'allosonic', and between 'paradigmatic' and 'syntagmatic'. On a general level, though, remix is paradigmatic in that, most of the time, it aims at presenting a song in a different style for a number of purposes (such as dancing); it is autosonic to the extent that most of the time we will hear autosonic material from the hypotext. However, as we have seen, there are a very large number of remixing possibilities. Accordingly, in a more complex analysis remix would be broken down into a large number of subcategories distributed throughout the table.

Similarly, allosonic parody appears as the only hypertextual practice within its cell (allosonic quotation and allusion being intertextual practices); it is possible, however, to think of a couple of other hypertextual practices that I have not discussed and which could fit in there. For example: relyricisation, which would consist of writing new lyrics to an existing song. This looks very much like translation but is significantly different because translation acts paradigmatically on its hypotext (same subject using a different system), whereas a relyricisation would transform its hypotext syntagmatically (different subject/content). A number of additional practices could appear there (such as remusicalisation), but we will end our discussion here for the moment.

IV

In this essay I have been exploring the possibility of applying Gérard Genette's theory of hypertextuality to recorded popular music. To try to apply literary theory to music is always a difficult task (ask semioticians!), but I believe it can be very fruitful. Hypertextuality (and transtextuality as a whole) can offer us a new perspective when looking at, and listening to, music: different pieces of music are linked in a number of ways; they thus share certain features. Among other things, a knowledge of this network of interaction enables us to 'understand' a given piece better.

But as well as being explored in much greater depth, transtextual practices should also be studied from the listener's point of view. It should then become evident that the listening process is a very complex and refined social practice. Of course, each listener has his or her own, unique transtextual network; but it should be possible also to look at an entire group's transtextual network, which would obviously be more intricate but might contain a number of identifiable common paths and milestones. On a more general level, it would be useful to extend the whole process to the whole of musical styles and practices, including non-Western ones.

During Lucien Poirier's seminar, in which we mostly dealt with classical music, much time was spent discussing important issues that arose automatically when one examined the relations existing between different pieces of music: the status of notation vis-à-vis the sonic nature of music; the performed version of a work in relation to its (presumably) ideal condition; and many other questions leading invariably to the problem of the ontological status of music. It would be interesting to observe how some conceptions of the 'Work of Art' might relate to the above table of hypertextual practice. For instance, if we consider the allosonic/autosonic division attempted here, we can see that the autosonic practices deal, by definition, with concrete manifestations of music (that is, actual sound events), whereas allosonic practices relate to a more abstract conception of music. This sends us back to a conceptualistic versus nominalistic debate around the question of the ontological status of the work of art. I am not sure who is right in the dispute between nominalists and conceptualists (although I find the conceptualistic view, paradoxically, more 'practical'), but transtextual practices show that it is possible to act both on the abstract elements of music (melody, lyrics, form, style, etc.) and on its concrete aspects (sound, performance, etc.). This calls, in turn, for a dual conception of the recorded popular song: (a) the song viewed abstractly in some 'ideal' form, and (b) its recorded incarnation viewed as a concrete manifestation of the same song.[63]

The musical work: reality or invention? I do not think it is possible to answer the question directly. What I believe, though, is that the very fact that we are able to trace back transtextual links means that we are able to link some 'things' together. But, in any circumstances, the decision to name these things 'works', 'pieces', 'songs', 'manifestations' or 'performances' becomes relevant only if it forms part of a more important project: to describe and understand the intricate interactions of music with human beings, along with other human activities. Transtextuality might provide us with a (quite) new interesting tool for doing so, since it already contains within itself the very idea of interactivity.

63. See Gérard Genette, *L'Oeuvre de l'art: immanence et transcendance*, Vol. 1, Paris, Seuil, 1994. This volume is available in English as Gérard Genette, *The Work of Art: Immanence and Transcendence*, trans. Gary M. Goshgarian, Ithaca and London, Cornell University Press, 1997.

[10]

From refrain to rave: the decline of figure and the rise of ground[1]

Philip Tagg

What, you may well ask, does a polemical piece about rave music have do to with Wilfrid Mellers? A lot, because not only is Mellers one of the first scholarly writers to take pop music seriously while also clearly enjoying it; he is also one of the few scholars to write about pop as though it had something to do with music and as though the music – not just its lyrics or social functions – were instrumental in vehiculating ideas, ideologies, attitudes and patterns of behaviour in a way no other symbolic system can. In fact, without Mellers, I doubt very much whether I would have ever dared write either this or any other piece in which I try, with varyingly limited degrees of success, to relate the structures of music to the society and culture in which and for which that music is produced and used. I underline this aspect of Mellers' work because I am certain I would have abandoned my studies of music in the early 1960s at Cambridge if I had not stumbled upon the Mellers parts of *Man and his Music* (Mellers & Harman, 1962), an extensive history of European art music which had the audacity to suggest that classical music actually meant something outside itself. In that book, Mellers managed to make links not only between music as sound and the personality of that music's composer, but also between the music, the composer and the world of ideas and society in which classical composers and their music were active. My Cambridge teachers poured haughty scorn on *Man and his Music* and on Mellers but I had found an intellectual ally in musicology, knowing full well, from my experience then as church organist, rock musician and pub pianist (even at the age of twenty), and if I played *a* and not *b* the old Methodist ladies were more likely to cry and that if I played *y* and not *z* the dancers would be far more likely to boogie on down. The choice was between, on the one hand, Palestrina crosswords plus Schenker and the aesthetics of musical absolutism and, on the other, making some sense out of the music. Mellers clearly represented the latter for me. Therefore, when trying to make sense out of the 'Kojak' theme, Abba's 'Fernando', the representation of 'Nature', 'Time Sense' or 'Death' in music, etc. I have written willy-nilly under the influence of Mellers. Even this piece owes a lot to Wilfrid Mellers because I hope to show how studying the structural characteristics of a certain type of music can tell us about the culture of which that music is such an important part.

More specifically, I want to suggest that rave music – especially techno – differs so basically from rock and roll as regards its musical structuration that old

210   *Middle Eight*

models for explaining how popular music interacts with society may need radical revision. This presentation is polemical rather than authoritative or scholarly: it simplifies and polarises issues that will definitely require further discussion and investigation. The article falls into two interlinked parts: (1) a critique of the 'rockologist' rationale of individuality and (2) a tentative enumeration of rave music's main structural traits. In what follows, I just want to raise questions that I think need to be asked and, eventually, answered. In fact, since this paper follows very few of the precepts I lay down for students, I might as well cast the scholarly mask entirely and start off on a personal note.

In one of our expensive phone calls across the North Sea, my daughter, aged eighteen, told me recently that well-meaning parents in Gothenburg, where she still lives, were pressuring local police to put an end to their parties. The musical fare of those parties consists to a large extent of sounds like these:[2]

Stereo MC's: 'Everything [Sabres on Main Street Mix]'[3]
Usura: 'Open Your Mind'[4]
Frequency-X: 'Hearing Things'[5]
Snap: 'Exterminate! [Endzeit 7"]'[6]
B.M.O: 'Mastermind'[4]
Capella: 'U Got 2 Know'[3]

I shall return to this music later because I think it is highly indicative of recent and important developments in our society and its music. I shall also try and give a few ideas as to how socialisation strategies might be read from the structures of the sort of music we have just heard. Before that, though, let me go on with my story.

The sort of parties my daughter was talking about are those organised semi-privately by individuals like herself and her peers in downtown premises such as vacant clubs, cellars or abandoned cinemas which they rent quite cheaply. They take a small fee at the door and make a modest profit selling beer and soft drinks at about half the price you have to pay in commercial pubs and restaurants. They often switch venues and in the summer they run such parties out in ample stretches of the Swedish countryside. In neither summer nor winter do they disturb the general peace because these are not house parties in the strict sense of the word: they are unofficial 'raves' – as such occasions are known in Liverpool or Manchester – held way clear of any residential buildings.

So, what do the Gothenburg elders really object to? Well, their panic is focused on the use of 'ecstasy' (MDMA), a non-hallucinogenic, amphetamine-based drug which enhances perception of colour and sound, increases body temperature and creates a relatively long-lasting feeling of accelerated euphoria. Regular use of the drug can cause serious psychosis, depression, lethargy and paranoia. MDMA-related death at rave clubs is connected with dehydration, insufficient ventilation, overcrowding and excessive body temperature.[7] There are, in other words, grounds for real concern. However, although 'ecstasy' can be a killer, it is unlikely that parents object to raves solely on the grounds that their own sons and daughters will all becomes junkies just because they may come into contact with those who do take ecstasy: that would be tantamount to suggesting that knowing someone who drinks whisky at the weekend means you will end up an alcoholic or that anyone who inhaled the smoke from someone else's joint in the 1970s ought to be dead by now from a heroin overdose.[8] It is probably fear of another 'high' that haunts those who would put an end to dance raves, the fear that their sons and daughters (and the society we all populate) are out of their control and that the young people, by organising and participating in these raves, have in fact started to take control over their own lack of control of society. This may sound cryptic, so let me explain.

Reaganisation, Thatcherisation, or whatever other label you attach to the brazen capitalism we have experienced during the last two decades, promotes greed as a virtue and propagates perverted notions of a non-cooperative individualism whose buzzwords are 'achievement', 'performance' and 'competition'. Our generation has been encouraged, often against our own will and collective self-interest, to elbow each other out of jobs and positions, to live up to outmoded ideals of family existence, to amass consumer commodities, to run at least one car, to be up to date, etc., etc. This sort of socialisation strategy is, of course, inherent in the totally illogical ideology of today's political economy and has resulted in more than one type of bankruptcy. For not only do thousands of businesses go bust every week, not only do professionals like computer programmers find themselves on the dole with a crippling mortgage and plummeting property prices, not only are the infrastructures of health, social welfare and public transport dismantled in front of our very eyes, we are *also* faced with an intellectual and spiritual bankruptcy in studies of contemporary culture. In the field of popular music studies I am referring to the corporealist precepts of rockology, to such statements as:

Music excites the body to automatic movement, an exhilaration that defeats boredom and inspires insight. . . . Music gives the body control over itself, granting personal freedom and revealing sexual potential. When Madonna says 'You can dance', she *truly* empowers her fans. (Lull 1992, p. 29–30)[9]

Today, in the post-gymnastic disco, post-AIDS era, what with the arrival of jogging, macrobiotic food, aerobics, work-outs and Californian-style body cult, we have witnessed the obvious promotion of the corporeal from youth subcultural division four to the premier league of capitalist culture. Young US-Americans are not recruited into the marines by Sousa marches but by Van Halen's melodically heavy-metal 'Iron Wings' and to the air force by Tom Cruise's crew-cut, bomber jacket and Berlin's melodious 'Top Gun' anthem. Vauxhalls are sold to the tune of 'Layla', Fords to ex-Queen guitarist Brian May's 'Driven By You', with all its mega-melodic electric guitar overdubs in parallel thirds.[10] Similarly, Bodyform Plus – one of those items of female hygiene consistently exposed on television as though it were blotting paper – sells neither to the tune of some pleasantly fresh acoustic guitar, nor flute, nor romantic strings, nor women's choir, but to a quasi-orgasmic, melodic line of ecstatic gospel rock that makes Nile Rodgers' pastiche of the genre in Eddy Murphy's *Coming to America* sound quite bland.[11]

Despite the rise of the rock-corporeal to a hegemonic status during the 1980s, it was, until very recently, still possible for respected scholars of rock to write as follows:

To find out how rock functions, it is necessary to explore effects that are not necessarily signifying, that do not necessarily involve the transmission, production, structuration, or even deconstruction of meaning. Rock and roll is corporeal and 'invasive'. For example, without the mediation of meaning, the sheer volume and repetitive rhythms of rock and roll produce a real material pleasure for its fans (at many live concerts, the vibration actually might be compared to the use of a vibrator, often focused on the genital organs) and restructure familial relations (by producing immediate outrage and rejection from its non-fans, e.g., parents). (Grossberg 1990, p. 113)[12]

212   *Middle Eight*

Since 1990 Grossberg has modified this view considerably, suggesting that our own generation's monopolisation of the aesthetics of youth culture, not least through the romanticism of rockology, may well have contributed to the reactionary ideology of the Thatcher and Reagan years.[13] My critique is therefore directed at the ideas just cited, not at the present position of their authors. Nevertheless, the last quotation is quite symptomatic of much sociological writing on rock in its mystification of musical signification and in its avoidance of the relationship between music as structure and experience. Apart from the 'wink-wink-nudge-nudge' fashion in which it assumes we, readers as well as listeners, all have intimate experience of vibrators, the statement also makes musicological nonsense, as Garry Tamlyn points out.

It implies that the 'vibrator' effect should logically arise when walking next to the bass drum and cymbals in a marching band or when standing at the assembly line in a packaging factory, or when listening to the final scene of Berlioz' *The Damnation of Faust*, because all those soundscapes feature generally high levels of volume and loud, regularly articulated beats in the form of strong bass thuds, sharp crashes etc.[14]

Now, rockologists may profess to some knowledge of factories but they would be unlikely to own up to any carnal knowledge of marches, let alone of Berlioz' music, so how rock's rhythms and sounds can be determined as inherently more sexual and corporeal than those of other structurally comparable musics or soundscapes remains a mystery to me. More seriously though, the quotation from Grossberg actually posits that there is such a thing as 'sheer sound' – some sort of bio-acoustic universal?[15] – that 'does not necessarily involve the transmission, production, structuration, or even deconstruction of meaning'. I take this to mean that rock rhythms and sounds need not be regarded as part of a culturally specific symbolic system and that they vehiculate neither primary nor secondary meanings of any cultural or political value. If this is so, the passage just quoted is an insult to every rock or pop musician and to all the time and energy they spend rehearsing, doing sound checks, studio retakes and different mixes to obtain *the* sound that says *a* and not *b*. It is also an insult to my daughter and her friends and to the time and energy they spend selecting tracks meticulously for their raves. Asked which records they would put on, she told me:

No, Dad, we wouldn't play 'There's No Limit', even if it's easy to dance to, because it's cheap and commercial. Real rave-goers aren't just fourteen-year-olds at a disco. They want to feel music has some point to it as well.[16]

In short, vast quantities of the cultural-theoretical verbiage I am expected to take seriously about rock music's 'rough', 'raw', 'anarchic', 'oppositional', 'body-emancipating' qualities may have had some value in the late 1960s or early 1970s but, please, it is now 1994.[17] Since 'Jumping Jack Flash' we have had to suffer two decades of cynical capitalism and serious unemployment, all to the marketing tune of yuppies jogging in designer track suits, of aerobic women sprattling about in pastel-shaded leg-warmers, of misunderstood steroid-inflated men on dubious vendettas and of AIDS-scares. Meanwhile, Madonna exposed her body umpteen times, the media went berserk about Michael Jackson's vitiligo[18] and the unemployment rate went up again. We have also seen the aimless Indiana Jones, the gaudy sado-masochistic acrobats of all-star wrestling, anorexic fashion models, Aryan male bodies with Hitler haircuts in synth pop videos or Calvin Klein adverts and we have been exposed to all those martial-arts-practising career goddesses who wash-and-go with their shiny hair and phoney body confidence (with wings?). All this amounts to a sort of health-and-action fascism or ideological body terror (and provides me with an oppositional excuse for continuing to smoke). Since the Sex Pistols we have had to witness television's Nintendo presentation of missiles cornering streets to enter Iraqi bomb silos, the demise of the world socialist system and more unemployment. It would be strange indeed if young people ready to take their place in this brave new world needed the same sort of socialisation expressed through the same sort of music and attitude to both body and emotions that rockology saw fit to canonise and to mystify.

Anyhow, rather than rant on at colleagues and what I see as both the ethical and intellectual bankruptcy of the rockologist and postmodernist mystifications of popular music, I will put my own neck on the academic chopping block in the sense that I have chosen to talk about something I know very little about – rave music. The reasons for my interest in the subject at this stage are (a) that rave is the first type of pop music since reggae and punk to provoke me into learning it actively as a musician; (b) that I don't have to find a guitarist, drummer and vocalist to make the music: I can do it all at home on my synthesizer and computer; (c) that rave music means a lot to my daughter and her peers and she means a lot to me; (d) that as a musicologist I find its musical structuring differs more radically from that of its precursors than most previous forms of pop. In fact, I think you almost have to go back to the change from Leroy Anderson's 'Blue Tango' into Presley's version of 'Hound Dog' to find such an essential musical shift in the world of Euro-American popular music. This is quite a claim, so what are the musical common denominators of rave that make it so special?

All rave music has certain stylistic and generic common denominators. Generically, rave is intended for energetic individual dancing in discos or at rave parties. You can dance 'with' someone by just facing them but you do not touch. There should be a powerful hi-fi system, the DJ should say as little as possible and get on with the music. If indoors, there should be plenty of rhythmic laser light effects – at some raves there is even colour coding so the evening will start with a relatively mellow yellow accompanying tracks set at a leisurely 116 b.p.m. and pass via blue and green to a frenetic red at 144 b.p.m by the end of the night.[19] Asked 'what do you think the main point of a rave is?' my daughter replied:

It's Friday and you've been out socialising, chatting away with your friends. Around midnight a lot of people go to a rave just to shake their bum off. It's much less dangerous a sort of intoxication than drinking or taking dope and as long as there's either plenty of water or soft drinks there and somewhere where you can cool off now and again, you just bop till you drop.[20]

Expounding energy all together to exciting sounds seems to be order of the day (or night).[21] Rave compilations are qualified by terms like 'urban', 'manic', 'megadance', 'power', 'ultrasonic', 'energy', etc. Most rave runs in regular two-bar periods of 4/4 (or four bars 2/4, if your prefer – it is really *alla breve* in classical terms). These periods are about half the length of those found in an average rock number and more akin to the short modules of fast disco. Tempos generally range between 116 and 144 b.p.m., the most common pulse rate being around 132, i.e. much faster than a march and quicker than most disco.[22] It is about the same basic pulse as up-tempo 2/4 gospel, or as fast jump numbers from the 1940s and early 1950s. This is also the same sort of speed as a bluegrass breakdown or as the polka. However, of all older forms of fast dance, it is probably most like the reel and breakdown because, like these, rave music also has a semiquaver surface rate in 2/4 (4/4). But whereas a constant banjo, fiddle or whistle run the reel's semiquavers melodically, rave puts them over percussively or as fast minimal riffs on sampled hi-hat or, more frequently as sequenced figures assigned to some distinct sampled sound like the Korg M1's Technoblock or a precise synthesized saw-tooth or square wave sort of sound. Rock and disco's snare drum backbeats seldom occur in rave which goes too fast to let the sound's attack and decay run its full course effectively. Bass riffs, if they occur at all, are usually quite simple, and seem to consist of either repeated or single notes sounding the root position of the overlying chord (usually a triad) or circling stepwise round it. Unlike those of rock and disco, rave bass tracks are rarely prominent features of the music.

Apart from the almost continually metronomic kick-drum knocking out the crotchet pulse (a trait of much disco but not of rock and roll), rave's most distinctive melodic feature is the almost obligatory syncopated keyboard chordal rhythm figure, frequently assigned to sampled piano but also given to other sounds – something xylophonish, guitaral or resembling a fat Oberheim preset, maybe.[23] Unlike rock music but like disco, rave syncopations run at a micro level, usually over half or one-bar units, rarely over two and never over more.

The instrumentation of rave is, to all intents and purposes, 100 per cent synthesized and/or sampled. Most of the material is also MIDI-sequenced, thus enabling the musician to set up more or less endless repetitions of the same figures which can then be deleted, copied, transposed, quantised, offset, inverted, retrograded, delayed, inserted or otherwise adjusted on-screen to manage breaks, fills, effects and, if required, vocals. Just as stylistically essential to rave is, however, the sampler which allows the musician to insert short units of sound from other music or from sounds outside traditional musical discourses altogether into the composition. The sampler is central to rave music's originality because it allows musicians to get out of the rut of just singing and playing by providing them with easy access to practically manageable sonic building blocks of aesthetic and ideological potential that are not just chords, timbres, rhythm patterns, riffs and so on. The sampler allows the composition to interact with the world outside its own discourse, not in the usual way of including lyrics to concretise some idea that is not necessarily primarily musical, but by incorporating not-necessarily musical sounds *into* the musical discourse, thus broadening the concept of what music can and cannot be on a highly popular basis. Recurrent sampled effects that I have heard so far have been the spoken word, the human voice, sirens, howlers and animals (the latter including sheep, cows, elephants and, of course, the little dog in Usura's *Open Your Mind*).[24] It should also be borne in mind that samplers are also often used in rave, not so much for making realistic carbon copies of acoustic instruments as for recreating the obviously synthetic sounds of otherwise obsolete analog synths from the 1970s and early 1980s.[25] 'Syntheticness' as reality and sounds from the world outside traditional notions of music are in other words just as characteristic of rave music's aesthetics as the metronomic onbeat kick-drum, the frenetically sequenced semiquaver surface rate, the ultra-short periodicity and fast crotchet pulse in 4/4 (or 2/4) time.

Vocals are not an essential ingredient of rave music, but when they do occur in standard dance numbers they are of two basic types. You will find either a female vocalist in quite a high register singing one-bar phrases whose lyrics consist of short, simple repeated phrases or just single words or even just 'oo-s' and aa-s';

or, alternatively, you will find a male voice, often sampled, reciting – not singing – single words or short phrases at regular intervals. Rave numbers featuring *sung* male vocal figures are quite rare.

As rave devotees will have gathered by now, I am restricting my account to the core of styles referred to by such labels as 'techno-rave', 'techno-house', 'altern-ative dance' or 'progressive dance' because in the rave substyles or 'dance rap' and 'hip house' (a.k.a. 'black urban'), male recitations are quite continuous and verbally coherent while the tempo is slower and the drum track less onbeat metro-nomic and more snare-drum/backbeat oriented – more 'funky', if you like. Sim-ilarly, the set of rave substyles labelled as 'R&B dance' – really more a sort of synthesized up-tempo soul-gospel-disco – features melodic vocals, usually sung by women, and phrases encompassing two bars rather than one.

Sung vocals are the only tracks in rave mixes that seem to be consistently given much echo, usually in the form of quite a generous reverb with Echoplex delay effects added at suitable junctures. Other tracks seem generally to be mixed up quite loud without much reverb, this producing a close, distinct, compact and busy effect over which the women wail in what seems like another acoustic dimension.[26]

The tonal language of rave music also shows some interesting traits. Whereas 'R&B dance' uses a lot of disco's major and minor seventh sonorities and whereas 'dance rap' sticks to the basically percussive backing tracks of rap music in general, European and North American techno-rave seems to go in a big way for the Aeolian and Phrygian modes, not as harmonic padding for blues pentatonicism, but as straight sets of minor mode triads or bare fifths without much trace of a seventh, let alone ninth, eleventh or thirteenth. With the exception of a few rock songs from the early 1980s which sported lyrics expressing alienation, hope-lessness and a sense of doom, no internationally popular music of this century has shown such a leaning toward these modes with their downward pulling minor sixths and/or seconds.[27]

Particularly remarkable is rave music's penchant for the Phrygian, a mode virtually unused previously in any form of internationally well-known music apart from what came out of Spain in the form of *malgueñas*, *farrucas*, *fandangos* and flamenco music. From a Eurocentric viewpoint, this is the mode of Spain, gypsies, Balkans, Turks and Arabs (possibly of the *mezzogiorno* also). Why Phrygian? Have British rave musicians taken a stand for the new-age travellers and gypsies?[28] Have European and North American bedroom boffins started to support the pan-Islamic movement or is the Phrygian thing a musical 'up yours' to the powers that sent the Nintendo missile through the Iraqi bomb silo window and smashed the lives of thousands of civilians in Baghdad, i.e. the same powers that condemn half the rave-going youngsters to unemployment? Or has everyone been listening to rai music? Or is the Phrygian mode just new and different? If so, why that particular difference and not another? What about the Lydian mode? It is just as rare in pop as the Phrygian.

Rave tracks seem to have an average duration of around five minutes. In formal terms they sometimes divide into two identifiable sections containing slightly different tonal material and variations in instrumentation, at least in the sense of altered presets, muted tracks, etc. Just as often, however, techno-rave tracks are horizontally (not vertically) monothematic. Other variation comes from the way in which tracks enter and exit and sound together with (or separate from)

216 *Middle Eight*

other tracks. Rave numbers rarely start with all tracks sounding simultaneously and often build up several two-bar units of other tracks before the quantised kick drum sets in. All rave numbers feature at least one obligatory break in which the harmonic-rhythmic one or two-bar riff, often heard as sampled piano, plays solo. Sometimes breaks feature other tracks or sounds – a sampled human voice, animals, a siren, etc.

When the bass drum stops people do different things. If it's an effect or the 'tssk-tssk-tssk' noise, some people just stand still; others go round like in slow motion. If it's the piano or another 'da-daa-da-dee-da' sort of thing, a lot of people kind of wave their arms about. When the break's on, no-one moves their feet or bums much. They do that when the bass drum starts again. Breaks are dead good: quite dramatic and exciting, because everybody stops and starts again.[29]

From this cursory glance at rave music's stylistic characteristics, several traits stand out as unique. There is a high rate of basic pulse combined with the high surface rate all sounding intentionally 'artificial' in the sense of obviously synthesized, sequenced and sampled. All this is then often tonally packed in the Aeolian or minor (gapped) pentatonic or Phrygian mode with little acoustic space given to anything except the female vocalist's short, high-pitched wails.

In the study of this recent development in rock music ('rock' in its widest sense) we need to ask a lot of structural and semiotic 'whys', as I did with the Phrygian aspects of the music.[30] Why the breakneck tempo? Why the explicit metronomic pulse on kick-drum? Why the constantly dense but distinct acoustic close-up? Why no prominent bass line? Why so many effects of the film soundtrack type? Why do tracks last five minutes and not three? Why so few sung male vocals? Why so many women singing short phrases in quite a high register with so much reverb? What does this male-female division of vocal 'labour' signify in terms of gender role ideals? Or, as the title of this paper implies, why is there so little tune and so much accompaniment? I cannot answer any of these questions satisfactorily here. What I hope to do, however, is to point our thoughts as scholars of popular music in a direction that takes account of radically new musical and social conditions influencing the production and use of rave music. One way of doing this is to concentrate on the musical expression of figure and ground.

I have on several occasions explained the relationship between, on the one hand, the advent of the figure/ground dualism in European visual art, with its central perspective, and, on the other hand, that of the melody/accompaniment dualism in European music. These developments in European art prefigure and/or accompany the rise of the bourgeois notion of the individual. Put crudely, Breughel, in works like *Children's Games* or *The Slaughter of the Innocents*, painted dozens of different human scenes into one and the same picture.[31] By the same token, William Byrd let eight non-hierarchically organised voices sing his *Great Service* as contrapuntal polyphony, not as a tune with a backing. The visual version of tune-versus-accompaniment can be seen in any Vermeer *Stilleben* – let us say the one where you see a flower in a vase at the front of the picture and a room and a window behind it (central perspective) – or in Da Vinci's *Mona Lisa* – a woman's face close up front and a bit of Italian scenery behind. From the Florentine *Camerata* and onwards, we are told, monody, (i.e. a melody with an accompaniment or 'backing') became the main dynamic of European composition. To put it crudely again, Haydn and AC/DC may not have much else in common but they both made music on the basis that there has to be some sort of melodic line – be it Angus Young on guitar or a solo aria line in *The Creation* – and some sort of accompaniment of that figure – be it drums, bass and rhythm guitar or second violins, violas, cellos and chordal woodwind.

Given this historically verifiable dual relationship (a) between themes as musical figures and the foreground individual and (b) between accompaniment or backing and the environment in which the figure/ground moves and has its being, it is possible, using the basic tools of musematic analysis, to come up with quite reasonable hypotheses as to how music encodes different patterns of socialisation. In this context you need to know if the music contains any melodic figures and, if so, how many occur at the same time. You also need to identify the backcloth, if any, against which those figures stand out in sonic relief. Then you have to find out how the figures interact with each other and with the background and establish any connotative meaning you might find in (a) the figure, (b) the ground and (c) in the relationship, if any, between figure and ground.

There are obvious differences between the figure/ground properties of different types of music, for example between traditional jazz, on the one hand, with its more collective forms of improvisation and shorter solo sections and, on the other hand, bebop, with its short collective sections and extensive solo improvisation. Another example would be the difference between European popular song and West African polyrhythmic music about which my mother once said 'it's nice and rhythmic, dear, but where's the tune?' Many forms of West African polyrhythmic music consist of a multitude of short, repeated, rhythmically and timbrically varied figures, all played simultaneously. Such musical structuring can also be read as social structuring: each individual part is required to differ from and yet interact with all the other individual parts. The successful musical event is in this sense homologous with the successful and immediate interaction of individuals in society. The music expresses a role for individuals in a social and natural environment that differs radically from that encoded in the European melody/accompaniment paradigm. Misunderstanding these essential elements of musical structuring also belies a more general, cultural confusion about the role of the individual in different populations. For example, during a visit to Cuba in the mid-1970s, some Swedish jazz musicians, accompanying the Gothenburg chamber choir on tour, came back to their hotel to discover a group of old men laying down really exciting rhythms on various percussion instruments in the hotel bar. The old men were delighted that guests from so far away wanted to join them in their music-making and things went fine in the collective rhythmic-motoric-harmonic jam until the Swedish saxophonist launched into an enthusiastic Cubop solo.[32] The old men all stopped playing after a few bars because their compositional norms, homologous to certain social norms governing the interaction of individuals, had been transgressed. The saxophonist's first thoughts were 'does no-one get to be free here?', and those of the old men 'who does he think he is barging in like that, drowning us and bulldozing our groove out of existence?' I am not trying here to make a case for one sort of music being intrinsically more progressive and collective than another: I merely want to suggest that different ways of organising musical figures, be it as figure/ground (as in most European and North American music), as mostly ground (as in West African polyrhythm) or as mostly melody (as in much Arabic music) may correspond to different general ideals of socialisation in different cultures.

In order to make this model a bit clearer and to insert some of rave music's unique properties in their historical context, let us take a quick semiotic look at the figure/ground structuration of one of rave music's most popular precursors in the Anglo-Saxon world – heavy metal. The obvious figures of heavy metal are the lead singer and lead guitarist: they literally 'lead' and they are either the star or the (guitar) hero of the band, providing the obvious foreground identification, both visually and sonically 'up front'. Behind them, both visually and sonically, are the instruments providing the backing tracks on their recordings: drums, bass, rhythm guitar and/or keyboards. What does heavy metal backing 'say'? What does the foreground 'mean'? What does the relationship between these two express?[33]

There is no room here to provide more than the most general answers to these questions. Heavy metal backing has several functions: (1) using sonic ana-phones, it stylises, humanises and culturally encodes (by sonic anaphones) certain aspects of the contemporary soundscape (broad-spectrum, consistently lo-fi noise, as in the rumble of traffic or mains hum); (2) using transmodal anaphones, it stylises, humanises and culturally encodes a particular sense of time as experience in contemporary society.[34] To cut a long story short (and omitting most links in a lengthy chain of argument), heavy metal backing presents the humanised sonic image of a fascinatingly overbearing electromechanical society containing very little room for manoeuvre and subjected to almost metronomic time slavery. It is all so loud and powerful that you can only make yourself heard if you raise your voice, like trying to talk to a friend on the other side of a city street containing a constant stream of noisy traffic. The musical equivalent of this is to scream like any self-respecting male rock vocalist over the top of all that other noise. Another strategy is to get a motor-bike that will let you weave in out of all that traffic and take you where you want to go much faster and sooner than Smith, Jones and Robinson in their silly little cars, with the added kicks of (a) feeling the speed hit you physically and (b) making a more piercing, roaring sound than others. Of course, what with Marlon Brando, James Dean and Co., the motor-bike often turns up as a social symbol of freedom and oppositionality, as, indeed, it does on lead guitar (with overdrive) in rock music.[35]

What sort of socialisation strategy is encoded in this type of rock? It seems to me that we are hearing individuals who beat the fascinating but overbearing system by screaming louder than it, by roaring or chain-sawing their way through it. These are individuals who issue from within that system and who beat it on its own terms by being louder than the loud, sharper than the sharp, harder than the hard. Hence the heavy-metal audience's arms raised high in a collective V-sign as the singer or lead guitarist rides away into another heroic urban sunset. Unfortunately, the emancipatory potential of this monocentric socialisation strategy can degenerate into the vulgar entrepreneurial egoism of the Thatcher and Reagan era and into its musical equivalent – hyper-melodic pomp and its elevation to a hegemonic position, as in the soundtrack of *American Anthem*, as in much of Queen's music, as in 'Iron Wings' and as in the Ford adverts.[36] Degenerated or not, mono-centric types of socialisation strategy are clearly less popular with today's ravers because, as our cursory enumeration of their music's main traits reveals, they do not go much for cohesive melodic statements and seem to eschew, both musically and socially, big figures. On the other hand, rave music contains plenty of small figures constituting plenty of ground, plenty of 'environment' . . .

If I have not totally misinterpreted the behaviour of dancers at the few raves and rave discos I have attended and if I am allowed to regard my daughter and her peers as in any way representative informants, rave is something you immerse yourself into together with other people. There is no guitar hero or rock star or corresponding musical-structural figures to identify with, you just 'shake your bum off' from inside the music. You are just one of many other individuals who constitute the musical whole, the whole ground – musical and social – on which you stand. The music is definitely neither melody nor melody plus accompaniment. Nor is it just accompaniment any more than West African polyrhythm, William Byrd's *Great Service* or Breughel's *Slaugter of the Innocents*. Polarising the issue, you could say that perhaps techno-rave puts an end to nearly four hundred years of the great European bourgeois individual in music, starting with Peri and Monteverdi and culminating with Parker, Hendrix and – Lord preserve us – Brian May, Whitney Houston and the TV spot for Bodyform sanitary towels.[37]

This is one important, musicologically founded reason for taking rave music seriously. Are we really witnessing a radically different musical expression of a radically new socialisation strategy amongst certain groups of young people in our society? If so, does this prefigure a new form of collective consciousness or does it mean the end of oppositionality and individualism? Are ravers hedonistic defeatists who have abandoned all hope of being heard as individuals in this oppressive society or does their music encode a protest against a totally compromised notion of individual freedom? Perhaps ravers have so conformed and identified with this system that their music expresses no distance to or quarrel with the inexorable pulse and automated march of society? Or does rave music say 'up yours' to 'performance', 'achievement', 'competition', 'enterprise' and all those other nauseous Thatcheritic buzzwords? Perhaps rave music at least criticises society by juxtaposing elements of music and sound that outside the musical event are traditionally supposed to belong to separate categories? Bearing in mind that real rave credibility consists of anonymously recording tracks on white labels, is it possible to suggest that the non-individualist character of the music actually does express a rejection of degenerate, hegemonic notions of the individual? Bearing also in mind the often semi-illegal, cooperative way in which raves are organised, is it going too far to hypothesise that rave music prefigures new forms of collective consciousness? Or are rave organisers another variation on the old 'hip capitalist' theme and rave DJs a mere variation on the old theme of central figure against general background?

The main aim of this article has been to raise questions, not to answer them. In so doing, I have had to be quite polemical and to polarise issues quite radically. I have also had to simplify, skip major steps in lines of reasoning and pass over gaping lacunae in both my own and in collective knowledge about techno-rave. This article may also give the impression that I consider all rave to be 'collective and good' and all rock to be 'individualistic and bad', a view to which I certainly do not subscribe. In polarising and simplifying issues, I have tried to formulate a few hypotheses (some more speculative than others) about how we, as scholars of popular music, could start trying to understand rave music's radical departure from the old rock canon. If we think this a subject worth studying, I am sure we would be well advised to ignore the unresolved Oedipal conflicts of cultural theorists who still seem to be battling with their own emancipation from a previous, unjust authority and who cannot see their own canonisation of rock as 'absolute' fun and corporeality as equally unjust and as one of late capitalism's most efficient ideological weapons.[38] Nor does it help us as popular scholars, let alone my daughter and her peers, to be told by politically 'correct' metatheorists that rave is a postmodernist collage of sound with no coherent structure, narrative or direction – another insult to rave musicians and organisers who want *a* and not *b* to happen and be felt. What we *do* need in the pop academy are people prepared to do some musicological, ethnographical and sociological donkey work. In my opinion that musicological work would be well-served if carried out in the spirit of Mellers rather than according to the gospel of the most recent French fashion of 'postmodernism'.

Endnotes

1 This article is dedicated to Maria Tagg, her rave accomplices and their right to party. It was first presented as a paper at the conference *Rock Steady/Rock Stydy: sulle culture del rock*, held at the Gramsci Institute in Bologna, 6–7 May 1993. With hindsight, perhaps it would be more correct to call the sort of music discussed here 'dance' or 'house' rather than 'rave'. Since the generic name of the sort of music discussed later still seems to fluctuate, I have kept the term 'rave' as not only referring to the functions at which such music may be played but also to the music 'itself'.

2 Thanks to the following persons for help, information, materials and opinions: Expanded Music (Paulino & Alessandra in Bologna), Paolo Ferrario (Bologna), Margit Kronberg (Göteborg), Liverpool Music House (Colin Hall and Gary McGuiness), Angela MacRobbie (London), Maria Tagg (Göteborg), Garry Tamlyn (Townsville) and Sheila Whiteley (Manchester). Thanks to Martin Cloonan and John Lovering (Liverpool) for their frank and brotherly criticism without which this article would have turned out even less convincing that it is anyhow.

3 On *Megadance – The Power Zone*. Virgin/EMI CDEVP 4, 1993.

4 On *Megadance – The Power Zone*. Virgin/EMI CDEVP 6, 1993.

5 On *This is Urban*. Pop & Arts (UK) CD 101, 1990.

6 On *Madman's Return*. Logic Records CD 74321 12851 2, 1992.

7 Information from the Merseyside Drug Training and Information Centre (phone call 17 May 1993). Massive amounts of the drug are in circulation in the Liverpool area. The drug is sold in the form of capsules, tablets and, occasionally, as powder. Capsules are marketed with different colours and names (e.g. red and black as 'Dennis the Menace', red and cream as 'Rhubarb and Custard') while tables are stamped with different images, e.g. doves ('love dove'), shamrocks or (as in Sweden)

Donald Duck. For a more detailed run-down on rave regulation in Britain, see chapter 'Raving in the Free World?' in Cloonan (1993).

8 My daughter assures me that she is aware of ecstasy having been present at only one of the twenty raves she has attended or organised in the Gothenburg area.

9 As Garry Tamlyn (Townsville, Australia) points out in the draft introduction to his doctoral study (see Note 14 below), cultural-theoretical writing on rock owes a lot to earlier, more journalistic and fan-oriented literature on the subject. A recurrent problem with all this literature, both academic and not, is its musicological inaccuracy. Tamlyn cites accounts of the same musical reality described in incompatible terms and cites numerous passages in which the sounds of rock music are labelled or described in affective or corporeal terms for which no empirical evidence exists.

10 Referring to original 1991 music track of British TV commercials. 'Layla' was rearranged classically and minimally for subsequent Vauxhall spots and 'Driven By You' was later rearranged semi-classically to sell the Ford Mondeo (1993).

11 The 'Soul Glow' hair spray spot in *Coming to America*, Paramount, 1988. CIC video (VHS). It is interesting to note that whereas the 1993 spot for Bodyform Plus concentrates visually on *one* woman and uses such an over-the-top melodic line (in fact the 'Bodyform for you' hook also resembles the well-known pomp-rock mega-melodics of 'Gillette, the best a man can get'), the 1993 spot for Tampax shows *groups* of women (pushing a yellow Volkswagen on a beach and playing volleyball) to the accompaniment or rave-style dance music.

12 Thanks to Garry Tamlyn for digging out the last two quotes.

13 The last section of Grossberg's paper at the *Rock Steady* conference seemed to me to express such a critique of the rockologist aesthetic.

14 Garry Tamlyn's doctoral work, provisionally entitled 'Rhythmic organisation in rock and

roll', is in progress at the the Institute of Popular music, University of Liverpool.

15 For description of 'bio-acoustic universals', see Tagg (1990b).

16 Conversation with Maria Tagg, 2 May 1993, referring to 'No Limit' (7″ mix) by 2 Unlimited on *Megadance – The Power Zone* (Virgin/EMI CDEVP 4, 1993). 'In this context the inverted snobbery of the rave scene should also be acknowledged, just as snobbish as the rock aestheticist's desire for authentic blackness (and Black Chicks' Man) . . . Maria may not have liked 'No Limit' and bands like Prodigy get very snooty about how exclusive and non-commercial they are really. Great though this assertiveness is at first, it easily becomes the kind of tedious and anti-musical tribalism we have seen all too often before . . . (If *I* don't like it, it's Shite). Relatedly, there's a lot of individualism in the rave scene . . . Here the individual spotlighted is not a musician but a DJ or the club organiser'. (Comments – with which I wholeheartedly agree – from John Lovering about the original version of this paper.)

17 'Rough', 'raw', 'anarchic', etc. are recurrent adjectives describing rock, as opposed to earlier forms of popular music, in much fan-oriented or journalistic literature on the subject.

18 Jackson's genuine depigmentation disorder was often reported as if he had undergone plastic surgery to make him look whiter.

19 Thanks to Sheila Whiteley (Manchester) for this observation.

20 Maria Tagg in phone conversation, 2 May 1993.

21 Maybe sweating through the night at raves is one way of avoiding sexual showdowns of the post-AIDS era (fiddling about with condoms, discussing HIV tests, etc.). As youngsters of the rock age we never had to worry about sex as a killer. Michelle of the Merseyside Drug Training and Information Centre also remarked that wereas people used to arrive at clubs and dances in groups of young men or women and then gradually pair off and disappear into the night progressed, people arrive at rave clubs in mixed groups and only rarely leave the venue as individual couples (phone conversation, 17 May 1993)

22 The DJ Ricci 'Rave Mix' of Ramirez's *Terapia* (DFC 124, 1993) runs at 163 b.p.m. This is, however, exceptionally fast, even for techno-rave tracks.

23 As the 'Fat Obie' sample track on *Future Music CD Vol. 1* (published with *FM* Magazine, UK, Spring 1993). Thanks to Gary McGuiness

(Liverpool Music House studio) for loan of the record.

24 I have subsequently learnt that the dog and elephant are in fact effects using presets on an old type of Roland. Thanks to Paolo Ferrario, Bologna for this observation.

25 On the *Future Music CD Vol. 1* there are several 'good old' synthesizers sampled ready for rave use (see endnote 21).

26 As stated earlier, wordless vocals also occur frequently. A particularly suggestive example of sampled female 'ooing' and 'aaing' can be found on Morenas' *Cuando brilla la luna*, DFC 067, 1992.

27 The signification of the Aeolian pendulum in rock music has been dealt with at some length in Alf Björnberg's '"There's Something Going On" – om eolisk harmonik i nutida rockmusik', in *Tvärspel – 31 artiklar om musik. Festskrift till Jan Ling*. Göteborg, Skrifter från Musikvetenskapliga institutionen, 9, 1984, 371–6. See also Tagg 1990b.

28 Thanks to Sheila Whiteley for the 'new age traveller' connection. At this point I played some examples of Phrygian mode rave, including: BMO's *Mastermind* (see endnote 4) and Capella's *U Got 2 Know* (see endnote 3).

29 Phone conversation with Maria Tagg, 2 May 1993.

30 i.e. why has so much rave music opted for that and not for, say, quartal harmony, atonality or the Lydian mode?

31 Breughel also let Icharos plop virtually unseen into a corner of the Aegean sea on a painting called *The Fall of Icharos*.

32 *Cubop* – the sort of Cuban-Caribbean inspired bebop music played by the Dizzie Gillespie big band in the late 1940s.

33 In what follows I am not considering the metal subgenres of thrash, speed and death which, with their lack of melody in the traditional sense of the word and as recent rock phenomena, might be worth considering from the same structural and ethnographical viewpoint as rave.

34 For explanation of anaphones Tagg (1992). For further discussion on musical expression of time, see Tagg (1984).

35 For a more extensive account of heavy metal's figure-ground dualism, see (1990a). The clearest example of the 'motor-bike = overdriven electric guitar solo' equation is perhaps the 1988 advert for the Philishave Tracer, in which the sound effect and visual image of a 'real' motor-bike is virtually indistinguishable from the electric guitar of the music track, highly similar to the start of Dire Straits' 'I Want My

222

MTV' (on *Brothers in Arms*, Vertigo 824499-4, 1985).

36 See tracks sung by Mr Mister and John Parr on *American Anthem* (Atlantic 781661-1, 1986). The cover features a mini-Travolta or Ralph Macchio type in leather jacket and a blonde young woman in aerobic clothing, a pastel-pink towelling ring securing her pony-tailed hair. We were happily spared from distribution of the film in Sweden. See also endnote 9.

37 The Bodyform sanitary towel advert referred to is the one in which vast quantities of the commodity are spilled, accidentally on purpose, by one woman. One sanitary towel is then picked up by the other woman and held up against the light coming through the Venetian blinds (they are so thin!). The vocal line is extremely ecstatic, rather pompously anthemic and quite florid piece of gospel rock celebrating the commodity ('whoa! . . . Bodyform for you!). The music makes Nile Rogers's pastiche of the style – the 'Slow Glow' advert from Eddy Murphy's *Coming to America* – sound quite bland by comparison. It is difficult to imagine anything more fraught with the double standards of individuality and commerce than a sanitary towel (menstruation is supposed to be a private issue and yet a majority of the population – women – experience the phenomenon for over a thousand days of their life). In fact it may be quite logical that the perverted 'mega-individual' of rock should be used to perpetuate such double standards.

38 Of course, the whole problem of cultural theory's idealisation, especially in 'postmodernist' terms, of rock-related genres, is a far more complicated issue than I can present here. Apart from the question of body-idealisation and its inverted racist consequences (see Tagg 1989) there also seems to be a notion that non-logocentric (including the affective, gestural and corporeal) systematisation of experience and meaning starts with Elvis Presley. This assumption falsifies European music history far more radically than the worst type of 'absolute music' aesthetics as applied to the bourgeois Central European 'classics'. Thankfully, music and dance have been around for some time on our continent making 'irrational' systematisations of individual and collective experience of body and emotions. Birgit Nielsen, fully garbed as Aïda, making Ziggy Stardust look like a bank clerk and bellowing a four-minute aria as she dies, makes no 'logical' sense as narrative in a classical novel and is certainly untrue, not to say physically impossible, from a 'rationalist' viewpoint, but it makes perfect sense musically and emotionally. According to some cultural-theoretical rockologists, then, Verdi ought to be labelled 'postmodern'. Why rationalism is so irrational about the irrational strikes me, as an 'irrational' musician, as irrational. Or, as Jung quipped in one of his less metaphysical moments: 'we complacently assume that the conscious makes sense and that the unconscious is nonsense' (1968, p. 54). I suppose the inability to make sense of the symbolic systems relating to our collective 'irrational' will inevitably lead to recurring fads of the 'postmodernist' type in such a logocentric tradition as that of our universities.

References

Cloonan, M. 1993. 'Banned: censorship of popular music in Britain, 1967–1992', unpublished Ph.D. dissertation, University of Liverpool

Grossberg, L. 1990. 'Is there rock after punk', in *On Record*, ed. S. Frith & A. Goodwin (London) pp. 111–123

Jung, C. 1968. *Man and His Symbols* (New York)

Lull, J. (ed.) 1992. *Popular Music and Communication* (Newbury Park)

Mellers, W. & Harman, A. 1962. *Man and His Music* (London)

Tagg, P. 1984. 'Understanding "time sense"', in *Tvärspel: Festskrift till Jan Ling* (Göteborg) pp. 21–43

1989. 'Open letter: Black music, Afro-American music and European music', *Popular Music*, 8/3, pp. 285–98

1990a. 'Reading sounds', *Recommended Recorded Quarterly*, 3/2, pp. 4–11 (published in Italian as 'Leggere i suoni', *Quarderni di Musica Realtà*, 23, 1989, pp. 168–183)

1990b. '"Universal" music and the case of death', in *La musica come linguaggio universale*, ed. R. Pozzi (Florence) pp. 227–66

1992. 'Towards a sign typology of "music"', in *Secondo convegno europeo di analisi musicale*, ed. Dalmonte & Baroni (Trento) pp. 369–78

[11]

What Does It Mean To Analyse Popular Music?

ADAM KRIMS

Taken together, the four publications reviewed here pose a question that penetrates to the heart of this journal, namely: what does it mean to analyse popular music?[1] The ambiguous and still-developing status of popular music as a disciplinary object cannot be lost on anyone who has ventured into the field as a researcher; moreover, the surprisingly different constructions of 'popular music' presented in this group of texts point both to a present fragmentation and also to a possibility only partially realised in any one particular source. On the one hand, the historical failure of music theorists and historians to engage seriously with 'unserious' music has left a vacuum happily filled by scholars from such disciplines as communications, sociology, media studies, area studies, gender studies and geography, to name just a few. Yet, on the other hand, the impressive range and theoretical diversity emanating from popular music scholarship over the past decade or two has only occasionally deployed what most readers of this journal would recognise as 'music analysis'. The few musicologists who to date have attempted structural analyses of post-Second World War popular music – for instance, Richard Middleton, Allan Moore, Walter Everett and Robert Walser – have traditionally found themselves in a liminal territory: limiting their audience in their own disciplines, they also enter into disciplinary terrain whose procedures lie far from those recognised in the domain of traditional music studies. But there are undoubtedly signs of change in both historical and analytical musicology, with a good number of (mainly younger) scholars preferring to specialise in a field whose cultural caché within academia has at last begun to flourish during the years since studies of popular culture generally took hold in (initially North American) academia. Dedicated sessions at meetings of the Society for Music Theory, the American Musicological Society and other professional bodies have been common for some years now, and many journals have chosen to follow suit. Such activity can still legitimately be labelled nascent, yet it can at least be hoped that, for all but the most dogmatically minded, the venture into popular music studies will render significant the accompanying range of interpretative perspectives.

This much said, any music theorists wishing to become involved in popular music studies should expect to have to acquaint themselves with the eclectic conceptual and terminological currency circulating among its more experienced participants. The first two books to be examined here (by Roy Shuker and Keith Negus) offer primary guidance from experts in the fields of media studies and sociology respectively, all the more needed because of the continuing (and in some respects surprising) paucity of relevant training in music departments. The other two (Allan Moore's single author handbook and the essays assembled under the co-editorship of John Covach and Graham Boone) are studies by music theorists and historians, and hence may be taken as representative of the current state of acclimatisation within the musicological sphere. Each book plainly aligns itself with one of the accepted disciplinary constructions of 'popular music'. At the same time, however, elements of different (and sometimes under-theorised) disciplines register their presence in each book, thereby engendering the potential for productive – if occasionally remedial – dialogue. It is to be hoped that some of the remarks made here will suggest ways in which the various texts might be taken to open onto each other – in spite of the fact that one or more of them may work unwittingly to foreclose alternative facets of musical engagement.

In the light of these latter observations, Roy Shuker's *Key Concepts in Popular Music* may come to stand as a crucial landmark in popular music studies; in short, it is the first major dictionary of popular music terminology conceived specifically for scholarly use. Shuker is an excellent choice for authoring such a resource, as his broad knowledge of both the theoretical and more 'concrete' aspects of popular music studies endows the book with a scope and facility that extends over multiple levels. There are very few students of popular music who will not find the dictionary useful; even those confining themselves to music analysis, for example, will find it indispensable for expanding terminological horizons. Entries are presented alphabetically, with extensive cross-referencing included at the end of each one; they range in length from a short paragraph to several pages, the latter characterising those entries which have received extensive treatment in scholarly literature (for instance, music video, youth cultures, radio, cultural imperialism and so on). Terms within the discussions that have their own entries appear in bold print, and Shuker includes, most usefully, both extensive references within the entries to pertinent scholarly literature and suggestions at the end of each entry for further reading and (where relevant) listening. Some solecisms do occur: for example, cross-references will occasionally direct the reader to a listing which itself simply refers back to the original entry (for instance, from 'Gender' to 'Riot grrl' and back again). In addition, while some omissions from the lists of citations border on the glaring (for example, there is no reference to Peter Manuel (1993) in the entry on 'Cassettes'), others seem inopportune (for instance, a reference within the entry on 'Ethnicity' to Jon Michael Spencer's edited collection as a source documenting the international spread of hip-hop (Spencer 1991) when that volume is flawed precisely by its lack of international focus). Nevertheless, such problems are not unduly pervasive and could well be corrected in a second edition. Supported by Shuker's admirably thorough bibliography, this dictionary is set to become an indispensable research tool. At the same time, Shuker is careful to delineate what the dictionary is *not* meant to do: hence it is not intended to encompass pre-rock popular musics, nor does it cover most specifically non-Western genres. Those with interests in these areas will clearly have to wait for similarly comprehensive and well-produced dictionaries to appear, or to act as entrepreneurs in a comparable vein.

All in all, it is difficult to read through *Keywords* without being impressed by the scope of Shuker's (almost literally) encyclopaedic knowledge, and the comprehensiveness with which he treats topics such as media policy, the music industry, the history of rock and so on. In this respect, he is plainly aware of sources drawn not only from the scholarly world, but also from more popular publications, as well as some of the specifically business-orientated surveys that many popular music scholars might have missed. Furthermore, given the revival of interest in Adorno over the past few years, it is also fortunate that Shuker is far from dismissive of Adorno's contributions to the field. In particular, he adroitly avoids the unfortunate oversimplification of ideas that characterises some of the reflex responses to Adorno's work, while still acknowledging (just as importantly) the reactions against the latter's theories which are currently prevalent in communications and cultural studies approaches to popular musics. Shuker also marks himself out from other scholars by not allowing the figure of Adorno to dominate his entry on Marxism (in which field Adorno's status remains highly questionable),[2] recommending instead the pertinence of political economic studies alongside the work of researchers like David Harker. By comparison, while self-contained entries on such loosely knit areas of activity as 'Locality' cannot do justice to the complexity of the attendant issues surrounding them, Shuker still provides an admirable synthesis of orientation and evaluation.

As with any such volume, one may of course find deeper fault with some of Shuker's synopses. Hence, while his account of rap sub-genres is intriguing, albeit puzzling at times (for instance, is the bass more prominent in gansta rap than in other sub-genres?; and why are only West-Coast artists named and not, for example, Mobb Deep and any number of No Limit MCs?), the prominence afforded to Russell Potter's uneven *Spectular Vernaculars* (Potter 1995) is odd, especially alongside the less extensive discussion of Tricia Rose's far more canonical and influential *Black Noise* (Rose 1994). Elsewhere, one might bristle at his seemingly uncritical acceptance of the notion that alternative rock 'emerged in response to the co-option of rock music by the record industry in the late 1960s and through the 1970s' (pp. 6–7). Any account of rock's history along these lines would seem to imply that a 'genuine' and popularly based folkish movement was ultimately supplanted by a process of commodification – a properly Hebdigeian account, perhaps, and one widely recounted by those for whom punk constituted a salvation of sorts. But what could then be said of any counter-narrative which seeks to allow for the prospect of rock music having *always* been a commodity, even if hundreds of thousands, perhaps millions, of middle-class (mainly white) youth had for a time invested it with an imagined status as anti-systemic? Or, conversely, could one reasonably expect to ignore more recent perspectives, both popular and scholarly, by which the popular music of the 1970s is currently being reinvested with libidinal energies and accounts of social significance? The narrative of the initial 'resistance' and later co-option of rock in the 1960s and afterwards is certainly one that would bear mention and explication (especially if one wished to understand the often exaggerated claims made for punk rock), but it need not be swallowed whole, particularly in the course of performing such an important task as explaining the meanings invested in the term 'alternative rock'. Issues of this kind, however, arise at a level of theoretical contention for which a dictionary could hardly bear a major burden; and it could even be argued that Shuker may claim the advantage of reflecting a mainstream view on such points in the fields of communications and cultural studies, in which acts of popular co-option and re-articulation (and popular 'resistance' in general), remain hallmarks by which popular musics are theorised and, for that matter, validated. Shuker says as much in his introduction, observing that concern in popular music scholarship 'has shifted from a focus on production and textual issues to a concern with consumption' (p. x). Shortly after this remark, Shuker is moved to explore the gap which exists between 'musicological and sociological approaches' – a gesture to which I shall return towards the end of this article.

Omissions are also inevitable in any such enterprise conducted on this compact scale. 'Relative autonomy', despite being frequently mentioned as an object of explicit contention in popular music studies, has no dedicated entry. In fact, it is generally the case that entries related to aspects of Marxist theory are less precise and well documented than those closer to the mainstream of contemporary media and cultural studies: discussions of 'Mediation' and 'Commodification', for instance, suffer from a vagueness which will be familiar to those with a background in Marxism who have traced representations of the latter in 'post-Marxist' scholarship. But any reflection of this kind undoubtedly extends to the field as a whole; in fact, Shuker's discussion of these and other concepts at least offers the advantage of reflecting the great variety of deployments which their associated terminology has enjoyed over the years, ranging from Birmingham (and related) cultural studies, to post-Foucauldian discourse analysis and beyond. Arguably, the purpose of a dictionary might dictate that the matter of terminological application ought to outweigh any bias in favour of rigid theoretical precision; even so, greater historical perspective could have been afforded in the present context by indicating some of the ways in which current approaches have tended to veer from a still deeply felt, if often unacknowledged, shadow.

By comparison, the volume is gratifyingly strong in a number of other important critical respects; entries on 'Audiences' and 'Postmodernism', for example, introduce the reader in a knowing and sophisticated manner to the major currents in the field. In particular, Shuker's native expertise grants the reader access to some of the important scholarship coming out of Australia and New Zealand over the past decade or so. Above all, the author proves extremely adept at writing clearly and concisely, packing surprising amounts of information into small paragraphs or whole pages and doing so in a way that even novices will find accessible. This last property is likely to render the dictionary particularly suitable as a supplement to introductory courses on popular music studies. For that matter, I suspect that Shuker has managed to produce a volume that will quickly become a standard reference text for courses in contemporary popular culture within just about any discipline. Even those for whom 'music theory' still carries the strict meaning of mapping 'internal' musical relationships owe their most serious students of popular music the opportunity to familiarise themselves with some basic terms from the (inter)discipline they may wish to enter. Shuker's dictionary is an excellent tool for accomplishing that task.

If Shuker's dictionary seems set to fulfil a valuable didactic purpose, then the same could be said of Keith Negus's *Popular Music in Theory: an Introduction.* The 'theory' referred to in the title is meant in the broadest sense of the term – in other words, it relates to a variety of reflective, if not altogether systematic, critical positions drawn variously from the realms of media studies, cultural studies and critical theory. Significantly, it would seem to include all kinds of music theory *except* for that branch of 'musicological' inquiry which focuses on musical poetics.[3] Moreover, as Negus acknowledges in his introduction, 'formal musicology' represents 'an area of knowledge and technique which for a sociologist has to be approached over one of the great disciplinary divides' (p. 4). Nonetheless, rather like Shuker, he proceeds to devote a great deal of space to issues of genre and style. While this means that those wishing to instruct students in the close reading of popular music may of necessity find the book wanting, there are at least important points of contact with such concerns.

Indeed, such caveats aside, Negus's text must be signalled as a major advance in the task of training professional popular music scholars: it stands as the kind of well-written, authoritative, comprehensive and topical introduction to issues in the field which simply did not exist until recent times. Of course, a number of single-volume studies have been available for some time, among them the by now familiar contributions from Richard Middleton (1990), Roy Shuker (1994), David Brackett (1995) and Brian Longhurst (1995). However, Negus's study is the first to offer a systematic and topical presentation of the various issues and debates that have taken place within the field, and especially over the past two decades. In particular, the author takes great pains to highlight the multiple criss-crossing critiques and counter-gestures which have characterised popular music scholarship in that time. To some extent, the separate chapters on 'Audiences', 'Industry', 'Mediations', 'Identities', 'Histories', 'Geographies' and 'Politics' engender a degree of repetition at the theoretical level, in spite of such meticulous organisation; issues of audience reception and inflection, for example, are inseparable from complementary considerations of the music industry and its levels of mediation, the identities of artists and consumers, the role of rock historians, the formations of place and the nature of political effects. However, the advantages of such repetition may outweigh the drawbacks of *déjà vu*, as the reader learns to negotiate the constellation of topics and is thereby equipped to form a more unified overview.

The 'Audiences' chapter sets out a usefully broad and resourceful approach for the book as a whole, exemplifying through its own design and content what might also be regarded as a microcosm of the history of popular music studies. Beginning with an exposition of Adorno's views on reception, it goes on to develop what Negus calls 'a tale about an increasingly active audience' (p. 8). A growing validation of modes of reception, coupled with social theory that portrays the activity of reception as potentially powerful (and resistant), is typical of recent scholarly interpretations of this topic (as in, for example, the work of John Fiske (1987) and Iain Chambers (1990)); consequently, there is a suggestion that the chapter is included less to lay out a neutral template, than to allow the book to unfold its own subtle teleology, one which sanctions a gradual process of enlightenment in favour of poaching, hybridity and other comparable values enshrined in postmodern cultural theory. Nevertheless, Negus is also careful to complicate any privileged reading, preferring instead to weave an appropriately tangled web of contested positions. The shadow of Adorno's pessimistic account of increasingly manipulated and regressive listeners, which still holds a surprisingly tenacious grip on the minds of popular music scholars to this day, can too easily stimulate a knee-jerk rejection; however, Negus deftly avoids that pitfall, choosing instead to provide a sympathetic account of Adorno's major theses. His survey of subsequent scholarship begins by traversing some work from the 1950s and early 1960s, usefully filling in terrain often missing from accounts of popular music studies. Examining scholarship on gender and homology, as well as more intellectually fragile and moralising critiques such as those of elitism, Negus does the reader the favour of including some recent and theoretically innovative approaches to subculture such as that of Sarah Thornton (1996). The chapter culminates in the various incarnations of 'active audience' theory, commencing with some moral precepts of the kind advanced by Joli Jensen (1992) and proceeding through a range of theoretically and ethnographically grounded arguments put forward variously by

Chambers, Ruth Finnegan, Jocelyn Guilbault, George Lipsitz and Sara Cohen. In all these instances, Negus renders clear and sympathetic accounts, developing issues and responses in ways that allow the theoretical worlds of the authors discussed to become more accessible to the reader. A pedagogically useful balance develops between earlier theories of ideology critique, which receive the bulk of Negus's attention, and more optimistic and validating scenarios of active and resisting audiences, which enjoy not just contemporary currency, but also the benefit of hindsight. Negus's own contribution to the chapter elects to temper the optimism of recent cultural studies and the validation of creative everyday life and bonding, citing David Morley (1993) on the important point that 'for viewers and listeners to reinterpret meanings is hardly equivalent to the discursive power of centralised media institutions to construct the texts that the viewer then interprets' (p. 33). In a scholarly climate where earlier analyses of political economy and conceptions of ideology are too easily dismissed in favour of voluntaristic views of reception and reinflection, Negus comes as a breath of fresh air, enabling students to grapple with the struggles which persist between social forces, rather than celebrating the infinitely localised pathways of the 'everyday'.

The 'Industry' chapter again begins with Adorno, whose presence in popular music scholarship is once more faithfully recorded as something of a scene of trauma, infinitely relived and denied, while never losing its status as some sort of awful and exaggerated truth. The chapter departs from Adorno sooner than the initial one, however, into the classic (and popularly disseminated) issues of co-optation and control. Here, as in the first chapter, Negus begins by traversing views of centralised power and the cultural effects of capital: Steve Chapple and Reebee Garofolo (1977), David Harker (1980), Nelson George (1988) and Peter Manuel (1991) all contribute to the narrative, be it for the music industry as a whole or, in the cases of George and Manuel, for specific segments and genres. Negus then turns to a related topic, one sometimes proposed as a way around the power of capital, namely the dichotomy of 'majors' versus 'independents' in the popular music industry (in which the latter is occasionally proposed as a route towards greater artistic freedom and a proliferation of stylistic diversity and political resistance). Setting views of a tension against perceptions of a symbiosis between these two poles, Negus develops the key issues in the context of an article by Stephen Lee (1995), which has the unusual virtue of being simultaneously an insider account (of Wax Trax! records) and a theoretically informed piece of academic scholarship. Negus helpfully draws out Lee's lesson that independents form part of an overarching system that includes their relationhips to the majors, and furthermore that the status of 'independent' is, in that case, largely one of symbolic identity and ideology. Although he rightly points out that such a study does not answer the questions of whether independent companies are 'more creative' than majors (however such a thing would be measured), the author unfortunately does not choose to engage with more recent developments in the music industry which might render these questions – at best – obsolete (if, indeed, they ever held much substance). Such new strategies of the music industry, majors and indies alike, proliferate ethnic/ geographic identities rather than 'mainstreaming' or standardising them, marketing the local, marginal and exotic in a revitalisation of ideas of authenticity. As one can see from rap (now, according to Christopher Farley (1999), the largest-selling musical genre in the United States) through Ricky Martin to the Afro Celt Sound System, the music industry can begin to take advantage of changes in technology and global communications to market product diversity for audiences that increasingly look to consume the global in the forms of the local.

These developments are better documented in the popular press than in scholarly research, though such contributions as those by Christopher Mele (1996) and Timothy Taylor (1997) do take us some way towards establishing differing perspectives from the ones outlined in Negus's chapter. Any simple updating would nonetheless be problematic, since recent developments might well yet lead to a more profound rethinking and historicising of the issues surrounding standardisation and diversity in the music industry. For his part, Negus presents a range of valuable insights deriving from his own observations on the day-to-day activity and 'cultural-aesthetic strategies' (p. 49) adopted by workers within the industry. Concerned to credit 'the people who are ... struggling towards the possibility of some form of critical distance from the commercial machine' (p. 54), he invites the reader to look more critically at the varying levels of music-industrial management. As Negus seems to be well aware, taking capital seriously means studying in detail both the workings of the commercial machine and the cultural parameters of economic processes. Such work need not seek to validate the industry as somehow 'less economic' or 'more human' than the constructions of political economy, so much as aim to stress the inseparability of commerce and culture. Indeed, assuming one is more daring, the prospect of permitting scholars to discuss cultures of the aesthetic as something other than a loosely conceived negation of the commercial would appear to be an even more desirable outcome. To this end, Negus's careful exposition of creation within the music industry is one of the signal advantages of this book, and his own interventions in the debates with which he engages succeed repeatedly in enriching and elaborating the constituent dialogues. Admittedly, there are some weaker moments, as for instance when he attempts to develop a critique of Simon Frith's 'pessimistic' view of 'all-powerful' capital (p. 54) in a way that seems to suggest that moral/ psychological categories – such as pessimism – or metaphysical categories – such as autonomy or freedom – should themselves be allowed to delimit the possibilities of critique. One may certainly recognise the efforts of music industry workers to pursue notions of creativity and autonomy without departing from the projects of political economy and ideology critique (indeed, such projects demand that one take seriously cultures of corporate production). Furthermore, Negus's recommended shift from examining the production of culture to examining the 'culture of production' (pp. 61–2) is probably a good deal less dramatic than his prose implies. However, such questions provide a helpful transition through to the next section of the book by addressing the status of music industry personnel as intermediaries in line with several models of culture production, as well as one or two arguments taken from Pierre Bourdieu.

The following chapter, 'Mediations', offers a significant shift of perspective as the conception of 'mediation' on which Negus chooses to concentrate is less that of a strictly Marxist derivation than an analysis of the role of media (especially radio and music video) in inflecting and transmitting popular music. The theoretical issues he examines are unquestionably familiar, in particular the overarching conflict between cultural powers and those of (a presumably resistant or liberatory) reception; but the chapter also offers thoroughly refined summaries of scholarship on radio and media institutions (the former especially being too often overlooked in discussions of the music industry), as well as a detailed discussion of Andrew Goodwin's ground-breaking work on music video (Goodwin 1992). By comparison, the 'Identities' chapter, focusing as it does on arguably the central current problematic of cultural studies, foregrounds the enabling theoretical supposition which could lend significance to just about any angle, namely the notion that 'identities [are] constructed, actively made and open to further change' (p. 133). This last phrase is, of course, the crux of where Negus claims studies of identity are heading, as the premise that identities are *contested* in both production and reception remains, to some extent, the nub of his topical overviews. In this case, the focal issues are black music (in which the influential work of Paul Gilroy most prominently structures the discussion), salsa and gender. This last item is particularised in discussions of heavy metal (in which Robert Walser emerges as the only musicologist other than Richard Middleton granted an extended individual appraisal throughout the book), k. d. lang, disco and Riot Grrrl. In each case, the privileged standpoints (and they are, of course, closely related) are notions of identity as an object of constant struggle and change, coupled with the question of *articulation*, by which Negus means the ways in which particular musical practices reach particular audiences and find their own places in those audiences' lives, concerns and social strategies. Negus adopts the term 'articulation', which he prefers because it 'enables us to ask questions about the relations *between* production and consumption' (p. 133; emphasis as original), from Stuart Hall's reading of Marx's *Grundrisse* (Hall

1974); and whatever reservations one might want to register about Hall as a reader of Marx, direct engagement with the latter's work in cultural studies is all but unavoidable. However, Negus goes even further, arguing (correctly) that Marx anticipated questions of consumption, thus reminding the reader that caricatures of Marxism are often contradicted by Marx himself. Moreover, his closing citation of Richard Middleton along with Lawrence Grossberg on this point also emphasises the conviction that an approach centring on 'articulation' need not exclude more explicitly musicological forms of engagement.

The 'Histories' chapter introduces some major shifts of focus, shifts which in turn can be taken as symptomatic of the unevenness apparent in popular music studies overall. For all the advantages of cultural studies, communications theory (including the question of active audiences) and the perspectives of gender and ethnic studies, it becomes especially apparent throughout this section of the book that the category of 'history' has been damningly fractured throughout the study of popular music. Negus's belief in historical knowledge as 'directly related to how different people develop a sense of identity' (p. 137), while patently true, nevertheless serves to underline just how difficult it is to reconstruct a category like 'history' from within the intensely localising pathways of identity studies. While the focus on identity quickly moves into the background of the discussion in any case – to some extent isolating the chapter from the rest of the book – Negus turns instead to the premise that history 'is *produced*' (p. 138; emphasis as original), and 'within quite specific circumstances' (p. 139).

Opposing such an approach to those (such as that of Peter Van Der Merwe (1989)) which take intrinsic determinations (especially style) as forming the substance of rock history, Negus then proceeds to sketch a range of 'multiple historical dialogues' (p. 139). From rock's allegedly 'revolutionary' status (often represented as being lost to the past), through 'race' crossover and male sexuality (concentrating on Elvis), he succeeds in fashioning as effective a survey from the shards of historical imagination as one could reasonably expect to find. His own contribution to the more narrowly stylistic conceptions of rock history follows as a tripartite subdivision of artist types into 'genericists' (who remain within established stylistic bounds), 'pastichists' (who adapt varied repertoires from different genres according to cultural demand) and 'synthesists' (who 'create new musical patterns' (p. 146) and thus become something like motors of stylistic history). While such a conception is certainly preferable to some of the hagiographies that populate many histories of rock, it is apparent that Negus seems less comfortable when obliged to address a more properly 'musical' issue of this kind. Consequently readers for whom musical poetics forms a central concern may well become frustrated with Negus's discussion here, as the implicit conception of the real subject of music history –

the 'music itself' – seems to form, if anything, an intellectual lapse in an otherwise admirably rigorous survey of the field. However, having moved onto the more familiar ground of Simon Frith's contentions (Frith 1983) about the end of rock (ideology) and subsequent notions broached by other commentators on the beginnings of 'postmodern' popular music, Negus is once again able to demonstrate his impressive command of shifting cultural formations.

The writings of Iain Chambers along with those of Chapple and Garofolo provide important pivots for a discussion of the profound transformations in the music industry, generations of listeners and the much-discussed moment of punk rock which took place between the 1970s and 1990s, while the work of Peter Wicke is introduced (Wicke 1992) to shore up the point that there are 'other histories of rock'. The chapter's closing gesture is a prolonged discussion of *Sgt. Pepper's Lonely Hearts Club Band*, focusing on the important discussions of Chambers, Ian MacDonald (1994) and Allan Moore (1993). A rare moment of unity in the rock historical imagination, this is the album that most often appears in narratives as a turning point, be it to an era of rock 'high art' (a notion to which we shall have to return later in this article), or to a degeneration into self-indulgence (as claimed, for instance, by David Hatch and Stephen Millward (1987)). Negus's own frame takes the chapter back to the broader themes of the book, pointing out how the album joined an '"ideology of rock" [that] was being codified by a new generation of writers who were legitimating "their" music in terms of an aesthetic tradition' (p. 155). Negus, too, acknowledges that the album 'both highlights and transcends the generic boundaries of rock' (p. 156). But, more to the point, he contends that much reception of *Sgt. Pepper's Lonely Hearts Club Band* has skirted important audiences, noting that if, on the one hand, 'the Beatles had and continue to have a great appeal for older people', then, on the other, 'there is perhaps a children's history of the Beatles' to be written (p. 156). If such suggestions might at first seem eccentric to some who study popular music, one should at least keep in mind the precedents established in certain recent critiques of sub-cultural theory (for example, by Gill Valentine, Tracey Skelton and Deborah Chambers (Valentine, Skelton and Chambers 1998)).

The 'Geography' chapter begins, most usefully, with a survey of arguments about cultural imperialism. Lenin receives a more thorough than usual discussion, and Oliver Boyd-Barrett (1977) is invoked to expand from a focus on economic relations to wider reflections on communication vehicles, industrial arrangements and media content. Negus underlines the important point that cultural imperialism can be multi-centred (and not, for example, simply American), while also emphasising the view that cultural imperialism does not preclude 'resistance' in relation to a fundamental unevenness of power (p. 171). Negus's primary argument here, not far from that of David Morley mentioned above, is that 'making use of music recordings in various ways is not the same as having the power and influence to direct the circulation of music products and recordings' (p. 171). Such an observation, in the face of some cultural studies approaches that seem bent on validating the force of 'resistant' musical practices, can only prove therapeutic in sober discussions of music and politics. Negus nevertheless surveys some of the more insistent objections to the cultural imperialism hypothesis, including those involving the globalisation of the music industry (to which he usefully counterposes Stuart Hall's famous 'self-presentation of the dominant particular' (Hall 1991, p. 67)); the hidden hybridity of presumably homogenous cultural forms; and the complexity (and thus presumed multi-directionality) of cultural globalisation.

The remainder of the chapter is devoted to that (relatively) new sub-field of popular music studies, place. Something like the geographical equivalent of 'identity' in cultural studies, 'place' has made an analogously successful impact in music studies, with two major collections (those by Andrew Leyshon, David Matless and George Revill (Leyshon, Matless and Revill 1998) and Thomas Swiss, John Sloop and Andrew Herman (Swiss, Sloop and Herman 1998)) and numerous essays appearing in rapid succession. Studies by Roger Wallis and Krister Malm (1984), Jocelyne Guilbault (1993) and in particular Sara Cohen (1994) are invoked to illustrate how it is that music can come to form cultural notions of place, and how its deployment may be strategic and contested (much like identity). Negus is, as usual, a sure guide through the thicket of musical geographies; and if the topic of place leaves one wanting for attention to objective spatial structures and relations of production rather than such a relentless focus on discourse, then such a lack is more attributable to the condition of popular music studies as a whole than any shortcoming on Negus's part.

By the time the reader arrives at the final chapter, 'Politics', the topic may already seem to have been extensively plotted throughout the remainder of the book. Yet the term narrows here to be confined to matters of the state itself. Negus privileges the concept of articulation, in which a given song is 'actively ... taken and given additional meanings and connected with a very particular political ideology and social agenda'. Further, he stresses the belief that 'songs and music *accumulate* and *connect* with new meanings and beliefs as they pass through time and travel to different places' (p. 195; emphasis as original). The enabling assumptions should be familiar by now: firstly, that meaning cannot be contained intrinsically within a musical text but rather is brought into being by an active audience for specific (often highly local) strategic purposes; and secondly, that such meanings are mobile and multiple, since the situation of audience articulation will vary greatly from place to place and from time to time. Taking John Lennon's 'Imagine' as an example, Negus shows how the song has been deployed for positions right across the (liberal democratic) spectrum, enabled precisely by its semantic vagueness (which he argues against the reading advanced by Middleton (1990)). The completion of Lennon's text by various audiences is taken as proof of the necessity that music's meanings be completed in acts of reception and re-articulation. And although one could suggest that Negus's intention of focusing on the song's vagueness works against his own argument about the universality of the need for audience completion – perhaps something by Ani DeFranco or Rage Against the Machine would have demonstrated the point better – the illustration forms a good basis for possible classroom discussion, given the cultural familiarity and resonance of the example. A prolonged consideration of Nazi music policies alongside some of the resistance they met serves to demonstrate both the power of music to become a rallying point and also how even the most oppressive of state forms can sometimes be made to manoeuvre against changing circumstances and audience preferences. A turn to more 'benevolent' state attempts to affect (normally national) music-cultural policy touches on issues of nationalism, media and state institutions and imagined communities. Such a discussion, though not new theoretically after the issues already conveyed throughout the book, is helpful as a means of connecting them to the critical corpus relating to the topic of local music scenes.

Like its predecessors, the 'Politics' chapter features a conclusion (pp. 219–24); and this one merits close examination, for it leads, perhaps surprisingly, into issues addressed by the two remaining volumes which form the basis of the present article. Throughout the book, Negus adopts what one might deem a mild political economy stance, which is to say that he emphasises some degree of institutional control and domination, against more properly postmodern validations of audience 'resistance' and re-articulation (the latter a position represented by, for example, Iain Chambers or John Fiske). His earlier endorsement of David Morley makes this general orientation plain, I believe, while more specific observations such as the repudiation of the belief that 'lyrics can have *any* meaning or that the intentions of the author play no part in shaping how a song is understood' (p. 194) consistently reinforce it.[4] Such a viewpoint is undoubtedly salutary, and although Negus also gives credit to the optimistic focus of postmodern cultural studies, his various arguments clearly entertain the possibility of formulating truly critical studies of domination and the force of capital. But equally encouraging (if surprising) is the fact that his conclusion also lends at least some tangential support to the study of music poetics. To this end, he draws on Lawrence Grossberg's assertion (Grossberg 1992) that music works its effects 'at the intersection of the body and emotions' (p. 220); and while such terms may be too vague to be of much help, he supplements them with his own view that 'while music is not a "universal language", the meanings of musical sound are not *that* "indecipherable"' (p. 221; emphasis as original). Admittedly, such a conviction is explicitly distinguished from sheer aesthetic appreciation (p. 222). Nevertheless, in respect of the political significance of the 'everyday world of music making' (p. 220), he deliberately holds out the worlds of musical sound as an unjustly neglected problematic for popular music studies.

If Negus's closing statements gesture towards the exploration of sonic structure as a site of negotiated meaning, then Allan Moore's *The Beatles: Sgt. Pepper's Lonely Hearts Club Band* appears to press resolutely ahead with such a mission by reinserting the album firmly into the disciplinary world of musicology, as a *work* of art. The first two chapters, respectively entitled 'Inheritance' and 'Preparation', present as fine a synopsis of the environment in Britain (and particularly Liverpool) as could be stuffed into the handbook format, aptly summarising research on social conditions, political situations, musical scenes and other aspects salient to the emergence of *Sgt. Pepper*. Moore's discussion of the emergence of the idea of the 'teenager' (pp. 4–7) provides important intersections both with studies of youth culture (for example, Tracey Skelton and Gill Valentine (1998)) and debates about sub-cultural theory (though Moore does not explicitly discuss the latter). His pinpointing of the importation of black music, while not mentioning major-label 'race records', at least insures that the important story will be told. The second chapter narrows the focus to the Beatles themselves, avoiding rehashing the well-known trajectory of their careers and beginning with a focus on the stylistic background of the Lennon/McCartney collaboration, the specificity of Liverpool and the early Beatles' participation in the development of rock 'n' roll in Britain. If the word 'development' seems to imply the historical paradigm of musical materials, and thus the aesthetic closure forsworn by Shuker and Negus, then such an impression is perhaps correct; even so, Moore's discussion relates the musical development to social situations in such a way as to deflect any criticism that his is 'merely' a teleological climb to *Sgt. Pepper*. On the contrary, the historicity of musical development is never in question in this chapter, and only an unthinkingly ascetic approach would expect to contradict his well-informed narrative.

At times, Moore ventures observations for which the reader will wish he had more room for explanation, such as where he asserts that the early to mid-sixties 'completed the change in capitalist emphasis from commodity production to the commercial and service sectors, expanding the working-class market for music of the 1950s into a middle-class youth market in the 1960s' (p. 11). Some kind of statistical or sociological support would have helped here, but Moore provides none. Hence, although such a compressed judgement may reasonably be attributed to the handbook format, the problematic he introduces is far too profound to merit such a lone statement. Regardless of this and other similar moments, Moore's discussion of the social environment of early rock in Britain remains clear, authoritative and admirable: the invention of youth culture, 'Swinging London', the mod and rocker battles, psychedelia and the specific bands implicated in these various terms are covered with a sweep and efficiency that renders the chapter suitable as a brief, generalised introduction to early rock in Britain.

In several passages – perhaps targeted specifically at musicologists – Moore examines the ways in which the Beatles might be said to cross the high/low cultural divide, as when he relates them to the tradition of musical expressionism established during the past century. In addition, Moore shows himself eminently capable of straddling the more localised historiographical lines that are seemingly intrinsic to the notion of a handbook. At one point, for example, he describes the relationship between the Beatles and the Rolling Stones as having become representative of the split between pop and rock, (pp. 14–15); detailing the dichotomy, he also underlines its discursive situatedness, citing Simon Reynolds and Joy Press's critique of the relevant gender context (Reynolds and Press 1995) prior to mapping the two musical groups onto its terms. The latter half of the second chapter is devoted to a traditional history of style in the development of mid-sixties rock, with particular emphasis being placed on the music associated with the 'mods', the Kinks, the Who and the Small Faces. Riffs replacing chord sequences, the focus on a vocalist and rhythm guitar, the adoption of various vocal styles and mixolydian harmonies are among the strands allowed to coexist in this narrative, and like any first-class scholar (including Negus), Moore is capable of convincing the reader that his approach is not only reasonable, but also crucial to comprehending the topic. The emergence of rock from pop as ground from figure is thus established, and Moore closes the chapter by returning to the development of radio, re-embedding what could have been too narrowly focused a discussion of style in the development of institutions. On the whole, the first two chapters afford a well-argued setting for *Sgt. Pepper*; and if Moore's own vision sometimes seems to burst out of the bounds of the book's modest format, frustrating the reader who needs a fuller discussion, then such is a small price to pay for the indication that, indeed, there *is* so much more to the story that one would hope he will tell elsewhere.

The third chapter, 'Inception', forms something of a transition between the historical background and the music analysis to come. In the course of relating the details behind the album's inception, Moore is committed to stressing the contingency and collective nature of the undertaking. In particular, he underlines a belief that the songwriter's concern while writing is neither to know what the song is about, nor to recount a narrative or relate a message, but merely to work. Indeed, for Moore, it 'is a mistake to attempt to find a definitive message hidden within every set of lyrics'; instead, what 'was always of primary importance was the way it sounded' (pp. 22–3). In this way, the conceptual grounding is clarified for the next section of the book: *Sgt. Pepper* should be allowed to register semantic ambiguity and over-determination, while the priority of sonic structure in turn centralises the problematic condition of music analysis. Such priorities and their supporting discourses are familiar from a good deal of musicological interpretation (for instance, in relation to the nineteenth-century Lied) and in that sense, *Sgt. Pepper's Lonely Hearts Club Band* is allowed to enter the canon in the strictest (and most Foucauldian) sense, not just as a collection of valorised 'texts', but also and at least as importantly, as a set of procedures for elaborating them.

A formalist approach is subsequently allowed to predominate throughout the fourth chapter which, in its single-minded focus on the songs, forms the heart of the book (and at thirty-two pages is by far the longest segment). Clearly aware of recent critiques pertaining to the practice of analytical close reading in popular music studies, Moore provides justification for proceeding with a structural interpretation on two counts: firstly, while granting that there may be visceral pleasures that transcend our reactions to formal design, he posits that they 'are not the only ones, nor are they ultimately the most significant' (p. 26); secondly, while granting that meanings are socially constructed by listeners, he maintains that a rigorous accounting of the *range* of possible meanings must be the object of any examination of the text. Comparison of Moore's arguments with, say, Negus's would not be altogether fair given the limitations of the handbook format; in any case, their attitudes are far from mutually exclusive. Moore also stipulates that, despite his Schenkerian-inspired graphic notation, he is not producing Schenker analyses *tout court*, specifically following Allen Forte's refusal (Forte 1995) to specify an *Ursatz* if appropriate. On a purely formal level, therefore, the author is evidently alert to the theoretical modifications entailed by his application of voice-leading principles. However, certain idiosyncracies are worth noting, such as the graph of 'Lucy in the Sky With Diamonds' (p. 31) in which bass progressions are taken to move in leaps of a fourth (for instance in the sequence e–B–F♯–B–e). Consequently, while one might well argue a loosening of the rules for rock, the question still arises as to what then remains of the orthodox notion that would justify retention of its standard notation. Similarly, the mention of a 'background' (p. 43), or suggestion that a melodic development depends on harmonic support to come into being (p. 38), might give rise to suspicion that Schenkerian-derived symbols almost inevitably bring with them Schenkerian assumptions.

Each of the songs on the album receives an average of two to three pages commentary by these interpretative means with the (perhaps interesting) exceptions of 'Within You Without You' and 'Sgt. Pepper's Lonely Hearts Club Band (reprise)'. A few additional qualifications should thus be noted in respect of Moore's analyses. They are intentionally less than comprehensive, often centring on semantic issues raised in a given song in relation to underlying harmonic features (for instance, in 'She's Leaving Home); the attainment of certain structurally important pitches (for example, in 'With a Little Help From My Friends'); aspects of texture and instrumentation (for instance, in 'Lucy in the Sky with Diamonds'); or rhythmic/metrical processes (for example, in 'Lovely Rita'). Usually, more than one of these parameters is brought to the reader's attention, with the priority determined *ad hoc* by the defining characteristics of the song. Moore also signals the importance of the recording as 'text' by picking up at certain key points on its stereo effect and the spatial placement of various sound sources (for example, the 'idiosyncratic' placement of voices in the title song (p. 28), or Lennon's positioning to the right in 'Being for the Benefit of Mr. Kite'). While such details might sometimes seem fortuitous, their implications can be crucial in helping to determine the unique nature of specific sound images for the album as a whole. In this, as in his readings of harmonic progressions and salient scale degrees, Moore proves enviably adept at illustrating the Beatles' compositional methods (sometimes personified as Lennon, McCartney, Harrison or George Martin); moreover, his broader arguments in favour of the complexity, subtlety and ingeniousness of the music rarely fail to impress. That said, if a song such as 'A Day in the Life' seems to inspire a more far-ranging and multifaceted treatment, then a number of others (for example 'Within You Without You') seem disadvantaged by the imposition of an implicit evaluative hierarchy. All the same, the breadth of his familiarity with each song is clear, and his discussion of more recent scholarship (especially that of Middleton) affords the reader a view of the conceptual field against which his own analyses emerge as eloquent figures.

On another note, the reader might wish that Moore had made more use of the earlier versions of certain songs released on the Beatles *Anthology*, Vol. 2 (The Beatles 1996). While these elicit occasional mention throughout the text, several of them give the kind of insight into working methods which is otherwise one of the author's more conspicuous concerns. Such sticking points, however, do not greatly diminish the value of his analytical efforts, which aim more at sensitive exegeses of the songs in question than at any grand theory of rock music. As one of the more eminent music analysts of rock, he displays consistent assurance in alighting on the processes he considers important for each song, and the indefinite status of certain voice-leading concepts does not substantially hinder the arguments which he supports from several levels simultaneously. What is more, there are several moments in the discussion where the reader will most likely regret that Moore was prevented from elaborating his thoughts at greater length. For instance, his suggestion of a gradual freeing of 'English popular music ... from its blues roots' (p. 82) – of which 'Penny Lane' would be emblematic – along with a proposed critical reorientation of 'Within You Without You' from the post-Thatcher perspective, are both highly intriguing. But, most provocatively, Moore chooses to end this phase of the commentary by underlining (to some extent via Middleton's notion of 'undercoding') the eventual indeterminacy of interpretation, or at least its pliability. While this gesture puts into question – to some extent – the structural analyses that precede it, it nevertheless succeeds in opening the field of inquiry to approaches drawn from the field of communications (for instance, audience studies and multiple articulations) that readers from the social sciences might be craving by this point. While Moore himself does not explicitly address this prospect, he is still thereby able to ensure that the book is capable of extending into future dialogues and scholarly interventions, which might in turn be approaching musicology from some rather more distant disciplinary location.

The final two chapters, 'Reception' and 'Legacy', re-embed the album historically, beginning with a reflection from the author as to how it is that *Sgt. Pepper* has been widely received as not the Beatles' 'best album musically . . . [but] culturally crucial' (p. 60). Such a dichotomy, of course, can easily be inserted in the symptomology of music analysis itself, both internally in respect of the issues of aesthetics and validation it inevitably embodies, and externally through the tensions it encounters with regard to socio-political concerns. One can gain a sure sense of Moore's outlook from his pronouncement that some of the standpoints adopted for *Sgt. Pepper* are simply 'not innocent' (p. 61) on ideological grounds (including David Harker's important contention (Harker 1980) that the album marked a transition to more private modes of listening). Moore helpfully outlines the contentious issues in the album's reception, such as its marking of a certain cultural legitimisation of popular music, its self-conscious sophistication (taken both positively and negatively, of course) and the purported musical unity of the album. On this last issue, Moore again wisely makes recourse to Middleton's notion of undercoding, translating it backwards into the aesthetic register in the form of various approving remarks on the album's 'richness'' (p. 65). Apparently as a means of reinforcing this judgement, he treats the reader to a fascinating critical survey of covers of the songs from the album, albeit one from which the 1978 film and soundtrack (Various Artists 1978) constitutes a conspicuous absence.[5]

Tracing *Sgt. Pepper*'s legacy in the 'concept' album, rock opera and 'progressive' rock of the 1970s (not to mention the well-known narrative of the punk reaction), Moore proposes the historiography of a 'dialectic' (presumably in a non-Marxist sense) of 'successive turns of sophistication and simplification' (p. 75). His criteria for both terms are not always clear, however, and the reader might wonder about other parameters (such as the rhythmic/timbral sophistication of funk or rap) that Moore might be leaving aside. Still, the idea does connect with quite a few other rock histories, and it is not difficult to see some value in the narrative as a means of situating *Sgt. Pepper*. Issues of authorship also arise, with Moore casting a sceptical eye towards the notion of the music as 'expression'. Preferring to analyse the historical determinations of the album's styles and themes, he takes the discussion full circle from the first two chapters in noting changes in audience from the working classes to the university and the bourgeoisie. The discussion is brought to a close by reviving the question of legitimisation, against which the album is felt to represent a 'failed striving' (p. 81). Moore nevertheless ends the book, perhaps tellingly, by reinserting *Sgt. Pepper* into the history of art music, suggesting some affinity (although in what sense is unclear) with the song cycle or even what Jonathan Dunsby (1983) has called the 'multi-piece'. In each case, questions of structural unity and art-historical lineage seem at least partly to have been prompted on text-generic grounds, such matters doubtless being thought relevant to the broader concerns of the target readership.

The paths that most obviously connect Moore's study to the collection edited by John Covach and Graeme Boone would appear to lie in two main directions: via close reading on the one hand, and questions of repertoire and canon formation on the other. The latter offers perhaps a more fruitful route, if for no other reason than because canon formation (itself not always a revelatory phenomenon, despite the quantity of ink spilled in studies of art music) can be deeply symptomatic of music-theoretical approaches to popular music. Joining this observation is an equally remarkable phenomenon, namely the small but dedicated and vocal group of (mainly American) music theorists such as Kevin Holm-Hudson and John Covach who have, in recent years, taken a scholarly shine to so-called 'progressive rock' of the late 1960s through to (approximately) the early 1980s.

Thus, in the Covach/Boone collection, Covach himself and Daniel Harrison fill in historical slots surrounding *Sgt. Pepper*, Covach with an examination of Yes's 'Close to the Edge' (Yes 1972) and Harrison with a survey of some aspects of the Beach Boys' production until around 1970 (in which, of course, *Pet Sounds* (The Beach Boys 1966) forms a legendary contribution to the formation of 'progressive rock'). Covach's essay argues the intriguing point that much progressive rock might incorporate not just 'surface' references to art music, but also some deeper interaction, sharing 'structural features and compositional practices with Western art music of the eighteenth and nineteenth centuries' (p. 9). Through a reading of 'Close to the Edge', he posits the view that even a composition which eschews any explicit reference to art music may still unfold 'a large-scale formal design reinforced by tonal, thematic, and rhythmic return and development' (p. 22). The musical examples are clear and resourcefully deployed, showing that the 'deeper interaction' with art music turns out, in this instance, to be based principally on motivic integrity (which is probably as good a criterion as any). The patient reader will find here an analytical means of modelling some of those gargantuan 1970s progressive rock poems (so to speak), whose terrible critical reputation could perhaps even lend a bit of 'bad-boy' pleasure to rehabilitative work (much as, in more mainstream popular music studies, some of the previously scorned 'pop' and disco repertoires of a slightly later period are being redeployed as sites of audience pleasure and engagement). The essay is only slightly skewed by an extended engagement with Hermann Hesse's *Siddhartha*, whose relevance the author argues for only on the grounds of its appearing to foreground themes similar to those of 'Close to the Edge' (a correspondence nonetheless given greater credence, though Covach overlooks the fact, by the cultural prominence of the novel at the time of the album's composition and recording). Those willing to confess (as I am) a former infatuation with and continuing interest in 'progressive rock' from this decade may find the essay thus still falls short of scholarly expectation, but this early publication in what may become a sub-specialty of rock music theory has to be regarded as intriguing.

Daniel Harrison's contribution may edge towards a similar canonical location but is ultimately more of a tragic history, the story of an artistically gifted Brian Wilson whom circumstances and (especially) commercial pressures conspired to wrestle into personal and professional submission. Harrison traces the waxing and waning of artistically innovative and ambitious work from its seeds in early Beach Boys efforts, through its apex in 'California Girls', 'God Only Knows', 'Good Vibrations', 'Wonderful' and 'Let the Wind Blow'. The last two also form part of a narrative of decline, in which *Smiley Smile* (The Beach Boys 1967a), *Wild Honey* (The Beach Boys 1967b), *Friends* (The Beach Boys 1968) and (especially) *Sunflower* (The Beach Boys 1970) marked less, and less ambitious, participation by Wilson. One of the more distinguished theorists of common-practice harmony, Harrison deploys his expertise to impressive effect in arguing for the harmonic and formal innovation of Wilson's classic compositions; and his more detailed discussions of individual songs manifest exemplary judgement in explicating features that are both palpable and subtle. Although he may be missing some social determinations when he suggests that a number of Wilson's aspirations retreated because 'few understand how to listen' to his songs (p. 53), Harrison nevertheless presents an impressive argument in support of the belief that listening to them in the ways he indicates indeed promises significant benefits.

Walter Everett's essay, 'Swallowed by a Song: Paul Simon's Crisis of Chromaticism', offers a similar story of compositional ambition and commercial frustration, significantly extending the historical parameters in question to the mid-1970s and early-1980s through a body of work less closely associated with the 'progressive' rock tradition. Everett's presence in the collection must itself be taken as significant, as he is one of the few theorists to have been analysing popular music long before it became at all fashionable (especially in his pioneering work on the Beatles). Schenkerian analysis is the order of the day here, as in his other work; and, in Everett's favour, a reasonable case could probably be made that in the music at hand (such as *Still Crazy After All These Years* (Paul Simon 1975) and *One Trick Pony* (Paul Simon 1980)) some conception of levels of chromaticism and diatonicism does indeed appear to be salient for a reasonable number of listeners (not to mention Simon himself). Less convincing, however, is Everett's additional supposition that Simon's turn to 'world music' represented a shift away from compositional complexity 'that required more inquisitive ears' to 'simpler' – in other words more diatonic – material (p. 117). Such a one-dimensional equation of chromaticism with difficulty and diatonicism with accessibility – particularly when conjoined with a lament that the latter represents a retreat from artistic ambition – appears to expose a number of uncritical assumptions on Everett's part. The same could be said of his decision to quote Paul Simon's comment praising Jamaican musicians on the grounds that 'They're not sophisticated and they're not phonies' (p. 117) in the midst of the main aesthetic argument; the racialisation of the issue is clearly not intentional on either Simon's or Everett's behalf, but especially in an era in which 'world music' enjoys an ever higher profile, the lesson might be inferred that what start out as methodological issues are never far from broader questions of social significance.

If Covach, Harrison and Everett concern themselves, to some extent, with the perennial tensions which are felt to exist between creativity and commerce, then the remaining essays take a more relaxed attitude to the products of the music industry. Graeme Boone's 'Tonal and Expressive Ambiguity in "Dark Star"' offers an extended consideration of design in the Grateful Dead's music, no easy project with compositions whose improvisational and free-flowing quality could well frustrate many a committed close reader. Positing a quasi-phenomenological quality of 'virtuality' (p. 202) to describe the group's unpredictable musical gestures (without, however, negating a certain organisational integrity), Boone offers his own free-form and flexible approach, carefully examining a particular recording of 'Dark Star' for tonal structure, rhythmic ambiguity and syntactic articulation. The final gesture of the essay, the only point in the entire collection that manifests an awareness of ethnomusicological issues or procedures, quotes a response from the band to an earlier draft of the author's analysis. On this count their blithe dismissal of the text (which less sympathetic readers will probably apply to the collection as a whole) as etic and uncomprehending, seems paradoxically to enhance the essay's enigmatic quality as a rare musico-poetic engagement with a difficult and understudied area of popular music.

A similar strength might be invoked concerning Dave Headlam's 'Blues Transformations in the Music of Cream', which maps the paths of various individual songs and musical style in general across the work of several blues artists and on into the work of the group. Headlam offers some engaging observations which, however, are difficult to generalise: on the one hand, in 'Crossroads', riffs are held to be isolated and concentrated within 'a simplified and regularised harmonic framework', while in 'Rollin' and Tumblin'', on the other hand, 'the Cream version actually takes the rhythmic implications of [Muddy Waters's] syncopated riff to a new level of complexity' (p. 79). Yet, in his conclusion, Headlam advances the rather sweeping view that Cream's music in general does tend to 'even out' aspects of both rhythm and form (p. 87). As inconclusive as his discussion may therefore appear, Headlam nevertheless succeeds in raising a range of issues important to those interested in blues/rock analysis, not least the virtue of proposing normative formal length and the enduring need to develop more 'systematic yet manageable' ways of describing sound.

Matthew Brown's '"Little Wing": a Study in Musical Cognition' and Lori Burns's '"Joanie" Get Angry: k. d. lang's Feminist Revision' both veer somewhat from the collection's more appreciation-oriented approach to attempt broader functions for analysing the musical poetics of rock. Brown takes Hendrix's classic recording as an occasion for mapping cognitive theories about a 'problem space' (p. 161) in which Hendrix, as a composer, must take 'some kernel of musical material' – in this case, pentatonic melodic figures – and expand it 'to create a coherent tonal work' (p. 157). Just what 'coherent' would mean in such a context is purportedly resolved by equating the point with harmonic logic and asserting that 'blues pieces essentially conform to the principles of common-practice tonality' (p. 161). Such an unargued assertion puts Brown squarely behind the eight ball, from which he never quite emerges, as the remainder of the essay is devoted to a fairly standard analysis of voice-leading and motivic levels in the song. Just how the graph and associated discussion demonstrate anything about musical cognition is not clear, as it is mainly about a scenario so generalised (namely, a starting-point and a structured environment in which to achieve a certain goal) as to be barely comparable with the more systematic work of Diana Deutsch and others, whose notion of science involves far fewer unestablished and far-reaching claims. Brown's essay can nevertheless be read as an interesting attempt to associate melodic motive in blues/rock with voice-leading levels, and the cognitive claims are easily enough set aside.

By comparison, Lori Burns's essay refers specifically to a lang cover of Joanie Sommer's 'Johnny Get Angry' of 1962 in which, Burns contends, lang 'problematises "the issue of violence against women" ' (p. 93). Instead of doing so by presenting a strong counter-figure to the thoroughly dominated and patriarchally minded figure of the earlier version, however, lang is seen here as dramatising and foregrounding the weakness of the female persona. While such an exercise in defamiliarisation may not go unrecognised by many readers, some informed feminists will surely take exception to Burn's conclusion that lang is asking 'what is the woman's role in the cycle of abuse'?, a question apparently to be answered by the suggestion 'that the woman is partly responsible for this social interaction' (pp. 110–11). The course of argument, however, is perhaps more interesting than the point of destination, and Burns offers some imaginative observations concerning voice-leading and, especially, harmonic alterations from one version to the other. Certainly, in a song so laden with (literally) violent gender politics and covered by such a prominent figure in that same political sphere, the musical recasting could hardly be free of gendered discourse, unless one would wish to maintain the improbable position that musical poetics simply is not (or cannot be) gendered at all. A more promising solution might, for example, have been to untangle the various harmonic and voice-leading revisions from questions of historical style, perhaps even considering the possibility that the process of rationalisation must then be re-problematised, since history itself may be gendered in significant ways. There lies a significant project in Burns's conception, whose imperfect realisation nevertheless suggests that some valuable work may yet be realised in the future.

Overall, the Covach/Boone collection assumes its place in the midst of an odd quandary. In one respect, it is likely that the majority of popular music scholars will simply find it irrelevant and mystifying, concentrating as it does on musical poetics regardless of any overriding social connection. Such an objection is, of course, not damning among many who associate themselves with the discipline of music theory, and who may well agree with Headlam's apologetics for rock-music analysis (by far the most extended and interesting in the book). Headlam shows more awareness than some of the contributors of the profoundly poor reputation of music analysis in popular music studies, and his concluding remarks offer far more substance than the introduction's testier attempt to portray those who question music analysts as unreasoning extremists. Yet Headlam's position on the poetics of popular music shifts within his essay in ways that may be taken as symptomatic. Initially, his framework would seem to validate musical poetics for their demonstrable social significance: his opening observations, in fact, assert that 'in view of the reception of rock music by audiences who knew little of its background or context but responded primarily to the music itself – the rhythm, volume, and timbres – it is clear that these features deserve serious consideration' (p. 59). Headlam here establishes an important point, though it surely invites some modification if it is to satisfy the sort of proper historicising treatment that he seems to outline. For example, however little background audiences may have known, there were (and are) certainly *discourses* (including 'racial' ones), if not any 'real' context of rhythm and volume in pervasive circulation; thus, the notion of a 'music itself', whose essential properties simply imprinted themselves on the listeners as a stamp in so much soft wax, is inconsistent with what popular music scholars can observe in both historical documents and, for that matter, in the world around them.

Yet this is not to swerve into the idealist stance that the music has *no* poetic design whatsoever; on the contrary, it is precisely the insertion of musical poetics into the world of discourse which is so difficult to accomplish, but which holds (including in this account by Headlam) the promise of formulating a compelling mode of popular music analysis. Headlam's actual analyses of Cream's music, in themselves quite good, do not deliver on his important introductory remarks, preferring to focus instead on purely intrinsic aspects of the music without engendering any particular arguments about their discursive salience. By the end of the essay, however, the grounds for mapping musical poetics have shifted dramatically as the author attempts to account for the conviction that there 'is only a small body of analytical writings on rock music worthy of the name' (p. 86). Yet, far from establishing a reasoned conclusion, his eventual assertion is simply that 'preliminary work has led me to a far deeper appreciation and understanding of both the source songs and Cream's transformed versions. In the end, this is my only truly defensible justification for advocating a greater role for musical analysis in the study of rock music' (p. 88). The more open-minded and interdisciplinary popular music scholars who might read this essay are bound to be disappointed by such a subjectively imposed resolution, and particularly in view of the promising nature of Headlam's project. The irony that possibly the most mystified argument is here presented as a bottom line ought to be an occasion for a thoroughgoing evaluation of the perceived need for disciplinary closure in any comparable context.[6]

A wholesale reflection of this kind could in fact succeed in generalising Headlam's apparent dilemma while at the same time furnishing a valuable perspective on all of the books discussed here. In short, the journey from Shuker – for whom the 'musicological' is virtually precluded, and in whose otherwise excellent effort the musico-poetic still stands as an outside and silent critique – to Covach/Boone – in whose contributions the musico-poetic becomes the occasion for disciplinary crowding-out of the worlds of discourse and society, despite sincere intention – can at least serve as an accurate representation of the severely fractured world of popular music studies as a whole. The rigid divisions into studies of the intrinsic and extrinsic are mitigated, to some extent, by Negus's surprising final placement of his problematic in the apparent vicinity of musical poetics (albeit a vast distance from the variety we would associate with traditional 'music theory'), not to mention Allan Moore's more eclectic mixture of appreciation and historical figuration. But the fact that the traditional boundaries taken to separate musical poetics from the world of the 'social' still seem to be recognisably in place for each of these authors cannot but dismay those for whom the critical blindspot central to either principal point of view forms an inevitably disabling consequence. Hence, while either standpoint is capable of bringing forth indispensible moments of truth, each also appears to obscure the other to the disadvantage of both. After all, the belief that the poetics of the music carries no social force is no less absurd than the notion that the music can be assessed (or 'appreciated') if divorced from the mediating effects of history and social life. A moment of true mutual recognition still lies in the future: the importance of musical poetics is generally acknowledged by scholars from (for example) communications and cultural theory, albeit often more by lip service than through serious engagement; while in most music theory (as in Covach and Boone's volume), more lip service towards cultural and social theory would be welcome. That said, a more appropriately sympathetic view might wish to emphasise the point that musical poetics (and, by extension, the field of music theory) is typically placed in a defensive posture by the generally poor reputation of music analysis within popular music studies.

The question then becomes whether it is more effective (not to mention intellectually respectable) for music theorists to cling to older models of music value, for which arguments, in the wake of both postmodern and Marxist critiques, seem increasingly threadbare;[7] or whether a far more involved but also more positive argument could be mustered for a musical poetics that would follow up on Headlam's initial intention to address the understudied entry of musical design into the world of social life (and, of course, its continual re-emergence). As long as music analysis maintains a negative outlook towards the changing (and ineluctably social) world around it, music theorists surely have no right to complain about our marginalisation. The current generation in the discipline is certainly suffering from a longstanding neglect of critical and cultural theory, but such cannot serve as an excuse for rejecting relevant critiques of (popular) music analysis; popular music studies is an elaborated field into which we now step as late-comers, and it is encumbent on us to learn the rules of that game. That is not to say that we cannot thereafter reaffirm the importance of music analysis – indeed, we can, and we should. But it should be an informed affirmation, not a blinkered activity in which we simply reinforce the intrinsic/extrinsic split that continues to blight popular music studies. Above all, music theorists need not assume that 'music theory' simply means the designation of models of pitch, rhythm or timbre; rather the term may also be invoked in order to reflect in a more broadly informed way about music. Even the embracing of 'cognitive science', whatever its ultimate defensibility, at least represents some progress by designating a situation for modelling musical poetics, other than simply closing one's eyes and purring about musical 'sophistication'.

All of the volumes reviewed here offer unquestionable value: Shuker provides a uniquely useful reference for (at least) recent Anglo-American pop music; Negus presents the best general theoretical introduction to the field;

Moore furnishes an evocative and eclectic model of rock musicology; and the Covach/Boone volume suggests some ways in which a largely unexamined repertoire might be fruitfully explored. But taken together as a symptomatic formation of popular music studies, these books suggest that the historical legacy of the intrinsic/extrinsic split – perhaps the most uniquely intransigent problem in the field of music studies – awaits the time when a proper demystification of musical design could bring about 'music theory' in the sense of, quite simply, theorising about music.

NOTES

1. Roy Shuker, *Key Concepts in Popular Music* (London: Routledge, 1998). xxiv + 365 pp. £12.99. ISBN 0-415-16104-5 (pb); Keith Negus, *Popular Music in Theory* (Cambridge: Polity, 1996). 243 pp. £15.99. ISBN 0-7456-1318-7 (pb); Allan F. Moore, *The Beatles: Sgt. Pepper's Lonely Hearts Club Band* (Cambridge: Cambridge University Press, 1997). xi + 98 pp. £10.99. ISBN 0-521-57484-6 (pb); John Covach and Graeme Boone, *Understanding Rock* (New York and Oxford: Oxford University Press, 1997). xiii + 219 pp. £15.50. ISBN 0-19-510005-0 (pb).

2. For more extensive examination of Adorno as an iconic Marxist figure within the sphere of music studies, see Henry Klumpenhouwer, 'Late Capitalism, Late Marxism and the Study of Music', *Music Analysis*, 20/iii (2001), pp. 367–405. See also Adam Krims, 'Marxist Music Analysis Without Adorno: Popular Music and Urban Geography', in Allan F. Moore (ed.), *Analyzing Popular Music* (Cambridge: Cambridge University Press, 2003), pp. 131–57.

3. I argue for a more comprehensive definition of 'music theory' in *Music/Ideology: Resisting the Aesthetic* (New York: Gordon and Breach, 1998), advocating that its narrower sense might be redesignated 'music poetics' (p. 7). A more elaborate discussion of this proposal appears in Chapter 1 of Krims, *Rap Music and the Poetics of Identity* (Cambridge: Cambridge University Press, 2000), where the latter term is taken to refer to the attempt to model any contextually salient aspect of musical sound.

4. If Negus's invocation of authorial control smacks too much of an individualising dead-end, then one can easily substitute terms such as institutional control, dominant discourse and so on.

5. Only some of the songs from the film/album were covers from *Sgt. Pepper*. However, Moore does survey covers of individual songs in other cases, and the attempt to resuscitate the album's story, whatever its commercial fortunes, would seem to merit at least some discussion.

6. In referring to closure in this sense, I have in mind the seemingly inexorable force that tends to press even the most well-meaning music analyst towards closing out the social world in the course of attempting a mapping of musical poetics. Headlam's reversal would appear to represent a clear case of this impulse at work.

7. The most enlightened Marxist approaches, in fact, are arguably of greatest benefit to music theorists, avoiding as they do the outright dismissal of musical poetics that sometimes mars more avowedly postmodern approaches. Henry Klumpenhouwer's 'Poststructuralism and Issues of Music Theory', in Krims (ed.), *Music/Ideology: Resisting the Aesthetic*, pp. 289–310, is helpful in this regard.

REFERENCES

Boyd-Barrett, Oliver, 1977: 'Media Imperialism: Towards an International Framework for the Analysis of Media Systems', in James Curran, Michael Gurevitch, Janet Woollacott, John Marriott and Carrie Roberts (eds.), *Mass Communication and Society* (London: Edward Arnold).

Brackett, David, 1995: *Interpreting Popular Music* (Cambridge: Cambridge University Press).

Chambers, Iain, 1985: *Urban Rhythms, Pop Music and Popular Culture* (London: Macmillan).

_____, 1990: *Border Dialogues: Journeys in Postmodernity* (London: Routledge).

Chapple, Steve and Garofolo, Reebee, 1977: *Rock 'n' Roll is Here to Pay: the History and Politics of the Music Industry* (Chicago: Nelson-Hall).

Cohen, Sara, 1994: 'Identity, Place and the "Liverpool Sound"', in Martin Stokes (ed.), *Ethnicity, Identity, and Music* (Oxford: Berg).

Dunsby, Jonathan, 1983: 'The Multi-Piece in Brahms: *Fantasien*, Op. 116', in Robert Pascall (ed.), *Brahms: Biographical, Documentary and Analytical Studies* (Cambridge: Cambridge University Press).

Everett, Walter, 1999: *Expression in Pop-Rock Music: a Collection of Critical and Analytical Essays* (New York: Garland).

Farley, Christopher, 1999: 'Hip-Hop Nation', *Time*, 153/v, pp. 44–54.

Fiske, John, 1987: *Television Culture* (London: Routledge).

Forte, Allen, 1995: *The American Popular Ballad of the Golden Era, 1924–1950* (Princeton: Princeton University Press, 1995).

Frith, Simon, 1983: *Sound Effects: Youth, Leisure, and the Politics of Rock 'n' Roll* (London: Constable).

George, Nelson, 1988: *The Death of Rhythm and Blues* (New York: Pantheon).

Goodwin, Andrew, 1992: *Dancing in the Distraction Factory: Music Television and Popular Culture* (Minneapolis: University of Minnesota Press).

Grossberg, Lawrence, 1992: *We Gotta Get Out of This Place: Popular Conservatism and Postmodern Culture* (London: Routledge).

Guilbault, Jocelyn, 1993: 'On Redefining the "Local" Through World Music', *The World of Music*, 35/ii, pp. 33–47.

Hall, Stuart, 1974: 'A "Reading" of Marx's 1857 Introduction to the Grundrisse', unpublished paper.

_____, 1991: 'Old and New Identities: Old and New Ethnicities', in Anthony King (ed.), *Culture, Globalization and the World-System: Contemporary Conditions for the Representation of Identity* (London: Macmillan).

Harker, David, 1980: *One for the Money: Politics and Popular Song* (London: Hutchinson).

Hatch, David and Millward, Stephen, 1987: *From Blues to Rock: an Analytical History of Pop Music* (Manchester: Manchester University Press).

Holm-Hudson, Kevin (ed.) 2001: *Progressive Rock Reconstructed* (New York: Garland).

Jensen, Joli, 1992: 'Fandom as Pathology: the Consequences of Characterization', in Lisa Lewis (ed.), *The Adoring Audience: Fan Culture and Popular Media* (London: Routledge).

Lee, Stephen, 1995: 'Re-examining the Concept of the "Independent" Record Company: the Case of Wax Trax! Records', *Popular Music*, 14/i, pp. 13–32.

Leyshon, Andrew, Matless, David and Revill, George (eds.), 1998: *The Place of Music* (New York: Guilford Press).

Longhurst, Brian, 1995: *Popular Music and Society* (Cambridge: Polity Press).

MacDonald, Ian, 1994: *Revolution in Head: the Beatles' Music and the 1960s* (London: Fourth Estate).

Manuel, Peter, 1991: 'Salsa and the Music Industry: Corporate Control or Grassroots Expression?', in Peter Manuel (ed.), *Essays on Cuban Music* (Lanham, MD: University Press of America).

_____, 1993: *Cassette Culture: Popular Music and Technology in North India* (Chicago: University of Chicago Press).

Mele, Christopher, 1996: 'Globalization, Culture, and Neighborhood Change: Reinventing the Lower East Side of New York', *Urban Affairs Review*, 32/i, pp. 3–22.

Middleton, Richard, 1990: *Studying Popular Music* (Milton Keynes: Open University Press).

Moore, Allan, 1993: *Rock: the Primary Text* (Milton Keynes: Open University Press).

_____, 1995: 'The So-Called "Flattened Seventh" in Rock', *Popular Music*, 14, pp. 185–201.

Morley, David, 1993: 'Active Audience Theory: Pendulums and Pitfalls', *Journal of Communication*, 43/iv, pp. 13–19.

Potter, Russell, 1995: *Spectacular Vernaculars: Hip-Hop and the Politics of Postmodernism* (Albany: State University of New York Press).

Reynolds, Simon and Press, Joy, 1995: *The Sex Revolts: Gender, Rebellion, and Rock 'n' Roll* (Cambridge, MA: Harvard University Press).

Rose, Tricia, 1994: *Black Noise: Rap Music and Black Culture in Contemporary America* (Hanover, NH: University Press of New England).

Shuker, Roy, 1994: *Understanding Popular Music* (London: Routledge).

Skelton, Tracey and Valentine, Gill (eds.), 1998: *Cool Places: Geographies of Youth Cultures* (London: Routledge).

Spencer, Jon Michael (ed.), 1991: *The Emergency of Black and the Emergence of Rap* (Durham, NC: Duke University Press).

Swiss, Thomas, Sloop, John and Herman, Andrew (eds.), 1998: *Mapping the Beat: Popular Music and Contemporary Theory* (Malden, MA: Blackwell).

Taylor, Timothy, 1997: *Global Pop: World Music, World Markets* (New York: Routledge).

Thornton, Sarah, 1996: *Club Cultures: Music, Media, and Subcultural Capital* (Hanover, NH: Wesleyan University Press).

Valentine, Gill, Skelton, Tracey and Chambers, Deborah, 1998: 'Cool Places: an Introduction to Youth and Youth Cultures', in Tracey Skelton and Gill Valentine (eds.)., *Cool Places: Geographies of Youth Cultures* (London: Routledge).

Van Der Merwe, Peter, 1989: *The Origins of Popular Style: the Antecedents of Twentieth-Century Popular Music* (Oxford: Oxford University Press).

Wallis, Roger and Malm, Krister, 1984: *Big Sounds from Small Peoples: the Music Industry in Small Countries* (New York: Pendragon).

Wicke, Peter, 1992: 'The Times They Are a-Changing: Rock Music and Political Change in East Germany', in Reebee Garofolo (ed.), *Rockin' the Boat: Mass Movements and Mass Music* (Boston, MA: South End Press).

DISCOGRAPHY

The Beach Boys, 1966: *Pet Sounds* (DCC GZS–1035).

_____, 1967a: *Smiley Smile* (Capitol ST–82891).

_____, 1967b: *Wild Honey* (Capitol T–2859).

_____, 1968: *Friends* (Capitol St–2895).

_____, 1970: *Sunflower* (Reprise RS–6382).

The Beatles, 1996: *Anthology*, Vol. 2 (Capitol 34448).

Paul Simon, 1975: *Still Crazy After All These Years* (CBS 33540).

_____, 1980: *One Trick Pony* (Warner Brothers 3472).

Joanie Sommers, 1962: *Johnny Get Angry* (Warner Brothers 1470).

Various Artists, 1978: *Sgt. Pepper's Lonely Hearts Club Band* (RSO 24100).

Yes, 1972: *Close to the Edge* (Atlantic 7244).

Music Theory

[12]

The Formation of a
Musical Style: Early Rock

RONALD BYRNSIDE

The term *style* is often used in discussions of music, as indeed it is used in discussions and assessments of many areas of life. In fact, we often use the term *life-style* to designate a particular mode and manner of existence. To attach the word style to a given phenomenon or set of phenomena is to suggest that it possesses something that is distinctive and individual to such an extent that it may be isolated from other generically similar phenomena. For example, in discussing footwear we can fairly easily separate the sneaker from the boot, the sandal, the thong, and several other types of shoes, on the basis of their distinctive qualities. In doing so we are consciously or unconsciously involved in one of the rudimentary procedures of style analysis.

As used in the arts, the term style refers to various levels, from the very general to the very particular. For instance, on a very general level one can refer to a Western style of music (as opposed to a non-Western style), or to a Renaissance style (as opposed to, say, a baroque style), or to an operatic style (as opposed to, say, a symphonic style). On a more particular level one may speak of a dixieland jazz style, as distinct from jazz style in general. On a still more particular level one can deal with the style of a given composer, or even a specific composition.

160   THE FORMATION OF A MUSICAL STYLE: EARLY ROCK

On any level the term style usually involves a description of the technical elements of the music. But a more complete assessment of a style takes into account certain things in the music that are not readily illustrated, verbally or graphically—certain aspects of performance, for instance, that are associated with, but not notated in, the music. A full assessment of a style also includes information and sometimes even speculation about the various relationships among the composer, the music, and its audience. A description of technical elements and performance idiosyncracies informs us about *what* is in a style; statements concerning the above-mentioned relationships attempt to inform us *why* the music is the way it is.

An analysis of a piece of music is useful to the extent that it instructs the reader about how the music is made and how it works, and provokes him to more deeply consider the music. But no stylistic analysis, however complete and sophisticated, can substitute for the music being analyzed; the analysis is not the same thing as "having" the piece. In trying to understand the uniqueness of a composition we must keep alive the distinction that exists between analysis and experience, but at the same time, be ready to accept stylistic analysis as something that can feed and broaden a musical experience.

In this chapter we will deal specifically with the formation and development of Rock 'n' Roll style, and also, more generally, with the formation of several other styles that have evolved in the course of Western music. We will be as concerned with the formative process of a style as we will with discovering and isolating its identifying characteristics.

Once formed, some musical styles remain relatively stable; that is, they do not continue to evolve. South Indian classical music, for example, has used the same body of basic melodies and rhythms, the same instruments and approaches to performance for more than two hundred years. Many generations of South Indians have performed this music over the years, and the only aspect of it that has changed has resulted from the differences among performers in improvisational skill and idiosyncrasy. Thus, there is an unmistakable and longstanding continuity to this musical style.

Some musics have undergone a change in style as a result of contact with the music of another culture. For example, the music of the Mbuti Pygmies of the Ituri forest in central Africa remained stylistically fixed for many generations, but early in the twentieth century this once completely isolated tribe made contact with other African tribes and with European explorers and settlers. As a result of these contacts the musical style of the Mbuti began to incorporate the sounds of certain instruments that had never previously been part of Mbuti music. There are numerous other examples of this kind of stylistic change.

The history of style in Western music is of a somewhat different pattern. Though some styles of Western music have remained stable for long periods of time, and though some styles have been transformed as a result of assimilating non-Western musical elements, the overriding tendency of Western music has been evolutionary. It seems a basic urge in Western man to change and reshape things, and this is reflected in the history of his music. For many centuries Western music has periodically involved itself in stylistic change. Some styles last longer than others, but whatever their longevity, they generally follow a pattern of formation, crystallization, and decay.

During its formative process a new style somehow detaches itself from its predecessor and, wittingly or unwittingly, emerges as a reaction to the older style. Ordinarily, this reaction to and breaking away from the older style is not clear-cut. In fact the new style usually borrows and/or adapts some element from the older style. After the formative process, the new style becomes crystallized and establishes itself, and its audience begins to recognize the boundaries of it. Finally, having been represented in a substantial body of compositions over a certain amount of time, the style becomes so familiar and certain things about it become so predictable that both composer and audience begin to lose interest. The entire process is then repeated, as another new style forms itself and breaks away from the decaying style.

Why Western man has chosen to create new musical styles for himself and why he has done it so consistently is a complicated and manifold question, to which only part of the answer can be found in the field of music. This is because music is a human activity, and the particular shape that a musical style assumes must be understood not only in the abstract, but in terms of the sociology of the composers of and the audience for that style.

There is a relationship between the human condition in a particular society and the artistic tastes of that society: political events and climates, and economic and sociological conditions shape the basic attitudes of a society, and these attitudes are, in turn, reflected in the arts. As the complexion of a society changes, different attitudes and tastes are formed. It sometimes happens that the basic attitudes of a given generation or age do not (and perhaps cannot) carry over to the next generation or age; many things, including a style of music, that were meaningful to the former, fail to be significant to the latter, which has developed its own attitudes based on its own experiences.

Perhaps unconsciously, or perhaps quite deliberately, new composers and a potentially new audience begin groping for ways to give musical shape and expression to newly emerging attitudes. This groping process is an integral part of, indeed, the first step in, the formation of a musical style.

Probably no one single factor prods a composer or group of composers to create a new style. It is by far more likely that a new style is formed for a combination of reasons and in response to a variety of needs. As a prelude to our investigation of the formation of rock 'n' roll style we will briefly discuss some other examples of musical styles in their formative stages. In

162   THE FORMATION OF A MUSICAL STYLE: EARLY ROCK

each case we will focus on only one aspect, one causal factor in the formation of the style, whether it be the rejection of an inherited style, the adoption of an alternative to an older style, or some other technological, aesthetic, or functional consideration. Eventually, as we examine the formation of rock 'n' roll style, we will take into account all of these factors.

A Style Formed in Response to New Musical-Aesthetic Needs

The formation of opera resulted in part from the desire to create a musical-dramatic kind of composition that simply could not be accommodated within the bounds of the inherited style. The *Camerata,* an early seventeenth-century group of Florentine noblemen, developed their musical style of opera in the shadows of the then prevalent Renaissance style of elaborate choral poly-phony. The desire of the *Camerata* composers and dramatists for a clear and affective presentation of drama through song led to the creation of a musical style that emphasized solo singing, virtually eradicated counterpoint, and treated harmony as an accompanimental, supportive force.

This new musical style was also an attempt to recreate the declamatory singing style in ancient Greek drama. Thus, while the *Camerata* style was new, it purported to be based on a very old model. Nevertheless, so many aspects of this style were so new and different from the late sixteenth-century style that composers, critics, and theorists found it appropriate to call the two styles by different names. The older style came to be known as the *prima prattica* ("first practice"), and the new style was called the *seconda prattica* ("second practice"). To some people, one of the implications inherent in this differentiation was that music written in the style of the *prima prattica* was appropriate for sacred purposes, but the *seconda prattica* was suitable only for secular purposes. The general notion that one style of music is acceptable for church use, while another is strictly secular, has persisted for several centuries and, with some exceptions, remains today.

However, jazz and rock, two traditionally secular musical styles, have, since the mid-1960s, been used in sacred contexts—the jazz mass and the rock service. This fact suggests some interesting questions that we will merely pose rather than attempt to answer here: Is there no longer a stylistic differ-ence between sacred and secular music? Was this distinction between the two styles originally based upon something concrete, or was it then, and has it been since, an artificial separation?

The separation of the *Camerata* style of music from other music was not, however, simply a matter of categorizing one as secular and the other as sacred; this new musical style was recognized as something new, above and beyond the question of its presumed secularity or its alledged non-sacredness.

In 1602 Giulio Caccini, a *Camerata* member, published some songs written in this new style, which bore the title *Le Nuove Musiche* ("the new music"). Jacopo Peri, another member of the group, recognizing that his music would strike most listeners as being different, and perhaps even strange, offered an apology for the new style, which begins:

> Before laying before you, gracious readers, these my compositions, I have thought it fitting to let you know what led me to seek out this new manner of music.[1]

The following recorded examples should make obvious some of the major differences between the older style and the new monodic style. In addition to gross differences in texture and harmony, one of the major differences, and indeed one of the dominant concerns of the *Camerata* composers, was in the setting of the text. The aim of the *Camerata* composer was that the text should be understood, and not cluttered up or lost in a web of several contrapuntal lines. It is suggested that the listener follow the texts in translation as he listens to the examples.

Examples in the new monodic style:

Giulio Caccini, "Dovrò dunque morire" from *Le Nuove Musiche. Masterpieces of Music Before 1750,* Vol. 2, No. 30, Haydn Society Records, HS 9039.

Claudio Monteverdi, excerpt from *Orfeo. History of Music in Sound,* Vol. 4, side 4, band 3, FCA Victor, LM 6029.

Giulio Caccini, *Pien D'Amoroso Affete and Amarilli. Masterpieces of the Italian Baroque,* The Bach Guild, BG 565, side 1, bands 1 and 3, respectively.

Examples in the older style:

Palestrina, "Sanctus," from Mass *Aeterna Christi munera.*

De Monte, "Benedictus" and "Agnus Dei," from Mass *Benedictus es.*

Lassus, "Benedictus" and "Hosanna" from Mass *Puisque j'ay perdu.*

(All of the above are found in *History of Music in Sound,* Vol. IV.)

Josquin Des Pres, "Sanctus," from Mass *L'homme armé. History of Music in Sound,* Vol. III, side 3, band 4, FCA Victor, LM 6016.

————, *Ave Maria. Masterpieces of Music Before 1750,* Vol. 1, No. 19.

During its formative stages a new musical style in the Western world almost always has its detractors as well as its practitioners and advocates. We are told by Pietro de Bardi, son of one of the founders of the *Camerata,* that this new singing style was at first "considered almost ridiculous." It is clear that the monodic style of the *Camerata* constituted a distinct reshaping of music. In Western man the strong urge to change and reshape is, ironically,

---

[1] Quoted with permission of W. W. Norton & Company, Inc., from *Source Readings in Music History,* p. 373ff, Compiled and Edited by Oliver Strunk. Copyright 1950 by W. W. Norton & Company, Inc.

balanced by a formidable resistance to change. This accounts for the condescension, skepticism, and derision to which every musical style is subjected during its formative process. Perhaps the audience for an established musical style initially views a new style as inimical not only to traditional musical and aesthetic values, but also to its entire system of values. Part of this attitude was expressed by G. M. Artusi in his essay, *The Imperfection of Modern Music* (1600):

> ...insofar as it [the new music] introduced new rules, new modes, and new turns of phrase, these were harsh and little pleasing to the ear, nor could they be otherwise; for so long as they violate the good rules—in part founded on experience, the mother of all things, in part observed in nature, and in part proved by demonstration—we must believe them deformations of the nature and propriety of true harmony, far removed from the object of music.... They [the composers] and their activities die together. By the general judgment of the wise and learned, ignorance, more than anything else, is considered the greatest of the many accidents which makes uncertain for every workman the road of good work.... Of ignorance, then, are born compositions of this sort, which, like monstrosities, pass through the hands of this man and that, and these men do not know themselves what the real nature of composition is. For them it is enough to create a tumult of sounds, a confusion of absurdities, an assemblage of imperfections, and all springs from that ignorance with which they are beclouded.[2]

The composers of the *Camerata* circle were interested first and foremost in the drama, and the personality of their musical style was shaped by this overriding interest. The texture, harmony, and form of this style were designed to serve and heighten the effect of the language of the drama. In the end, their reaction to and rejection of the old musical style stemmed from a knowledge that the old style could not accommodate the kind of drama-centered music they wanted to create.

A New Style Created by the Expansion of Elements from the Old Style

No less obvious a break with a stylistic tradition occurred near the beginning of the fourteenth century. In France and Italy some composers began to write a kind of music that was in some respects noticeably different from the general musical style of the thirteenth century—in fact, it was so different that some composers and other spokesmen referred to it as the *Ars Nova* (new art). In the same breath they referred to the thirteenth-century style

---

[2] Quoted with permission of W. W. Norton & Company, Inc., from *Source Readings in Music History*, pp. 393–404, Compiled and Edited by Oliver Strunk. Copyright 1950 by W. W. Norton & Company, Inc.

as the *Ars Antiqua* (old art). This conscious labeling of styles in terms of old versus new is one of a number of ways in which the formation of the *Ars Nova* style was similar to the formation of the seventeenth-century style just discussed.

The fourteenth century is often, and with good reason, referred to as an essentially secular age. Most of the *Ars Nova* composers of whom we have knowledge invested a considerable share of their energies in the production of secular music. This constituted a major shift, for, in earlier centuries, the church was the principal patron of music, and composers generally spent their time providing the church with music—obviously, sacred music. In a sense, then, beginning with the *Ars Nova* the church relinquished its role as the primary director of musical style.

We have already noted that one of the issues in the formation of the seventeenth-century monodic style was the question of its suitability (or lack thereof) for sacred purposes. That issue was directly anticipated as the music of the *Ars Nova* developed. In contradistinction to the *Camerata* composers, whose need to break with the established style grew out of dramatic rather than strictly musical concerns, the *Ars Nova* composers built from the style they inherited, altering and expanding the rhythmic and harmonic parameters of that style, and at the same time creating musical forms designed to serve secular rather than sacred functions.

We have seen that in their formative years new styles have their detractors; that was the case in the seventeenth century, and it was the case during the formation of the *Ars Nova* style in the early fourteenth century. The composers of this new style incurred the wrath of certain spokesmen for the older style. Notice how Jacob of Liége, the author of the statement below, implies that the new style affects not only musical but ethical values as well:

> Would that it pleased the modern singers that the ancient music and the ancient manner of singing were again brought into use! For, if I may say so, the old art seems more perfect, more rational, more seemly, freer, simpler, and plainer. Music was originally discreet, seemly, simple, masculine, and of good morals; have not the moderns rendered it lascivious beyond measure?[3]

Ultimately, *Ars Nova* style may be viewed as a expansion of certain technical features of the old style, a stretching of these features severe enough to render them unrecognizable in terms of the practices of the old style, and an organization of them consistent enough to justify referring to them as practices of a new style.

---

[3] Quoted with permission of W. W. Norton & Company, Inc., from *Source Readings in Music History,* p. 189, Compiled and Edited by Oliver Strunk. Copyright 1950 by W. W. Norton & Company, Inc.

166 THE FORMATION OF A MUSICAL STYLE: EARLY ROCK

A New Style Resulting from a
Rejection of the Inherited Style

Western art music experienced another major stylistic change in the early years of the twentieth century; in fact, it broke from some of the basic musical procedures of art music of the seventeenth, eighteenth, and nineteenth centuries. The most drastic change occurred within the field of harmony: the most unequivocal difference between baroque, classical, and romantic music and a good deal of early twentieth-century music is the absence or distortion of functional harmony in the latter. At this point the reader should listen to as many of the following compositions as he can, so that he may have some idea of the nature and extent of this fundamental difference.

Claude Debussy: "Brouillards," from *Preludes,* Book 1
    "Pagodes," from *Estampes*
    "Et la lune descend sur la temple qui fut," from *Images* (1907)
    "Voiles," from *Preludes,* Book 1

Charles Ives: "Halloween" and "Over the Pavements," from *A Set of Pieces for Theater Orchestra*

Anton Webern: Five Movements for String Quartet, Op. 5

Arnold Schoenberg: Suite for Piano, Op. 25

Igor Stravinsky: *The Rite of Spring* (opening section)

Darius Milhaud: *Bull on the Roof;* Suite Provencale

Paul Mindemith: Piano Sonata No. 3

Edgar Varèse: *Ionisation*

Though baroque, classical, and romantic musics may, on a general level, be easily understood as separate styles, all three, despite their differences, exhibit the principles of functional harmony. In other words, for about three centuries there was continuity to Western art musics—a common central nervous system. Thus, the break from tonality in the early years of the twentieth century represented one of the most radical departures from tradition in the history of Western music.

Many composers continued to write in tonal idioms, and thus extended the long history of functional harmony. In assessing the music of those who did not continue this tradition, one discovers a variety of alternatives to tonality, and a variety of personal styles. But despite different stylistic bents, these composers were united in the belief that the system of functional harmony was exhausted, and that alternatives to this system had to be found.

Debussy's alternative was, at least on the surface, much less radical than some of the others; his approach was not to destroy tonality completely but, rather, to distort it. This he accomplished by organizing his music in such a way that chords became significant more for what they were, in a purely sonorous sense, than for what they did, in a functional sense. (It can be assumed that all composers working within the system of functional harmony were interested to one degree or another in the sonorous qualities of chords. Thus, the suggestion is not that this fascination was invented by or unique to Debussy.)

To remain within the realm of functional harmony, a composer must necessarily select and arrange his chords in such a way that there will emerge from his music that special hierarchy of harmonies described in Chapter 1. If we understand tonality as a musical syntax—a sense-giving, form-giving system—then we can understand that chords in tonal music have a dual nature—functional and sonorous. The composer of tonal music regards his chords primarily as functional elements, restricting himself to using the number, type, and placement of chords that will establish this syntax. The sheer celebration of sonorities is not permitted to damage functionality.

Many of Debussy's compositions are in contrast with this. In such compositions sonorities are used as ends in themselves; they are directionless, and the chordal relationships and progressions that characterize functional harmony are absent. Notice in "Brouillards" how several of the sections—the first section, for example—seem to dwell upon one basic sound; notice, further, that these sounds are devoid of any urgency to progress to some other particular sound. This non-progressive, non-functional harmony might well be described as successive harmony: one sound or section precedes or follows, but does not lead to or result from, another sound or section. This is not true of all of Debussy's music, but it is characteristic of the pieces listed above, and of several of his other works.

The Ives piece, "Halloween," represents a different kind of alternative to functional harmony, for, unlike the Debussy compositions in which tonality is distorted rather than destroyed, this piece abandons tonality altogether. In it, Ives focuses on a body of sounds that are not typical of tonal music; furthermore, the piece consistently avoids arrangements of chords from which traditional functionality would emerge. This kind of music is sometimes referred to as *atonal*—outside the realm of tonality.

We have discovered that on a general level tonality is a musical system organized around a set of basic functional principles, but that on a particular level a great and diverse range of styles has been created within the system. The same is true of atonal music. For example, both the Ives the Webern compositions can be classified as atonal, but as we examine the particularities of these compositions we discover that they sound quite different from each other. Though these composers were united in their desire to avoid tonality, their separate musical personalities suggested different ways of accomplishing this.

Arnold Schoenberg is the inventor of the twelve-tone musical system, within which all pitches are related only to one another, not to a group of hierarchical and functional chords. This system has proved to be a viable and very influential alternative to tonality. Schoenberg's Suite for Piano, listed above, was one of the earliest compositions to. employ systematically the principles of the twelve-tone system.

During the early decades of the twentieth century various other alternatives to tonality emerged, such as bitonality and polytonality—double or multiple tonalities whereby the feel of simultaneously functioning tonal centers was created. Milhaud is one of a group of twentieth-century composers who have from time to time explored these alternatives.

For some composers the loss of interest in tonality led to a de-emphasis on pitches in general, and, concomitantly, to a special and exaggerated interest in other parameters of music, such as rhythm, texture, and timbre. *Ionisation,* by Varèse, is scored for a large battery of percussion instruments, most of which are instruments without definite pitch. The piece is a clear and unequivocal rejection of tonality.

Of course, the above is neither a complete catalogue of early twentieth-century alternatives to tonality, nor a complete list of composers who sought to incorporate these alternatives in their music; it indicates sufficiently, however, that Western art music experienced a dramatic stylistic change early in this century. More than anything else, this change was occasioned by the belief that the old system—tonality—was exhausted, and could not accommodate the aims and intentions of certain composers.

The Role of Economics
in the Formation of a Style

The personalities of some musical styles have been determined to a surprisingly large extent by economic considerations. Since the nineteenth century, some musics have been created, in part, as salable products. To varying degrees, these may be considered commercial musics. The term commercial, as it is herein applied to music, does not necessarily carry with it derogatory overtones, nor is the term restricted to popular musics. The notion of the composer making his living through the sale of his compositions, either to a ticket-buying concert audience, or to purchasers of printed music, is one that developed early in the nineteenth century. (There were, however, numerous, scattered precedents.) With the demise of the patronage system of the eighteenth-century musical world, and with the rise of nineteenth-century industrialization and economics, the role of the art music composer shifted from employee to free agent.

Using industrial terminology in a musical context, we may speak of producer (composer), product (the composer's music), and consumers (the audience). Again, this in no way implies that when a composer attempts to sell his music, he stoops to some kind of crass commercialism, and of necessity forfeits his artistic integrity. We would not, for example, suggest that Renoir, who sold many of his paintings during his lifetime, had less artistic integrity than did Van Gogh, who could sell very few of his. The suggestion here is simply this: beginning in the nineteenth century, many composers adapted themselves to new economic facts of life.

In the early 1800s the piano became a mass-produced instrument, used by professional concert pianists, and purchased in significant numbers by institutions, and by the public for home use. The rising popularity of the piano, as both a solo and an ensemble instrument, called, in turn, for a repertory—one diverse enough to exercise the several functions of the instrument. A number of nineteenth-century composers answered this call with concertos, and chamber and solo music for the piano.

Piano instruction also began to assume the proportions of a business: composers supplied the demand for instructional and exercise books and for piano transcriptions of folksongs, marches, waltzes, and excerpts from popular operas. The financial success and, in fact, the very life of this repertory resulted from the technological development of the piano. At the same time, the commercial success of the piano depended upon an economic scene healthy enough to permit large numbers of people to purchase pianos, piano music, piano instruction, and tickets to concerts of piano music.

The latter point is worthy of further discussion. Perhaps the most obvious area in which economy can affect musical style is the size and scale along which a musical style develops, a process often determined by the relative affluence or depression characteristic of the potential audience. For example, all other things being equal, an audience might welcome, say, a large-scale, theatrical operatic style, featuring a large cast and orchestra, and elaborate stage machinery and costumes. The success of such a production depends upon the price of tickets, as compared with the wages of the potential audience. The price of tickets is determined by production costs. One can readily see that under certain economic conditions an operatic style on this scale could not thrive. In a depressed economy composers and audience of opera would have to content themselves with a much smaller, chamber-like operatic style.

The Role of Technology
in the Formation of a Style

On the surface, the 'echnology of an age may seem far removed from music, but surprisingly often, technology has been a factor in the development of a musical style. Sometimes it directly and obviously affects this process, as, for example, in electronic music, the very sounds of which are produced by instruments from the field of technology. The electronic hardware used in making this music became available to the public only as recently as the early 1950s; thus, electronic music and its several particular

170   THE FORMATION OF A MUSICAL STYLE: EARLY ROCK

styles could not have been created prior to the mid-twentieth century. From one point of view it may be said that electronic music had to wait for the appropriate level of technology to develop; from another, one might hold that the theory of this music developed from the technology, and that composers found out what they wanted to say only after experimenting with the hardware. From any viewpoint it is obvious that electronic music styles have a fundamental relationship with technology.

One of the basic ingredients of the sound of rock music is the electric guitar; here again, a musical style, or a significant aspect of it, was directly affected by a technological development.

The style of American popular music in this century has been effected by technology in another, somewhat more oblique manner. The success of any popular music depends on the mode of its dissemination. Prior to this century the available modes were sheet music or, more frequently, live performances. Today live performances persist, but recordings have replaced them as the mode of dissemination most responsible for the popularity of a piece of music. In fact, today's mechanized modes of dissemination are inseparable components of the popularity of a song. Of course, this is not to imply that every song that is recorded achieves popularity—that is far from being the case. The suggestion, however crass it may have seemed in the past, is that mechanization is as important to the popularity of a given song as are its musical and textual components.

Because the mode of dissemination of much music has shifted from live performance to mechanized reproduction, the idea presents itself that popular music has, in a sense, become dehumanized. Perhaps the loss of live contact between performer and audience should be considered one of the liabilities of mechanization. However, there are other factors that, depending upon one's disposition, could be counted as either assets or liabilities. For example, mechanization in the form of the recording guarantees a performance that is always the same, and, we must assume, the ultimate rendition as a given performer envisions it. Furthermore, mechanization eliminates such human variables as a cracking voice or a momentary loss of memory.

Mechanization has affected the *content*, as well as the form, of some popular music. Over several decades a body of popular songs has been built, which takes as its subject matter certain facets of the mechanical-technological world. Let us direct our attention to a particular category of such songs—those dealing with mechanized modes of travel: trains, cars, airplanes, and so on. A wide range of attitudes towards instruments of travel exists within these songs. Some merely view means of travel as novelties, or they celebrate them as newly found conveniences and luxuries. Other songs tend to romanticize instruments of travel, as, for example, the song in which a man speaks of a locomotive as if it were a friend. Other songs suggest a psychological dependency on modes of travel. Still others mostly of recent vintage, mention instruments of travel, celebrating not the instruments but, rather, travel itself, or the escape or motion therein.

In the first type of travel song mentioned above, the journey usually terminates at home; thus, there is a circular motif to such songs. This is evident in such songs as "Chattanooga Choo-Choo, Won't You Choo-Choo Me Home?" (1941), "In My Merry Oldsmobile" (1905), and "Come Josephine in My Flying Machine" (1910).

In the second kind of travel song the poet often seems to be counting on the instrument of travel to do something for him, to somehow change his situation for the better. This is evident in songs such as "When My Dreamboat Comes Home" (1935).

> When my dreamboat comes home,
> Then my dreams no more will roam
> I will meet you and greet you
> Hold you closely my own.
> Moonlit waters will sing
> Of the tender love you bring
> We'll be sweetheats forever
> When my dreamboat comes home.*

* © 1936 M. Witmark & Sons. Copyright Renewed. All Rights Reserved. Used by permission of Warner Bros. Music.

In this kind of song the poet does not do the traveling. He waits. The same is true of "I'm Waitin' for the Train to Come In" (1948), in which the poet not only waits, but also draws a parallel between the instrument of travel and his life.

> I'm waitin' for the train to come in
> Waitin' for my life to begin.
> I've counted every minute of each live long day,
> Been so melancholy since you went away.
> I've shed a million teardrops or more,
> Waitin' for the one I adore.
> I'm waitin' in the depot by the railroad track,
> Waitin' for the choo-choo train that brings you back.
> I'm waitin' for my life to begin,
> Waitin' for the train to come in.

Copyright © 1945 Martin Block Music. Copyright Renewed 1972 Dorsey Brothers Music, A Division of Music Sales Corporation, New York. Used by Permission.

In certain lines of "The Trolley Song" (1944) we sense a connection between the "nervous system" of the trolley and the nervous system of the poet:

> Clang, clang, clang went the trolley,
> Ding, ding, ding went the bell,
> Zing, zing, zing went my heartstrings...
>
> Chug, chug, chug went the motor,
> Bump, bump, bump went the brake,
> Thump, thump, thump went my heartstrings...
>
> Buzz, buzz, buzz went the buzzer,
> Stop, stop, stop went the wheels,
> Stop, stop, stop went my heartstrings. . . .*

Some recent songs suggest that travel has become a fact, even a way of life. In his book, *Future Shock* (New York: Random House, 1970), Alvin Toffler tells us that "Transcience is the new 'temporariness' in everyday life." "It results in a mood, a feeling of impermanence" (p. 42). Jerry, in Edward Albee's *The Zoo Story*, characterizes himself as a 'permanent transient' (p. 42). Elsewhere in Toffler's book (p. 69) we are told that in 1914 the average American traveled about 340 miles per year by mechanized means. In 1967 the average American travelled 10,000 miles per year by automobile alone. Implicit in statements and statistics of this kind is that mechanization (in this case, only in the form of travel) is with us, around us, and in us; this is a state of affairs that has developed not suddenly, but more like a crescendo. It seems our increasing involvement with technology has changed society in more than merely mechanical ways.

The nature of these changes is reflected in several recent songs dealing ostensibly with mechanized travel, but actually with much more than that. In contrast with earlier types of travel songs, these recent ones view instruments of travel neither as luxuries nor as means to improve life. The impression one gets from these songs is that travel *is* life. In these songs travel is not circular, nor does the poet wait while someone else travels to him. The path is linear; travel doesn't really have a destination; its only direction is out. Consider the lyrics of the song "So Far Away," by Carole King:

> So far away,
> Doesn't anybody stay in one place anymore?
> It would be so fine to see your face at my door.
> Doesn't help to know you're just time away.
>
> Long ago I reached for you and there you stood,
> Holding you again could only do me good.
> How I wish I could,
> But you're so far away.

One more song about moving along the highway,
Can't say much of anything that's new.
If I could only work this life out my way,
I'd rather spend it being close to you.

But you're just time away,
Doesn't anybody stay in one place anymore?
It would be so fine to see your face at my door.
Doesn't help to know that you're so far away.
Yeah, you're so far away

Traveling around sure gets me down and lonely,
Nothing else to do but close my mind.
I sure hope the road don't come to own me,
There's so many dreams I've yet to find.

But you're just time away,
Doesn't anybody stay in one place anymore?
It would be so fine to see your face at my door.
Doesn't help to know that you're so far away.*

Thus, the effects of mechanization are more than merely technical; they are seen in the attitudes and aesthetics of both the composers of travel songs, and the audience, and are clearly reflected in their music and poetry.

All the topics thus far touched upon—the rejection of an inherited style; an alternative to that style; economic, aesthetic, functional, and technological considerations—are factors in the formation of rock 'n' roll style.

The Formation and Development of Rock 'n' Roll Style

Since the late 1950s, rock music of one kind or another has dominated the American popular music scene. It is a music that differs substantially from the predominant popular music of the 1930s and 1940s. Partly for that reason, rock 'n' roll (as rock music was called in the mid to late '50s) was viewed as a very short-lived fad by the practitioners of and the audience for the older style of popular music. During these early years of rock there were numerous predictions that rock 'n' roll was about to die, and that the older style was coming back.

As reported in the April 18, 1957, edition of *DOWN BEAT* magazine, Louis Brecker, owner of New York's Roseland Dance City Ballroom (a kind of temple for the old-style dance music), said: "The people are dancing and *will* turn to enjoy a good danceband. . . . Bands are on the upbeat in popu-

174   THE FORMATION OF A MUSICAL STYLE: EARLY ROCK

larity. You can almost sense it." Mr. Brecker was so convinced of the truth of this notion that he reportedly spent 2½ million dollars remodeling and refurbishing his Ballroom.

In the same magazine The Rev. Norman O'Connor, a jazz enthusiast, suggested not only that rock 'n' roll was a fad, but also that its popularity was nearly finished, and that it was about to be replaced by a new fad. He said: "Calypso music is gradually edging rock 'n' roll out of the popular music scene . . . rock 'n' roll is a stage in popular music . . . and is now on the way out."

A little earlier (*DOWN BEAT,* May 30, 1956), jazz musician John Lewis said, in reference to rock 'n' roll: "I think it's a transitory thing because you can only take so much of it no matter who you are, because the music is so limited in scope. It's a formula. . . ."

As we have seen, these predictions proved to be erroneous. And rather than remaining the same, rock music has continued to evolve. Indeed, several individual styles of rock have developed. In other words, we may view rock music from the mid '50s to the present as a new style in general (in effect, the new popular music style), but in particular we may say that rock is many styles. The earliest of these, and the subject of our present investigation is rock 'n' roll.

For reasons with which we shall deal presently, it is not possible to assign a specific date of birth to rock 'n' roll, or to single out an "inventor" of the style; we can say that rock 'n' roll became the generally accepted label for a specific musical style sometime in the mid '50s.

The etymology of the term rock 'n' roll leads us back to the earlier blues, where it was often used to describe the sex act. The term "rocking and reeling" was used to describe a particular kind of rural black religious song that called for a very animated and physical performance. Rock 'n' roll seems always to have implied physicalness, excitement, and frenzy. The late '40s and early '50s saw the emergence of several songs that were meant to be danced to, the titles of which use the word rock: "Good Rockin' Tonight" (1948), by Wynonie Harris; "Rock All Night Long" (1950), recorded by the Ravens; and "We're Gonna Rock" (1951), by Gunther Lee Carr. In fact, the closer we approach the time when rock 'n' roll style was formed, the more consistently we find the term rock 'n' roll associated with a dance beat.

One of the earliest to popularize the term among a mass audience was Alan Freed, a Cleveland disc jockey whose radio program, begun in 1952, was called "Moondog's Rock 'n' Roll Party." But it was not until about 1955 that rock 'n' roll style, as it is herein described, fully formed itself and took command of its audience. Also in 1955 the first rock 'n' roll movie premiered —*Rock Around the Clock,* starring Bill Haley and his Comets, and featuring Little Richard.

The influences on and the lineage of rock 'n' roll style can be traced to some earlier musics. Of these, the most closely related to it is the style known as rhythm and blues. Less closely related, but nevertheless very important in the formation of rock 'n' roll, are certain elements from a broad style once known as hillbilly music, but now called country and western music.

Before describing rhythm and blues style, we must first deal with a certain confusion that has grown up around this term. For about two decades prior to 1948 the term "race records" was used by record companies and music trade journals as a label for black popular music. Since several kinds of music were popular among black audiences during these years, "race" did not refer to a single, particular style, but was loosely applied to traditional blues, country blues, some gospel music, some jazz, and some more or less "white-style" ballads as performed by black musicians. Several of the major record companies even had subsidiary labels that recorded songs designed to be popular among and purchased by black audiences. *The Billboard* magazine, one of the principal music trade journals, published lists of the most popular "race records." An examination of these lists reveals the diversity among the musics that were included under the blanket label of "race records."

The Billboard's list of the most popular "race records" for the week ending July 30, 1948, contains the following:[4]

1. "I Can't Go On Without You," Bullmoose Jackson.
2. "Good Rockin' Tonight, Wynonie Harris.
3. "Run, Joe," Louis Jordan.
4. "Long Gone," Sonny Thompson.
5. "My Heart Belongs to You" Arbee Stidham.
6. "Tomorrow Night," Lonnie Johnson.
7. "Messin' Around," Memphis Slim.
8. "Pretty Mama Blues," Ivory Joe Hunter.
9. "Send for Me if You Need Me," The Ravens.
10. "Lollypop Mama," Wynonie Harris.
11. "All My Love Belongs to You," Bullmoose Jackson.
12. "Tell Me Daddy," Julia Lee and Her Boyfriends.
13. "Fine Brown Flame," Nellie Lutcher.
14. "King Size Papa," Julia Lee and Her Boyfriends.
15. "Recess in Heaven," Dan Grissom.

The list includes straight blues (number 8), white-style ballads (1, 11), a jazz group (3), a religious song (15), and some examples of what eventually came to be known as rhythm and blues style (2, 9, 13).

In 1949 *The Billboard* dropped the term "race" and substituted for it the term "rhythm and blues." Thus, rhythm and blues became the general label for the several kinds of music popular with black audiences. Undoubtedly,

---

[4] Quoted with permission of *Billboard* Magazine.

one of the reasons for dropping the term "race records" at that time was the growing social consciousness of many whites, which suggested that the term was unfair, discriminatory, and certainly racist. Rhythm and blues was, no doubt, a fairer term than "race records," but it was an only slightly more accurate label for this diverse body of music. Lame as it is, this is the term that has been passed on to us. Speaking of it in the most general sense, we can say that there was a slow rhythm and blues music—the blues—and a fast rhythm and blues music—jazz-derived forms.

At about this same time (late '40s), a new and different style of music, which brought together certain elements of both fast and slow rhythm and blues into a dance or "jump" blues, began to develop. This newly emerging musical style added to the existing amalgamation certain elements and accessories of its own, and ultimately resulted in a kind of music that was identifiable and recognizable in its own. Confusing though it is, *this* style should be called rhythm and blues. We must now emphasize that hereinafter, unless otherwise specified, the term rhythm and blues will refer to this particular style, not to the large and diverse body of black popular music, which some of the music trade journals continued to call rhythm and blues.

The Billboard continued to publish a listing of rhythm and blues hits until August 16, 1969. In its next issue (August 23) *The Billboard* carried an editorial that stated, in part:

> Beginning with this issue *Billboard* uses the designation "soul" in place of rhythm and blues. . . . The term soul more properly embraces the broad range of song and instrumental material which derives from the musical genius of the Black American. . . . The term, too, has relevance to a style of performance as well as to musical form.[5]

The first four songs in *The Billboard*'s rhythm and blues chart of August 16, 1969, were:[6]

> "Choice of Colors," The Impressions.
> "Mother Popcorn," James Brown.
> "Share Your Love With Me," Aretha Franklin.
> "Nitty Gritty," Gladys Knight and the Pips.

The first four songs in *The Billboard*'s soul chart of August 23, 1969, were:[7]

> "Share Your Love With Me," Aretha Franklin.
> "Choice of Colors," The Impressions.
> "Nitty Gritty," Gladys Knight and the Pips.
> "Your Good Thing," Lou Rawls.

[5] Quoted with permission of *Billboard* Magazine.
[6] Quoted with permission of *Billboard* Magazine.
[7] Quoted with permission of *Billboard* Magazine.

This means that on August 16, 1969, "Share Your Love With Me" was a rhythm and blues song, and Aretha Franklin was a rhythm and blues singer. But one week later, "Share Your Love With Me" became a soul song (soul being "relevant" to the form of the song), and Aretha Franklin became a soul singer (soul being "relevant" to her style of performance). This is one of the many ways in which terms that are not based on musical-analytical criteria can be confusing, even misleading. We will, therefore, examine rhythm and blues, this ancestor of rock 'n' roll, as a musical style, not as a marketing label.

The stylistic terms rhythm and blues and rock 'n' roll have on occasion been used interchangeably; in fact, to a considerable extent the former term overlaps the latter both chronologically and stylistically. In the case of some songs from the period around 1953 to 1956, it becomes somewhat academic to argue which of the two terms is more appropriate. To complicate the confusion, we must remember that the term rock 'n' roll is considerably older than the style of music it embraces. And, potentially more confusing, the term rock 'n' roll is older than the term rhythm and blues, though the style of pure or archetypal rhythm and blues is, as has already been suggested, older than rock 'n' roll style. Keeping these semantic and chronological difficulties in mind, but without allowing them to thwart our investigation of the formation of rock 'n' roll style, let us proceed.

The prototypical rhythm-and blues piece is an amalgamation, in that it is music "with a beat," set in the harmonic language and formal structure of the blues, especially the twelve-bar blues. In general, this fascination with beat resulted from the jazz with which the creators of rhythm and blues style were familiar. Rhythm and blues developed a pattern of accents within the 4/4 meter that eventually became a trademark of the style:

$$4/4 \quad 1 \quad 2 \quad 3 \quad 4 \quad / \quad 1 \quad 2 \quad 3 \quad 4$$
$$ \quad X \quad * \quad \circ \quad * \quad \quad X \quad * \quad \circ \quad *$$

The X indicates that the metrical downbeat is stressed; the * means that beats 2 and 4 are sharply accented with hard "socks"; and the ° refers to the unaccented or ignored beat in this rhythmic pattern. The following recorded example illustrates this pattern: "Honky Tonk," Part II, by Bill Doggett (*Great Hits of Rhythm and Blues,* Columbia G 30503, side 1, band 1).

Rhythm and blues was dance music, and the accent pattern diagrammed and heard above affords an almost choreographic description of the bodily movements in the dancing: arms extended, hands rigidly slapping the air on beats 2 and 4; a shuffling motion with the feet at beat 3; all accompanied by undulating and snapping movements of shoulders, elbows, and torso.

178   THE FORMATION OF A MUSICAL STYLE: EARLY ROCK

Many rhythm and blues songs superimpose upon this accent pattern another pattern, which further energizes the music. This pattern is the so-called eight-to-the-bar, or boogie beat, borrowed from the jazz style known as boogie woogie, which enjoyed its greatest popularity in the 1940s. The boogie beat activates all four basic beats in a 4/4 measure by dividing each of them into two, so that there are eight rather than four pulses to the bar:

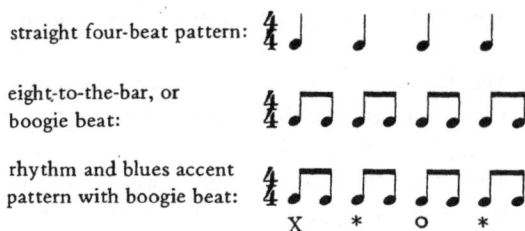

Inasmuch as rhythm and blues was a dance music, it could not borrow or adapt anything from the experimental jazz (such as bop) of the late '40s and early '50s—music that was meant essentially to be listened to, rather than danced to. But boogie woogie provided an eminently inflexible and danceable beat. Pinetop Smith, an early practitioner of boogie, and the man most responsible for the popularization of the term boogie woogie, conceived of it as a dance music. This is made clear in his recording, "Pinetop's Boogie Woogie" (*Encyclopedia of Jazz on Records,* Vol. III—"Jazz of the Forties," Decca DXF 140).

The blues has several forms, of which one of the most frequently encountered is the twelve-bar blues. Its pattern is illustrated below:

A (4 bars) "Oh, I'm feelin' so sad all the live long day."
A(1) (4 bars) "Oh, I'm feelin' so sad all the live long day."
B (4 bars) "Think I'll go down to the river and throw my poor self in."

In terms of text and melody, phrases A and A(1) are identical (they differ in harmony, as you can see below). The first A makes a statement, which the second A repeats and reinforces. The B phrase has a different melodic line, and is usually a lyric that in some way comments upon or draws a conclusion from the statements made in A and A(1). Though there are many possible variations on the harmonic scheme below, it may be taken as a norm for the twelve-bar blues:

	A	A(1)	B
4/4	1 2 3 4	1 2 3 4	1 2 3 4
	I7	IV7 I7	V7 I7
	Tonic	Subdominant Tonic	Dominant Tonic

The following recorded example illustrates the "X * ○ *" beat pattern of prototypical rhythm and blues, the twelve-bar blues format, and (with very minor exceptions) the harmonic scheme outlined above: "Work With Me Annie," by Hank Ballard and the Midnighters (*Great Hits of Rhythm and Blues,* side 1, band 2).

Also present in this example and in many other examples of prototypical rhythm and blues (and also in rock 'n' roll) is an ostinato-like figure that we will hereinafter refer to as an incantation. It is a short, repetitive figure performed by the group supporting the lead singer, and is designed to create a kind of mesmerizing effect. Sometimes, an incantation is the repetition of a few words; just as frequently, it repeats neutral syllables, as in the Ballard song above, where the incantation is "Ah-oom, Ah-oom," etc. The element of incantation is not as crucial to the personality of archetypal rhythm and blues as are the beat pattern and the blues format, but it is used often enough that we might consider it an accessory of the style.

The texts of rhythm and blues songs are usually about love. But by the standard of white radio stations in the '40s and '50s, many of these texts were either (1) downright dirty, (2) heavily and obviously laden with sexual innuendoes, or (3) grammatically unacceptable. By such standards, any or all of these "facts" rendered these lyrics unsuitable for mass public consumption. It is not our purpose here to even attempt to suggest what makes a text dirty or obscene. We can say, however, that many rhythm and blues lyrics speak of love in basic, earthy terms, and that certain words that are consistently used in certain contexts are quite likely sexually connotative. Consider this, and then consider the fundamental differences in approach to the subject of love in the two texts below. The first is the beginning of "Work With Me Annie"; the second is from a roughly contemporaneous song, but one written in the style of popular white ballads.

     1.

Work with me Annie,
Work with me Annie,
Work with me Annie,
Work with me Annie,
Work with me Annie,
Let's get it while the gettin' is good
(so good, so good, so good, so good)
Annie please don't cheat,
Give me all my meat.
Ah   oo   oo   oo   oo   oo,
So good to me.
Work with me Annie,
Let's get it while the gettin' is good. . . .

180 THE FORMATION OF A MUSICAL STYLE: EARLY ROCK

2.

Take my hand, I'm a stranger in paradise.
All lost in a wonderland/ A stranger in paradise.
If I stand starry-eyed/ That's the danger in paradise.
For mortals who stand beside/ An angel like you.
I saw your face and I ascended/ Out of the common place into the rare.
Somewhere in space I hang suspended/ Until I know there's a chance that you care.
Won't you answer the fervent prayer of a stranger in paradise,
Don't send me in dark despair/ From all that I hunger for.
But open your angel's eyes/ to the stranger in paradise,
And tell him that he need be/ A stranger no more.*

* From "Stranger in Paradise" By Robert Wright & George Forrest. © 1953 Frank Music Corp. Used By Permission.

In spite of its earthiness and its use of rather obvious innuendoes, the rhythm and blues language does not incorporate words that are commonly recognized as obscene (i.e., four-letter words). Generally speaking, rhythm and blues texts are not violent, nor are they morose (as is often the case in the blues). The lyrics may deal with sex, or perhaps with excessive drinking, or with other topics, but essentially, rhythm and blues texts express a good mood.

The vocal style of rhythm and blues calls for heavy, raspy sounds, but not the moaning quality often associated with blues singing, nor practically any of the crooning of vocalists of white popular music of the late '40s. In addition, rhythm and blues delivery is marked by the occasional use of falsetto, shouts, and growling sounds. Vocal ornamentation and melismas are few in comparison with blues singing, where great melodic and rhythmic freedom and improvisation are expected of the singer.

The typical rhythm and blues instrumentation consists of drums, piano or organ, bass guitar, optional lead guitar, and honking tenor sax. The principal duty of the drums is to keep time and to enunciate the accent pattern. The piano or organ supplies the harmonic background and enunciates the boogie beat, if present; occasionally, it plays solo lines. The bass guitar provides the bass line. If a lead guitar is present, it functions as a solo instrument or as harmonic support, and/or assists the drums in stating the beat pattern. The primary role of the growling. or honking tenor sax is to provide a fairly extended solo between stanzas, while the singer rests. In addition, it may supply simple, unobstrusive countermelodies to the singer or singers. The solos and the countermelodies are, like jazz solos, improvisational in nature, though ordinarily not as intricate and complicated. The sax may also be a lead instrument in introductions and closing formulas. Although there are variations on this basic makeup—for instance, a larger instrumental group—

prototypical rhythm and blues rarely calls for a group smaller than or very different from this one.

Some songs use the standard accent pattern of archetypal rhythm and blues, but have no direct connection with the blues. For these pieces the label rhythm and blues is something of a misnomer; nevertheless, some of their characteristics may persuade us to accept these pieces as members of the family. For example, they may utilize several other elements or accessories of rhythm and blues style, such as its instrumentation, vocal style, kind of text, and incantation. Such songs might be referred to as generic rather than archetypal rhythm and blues. It is with this kind of song that the lines between pure rhythm and blues and rock 'n' roll begin to blur.

Rhythm and blues style crystallized sometime in the early '50s. It was almost exclusively a black American music, made by black musicians, and intended for and listened to by black audiences. In the mid '50s, as it moved from an exclusively black audience to a black and white audience, it was modified, and it acquired some new features, and a new name: rock 'n' roll.

Rock 'n' roll borrowed or adapted a number of technical elements from the rhythm and blues style. In most cases, what was borrowed was modified: it was either exaggerated or simplified. For example, a large body of rock 'n' roll songs (though not all exhibited as many rock 'n' roll elements as others) retained the accent pattern of rhythm and blues. But in these songs there was a tendency to emphasize the downbeat and the hard socks even more than was the case in most rhythm and blues. In rock 'n' roll the downbeat literally became exaggerated.

One way of doing this was to precede the downbeat with some kind of rhythmic confusion or disturbance on the upbeat (or before the theoretically correct place for the upbeat) ; when this confusion is suddenly resolved on the downbeat, the resulting tendency is to make the downbeat seem much clearer and more emphatic. The drummer in a rock 'n' roll group is usually responsible for accomplishing this. If he begins rhythmic disturbance earlier than the fourth beat, he in effect creates a longer upbeat—he stretches the beginning of the upbeat further back into the measure. Graphically illustrated, this is what happens:

```
1  2  3  4                      1  2  3  4          1
X  *  ///////////////////////   X  *  ///////////// X
      fast drum activity, crea-
      ting a rhythmic disturb-
      ance which is resolved HERE!
```

This device can be heard in the following recordings:

"More Than One," by Phil Marks and the Originals. *Roots: the Rock and Roll Sound of Louisiana and Mississippi,* Folkways FJ 2865, side A, band 1. (The device is heard almost every eight bars throughout this song.)

"Lucille," and "The Girl Can't Help It," by Little Richard. *Little Richard Cast a Long Shadow,* Epic EG 30428, side 1, band 1, and side 1, band 2, respectively.

The drummer can elongate the upbeat even further. In doing so, he creates added tension and increases further the anticipation we feel for the downbeat, so that it arrives with even more of a crash. Notice in "Check Up," by Lawrence Bruce (*Roots,* side B, band 4) that the rhythmic confusion, or elongated upbeat, lasts almost an entire measure is some instances.

Rock 'n' roll makes use of other devices that tend to exaggerate the downbeat. One of these is what we might call the ensemble swoop, in which the ensemble pays a small upward slurring motive that, again, begins somewhat ahead of the fourth beat:

$$1 \quad 2 \quad 3 \quad 4 \quad / \quad 1 \quad 2 \quad 3 \quad 4 \quad / \quad 1$$

One, two, and three are played on the beat, but the pulsation of beat four begins early (after three, but before the theoretically correct time for four).

The eight-to-the-bar approach toward activating all the beats in the measure was carried over to rock 'n' roll from rhythm and blues. Many rock 'n' roll songs use this device, but perhaps an even more typical rock 'n' roll technique is to divide the beats into triplets, creating a hammer-like effect:

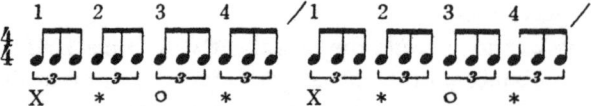

This penchant for triple rather than the duple division of the beat may also be regarded as a borrowed element that is subsequently exaggerated.

A smaller group of rock 'n' roll songs use Latin or quasi-Latin rhythmic patterns, as in "Rome Wasn't Built in a Day," by Al White and his HiLiters (*Roots,* side A, band 3). Here the pattern is:

Notice that beats one, two, and four are played on the beat, while beat three, the ignored beat of rock 'n' roll, is not. The use of such rhythmic patterns may be considered another means of activating the rhythmic life of the music without damaging its danceability.

The instrumentation of early rock 'n' roll was very much like that of rhythm and blues. The biggest exception was that in rock 'n' roll the guitar rose in status; it not only became more important than it had been in arche-typal rhythm and blues, it became louder—to the point of exaggeration, due to the increased use of electronic amplification.

It developed with rock 'n' roll that the more generally public it became, the more exaggerated and theatrical it became in certain respects. The hip-swinging of Elvis ("The Pelvis"), and the stand-up piano thumping and exaggerated pompadour of Little Richard became significant accessories of the style, as did sequined suits and other (at the time) bizarre costumes.

The vocal style of rock 'n' roll resembles that of rhythm and blues, but again, the former modified the latter in some respects. The biggest difference between the two is the introduction of certain white elements into rock 'n' roll vocals. Elvis Presley offered a vocal style that was, in a way, tamer than the sound we associate with rhythm and blues. The shout and falsetto ele-ments of much rhythm and blues were not present in his delivery, and the raspy and growling sounds were watered down. In the pronunciation of many words, Presley compromised between a basic southern black delivery and a basic white vocal style—his was a rural southern voice that partook of both.

Presley and Bill Haley, two of the leading white performers of rock 'n' roll, both came from country music backgrounds. Taken as broad styles, rhythm and blues country and western music of the late '40s–early '50s were more closely related to each other than either was to white popular music of the same era. In the first place, country and western music and rhythm and blues were styles outside the mainstream of popular music. The instrumenta-tion of the two styles was roughly similar, though not exactly so, and both were decidedly different from the instrumentation of mainstream popular music. The vocal style, delivery, and accent of the country and western singer was decidedly different from his counterpart in popular music. In terms of accent the white country singer and the black rhythm and blues singer had something more or less in common: certain pronunciations that were not shared by the white pop singer. Also, the yodelling and hooting of the country and western singer may be considered the counterparts of the falsetto and shouting of the rhythm and blues singer.

In country and western lyrics the treatment of romantic love departed, as it did in rhythm and blues texts, from the idealized, "sophisticated" love lyrics of mainstream popular ballads. In addition, the archetypal rhythm and blues beat is found, though in a slightly softer version, in a large number of country and western songs of the late '40s. Hear, for example, "Walkin' the Floor Over You," by Ernest Tubb (Decca DL 4118), which was popular with "hillbilly" audiences during this time.

Hear also the "X * o *" pattern (with triplets) in a slightly later "hill-billy" song, "A Poor Man's Roses," by Patsy Cline (Starday SLP 291).

During the years in question, these two styles—rhythm and blues and hillbilly (or country and western) music—were, in terms of technical elements and performance practices, surprisingly similar; it must be remembered, though, that the audiences for these two musics were separated by a wide sociological gulf.

In the formation of rock 'n' roll some elements borrowed from rhythm and blues were simplified rather than eraggerated. On the whole, rock 'n' roll lyrics represent a simplification or softening of the texts and sentiments of rhythm and blues. A great many rock 'n' roll songs deal with love, just as rhythm and blues songs before them had done. But in rock 'n' roll, earthiness and blatant sexual references were largely eliminated from the lyrics. In fact, in many rock 'n' roll songs love is spoken of in terms that can be called frivolous.

Herbert Reed of the Platters, a very successful rock 'n' roll group (their "The Great Pretender" sold over two million records, and "Only You" sold over a million and a half), said in an interview in *DOWN BEAT* (May 30, 1956):

> I think that one reason for its popularity is that most rock and roll is really simple thoughts about how people feel. . . . Criticism concerning objectionable lyrics is no longer valid since, in the majority of new records, the lyrics are , clean.

One of the earliest vehicles for rock 'n' roll was the "cover record," in which a performer (usually white) offered a vocally softer and textually less objectionable version of a song previously recorded by a black rhythm and blues performer. A typical "cover" version of a rhythm and blues song removed sexual suggestiveness from the text. For example, Hank Ballard's rhythm and blues song, "Work With Me Annie," with its sexual connotations, was rendered harmless in a "cover" version," Dance With Me Henry," recorded by Georgia Gibbs and others.

Most of the best known performers of rhythm and blues had backgrounds in straight blues and/or jazz of one kind or another. As pure rhythm and blues began to be modified into rock 'n' roll, some of these performers returned to their former backgrounds, some were able to make the stylistic transition from black-based rhythm and blues to black-and-white-based rock 'n' roll. The earliest successful white rock 'n' roll singers—Presley, Haley, Jerry Lee Lewis, and others—broke from their hillbilly music background, but they also brought it with them into rock 'n' roll. It is not surprising that for a short period of time, the music of these people was sometimes called "rockabilly."

Some post-rhythm and blues music moved closer to mainstream white popular balladry while retaining many of the essential ingredients of rock 'n' roll, thereby creating a softer brand of rock 'n' roll. To distinguish between rock 'n' roll and this offshoot, as they existed around 1955–57 or so, we might call the latter by the slightly less colloquial name of rock *and* roll.

Among white performers, the most financially successful of the very early practitioners of this style was Pat Boone, a white crooner, who sang rock 'n' roll lyrics, frequently accompanied by soft strings and a rhythm section mildly enunciating the rock 'n' roll beat pattern. Some black singers also were successful with this softer brand.

Many slow or ballad-type rock and roll songs moved further away from both the lyrics and the formal structure of rhythm and blues, and closer to the sentimental lyrics and formal design of mainstream popular ballads, without, however, becoming mere imitations of such ballads. A case in point is Clyde McPhatter's "Long Lonely Nights" (*History of Rhythm and Blues: Rock and Roll, 1956–1957*, Atlantic SD 8163, Vol. 3, side 2, band 6). Notice the use of eight-bar phrases, and a harmonic language that is more typical of white ballads than of rhythm and blues or rock 'n' roll. Notice also the use of instruments that were foreign to rhythm and blues. Nevertheless, the singer does have the vocal quality and delivery associated with rock 'n' roll; in fact, he makes use of something that we have not yet mentioned, but which is an accessory to rock 'n' roll style. Notice that at the ends of several phrases, he uses a vocal gimmick: a kind of exaggerated whooping falsetto. This is not the raucous shout of rhythm and blues, nor is it the high but masculine yodel of the country and western singer. This seems to be much tamer and simpler, and it has something about it that is almost childlike. Other uses of this device may be heard in two other songs from the above-mentioned album: "Fools Fall in Love," by The Drifters, and "Young Blood," by The Coasters.

The managers and disc jockeys of radio stations that played rock 'n' roll were generally middle-aged men; so were the producers of rock 'n' roll records, and in some cases, the writers of rock 'n' roll songs. But the audience for rock 'n' roll was decidedly, almost exclusively, teen aged. Much has been written about the personality of this audience—its general rebelliousness; its disinterest in the values and habits of its parents; its clannishness, and lack of rapport with its elders. It is possible that this audience, which so enthusiastically adopted rock 'n' roll, took a special delight in the belief that this music belonged only to them. To their elders, rock 'n' roll was either incomprehensible, immoral, or simple-minded.

On April 18, 1956, *DOWN BEAT* carried a feature story under the headline, "Teeners Riot in Massachusetts and Cause Rock and Roll Ban." The disturbance resulted from a misunderstanding between the promoters of a concert at the Massachusetts Institute of Technology and a large group of teenagers who paid their admissions believing they would be permitted to dance. When they were not allowed to do so, a riot erupted. The chairman of the Boston Licensing Board said: "Some of this music is crazy . . . some rock and roll is very acceptable to me, but its exciting tempos could endanger the morals of our youth. The then mayor of Boston said he felt that "Rock and roll concerts incite something that causes a lot of trouble with kids." And a Cambridge police sergeant said, "Modern music apparently has an unwholesome effect on teenagers."

The more the music was ridiculed (in the above instance it was even outlawed), the more firmly welded together the audience became, and the more desperately it attached itself to rock 'n' roll. In fact, several rock 'n' roll songs that became hits were sheer celebrations of rock 'n' roll itself; one of these, "School Days," by Chuck Berry, contains the line, "Hail, hail rock 'n' roll."

The transistor radio became standard equipment for this audience. This inexpensive little box was the source of the rock 'n' roll sound and message, and its portability allowed the audience to take the sound-message anywhere it wished. Even the frowns and complaints of those outside the audience could not silence it, for the transistor was frequently equipped with an earplug amplifier.

In this respect, the audience for a particular musical style had an impact on a certain area of the economy. According to the *Electronic Industries Association Yearbook of 1969*, 1,690,000 portable radios were sold in the United States in 1950. By 1958 sales reached 5,105,000; by 1961 the figure was 14,651,000.

"Nobody likes rock and roll but the public," said Bill Haley (*DOWN BEAT*, May 30, 1956). The public to which he referred was, in fact, the increasingly large teenage audience for rock 'n' roll.

Exactly why this audience was attracted to rock 'n' roll does not admit of a simple answer. In his article, "Popular Music versus the Facts of Life,"[8] S.I. Hayākawa may have touched upon part of the answer when he suggested that the rock 'n' roll audience was reacting negatively to the phony, artificial view of life and love expressed in the white ballads popular among older generations. On the other hand, there is much to be said for the idea that people do not live by facts alone, and that they require a certain amount of fantasy and artificiality.

The lyrics of rhythm and blues songs do deal with the subject of romantic love in a factual, unsophisticated, and unartificial way, especially so in comparison with the lyrics of white popular ballads. But the rock 'n' roll audience was much larger and heterogeneous than the audience for pure rhythm and blues; and as we have seen, the lyrics of rock 'n' roll songs are in general not as hard-nosed, factual, and graphic as are the lyrics of the typical rhythm and blues song. They are a compromise between the sentimental and artificial tone of the lyrics of white ballads, and the gutsy, realistic lyrics of rhythm and blues.

[8] Bernard Rosenberg and David M. White, eds., *Mass Culture* (Glencoe: The Free Press, 1957), p. 400.

This compromise was the result of several factors, probably the most important of which was an economic one: the suggestive lyrics of rhythm and blues could not be put up for sale to the mass public. It may be true that during these years the adult population was losing a certain amount of control over its children; nevertheless, it was by no means a powerless group, and its economic power coupled with its essentially puritanical views had to be reckoned with by the music industry. This puritanical element and the network radio stations which grudgingly (at first), then enthusiastically, "pushed" rock 'n' roll probably precluded the further development of love lyrics in a truly earthy vein.

As we have seen, rock 'n' roll tended to exaggerate a number of things it borrowed from rhythm and blues; it did the same with incantation and nonsense syllables. The same group that was opposed to suggestive lyrics seems not to have opposed lyrics that were grammatically impure, or textual incantations made of nonsense syllables. Partly for this reason, rock 'n' roll seized upon and exaggerated these elements to such an extent that phrases such as "A wop bam a lu ah, A wop bam boom "became an integral part of its style.

Cleaning up the lyrics and making them apparently harmless seemed to assuage the angers and fears of the adult population. For the most part they still, it seems, did not like the music, but in the end they did not prevent it from becoming an enormously successful business.

The rock 'n' roll audience was born at the beginning of the population explosion in this country during World War II. By 1955 there were many more people under the age of 21 than there had ever been in twentieth-century America. If for no other reason than by sheer force of numbers, this segment of the population would have to be catered to. This emerging audience was young, vast, and as a result of the relative affluence of the immediate postwar years, it had some money, and a belief that more money was on call if needed. How different such a belief was from that held by teenagers and young parents during both the depression years of the '30s and the ration-haunted years of the early '40s.

The rock 'n' roll audience also accumulated a kind of independence unknown to earlier generations of teenagers, an independence traceable to a number of things. It was the first generation to grow up with television. Whatever else television may or may not have done to and for this audience, it can safely be assumed that it offered its audience a firsthand, visual acquaintance with many people and things beyond its home towns, and at an earlier age than had previously been typical.

Then, too, for many of this group there was no permanent home town, but rather a series of temporary places to live. This migratory pattern became a fact of life in the '50s for the corporate businessman, or "organization man," and his wife and family. In his book, *The Organization Man*

188   THE FORMATION OF A MUSICAL STYLE: EARLY ROCK

(1957), William H. Whyte informs us that many of these families moved to different locations as many as seven or eight times in a ten-year span. It is an immensely complicated problem, and one far beyond the province of this book, to try to assess the many possible effects of this pattern upon the rock 'n' roll generation. But one reasonable guess is that it produced in it a feeling or a spirit of rootlessness.

For those not involved in the world of the corporate organization man and the migratory nature of such an existence, many did remain in more or less permanent home towns. However, some of these were exposed to the working mother syndrome that was so much in evidence in the '50s.

From all of this, it is possible to speculate that the new generation may well have been developing a set of attitudes about home, roots, and family that was different in some ways from the attitudes of its elders. In fact, it seems that at about mid-century many new attitudes on many different fronts were being formed, all of which were precipitated by conditions and events peculiar to that time.

But from a musical point of view, why the emergence of rock 'n' roll style at this particular time? A study of popular music in the '40s occupies another chapter of this book. A reading of that discussion reveals that many love songs from the early '40s dealt with the happiness, dreams, longings, and tragedies of young men and women in love, but caught in a wartime situation that necessarily kept them separated, either for the duration of the war (as expressed in songs such as "I'll Be Home for Christmas, if Only in My Dreams"), or—in the most tragic cases—forever (as expressed in, for instance, "I'll Never Smile Again").

The rock 'n' roll generation had no personal experience with such situations; the sentiments and tone of such lyrics were without real meaning to them. Their joys and their tragedies were of a different order: perhaps simpler, thus calling for simpler words; or less dreamy, demanding more realistic, down-to-earth terminology; and more adolescent (they were, of course, younger than the wartime generation mentioned above, but they were also forced to deal with some adult situations at comparatively younger ages), thereby calling for a more direct, less sophisticated expression of sentiments and feelings.

Swing, the jazz style that had been so popular with the parents of the rock 'n' roll audience, was also outside the direct experience of the latter group. By about 1950 or so, big band jazz, and big dance bands in general, were practically out of business. They simply weren't available to the 10- to 13-year-olds who in just a few years would form the core of the rock 'n' roll audience. At this time jazz splintered into smaller groups; the most significant of these dedicated itself to bop and other forms of experimental jazz, which for a variety of reasons appealed neither to the very young teenagers nor to their parents. Thus, a line of continuity, in the form of an interest in jazz, that might have developed between the two generations did not.

The remaining significant body of popular music from the late '40s was either of the topical novelty type (which becomes dated in a hurry), or belonged to a group for which it is difficult to supply a suitable label: the narrative and quasi-folksongs, such as "Mule Train," "The Old Master Painter," "Lucky Old Sun," "Ghost Riders in the Sky," and others. Both types lacked a danceable beat, and it is probably because of this that they failed to capture the imagination of the younger generation.

It is fair to argue that in several ways the late '40s–early '50s was a rather dull time in the United States. The war had ended, and although no reasonable human being was sorry to see it end, the air of electrified tension that accompanies such a holocaust was also brought to an end. The servicemen gladly discarded their military uniforms, but many of them quickly attired themselves in the civilian uniform of the '50s: the grey flannel suit. Equally dull was the kind of newly emerging suburban community like Levittown, Pennsylvania, with its row after weary row of look-alike houses, its super-markets filled with uniformly packaged frozen foods, and the many chrome-encrusted and tail-finned automobiles that began to crowd the same streets at the same, predictable times of day.

With all of the above factors in mind, it is perhaps not too difficult to see why rock 'n' roll became such a quick and smashing success with its new, young audience. It did everything that the old style of popular music did not do for it. It used the right kinds of texts, expressed the right sentiments in an easily approachable manner, was not cluttered up with virtuosity, and had an utterly consistent, danceable beat.

Moreover, it belonged to this audience—the whole audience. It was not rooted in one section of the country or a particular kind of background or even in one ethnic group. This fact was eventually one of considerable pride to the audience—this was one kind of ownership this somewhat rootless group understood. Furthermore, this style of music belonged to them because no one else wanted it. In fact, as we have seen, some people didn't even want them to have it, which probably made it all the more appealing. Finally, at a time when many things, musical and otherwise, seemed rather dull, the audience found that rock 'n' roll music was exciting.

DISCOGRAPHY

Many recordings of rhythm and blues and rock 'n' roll songs are still available; however, as time goes by, they become more difficult to locate and, in many cases, much more expensive than they were several years ago. The recent revival of interest in this music has prompted record companies to reissue many of the biggest hits in albums. However, such albums usually include non-hits and sometimes, irrelevant material. But in the long run, the albums provide the best, most practical, and least expensive introduction to this music. Below is a very selective list of albums devoted to this music, as performed by several of the most significant practitioners of the styles. In the interest of economy, no attempt has been made to include every important performer and song. Instead, the list aims to be representative. The albums are divided into three groups: indispensable, important, and very useful. Following this is a supplementary list of recordings that are useful in the study of rhythm and blues, rock 'n' roll, and rock and roll.

Indispensable

Great Hits of R&B, Columbia G 30503. In addition to the selections already mentioned in this chapter, this album also contains other crucial performers and songs, such as "Fever," Little Willie John (Peggy Lee made a successful "cover" version of this song); "Sixty Minute Man," Billy Ward and the Dominoes; "Only You," The Platters; "Trying," LaVerne Baker.

ELVIS PRESLEY, *Elvis' Golden Records* (March, 1958), Volume I, RCA Victor. There is also a Volume II to this set, but it is this first volume that is crucial. The album includes, among others, "Hound Dog," "All Shook Up," "Heartbreak Hotel," "Teddy Bear," "Jailhouse Rock."

History of Rhythm and Blues, 4 volumes, Atlantic SD 8161, SD 8164. Volumes 2 and 3 are crucial; Volumes 1 and 4 are useful. In addition to the selections already mentioned in this chapter, Volume 3 has several important rock 'n' roll songs. "Corrina, Corrina," Joe Turner; "Ruby Baby," The Drifters; "Jim Dandy," LaVerne Baker; "C.C. Rider," Chuck Willis. Especially important in Volume 2 are: "Money Honey," The Drifters; "Shake, Rattle, and Roll," Joe Turner; "Tweedle Dee," LaVerne Baker.

Bill Haley's Greatest Hits (June, 1968), Decca DL 5027. Particularly important are: "Rock Around the Clock"; "See You Later Alligator"; "Shake, Rattle and Roll."

Little Richard: Cast A Long Shadow 4 sides, Epic EG 30428. The album contains a number of Little Richard's most important early rock 'n' roll hits, plus some later material. Hear especially: "Lucille"; "Tutti Frutti"; "Long Tall Sally"; "Good Golly Miss Molly"; "Whole Lotta' Shakin' Goin' On."

Important

Chuck Berry's Greatest Hits (April, 1964). The album contains many important rock 'n' roll songs, such as "School Days"; "Roll Over Beethoven"; "Maybelline"; "Johnny B. Goode."

PAT BOONE, *Pat's Greatest Hits,* Dot 3071, S 25071. The album contains several of the singer's rock and roll best-sellers from the mid '50s.

FATS DOMINO, *Rock & Rollin'* Imperial 9004, 9009. The album contains several of the best songs of one of the central figures in rock 'n' roll, including 'Aint It a Shame" (Pat Boone made a very successful cover version of this song); "You Said You Love Me"; "Fat Man."

Very Useful

PAUL ANKA, *21 Golden Hits* (1963). Most typical of this rock and roll performer are "Diana," and "Puppy Love."

FRANKIE AVALON, *15 Greatest Hits* (1964). Avalon and Anka are very much in the same (soft) vein. Hear especially: "Bobby Sox to Stockings."

BIG BOPPER, *Chantilly Lace* (1958). The title song from this album was a big rock 'n' roll hit in 1958.

Bo Diddley's 16 Alltime Greatest Hits (1964). The album contains several songs typical of the style of this important early rock 'n' roll singer.

THE DRIFTERS, *Rockin' and Driftin'* (1958). "Ruby Baby" and "Fools Fall in Love" are included in Vol. 3 of *History of Rhythm and Blues,* but this album also includes several of their other hits, such as "Drip Drop."

BUDDY HOLLY (1958). Another important early rock 'n' roll performer; this album includes his two biggest hits: "Ready Teddy," and "Peggy Sue."

Golden Hits of Jerry Lee Lewis. The album includes "Whole Lotta' Shakin'," and "Great Balls of Fire."

RICKY NELSON (1958). Very typical of the lyrics and singing style of the soft rock and roll style of the late '50s.

CARL PERKINS. Another rock 'n' roll performer with a country music background. This album contains his biggest hit, "Blue Suede Shoes," also made famous by Elvis Presley.

JOE TURNER. This well known and highly respected blues singer had some success as a rock 'n' roll performer. "Chains of Love" and "Corrina, Corrina" are included in *History of Rhythm and Blues.* In addition to these, this album contains "Shake, Rattle, and Roll," "Flip Flop," and "Honey Hush."

Richie Valens Memorial Album. Hear especially "Donna" and "Come on, Let's Go Rockin' All Night."

BIBLIOGRAPHY

In the past four or five years a great many books on various aspects of rock have been published. The quality of these sources is very uneven. Moreover, the majority of them either discuss the history of rock, giving general attention to each style, or concentrate on rock from the Beatles to the present. Below is a very selective list of sources that deal in useful ways with early rock and/or its ancestors.

BELZ, CARI, *The Story of Rock.* New York: Oxford University Press, 1969.

COURLANDER, HAROLD, *Negro Folk Music, U.S.A.* New York: Columbia University Press, 1963.

GILLETT, CHARLIE, *The Sound of the City.* New York: Outerbridge & Dienstfrey, 1970.

KEIL, CHARLES, *Urban Blues.* Chicago: University of Chicago Press, 1966.

ROXON, LILLIAN, *Rock Encyclopedia.* New York: Grossett & Dunlap, 1969.

192   THE FORMATION OF A MUSICAL STYLE: EARLY ROCK

SHAW, ARNOLD, *The Rock Revolution*. London: Crowell-Collier Press, 1969.

SHELTON, ROBERT, *The Country Music Story*. New York: Bobbs-Merrill, 1965.

The following items provide many useful insights into the sociology of the rock 'n' roll era:

JACOBS, NORMAN, *Culture for the Masses?* Princeton, N. J.: Van Nostrand, 1959.

MCLUHAN, MARSHALL, *Understanding Media*. New York: McGraw-Hill, 1964.

ROSENBERG, BERNARD, and DAVID M. WHITE, eds., *Mass Culture*. Glencoe: The Free Press, 1957.

WHYTE, WILLIAM H., *The Organization Man*. Garden City, N. Y.: Doubleday, Anchor Books, 1956.

[13]

Toward a Theory of Popular Harmony

Peter K. Winkler

I

In this paper, I wish to examine some samples of jazz and popular music
with this question in mind: How does this music go? What is its
harmonic syntax?

The question may seem naive; don't we know all too well how pop music
goes? Its harmonic language is that of classical European tonality,
only-more simple-minded. Our ears are daily assaulted by its harmonic
commonplaces, ready-made formulas, easy clichés. We have to live with
this stuff; must we study it as well?

Jazz historians, especially, seem to deal with popular harmony with a
certain sense of embarrassment. André Hodeir, in *Jazz: Its Evolution
and Essence*, writes:

> Jazz musicians have no special reason for taking pride in an
> harmonic language that . . . does not really belong to them but
> rather to a "light harmony" that North America borrowed from
> decadent Debussyism. . . . [They] do not have strict enough
> standards of harmonic beauty to know how to avoid certain chords
> or progressions. (David Noakes, trans. (New York: Grove Press,
> 1956), pp. 141, 143)

Presumably, what bothers Hodeir is that pop harmony (and jazz harmony
with it) is a kind of musical slang: it falls naturally into predictable,
familiar patterns -- clichés, if you will, or to use a more fashionable
term, *paradigms*. Writers on jazz have often noted the existence of such
patterns in passing, but with little curiosity. In *Early Jazz*, Gunther
Schuller occasionally alludes to "standard chord progressions and forms",[1]

---

1. *Early Jazz: Its Roots and Musical Development* (New York: Oxford
   University Press, 1968), p. 134.

---

but he never troubles to tell us what they are. As a result, his analyses
of solos and whole compositions, insightful as they are, often seem to
exist in a vacuum, sealed off from the musical environment that shaped
jazz. Schuller apparently assumes either that we all know what the
standard chord progressions are, or that we don't really need to know.

Instead of ignoring harmonic clichés, like Schuller, or wishing they would
go away, like Hodeir, I propose to single out one of these clichés and
stare it straight in the face. By applying Schenkerian analytic
techniques, I intend to find out what exactly this cliché is, how it is
used, and, more importantly, *why* it is used. Since my discussion will be

Winkler, Popular Harmony

limited to this single pattern, my conclusions will not be global: I am
not trying to construct a theory that will explain every chord succession
in pop. But I believe we can infer some general principles from this
test case. If we view such a cliché as a harmonic condensation or
summary, the way in which the harmony moves within it can be taken to
represent the way in which pop harmony moves in general.

                                II

Let me quote from one of the first authors who seriously attempted to
investigate the syntax of jazz harmony: Winthrop Sargeant. In *Jazz:*
Hot and Hybrid, first published in 1938, Sargeant wrote:

> The bread-and-butter basis of jazz harmonization exhibits the
> influence of two very important musical factors. The first of these
> is the type of close chromatic harmony known as "barbershop." The
> second is our old friend the blues scale. (3rd ed., enlarged (New
> York: Da Capo Press, 1975), pp. 197-198)

Sargeant's notion of "barbershop harmony" is applicable to the cliché
I wish to study. Here is his description of the phenomenon:

> In "barbershop" harmony the voices tend to stick close together and
> to move in parallel formations. As often as possible the movement
> is by chromatic half-steps. Seventh- and ninth-chords are as common
> as, if not more common than, triads -- especially seventh- and
> ninth-chords of "dominant" formation. These latter often succeed
> each other by parallel chromatic movement, and by such cyclical
> progression through related keys as the following:

                        (Sargeant, p. 198)

Example 1 (p. 6) is a collection of instances of the cliché Sargeant
describes. All of these examples are short, self-contained patterns that
elaborate a progression from tonic to dominant. They can be repeated as
ostinatos, or serve as introductions or "vamps". They can also serve
within a piece as formal articulations, connecting the end of one section
to the beginning of the next; in such a case they are called "turnarounds".
Thus they are parenthetical, bracketed off, so to speak, from the
harmonic argument of the tune proper. They tend to be stereotypes,
applicable to an infinite number of tunes. The Inkspots provide us with
the ultimate case: they used the same cliché to begin every song they
performed (Example 1f).

I find Sargeant's description of this cliché interesting not because he
is the only one to have noticed this phenomenon -- it is mentioned at

In Theory Only 4/2   5

least in passing by many writers -- but because he emphasizes
voice-leading. This approach is rare in the literature; jazz and pop
theorists tend to think solely in terms of the structure and function
of individual chords. Pop chord notation encourages such thinking,
since it consists of the letter-name of the root plus numerals to
indicate the intervallic character of the chord built on that root.
Such notation is convenient because it can describe the chord without
resorting to staff notation, and without pinning down the actual
distribution of the parts (the "voicing"), thus allowing a variety of
realizations. But the notation tends to perpetuate Rameau's view of
harmony: chords are discrete entities, which we study and classify by
type. How they are connected is a separate problem. Such thinking,
as I hope to show, can be inefficient and misleading.

For instance, the notation for Example la would be something like this
(^{6} means "with added sixth" and ^{7} means "dominant seventh"):

$$D^\flat - B^\flat 7(^\flat 9, ^\flat 13) - E^\flat 9 - A^\flat 7(^\flat 9, ^\flat 13) - D^{\flat 6}$$

Although this notation clearly indicates the bass line, it obscures the
fact that the upper parts move downward in parallel chromatic motion.
The notation outlines the structure of each chord, but fails to specify
how one chord connects to the next. Yet it is clear that in this
example voice-leading determines chord structure, not the other way
around.

In order to see the voice-leading more clearly, I have stripped these
examples of their foreground embellishment and transposed them all to C
(Example 2, p. 7). No two of them are identical, but all of them can
be related to Sargeant's "barbershop harmony" pattern.

Let us continue examining the first example (Example 2a). It closely
resembles Sargeant's pattern: the motion from tonic to dominant is
filled in with a chain of secondary dominants. The voices that
determine the function of each chord are shown in the bass clef: they
include the root, third, and seventh of each chord. The bass moves
through the circle of fifths, while the two upper parts form tritones
which move downward in parallel chromatic motion. This motion is
possible because of a pun of which the tritone is uniquely capable:
since it is the only interval that inverts into itself, a given tritone
can supply the third and seventh degrees to two different dominant-
seventh chords whose roots are, themselves, a tritone apart. If the
bass moves by fifths, the third of one chord can move chromatically
to the seventh of the next, and vice versa. The upper voices (shown as
black notes in the treble clef) would traditionally be described in
terms of *extension* (adding ninths, elevenths, or thirteenths) and
alteration (chromatically raising or lowering some voices) of the chords.
Although these notions cannot be dispensed with completely, it would
seem more efficient to view the upper parts contrapuntally, as
reinforcements of the chromatic tritone progression.

Example 2b, from Duke Ellington's "Reminiscin' in Tempo", seems to be an
exception to my statement that all of these clichés move from tonic to
dominant: here the motion is to a dominant chord built on the flatted
supertonic. Yet our ears tell us that Examples 2a and 2b are very

6   Winkler, Popular Harmony.

Ex. 1: Clichés

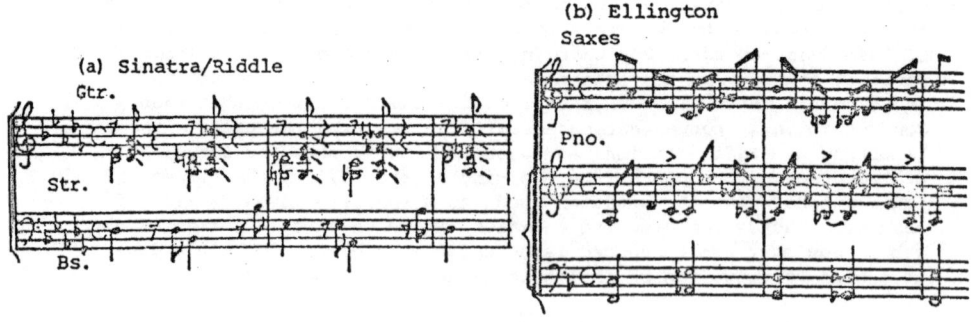

(a) Sinatra/Riddle

(b) Ellington

(c) Beatles

(d) Mathis

(e) Five Satins

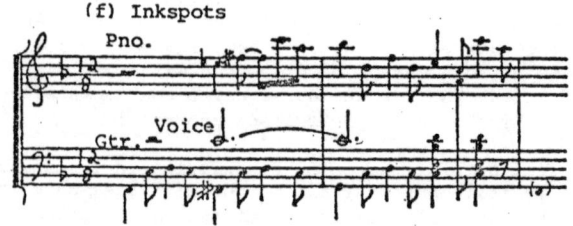

(f) Inkspots

In Theory Only 4/2   7

Ex. 1: (continued)

(g) Ray Charles

(h) Claude Thornhill

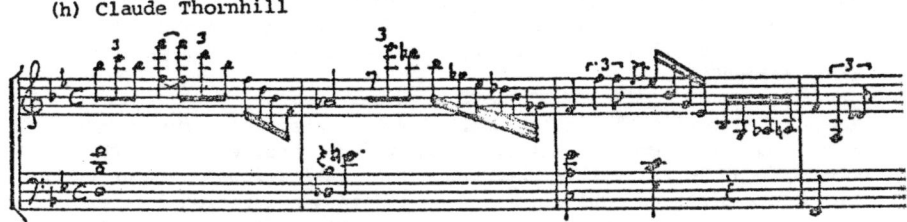

Ex. 2:   Clichés analyzed

(a)   (b)   cf:

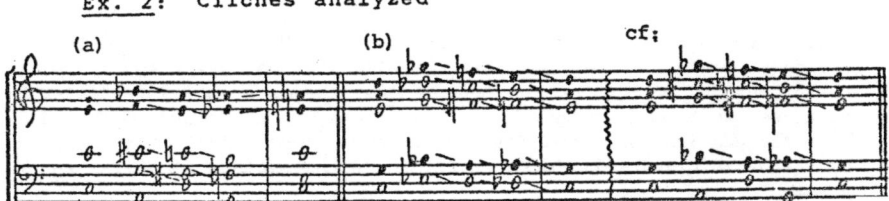

(c)   (d)   (e)

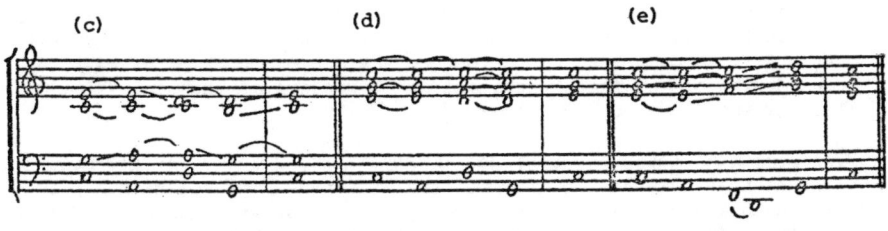

(f) Inkspots   (g) Ray Charles   (h) Claude Thornhill

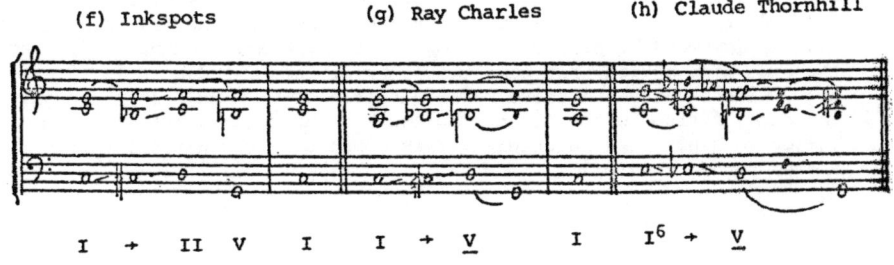

I → II V   I   I → V   I I^6 → V

similar. In what sense can these two progressions be seen as related?
Orthodox jazz theory would invoke the notion of *chord substitution*. It
would explain the Db^7 chord in 2b as a substitution for a G^7, and the
Eb^7 chord, similarly, as a substitution for an A^7. According to this
notion, a given chord may be replaced by any one of a number of others
without disturbing the sense of the progression, rather like substituting
bulbs of different colors on a string of Christmas lights. Of course,
any old chord won't do: the substitute must have the same function
(tonic, dominant, subdominant, etc.). Jazz textbooks often confront
the student with a complicated-looking table of possible substitutions
which must be memorized like multiplication tables: a dominant may be
replaced by a dominant a tritone away, or a diminished or half-diminished
chord built on one of several possible roots; a supertonic may be
replaced by a subdominant; a tonic may be replaced by a mediant or
sub-mediant, etc. Is there a simple principle that could replace all
these tables?

Rather than taking the isolated chord as our starting-point, let us
return to voice-leading patterns. The tritone progression in 2b is the
same as that in 2a. It is this connection that allows us to hear the
two progressions as equivalent. A Db^7 chord can function like a G^7 chord
because the two share the same functional tritone (B-F), by virtue of the
tritone pun I mentioned above. In fact, we could easily "re-substitute"
a I-VI-II-V bass in Ellington's progression.

What of the next three examples (2c, 2d, 2e)? Here there is no tritone
motion -- in fact no chromaticism at all. Yet we hear these as related
to Sargeant's "barbershop" pattern because the bass motion I-VI-II-V is
retained, so that even though the "functions" of the chords on A and D
have changed (they are not dominants), the strong effect of root motion
by fifths is still felt (even in 2e, where this motion is filled in by
a third).

Perhaps we can redefine substitution as *the act of altering some
details of voice-leading while retaining others*. This definition has
the advantage of focusing on the *context* in which a chord occurs rather
than on the structure of the chord itself. But it will be a maddeningly
vague definition unless we can define the context more precisely. By
considering all of these progressions as members of the same "family",
I am attempting to do just that.

The remaining three progressions (Examples 2f, 2g, and 2h) are more
distant relatives of the ones we have examined. The relationship is
best seen if we view them as a series of successive transformations.
The Inkspots' cliché (2f) transfers part of the chromatic voice-leading
to the bass: the chord on D is approached by a diminished seventh chord
instead of a dominant. Because of the bass motion, the tritones do not
resolve downward by parallel motion. The Ray Charles example (2g) has
the same bass motion, but here the minor seventh chord on D is deleted:
the diminished seventh chord moves directly to V, with D in the bass.
The same is true in the Claude Thornhill example (2h), but here the
motion to D has been inverted: it is approached chromatically from
above, rather than below.

I have tried to show how all these clichés belong to the same "family" --
how they could be said to fall under the rule of a single paradigm. But
what, precisely, is this paradigm? No single element links these
progressions; instead, we can see two independent but related phenomena:
parallel chromatic motion (usually involving tritones), and root motion
by the circle of fifths. Both phenomena are associated with tonic-to-
dominant progressions. If we stretch our definition of "dominant" a bit,
we could say that each chord in these progressions (except, of course,
the framing tonics) acts as some sort of dominant to the next. Perhaps
the appeal of this paradigm lies in its simplicity: the dominant
function has been generalized to the point of governing nearly the
entire harmonic environment.

I feel the paradigm needs a new label; "barbershop harmony" suggests
chromaticism, which, as we have seen, is not necessarily present.
Perhaps we could call it the "circle-of-fifths paradigm", with the
understanding that a progression can be "circle-of-fifths-y" even when
the root doesn't move by fifths.

III

Our clichés have allowed us to isolate and study the paradigm in a
test-tube; now we must see how its influence is felt on larger musical
units. The paradigm can be expanded or generalized in a number of
different ways:

(1) It may be extended through simple repetition. The examples from
the Beatles (1c), Ellington (1b), and the Five Satins (1e) are not
introductions but beginnings of phrases, and the phrases continue with
repetitions of the pattern until it is interrupted to make a cadence.
This has been a very common way of beginning a song ever since the late
1920's, and the tendency reached a peak with the black vocal group style
of the 1950's, in which nearly every song is built on this formula.

(2) The paradigm can be prolonged through the addition of passing
harmonies and the insertion of additional structural articulations; in
Schenker's terms, it can serve as a background or middleground structure
which is subject to further foreground elaboration. In George Gershwin's
"The Man I Love" (Example 3, p. 10) a motion from I to VI is prolonged
by descending chromatic motion in the first four measures, and this is
answered by II-V-I in the remainder of the phrase.

(3) Conversely, the paradigm is extremely useful as a foreground device
elaborating simpler background structures. This was a discovery of the
be-bop musicians, who quickened the harmonic rhythm of old tunes by
inserting circle-of-fifths patterns. Not even the blues was immune to
this treatment. In Charlie Parker's "Blues for Alice" (Example 4, p. 10),
circle-of-fifths progressions are used to articulate a bass pattern that
descends stepwise from the tonic to the low supertonic. Though the
pattern coincides with the harmonic changes of the blues at the crucial
points, it perhaps resembles progressions like the Five Satins' cliché
(Example 2e) more closely, since the return to the tonic in m. 7 functions

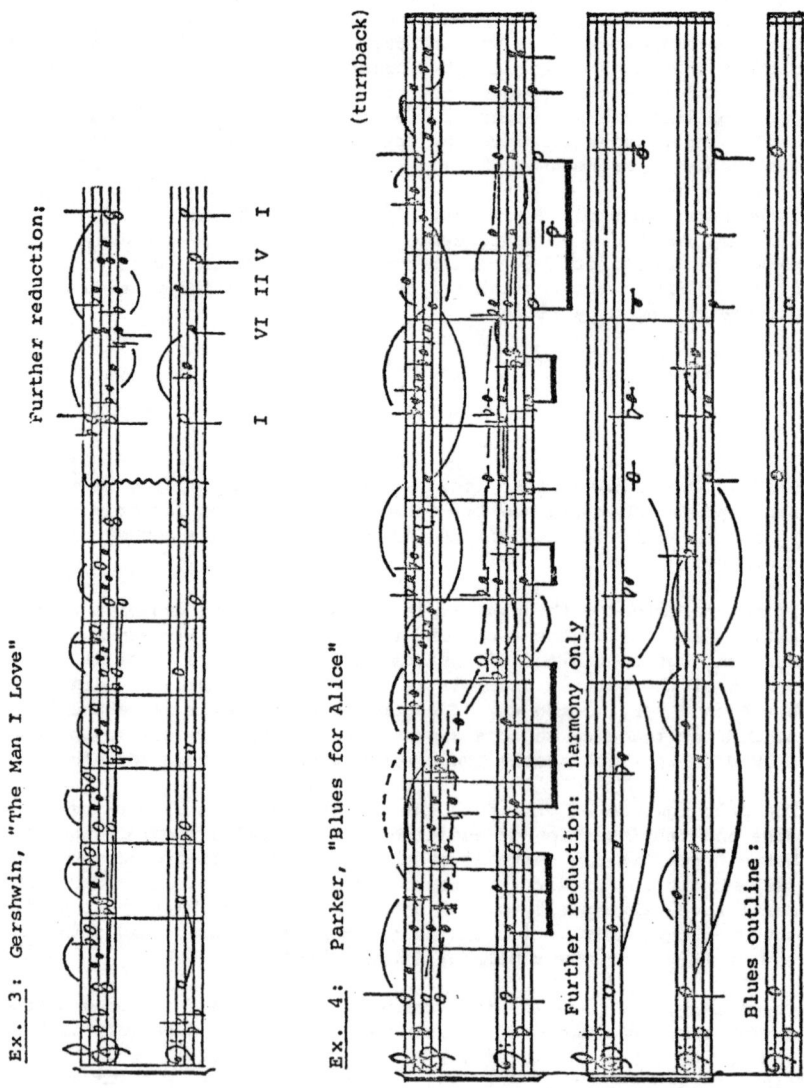

Ex. 3: Gershwin, "The Man I Love"

Further reduction:

I   VI II V I

Ex. 4: Parker, "Blues for Alice"

(turnback)

Further reduction: harmony only

Blues outline:

as a passing harmony between IV and II.

(4) Finally, the paradigm offers a smooth way of traveling into distant
keys for harmonic variety. A classic example is Jerome Kern's "All the
Things You Are", which I will discuss later.

A list of the songs in which this paradigm can be found would be
practically endless. From early Tin Pan Alley through the beginnings of
modern rock, from the music of backwoods jug bands to the most
sophisticated theater music, from the most banal commercial hit to the
most arcane and forbidding be-bop improvisation, the influence of this
paradigm can be found everywhere.

Obviously, this includes a lot of bad music. And the charge could still
be made that jazz and pop musicians are attracted to this paradigm simply
because they don't know any better. How can we speak of critical
standards when dealing with a pattern as basic and predictable as this?
Clearly there is no intrinsic merit in the paradigm. The value lies in
what a great composer or soloist makes of it.

"Making something" of the paradigm does not necessarily mean varying or
extending the pattern in sophisticated or subtle ways, for artistic merit
in pop and jazz does not always lie in complexity. Take, for example,
the trio from James P. Johnson's "The Mule Walk" (Example 5, pp. 12-13).
An ostinato version of the paradigm serves as the first half of each
eight-measure phrase. The first phrase continues with a shift to
G major, confirmed by a cycle of dominant sevenths. But the cycle
continues past G to form a turnaround back to Eb. The second phrase
concludes with another circle-of-fifths pattern, which is slightly
obscured by a bass line which connects II and V chromatically, and
cadences on a first-inversion tonic.

There is certainly nothing innovative in all this -- even the move to
a major chord built on III is a common device. Nevertheless, I think
this is a splendid piece. I like the way the melodic line "bounces" up
to the sixth degree in m. 2, the way this upward tendency is continued to
D in m. 5, and the way the second ending takes care of the high D in
m. 14, moving it back to Bb. I also admire the pell-mell manner in
which the turnaround undercuts the G major cadence in m. 8. The use of
the circle of fifths creates a sense of streamlined efficiency; the
design is just enough to create a satisfying harmonic structure, no more.
It has been argued that in pieces like this the harmonic structure is no
more than a passive vehicle for the rhythm, but I can't imagine a
harmonic structure that would have more momentum than this one. For me,
the beauty of pop music often lies in doing the perfectly obvious as
simply and elegantly as possible.

IV

The great master of such minimalism was Count Basie, so it is
appropriate to turn to one of his recordings to see what use a jazz
soloist makes of our paradigm. Most of the tunes in the Basie repertoire

12   Winkler, Popular Harmony

Ex. 5: James P. Johnson, "The Mule Walk", Trio

Ex. 5: (continued)

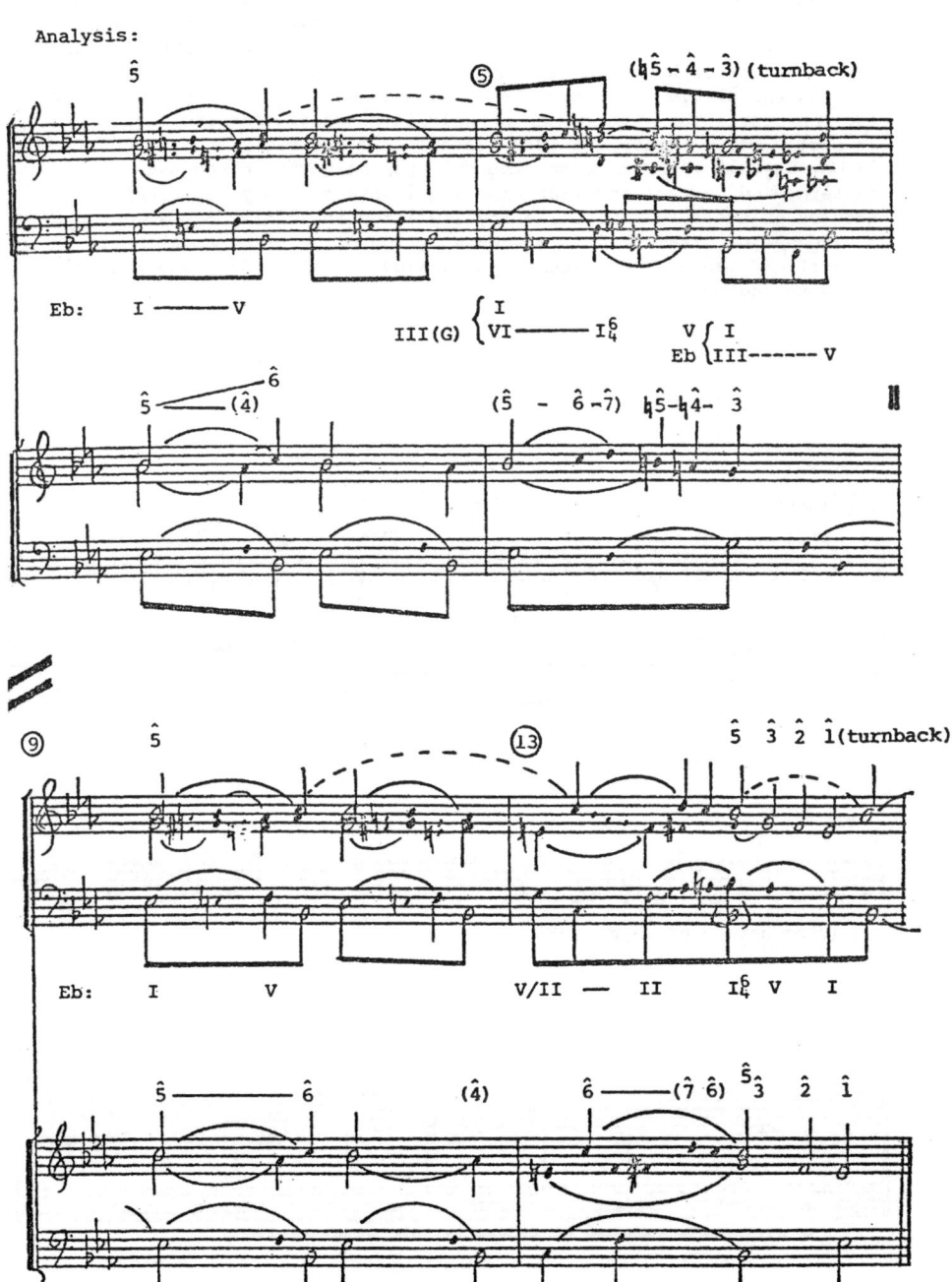

of the late '30's and early '40's were based either on the blues or on a
pattern commonly referred to as the "I Got Rhythm" changes. This is a
standard 32-bar AABA pop song form, whose A sections are built on an
ostinato 2-bar version of the circle-of-fifths paradigm, with alterations
at the end of each phrase to make a cadence. The bridge also moves
through the circle of fifths, but at the slower rate of one chord every
two measures. The pattern as a whole is so consistent and logical that
it easily becomes second nature, rather like the blues. Gershwin's
"I Got Rhythm" is by no means the only pop song that makes use of this
pattern, and in fact the improvisation I wish to study is actually
modeled on the tune "Shoeshine Boy", written in 1936 by Sammy Cahn and
Saul Chaplin. Example 6 is a transcription of solos by Count Basie
(piano) and Lester Young (tenor sax), from Basie's 1937 Decca recording
of "Roseland Shuffle".

Ex. 6:   "Roseland Shuffle ["Shoeshine Boy"]"

CHORUS I

(Basie)

(same harmonies as m. 1-8)

(BRIDGE)

(Young)   (Basie)

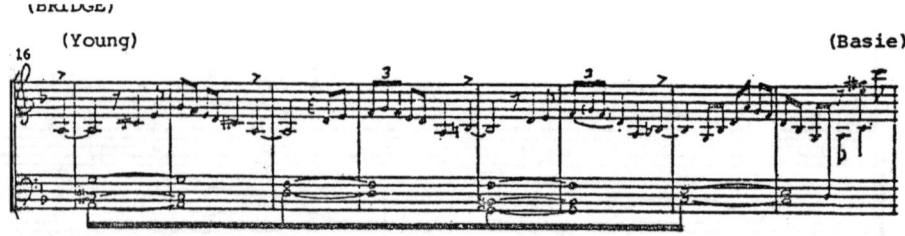

Ex. 6: (continued)

(Basie)

(same harmonies as m. 1-8)

CHORUS II

(Basie)   (Young)   (Basie)

(Basie)   (Young)

(BRIDGE)

(Basie)   (Young)

(Basie)   (Young)

*(chromatic smear)

16   Winkler, Popular Harmony

A common view of what a jazz soloist does could be expressed thus: as
the harmonies go by, he selects notes from each chord, out of which he
fashions a melody. He is free to embellish by means of passing and
neighbor tones, and he may add extensions to the chords, but at all times
a good improviser must follow the changes.

This description certainly fits Young's solo on the first bridge (see
analysis, Example 7a): his lines are clearly based on arpeggiations of
the chords, with some extensions added to the dominant. But what are we
to make of Basie's approach to m. 9-13 of this chorus (Example 7b)?
He plays a simple blues lick in polyrhythms; the pitches do not change
and clearly clash with the underlying harmonies (clashes are indicated
by "?" in Example 7b). There are similar clashes elsewhere, for example,
m. 29-30 in the first chorus, and m. 5-8 and 25-32 in the second.

We could attribute this to the vagaries of improvisation, but in fact
one encounters similar effects in notated ragtime, for example at the end of
the first strain of Joplin's "The Entertainer" (Example 7c). Here the
left hand outlines a descending progression while the right hand repeats
an ostinato figure centering around C and E. The blues are full of such
examples: the melodic line often hovers around the fifth or the tonic
regardless of whether it is supported by the harmonies. Does this mean
that ragtime and jazz musicians are ignorant or careless about the proper
resolution of dissonances?

An answer can be found by invoking Schenker's notion of structural levels.
In the Joplin example, the descending progression is a way of elaborating
a motion from the tonic chord in root position to the tonic chord in
second inversion. The melody simply treats this background harmony as
if it were foreground, and elaborates it directly. Thus, the background
is elaborated in two different ways simultaneously. The ear accepts the
clashes along the way because the two parts coincide at the crucial
points, and because each part makes sense by itself.

The same can be said of the Basie passage (Example 7b): the circle-of-
fifths ostinato is, in the last analysis, just a way of prolonging the
tonic harmony, which Basie's right hand riff is elaborating directly.

The melodic elaboration in both of the above cases is static, but it need
not be. At the end of the second chorus (Example 7d), Young plays a line
that clearly implies a moving voice: D-Db-C. The motion from D to Db
fits easily into the harmonies, but Db lasts too long; it clashes with
the D^7 harmony, and resolves to C too late, since the harmony has already
moved to G^7. But the line makes perfect sense in itself, strongly
implying its own chord progression. The effect could be described as a
syncopation on the level of harmonic rhythm: Young deliberately delays
the resolution of the Db until it is too late. Such a syncopation adds
greatly to the momentum of the music, since the ear must reach ahead,
so to speak, to accommodate the odd dissonance treatment.

When soloing over a given set of chord changes, then, a jazz musician
really has several options: he may reflect the chord progression
exactly, he may "skim over" the progression and simply elaborate the
background harmony, or he may fashion his own voice-leading which may

In Theory Only 4/2   17

Ex. 7: "Roseland Shuffle"   Analyses

(a) Young: CHORUS I, m. 17-24 (BRIDGE)

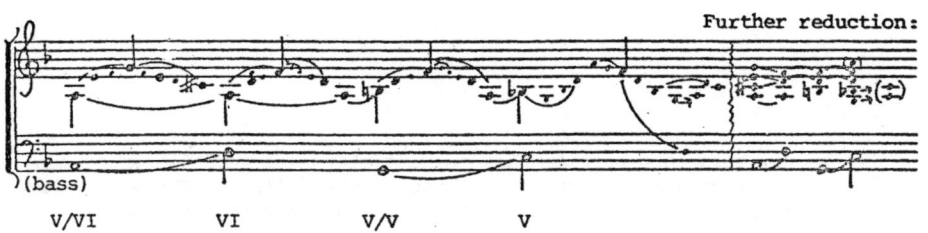

(b) Basie: CHORUS I, m. 9-13

(c) Scott Joplin, "The Entertainer", 1st strain, m. 13-16

(d) Young: CHORUS II, m. 29-32

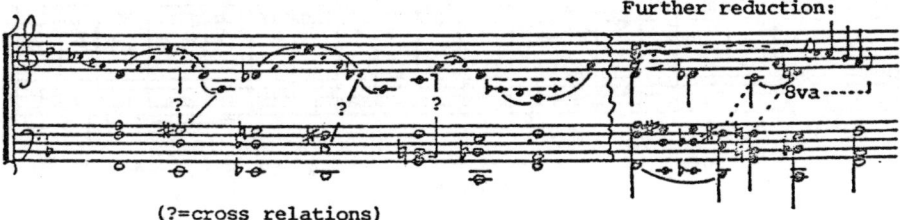

18   Winkler, Popular Harmony

clash at some points with the chords the rhythm section is playing. Much
of the interest and variety in Basie's and Young's soloing lies in the
ways they contrast these different approaches. What they adhere to at
all times is not the foreground of the harmonic structure, but its
background.

V

Let us now turn to a more complex soloist playing a more elaborate tune.
It is said that Jerome Kern was astonished when "All the Things You Are"
became a hit, because he assumed that such far-reaching modulations
would be beyond the grasp of the general public. But the circle-of-fifths
patterns work so smoothly that the tune is easy to follow. The most
startling moment is the enharmonic transition from the end of the bridge
to the return of the first phrase (Example 8, m. 23-25). But this shift
has been carefully prepared by the earlier shifts of key center. The
move to C major at the end of the first phrase (m. 7-8) is achieved by
taking the Db major chord (IV in Ab major) as a chromatically altered
II in C major (some musicians spell out the shift by moving the Db to a
D -- see the note in parentheses in m. 5). The transition between
m. 8 and m. 9 is a shift of the opposite sort: the bass sustains C as
the upper parts move down chromatically. The shift at the end of the
bridge is basically just a matter of moving the bass upward chromatically

Ex. 8: Jerome Kern, "All the Things You Are"

Harmonic analysis

In Theory Only 4/2   19

Ex.9: Charlie Parker, solo on "All the Things You Are"   (Massey Hall Concert; 2nd Chorus)

20   Winkler, Popular Harmony

Ex. 9: (continued)

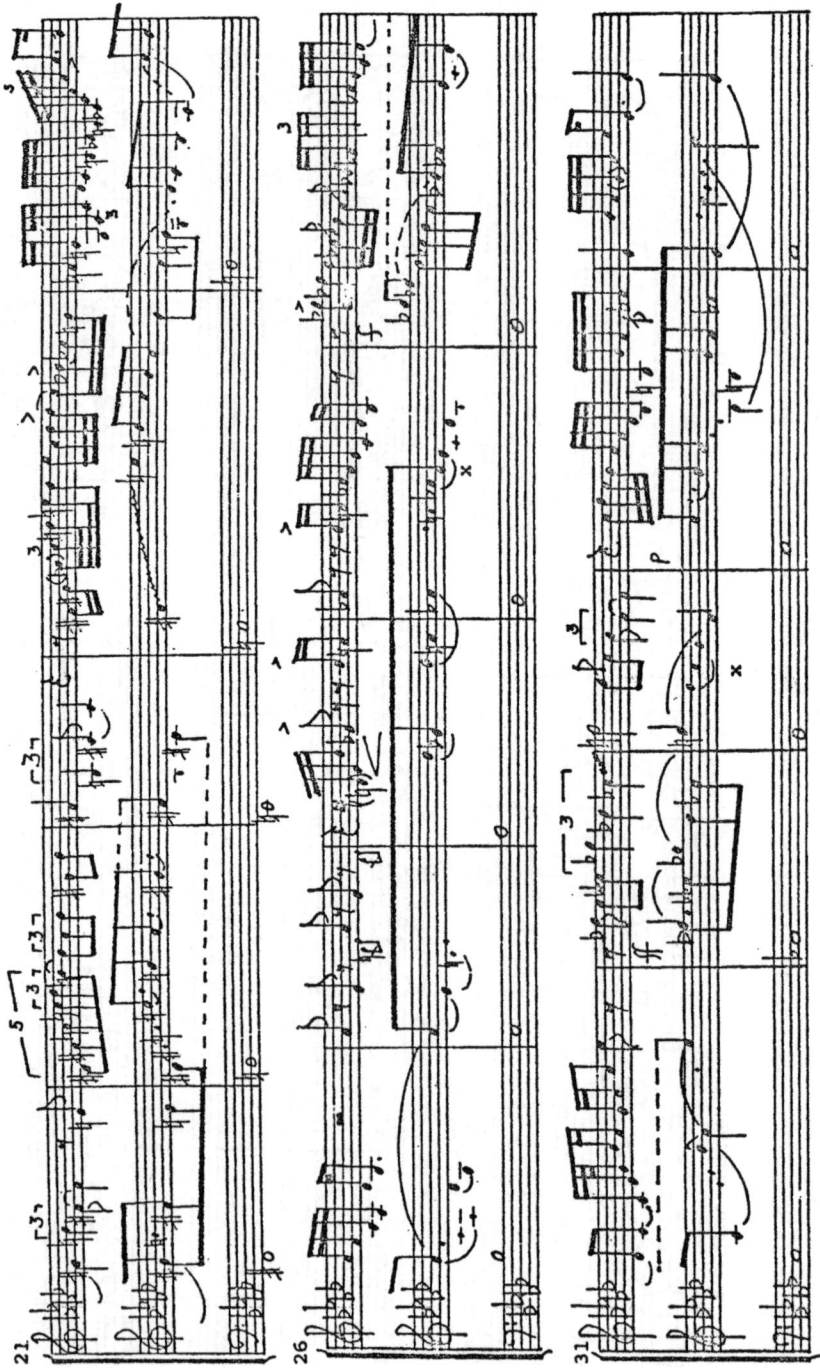

from E to F as the upper parts sustain the same pitches; the augmented chord is inserted to help prepare the listener for the succeeding passage.

Charlie Parker's solo on this tune (transcribed in Example 9, pp. 19-20) seldom "skims over" the chord changes (except perhaps in m. 7-9), though ne sometimes arrives at a harmony behind or ahead of the rhythm section, and interpolates additional harmonies. A clear example is the phrase rrom m. 24 to m. 26, which begins with the transitional augmented chord and continues with the return of the opening harmonies. Parker shifts from the whole-tone scale on C to the F minor scale on the last beat of m. 24, a beat ahead of time. And within m. 25 he suggests an additional V-I progression in F minor.

This solo, like many by Parker, is filled with such a wealth of melodic ideas that it would seem improbable that there could be any unifying conception behind it. But if we ask how Parker makes use of the circle-of-fifths paradigm, how he connects chord to chord, a pattern emerges. It is a pattern that is frequently used in the accompaniment to this tune (Example 10a): the stepwise filling-in of the interval of a falling fifth. It is an obvious contrapuntal possibility whenever a bass moves by fifths (see the species counterpoint abstraction, Example 10b), and we can find it frequently in the classical literature (Example 10c).

The second staff of Example 9 is an analysis of Parker's solo in terms of the use of this pattern. This is something of a one-sided view; the four-note descending pattern is clearly not the *only* thing happening in the solo, but to trace it through provides an interesting perspective.

Ex. 10:

(a) Models

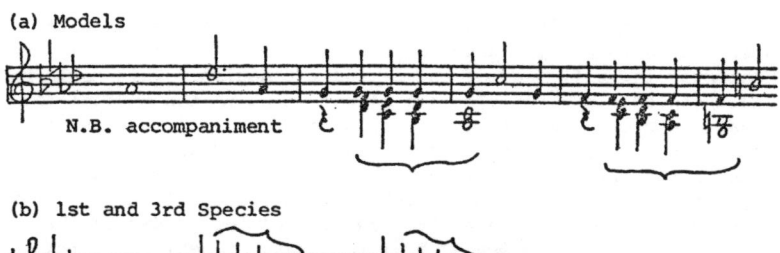

N.B. accompaniment

(b) 1st and 3rd Species

10 9 8 7   3

(c) Mozart,
Rondo, K. 494
m. 95 ff.

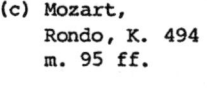

22   Winkler, Popular Harmony

We can see most if not all of our species counterpoint abstraction
(Example 10b) in the first five measures of Parker's solo. What is
remarkable is not the fact that the pattern is used so consistently, but
the astounding variety of ways in which it is articulated. In m. 1-2
Parker breaks the four-note motive into two decorated appoggiatura
figures. The second of these appoggiaturas is connected directly to the
beginning of the next statement of the motive. In the flurry of notes
in m. 4-5 we can see the stepwise motive expanded to span the distance
between Db and F, with the additional interpolation of a lower statement
of the motive (spanning Eb-Bb). Both ideas -- that of breaking the
motive into two appoggiaturas, and that of extending the stepwise motion
(or stringing successive statements of the motive) into long, scalewise
descents -- are developed through the rest of the solo. To me the most
beautiful moments are the cadence at the end of the bridge (m. 20-23)
where the motive is extended an extra step to arrive on the ninth of the
chord, and the tortuous twist the motive is given in m. 32, just before
the final cadence.

Seeing Parker's extraordinary rhythmic and melodic invention as an
elaboration of simple contrapuntal models is not just an analytical game.
I am suggesting that this approach provides insights into the very nature
of improvisation. It can show what it means for an improviser to know
where he is going. More important, it can show that he knows *how to get
there*, because he knows how to use the contrapuntal possibilities
implicit in a given harmonic paradigm.

                                VI

The influence of the circle-of-fifths paradigm has declined since the
mid-1950's. The harmonic languages of rock and soul have moved away from
the all-encompassing influence of the dominant function. This could be
due to the increased importance of the blues, in which the subdominant
function has, to a certain extent, replaced the dominant function as a
structural basis. Such harmonic habits are encouraged when composers use
guitars rather than pianos to work out their harmony. In rock we
frequently encounter the progression I-bVII-IV-I, which virtually turns
our paradigm upside-down (for example, the coda of "Hey Jude" by the
Beatles or "Sympathy for the Devil" by the Rolling Stones). But this
progression is not nearly so pervasive as the circle-of-fifths paradigm
had been earlier. In fact, root motion by fifth in either direction no
longer seems to have a privileged position; the strong functional
implications of such motion are not always desired today. There are
other tendencies (perhaps also traceable to the use of a guitar as a
composing instrument) -- pedal-point harmonies, root motion by diatonic
step, modal harmonic and melodic organization -- that point away from
functional tonality and toward a tonal sense that is less directional,
more free-floating.

We can hear these tendencies along with echoes of the circle-of-fifths
paradigm in the tune, "That's the Way of the World", by members of the
progressive soul group, Earth, Wind, and Fire (Example 11). The central

harmonic idea in the song is a four-measure progression that contrasts
pedal points with a chromatically descending line from the seventh degree
to the fifth -- not unlike the descending line in "The Man I Love", but
with a harmonic coloration that points to the subdominant side. As is
typical of many songs today, this four-measure progression is an ostinato
that underpins the introduction, verse, and refrain. For relief there is
a bridge whose bass slowly moves through a circle-of-fifths progression.
The melodic lines are brief, pentatonic calls that reflect none of the
chromaticism of the harmony. The bass part is one of the most attractive
aspects of the piece; in an ostinato rhythm that recalls the pedal parts
in Bach's chorale preludes, the bassist (Verdine White, one of the song's
composers) subtly inflects the descending progression by supplying
several different root motions (Example 11b).

Ex. 11:   Earth, Wind and Fire, "That's the Way of the World"

(a) Harmonic Outline

Introduction, Refrain, Verse: ("Hearts of Fire)

Bridge: ("You will find peace of mind")

Varied Refrain (and pattern for guitar solo):

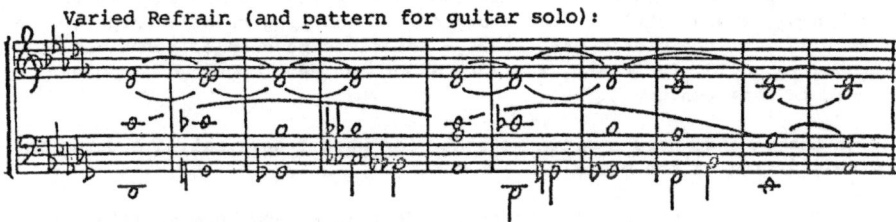

(b) Transcription of Verdine White's bass part

(1) Refrain: ("Hearts of Fire")

24   Winkler, Popular Harmony

Ex. 11b: (continued)

(2) Varied Refrain:

VII

My investigation has been shaped by two theoretical notions. The first
is Schenker's idea that harmony is best seen as the result of contrapuntal
voice-leading, not the other way around, and that harmonic syntax is best
understood in terms of the contrapuntal elaboration of a simple background
progression.

The second notion is the idea of a "paradigm". I have tried to see the
circle-of-fifths paradigm as a bundle of harmonic habits, reflexes, and
tendencies that are employed (consciously or unconsciously) in a wide
variety of ways. The blues is another paradigm, of a rather different
sort. A complete theory of popular harmony would involve the isolation
and description of many paradigms, and descriptions of how they interact
within particular styles. The story of the shifting relationship between
the blues and the circle of fifths -- sometimes peaceable, sometimes
uneasy -- could, in itself, say much about the development of popular
music in this century.

John Lennon once used a vivid metaphor for what I have called a paradigm,
when speaking of the blues:

> The blues are beautiful because it's simpler and because it's real.
> It's not perverted or thought about: It's not a concept, it is a
> chair; not a design for a chair but the first chair. The chair is
> for sitting on, not for looking at or being appreciated. You sit on
> that music. (Jann Wenner, "The Rolling Stone Interview: John Lennon",
> *Rolling Stone*, January 7, 1971, 74:41)

(SUNY at Stony Brook)

In Theory Only 4/2 25

ACKNOWLEDGEMENTS

Example 1a   "I Get a Kick Out of You" by Cole Porter. Arranged by Nelson Riddle. Copyright 1934 by Warner Bros., Inc. Copyright renewed. All rights reserved. Used by permission. [from Frank Sinatra, *Songs for Young Loves* (Capitol W 587), 1950's]

Example 1b   "Reminiscin' in Tempo" by Duke Ellington. Copyright 1935 by American Academy of Music, Inc. Copyright renewed. Used with permission. All rights reserved. [from *The Ellington Era, Vol. II* (Columbia C3L 39), 1935]

Example 1c   "Ringo's Theme (This Boy)" by John Lennon and Paul McCartney. Copyright 1963 by Northern Songs Limited. All rights for the U.S.A., Canada, and Mexico controlled by Maclen Music, Inc. c/o ATV Music Corp. Used by permission. All rights reserved. [from *Meet the Beatles* (Capitol 2017), 1963]

Example 1d   "Let's Love" by Richard Ferraris and Norman Kaye. Arranged by Ray Ellis. Used by permission of Andrew Scott, Inc. [from Johnny Mathis, *More Johnny's Greatest Hits* (Columbia CL 1344), 1950's]

Example 1e   "(I'll Remember) In the Still of the Nite" by Fredricke Parris. Copyright 1956 by Llee Corp. International copyright secured. Used by permission. [from The Five Satins, *In the Still of the Nite* (Ember), 1956]

Example 1f   "Street of Dreams", words by Sam M. Lewis, music by Victor Young. Copyright 1932, renewed 1960, by Miller Music Corp., New York, NY. Used by permission. [from *The Inkspots Greatest Hits* (Decca DXB 182), 1940's]

Example 1g   "Makin' Whoopee" by Gus Kahn and Walter Donaldson. Used by permission of Donaldson Music Co. [from Ray Charles, *Ray Charles, A Man and His Soul* (ABC 590), 1960's]

Example 1h   "Getting Some Fun Out of Life", words by Edgar Leslie, music by Joe Burke. Copyright 1937 by Ahlert-Burke Corporation and Edgar Leslie. Used by permission. All rights reserved. [from *The Golden Years, Vol. 1* (Columbia C3L 21), 1937]

Example 5   "The Mule Walk" by James P. Johnson. Publisher unknown. [from (Columbia CL 1780), 1939]

Example 6   "Roseland Shuffle" ["Shoeshine Boy"], words by Sammy Cahn, music by Saul Chaplin. Copyright 1936 by Mills Music, Inc. and Dorsey Bros. Music, a Division of Music Sales Corp., New York. All rights reserved. Used by permission. [from *The Best of Count Basie* (Decca DXSB 7170), 1937]

26   Winkler, Popular Harmony

ACKNOWLEDGEMENTS (continued)

Example 7c   "The Entertainer" by Scott Joplin. Used by permission of
               Shattinger International Music Corp.

Example 9   "All the Things You Are", words by Oscar Hammerstein II,
               music by Jerome Kern. Copyright 1939 by T. B. Harms Co.
               Copyright renewed. International copyright secured. All
               rights reserved including public performance for profit.
               Made in U.S.A.
               [from Charlie Parker, *Jazz at Massey Hall* (Fantasy 86003),
               1953]

Example 12   "That's the Way of the World" by Maurice White, Charles
               Stepney, and Verdine White. Copyright 1975. Used by
               permission of Saggifire Music.
               [from *That's the Way of the World* (Columbia PC-33280), 1975

*****

TRUE QUOTES FROM REAL CONDUCTORS DEPT.

"Bach was one of the greatest melodists of all times; he couldn't
even write a fourth cornet part without it being melodic!"

                    -- An Anonymous Band Conductor

[14]

On Aeolian harmony in contemporary popular music
Alf Björnberg

Looking at the complex of musical styles, evolved during the last three decades, which today are brought together under the term rock music, one might ask whether it is justified to speak of a special kind of "rock harmony". For several reasons, such a concept is problematic. In general, it can be argued that harmony is a less important parameter of musical expression in rock music than, for instance, rhythm, melody and timbre. Furthermore, one of the most characteristic traits of rock music is its eclecticism; most musical styles, folk, art or popular, have served as sources of musical material for some rock style or other. Thus most authors dealing with rock music, even those with a musicological approach, tend to treat the matter of harmony rather briefly: it's not important, and there's nothing particular about it.[1] One further reason why few attempts have been made to describe the harmonic practice of rock might also be the fact that rock musicians are, to a great extent, bearers of an "oral-electronic tradition", and thus have little need for an explicitly formulated music theory. Nevertheless, this article is an attempt to analyse one distinct type of harmonic practice which has become increasingly frequent, both in different rock styles and in other popular music genres, during the last decade. The purpose of the analysis is not only the establishment of intramusical relationships, but also the determination of, on the one hand, the social and affective meaning of this harmonic practice and, on the other, the musical-structural correlates of this meaning.

Generally speaking, harmony in rock music is less strictly governed by the rules of traditional functional harmony than is the case in jazz music, at least in pre-1960 jazz. Peculiarities pertaining to harmony in rock music have often been described as "modal"; however, the somewhat contradictory juxtaposition of the terms modal and harmony needs some explanation. Many chord sequences used in rock music are modal in the sense that they derive from melodic formulae, in which each note is coloured with a (usually major) triad, resulting in "unfunctional" progressions (examples of this will be given below). Another type of harmonic structure which may also be termed modal occurs when all chords used are based on one and the same modal scale. This is the case for instance in the "modal jazz" of the early 1960s, but also in many rock songs. There are, however, some crucial differences between the types of modal harmony used in jazz and rock music, respectively. While in modal jazz the repudiation of functional harmony is emphasised by the use of non-triadic chords, such as combinations of fourths, the traditional triads are usually retained in rock music. Furthermore, in jazz the modal scale being the basis of the music is explicitly stated and consciously conceived of as material for melodic as well as harmonic elaboration, while this is far from always the case in modal rock where, in fact, the scale is often only implicitly stated in the chordal material. It may seem that in such cases the notion of "modal harmony" amounts to nothing more than a theoretical construct. As a rule, however, the actual use of such a set of chords also involves a number of characteristic progressions differing from "regular" functional harmony, bringing about an effect in many respects similar to the consistently applied modality in modal jazz (and also making evident the affinity between the two kinds of modal harmony outlined above).

Aeolian harmony is the term adopted here for a certain type of modal harmonic practice which, as has already been hinted at, has gradually become more frequent in rock music in the last ten years. This term refers to a chordal material of triads exclusively using the notes of an Aeolian or "natural minor" scale; that is, the chords i, ♭III, iv, v, ♭VI and ♭VII (formally also the seldom used diminished chord ii°). The music from which this abstract concept is derived is tonal in the sense of the existence of an unambiguous keynote/tonic chord, but at the same time it includes some essential features which separates it from traditional functional harmony. The dominant major chord is not used, and thus the fundamental progression of functional tonality, V-I, with its onward-directed resolution of leading-note to tonic, is refrained from and replaced by a number of other chord progressions. These fall into two main categories: those using the chords i, ♭VI and ♭VII, and those using i, iv, and v. The three latter chords are of course nothing but the basic sonorities of functional harmony, apart from the exchange of the dominant major chord for the minor variant. The reason for including progressions of this kind in the present discussion is, however, not mere theoretical formalism; besides the fact that chord sequences involving v instead of V have become more common, the affective meanings associated with the two main types of Aeolian progressions as defined above appear to be similar, and in many instances progressions combining all the above-mentioned chords are used.

The Aeolian progressions are often used as short harmonic ostinatos, perpetually repeated to the effect of creating an "Aeolian harmonic field". This can be clearly heard in songs like Dylan's *All along the watchtower* (1968) and Eric Clapton's *Layla* (1970), using the chord sequences i♭VII-♭VI-♭VII and i♭VI-♭VII-i, respectively. Other early examples of the same kind include David Bowie's *1984* (1974), 10 C.C.'s *Wall Street shuffle* (1974) and *Phoenix* by Wishbone Ash (1970). A further example of the use of Aeolian ostinatos is featured in the final from the Swedish left wing music movement's musical theatre play *Vi äro tusenden* ("We are thousands"), where a melodic ostinato is accompanied by four different alternating harmonic ostinatos using Aeolian harmony. Since the middle of the 1970s rock songs entirely or mainly based on Aeolian ostinatos, built on the chords i, ♭VII and ♭VI have appeared with increasing frequency: Dire Straits' *Sultans of swing* (1978), *Message in a bottle* (1979) by The Police, Phil Collins' *In the air tonight* (1981), *I know there's something going on* (1982) by Frida (from ABBA), ABC's *The look of love* (1982) and Kim Wilde's *The second time* (1984), to mention only a few. A perhaps even larger number of songs are to a larger or smaller extent characterised by the use of Aeolian harmony, without this taking the form of harmonic ostinatos; some examples are Kim Carnes' *Voyeur* (1982), Irene Cara's Flashdance (1983) and *Let's dance* (1983) by David Bowie. The progression ♭VI-♭VII-i also often assumes the function of a cadence, more or less replacing the iv-V-i cadence. This can be heard for instance in the above-mentioned *Sultans of swing*: while the dominant major chord actually does appear in the song, all full cadences are of the (♭VI-)♭VII-i type.

The descending fifth cadence is still maintained where sequences involving the v chord are used, but the tension-resolution effect of the cadence is weakened by the absence of the leading-note in the v chord. Examples of i-iv-v harmony can be found prior to the "age of rock" in many blues songs, like, for instance, Willie Dixon's *All your love*; all minor blues choruses are also used in rock numbers like Pink Floyd's *Money*. In many rock songs of the last decade, however, the v chord is used also in other contexts, generally replacing the V chord or entering into harmonic ostinatos like i-v or i-♭VII-v. Examples of this can be heard for instance in Fun Boy Three's *We're having all the fun* (1982) and *Der Kommissar* (1982) by the Viennese rapper Falco.

What has been said thus far might give the impression that the harmonic models described are seen as radically new and peculiar to music in certain genres of recent origin. Of course this is not the case; however, the question of the relationship between Aeolian harmony and previously occurring harmonic patterns within rock and other musical styles is a complex one, and only a few aspects of this problem will be dealt with here. The following discussion will be focussed upon similarities and differences in Aeolian harmony as compared to some other harmonic practices typical of 1960s and 1970s rock music.

As was hinted at above, harmonic progressions modal in the sense of deriving from melodic formulae "coloured" with major triads, are not unusual in rock music from the mid-1960s onwards. The most important melodic substrata for such progressions are those derived from the so called "blues-pentatonic" or "pentatonic minor" scale. Without entering here into the discussions concerning the origin and exact nature of "blue notes", and the most valid representation of the "blues scale", it can be asserted that in jazz, and particularly in rock, the ambiguous pitch patterns of the blues are often stylised into this pentatonic scale. In this process the blue notes are identified with the flat third and seventh degrees, respectively, of the well-tempered scale; here the typically "white/rock" (as opposed to "black/blues") interpretation of blues pieces as being in the *minor* mode is involved. As can be expected, this stylisation, being the result of an adaptation to the well-tempered system, is more pronounced in instrumental than in vocal lines. Pentatonic riffs using this scale are familiar both in jazz and rock music, but the formation of chord progressions based on such melodic formulae (that is, progressions involving the ♭III and ♭VII chords, like I-♭III-IV and IV-♭VII-I) is specific to post-1960 rock; chord sequences of this kind are common enough in 1960s and 1970s rock for examples to be unnecessary. Besides these, other "mediantic" progressions are also often used; two frequently occurring types are I-II-IV (e.g. in The Beatles' *Sgt. Pepper's Lonely Hearts Club Band* (1967)) and ♭VI-♭VII-I (e.g. in Stevie Wonder's *I was made to love her* (1967) and Jimi Hendrix' *Voodoo chile* (1967)). It is possible that these latter variants can also be traced back to the blues-pentatonic scale.[2] As can be seen, obvious resemblances exist between Aeolian harmony and these "blues-mediantic" progressions. The Aeolian chord material, as presented above, could theoretically be derived by adding the flat submediant ♭VI to the set of chords I-♭III-IV-V-♭VII and changing the I, IV and V chords from major to minor (whether this reconstruction is the most valid explanation of the use of Aeolian harmony is a question left open at this point; certainly other influencing factors, like modality in different folk styles, in classical art music and in film/TV background music, must be taken into consideration). In this process two things are accomplished: the main ethos of the harmonic system used changes from the major prevalent in most previous rock to minor, and a higher degree of unity in the chord material is attained, making the harmonic progressions more "static" and "tension-less".[3]

Here the problem of the meaning of Aeolian harmony is approached, i.e. the question of what, if any, specific affective and social meaning is associated with Aeolian harmony as it has been used in popular music of the last decade. As is always the case in analysing the meaning of musical messages, the justification of singling out one parameter (in this case, the harmonic) can be called in question; as a matter of fact, the increased use of Aeolian harmony in modern rock is accompanied by various other important changes, affecting melody, rhythm, instrumental technique, mixing etc., of which nothing has been said here. Nevertheless, some suggestions as to the possible ways of interpreting this harmonic practice will be made.

Although the harmonic parameter is not the one usually connected with direct, subjectively expressive messages in music, harmonic formulae and the general harmonic language may play a certain role in determining the affective meaning of a piece of music. Harmonic processes constitute a part of a mood-creating and -defining background to the overtly subjective-expressive statements of melody, partly through their relationship to melodic processes (as for instance in appoggiaturas), but also in their own right. Aeolian harmony, as defined above, forms a unitary closed system with few components, generally pervading an entire piece of music; therefore, it can be argued, Aeolian harmony may be treated as one generalised unit of musical expression, or *museme*, in the sense that this term is used by Tagg (1982). A conceivable way of finding out the affective meaning of this museme would be to examine the extramusical associations connected with pieces using Aeolian harmony, in order to establish the possible common denominators (cf. Tagg's "interobjective comparison" method). Since all examples quoted here are pieces of vocal music an obvious place to look for extramusical associations is in the lyrics of the songs; if the verbal messages associated with the use of Aeolian harmony show some measure of consistency, it may be concluded that they also form a verbal representation of the affective meaning of this musical practice.

Refraining here from the space-demanding citing of lyrics excerpts, it is nevertheless maintained that a considerable degree of such consistency exists. A notably large part of the rock songs making extensive use of Aeolian harmony have lyrics dealing with subject matters such as historical and mythical narratives, static states of suspense and premonition, alienation in life and in personal relationships and fear of, but also fascination by, the future and modern technology and civilisation. Altogether these lyrics define a field of associations which might be characterised by keywords such as "vast stretches of time and space", "staticness", "uncertainty", "coldness", "grief" and "modernness". These keywords could consequently be used to describe the affective meaning of Aeolian harmony.

Provided that this interpretation is valid, a number of questions arise. Why is music expressing such affective states becoming more frequent? In what popular music genres, besides the more or less youth-oriented rock music discussed here, is this harmonic practice occurring? Does the affective meaning of Aeolian harmony change, and if so, how, when it is used in connection with a lyrical content different from the ones described, and in other functional contexts? Here only a few tentative answers to these questions can be given.

It is not difficult to establish the fact that today the use of Aeolian harmony is frequent not only in youth-oriented rock music, but also in different genres of the popular music mainstream. To take one example, among the songs entered in the Swedish Eurovision Song Contest qualifications, which in many respects can be considered an epitome of Swedish mainstream music, since the end of the 1970s many songs to a greater or lesser extent based on Aeolian harmony have appeared. This is not very remarkable, bearing in mind the fact that during the 25 years these contests have been arranged, the musical changes occurring have mainly consisted in the absorbing of rock elements with a time lag of a couple of years. In this process, elements of an allegedly structural rather than expressive nature (like those pertaining to harmony) are absorbed more easily and quickly. The lyrics used with Aeolian based music in this context are in some cases consistent with the associational field depicted above, like for instance in the 1980 songs *Låt solen värma dig* ("Let the sun warm/heat you")[4] and *För dina bruna ögons skull* ("For the sake of your brown eyes"); in other cases lyrics are based on traditional love song or novelty formulae. It may seem that the appearance of songs of the latter kind implies that in this context the affective meaning of Aeolian harmony is not the specific one proposed above, and that this harmonic language merely carries with it a general aura of musical novelty, having been taken over from the "more contemporary" youth-oriented rock music. However, there is yet another less manifest level on which Aeolian harmony can be argued to carry meaning and significance, regardless of the lyrical content associated with it.

If it is true that, as John Shepherd has argued, "different forms of 'popular' music articulate *from within their very structure* the socially mediated subjective experiences of differently situated groups, subcultures and counter-cultures" (Shepherd 1982: 150; my italics), a further interpretation of the meaning of Aeolian harmony in contemporary popular music, clearly related to the associational field described above, may be suggested. First, however, the particular characteristics of this harmonic practice, regarding on the one hand its musical-structural attributes, and, on the other, its "subcultural status", will be recapitulated. Although not transcending the framework of functional tonal harmony, the Aeolian ostinatos lack the strongly forward-directed, teleological character typical of the tension-resolution progressions of "regular" functional harmony. Further, the increased use of Aeolian harmony also implies an increased presence of a minor ethos in popular music; however, this is not the subjective-emotional ethos of functional tonal minor.[5] Concerning the relation of Aeolian harmony to specific social groups, it has been indicated above that today no strong such relation exists, this harmonic practice having spread from youth-oriented rock to different genres of mainstream popular music.

Thus, it may be suggested that the use of Aeolian harmony signifies a change in the way life in contemporary Western industrialised societies is experienced, a change affecting large and heterogeneous social groups. The ideology of industrial capitalism dominant in these societies has, as has been argued in several contexts, a musically encoded representation in functional tonal music, which in its structure reflects the assumptions, inherent in the ideology, of the naturalness of an orderly, progressive societal development. The alternative to the uni-directional, goal-oriented progressions of functional harmony which Aeolian harmony constitutes, may in its turn be seen as the musical coding of a conflict between important traits of the dominant ideology and the way in which reality is actually experienced. Faced with the growing threats affecting Western industrialised societies today: atomic war, environmental pollution, increasing unemployment, the rapid dissolution of traditional social values and institutions, people in widely differing social situations, it can be argued, experience a more or less conscious distrust in the optimism for the future contained in the dominant ideology. Due to the relatively marginal status of young people in these societies, the awareness of crisis is first expressed in youth-oriented music, where it is also often verbally formulated in the lyrics (cf. above). However, since these symptoms of crisis affect much larger social groups, they now appear in musically encoded form also in mainstream popular music. Although such topics are rarely directly addressed in the lyrics of mainstream pop, their presence is manifest on a musical-structural, non-verbal level.

Thus, with the use of Aeolian harmony, the carefree letting out of youthful energy in "three-chord rock" and the confirmation of a secure and cosy existence in mainstream pop have both assumed a problematic dimension, reflecting currently manifest contradictions and conflicts in Western industrialised societies.

In the music dealt with here, tendencies both of critique and formulation of alternatives to the dominant ideology, and of resignation and the romanticising of destruction can be detected. Which of these tendencies will prevail remains to be seen.

Notes

1   Except, of course, when it is described as downright deficient, more or less explicitly judged according to the standards of traditional functional tonal harmony. For examples of this position see, for instance, Hartwich-Wiechell 1974.

2   That is, the chord sequences stated can be seen as parts of transpositions of the "blues-pentatonic chord material" to the fifth and fourth degrees, respectively, yielding the sequences V-♭VII-I-II-IV and IV-♭VI-♭VII-I-♭III. Even if this argument amounts to nothing more than a theoretical construct it may serve the purpose of illustrating the musical principles underlying this harmonic practice.

3   The relationship of Aeolian harmony to blues-based harmonic practices might perhaps be illustrated by Dave Marsh's comment on Clapton's Layla: "... with Layla Clapton composed his own perfect blues without resorting to the traditional blues form. It's an epiphany few white men have experienced..." (Marsh 1976: 274).

4   The lyrics of this song in an obvious fashion link in with the fact that the qualification contest was held two weeks before the plebiscite on the future use of nuclear power in Sweden. The song expresses vague worries about the future in general, and the suggested solution to the (not clearly stated) problem is to rely on the warmth of the sun, with both literal and figurative interpretations lying close at hand.

5   Cf. Adorno's comment on the minor mode being used as a sparsely applied sentimental spicing of the prevalent major in entertainment music (Adorno 1976: 52). Obviously the music dealt with here has a function quite different from the one described by Adorno.

References

Adorno, T. W. 1976. Musiksociologi: tolv teoretiska föreläsningar (Sociology of music: twelve theoretical lectures) (Kristianstad)

Hartwich-Wiechell, D. 1974. Pop-Musik: Analysen und Interpretationen (Köln)

Marsh, D. 1976. 'Eric Clapton', *The Rolling Stone illustrated history of rock & roll*, ed. J. Miller (New York), pp. 272–75

Shepherd, J. 1982. 'A theoretical model for the sociomusicological analysis of popular musics', *Popular Music*, 2, pp. 145–77

Tagg, P. 1982. 'Analysing popular music: theory, method and practice', *Popular Music*, 2, pp. 37-67

[15]

The so-called 'flattened seventh' in rock

ALLAN MOORE

Preamble

This article began,[1] quite simply, as the presentation of a stage in the mapping-out of those harmonic practices which serve to distinguish rock and closely cognate styles (hereafter simply 'rock') from those of common-practice tonality on one hand, and jazz on another. It soon became apparent, however, that such a task necessitated some detailed consideration of the means by which the conclusions might be presented and, therefore, some careful consideration of analytic method. To my knowledge, there is as yet very little concern for theorising analytic method in rock music[2] and, therefore, what follows may act as a tentative opening of a difficult debate. The issue at present is, simply, whether or not Schenkerian theory can be adequately applied to this music. My conclusion is that as yet it cannot, and I shall present my findings in that light, but the reasons for my position must, I think, be spelt out. Thereafter, my specific concern will be to investigate varieties of the use of the diatonic 'flattened seventh' in rock, which I shall do by focusing in turn on three issues, investigating them through the analysis of particular examples rather than through any larger generalisations.

The first of these issues is the use of the flattened seventh scale degree (i.e. $b\hat{7}$, e.g. the note B^b in the scale of C major) in melodic patterns, particularly in laying out a theoretical derivation of rock from blues practices. The second is the local articulation of flattened seventh harmonies (built on $bVII$ in the diatonic major scale, e.g. the chord of B^b in C major or, indeed, C minor), through appropriation of the concept 'cadence'. The third is the more global articulation of the same flattened seventh harmonies, approached through 'modulation'.

I have made no attempt to put into historical context the changes in articulation that I note. Indeed, as practices covering a range of barely forty years, I perceive them less as changes than as various realisations of a potential. My model is that of a simple terrain, specific features of which are represented by the examples I shall present. This is not an *essentialist* argument, since my terrain is actually no more than the sum of its features, and does not exist before the invention and identification of those features, but neither does it accept any crude linear causal chain of stylistic development.

Analytic method

There is a growing acceptance of the relevance of Schenkerian methods and assumptions for much of this repertoire,[3] due both to the training of those undertaking the analytical work, and also the evident superiority of Schenkerian techniques over others (see e.g. Bent 1987, pp. 38–41, 49–52, 81–5; Cook 1987, pp. 237–45) for the analysis of classical tonal music. Although his work did not become widely influential until the 1960s, the German theorist Heinrich Schenker formalised, between about 1925 and 1935, an analytical method for the music of the tonal era (broadly music for opera houses, concert halls, cathedrals and courts of Central and Northern Europe *c.*1750–1900). Its most notable feature was its replacement of taxonomic (the identification and classification of a piece's form and harmonies) and emotive (the finding of extra-musical, 'emotional' qualities in the pattern of a piece's changing states) approaches with a non-logocentric, formal-ist[4] approach. His underlying, though unstated, aim is now accepted as having been the promotion of the music of the (Germanic) 'great masters' at the expense of the modernism (both German and French) which had hijacked the development of the musical language of 'high art'. His influence has become so pervasive that there are now theorists who suggest that '. . . Schenkerian analyses *are* the tonal pieces of the decades since the nineteen-fifties . . .' (Benjamin 1981, p. 168). This influence is such that it now forms part of the training of all musicologists in at least the UK and USA, and also through the rest of Europe, Australia and elsewhere.

Schenker's method is concerned with understanding pieces of music as auto-nomous entities, with little regard even to the stylistic habits of their composers, and certainly with no concern for the cultural conditions of their production, trans-mission and reception. It is also concerned with understanding them as *tonal objects*, i.e. as the instantiation of sets of rules (which Schenker undertakes to elucidate) which combine to define tonality. Thus, the employment of Schenkerian techniques in rock analysis necessarily carries with it the assumption that rock also uses the language of classical tonality, and this forms my first main objection. A Schenkerian approach to rock requires us to identify rock's harmonic language as a flexible major/minor system, but rock practice is to make ubiquitous departures from such a system – departures which orthodox Schenkerian theory would accommodate as aberrant. And yet it is *intrinsic* to what rock music has been, that the use of the 'flattened' diatonic seventh scale degree (and sixth, third, second and occasionally fifth, and also 'sharpened' fourth), far from being aberrant, should not even be viewed as *departures*. Such a view leads inevitably to the model of rock as a deformed offspring of classical tonality. Thus, in arguing against the use of Schenkerian methods for rock, I am arguing that this is not its relationship with classical tonality. However, this does not mean that I have preference for a taxonomic, rather than a linear analysis; indeed, it seems to me that any music which makes use of linear modes of continuity, i.e. where successive pitches are found to lie within the range of what we term a tone, demands a linear analysis. My melodic reductions will employ stems to indicate this largely linear motion.

One of the strongest aspects of Schenker's method is its concentration on the types of elaboration used to develop a surface from a background harmonic structure, and this remains a concern for studies of rock practices. Here, however, elaboration develops a surface from *repetitions* of harmonic patterns within the single song: Schenkerian theory is largely unhelpful here, and this is my second main objection. The strophic and open-ended forms which constitute rock are not the deviant things which, in my reading, Schenkerism would have them be. This is the issue of the closure of the fundamental line. Schenker demonstrates that, in the *background* of a tonal piece, there is a stepwise melodic descent all the way to the tonic. Once this has been achieved, the structure of the piece is closed and, to all intents and purposes, the piece is over. My concern over the employment of this mechanism in rock analysis is illustrated by a song like Supertramp's 'Crime of the Century'. Each of two verses closes on a middleground VI-I cadence (locally articulated by a III-I cadence) in a natural A minor (or A Aeolian), under 4–3.[5] This harmonic formula (VI-I) is then repeated for an extended coda (nearly two-thirds of the length of the song) and the unorthodoxy and inconclusivity of the cadence is, to my ears, what the song is about.

A third, related objection, is directly pertinent to the issues raised in this paper. Schenkerian orthodoxy expects 2 (the second scale degree, preceding the final drop to the tonic) to be underpinned by V, leading to a final I (beneath 1). It is my aim here to identify the widespread occurrence of VII leading to I. My ears refuse to hear VII as merely a substitute V, and this is perhaps the crux of the matter. While I am happy to leave open the possibility that Schenkerian methods may be *adaptable* to this repertoire (this proposal has been made by Middleton 1990, pp. 195–6), that position would need more careful theorising than it has yet received, and I do not undertake that task here.

I suggested earlier that there is a growing acceptance in some quarters of the use of Schenkerian methods for popular music. I also noted that Schenker's approach was strictly formalist in nature. Despite the fact that, in recent years, popular music scholarship has properly taken an interdisciplinary approach (see, for example, Middleton 1990; Tagg 1991; Walser 1993; Whiteley 1992), there is now a danger of beginning to treat popular music without reference to its cultural and social contexts. This was, indeed, the thrust of Hauenstein's Schenkerian study of Abba (1993), which determined not to see the pertinence of cultural context. It is also implicit in some of the work of Walter Everett: indeed, the suggestion in Everett (1993) that 'learned' and 'vernacular' repertoires can be directly equated by way of Schenkerian analysis at the level of 'expression' implies that examples of the latter repertoire function autonomously. It does not follow, however, that to utilise Schenkerian methods *forces* one into formalism: the discussion in Griffiths (1992) of Elvis Costello's 'Sleep of the Just' ably interprets it as a *political* statement. Indeed, the analytical discussion which follows may equally be criticised for its formalist tone, but I believe this approach to be necessary at this point in the history of popular music scholarship precisely in order properly to distinguish the harmonic practices of distinct repertoires, a distinction which is still poorly understood. I shall return to this point in my conclusion.

Rock as a modal harmonic system

I take the presence of the leading-note[6]/tonic relationship as axiomatic to the definition of common-practice tonality, particularly in respect of the existence of cadential functions and modulations. I have argued elsewhere[7] that the harmonic practices of rock, while sharing many features with classical tonality, are nonetheless distinct. This can extend from a minimal divergence at one extreme (those rock songs which use triadic harmonies to give substance to a conventional period structure) to a maximal at the other (riff- and drone-based songs). But for both these extremes, one fundamental site of this separate identity is the frequent absence of a diatonic scalic leading-note. I approach discussion of this site through constructing rock as a modal system. This construction, while my own in the working out of its details, nevertheless takes as its starting-point the conscious practices of many performers which are found articulated in guitarists' magazines. This in itself is no necessary justification for it, but I do want to retain a sense of dialogue between theory and practice, in response to a desire to ensure that theory remains *pertinent* (I shall return to this point below). According to this modal system, triads are erected on each degree of the mode within the established (mis-)identification of the medieval church modes: thus, the Lydian mode is the white-note scale beginning on F, the Ionian mode likewise on C, the Mixolydian mode on G, the Dorian on D, Aeolian on A, Phrygian on E and Locrian on B. Thus, only two modes (the rare Lydian, and the Ionian) include a leading-note: the remaining five all have the 'flattened' seventh. This system also minimises the occurrence of root-altered harmonies, as can be seen in Moore 1992, pp. 83–106.

These modes may themselves afford particular (emotive/)somatic baggage: to take one striking metaphor, whereas the Aeolian sixth degree implies resignation, anthropomorphised as a fly caught on flypaper, the Dorian sixth, in its greater distance from the Fifth, at least carries the illusory possibility of escape, the effort expended to constantly raise the leg, etc. Although this suggests the basis for a more thoroughgoing investigation of the meaning of individual songs, I have as yet found insufficient evidence to support the argument that this 'baggage' really strengthens the interpretation of the lyrics of songs using the relevant modes.[8]

My questions thus are, how are cadence and modulation articulated without the use of the leading-note?

Example 1. Howlin Wolf: 'Somebody Walkin' in my House'

Melodic patterns

As stated above, I propose to investigate these questions using specific examples, introducing them through limited discussion of the melodic diatonic flattened seventh. Inevitably, many of my examples will be unfamiliar to many readers; I have made no attempt at providing transcriptions, contenting myself with analysis. I can only hope that the thrust of my demonstration is sufficiently convincing. In Examples 1 to 6, I have summarised melodic motions in a sort of compressed contour analysis, rather than quoted entire melodies, in order to draw out common features from successive phrases. Thus, in Example 1(a), the motion e2-d2-b1-g1-e1 is common to all phrases,[9] while the bracketed b1-a1-g1, g1-a1-g1-e1 and g1-a1-b1-a1-g1-e1 summarise the main 'intensions'.[10] The melody of Example 1, Howlin' Wolf's 'Somebody Walkin' in my House', describes what I would suggest is an unambiguous blues pattern: Example 1(a) is a descending 'blues' pentatonic, i.e. of the form e-d-b-g-e (which could be analysed as either Aeolian or Dorian lacking sixth and second degrees), while Example 1(b) provides an impetus for descent. This melodic motion takes place over an alternating E Ionian I-IV harmonic pattern (i.e. the chords of E and A), serving an ornamented drone function. Example

Example 2. *Howlin Wolf: 'Goin' Down Slow'*

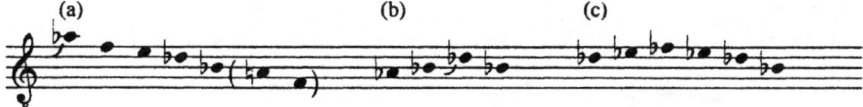

2, Howlin' Wolf's 'Goin' Down Slow', is similar. Here, the melodic outline is underpinned by a conventional twelve-bar harmonic pattern in Bb. Examples 2(b) and 2(c) appear only once, as bars 1–4 of the opening verse. *Every* other melodic phrase (including the first four bars of the other sung verse) uses Example 2(a). Both these songs exemplify the 'divorce' between melodic and surface harmonic schemes which we might characterise as 'historically mediated slippage' following van der Merwe (1989, pp. 225–32), or as 'concurrent alternative elaborations of background harmonies' following Winkler (1978, pp. 16–18). My own preferred explanation comes closer to that of Winkler, although for reasons far beyond the scope of this article.

Example 3. *Fleetwood Mac: 'Black Magic Woman'*

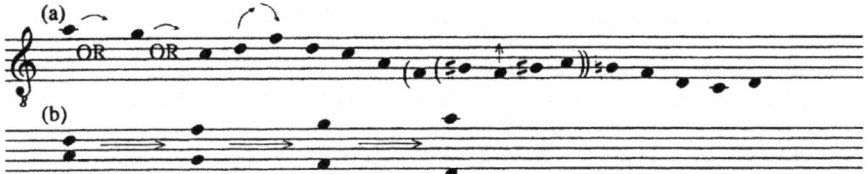

The differences between these two examples and Example 3 are instructive. Fleetwood Mac's 'Black Magic Woman' is much more securely described as a 'rock blues'. Structurally, it is an Aeolian twelve-bar blues on D with substitutions.[11] Example 3(a) extends through an entire verse, which consists of four vocal phrases (2 bars, 2 bars, 4 bars, 4 bars). The first two phrases ornament d2, while the descent closes on g1 in phrase 3 and d1 in phrase 4 (each approached directly via lower neighbour-notes). Example 3(b) traces the expanding *range* of each of the four phrases in the most melodically elaborate verse. This suggests a measure of planning conventionally understood as lacking in earlier blues, and clearly lacking in Examples 1 and 2.

Example 4, Led Zeppelin's 'You Shook Me' suggests an alternative expansion of this paradigm into rock practice. This is a standard Ionian twelve-bar on E, with two melodic phrases per four bars of harmony: the first four phrases are founded on Example 4(a), the last two on Example 4(b). The independence of melodic and harmonic patterns remains evident, although the predominantly falling nature of the melodic line is tempered by a strongly rising upbeat.

Example 4. *Led Zeppelin: 'You Shook Me'*

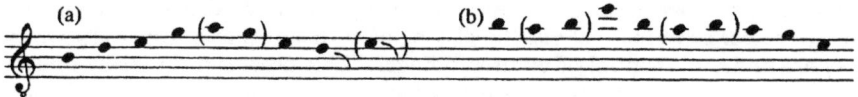

190   *Allan Moore*

Example 5. Led Zeppelin: 'Bring it on Home'

A further Led Zeppelin example, 'Bring it on Home', neatly suggests a potential pathway from the blues pentatonic scale to the widespread, orthodox rock
Mixolydian. The song has a slow introduction and coda surrounding the uptempo
song proper. The introduction uses an E Ionian twelve-bar sequence on guitar
(with a greatly extended I), under a melodic, E Aeolian pattern. This is found as
Example 5(a), which represents an extreme melodic reduction; I have ignored local
repetitions articulated as momentary reversals of contour. The 'song proper' takes
place over a held I, with the vocal phrases taking the form of Example 5(b).
Example 5(c) transcribes the two-part E Mixolydian guitar riff which separates the
verses of which these latter vocal phrases consist. Note that the song therefore
makes structural use both of a blues pentatonic scale in the outer sections, and of
a standard Mixolydian in the central portion.

I have already declared my intention not to place into a historical context the
transition from blues pentatonic to rock Mixolydian. Any subsequent attempt
would also need to take into account the influence of other styles. The Mixolydian/
Dorian nature of much English traditional song, and its influence on 'folk rock' is
widely accepted. Taking another route, Neil Young's 'Oh Lonesome Me' is far
closer to southern US country music. The melodic motion of Example 6(a) underpins the verse: the first half is repeated over an E Mixolydian I-IV, acting as an
ornamented drone, reaching V beneath e2 and closing on IV. Example 6(b) concludes the verse, over an E Mixolydian VII-IV-I. It is to the role of VII in these,
cadential, contexts that I now turn.

Example 6. Neil Young: 'Oh Lonesome Me'

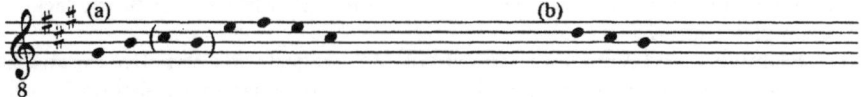

Cadences

I have argued elsewhere[12] that the harmonic practices of rock encourage the identification of harmonies as discrete entities not subject to voice-leading[13] processes.
Part of the reason for this lies in instrumental practices themselves. Guitar chords
tend to be held in a convenient position with bass and treble pitches possible
determinants: inner parts rarely have a linear role, merely existing to fill out the
chord. Similar concerns underlie the playing of keyboard chords, especially when
they are under the control of untutored fingers. This observation actually underpins a further objection I have to the indiscriminate application of Schenkerian

methods to this repertoire, namely that voice-leading frequently does not determine harmonic succession, which may, therefore, be entirely 'dissonant'. Again,
Schenkerian analysis of rock needs careful theorising.

This view of rock harmony determines the manner in which the remainder of
the examples are laid out. I have summarised essential melodic and bass motions,
bringing rhythm into analytical play by barring these examples. This provides a
clear sense of the speed of harmonic movement. Melodic pitches have been
adjusted to the tempered scale for ease of reference only. It should be noted that
chordal inversions[14] are rarely used in rock: they tend to appear only within certain
(more aesthetically motivated) styles, where their role is usually to allow the construction of a stepwise bass line.

Example 7. Icicle Works: 'Don't let it Rain on my Parade'

(I   IV ...)   VII V   VII IV   I
D Mixolydian

Part of the heritage of rock lies within common-practice tonality: this should
alert us to the expectation that we will find both parallels and more distant relationships between cadences in the two practices. Example 7 summarises the harmonic
material of the refrain to the Icicle Works' 'Don't let it Rain on my Parade', a song
which heavily pastiches mid-1960s US West Coast pop. The refrain employs a
standard 'half close/close' period structure within a D Mixolydian context, but the
contrast between the imperfect[15] (VII-V$^{\#3}$) and extended plagal[16] (VII-IV-I) cadences
is particularly notable: this is the only occurrence of V in the entire song. The
extension of the plagal cadence in this way is by no means unusual in rock, but
it does appear to be less common than the simple VII-I. This latter may frequently
invite interpretation as a contraction of that extended plagal cadence. It is also
commonly interpreted as the pragmatic result of the technically easy motion of
sliding a guitar barre[17] chord up two frets, but Example 8 makes it clear that it
may be employed in other instrumental contexts, for the basis of The Beatles'
'Lady Madonna' is the piano, and the cadence is not simply articulated by full
parallel motion. In this case, the VII-I is itself extended, being approached via VI.

Example 8. Beatles: 'Lady Madonna'

D Aeolian   VI VII   I$^{\#3}$

192   *Allan Moore*

Example 9. Secret Affair: 'Time for Action'

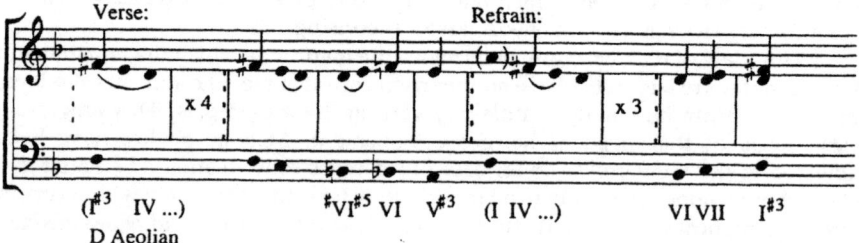

$(I^{\#3}$ IV ...) $^{\#}VI^{\#5}$ VI $V^{\#3}$ (I IV ...)   VI VII $I^{\#3}$

D Aeolian

Example 10. Clannad: 'Backstairs'

(VII)   VI VII I

D Aeolian

In contrast, note that the bridge section ends with a half close Ionian II^7-V, landing on I at the repeat of the refrain.

Examples 9 and 10 present further examples of the same type of cadence, but from markedly different styles. Secret Affair's 'Time for Action' was a cult mod single from the time of the English mod revival in the late 1970s, while 'Backstairs' is by Irish group Clannad, whose work is shot through with Celtic imagery and pastiches of Irish traditional music. Example 9 presents the harmonic material of verse and refrain (the bridge has the character of a relative minor episode), while Example 10 presents the refrain only. In this latter example, the melodic line suggests the flexibility often associated with the use of the harmonic 'flattened' seventh.

Both Examples 11 and 12 are by Peter Gabriel, respectively the cadences to the verse of 'Waiting for the Big One' and the refrain of 'I Don't Remember'. Both exhibit extended versions of this same cadence over a scalic bass but, whereas the first is rising (as we might expect), the second is falling. Example 12 is particularly interesting, because it seems to be asserting the functional equivalence of Aeolian VII^6_5-I and Phrygian II-I (which latter *does* seem to act as a substitution). I have encountered few examples of this latter cadence in rock, but its presence here

Example 11. Peter Gabriel: 'Waiting for the Big One

C Aeolian   VI   VII   I

Example 12. Peter Gabriel: 'I Don't Remember'

D Aeolian   VII   I   (Phrygian)   II   I

seems to suggest that the essential feature is to approach the tonic by linear motion in the bass.

Clearly, the VII-I cadence does not have the finality of the traditional V-I, although it is articulated as a full close in all the examples I have presented. In terms of poetics, it seems to me to qualify the certainty of V-I with 'nevertheless'.

Modulation

In a harmonic modal system, a tonic cannot be identified by scale collection (i.e. a simple listing of the non-ornamental pitches in use at any point) as it would be for the tonal system, since each collection is shared by seven separate modes. I have described elsewhere the (largely rhythmic) factors which seem to define tonic functions[18] in rock, but here I wish to move beyond that argument, in order to identify how, in the absence of clues given by collection, modulation is effected. The device I shall focus on is that of the pivotal use of particular chords. I shall demonstrate a number of different contexts for this feature, with the purpose of documenting something of the variety of its appearance in rock. All my examples here use *b*VII to effect the modulation: I am not arguing that rock does not use other pivots (some of these examples could be reinterpreted in favour of other pivotal chords), but my context here is simply the use of *b*VII. It should be noted at this point that such modulations are frequently not accompanied by an unambiguous cadence within the new mode – in those cases where ambiguity as to mode is avoided, this tends to be the result of the use of a 'hook' rock progression in the new mode. Example 19 will provide a clear example.

Another, minor, point of disagreement with Schenkerian theory comes about here. Although traditional, taxonomic, tonal analysis identifies within a piece a series of keys through which the music modulates or passes, this concept was largely replaced by Schenker with the notion that these modulations are but local disturbances of a single key (the tonic key) which exerts control over an entire piece. Modulations are seen, therefore, to be simply local departures. This is by no means so in rock, where an initial mode can be no more than a convenient starting-point, carrying no necessary implication of return. Modulation, therefore, as the moment of the change of modal focus, has a far higher priority.

I start with two simple examples. In Peter Gabriel's 'Here Comes the Flood' (Example 13), the verse begins in C# Aeolian, with B as VII prominent both in the opening I-VII-VI progression and also as the starting-point for the passage which modulates in a standard way to the 'relative major' (i.e. E Ionian). The refrain then sits astride E Ionian/Aeolian, within which B (as V) remains prominent. In John Farnham's 'You're the Voice' (of which Example 14 supplies the pertinent

194   *Allan Moore*

Example 13. Peter Gabriel: 'Here Comes the Flood'

Example 14. John Farnham: 'You're the Voice'

refrain and bridge), the modulation has a pragmatic rationale. The song is simpler than many chosen here, and might not be expected to modulate. Both verse and refrain are in an unambiguous F Mixolydian with prominent VII (chord of E♭). The bridge introduces Scottish highland bagpipes on the melody, but bagpipes are tuned to B♭ Mixolydian.[19] Thus, E♭ becomes reinterpreted as the limit chord of the progression (i.e. IV) before the original mode is recovered.

I now move on to some more complex examples. The verse of Jethro Tull's 'This is not Love' (Example 15) broadly falls into an A Aeolian framework, with the extended VI-VII-I cadence we have already noted: VII is represented by the chord of G. In the bridge, this G then acts pivotally as IV of D Aeolian, inviting interpretation as a plagal-related cadence (with the momentary interpolation of VI at point 'a'). I is now reinterpreted as II in C Aeolian (at point 'b'), wherein G appears as V in perfect cadences (point 'c'), before being reinterpreted as VII in A Aeolian (point 'd') leading us back to the repeat of the verse. Note especially the two occurrences of the refrain. At the end of the verse, its context is clearly that of A Aeolian, but at the end of the bridge, its context is much more that of a C

Example 15. Jethro Tull: 'This is not Love'

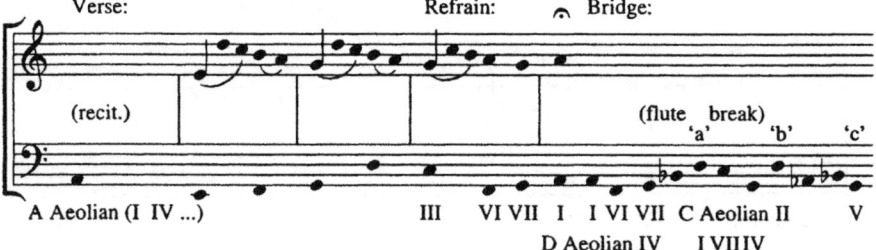

Ionian interpolation within a C Aeolian context. In other words, in the latter case it is now situated on the tonic, a strength which is attested to both by its immediate repetition and by its articulation (broadly a crescendo which leads, via chords on E*b* and B*b*, climactically back to A Aeolian).

The richness of this example is by no means unusual. Led Zeppelin's 'Out on the Tiles' (stylistically rather distant) moves similarly between three modes by the use of an equivalent device. As Example 16 shows, the introduction is founded on A Dorian. F# is then reinterpreted as I Mixolydian for the verse, with an emphasis on E as VII. This E is in turn reinterpreted as I Ionian for the refrain, with an emphasis on IV (the tonic of the introduction). The E returns as Mixolydian I for the coda.

An earlier Jethro Tull song, 'Queen and Country', makes use of a slightly simpler scheme (Example 17). The verse settles onto E Aeolian, with a prominent VI-VII-I progression. The refrain begins as a simple upward melodic and harmonic

Example 16. Led Zeppelin: 'Out on the Tiles'

Example 17. Jethro Tull: 'Queen and Country'

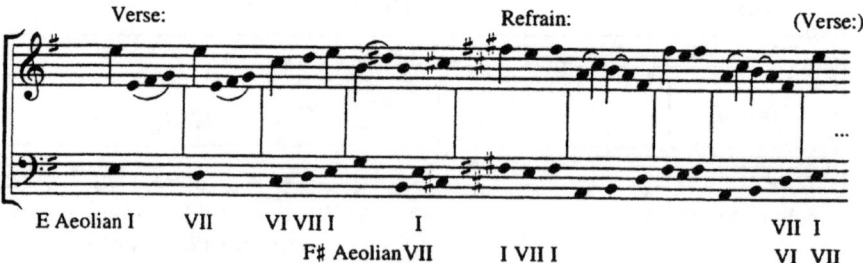

transposition to F# Aeolian, with E reinterpreted as VII. The refrain ends on VI-VII (D-E), the latter chord also serving as I of the next verse. The force of this progression becomes plain at the end of the song, where the refrain is repeated, such that the final VI-VII leads straight back to I in F# Aeolian: the finality of this gesture (a very common closing gesture for the 'rock song') is thus retrospectively signalled by the VI-VII-I progression of the verse. The neatness of this construction is self-evident. Although these examples from Led Zeppelin, Jethro Tull and Peter Gabriel are insufficient to prove the case, I would argue that there is no actual correspondence between the richness of a modulatory scheme and the relative stylistic maturity of particular artists.

    I conclude this short survey with discussion of three further examples. As Example 18 suggests, in 'Kite', Kate Bush's approach to harmony has a virtuoso character frequently considered beyond the capacity of rock musicians. Modulations are effected by twice using VII pivotally. The first is a move from C Aeolian with VII on Bb (for the verse) to Bb Mixolydian for the first part of the refrain. VII

Example 18. Kate Bush: 'Kite'

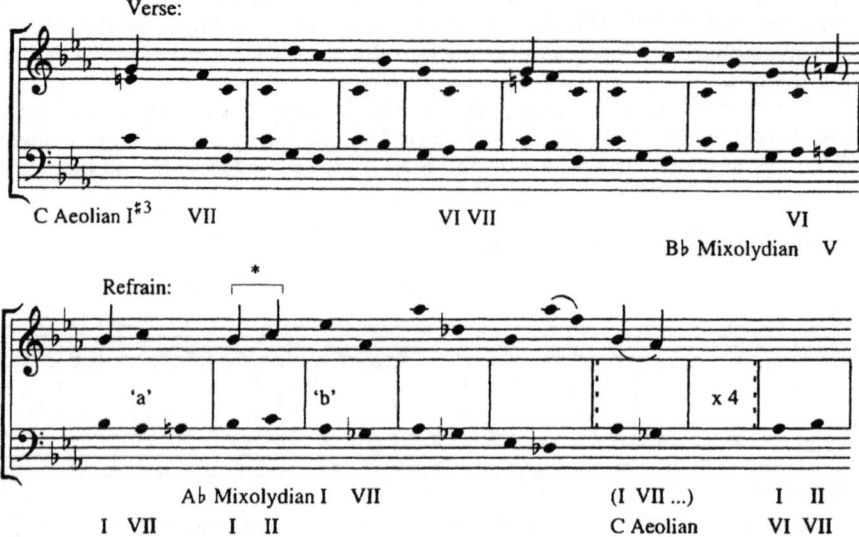

Example 19. David Bowie: 'Ashes to Ashes'

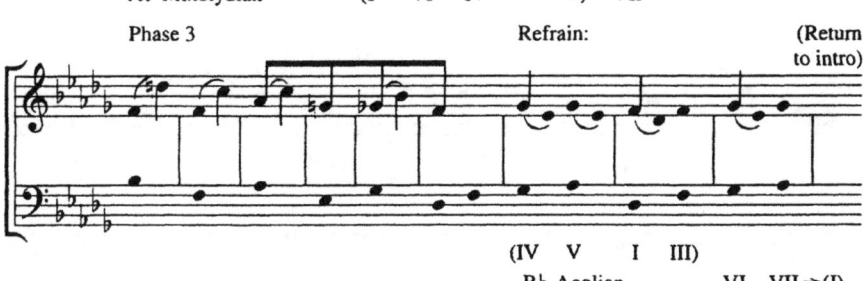

(i.e. A♭) is then itself reinterpreted (points 'a' and 'b') to form I of A♭ Mixolydian for the remainder of the refrain, returning to the verse by way of the VI-VII-I (C Aeolian) cadence discussed above. Ambiguities persist, for the asterisked succession in the refrain also lends itself strongly to interpretation as a VII-I modulation returning to C.

Example 19 summarises David Bowie's 'Ashes to Ashes' in its entirety. The verse falls into an instrumental introduction and three distinct phases. The introduction uses a stock B♭ Aeolian I-VII-IV repeated succession, reinterpreting VII as I of A♭ Mixolydian in the first phase of the verse. This phase is underpinned by another stock formula, i.e. I-VI-IV-V (the 'Stand by Me' changes). The second phase reinterprets VII (i.e. chord of G♭) now as IV of D♭ Ionian, using yet another stock pattern (I-III-IV-V). The third phase suggests in succession Mixolydian B♭, A♭ and G♭. The refrain returns to D♭ before A♭ (as V of D♭) returns to its initial function as VII of B♭ Aeolian returning to the verse. It should be noted that the refrain employs a stock formula related to that of the second phase, i.e. IV-V-I-VI. Because the harmonic language of this song seems paradoxically so limited (at least in its actual articulation), it raises the question of how successive tonics can be articulated. It seems to me that this is achieved by their appearance at stressed points within a stock or 'hook' formula, particularly marked also by a change of harmonic movement (double speed in this example). These patterns I have identified as 'stock' will be found explored in Moore (1992)[20] – their function in rock is normally to act as the basis for 'open-ended repetitive gestures'.[21]

The final example is both exceedingly rich and interesting: Nik Kershaw's 'One and Only', as sung by Chesney Hawkes; it was this song which originally fired my investigation. Example 20 summarises the harmonic material of the entire song. Its formal articulation can be simply described: introduction, verse/refrain

Example 20. Chesney Hawkes: 'The One and Only'

(twice), bridge, instrumental, refrain repeat to fade. The introduction is in C Ionian, with an emphasis on VI. This VI becomes I for the first half of the verse, which settles into A Aeolian. The final chord, VII (point 'a'), is now reinterpreted as V of C Aeolian for the second half of the verse. Again, the final chord is VII, which is now interpreted as (Mixolydian) VII for the refrain, which itself repeats the material of the introduction. The direct transposition within the verse is itself unusual in rock, but rarer developments are to follow. The bridge begins in C Aeolian, the first half ending on IV (point 'b') which becomes V of Bb Aeolian leading to the second half of the bridge. This, although now in Bb Aeolian, repeats the entire sequence of the verse, leading on to an instrumental version of the refrain now based on Bb. The V with which this ends is then reinterpreted as IV of C Ionian for the refrain, with which the song plays out. The appearance of one chord sequence (that of the refrain) at two different levels is not unknown in rock, but the appearance of a second (that of the verse) at three separate transpositional levels, and with structural consequence, is rare indeed. This suggests a level of abstraction far removed from the stereotype I have referred to above, of composing at the guitar or piano, wherein harmonic patterns are largely determined by the instrument's construction and the player's physiology, although it does not undermine the interpretation of harmonies as 'givens'. Indeed, Kershaw's general harmonic practices are so notable that I intend to pursue them elsewhere.

With all these examples of the use of the 'flattened' diatonic seventh chord in modulatory situations, the most important feature seems to me to be not that the chord can act pivotally in theory, but that it also does so in practice. As Richard Middleton implies in stressing not only issues of competence, but also of pertinence (1990, p. 173), we cannot afford the luxury of a theoretical exposition of rock's musical practices which cannot be directly related to the music-as-heard.

Conclusion

It is of the nature of the research summarised here that it does not support a conclusive argument. I have merely attempted to demonstrate the importance of the chord built on the 'flattened' seventh degree in particular contexts, those of the cadence and the modulation. I think the richness of the range of examples of the latter that I have identified is worthy of note, particularly since it strengthens the view that this degree is as normative in rock as the 'diatonic' seventh, and that it is certainly not aberrant. In the 1990s, it is becoming abundantly clear that the split between 'classical' and 'popular' musics is fast diminishing, whether this is judged with reference to use, to marketing and dissemination, to production, or to any other of a multitude of criteria. The danger attendant on this is that we may come to overlook the real differences inherent in the ways different styles are constituted. An account of rock's harmonic practices derived from those of common-practice tonality misrepresents, I believe, much of its distinctive quality.

Endnotes

1 Many thanks to Dai Griffiths and Stan Hawkins for perceptive comments and difficult questions raised against an earlier version of this article.

2 Although see Tagg (1982), Middleton (1990), Moore (1993) and Hawkins (1993).

3 See e.g. Griffiths (1992), Everett (1993), Hauenstein (1993), for some of the most recent examples.

4 Some writers prefer to describe Schenker's as a *structuralist*, rather than a *formalist* approach, especially since Schenker's primary analytic concern is with distinguishing between a piece's *foreground* (i.e. surface), *middleground* and *background* (i.e. structure). I prefer the description *formalist* purely because Schenker has no recourse to the linguistic theory of Saussure, from which *structuralist* theory emanates.

5 The caret is used to indicate a background, 'structural' scale degree. Thus, the melody here comes to rest on the third degree of the scale, never falling to the tonic.

6 The seventh scale degree, a semitone below the upper tonic. Chew (1983) argues strongly for the rehabilitation of the leading-note within Schenkerian theory, focusing not only on the way $\hat{1}$ is approached from above via $\hat{2}$, but also the way it is approached from below via $\hat{7}$. Whatever the benefits of this position, it only compounds the difficulties encountered in rock, where $\hat{7}$ is widely absent.

7 See Moore (1992, 1993).

8 Björnberg (1989) makes a start in this direction.

9 References to specific melodic pitches follows the standard nomenclature: 'c' represents the c of the viola, rising to 'b' at the top of that octave; 'c1' is middle c, rising to 'b1', 'c2' is the note an octave above middle c, etc.

10 By this, I mean deviations from the melodic structure, by analogy with 'extension', but using Chester's (1970) formative distinction between 'intensional' and 'extensional' (see also Moore 1993, p. 21). Whereas 'extension' suggests temporal expansion beyond prior set boundaries, 'intension' signifies 'internal'

200   *Allan Moore*

development, recognisable on repetition, and, which I think, distinguishable from both 'ornamentation' and 'elaboration'.

11 Harmonically, it follows the rarer I-V-I-IV for its first eight bars. This pattern would not be generated by Steedman's (1984) rules for the jazz 'twelve-bar'. He, moreover, sees minor twelve-bar patterns necessitating a dominant major. His theory may work for jazz, but not for other uses of the twelve-bar structure.

12 See Moore (1993, p. 48).

13 'Voice-leading' conceptualises the understanding that music is built entirely from superimposed middleground melodies which move, at different rates, entirely by step.

14 I.e. the practice of placing in the bass of the texture any note *other* than the root of the chord.

15 In traditional theory, an 'imperfect cadence' (or half close) ends on chord V rather than the expected I (which is understood as a 'perfect cadence', or full close).

16 Again in traditional theory, the 'plagal cadence' is marked by the harmonic succession IV-I. It conventionally underpins settings of the word 'Amen', and is also considered a full close.

17 To play a barre chord, a guitarist holds the index finger across all six frets, making it very simple to bring the whole hand up or down the fretboard in one movement.

18 See Moore (1992, p. 77) where I suggest that a tonic is likely to exhibit persistence, laterality and/or emphasis within any harmonic pattern.

19 The fundamental of bagpipes is called A, but with a frequency of about 463 c/s, i.e. far closer to concert Bb (MacNeill and Richardson 1987, pp. 34, 37) – these seem to have been sampled and transposed. To have transposed the sample up to F would have changed the timbre of the instrument too much.

20 See Moore (1991, pp. 82ff.).

21 See Moore (1993, pp. 47, 50–1).

References

Benjamin, W. 1981. 'Schenker's theory and the future of music', *Journal of Music Theory*, 25, pp. 155–73

Bent, I. 1987. *Analysis* (Basingstoke)

Björnberg, A. 1989. 'On aeolian harmony in contemporary popular music', *IASPM Nordic Branch Working Paper No. 1*

Chester, A. 1970. 'Second thoughts on a rock aesthetic: The Band', *New Left Review*, 62, pp. 75–82

Chew, G. 1983. 'The spice of music: towards a theory of the leading-note', *Musical Analysis*, 2, pp. 35–53

Cook, N. 1987. *A Guide to Musical Analysis* (London)

Everett, W. 1993. 'Musical expression at deep structural levels in learned and vernacular repertoires (I)', paper presented at 5th British Music Analysis Conference/28th Annual RMA Conference, Southampton (March)

Griffiths, D. 1992. 'Talking about popular music (4): politics', paper presented at Popular Music: the Primary Text, London (July)

Hawkins, S. 1993. 'Perspectives and problems within the analysis of popular music: "Lost in music" ', paper presented at 5th British Music Analysis Conference/28th Annual RMA Conference, Southampton (March)

Hauenstein, P. 1993. 'Principles of melodic construction in the songs of ABBA', paper presented at 5th British Music Analysis Conference/28th Annual RMA Conference, Southampton (March)

MacNeill, S. and Richardson, F. 1987. *Piobaireachd and its Interpretation* (Edinburgh)

Middleton, R. 1990. *Studying Popular Music* (Buckingham)

Moore, A. 1992. 'Patterns of harmony', *Popular Music*, 11, pp. 73–106

    1993. *Rock: the Primary Text* (Buckingham)

Steedman, M. 1984. 'A generative grammar for jazz chord sequences', *Music Perception*, 2, pp. 52–77

Tagg, P. 1982. 'Analysing popular music: theory, method and practice', *Popular Music*, 2, pp. 37–63

    1991. 'Fernando the flute', unpublished research report, Institute of Popular Music, Liverpool University

van der Merwe, P. 1989. *Origins of the Popular Style* (Oxford)

Walser, R. 1993. *Running with the devil: Power, Gender, and Madness in Heavy Metal Music* (Hanover, NH)

Whiteley, S. 1992. *The Space between the Notes* (London)

Winkler, P. 1978. 'Toward a theory of pop harmony', *In Theory Only*, 4, pp. 3–26

Discography

The Beatles, 'Lady Madonna', Parlophone, 1968

David Bowie, 'Ashes to Ashes', *Scary Monsters*, RCA, 1980

Kate Bush, 'Kite', *The Kick Inside*, EMI, 1978

Clannad, 'Blackstairs', *Macalla*, RCA, 1985

John Farnham, 'You're the Voice', RCA, 1987

Fleetwood Mac, 'Black Magic Woman', *The Pious Bird of Good Omen*, Blue Horizon, 1969

Peter Gabriel, 'Here Comes the Flood', *Peter Gabriel*, Charisma, 1977

Peter Gabriel, 'I Don't Remember', *Peter Gabriel 3*, Charisma, 1980

Peter Gabriel, 'Waiting for the Big One', *Peter Gabriel*, Charisma, 1977

Chesney Hawkes, 'One and Only', Chrysalis, 1991

Howlin' Wolf, 'Somebody Walkin' in my House', *Golden Classics*, Astan, 1984, original issue not identified

Howlin' Wolf, 'Goin' Down Slow', *Golden Classics*, Astan, 1984, original issue not identified

Icicle Works, 'Don't let it Rain on my Parade', *If You Want to Defeat the Enemy Sing His Song*, Beggars Banquet, 1987

Jethro Tull, 'Queen and Country', *Warchild*, Chrysalis, 1974

Jethro Tull, 'This is not Love', *Catfish Rising*, Chrysalis, 1991

Led Zeppelin, 'Bring it on Home', *Led Zeppelin II*, Atlantic, 1969

Led Zeppelin, 'Out on the Tiles', *Led Zeppelin III*, Atlantic, 1970

Led Zeppelin, 'You Shook Me', *Led Zeppelin*, Atlantic, 1969

Secret Affair, 'Time for Action', I-Spy, 1979

Supertramp, 'Crime of the Century', *Crime of the Century*, A&M, 1974

Neil Young, 'Oh Lonesome Me', *After the Goldrush*, Reprise, 1970

[16]

Making Sense of Rock's Tonal Systems

Walter Everett

ABSTRACT: Despite frequently voiced assertions and their underlying presumptions, there is no single sort of tonal behavior common to all rock music, but rather a spectrum of approaches to scales, harmonic function and voice leading. This essay addresses the issue from two perspectives. The first suggests an array of six tonal systems ranging from the traditional major mode through modal (including minor-pentatonic) practices having increasing structural value, to chromatic relations with little basis in any deeper diatony. The second perspective studies the varied degrees of interaction between harmony and voice leading evidenced in samples of rock music from two historically opposed timeframes, the more homogeneous span of 1957–58 and the more radically experimental period of 1999–2000. Finally, Beck's "Lonesome Tears" (2003) serves as a model for an analytical approach to one iconoclastic combination of voice leading and harmony.

POTENTIAL KEYWORDS: rock music, tonality, harmony, voice leading, Schenkerian analysis, modal theory, blues, popular music, Beck.

In its history now spanning half a century, rock music has found expression in dozens of styles and sub-styles, each characterized in part—sometimes in large part—by its own approach to a preexisting tonal system, or sometimes by its unveiling of a seemingly novel tonal system.[1] Of course there are many other musical and poetic traits of importance in marking style distinctions (including rhythm at surface, phrase, and sectional levels, tone color, performance practices such as phrasing, articulation, and dynamics, and recording techniques), but in this essay we will focus solely on matters of tonal structure, in hopes of addressing in a brief space an underlying context for the wide variety of systems that exist.

Whereas several other writers have discussed harmonic issues in rock music, they have either focused upon a particular piece or style and not attempted a global perspective, or attempted such a view but come up short of a useful approach.[2] The full history of tonal

---

1 Various portions of this paper had been presented at the following conferences: Society for Music Theory/"Musical Intersections" megaconference, Toronto (November, 2000), "Music Analysis and Popular Music" conference, University of Cardiff, Wales (November, 2001), and the Florida State University Forum (March 2002).

2 I have elsewhere had to discuss the approaches of other writers who hold the entire rock literature to be "monolithic," altogether the product of an unvarying application of harmonic principles; see Everett 2000, 303. Most investigations into the harmony of rock treat every chordal root as of equal

behavior in rock music is barely to be sketched in this essay, but perhaps we may lay the groundwork for what directions such an encyclopedic project might explore. At the core of this study is the proposition that while rock music grew from the common-practice-bound norms of the popular music of the 1950s and 1960s, it has subsequently ventured into many different styles, some with highly experimental approaches to tonal issues, and that some of these new directions have led even further over time from the normally interrelated roles of voice leading and harmony exhibited in the common practice of rock's roots, eventually landing in very strange tonal terrain indeed. Whereas differing tonal approaches may have evolved initially as an aspect of new stylistic differentiations, in subsequent years they would be appropriated from one style to another, so that today's rock music evinces a multitude of tonal values that are no longer consistently tied to particular styles; many different tonal systems are now practiced by the same artist, on the same album. This article proceeds in three parts, moving from the general to the particular: a proposal for the large-scale classification of six different harmonic systems common in rock music, with illustrations taken from throughout its history, is followed by a more narrowly focused study of particular tonal behaviors exhibited in two two-year periods spanning rock's history, and the essay concludes with a detailed analysis of some difficult tonal issues as presented in a single recent song, Beck's "Lonesome Tears." Examples are chosen from a wide range of rock music and closely related popular styles marketed in the U.S., though originally produced in the U.S., U.K., and elsewhere.

It is my contention (supported by a close study of more than 6,000 popular songs produced in the 1950s and 1960s) that the tonal norms basic to the pop music from which rock emerged are the same norms common to the system of common-practice tonality.[3] These norms are still adhered to, in varying degrees, in most current popular music, although we also find today many competing approaches to "normal" tonality. This current multiplicity is likely in part a reflection of the increasingly diverse social identities represented by today's listeners as opposed to the more homogeneous audence of a half-century ago. Through the mid-1950s, nation-wide marketing was aimed at that audience by five major record labels; soon thereafter and in the decades to come, the rise of countless independent labels was to introduce the country to a profusion of new styles. The devotees of any given sub-style need not realize how their preferred tonal behaviors relate to the totality of other practices, much less have a conscious appreciation as to what tonal attributes are statistically normal or deviant. Nonetheless, there are indeed strong listening preferences, reflected in the changing popularity over time of various tonal systems as suggested in the precisely calculated histories of local, regional and national sales and radio play documented in such trade magazines as *Billboard, Record World,* and *Cashbox.*

---

value, set aside inverted chords as "rare" and thereafter ignore them, rely upon discredited concepts such as "retrogression," and leave unconsidered the ramifications of voice leading upon chord identity, function, embellishment and harmonic expansion. I will here cite Stephenson 2002 as perhaps the most developed of all such studies, for all its good points in other domains. It is my belief that a Schenkerian understanding of tonal relationships allows for a clearer hearing of the variations among rock's tonal approaches than what has been afforded by methods thus far appearing in other analyses.

3 I am grateful to the National Endowment for the Humanities for a Fellowship that allowed me a year of released time to pursue the study referred to above, undertaken in order to write a book on rock music for the general public. Any views, findings, conclusions, or recommendations expressed in this publication do not necessarily reflect those of the National Endowment for the Humanities.

The reader should understand at this point that I do not recognize any strict boundary between rock musics and their stylistically related siblings, and therefore do not wish to attempt to define what separates rock from other pop-music forms—I do not believe a workable definition to be possible. I think we all realize that Led Zeppelin, with its loud guitars, flamboyant drums, and sometimes shouted vocals clearly represents rock music whereas the more temperate McGuire Sisters do not, but then what of the contemplative songs of Simon and Garfunkel? Many popular genres, including doo-wop, country, rap, disco, r&b/soul, gospel, hip-hop, fusion, new wave, funk, film score, ballad, folk, reggae, techno, Broadway, Tin-Pan Alley and others have important intersections with rock musics and yet have exemplars at quite a remove as well. Other genres, such as prog, punk, metal and grunge, probably have no significant life outside of rock music, but that does not necessarily put their defining characteristics at rock's core. I don't agree with the currently popular ideological notion of "authenticity" as a fully useful guideline either, because there is a great deal of commercial top-forty music written, performed, produced and consumed with great sincerity, and because the value of appearances can be countered in central ways based on the distance between authorial voice and rock singer's biography. Two instances of the latter would be Bruce Springsteen's having lived for many years now in that mansion on the hill while he remains convincing as the underdog's advocate, and Eminem's posturings as Slim Shady and Marshall Mathers deliberately turning the nature of authenticity on its head. I leave the fine points of stylistic demarcation to others even though I will at times distinguish tacitly between rock and its somehow tamer, perhaps simply more institution-oriented, pop background.

I. Classifying Rock's Tonal Systems

The tonal systems of rock can be classified according to certain characteristics, ordered in Table 1 as somewhat progressively further removed from common-practice tonal behaviors. These normal behaviors should be understood not only as those characteristic of historical stylistic forebears in pre-rock popular-music genres, but also as basic, ageless principles of tonality that are more or less reflected in all subsequent styles. To state this central point another way for clarity's sake: while the underlying principles of tonality are unchanging, rock has evolved several different ways of relating to that tonal background. It is these different relationships with the unchanging tonal background that is presently under investigation. Each classification in Table 1 is defined in terms of its dependencies upon harmonic and voice-leading functions, for these are the two means by which tonal centers are supported and clarified in the ears of all listeners, whether or not these listeners are consciously aware of the technical reasons they hear the way they do. Of all the ten-to-fifty thousand best-known works from all of the pop-rock literature, the vastly overwhelming majority—no doubt more than 98%—would be classified as tonal; Table 1 indicates in a broad manner the ways in which such tonal behaviors are expressed. The systems arranged in Table 1 progress from traditional major-minor and modal systems through pentatonic patterns, ultimately ending in chromatic relationships that may bear little resemblance to any normal establishment of tonal centricity.

4   *Making Sense of Rock's Tonal Systems*

Table 1. Classifications of Rock's Preeminent Tonal Systems

1a   Major-mode systems with common-practice harmonic and voice-leading behaviors. May be inflected by minor-mode or chromatic mixture.

1b   Minor-mode systems with common-practice harmonic and voice-leading behaviors. May be inflected by major-mode or chromatic mixture.

2   Diatonic modal systems with common-practice voice-leading but sometimes not with common-practice harmonic behaviors.

3a   Major-mode systems, or modal systems, with mixture from modal scale degrees. Common-practice harmonic and voice-leading behaviors would be common but not necessary.

3b   Major-mode systems with progressive structures. Common-practice harmonic and voice-leading behaviors would be typical at lower, but not higher, levels.

4   Blues-based rock: minor-pentatonic-inflected major-mode systems. Common-practice harmonic and voice-leading behaviors not always emphasized at the surface, but may be articulated at deeper levels and/or in accompaniment.

5   Triad-doubled or power-chord minor-pentatonic systems unique to rock styles: I - $\flat$III - IV - V - $\flat$VII. Common-practice harmonic and even voice-leading behaviors often irrelevant on the surface.

6a   Chromatically inflected triad-doubled or power-chord doubled pentatonic systems of early metal. Common-practice harmonic and voice-leading behaviors often irrelevant on the surface.

6b   Chromatically related scale degrees with little dependence upon pentatonic basis. Common-practice harmonic and voice-leading behaviors often irrelevant at deeper levels as well as surface.

The tonal system itself, because of the nature of the triad and the scale it inhabits, depends upon such concepts as fifth-based harmonic relationships, consonance and dissonance, and stepwise passing and neighboring functions. It is precisely these properties singular to the diatonic system that make purely pentatonic music tonally ambiguous in comparison, devoid of counterpoint and harmonic drive, its tonal centers dependent primarily upon assertion rather than upon syntactical relationships. But not all rock music is singularly blues-born pentatonicism; much of it is subject in its underlying structure to the same fundamental harmonic and voice-leading principles as those that govern the tonal structures of any prior tonal style.[4]

---

     4 It has been argued that "every early rock 'n' roll song is based on the twelve-bar blues form" (Hamm 1979, 396), but this leaves unconsidered a largely diatonic 16- and 32-bar doo-wop tradition just as important to very early rock and roll. And while the likes of Buddy Holly and the Everly Brothers did not achieve national prominence until a year after Elvis Presley did, the centrally diatonic nature of their south(west)ern and Appalachian folk-country styles was just as characteristic of Presley's repertoire as

Now to present examples that illustrate the relationships classified in Table 1 in some detail. First, the thoroughly major-mode or minor-mode systems given in the table as Types 1a and 1b. The greatest percentage of all songs succeeding on the pop charts falls into the first group in this conservative pair. Examples in the pure minor are far less common than major-mode songs, but they may be found in such unexpected places as Ozzy Osbourne's "Revelation (Mother Earth)." With few if any deviations from classical harmonic and contrapuntal norms, the tonal relationships basic to this music are certainly amenable to a standard Schenkerian treatment. This is why I have argued that most of Billy Joel's writing is closer to that of Brahms than it is to Howlin' Wolf's, and Figure 1, a sketch of the voice leading and harmony in Joel's "She's Always a Woman," confirms that all of Joel's patterns here, despite a surprising chromatic turn halfway through the bridge, fall within the classical common practice at which he worked so hard as a young piano student composing in the styles of Beethoven and Chopin.[5] Incidentally,

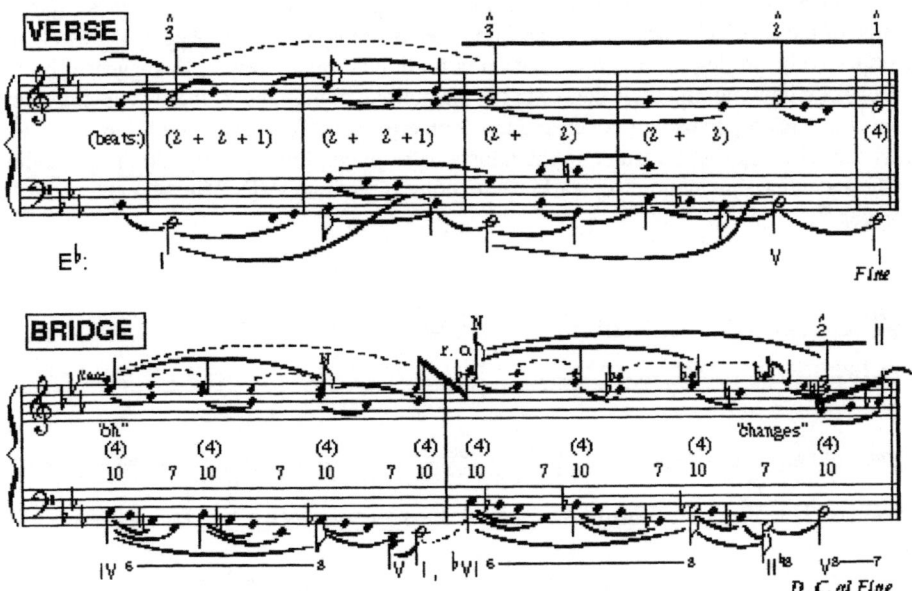

Figure 1. Analysis of "She's Always a Woman" (Billy Joel), *The Stranger,* **1977**

an understanding of the tonal structure in Joel's song, particularly involving its dominant-functioning anacruses, provides a firm understanding of its quincuncial rhythmic expansions, disproving I think the baseless yet frequently repeated charge among rock researchers that

---

was the blues. Another of the earliest r&b/rock groups, The Platters, owes more by far to Jerome Kern ("Smoke Gets in Your Eyes") and to the major/minor tonal traits of Tin-Pan Alley than to the blues.

5 The Brahms vs. Howlin' Wolf characterization is made in Everett 2000, 303. The graph of "She's Always a Woman" is from my unpublished paper, "Musical Expression at Deep Structural Levels in Learned and Vernacular Vocal Repertoires," presented to the March, 1993, joint meeting of the Society for Music Analysis and the Royal Musical Association, Southampton.

Schenker says nothing about rhythm.[6] I have published similarly conventional analyses of the Beatles' "I Should Have Known Better" and "Nowhere Man," both of which songs follow normal Schenkerian paradigms in ^5-line descents that describe in the first case a tonal expression of hindsight through ingenious motivic relationships and, in the latter, an ironic view of one who doesn't realize how much he has achieved and how highly he is valued by others.[7]

But pop music need not exemplify all of the voice leading patterns typical of 18th- and 19th-century instrumental music, particularly at deep levels, and so the three genera of fundamental lines commonly associated with late Schenker—the ^3-line, the ^5-line, and the ^8-line, all structural descents—need not be expected in this repertoire any more than they would be in vocal music by Berlioz or Wolf. In other words, Schenker's methods are useful not only for showing how songs are tonally normal, but in showing precisely in what ways songs deviate from conventions. Thus, songs not expressive of direct approaches to goals, as true of the Beatles' "Julia" and "The Long and Winding Road," graphed in Figures 2 and 3 respectively, are led by structures with non-traditional upper voices, as suggested by the trancelike unmoving fifth scale degree in the meditative "Julia," and by the always-digressing away-and-back-again pattern governing the counterpoint in "The Long and Winding Road." This sort of comparison against norms allows us to judge, for instance, that "the sounding of the cadential V is minimized nearly to the point of not happening" in "Strawberry Fields Forever."[8]

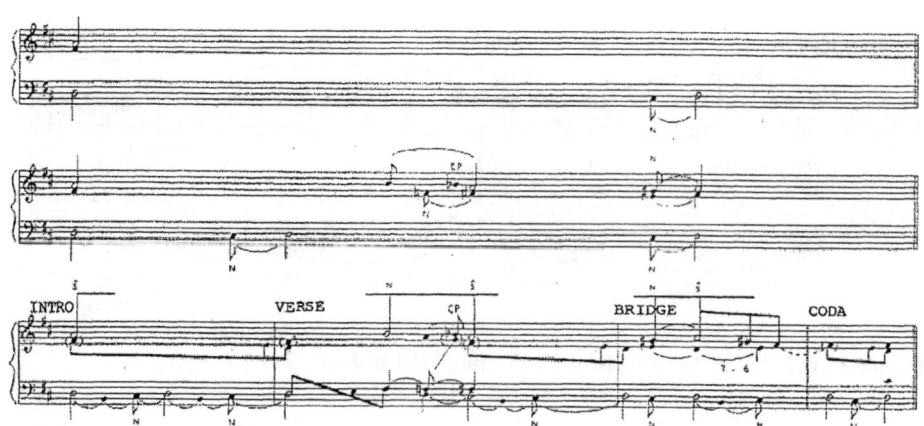

Figure 2. Analysis of "Julia" (John Lennon), *The Beatles,* **1968**

---

6 Middleton 1990, 193, is probably the most prominent and influential accusation in the rock-analytic world that Schenkerian analysis "ignores" rhythmic (as well as motivic) features. He cites Narmour 1977 as his source of understanding.

7 The Beatles analyses appear in Everett 2001, 226–29 and 322–23, respectively.

8 The "Julia" graph first appeared in Everett 1986, 383, the "Long and Winding Road" sketch in Everett 1999, 228. The statement as to "Strawberry Fields Forever" is from Everett 1986, 372.

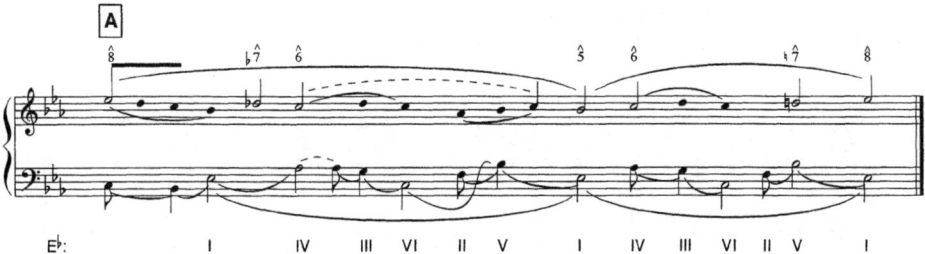

Figure 3. Analysis of "The Long and Winding Road" (Paul McCartney), *The Beatles*, 1969

It must be borne in mind that the relevance of normal backgrounds lies in direct proportion to the degree to which all other aspects of the tonal system are invoked, whether or not that background is actually articulated in the song in question. The background is the context-providing vessel, whereas the material of the song itself is the content. When the deepest harmonic structure is articulated, it appears in conventional goal-directed cadences, whereas the interesting, novel early and middle parts of phrases, and the early parts of mid-sections of pieces as a whole, are the contents that embellish those familiar structures. The expressive aim of that material may for instance argue in a given song that closure is irrelevant, and so will avoid the statement of a final V-I cadence or a melody that steps down to the first scale degree. The lack of these elements in the song does not suggest that they are not manifestations of the governing system from which the individual song takes its meaning. When Richard Middleton (1990, 195-96) argues that in the "Twist and Shout" retransition the circular lack of closure suggested by the great dominant-seventh arpeggiation proves the irrelevance of Schenker, he's got it half right; any Schenkerian would argue that this V-harmony is a structure-<u>interrupting</u> dominant, just like that shown at the end of the bridge of "She's Always a Woman" in Figure 1, not a cadential <u>goal-approaching</u> dominant. The Schenkerian hearing explains precisely the nature of that closure-defying circle. Those who argue that Schenker distorts a structure, or that a Schenkerian forces the round peg into the square hole are focusing in the wrong direction; one must appreciate just how much can be learned from the gentle comparison of the example to the convention; the object is not to ignore the song's salient moments or to whitewash-over the differences between individual song and convention, but to understand just what's unusual in the piece at hand. Comparison to the norm and to a history of related approaches is what provides that information.

Turning to our second type, we encounter numbers throughout the history of rock with modal backbones. Some have well-directed melodic lines, often exemplifying even classical descents that are supported contrapuntally, but—especially when the leading tone is absent—there is often no harmonic pull to the tonic. All of this is true of Paul Simon's "The Sounds of Silence," sketched in Figure 4. This is an Aeolian example with no harmonic function at all, yet the voice leading is based on a clear descent supported by counterpoint that turns from dark parallel fifths to hopeful imperfect consonances, only to return to the duo's stark final unison. Other modal examples are not nearly so conventional with their voice leading—consider the very non-Western Mixolydian "Tomorrow Never Knows," the upper voice of which carries only the simple I - bVII -I neighbor motion over a transcendental yet unmoving tonic pedal. The entire song's counterpoint is given in Figure 5.

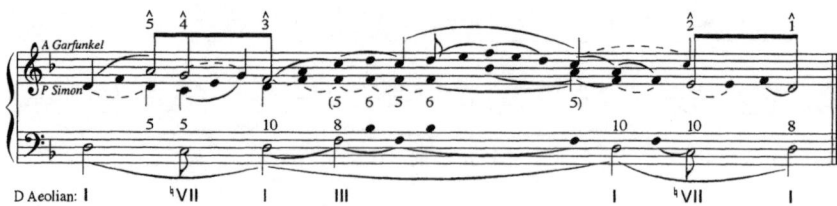

Figure 4. Analysis of "The Sounds of Silence" (Paul Simon), Simon and Garfunkel, 1964–65

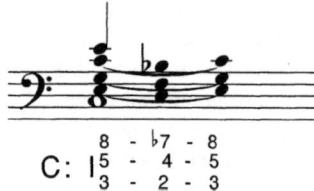

Figure 5. Analysis of "Tomorrow Never Knows" (John Lennon), *Revolver*, The Beatles, 1966

One must not be too quick to ascribe chromatic events to modal function, particularly where bVII is involved. The bVII - IV - I progression, the double-plagal cadence as articulated in the celebrated "Hey Jude" coda, is often incorrectly said to have a modal basis. Following its late-summer, 1964, appearance in the introduction to the Four Tops' "Baby I Need Your Loving," this function jumped into rock music from various directions, all in the first three months of 1965, in Martha & the Vandellas' "Nowhere to Run," the Who's "I Can't Explain," the Rolling Stones' "The Last Time," and the Beatles' "The Night Before."[9] Amid apparent confusion, bVII - IV - I is variously referred to as an Aeolian, Dorian, or Mixolydian pattern. But such a modal basis cannot be any more necessary for this relationship than it would be for fifths circling in the opposite direction, as with the long sequence of applied dominants in, say, "Sweet Georgia Brown," the verse of which repeats the progression, E^7 - A^7 - D^7 - G^7 - B^7. Both sequences—that in descending fifths and that in descending fourths— should be heard as chromatic functions, involving the use of notes from outside the scale, sharps in the applied-dominant case, and flats in the double-, triple-, or quadri-plagal example. For, just as can a sequence of descending fifths, a passage involving descending fourths can carry on for quite an extended run, as in the verse of "Hey Joe," the bridge of "A Day in the Life," or the chorus of "Jumpin' Jack Flash." The counterpoint of continual downward-resolving neighbors is strongly functional even if the harmony is not, even if no tonal center can be suggested by

---

9 Thanks to Jonathan Bernard for reminding me of the Who example in an exchange on the smt-list, c. 2002. I discuss the double-plagal cadence in some detail, with accompanying voice-leading graphs, in Everett 2000, 323–26.

this sequence in and of itself. If one more descending fourth is added to one end or another of the string, it does not change the entire mode in which the passage is based, but simply adds or cancels another chromatic flat. This sequence establishes neither scale nor tonal center, so no mode can be suggested.

The Type-3 system illustrates further decomposition of the major mode. According to 3a, the major scale would be infiltrated by mixture from outside the major-minor system. This is the sense in which the Beatles' "P. S. I Love You," shown in Figure 6, is predominantly in D major and featuring its I, IV, and V chords, but is given a cadence in the refrain that seems drawn from Aeolian practice, allowing for rising major passing triads on the bVI and bVII scale degrees. Note that the major section employs some rudimentary counterpoint, although one could not find the voice leading coherent; the parallel octaves and fifths suggested in the verse foreshadow triads in the modal cadence that if not downright parallel, are at best heterophonic. The Stones' "Brown Sugar" is closely related; this song has a verse and chorus strongly in C major, featuring a backbone of I, IV, and V chords. But the instrumental break, whose chord changes are given as Figure 7, takes the Aeolian mixture of "P. S. I Love You" one step further by involving a bIII chord as well as the bVI - bVII - I cadence. Note how the 4-3 suspensions create a surface illusion of counterpoint, but parallel fifths and octaves keep structural voice leading at bay.

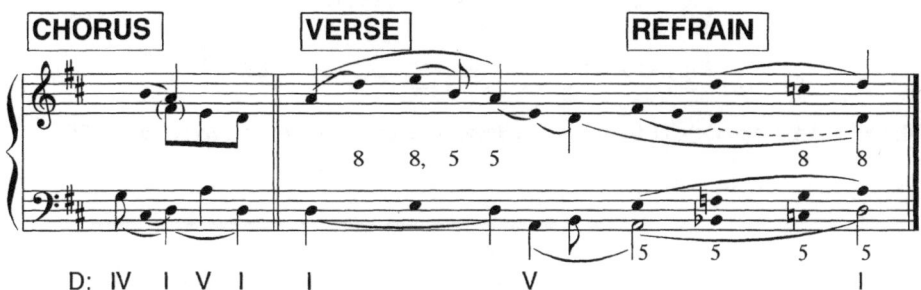

Figure 6. Analysis of "P. S. I Love You" (John Lennon - Paul McCartney), The Beatles, 1962

CM: bIII - I $^{4\text{-}3}$ - bVI - bVII - I $^{4\text{-}3}$ [repeat for sax break]

Figure 7. Chords of instrumental break of "Brown Sugar"
  (Mick Jagger - Keith Richard), *Sticky Fingers*, The Rolling Stones, 1971

Type 3a also includes quasi-modal scales affected by mixture. Though regular Dorian, Mixolydian, and Aeolian modes are represented in rock examples most often and even the Phrygian mode is heard in Björk (see "Army of Me"), scales need not be so conventional.[10] Figures 8 and 9 illustrate. Beck's "Get Real Paid," for instance, is clearly in an asserted C, despite minimal contrapuntal interest and the lack of any harmonic division whatsoever; tonal variety is afforded mostly by the coloristic contrast of minor-pentatonic, whole-tone, octatonic, major-pentatonic and chromatic vocabularies. Radiohead's "Everything in Its Right Place" is in a strongly asserted F, supported by a big fifth divider of structural value with arpeggiations to C's in both bass and vocal parts, and also featuring tonic-defining neighbor motions. But the scale consistently combines the major lower tetrachord with the Aeolian upper tetrachord.

Figure 8. Analysis of "Get Real Paid" (Beck Hansen), *Midnite Vultures***, Beck, 1999**

Figure 9. Analysis of "Everything in Its Right Place" (Thom Yorke), *Kid A***, Radiohead, 2000**

---

10 The Phyrygian mode is extremely rare in rock music, but Robert Walser points out that "speed metal is usually Phrygian or Locrian" (Walser 1993, 46). The guitar work in Megadeth's "Psychotron" features a second scale degree a half-step above tonic that may be diatonic, rather than a chromatic passing tone, and the guitars in their "Ashes In Your Mouth" feature second and fifth scale degrees that sound Locrian. The overall effect of these numbers, however, especially with their power-chord vocabulary, their lack of harmonic function, and their fully minor-pentatonic vocal parts, would seem to situate these examples in Type 6a, discussed below.

Type 3b would allow for songs with progressive structures, where true modulation creates a movement to a key area that never need return to tonic. This is most commonly expressed in rock's "truck-driver's modulation," where verses or choruses may appear in successively higher keys, normally a half-step or whole-step apart, motivated by various expressive needs.[11] In some cases, a bevy of shifts serves only to attempt to compensate for a brief song's lack of structural interest, and the effect can be one of an arranger trying to salvage a weak idea, even if the arranger and composer are one and the same person. The effect has loads of gravitas, and perhaps has been largely put to rest with Barry Manilow's larger-than-life production numbers, although divas like Mariah Carey ("I Don't Wanna Cry") keep it alive.

Type 3b would also include more experimental tonal devices, such as that heard in Paul Simon's "Still Crazy After All These Years." Here, as shown in Figure 10, modulations within the saxophone interlude and within the final verse produce, respectively, expanded and contracted forms of a governing upper-voice fifth-progression, thus the upper voice governing the interlude labelled an X-5 progression and the contracted 5-line of the third verse moving from a third-scale degree B to a third-scale degree C-sharp resulting in a five-line crammed into the space of a fourth.[12] In a related way, XTC's "I'd Like That," sketched in Figure 11, first presents the vocal E as fifth scale degree of A major, and then twists the tonal scheme to allow it to become first scale degree. The resulting harmony is structurally wild, even though sensibly functional on the surface, and the voice leading is clean yet structurally unconventional, at least in any classical sense.

As indicated under Type 4, the blues has an essentially major-mode structure. In the twelve-bar-based "School Days," Chuck Berry's vocal and lead guitar parts are thoroughly pentatonic, but the structure-expressing bass and piano boogie in the major mode. The rarity of exceptions, as found in B.B. King's minor-mode "The Thrill is Gone," proves the rule. If this seems out of line with prevailing descriptions, which typically rely on reference to a "blues scale" and don't seem to discriminate between tonal characteristics of melody and backing, consider the rhythm section's accompaniment aside from all vocal and solo melodic lines. It is in the supportive major-mode instrumental chordal backing, not in the soloistic melodic material, that structural harmony is expressed.[13] Listen to Robert Johnson's guitar in the last verse of "Walking Blues." As in many others of his recordings, the I, IV, and V triads are all given as they occur in the major scale, without the chromatic blues inflections that mark the melodic parts. It is the spirit of mixture among the upper partials through which the tonic and subdominant triads can take on embellishing minor sevenths, just as does the dominant; this is heard in the blues boogie of Johnson's "When You Got a Good Friend." This mixture comes from the minor-pentatonic scale, which also provides pitch inflections, sometimes including bent notes, for solo melodic parts including vocal lines and lead instrumental riffs. There may be such a thing as a blues scale (with or without a lowered fifth scale degree), as in Gershwin

---

11 Several of these expressive reasons for employing the truck-driver's modulation are given in Everett 1997, 151, nn. 17–18. The term "pump-up" modulation has been proposed for the same technique, as part of a deep investigation into the effect, in Ricci 2000, 130–33.

12   The graph in Figure 10 first appeared in Everett 1997, 124–25.

13 The blues scale is basic to the tonal nature of the blues, and so of blues-based rock, in the understanding of many researchers; see, for instance, Van der Merwe 1989, 118–29. Nowhere have I seen a reliance on the major mode (with melodic inflection based on minor-pentatonic embellishment), as I propose here.

examples, but this has nothing to do with rock music, which borrows only from a blues that colors a structural major mode with minor-pentatonic melodic borrowings. Sometimes in blues-based rock music, the melodies make deliberate contrasts of major-vs.-pentatonic tunes, all over a major-mode accompanimental support; I have written elsewhere of the expressive effects resulting from this technique in Bill Haley's "Rock Around the Clock," Nirvana's "Lithium," and the B-52s' "Channel Z."[14]

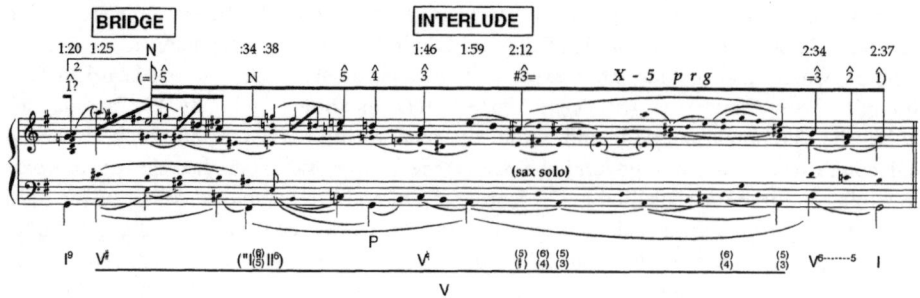

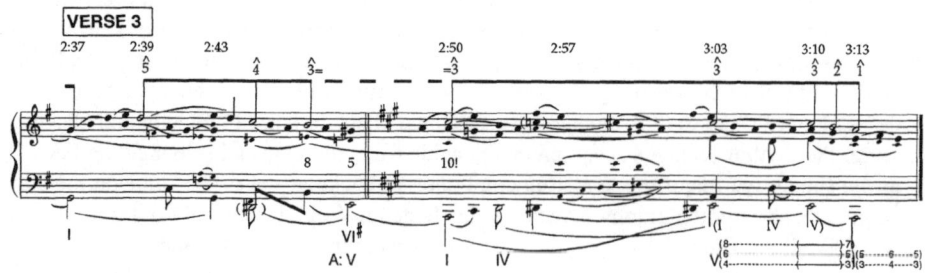

Figure 10. Analysis of "Still Crazy After All These Years" (Paul Simon), *Still Crazy After All These Years*, 1975

---

14 The modal inflections in these three songs are discussed in Everett 2000, 329, 329–30, and 284–86, respectively. Haley's 1954 hit, "Dim, Dim the Lights (I Want Some Atmosphere)," contrasts major and pentatonic-minor modes in its melody so as to represent light and dark to suggestive ends just as does his later "Rock Around the Clock."

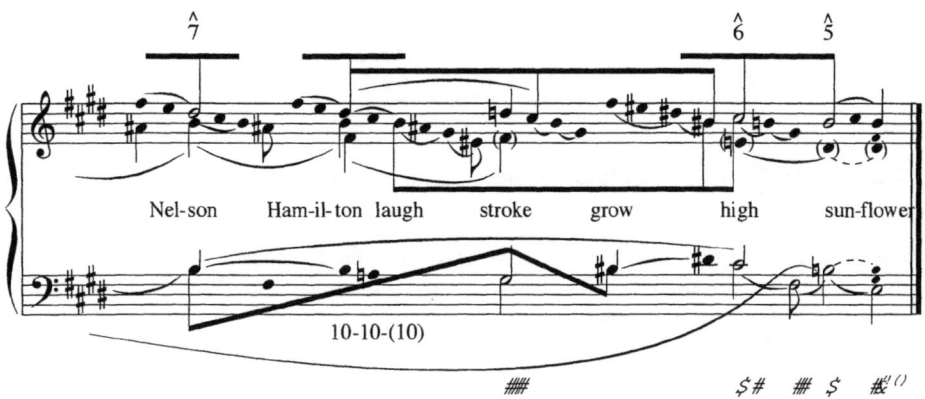

Figure 11. Analysis of "I'd Like That" (Andy Partridge), *Apple Venus Volume 1***, XTC, 1999**

The wonderful thing about the minor-pentatonic scale, and the main reason it is so amenable to extensive improvisation, is that there is no regular relationship of dissonance to consonance, partly because the scale lacks intrinsically dissonant tritones and half-steps, but also because of the relatively large number of times that thirds are represented in the scale. The three-note collection [0-2-5], for instance, appears at four different places in the five-note scale. This means that position-finding is much more ambiguous here than in the major scale, where every interval appears a unique number of times. And as a practical matter, a blues in E-flat can feature the free and easy melodic use of any and all black keys on the piano, unencumbered by suggested resolutions of purported dissonances. Children have particular fun with this—play an E-flat-major blues structure in the piano's bass and tenor registers while they improvise on black keys above—anything at all works just fine because there can be no bad counterpoint!

It is commonly remarked that dominant harmony is not of structural value in the blues. Given individual cases, this may or may not be true; whether or not the dominant is articulated in any given piece of music, it is of structural value in the major system that is inhabited by that blues. In fact, the dominant is usually the basis of the interrupting turnaround between verses, and then usually resolves directly to I in any cold ending. But the V chord is also usually present in the third of the three lines in each verse, where its resolution to I is often mitigated by an intervening subdominant, which of course has no harmonic value but merely softens the resolution to tonic with its contrapuntal stepwise descents. The contrapuntal functions of this "softened" authentic cadence in the blues are shown in Figure 12. A different sort of compacting of the harmonic value of V with the neighbor functions of IV is heard in the simultaneity of fa-la-do over sol, as heard in Paul McCartney's "The Long and Winding Road" (see the C over the second bass note in Fig. 3), a sonority he would recall eight years later in the introduction of "With a Little Luck," and would appear in many other gospel-tinged keyboard numbers by McCartney, Stevie Wonder (as in "Knocks Me Off My Feet"), and others.

C: V 8----7   I

Figure 12. "Softened" V - I blues cadence

Type 5 is new with rock music. Here, each member of the minor-pentatonic scale is treated as the root of a major triad, in effect doubling the scale in major thirds and fifths as well as octaves.[15] The five major chords that result are not functionally related, and do not normally lead to each other in progressions—even though both the first and fifth scale degrees are represented as roots—any more than melodic events in the minor-pentatonic scale are expected to resolve in any particular way. There is no regular basis in the major mode, although mixture can bring major-mode elements into a song's different sections for contrast. Despite the presence of chords, the patterns that result are thoroughly melodic. Such doubling rarely occurs in other scales—the deliciously ludicrous chords of "I Am the Walrus" do result from a major triad doubling of the Aeolian scale, and some semblance of chromatic function lies behind the pugilistic triad-doubling of major-mode scale degrees in "Bad, Bad Leroy Brown," but the line in that song progresses only from the first to the fifth scale degree. Sometimes, as illustrated in Figures 13, 14, and 15, a grouping of four chords seemingly taken from the Aeolian mode, I, bIII, IV, and bVI, have actually been selected from the minor-pentatonic scale; it is the interlocking of [0-2-5] trichords heard as relationships between non-functional roots of major triads on I, bIII, IV, and bVI in such songs as the Monkees' "I'm Not Your Steppin' Stone," the Knack's "My Sharona," and Nirvana's "Smells Like Teen Spirit" that create this blues-like effect, but notice that there is just as often an interesting counterpoint between upper voices and bass, as there are strict parallel doublings, in this modal procedure that also admits of some chromaticism. The chorus of "Steppin' Stone," for instance, features a prominent inner voice that descends ^8 - ^b7 - ^6 - ^b6 over the triads indicated in Figure

---

15 This concept has apparently been explored previously by Alf Björnberg in an unpublished 1985 presentation to IASPM in Montreal entitled, "On Aeolian Harmony in Contemporary Popular Music"; this work is cited in Middleton 1990, 198.

13. Examples truly in the Aeolian mode would typically use a minor dominant; such a chord would have no place in these pentatonic-system songs.

I ♭III IV ♭VI [repeat]

I - I - I - I - I'm not your steppin' stone.

Figure 13. Chords of chorus of "(I'm Not Your) Steppin' Stone"
(Tommy Boyce - Bobby Hart), The Monkees, 1966

I
Never gonna stop, give it up—such a dirty mind

♭III

I always get it up for the touch of the younger kind.

IV ♭VI I

My, my, my - y - y, whoa!

Figure 14. Chords of refrain of "My Sharona"
(Doug Fieger - Berton Averre), The Knack, 1979

I IV ♭III ♭VI

Load up on guns, bring your friends . . .

Figure 15. Chords of verse of "Smells Like Teen Spirit"
(Kurt Cobain - David Grohl - Chris Novoselic), Nirvana, 1991

In the triad-doubled minor-pentatonic mode, expressed in I, bIII, IV, V, and bVII chords, harmony is non-functional, and voice-leading is severely compromised; all voices, again, tend to move in strictly parallel doublings of root-position triads or empty power-chord fifths. Sometimes, as in "Bo Diddley" or "My Generation," the tonic is established simply by neighbor motions from I to bVII and back again. In many cases from the 1960s, beginning with "On Broadway" and extending through "Uptight" and "Got to Get You Into My Life," these chords alternate over a stationary tonic pedal. Whereas a rudimentary Schenkerian graph like that in Figure 5 could indicate the counterpoint here despite a lack of harmonic function, such an attempt would be useless in more involved ventures into the minor-pentatonic system, where the scale's gaps and lack of traditional relationships between dissonance and consonance are tonally limited. Here such [0-2-5]-based groups as I - bIII - bVII - I and the I - bIII - IV - I of the "Sgt. Pepper" chorus are functionally equivalent; in fact, both patterns appear back-to-back in Living Colour's "Cult of Personality," the chords and lyrics of which are indicated as Figure

16. Tonic status is suggested by metric assertion and often by melodic goal-directedness, with some support added if all five scale degrees are presented as "roots."

      G5 -   B♭5   F5 - G5

Look in my eyes, what do you see? The Cult of Personal -i - ty.

I know your anger, I know your dreams. I've been everything you wanna be, oh;

    B♭5   C5 - G5

I'm the Cult of Personal - i - ty.

Figure 16. Chords of verse / refrain of "Cult of Personality" (Living Colour), *Vivid*, 1988

The pentatonic nature of blues-based rock was loudly announced in Memphis, where the introduction to "In the Midnight Hour," shown in Figure 17, was arranged.[16] Note the parallel major triads arranged along the minor-pentatonic scale in Figure 17, E: bVII - V - IV - bIII (answered immediately by the major-mode verse, I - IV - I - IV, etc.). Note also the potential colorful cross relations that could result from parallel major thirds in moving from bVII to V and from bIII to I. Articulation of these, through thoughtful guitar voicings, led to the signature riff of "Proud Mary," C - A - G - F - D. (Although the triads are generated from parallel doublings of the scale steps, their ultimate voicings lead to stark pairings in two relative-parallel progressions, in neo-Riemannian terms, from C to A and from F to D.[17]) But despite the momentary emancipations from the major-minor system, both of these intros lead to songs locked right back into that major mode. The Kinks come to mind for their minor-penatonic doublings, but they also sought contrast through counterpoint and chromaticism. In "All Day and All of the Night," shown in Figure 18, the verse moves from an [0-2-5]-based pattern with completely parallel I - bVII - bIII - I chords, to the same pattern transposed up a fifth for the chorus. But the two areas are joined by a transition that introduces both contrary motion and applied-dominant chromaticism, for a nice mix of assertive elegance and pure raunch. More typically, a major-mode song like "Please Please Me," or Carl Perkins's "Lend Me Your Comb" before it, will interject a blues-based parallel minor-pentatonic riff such as bIII-IV-V into an otherwise major-mode song.

Chord roots that could be interpreted as minor-pentatonically related do not necessarily mean any break from tonal tradition. The Left Banke's follow-up hit to "Walk Away Renée," called "Pretty Ballerina," is unusual for its brilliant Lydian tendencies on the surface. A bit deeper, all chords are major triads with roots on each of the piano's black keys, with E-flat as tonic; see the chords as indicated between the staves in Figure 19. In that, it would seem we'd

---

16 Figure 17 appeared first in Everett 2002, 33.

17 Thanks to Guy Capuzzo for suggesting to me the possible role of parsimonious voice leading in this example in a February, 2001, conversation.

have an E-flat minor-pentatonic system. But because of the vocal counterpoint mixing octaves, fifths and tenths against the bass, and because the roots in that bass clearly arpeggiate the I - bIII - V triad for an Aeolian-inflected but direct harmonic function, the song's context is the major mode with modal mixture (Type 3a). Note the same structure, colored very differently by the foreground chords, governing the "Sweet Georgia Brown" example discussed above.

Figure 17. Introduction to "In the Midnight Hour" (Wilson Pickett - Steve Cropper), Wilson Pickett, 1965

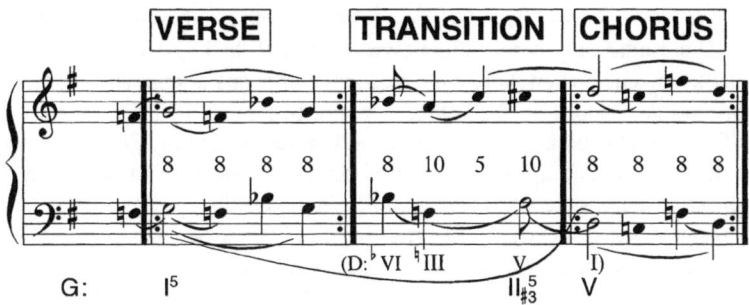

Figure 18. Analysis of "All Day and All of the Night" (Ray Davies), The Kinks, 1964

We end with Type 6, in which cases we trace a further departure from normally articulated tonal centricity. Here, the pentatonic scale is liberated from its tonal clutches in a process of chromatic embellishments that free the scale from suggested harmonic relationships to the point where, if tonic is supported at all, it may be so primarily by assertion rather than by syntax. This departure is easily traced through the history of heavy metal, whose emphasis on open-fifth power chords begins with doublings of the minor-pentatonic scale and by the decade grows progressively embellished by half-step passing tones and neighbors to the point where it often becomes difficult to determine what are authentic scale degrees and what are not. The distinction between Types 6a and 6b is a slight one made in attempting to separate those structures whose integrity is questioned by the half-step embellishment from those structures whose integrity is so destroyed.

Figure 19. Analysis of "Pretty Ballerina" (Mike Brown), The Left Banke, 1967

In the psychedelic blues of "Spanish Castle Magic," Figure 20, Jimi Hendrix distracts the ear from the underlying minor-pentatonic scale with chromatic passing tones, all treated the same as structural tones in forming root-position open fifths.[18] The underlying pentatonic descent, C- B-flat - G - F - E-flat - C, is presented vocally and clarified metrically but is disguised by a series of chromatically descending power-chords, B-flat5 - A5 - A-flat5. We are aware that C is the tonal center, even though the reason we hear this is somewhat obscure. In Deep Purple's primordial "Smoke on the Water," a minor-pentatonic [0-2-5] pattern, I - bIII - IV, that could have been the basis of a number by the Temptations (as in "I'm Losing You"), leads to a chromatic ornamentation, bV-to-IV, that is not at all at home in Motown. (In "Nobody's Fault," Aerosmith inserts the chromatic complete-neighbor figure, IV5 - bV5 - IV5, into an otherwise major-mode context.) In "Electric Funeral," Black Sabbath goes a step further in using that bV as a non-functional chromatic passing tone in the chords I - V - bV - IV - bIII - I. (Similarly, Guns 'n' Roses passes V5 - bV5 - IV5 - I5 in "My Michelle.") In all these examples, the minor-pentatonic scale is given chromatic development, but the absence of oblique or contrary motion through all of these parallel fifths tends to assert emphasis more or less equally among the embellishing and the structural tones.

By the time we reach type 6b, tonal centers are given little or no syntactical support. Thus, in Alice in Chains' "Them Bones," half steps take over the chord relationships in the initial filling-in of a minor third, C-sharp-to-E, as shown in Figure 21. As did the Kinks, Alice breaks away from the parallel chords with some counterpoint in a "Day Tripper"-like suggestion of a German augmented sixth. The same filled-in minor third with which "Them Bones" begins also forms the verse of King's X's "Fish Bowl Man." But metal-based styles are not the only ones now infected with functionless half-steps among roots. The air of disorientation achieved by Portishead owes a lot to the open-fifth chords related by half-step, without any sort of harmonic, or even normal contrapuntal, syntax. Figure 22 gives the lyrics and chords in upper case, and also the principal vocal pitches in lower case, for one verse of Portishead's "All Mine," whose E-flat tonic is suggested largely by vocal assertion. Notice the occasional [0-2-5] minor-pentatonic vocal licks, lending the track a bluesy air, despite the lack of pentatonic

---

18 Figure 20 appeared first in Everett 2000, 334.

Figure 20. Verse of "Spanish Castle Magic" (Jimi Hendrix), *Axis: Bols as Love,* **1968**

root relationships. The roots, in fact (E-flat, D, a passing C-sharp and B), strongly suggest a rather atonal [0-1-4] and [0-1-2-4] quality; in the first two lines of the verse, the chord changes seem to support the joining of two unrelated pentatonic-like melodies so as to create melodic [0-1-4] and [0-1-2-4] collections, which are marked as such in the figure. The verse's third and last line gives up the pentatonic pretense, largely wallowing in the half- and whole-steps that occasionally remind us of the [0-1-4] and [0-1-2-4] sets. Even farther out along the scale are a number of tracks on KoRn's album, *Issues*, where the octatonic scale forms the reference for melodic lines and power chords, burying the pentatonic and major scales in the distant past. The introduction and verse of their song "Hey Daddy" is made from five pitches of the 23 octatonic scale on B.[19]

$$C\sharp5 \; - \; D5 \; - \; D\sharp5 \; - \; E5 \; \text{[eight times]}$$

$$A5 \; - \; G\sharp^7_5 \; - \; B5 \; - \; B\flat5 \; - \; [C\sharp5]$$

Figure 21. Chords in "Them Bones"
    (Layne Staley - Jerry Cantrell), *Dirt*, **Alice in Chains, 1992**

---

19 I am grateful to Jonathan Pieslak for introducing me to the tonal world of KoRn.

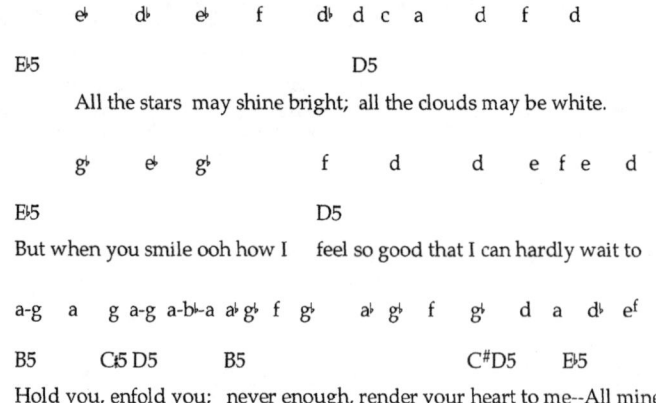

Figure 22. Melodic pitches and Chords in verse / refrain of "All Mine"
        (Geoff Barrow - Beth Gibbons), *Portishead*, 1997

II. Comparing Tonal Behaviors in Two Historically Removed Periods

In order to support the notion that the tonal systems evident in rock music have in fact expanded over the years, it would be useful to measure tonal relationships exhibited at different points in its history. To this end, I have chosen a pair of two-year periods for a preliminary study: 1957–58 (most likely the two-year block of popular music enjoying the heaviest saturation of rock 'n' roll) and 1999–2000 (arbitrarily fixed upon as the last two-year span in rock's first millenium).[20] Because the musics and the audiences that support them are so very different in kind between these two samples, a word on sample selection is in order before the study's design is outlined. Before the late-1960s rise of the LP as the leading vehicle for rock music, the 45-r.p.m. single (by which a song would be marketed for radio play, jukebox exposure, and home use) was the industry standard. Focusing on such a time when commercial appeal and critical praise were not necessarily attributes of different popular styles, it makes most sense to consult the upper reaches of *Billboard*'s weekly "Top 100" and "Hot 100" singles charts to determine a worthy sample of study. It happens that fifty records peaked within the top four positions of these charts in 1957 and the same number did so the following year, and so the 100 most popular recordings of 1957–58 were those to reach the top four chart positions in those years. In the late 1990s, such a sample would not be representative of the same things. Rock music was then marketed primarily through compact-disc albums, rather than the promotional singles that have had a far less significant audience since the peak popularity of that format in the mid-1970s. But neither would *Billboard*'s weekly chart of the top 200 albums be a fully reliable standard; one of the highest-ranking CDs in the

---

20 It might be interesting to study the relationships among any, or many, other such samples from throughout rock history, but I leave this simply as a suggestion.

1999/2000 album charts was the Beatles' *1*, a repackaging of their hits from the 1960s (it was the number-one album for eight weeks beginning in 2000), and other compilations of older material also enjoyed #1 status as CDs in these two years. Additionally, many highly worthwhile albums by critically acclaimed artists—such as those espousing "alternative" rock—do not particularly seek the degree of chart success that any aspiring artist would have found necessary in the 1950s. So a more subjective approach was thought appropriate. To represent the years 1999–2000, it was decided to create a sample of fifteen albums released in each year, combining those new recordings with highest chart success (each of the two years is represented with seven #1 albums) with others earning critical acclaim (cult favorite Sleater-Kinney, for instance, enjoyed highly favorable notices and feature stories in the *New York Times*). An effort was made to reflect in the sample the most popular and/or significant styles of the day—hip-hop, hard rock, country, alternative rock, grunge, mainstream rock, arena rock, jazz-rock fusion, pre-teen idols, and catalog artists with new releases—just as the singles chart would have done in its day.

Table 2. Criteria for Establishing Voice-Leading and Harmony Values

Voice-leading:
1) stepwise melody in actual or implied lines; diatonic/chromatic linear progressions and other melodically connective tissue
2) strong, clear resolution of (vocal) melodic tendency tones
3) expected, transferred, implied, or ironic resolutions of non-harmonic tones
4) presence of linear-intervallic patterns
5) independence of bass from chord roots
6) independence of parts, particularly among outer voices

Harmony:
1) single all-consuming tonal center; strong identity of scale degrees
2) superficial predominance of functional relationships (falling fifths, thirds)
3) V-I for structural cadence
4) structural leading harmony for end of contrasting section (such as V^7 preparing I)
5) few non-functional chords or non-functional structural relations; no "truck-driver's" modulation or similarly "inorganic" large-scale relationships
6) no modally subjugated leading tone

Rather than simply voicing an assertion that the 1957–58 sample is hardly adventurous in exploring the classifications of Table 1 in comparison to the vital disparity of classifications heard in the later rock music, a more detailed study of the roles of voice leading and harmony in establishing tonal centers in both samples was thought to be in order. The chosen method is predicated upon a stipulation of the most important general characteristics of normal tonal voice leading and harmony, according to six criteria that concern both surface and structural events designated for each of these two tonal domains. The twelve criteria are listed in Table 2. For statistical purposes, all criteria were arbitrarily accorded equal weight. Each of the 100 hits from 1957–58, and each of the 382 tracks on the thirty 1999–2000 albums, was scored on twelve scales of one-to-ten, in recognition of the degree to which each of the criteria was observed the song's tonal composition. A total voice-leading score and a total harmony score were computed for each song, with up to sixty points awarded in each of the two domains. For instance, the deliciously deviant song "Hollywood Freaks" on Beck's *Midnite Vultures* album was given one point of an available ten for stepwise melody and linear progressions, two points out of a possible ten for resolution of vocal tendency tones, three points for resolutions of non-harmonic tones, and the song scored no other credit for voice-leading attributes, totalling out at six points of a possible sixty in this domain. In terms of harmony, this song earned six points for the strength of its tonal center and three more for its structural valuation of cadential dominant harmony. For the 1999–2000 sample, scores for all of the songs on an album were then averaged. In this process, each discrete song was weighted equally, to arrive at a total voice-leading score and a total harmony score for each album, each of these totals ranging from zero to sixty. Table 3 lists each of the top one hundred songs of 1957–58, indicating the degree of chart success and total voice-leading and harmony scores for each song, and Table 4 lists each of the song titles for all thirty albums of 1999–2000, along with the individual song scores and the average scores and chart peak for each album. I cannot claim that my scoring method has been applied with perfect consistency across all samples, or that it reflects a perfect hearing and evaluation in every case, but it does represent a single honest attempt. No doubt, such a study would be made more reliable by a large number of suitably educated subjects duplicating the scoring process for these 482 songs, but for practical purposes, my provisional hearing is our starting point.

Table 3. Top One-Hundred Hit Songs of 1957–58, according to *Billboard's* "Top 100" and "Hot 100" singles charts, [Their Year of Popularity and Chart Peak], and (Their Voice-Leading / Harmony Values)

Paul Anka: Diana [1957; #1 for 1 wk] (50/60)
Chuck Berry: School Day [1957; #3 for 3 wks] (34/53)
Chuck Berry: Sweet Little Sixteen [1958; #2 for 3 wks] (42/59)
Pat Boone: Love Letters in the Sand [1957; #1 for 7 wks] (48/60)
Pat Boone: April Love [1957; #1 for 6 wks] (55/60)
Pat Boone: Don't Forbid Me [1957; #1 for 1 wk] (50/60)
Pat Boone: A Wonderful Time Up There [1958; #4 for 5 wks] (31/46)
Pat Boone: It's Too Soon To Know [1958; #4 for 1 wk] (51/60)
The Champs: Tequila [1958; #1 for 5 wks] (40/49)
The Chipmunks: The Chipmunk Song [1958; #1 for 4 wks] (44/50)
David Seville [& The Chipmunks]: Witch Doctor [1958; #1 for 3 wks] (40/49)
The Chordettes: Lollipop [1958; #2 for 2 wks] (41/60)
Jimmy Clanton: Just a Dream [1958; #4 for 3 wks] (54/60)
The Coasters: Searchin' [1957; #3 for 1 wk] (26/54)
The Coasters: Yakety Yak [1958; #1 for 1 wk] (46/56)
Cozy Cole: Topsy II [1958; #3 for 3 wks] (52/49)
Perry Como: Round and Round [1957; #1 for 2 wks] (48/48)
Perry Como: Catch a Falling Star [1958; #1 for 1 wk] (52/50)
Perry Como: Magic Moments [1958; #4 for 1 wk] (47/50)
Sam Cooke: You Send Me [1957; #1 for 3 wks] (46/60)
Danny & The Juniors: At the Hop [1958; #1 for 7 wks] (44/59)
Bobby Darin: Splish Splash [1958; #3 for 1 wk] (43/60)
Bobby Day: Rock-in Robin [1958; #2 for 2 wks] (49/59)
The Dell-Vikings: Come Go With Me [1957; #4 for 1 wk] (37/60)
The Diamonds: Little Darlin' [1957; #2 for 8 wks] (37/60)

The Diamonds: The Stroll [1958; #4 for 1 wk] (34/60)
Fats Domino: Blueberry Hill [1957; #2 for 3 wks] (44/59)
Fats Domino: I'm Walkin' [1957; #4 for 1 wk] (40/60)
Jimmy Dorsey Orch: So Rare [1957; #2 for 4 wks] (53/50)
Tommy Edwards: It's All in the Game [1958; #1 for 66 wks] (51/60)
The Elegants: Little Star [1958; #1 for 1 wk] (51/60)
The Everly Brothers: Wake Up Little Susie [1957; #1 for 4 wks] (39/44)
The Everly Brothers: Bye Bye Love [1957; #2 for 4 wks] (49/60)
The Everly Brothers: All I Have to Do Is Dream [1958; #1 for 5 wks] (50/60)
The Everly Brothers: Bird Dog [1958; #1 for 1 wk] (36/58)
The Everly Brothers: Problems [1958; #2 for 1 wk] (46/56)
The Four Preps: 26 Miles (Santa Catalina) [1958; #2 for 3 wks] (42/60)
The Four Preps: Big Man [1958; #3 for 2 wks] (46/59)
Connie Francis: Who's Sorry Now [1958; #4 for 2 wks] (54/50)
Ernie Freeman: Raunchy [1957; #4 for 1 wk] (34/58)
Terry Gilkyson & The Easy Riders: Marianne [1957; #4 for 1 wk] (43/60)
Charlie Gracie: Butterfly [1957; #1 for 2 wks] (35/60)
Russ Hamilton: Rainbow [1957; #4 for 1 wk] (51/50)
The Hilltoppers: Marianne [1957; #3 for 1 wk] (45/60)
[Buddy Holly &] The Crickets: That'll Be the Day [1957; #1 for 1 wk] (39/60)
Buddy Holly: Peggy Sue [1957; #3 for 3 wks] (35/56)
Tab Hunter: Young Love [1957; #1 for 6 wks] (42/59)
Ferlin Husky: Gone [1957; #4 for 4 wks] (34/60)

Sonny James: Young Love [1957; #1 for 1 wk] (43/59)
Bill Justis Orch: Raunchy [1957; #2 for 1 wk] (33/58)
The Kingston Trio: Tom Dooley [1958; #1 for 1 wk] (43/60)
Buddy Knox: Party Doll [1957; #1 for 1 wk] (45/60)
Frankie Laine: Moonlight Gambler [1957; #3 for 1 wk] (42/57)
Jerry Lee Lewis: Whole Lot Of Shakin' Going On [1957; #3 for 2 wks] (35/58)
Jerry Lee Lewis: Great Balls of Fire [1958; #2 for 4 wks] (31/58)
Little Anthony & The Imperials: Tears On My Pillow [1958; #4 for 1 wk] (44/47)
Laurie London: He's Got the Whole World In His Hands [1958; #1 for 4 wks] (37/54)
Dean Martin: Return to Me [1958; #4 for 3 wks] (49/60)
Johnny Mathis: Chances Are [1957; #1 for 1 wk] (47/60)
The McGuire Sisters: Sugartime [1958; #1 for 4 wks] (48/49)
Domenico Modugno: Nel Blu Dipinto Di Blu (Volare) [1958; #1 for 5 wks] (58/60)
Ricky Nelson: A Teenager's Romance [1957; #2 for 1 wk] (48/60)
Ricky Nelson: Be-Bop Baby [1957; #3 for 1 wk] (40/60)
Ricky Nelson: I'm Walking [1957; #4 for 1 wk] (43/60)
Ricky Nelson: Poor Little Fool [1958; #1 for 2 wks] (37/60)
Ricky Nelson: Stood Up [1958; #2 for 3 wks] (29/58)
Ricky Nelson: Believe What You Say [1958; #4 for 1 wk] (41/60)
Patti Page: Old Cape Cod [1957; #3 for 1 wk] (53/50)
The Platters: Twilight Time [1958; #1 for 1 wk] (54/60)
The Playmates: Beep Beep [1958; #4 for 2 wks] (46/47)
Perez Prado Orch: Patricia [1958; #1 for 1 wk] (44/60)
Elvis Presley: All Shook Up [1957; #1 for 9 wks] (40/60)
Elvis Presley: Jailhouse Rock [1957; #1 for 7 wks] (34/55)
Elvis Presley: (Let Me Be Your) Teddy Bear [1957; #1 for 7 wks] (46/59)

Elvis Presley: Too Much [1957; #1 for 3 wks] (34/59)
Elvis Presley: Love Me [1957; #2 for 2 wks] (47/60)
Elvis Presley: Don't [1958; #1 for 5 wks] (49/59)
Elvis Presley: Hard Headed Woman [1958; #1 for 2 wks] (33/58)
Elvis Presley: Wear My Ring Around Your Neck [1958; #2 for 1 wk] (46/60)
Elvis Presley: One Night [1958; #4 for 2 wks] (46/60)
The Rays: Silhouettes [1957; #3 for 2 wks] (49/50)
Debbie Reynolds: Tammy [1957; #1 for 5 wks] (58/60)
Marty Robbins: A White Sport Coat (And a Pink Carnation) [1957; #2 for 1 wk] (51/49)
Jimmie Rodgers: Honeycomb [1957; #1 for 4 wks] (47/49)
Jimmie Rodgers: Kisses Sweeter Than Wine [1957; #3 for 3 wks] (39/43)
Jimmie Rodgers: Secretly [1958; #3 for 3 wks] (36/60)
The Royal Teens: Short Shorts [1958; #3 for 2 wks] (35/57)
Tommy Sands: Teen-Age Crush [1957; #2 for 2 wks] (54/60)
Jack Scott: My True Love [1958; #3 for 1 wk] (30/60)
The Silhouettes: Get a Job [1958; #1 for 2 wks] (31/58)
Frank Sinatra: Hey! Jealous Lover [1957; #3 for 1 wk] (47/49)
Frank Sinatra: All the Way [1958; #2 for 1 wk] (57/50)
Gale Storm: Dark Moon [1957; #4 for 1 wk] (50/60)
The Tarriers: The Banana Boat Song [1957; #4 for 1 wk] (49/60)
The Teddy Bears: To Know Him, Is To Love Him [1958; #1 for 3 wks] (49/60)
Conway Twitty: It's Only Make Believe [1958; #1 for 2 wks] (44/58)
Andy Williams: Butterfly [1957; #1 for 3 wks] (37/60)
Andy Williams: Are You Sincere [1958; #3 for 1 wk] (46/60)
Billy Williams: I'm Gonna Sit Right Down and Write Myself a Letter [1957; #3 for 4 wks] (54/50)
Sheb Wooley: The Purple People Eater [1958; #1 for 6 wks] (44/48)

Table 4. Thirty Selected 1999–2000 Albums [Their Year of Popularity and Chart Peak], Their Songs and (Voice-Leading/Harmony Values)

a   **Backstreet Boys: Millenium** [1999; #1 for 10 wks] (avg. score: 45.3/47.8)
        Larger than Life (33/33); I Want It That Way (38/50); Show Me the Meaning of Being Lonely
        (43/43); It's Gotta Be You (43/50); I Need You Tonight (56/50); Don't Want You Back (43/49);
        Don't Wanna Lose You Now (41/43); The One (43/55); Back to Your Heart (56/49); Spanish Eyes
        (49/55); No One Else Comes Close (48/46); The Perfect Fan (50/50)

b   **Beck: Midnite Vultures** [1999; #34] (avg score: 25.5/25.5)
        Sexx Laws (46/55); Nicotine & Gravy (27/24); Mixed Bizness (28/25); Get Real Paid (22/15);
        Hollywood Freaks (6/9); Peaches & Cream (12/18); Broken Train (33/33); Milk & Honey (28/26);
        Beautiful Way (41/48); Pressure Zone (41/27); Debra (22/26)

c   **Counting Crows: This Desert Life** [1999; #8] (avg score: 51.6/48.9)
        Hanginaround (51/51); Mrs. Potter's Lullaby(53/60); Amy Hit the Atmosphere (49/52); Four Days
        (57/43); All My Friends (52/56); High Life (51/44); Colorblind (55/45); I Wish I Was a Girl (55/59);
        Speedway (46/40); St. Robinson in His Cadillac Dream (47/39)

d   **Creed: Human Clay** [1999; #1 for 2 wks] (avg. score: 19.6/23.6)
        Are You Ready (20/16); What If (24/36); Beautiful (21/21); Say I (18/10); Wrong Way (12/10);
        Faceless Man (21/19); Never Die (14/9); With Arms Wide Open (19/27); Higher (20/46); Wash
        Away Those Years (28/35); Inside Us All (19/31)

e   **Dixie Chicks: Fly** [1999; #1 for 2 wks] (avg score: 43.3/58.8)
Ready to Run(47/56); If I Fall You're Going Down With Me (43/60); Cowboy Take Me
Away(51/60); Cold Day in July (47/60); Goodbye Earl(37/60); Hello Mr. Heartache (41/59); Don't
Waste Your Heart (47/60); Sin Wagon (40/54); Without You(48/60); Some Days You Gotta Dance
(43/58); Hole in My Head (27/58); Heartbreak Town (46/59); Let Him Fly (46/60)

f   **Eminem: The Marshall Mathers LP** [2000; #1 for 8 wks] (avg score: 23.8/33.6)
PSA 2000(0/0); Kill You(45/52); Stan(41/43); Paul (Skit) (0/0); Who Knew(20/36); Steve Berman
(Skit)(5/10); The Way I Am (38/60); The Real Slim Shady (38/60); Remember Me (13/6); I'm Back
(32/33); Marshall Mathers (34/54); Ken Kaniff (Skit) (7/8); Drug Ballad (42/37); Amityville (20/57);
Bitch Please II (23/20); Kim (20/37); Under the Influence (23/54); Criminal (27/37)

g   **Foo Fighters: There Is Nothing Left to Lose** [1999; #10] (avg score: 32.4/36.5)
Stacked Actors (17/20); Breakout (20/19); Learn to Fly (27/24); Gimme Stitches (39/39); Generator
(39/51); Aurora (37/42); Live-in Skin (27/22); Next Year (42/60); Headwires (38/22); Ain't It the
Life (37/49); M.I.A. (33/53)

h   **Macy Gray: On How Life Is** [1999; #4] (avg score: 32.6/36.1)
Why Didn't You Call Me (35/34); Do Something (32/34); Caligula (26/24); I Try (35/49); Sex-o-
Matic Venus Freak (27/23); I Can't Wait to Meetchu (29/30); Still (33/57); I've Committed Murder
(37/27); A Moment to Myself (31/27); The Letter (41/56)

i   **Jay-Z: Volume 3: The Life and Times of S Carter** [2000; #1 for 1 wk] (avg score:
20.1/33.2)
Hova Song (Intro)(35/45); So Ghetto (10/51); Do It Again (Put Ya Hands Up)(13/34); Dope Man
(28/56); Things That U Do (38/32); It's Hot (Some Like It Hot) (14/26); Snoopy Track (19/45); S.
Carter (29/32); Pop 4 Roc(22/19); Watch Me (15/17); Big Pimpin' (13/58); There's Been a Murder
(6/2); Come and Get Me (12/8); NYMP (13/28); Hova Song (Outro) (35/45)

j   **B. B. King and Eric Clapton: Riding with the King** [2000; #3] (avg score: 30.4/40.8)
Riding with the King (32/30); Ten Long Years (28/42); Key to the Highway (29/43); Marry You
(28/41); Three O'Clock Blues (31/42); Help the Poor (28/46); I Wanna Be (28/24); Worried Life
Blues (27/44); Days of Old (32/41); When My Heart Beats Like a Hammer (27/43); Hold On I'm
Coming (29/43); Come Rain or Come Shine (46/51)

k   **KoRn: Issues** [1999; #1 for 1 wk] (avg score: 14.1/11.0)
Dead (25/40); Falling Away from Me (14/11); Trash (11/7); 4 U (40/50); Beg for Me (20/6); Make
Me Bad (9/3); It's Gonna Go Away (14/21); Wake Up (14/4); Am I Going Crazy (7/3); Hey Daddy
(10/3); Somebody Someone (10/3); No Way (3/3); Let's Get this Party Started (19/6); Wish You
Could Be Me (5/3); Counting (2/2); Dirty (23/11)

l   **k. d. lang: Invincible Summer** [2000; #58] (avg. score: 38.3/41)
The Consequences of Falling (35/28); Summerfling (37/42); Suddenly (40/38); It's Happening with
You (42/51); Extraordinary Thing (39/42); Love's Great Ocean (30/30); Simple (57/54); What Better
Said (42/51); When We Collide (32/25); Curiosity (36/52); Only Love (31/38)

m   **Paul McCartney: Run Devil Run** [1999; #27] (avg score: 29.3/47.8)
Blue Jean Bop (31/42); She Said Yeah (36/50); All Shook Up (26/52); Run Devil Run (21/33); No
Other Baby (19/42); Lonesome Town (40/60); Try Not to Cry (27/41); Movie Magg (37/40); Brown
Eyed Handsome Man (24/40); What It Is (26/57); Coquette (27/60); I Got Stung (30/53); Honey
Hush (31/40); Shake a Hand (36/49); Party (28/58)

n   **N'Sync: No Strings Attached** [2000: #1 for 8 wks] (avg score: 39.7/48.1)
Bye Bye Bye(34/52); It's Gonna Be Me (46/56); Space Cowboy (Yippie-Yi-Yay) (27/33); Just Got
Paid (34/42); It Makes Me Ill(30/41); This I Promise You (52/50); No Strings Attached (43/48);
Digital Get Down (35/56); Bringin' da Noise (42/46); That's When I'll Stop Loving You (50/58); I'll
Be Good For You (33/35); I Thought She Knew (50/60)

o   **Nelly: Country Grammar** [2000; #1 for 5 wks] (avg score: 17.4/14.9)
Intro (0/0); St. Louis (29/37); Greed, Hate, Envy (29/22); Country Grammar (Hot . . .) (28/24); Steal
the Show(5/16); Interlude (0/0); Ride Wit Me - City Spud (44/34); E. I. (20/10); Thicky Thick Girl
(32/12); For My (8/10); Utha Side (17/23); Tho Dem Wrappas (14/13); Wrap Sumden (15/11);
Batter Up (13/11); Never Let 'Em C U Sweat (6/10); Luven Me (36/20); Outro (0/0)

p   **Notorious B.I.G.: Born Again** [1999; #1 for 1 wk] (avg score: 8.2/11.4)
        Born Again (Intro) (22/35); Notorious B.I.G. (12/16); Dead Wrong (3/1); Hope You Niggas Sleep
        (3/1); Dangerous MC's (4/1); Biggie(12/35); Niggas (12/20); Big Booty Hoes (13/13); Would You
        Die For Me (5/5); Come On (10/18); Rap Phenomenon (2/3); Let Me Get Down (1/13); Tonight
        (7/10); If I Should Die Before I Wake (7/6); Who Shot Ya (4/7); Can I Get Witcha (6/17); I Really
        Want to Show You (21/3); Ms. Wallace (Outro) (3/2)

q   **Oasis: Standing on the Shoulder of Giants** [2000; #24] (avg score: 26.2/31.4)
        Fuckin' in the Bushes (21/22); Go Let It Out (28/16); Who Feels Love? (38/15); Put Yer Money
        Where Yer Mouth Is (18/18); Little James (28/20); Gas Panic! (21/43); Where Did It All Go Wrong?
        (24/46); Sunday Morning Call (29/39); I Can See a Liar (29/40); Roll It Over (24/37); Let's All Make
        Believe (28/49)

r   **Pearl Jam: Binaural** [2000; #2] (avg score: 17.1/21.5)
        Breakerfall (15/18); Gods' Dice (20/16); Evacuation (10/13); Light Years (17/37); Nothing as it
        Seems (18/22); Thin Air (27/22); Insignificance (17/40); Of the Girl (15/14); Grievance (12/13);
        Rival (9/19); Sleight of Hand (9/2); Soon Forget (27/49); Parting Ways (26/15)

s   **Phish: Farmhouse** [2000; #12] (avg score: 33.4/31.7)
        Farmhouse (47/52); Twist (29/43); Bug (32/26); Back on the Train (38/31); Heavy Things (41/60);
        Gotta Jibboo (26/20); Dirt (37/30); Piper (31/12); Sleep (29/26); The Inlaw Josie Wales (34/33);
        Sand (25/16); First Tube (32/31)

t   **Radiohead: Kid A** [2000; #1 for 1 wk] (avg score: 34.8/20.6)
        Everything in Its Right Place(44/17); Kid A (35/27); The National Anthem (34/17); How to
        Disappear Completely (36/26); Treefinger (9/10); Optimistic (34/21); In Limbo (28/6); Idioteque
        (37/13); Morning Bell(50/40); Motion Picture Soundtrack (41/29)

u   **Rage Against the Machine: The Battle of Los Angeles** [1999; #1 for 1 wk] (avg score: 7.2/10.8)
        Testify (15/15); Guerrila Radio(7/13); Calm Like a Bomb(4/10); Mic Check (5/8); Sleep Now in the
        Fire (4/13); Born of a Broken Man(11/11); Born as Ghosts (10/10); Maria (2/12); Voice of the
        Voiceless (8/5); New Millenium Homes (5/11); Ashes in the Fall (6/10); War Within a Breath
        (9/12)

v   **Santana: Supernatural** [1999; #1 for 12 wks] (avg score: 29.3/37.5)

        (Da Le) Yaleo (24/34); Love of My Life (36/46); Put Your Lights On (30/51); Africa Bamba (41/48);
        Smooth (33/53); Do You Like the Way (15/10); Maria Maria (31/40); Migra (23/17); Corazon
        Espinado (31/47); Wishing it Was (17/25); El Farol (46/60); Primavera (32/44); The Calling (22/12)

w   **Sleater-Kinney: All Hands on the Bad One** [2000; #177] (avg score: 14.7/15.2)
        The Ballad of a Ladyman (24/23); Ironclad (14/11); All Hands on the Bad One (10/15); Youth
        Decay (10/8); You're No Rock n' Roll Fun (24/30); #1 Must Have (12/8); The Professional (9/7);
        Was It a Lie? (10/8); Male Model (3/6); Leave You Behind (30/54); Milkshake n' Honey (11/10);
        Pompeii (8/5); The Swimmer (26/12)

x   **Britney Spears: Oops! I Did It Again** [2000; #1 for 1 wk] (avg score: 40.1/45.9)
        Oops! I Did It Again (49/56); Stronger (32/57); Don't Go Knockin' on My Door (39/51); (I Can't Get
        No) Satisfaction (26/11); Don't Let Me Be the Last to Know (42/45); What U See (Is What U Get)
        (38/53); Lucky (38/45); One Kiss From You (52/53); Where Are You Now (46/41); Can't Make You
        Love Me (43/40); When Your Eyes Say It (34/39); Dear Diary (42/60)

y   **Steely Dan: Two Against Nature** [2000; #6] (avg score: 38.4/22.2)
        Gaslighting Abbie (50/27); What a Shame About Me (49/32); Two Against Nature (20/12); Janie
        Runaway (29/13); Almost Gothic (43/7); Jack of Speed (40/34); Cousin Dupree (29/45); Negative
        Girl (36/16); West of Hollywood (50/14)

z   **TLC: Fanmail** [1999; #1 for 5 wks] (avg score: 21.9/29.3)
        Fanmail(18/12); The Vice-E Interpretation (Interlude)(0/0); Silly Ho (10/12); Whispering Playa
        (Interlude) (0/0); No Scrubs (25/60); I'm Good at Being Bad (30/28); If They Knew (34/50); I Miss
        You So Much (53/52); Unpretty (34/60); My Life (34/43); Shout (19/45); Come On Down (32/14);
        Dear Lie (36/58); Communicate (Interlude) (0/0); Lovesick (10/9); Automatic (14/6); Don't Pull
        Out on Me Yet (24/49)

@ **Vertical Horizon: Everything You Want** [1999; #40] (avg score: 30.2/39.5)
We Are (30/19); You're a God (28/31); Everything You Want (27/23); Best I Ever Had (Grey Sky Morning) (39/52); You Say (29/50); Finding Me (29/45); Miracle (30/47); Send It Up (35/59); Give You Back (36/58); All of You (29/28); Shackled (20/23)

\# **Veruca Salt: Resolver** [2000; #171] (avg score: 29.7/33.0)
The Same Persion (32/28); Born Entertainer (26/30); Best You Can Get (29/38); Wet Suit (28/45); Yeah Man (31/40); Imperfectly (40/48); Officially Dead (35/22); Only You Know (32/22); Disconnected (26/48); All Dressed Up (39/45); Used to Know Her (22/18); Pretty Boys (30/21); Hellraiser (16/24)

\$ **XTC: Homespun / Apple Venus Volume One** [1999; #106] (avg score: 43.3/42.2)
River of Orchids (39/29); I'd Like That (58/55); Easter Theatre (44/45); Knights in Shining Karma (42/41); Frivolous Tonight (35/40); Greenman (33/31); Your Dictionary (52/57); Fruit Nut (44/50); I Can't Own Her (47/49); Harvest Festival (45/35); The Last Balloon (37/32)

% **XTC: Wasp Star (Apple Venus Volume 2)** [2000; #108] (avg score: 43.5/48)
Playground (48/47); Stupidly Happy (25/39); In Another Life (40/49); My Brown Guitar (50/43); Boarded Up (26/22); I'm the Man Who Murdered Love (46/59); We're all Light (40/60); Standing in for Joe (50/49); Wounded Horse (55/60); You and the Clouds will Still be Beautiful (52/45); Church of Women (32/45); The Wheel and the Maypole (58/58 [Wheel portion 26/23 as unstable intro to Maypole])

The values of each sample were then plotted as Cartesian coordinates on three scatter charts, shown as Figures 23, 24 and 25. (For the 1999–2000 sample, data is presented both in terms of individual songs—perhaps more comparable to the scores from 1957–58—and of whole albums, ostensibly the intended objects of latter-day listening.) In these graphs, higher voice-leading scores bring a song or album higher along the y-axis, and higher harmony scores lead further to the right along the x-axis. Note that scores progressively below 60 in either domain do not necessarily mean that a given work is that much more averse to a Schenkerian hearing, although some of the resulting graphs for songs approaching coordinates of 0/0 might include highly unconventional attributes. From the work of Harald Krebs, for instance, we have learned how to adapt Schenkerian analysis to the piece with more than one key center, and that certainly applies here to the truck-driver's modulation, the main reason the Backstreet Boys do not score a nearly perfect 60 in harmony, as well as to the other situations where a single key center is not absolute.[21] From the work of Carl Schachter, David Neumeyer, and Allen Forte, we have accepted Schenkerian ways of dealing with voice-leading structures not seemingly governed by upper-voice descents to the first scale degree, but by other sorts of stepwise lines to the tonic scale degree, or even to another member of the tonic triad.[22] Placement on the charts is not in any way a mark of complexity or value, and is not related to many style markers, as can also be said of common-practice era works more traditionally understood through Schenkerian ears. As far as complexity goes, hip-hop very often involves a simple uninterrupted repetition of short phrases that may be either highly tonal or not tonal at all, resulting in placements throughout the chart. Vying for the upper-right-hand corner of Figure 24 are both the utterly predictable Backstreet Boys (album "a") and the highly imaginative XTC ("\$" and "%"); approaching even more closely to that corner are the simply pleasing Counting Crows (c) and Dixie Chicks (e). One example from XTC (\$) is graphed in Figure 11 above; despite its very high scores, this song displays both a post-tonal modulation

---

21 See Krebs 1981 and 1985.
22 See Neumeyer 1987, Schachter 1994, and Forte 1995.

and an unconventional structural upper voice. In comparing Figure 24 with *Billboard*-chart information from Table 4, it can be seen that the average scores of the fourteen number-one albums chosen from these years reside in a remarkably even distribution among all the scattered placements, including a significant representation of their extremes, suggesting that the relatively "subjective" quality of the sample choice is not responsible for the resulting disparity of scorings.[23]

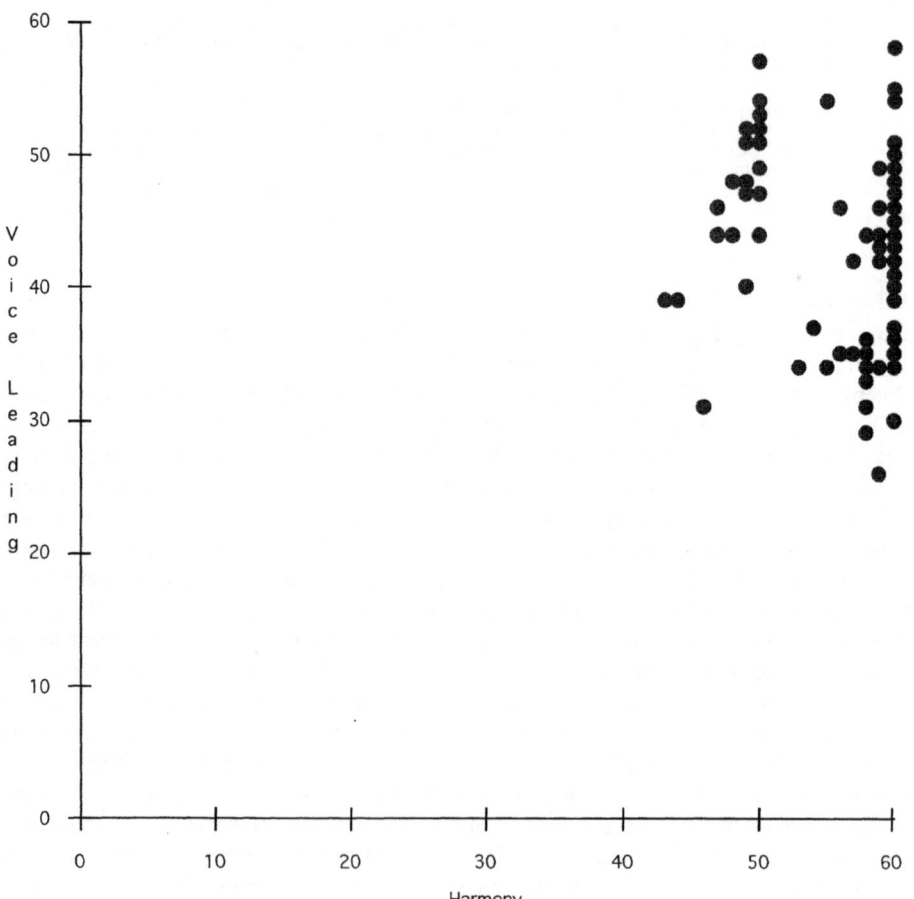

Figure 23. Voice-Leading and Harmony Values for Top One Hundred Songs of 1957–58

---

23 For the fourteen number-one albums, the voice-leading mean (26.1) and standard deviation (12.8), and the harmony mean (30.5) and standard deviation (15.8), are just slightly more outlandish in nearly every regard than are the corresponding numbers for the 1999-2000 population as a whole (mean and standard deviation respectively: 29.4 and 11.4 for voice leading, 32.9 and 13.0 for harmony), but not significantly so, given our indeterminate margin of error in scoring.

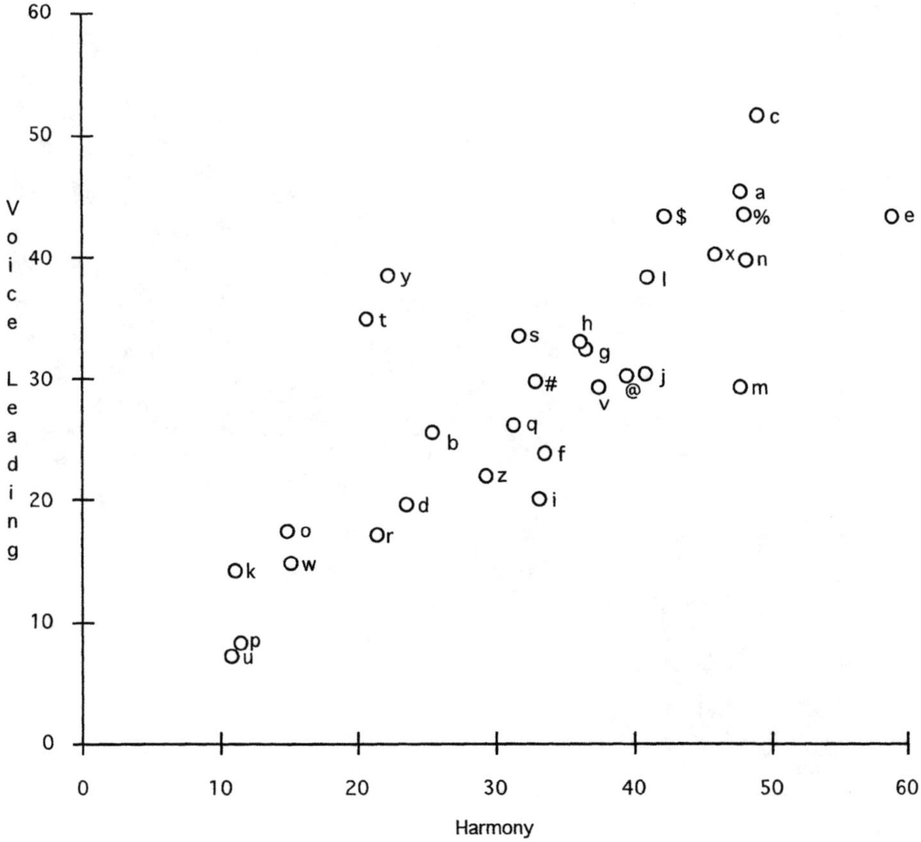

Figure 24. Voice-Leading and Harmony Values for Thirty Selected 1999–2000 Albums

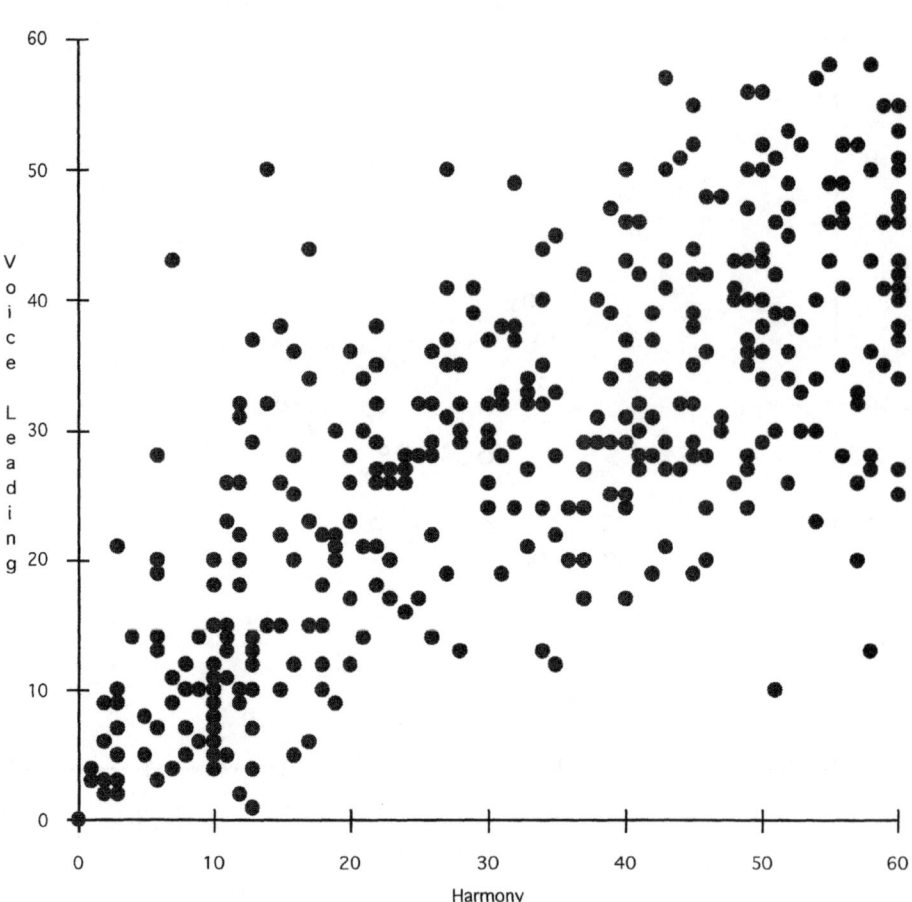

**Figure 25. Voice-Leading and Harmony Values for Songs From Thirty Selected 1999–
2000 Albums**

Of central interest is the relative homogeneity seen in Figure 23, as opposed to the great
variance registered in Figures 24 and 25. Significantly, more than a third of the population
of Figure 23 is not even evident on the chart—37 of the 100 scores duplicate those of others
already represented. The rough appearance of two vertical wedge-shaped bands corresponds
to the fact that a large segment of the population was given perfect scores in harmony, and
an echo of that group would have had perfect scores in that domain but for an automatic ten-
point loss due to the presence of at least one truck-driver's modulation. The means of scores
in Figure 23 (43.7 for voice leading, 56.6 for harmony) are significantly higher than those in
Figures 24 (29.4 / 32.9) and 25 (28.2 / 32.3), evidence of the full range of experimentation that
moves away from tonal normalcy (considered as an ideal 60/60) heard in 1999–2000 but not
in the earlier period. The rate of duplicated scores in Figure 25 is 14.9% (57 of 382), compared
to the 37.0% registered in Figure 23.

Focus for a moment on Figure 24. Given the possibility of inconsistencies in the scoring method from one album to another, perhaps just as significant as the wide range represented in the chart is the general inclination of albums to reflect the degree to which they adhere to, or deviate from, tonal norms in fairly equal values in terms of both voice leading and harmony. In other words, when an object receives low scores in one domain, it does similarly in the other, for the most part. This fact is reflected in the fairly straight line, given something of a margin of error, from bottom left to upper right (and seems to be predicted in the wedges suggested in Figure 23). Curious, however, is the line that transverses this one, running from Albums "y" and "t" to Album "m," with several others clustered in between. These three more extreme positions, clearly outside the standard deviation, seem intuitively correct, given the nature of those albums. "y" is Steely Dan's *Two Against Nature*, which typically evidences highly normative goal-directed voice leading and intensive counterpoint but jazz-based harmonies that may undercut function or otherwise refer to norms only obliquely through distant chromatic substitutions. Radiohead's *Kid A* ("t") has a similar strength of voice leading in the face of abandoned harmonic functions. Album "m" is Paul McCartney's *Run Devil Run*, a new-for-1999 collection of rock 'n' roll oldies; its nearly completely gapped pentatonic melodies that resist both linear connections and most pulls of dissonance to consonance, and its uncharacteristically root-bound bass lines, yield low voice-leading scores while its blues-centered tonal surety brings high harmony scores. Note that the B. B. King / Eric Clapton collaboration with a similar language, Album "j," is close by on the scatter chart. Continuing into the interior of the curious "y"-"m" vector, I suspect that Album "s," Phish's *Farmhouse*, rises a bit higher than the norm in its voice-leading position because of its relatively elaborate vocal counterpoint, and that Album "@," Vertical Horizon's *Everything You Want*, is lower on that same measure because its bass player does not abandon chord roots.

Also interesting is the wide variance in raw scores that can occur within albums. With KoRn's *Issues*, Album "k," the song "Counting" scores a reluctant 2 in each domain, while "4 U" achieves respective scores of 40 and 50. No question as to which of these two songs management would pull as the radio-friendly single, requiring a much broader appeal than would the niche-marketed album. (The marketing possibilities for such an analytic method might be intriguing!) The wide variety of tonal approaches within some albums accounts for the fact that the standard deviations of scores in Figure 25 (14.2 for voice leading, 18.2 for harmony) are significantly higher than those of the scores as averaged for albums in Figure 24 (11.4 for voice leading, 13.0 for harmony).

Now whereas I argue that an album need not achieve a paired score of 60/60 for Schenkerian treatment, the attributes of "low-achieving" albums can be quite unconventional when presented in a voice-leading sketch. Norms are rarely relied upon in albums starting in the lower-left corner, progressing upwards from hip-hop artist The Notorious B.I.G., and hard-rock KoRn and Rage Against the Machine, through post-punk Sleater-Kinney, to Nelly, Pearl Jam and Creed. Recall that Figure 8 presents a graph of Beck's low-scoring "Get Real Paid," which is triadic and embellishes the tonic sonority with clearly passing and neighboring relationships, but establishes no harmonic tension. Figure 9 shows a similar approach to these relationships in Radiohead's "Everything in its Right Place." Those scores around the middle of the chart would present various sorts of perhaps-surmountable interesting challenges to tonal norms for the seasoned Schenkerian, and those rising toward the upper-right corner would be loaded with good (more "normal") pieces for student analysis. For any of this, unless it is just impossible to determine degrees of consonance and dissonance—depending upon the nature of the tonal system represented—a Schenkerian approach would be perfectly appropriate to demonstrate just how normal or just how deviant a given work is in relation to tonal expectations that arise in the context of the entire literature. Obviously, if one listens only to post-grunge hard rock, one will not have these normal expectations. But I think this study suggests, in a manner that approches quantifiable significance, the argument that the majority of listeners who hear an array of tonal approaches in the hit records that reside in and out of today's mainstream also possess many of the same tonal-hearing mechanisms that were present one, two, and three hundred years ago.

III. A Complex Tonal Structure Yields Its Secrets

Most pop tunes and a good many rock records can be slipped into one of the "Classification" pigeonholes quite easily. Many rock songs, however, yield up their identity only very reluctantly. One recent song, Beck's "Lonesome Tears" from *Sea Change* (2003), is a case in point. Beck's often iconoclastic approach to chord succession (perhaps more obvious in *Odelay*, *Mutations* and *Sea Change* than in the intervening parody album, *Midnite Vultures*) demands an unusually deep penetration below the surface to appreciate the nature of harmony in many of his songs, "Lonesome Tears" included. A recognition of the forces of voice leading upon harmony is vital to an interpretation of chord succession here, and would thus make for a useful illustration of the factors considered thus far more abstractly.

[INTRO:] B♭m - A – C♯ (2x)

[VERSE:] C♯ - B - F♯ - A - C♯ - B - B♭m - F♯ (2x)

[CHORUS:] B♭m - A - E (2x)

[INTERLUDE:] G♯m - E - G♯m - G - B

Figure 26. Chords in "Lonesome Tears" (Beck Hansen), *Sea Change*, Beck, 2003

Because "Lonesome Tears," like nearly all other rock music, is unavailable in a reliable score, the resourceful analyst might first look for a cheat at OLGA, the Online Guitar Archive, a database of song lyrics and tabs (guitar parts written by amateur contributors either with chord symbols showing root and color or with full tablature), and may be lucky enough to find chord symbols such as those shown in Figure 26.[24] This information, with CD and guitar at the ready, will get the listener far into picking and singing through the pitch-world of "Lonesome Tears." But not too far. Even the pondering of the rectification of enharmonic spellings (B-flat minor = A-sharp minor?) and consideration of the clues offered by metric accent leave unanswered many questions regarding which pitch-class or pitch-classes might claim tonal centricity,

---

24   OLGA is found at http://www.olga.net/dynamic/search.php?search=.

which "chords" have harmonic function and which are embellishing, where harmonic syntax might be operating and where voice leading is purely or largely contrapuntal. Clearly, more work needs to be done before one could begin to classify the sort of tonal operations at work here.

Only a consideration of voice leading will lead to progress with this puzzle, and so the analyst might come up with a sketch such as that given as Figure 27. Many things then start to make sense: as confusing as the bass line may be at first, all vocal and string parts in the Introduction, Verse and Chorus clearly prolong C-sharp-major harmony. While the Introduction, for instance, does actually sound the triads, B-flat minor - A - C-sharp, the string lines allow this to be heard as a simple C-sharp major chord whose third and fifth are ornamented by a normally resolving chromatic augmented fourth, as shown in the two parts of Figure 27a. In the Verse (see Fig. 27b), the bass line can only be understood as support for the vocal and string parts: the bass A-natural is a leaping passing tone, supporting the chromatic passing tone in the tenor range (which clarifies how the vocal part omits the diatonic a-sharp^2). The first tenor a-sharp, neighbor to the following g-sharp, is supported by the bass F-sharp, which thus has the largest bass role other than C-sharp itself, functioning as a plagal IV. That makes the prior B-major sonority a double-plagal, working as IV of IV. The second bass B-natural passes to A-sharp, representing the unfolded third above a second plagal F-sharp, which is shown (by the arrow) to resolve only in the vocal e-sharp^2 that follows in the repeat. So every single bass tone of the Verse is present for contrapuntal reasons, mostly in support of motion among the complex of upper lines, leaving C-sharp the only tone of real harmonic value, and F-sharp the next-strongest sonority. Clearly, it would be senseless to try to evaluate the harmony of this song by studying its OLGA roots alone, which are nearly all of an illusory nature.

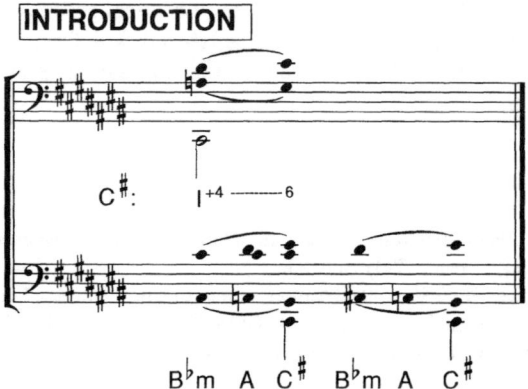

Figure 27. Analysis of "Lonesome Tears" (Beck Hansen), *Sea Change*, Beck, 2003

E-major harmony is prolonged in the Chorus, which plays both upon a variation of the chords heard in the Introduction and upon a continuation of the Verse's descending line through the C-sharp-major triad (replicating the Verse's "descant" part in unfolded thirds above). We also have here a neat tying-up of all the A-sharp - A-natural business, with the bass "explaining" that the singer's b^1 is a mere passing tone to an unrealized a-sharp^1, and that A-natural, once a tenor-register chromatic passing tone, now takes over the diatonic role once played by A-sharp. In fact, a local diatonic spelling here would show B-flat as bass neighbor to A, and the vocal part should then read d-flat^2 - c-natural^2 - (b-flat^1) - a^1 - g-sharp^1. The Interlude is somewhat ambiguous but its tonality can be interpreted as B major inflected with an Aeolian cadence, the final tonic of which side-steps up to the overall tonic of the next verse's C-sharp. (The song concludes with a minute-long passage with C-sharp-major scales in a contrary motion that tips the hat to "I Am the Walrus," all brought into some vertical synchronicity by the addition of a F-double-sharp passing tone in the upper ascending part and a repeated C-sharp in the lower descending part.) Overall then, the song presents us with the harmonic progression C-sharp (Intro - Verse) - E (Chorus) - B (Interlude) - C-sharp (Verse). Along with the Verse's important F-sharp chord, this series gives prominent voice to four of the five triads of the C-sharp minor-pentatonic scale, but such a construction seems as off-base as did the E-flat-minor black-note-scale argument for "Pretty Ballerina." Clearly, the voice leading argues for a key of C-sharp major colored by a touch of mixture in the Chorus, moving to a modal neighboring bVII as a substitute for V at the close of the Interlude. This hearing places Beck's innovative and recalcitrant song squarely into Box 3a.

If this essay has accomplished nothing else, I hope it argues successfully that there is no single monolithic style of rock harmony, that blues is not the basis of all modern popular music, and that there are gradations between and among approaches based on the interrelated roles of harmony and counterpoint. Even if many rock composers and performers seem to rely on chord changes with obsessive metric regularity and at great expense of the horizontal domain, there is in many styles quite enough contrapuntal interest and quite a strong enough hierarchy of harmonic values to reward the listener who likes a challenge here and there. The study of rock music can take any number of literary, historical or sociological directions, but it could keep quite busy an army of analysts charged merely with furnishing an understanding of its tonal behaviors. Fortunately, there are plenty of interesting recordings, and plenty of qualified listeners to make a go of it.

References

Everett, Walter. 1986. "Fantastic Remembrance in John Lennon's 'Strawberry Fields Forever' and 'Julia.'" *The Musical Quarterly* 72(3): 360–93.

———. 1997. "Swallowed By a Song: Paul Simon's Crisis of Chromaticism." In *Understanding Rock*, ed. John Covach and Graeme Boone. New York: Oxford University Press: 113–53.

———. 1999. *The Beatles as Musicians:* Revolver *Through the* Anthology. New York: Oxford University Press.

———. 2000. "Confessions From Blueberry Hell, or, Pitch Can Be a Sticky Substance." In *Expression in Pop-Rock Music*, ed. Walter Everett. New York: Garland Publishing.

———. 2001.*The Beatles as Musicians: The Quarry Men Through* Rubber Soul. New York: Oxford University Press.

———. 2002. "Detroit and Memphis: The Soul of *Revolver*." In *'Every Sound There Is': The Beatles'* Revolver *and the Transformation of Rock and Roll*. Aldershot, U.K.: Ashgate Publishing.

Forte, Allen. 1995. *The American Popular Ballad of the Golden Era, 1924–50*. Princeton, N.J.: Princeton

University Press.

Hamm, Charles. 1979. *Yesterdays: Popular Song in America*. New York: W.W. Norton & Company.

Krebs, Harald. 1981. "Alternatives to Monotonality in Early Nineteenth-Century Music." *Journal of Music Theory* 25(1): 1–16.

———. 1985. "The Background Level in Some Tonally Deviating Works of Franz Schubert." *In Theory Only* 8(8): 5–18.

Middleton, Richard. 1990. *Studying Popular Music*. Buckingham, U.K.: Open University Press.

Narmour, Eugene. 1977. *Beyond Schenkerism: The Need for Alternatives in Music Analysis*. Chicago, I.L.: The University of Chicago Press.

Neumeyer, David. 1987. "The Ascending *Urlinie*." *Journal of Music Theory* 31(2): 275–303.

Ricci, Adam. 2000. "A 'Hard Habit to Break': The Integration of Harmonic Cycles and Voice-Leading Structure in Two Songs by Chicago." *Indiana Theory Review* 21: 129–46.

Schachter, Carl. 1994. "The Prelude to Bach's Suite no. 4 for Violoncello Solo: The Submerged Urlinie." *Current Musicology* 56: 54–71.

Stephenson, Ken. 2002. *What to Listen For in Rock: A Stylistic Analysis*. New Haven, C.T.: Yale University Press.

Van der Merwe, Peter. 1989. *Origins of the Popular Style: The Antecedents of Twentieth-Century Popular Music*. New York: Oxford University Press.

Walser, Robert. 1993. *Running With the Devil: Power, Gender, and Madness in Heavy Metal Music*. Hanover, N.H.: Wesleyan University Press.

[17]

Incongruity and Predictability in British Dance Band Music of the 1920s and 1930s

Derek B. Scott

This article was prompted by a number of questions: How do we approach the study of British dance band music of these vintage years? Do they represent a golden age in quantity rather than quality? Is it possible to construct criteria for deciding what is good and bad in this music? I am particularly interested in asking these questions of dance band music of the 1920s and 1930s because, despite the enormous attraction dance bands held for a majority of people in the United Kingdom between the two world wars, and despite this period's mythic status as the "golden era" of the dance band (at least in the eyes of the publicists for the record industry), it is not uncommon to find dance band music neglected or despised (usually when compared to "real" jazz) even by writers normally sympathetic to popular music. How do we explain the contradictory response to an old dance band record summed up in the phrase "wonderfully awful"? Perhaps, in the latter case, the answer is that such things as humor and sentimentality are very period specific; they quickly become dated, and so an old record often seems to lend insight into the way people felt at a specific time, which, being past, in turn evokes nostalgia and a feeling of empathy with those whose lifetimes preceded our own. At the same time, it must be acknowledged that by responding in such a fashion the meaning of the music to us differs from its meaning to its original listeners—a neat illustration that history and aesthetics are not mutually exclusive categories.

Is it at all possible, then, to take any steps toward finding answers to the above questions in the present relativistic climate, or can we speak only of differences rather than aesthetic values? What methodology, distinct from that used in the study of Western classical music, is best suited to a consideration of the aesthetics of dance band music of the 1920s and 1930s? Two favorite attacks made by critics of commercial popular music are (1) to claim it is cliché ridden, and (2) to condemn it for being badly performed. The first can be parried by considering the music from the point of view of reception (for example, certain structural parameters may be "standardized," but how predictable does the listener find the music as a whole?). The second can be countered by considering matters of incongruity. Incongruity is produced as the effect of conflict between stylistic codes so that the conventional meanings of these codes are negated or thwarted. Alternatively, one might say that incongruity results when predictability is avoided by unstylish means. This may be unintentional, and therefore likely to produce purposeless conflict or confusion of meaning, or premeditated, as is the case with parody, where a clash of codes is used deliberately so as to provoke critical awareness of style.

Incongruous Mixing of Styles

By the turn of the century, the United Kingdom had long adopted a European classical perspective on what constituted qualitative norms in music and was restaking its own claims as a major player in this field with composers like Elgar, Holst, and Vaughan Williams. Moreover, the country had a history of importing elite French, Italian, and German music to satisfy the tastes of the English, Scottish, and Anglo-Irish aristocracy. Now, if we note that before the 1890s the only musical import associated with North America was blackface minstrelsy, and that this was followed by a variety of other popular styles, such as the songs of Tin Pan Alley, ragtime, and jazz, the complexity of the reception given to jazz and of the cultural environment within which British dance bands emerged can easily be imagined. An immediate way in which the contradictory welcome given to popular music from the United States becomes apparent is in the urge to mix elite and popular styles. Yet this desire to elude the vulgar often creates incongruity, since what counts as "good" in elite music may not be regarded as being so in popular music, and vice versa. Consider the incongruous effect of quasi-operatic singing on some early dance band records—for example, Stuart Robertson's singing on Ronnie Munro's recording of "Hello, Aloha, How Are You?"[1] Even as late as Henry Hall's 1936 recording of "It's a Sin To Tell a Lie," Elizabeth Scott is still "operatic" (perhaps an indication of how enduring an influence were the BBC's efforts to encourage "highbrow" taste).[2] The incongruous mix of styles is also found in the United States (The Silver-Masked Tenor). What does it tell us about style? Is it not simply *good* singing? These singers certainly possess the skills to excel in one kind of music, but that proficiency is no more apt for this idiom than is Frank Sinatra's for singing "On the Road to Mandalay" (Kipling-Speaks), which he once misguidedly did. The "classical" voice can be related to instrumental techniques and standards of beauty of tone production within that style. Dance band songs have their own range of associated vocal techniques that are not found in elite music—scatting, growling (both pioneered by Louis Armstrong), speaking, whistling, whispering, crooning, yodeling, and smearing or bending notes—and many of these can also be related to dance band instrumental techniques (for example, the use of a plunger mute to create a growling sound on trumpet or trombone). Even the singer's pronunciation may be a crucial part of style: many British singers in the 1930s felt the need to adopt American accents to sing dance band songs stylishly, just as British singers in the 1970s felt it necessary to use an American southern accent for country music.[3] Some singers adopted the new crooning style, or even a "dirty" jazzy style. Some performers developed more than one style of singing: Gracie Fields, for example, could sing in either her comic "cracked" voice or her "classical" voice—both with commercial success (her recording of "Ave Maria" was a best-seller).

Any criticism of vocal style that fails to take account of the problem of incongruity is going to misfire. The "classical" listener may accuse the dance band singer of unclear vowels, exaggerated vibrato, insincere accent, nasal production, and so forth, in the mistaken belief that excellence is to be attained by adopting "classical" practices. However, a musical style is a discursive code that has developed from the solidification of conventions; and although it may be subject to further development and change, that process cannot be achieved by rupturing, negating, or contradicting its most important and defining attributes.

The mix of jazz and folk was something else that was tried out in the '30s. This is a stylistic hybrid that returns periodically as a fusion that seems possible and indeed desirable to some.[4] Leonard Feather was the first to use the idea of jazzing English traditional airs, and recorded two arrangements in 1937. The next year he re-formed what he called Ye Olde English Swynge Band, which now included West Indian musicians Dave Wilkins (trumpet) and Bertie King (tenor saxophone), with the support of Harry Sarton at Decca.[5] Interest then faded, but further attempts along these lines were made by others after the war. The assumption was often made that because jazz and folk could both be fitted into the same ideological category of "authentic proletarian voice distorted by culture industry" there ought to be a similar fit between their musical idioms. The difficulty here is that, as Gino Stefani has pointed out, style codes are not only rooted in social practices but are also "a blend of technical features, a way of forming objects or events."[6]

Certain other stylistic fusions occurred as a result of shared repertoires, with varying degrees of incongruity in performance. The dividing line between the military band repertoire and that of the dance band or the light orchestra was not sharply drawn. In the '20s, for example, Léon Jessel's *The Parade of the Tin* [or *Wooden] Soldiers* (1911) was commonly played by all three. The music is described as a "Fox Trot or March" but bears little resemblance to the former (besides, the origins of the fox trot are normally traced back only as far as 1913). Even in the '40s, the Squadronaires[7] played the occasional military band piece, like "American Patrol" (Meacham),[8] and military bands sometimes played for dances (though they had to endure the grumbles and sarcastic comments of those dancers who found their style too rigid).[9] The light classics were another, and bigger, source of potential dance band repertoire: "Moonlight and Roses," for example, was adapted from Edwin H. Lemare's Andantino in D-flat (1892) by Ben Black and Neil Morét (1925). Ted Heath's band[10] played everything from "Olde Englyshe" airs to Debussy's *Clair de lune.*

Incongruity between Music and Lyrics

Occasionally, an element that might appear to be incongruous with the verbal content of a dance band number is nevertheless pertinent to the musical style. Take the strangely withdrawn quality of male trios even where the mood of the words seems to dictate exuberance, a striking example of which occurs in Jack Hylton's[11] recording of "Happy Days Are Here Again." How happy do the singers sound compared to the good-humored trombone and the effect of joyous tap dancing with musical pitches created by the sixteen-bar xylophone solo? And how are we to understand the meaning of a trio singing as one person, as in Lew Stone's[12] recording of "Zing! Went the Strings of My Heart"? Again, this occurs alongside some otherwise readily grasped instrumental word painting ("zinging" strings on the guitar). These trios, as well as duets such as that on the Savoy Orpheans'[13] recording of "Baby Face," challenge Peter Wicke's contention that it was the Beatles who introduced the collective "we" in opposition to the romanticized "I" of earlier love songs.[14]

Incongruity between Dance Band Style and "Classical" Style

One of the most radical departures from "classical" vocal style in dance band records was the amplification of a soft voice; in "classical" style, where balancing sound is a matter for composers, not technicians, such a voice tone would sound incongruous and suggest that an artificial remedy had been sought for a lack of projection techniques. The change from recording horn to microphone with the advent of electric recording in 1924–1925 made possible the birth of the crooners "Whispering" Jack Smith, Rudy Vallee, and, in the United Kingdom, Al Bowlly. "Whispering" Jack Smith was a frequent visitor to Britain between 1926 and 1930, recording with Bert Ambrose[15] and Caroll Gibbons.[16] His version of "My Blue Heaven" was an enormous success and established the new crooning style. It is still debated whether Smith crooned from necessity (a lung injury following a wartime gassing) or as a novelty (possible only with the new microphone technology). Crooning worked well for records, since it added to the intimacy of a musical commodity that could be personally consumed in the home.

It is, in general, incongruous with "classical" style for instruments to be given priority over voices, but that such priority was for a long time the case with dance bands is shown by the anonymity of the vocal refrains on record labels of the 1920s and by Lew Stone's trick, even well into the 1930s, of asking band members to take vocal refrains. The individual identity of singers was deemed relatively unimportant until Bowlly built a following of admirers.

Recording technology was most notably exploited in matters of balance: only with the arrival of the microphone was the double bass able to replace the tuba, the former being all but inaudible on acoustic recordings. The "artificial" balance of the microphone recording opened up a new world of possibilities that inevitably conflicted with classical orchestration, the fundamental skill of which was to create a "natural" balance of sound between instruments (and voices). Recording technology could be used to create novel effects. Billy Cotton's[17] record "I've Got Sixpence" (1941) has a fade-out ending; that is to say, it exploits the possibilities of sound recording to produce an effect that could not be reproduced in live performance. The impression given by this record is that Cotton's band is marching toward the listener at the beginning and away again at the end, playing all the while. Henry Hall's record "Rusty and Dusty" (1936) has a similar fade effect, but on that occasion the song remains a complete musical

entity: the fade is a technologically engineered crescendo and diminu-
endo that could just about be emulated live. It demonstrates, perhaps,
an initial reluctance to move beyond the bounds of what was possible
in live performance, the reason for such reluctance possibly being that
commercial music was at this time thought of as a literate culture
typified in commodity terms by the song sheet, and not as an electronic oral culture typified by records. Evidence for this is given by
the common practice of simultaneously releasing different band
arrangements of new songs: the consumer was expected to buy the
interpretation he or she preferred. Only when sales of records began
to overtake sheet music sales in the mid-1950s did a record that was
particularly successful come to represent the *Urtext* of a song. This, in
turn, gave rise to the practice of releasing budget-price recordings that
closely copied an existing record, rather than offering an alternative
interpretation.[18]

The Sociocultural Context of Dance Band Music

Since the problems of incongruity outlined above are as much
involved with the historical and social context of the production of
dance band music as with its technical features, we should seek to
understand what was peculiar about the cultural context in which this
new music emerged and established itself. For example, how important
for the emergence of a distinctive cultural epoch, characterized as the
Jazz Age, was the decline in infant mortality rates during the first
quarter of the twentieth century? After all, the "rock revolution" is
often traced to the post–Second World War baby boom that produced
the teenage market of the late 1950s. There were an unexpectedly
large number of young people around in 1918 to take the place of
those who had been slaughtered in the First World War, and many of
those born in the new century would have been too young to have
fought in that conflict. Furthermore, the psychological effect of being
born near the start of the new millennium must have contributed to a
sense of difference. A distinctive generation, therefore, was ready to
identify with a distinctive and in many ways consciously oppositional
music.

It is not surprising that this generation should favor songs with
romantic, escapist, even frivolous lyrics, in reaction to the improving
tone of drawing-room ballads and the association of the latter with the
call of morality, duty, and patriotism for which so many lives had
recently been shed in a questionable cause. Perhaps it explains why

Figure 1.   Bert Ambrose and his band at the Mayfair Hotel in 1932 (Photo © Hulton Deutsch)

dance music, unlike the music hall, succeeded in winning over a large fraction of the middle and upper classes. In consequence, a figure like Ambrose acted as a symbol of a broad class alliance that stretched from the wealthy clientele of the Mayfair Hotel to the working-class family listening to his band at home on the wireless. During the Depression, for example, Ambrose's "The Clouds Will Soon Roll By," recorded at the Mayfair Hotel, could have been interpreted symbolically as a plea for patience and restraint and, if so, would have performed the hegemonic function of urging people to resist being drawn into class antagonism. The years immediately after the First World War had witnessed some major political upheavals at home and abroad, troubling to both the Left and the Right: in the autumn of 1923, for example, Mussolini had consolidated his power (becoming Il Duce), and in December of that year Britain's first Labour Government (under Ramsay MacDonald) was elected. The dole and the means test had been the fate of many after the First World War, and consequently the emotional temperature of the United Kingdom was running high.

Predictability of Repertoire and Performance

The repertoire of some bands was more predictable than others. Accordion bands were inevitably drawn towards tangos, just as banjo bands found the blackface minstrel repertoire irresistible. Accordion bands were a feature of the '30s,[19] the most famous, Primo Scala (real name Harry Bidgood) and His Accordion Band, was formed in 1934. Accordion bands, mandolin bands, and banjo bands all featured a rhythm section of piano, bass (sometimes bass banjo in banjo bands), drums, and often a xylophone (which made a nice contrast with the accordion tone).

Black performers found themselves affected by predictability—the audience's expectation that they should perform in a certain way. The history of the involvement of black musicians in British popular music of this period has only recently been the subject of research.[20] Small black bands, however, were not uncommon in London clubs by 1920, and these bands included not only African Americans but also Africans and West Indians. The Versatile Four (two banjos, piano, and drums) performed in the clubs from 1913 and had some success in 1919 with their recording of "After You've Gone."

The history of blackface minstrelsy weighed heavily upon black performers at the same time as it accounted for the continuing attraction of blackface performers like Al Jolson and G. H. Elliot. Jolson was heir to the emotionalism and sentimentality of the postbellum minstrels, as Elliot was the inheritor of the "refined" style of minstrelsy that dated back to early troupes like the Virginian Serenaders and the Ethiopian Serenaders.[21] Much blackface minstrelsy and associated music had been misrecognized as a part of a real African American culture rather than as an ideological construct; for example, Alfred Scott Gatty's *Plantation Songs* (published in the 1880s) represented a realistic picture of plantation life for many Victorians. When Sam Hague's all-black, ex-slave minstrel troupe toured Britain in 1866, he emphasized their "naturalness." Yet, like succeeding black troupes, they were not "natural" but working within white expectations of the genre. Black bands at first found themselves judged by minstrel standards, and early jazz musicians found it almost impossible to disentangle themselves from the minstrel business. There was no obvious alternative to this way of performing to a white audience.[22]

As far as the music is concerned, however, it cannot be emphasized too strongly that while the score may appear predictable, the performance may not be so. The major figures in dance band music are generally performers rather than songwriters, a fact that indicates a particular musical emphasis. For we study the bulk of the commercial popular music of the 1920s and 1930s through recordings, whether live, radio, or studio recordings (the last often being one of several takes). In a survey of elite music we would examine scores; but even for a dance band record with little or no improvisation, the score of the arrangement is an inadequate representation of the music. To clarify the position, we might contrast the relative ease of studying a stage play from the printed page with the difficulty of studying a film from its screenplay. In the case of a film, the montage, the photography, the soundtrack, and an actor's performance may each at times take precedence over the script. There are those who, where dance bands are concerned, value recordings for the extent to which players *depart* from a literal reading of the score; this is a criterion for assessing value that is completely at odds with judgments on contemporaneous elite music. As Rose Rosengard Subotnik has remarked, "The ideal of structural listening has made our perceptions and analytical concerns as musicologists almost completely dependent on scores, as if the latter were books."[23]

Most importantly, the nature of jazz improvisation must be considered. If transcribed, it will often produce complex notation (for example, five against three) and awkward-looking syncopation. Of course, it could be argued that "expressive" playing produces a similar effect on the rhythm of other kinds of music: a computer transcription of a concert harpsichordist playing the C-major prelude from book one of Bach's *Well-Tempered Clavier* would not reveal a succession of even quavers. However, jazz flexibility differs in that it is part of a polyrhythmic structure. A predictable rhythmic pattern in an unchanging tempo may form the background to an unpredictable and rhythmically flexible improvisation. The question of how much of this flexibility is demonstrated by a dance band is therefore crucial for many jazz enthusiasts and can be used as a yardstick by which to judge the band's jazz credentials. In this connection such enthusiasts might cite the jazz attractions of Nat Gonella's improvised trumpet obbligato in Ray Noble's[24] recording of "Oh, You Nasty Man," or Bert Read's piano in Ambrose's recording of "Bye Bye Blues."

The Predictable, the Functional, and Extramusical Necessities

In order not to confuse the predictable with the functional, it is important to weigh the importance of differing extramusical necessities when considering the musical output of the palais band, the show band, and the radio band. In trying to understand how the popular music of this period was consumed, the importance of the dance is not to be underestimated. The primary function of much of this music was conative, its main object being the regulation of physical movement. Today the dance as a set piece with many prelearned movements has declined in importance, and people will often be seen dancing *at* bands rather than *to* them. This is not to say that the dances were so rigidly codified that space was unavailable for individual freedoms: quicksteps, for example, offered skillful dancers an opportunity for fancy footwork. Anyone who simply listens to old dance band records is not repeating the same experience of consumption as was had by those who found functional purpose in the music (even though there is no doubt that dance band records were also sometimes played simply to be listened to). As Dennis Potter's television drama (and, later, film) *Pennies from Heaven* demonstrated, it is when this music is choreographed that it really comes to life. It is significant that when the Original Dixieland Jazz Band first appeared in Britain, at the London Hippodrome on 7 April 1919, they performed with a male and female dancer.

The predictability of dance rhythms must also be weighed against their effect (deliberate or otherwise) as a counter to sentimentality. An illustration would be "Whispering" Jack Smith's recording of "My Blue Heaven," where the strictness of the tempo acts as a foil to the sentiment of the words. Instead of the text's being subjected to a range of conventional "classical" devices for evoking sentiment (for example, a generous rubato, or the lingering emphasis of a pause or ritardando), the unchanging pace (and, it must be added, Smith's crooning) creates an impression of understatement.

Show band numbers often involve a visual element that needs to be considered as a vital part of the experience. A show band was to be looked at, hence the routines: for example, Jack Hylton and His Band "sank on stage"[25] at the end of "He Played His Ukulele as the Ship Went Down" (le Clerq), and the members of Jack Payne's band[26] positioned themselves around a model of a locomotive to play "Choo Choo" (Trumbauer-Malneck). Billy Cotton's band evolved from palais band to show band and later moved from variety theater to television, where he was given his own show. Since people were watching, not dancing, show bands were less predictable in matters of tempo than the palais bands. They could, for example, perform numbers in flexible tempo, like "My Old Dutch" (Chevalier-Ingle).

The medium of radio was as important to the production and reception of items by BBC radio bands as was the visual element to

Figure 2.   Harry Roy and his band performing in Variety in 1934 (Photo © Hulton Deutsch)

show bands and the dance to palais bands. In Henry Hall's recording of "Rusty and Dusty," the fade-in beginning and fade-out ending are effective on radio and reminiscent of the listener's own activity of tuning into the station and turning the volume control. It also differs from a typical dance hall number in being a song for children. Like "The Teddy Bears' Picnic," it caters to the radio "family audience." Another obvious radio entertainment is Henry Hall's "I Like Bananas," the evidence here being the quantity of spoken humorous material.

Predictability of Lyric Content

Not all the lyrics of popular songs of this time were of the "moon and June" variety, which they are often caricatured as being. There were "jilt songs," such as "It's the Talk of the Town" (Symes-Neiburg-

Figure 3.   Henry Hall and his orchestra broadcasting from a BBC studio in 1932 (Photo © Hulton Deutsch)

Levinson) and "I've Got an Invitation to a Dance" (same songwriting team). Even the delicate subject of separation and divorce is touched upon in "In a Little Second Hand Store" (Pease-Dreyer-Nelson). There was the occasional song about current affairs. In 1931, as a result of the slump in world trade and the subsequent trade war, the economy had sunk into a deep recession, prompting President Hoover to propose a holiday from all war debts to achieve a world recovery. In England, Horatio Nicholls (Lawrence Wright) wrote a song about it, entitled "We're All Good Pals at Last." German anti-Semitism is criticized in "Leave Abie Alone" (Pearson) of 1933, a song which, unfortunately, does not entirely shake itself free of anti-Semitism, since it contains the unfortunate lines, "Tho' he's only a Jew / he's a man the same as you." It should be stressed, however, that care is needed when selecting songs to characterize responses to social upheaval: the anthem of the Depression in the United Kingdom was not "Brother, Can You Spare a Dime?" (Harburg-Gorney) but the buoyantly cheerful "Sing as We Go" (Parr-Davis). Gracie Fields, who made the last song famous, was resiliently and optimistically "one of us" in the eyes of the British working class.

Predictability and Musical Signs

Certain musical and verbal signs are used time and again to evoke a particular sociocultural location in the imagination of the listener. Since such signs rely upon a familiar association between signifier and signified, they can be adopted by any songwriter. Jimmy Kennedy and Michael Carr, one of Britain's most successful songwriting partnerships, furnish many examples. In Jack Harris's recording of "On Linger Longer Island," the presence of a Hawaiian guitar added to a melody suggestive of the sliding parallel chord shapes idiomatic to that instrument (Ex. 1), the mention of "wicky-wacky," the greeting "Aloha," and even the word "linger" in the title tell us instantly it is a South Sea island and not, say, a Hebridean island, even without our being given the confirmation of the place name Waikiki (itself the most popular choice in songs of this type).

The word "misty," on the other hand, in "Misty Islands of the Highlands," is just what one would expect to find as a description of the Hebrides. There are references to the glen, heather, and a crofter's cabin (*sic*) and lots of sentimental appoggiaturas in this song; in fact, it continues a "Scottish nostalgia ballad" tradition that dates back to the time of the Highland clearances.

In addition to the misty Celtic romanticism of Marjorie Kennedy-Fraser (*Songs of the Hebrides*, 1909–1921) and Duncan Morison (*Ceol Mara*, 1935), who had likewise turned Hebridean melodies into drawing-room ballads, there had developed another kind of pseudo-Celtic music, illustrated by the Jimmy Kennedy and Michael Carr song above and their "Did Your Mother Come from Ireland?" recorded by Billy Cotton, among others. An Irish song aroused certain expectations, and this one satisfies most of them: there are references to shamrock, blarney, Kerry pipers, and St. Patrick, and the music features a solo fiddle (in Cotton's version) and modulates to the relative minor for a contrasting middle section, a device that can be traced back to several well-known "Irish" ballads of the nineteenth century—for example, "Kathleen Mavourneen" (Crawford-Crouch, c. 1838), "The Rose of Tralee" (Spencer-Glover, 1847), and "Come

I met a   la - dy with a wick - y - wack - y way.

Example 1.   "On Linger Longer Island," Jimmie Kennedy and Michael Carr, refrain, mm. 2–4, transcribed from Jack Harris's recording

Back to Erin" (Claribel, 1866). "Did Your Mother Come from Ireland?" arrives as the continuation of a 150-year-old cultural history of commercial "Irish" song that brought its own necessities; Jimmy Kennedy, who actually *was* Irish, and Michael Carr, who moved to Ireland as a child, could no more ignore those necessities than Louis Armstrong could suddenly shake off a history of expectations associated with blackface minstrelsy. "If You Want to Touch an Irish Heart" (Castling), for example, treats Claribel's "Come Back to Erin" as an "authentic" Irish song. This type of pseudo-Celtic song has to be distinguished from deliberate attempts at caricature, as in Flanagan and Allen's "That's Another Scottish Story," where a "mean Scot" stereotype forms the running gag.

Some subjects prompt the production of an instantly recognizable chain of signifiers. In "The General's Fast Asleep" and "The Handsome Territorial," arpeggio shapes and repeated notes are used to connote bugle calls. "South of the Border" uses a bass pattern that signifies cowboys or horseback riding (Ex. 2).

Similar patterns are also found in their "Sunset Trail" and "Ole Faithful." The illusion of "South of the Border" being a cowboy song was enhanced when Gene Autry began to sing it—yet as a screen cowboy he was no more a real cowboy than the song is a real cowboy song. Ellington's band at the Cotton Club was often having to pretend to be in the jungle; British bands usually found themselves pretending to be in the Wild West or the South Seas.

Mixtures of Incongruity and Predictability

Predictability and incongruity mingle together when use is made of what Barthes, in *Mythologies*, labeled a "second order semiological system": "That which is a sign (namely the associative total of a concept and an image) in the first system, becomes a mere signifier in the second."[27] In the case of music, we need to consider how the associative total of a concept and a sound is made to function as a signifier.

Example 2. "South of the Border," Jimmie Kennedy and Michael Carr, opening of refrain

In Ambrose's recording of "Ho Hum," the opening quotation of Mendelssohn's "Spring Song" is not present simply as a sign that combines a signifier (a sprightly, "innocent," lyrical theme) with a signified (springtime). It is used, as a quotation of the music of the "classical" composer Mendelssohn, to signify an "arty," poetic, and "elevated" vision of spring. The effect is that Mendelssohn is sent up by what follows—music markedly different from his own; we are being told, with humorous effect, even a hint of naughtiness or subversion, that *that* music is nothing like *this* music. The technique could be compared to that of montage in film, although here it is a juxtaposition of two different sound images, or to the startling juxtapositions found in surrealism or subcultural bricolage.

In Jack Hylton's recording of "Meadow Lark," a similar effect to that described above is created by an opening quotation of Grieg's "Morning" from *Pier Gynt.* It is not intended simply to signify morning by using a conveniently already written pastoral pentatonic theme; it is intended to signify morning as represented in elite or art music. An immediate contrast again follows and draws our attention to its incongruity in this context, to the difference of what is Hylton's music —and the assumption is that the latter is also *our* preferred style of music. The "classical" quotation was by no means a peculiarly British affair; in the song "Bill," from Jerome Kern's *Show Boat* (1927), the introduction quotes from Beethoven's *Leonora* Overture no. 3, and does so with a certain sourness, since its connotations of heroism (associated both with Beethoven's opera and, indeed, with Beethoven's own character) only serve to emphasize that Bill is neither a hero nor a person who would "appreciate" Beethoven.

What has been written above concerning "classical" quotations should not be taken to apply to all quotations: for example, the quotation may be assimilated into the song as the same sort of music, as happens when Stephen Foster's "My Old Kentucky Home" (1853) is quoted in Jack Hylton's recording of "Speaking of Kentucky Days."

Sometimes audience expectations are challenged. In Lew Stone's recording of "My Old Dog," Nat Gonella is not singing in a Cockney accent for humor, even if the song (by comic songwriter Leslie Sarony) is in many ways a typical vehicle for a comedian in a "tearful clown" mood—and Cockney, Yorkshire, or Lancashire accents are usually good for a laugh in parody songs or songs concerning working-class manners. Many sublimely ridiculous things seem to have been introduced deliberately into this recording: for example, the romantic "virtuoso" piano accompaniment to words describing roses growing in the corner of the garden where the dog lies (dog roses?), and the chorus whistled in unison by several members of the band (you whistle dogs, of course). The band appears to be adopting the sophisticated strategy of sending up the song by being serious. This is a strategy well known from Gilbert and Sullivan operetta, but because the style of those works is incongruous with that of dance band music, the details of the strategy differ. For example, the use of a chorus to echo ends of lines is for Gilbert and Sullivan a common humorous device; but listen to Roy Fox's[28] recording of "Calling Me Home," where, in the sentimental context of boy treble, muted trumpet, and sustained saxophone chords, that same device is intended to be taken seriously.

Predictability of Rhythm and Harmony

Some additional words are necessary concerning predictability as it relates to rhythm and harmony. To the classically trained musician, much dance band music appears to consist of repetitive rhythmic patterns bound into a metrical straightjacket. Often the attention of the classical musician has been arrested by a kind of repetition that is used regularly in this style *instead of* the kind of repetition found in "classical" style. The device of the riff will serve to illustrate the point. Richard Middleton[29] takes up the term "museme," coined by Philip Tagg,[30] and refers to the riff as an example of a museme, a unit of musical expression that cannot be broken down further without losing meaning (this is not an exhaustive definition, and it is doubtful whether one can be found). Western music, Middleton explains, is normally characterized by "discursive" repetition, repetition that operates from the level of the phrase to longer units. "Musematic" repetition shows the influence of African-American music, and musematic techniques become increasingly common in twentieth-century dance music, reaching a peak in swing tunes and arrangements. There are earlier examples of musematic repetition ("Yes Sir, That's My Baby," Kahn-Donaldson, 1926), but what was rare in the 1920s became typical of the dance band music of the late 1930s and early 1940s.

There was a preponderance of heavy two-beat feel in 1920s dance music, which could prove unyielding, with little syncopation and a tuba remorselessly pounding roots and fifths of chords, as in Jack Hylton's recording of "Yes Sir, That's My Baby." Even complex syncopations may bounce off this basic pattern (for example, "Fascinating Rhythm," by Ira and George Gershwin); that is, they work around a divisive meter. The newness of the charleston was that it was not just that the melody was syncopated but that an additive meter (3 + 3 + 2) was created as a result of syncopating all parts (including those playing accompanying harmony) simultaneously. The Savoy Orpheans' recording of "Charleston" contains a spoken introduction by Ramon Newton pointing out its novelty: "This record is unique, in that it features a distinctly new syncopated rhythm called the charleston." The remark stands as testimony to the paradoxical value of unpredictability in a capitalist society; there are always potentially large profits to be made from a mass-marketed "unique" commodity. The additive rhythm used in the Charleston is not in itself "distinctly new"—it features, for example, in the introduction and elsewhere in "Peg o' My Heart" (Bryan-Fisher) of 1913—but it received greater emphasis than ever before.

Around 1930, there was a change from two-beat to four-beat,[31] a merging of ragtime two-beat and blues four-beat that offered greater swing. Duple meter of the 1920s was likely to be emphasized by a banjo as 2 semiquavers + 3 quavers per bar, or 2 quavers + 2 semiquavers + 1 quaver per bar (cf. Jack Hylton's recording of "Under the Ukelele [sic] Tree"). There was not yet the backbeat emphasis of 1 quaver + 2 semiquavers + 2 quavers. In 1933 Leonard Feather was complaining about the lack of jazz in triple meter, yet the Original Dixieland Jazz Band had $\frac{3}{4}$ tunes in their repertoire—for example, "I'm Forever Blowing Bubbles" and "Alice Blue Gown." It is not surprising that he should become the first to compose a $\frac{5}{4}$ blues ("Bass Reflex"); he has also written a "Twelve Tone Blues."[32]

While there often does seem to be a high degree of predictability regarding the overall shape of a song arrangement (introduction,

instrumental chorus, vocal chorus, instrumental chorus), it rarely
applies to the disposition and duration of instrumental solos. The
imagination shown in some arrangements is considerable: for example,
Lew Stone's moody arrangement of Reginald Foresyth's "Garden of
Weed" or Sid Phillips's many inspired arrangements for Ambrose.

However, the characteristic parallel motion of dance band harmonies can in some hands result in awkward voice leading; in such
cases, the unpredictability of individual parts is scarcely a matter for
praise. Consider the lowest part in the following section of "Down in
the Glen" (Gordon-Connor) in a dance-band arrangement made by
Cyril Watters (Ex. 3).

Note also the haphazard use of consecutive fifths in the phrase
"Across the moonlit heather." Consecutive fifths also feature as a
matter of contingency rather than deliberation in vocal trios; thus,
the unpredictability is again born of accident rather than imaginative
usage. See the extract from Jack Mason's 1938 arrangement of
"Alexander's Ragtime Band" (Berlin) given in Example 4.

In instances like these, the unpredictable elements are merely
random by-products of an overly rigid treatment of one musical
parameter at the expense of others. There is no purposeful design to
stimulate or delight; they issue instead from a pursuit of stylistic practice in which the mechanical has overridden the imaginative.

Absorbing the commercial thirty-two-bar Tin Pan Alley song
form into jazz did not have all ill effects, whatever some may have
feared: for example, it brought a more complex harmonic vocabulary
that extended the possibilities for improvisation and melodic affect,
thereby offering opportunities for imaginative avoidance of the predictable. "Honeysuckle Rose" (Razaf-Waller, 1929) shows how
melodic affect is transformed by the use of extended harmonies rather
than simple triads, which here (i.e., the predictable ones) would
steadfastly affirm the home key with alternating IV and I chords
instead of building expectation (by delaying the tonic) with alternating chords of II^7 and V^{13}. Note also that the tune continually outlines
a D-minor triad, yet Waller does not use this chord once in the entire
song. In this song unpredictability is clearly linked to musical imagination (Ex. 5).

As far as thirty-two-bar structures themselves are concerned, it
is possible for the overall number of bars to be predictable, but not
their phrasing within the thirty-two-bar chorus: in "Let's Put Out the
Lights," as recorded by Ambrose, for example, the thirty-two bars
divide into 8 + 7 + 9 + 8. Even songs that fall out as 8 + 8 + 8 + 8
do not necessarily have four-square phrasing within the eight-bar

Example 3. "Down in the Glen," Harry Gordon and Tommy Connor, arrangement by Cyril Watters, refrain, mm. 9–14

Example 4. "Alexander's Ragtime Band," Irving Berlin, arrangement by Jack Mason, opening of refrain

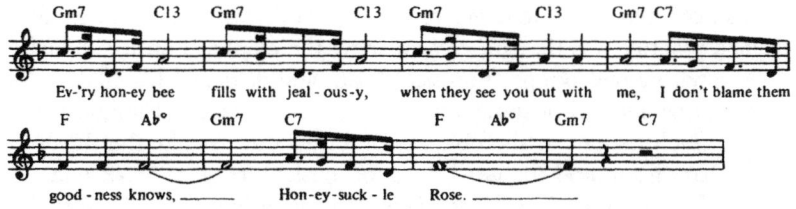

Example 5. "Honeysuckle Rose," Fats T. Waller and Andy Razaf, opening of refrain

periods. What is more, the effects of syncopation can be enormous: in Irving Berlin's "Puttin' on the Ritz" the opening four bars of the chorus contain a syncopated rhythm that metrically displaces the sixteen crotchet beats so that, instead of a grouping of $4 + 4 + 4 + 4$, they fall into $3 + 3 + 4 + 3 + 3$. Not all songs use the thirty-two-bar chorus: "Valencia," a one-step recorded by the Savoy Orpheans, is constructed in the main of ten-bar melodic sections (dividing into $2\frac{1}{2} + 7\frac{1}{2}$ bar phrases). Finally, if the thirty-two-bar chorus was in itself such a successful formula, why has it been of so little importance to rock?

Conclusion

Apropos of music hall, Raymond Williams remarked that some performers brought "new kinds and areas of experience which the 'legitimate' drama neglected or unreasonably despised."[33] It might be argued similarly that the dance band provided a musical experience the concert hall despised (though not all concert hall composers—Vaughan Williams entitled the third movement of his *Partita* "Homage to Henry Hall"). Some scorned this music for being riddled with musical "errors" and being poorly performed, when what was really at issue was the incongruity between its stylistic practices and the conventions of "classical" music. Others were content to condemn this music because they assumed, as did Adorno, that it epitomized in practice the kind of advice given in Abner Silver and Robert Bruce's *How To Write and Sell a Hit Song* (1939).[34] This second line of attack amounts to a condemnation of predictability, which is seen as the inevitable outcome of basing a musical practice on the notion that there is a formula for success. To draw a parallel in the classical field, no one was keen to suggest that the success of the second English musical renaissance was directly linked to the explanations of classical "good practice" given in Ebenezer Prout's *Applied Forms*, because classical good practice was thought of as placing the emphasis on individual, imaginative reworkings of musical forms and devices (this allows a fox trot to be accused of standardization, but not a classical minuet).

Such matters as the ubiquity of formal devices like the thirty-two-bar chorus and the need to tailor musical items to fit 78 rpm records have indeed raised the issue of standardization. It is better, though, to think of the problem from the angle of reception rather than production, as a problem of predictability rather than standardization, since the latter concept works against the perception of a dialectical relationship between the production and consumption of this music by suggesting that the listener's role is passive and that a formula for commercial success (if, indeed, such a formula were to exist) lies with the producer alone.

Discography

"After You've Gone" (Creamer-Layton). The Versatile Four. Recorded ? Sept. 1919 (6399).

"Alice Blue Gown" (Tierney). The Original Dixieland Jazz Band. Recorded 14 May 1920 (74104).

"Ave Maria" (Bach-Gounod). Gracie Fields. Recorded 25 Oct. 1934 (2EA 1011–3).

"Baby Face" (Davis-Akst). The Savoy Orpheans. Vocal: duet. Recorded 13 Oct. 1926 (matrix unknown).

"Bye Bye Blues" (Hamm-Bennett-Lown-Gray). Ambrose and His Orchestra. Vocal: Sam Browne. Recorded 13 Oct. 1930 (Bb–20237–3).

"Calling Me Home" (Wilfred). Roy Fox and His Band. Vocal: Bobby Joy. Recorded 12 June 1936 (matrix unknown).

"Charleston" (Mack-Johnson). The Savoy Orpheans. Recorded 7 July 1925 (matrix unknown).

"The Clouds Will Soon Roll By" (Woods-Dixon). Ambrose and His Orchestra at the Mayfair Hotel. Vocal: Elsie Carlisle. Recorded 22 July 1932 (OY–2376–2).

"Did Your Mother Come from Ireland?" (Kennedy-Carr). Billy Cotton and His Band. Vocal: Alan Breeze. Recorded 27 Oct. 1936 (CAR 4255–1).

"Garden of Weed" (Foresyth). Lew Stone and His Band. Recorded 24 Apr. 1934 (TB–1207–2).

"The General's Fast Asleep" (Kennedy-Carr). Joe Loss and His Band. Vocal: Chick Henderson. Recorded 22 Oct. 1935 (OEA 2000–1).

"The Handsome Territorial" (Kennedy-Carr). Jack Hylton and His Orchestra. Vocal: George Baker (?), Doreen Stephens. Recorded 25 May 1939 (OEA 7816–1).

"Happy Days Are Here Again" (Yellen-Ager). Jack Hylton and His Orchestra. Vocal: trio. Recorded 30 Jan. 1930 (Bb 18627).

"Hello, Aloha, How Are You?" (Gilbert-Baer). Ronnie Munro and His Dance Orchestra. Vocal: Stuart Robertson. Recorded Aug. 1926 (777–2).

"Ho Hum" (Suesse-Heyman). Ambrose and His Orchestra. Vocal: Sam Browne. Recorded 9 June 1931 (OB–972–2).

"I Like Bananas (Because They Have No Bones)" (Yacich). Henry Hall and the BBC Dance Orchestra. Vocal: Dan Donovan. Recorded 2 June 1936 (matrix unknown).

"I'm Forever Blowing Bubbles" (Kenbrovin-Kellette). The Original Dixieland Jazz Band. Recorded 10 Jan. 1920 (76754).

"In a Little Second Hand Store" (Pease-Dreyer-Nelson). Henry Hall and the BBC Dance Orchestra. Vocal: Les Allen. Recorded 8 July 1933 (matrix unknown).

"It's a Sin to Tell a Lie" (Mayhew). Henry Hall and the BBC Dance Orchestra. Vocal: Elizabeth Scott. Recorded 12 Sept. 1936 (matrix unknown).

"It's the Talk of the Town" (Symes-Neiburg-Levinson). Jack Hylton and His Orchestra. Vocal: Eve Becke. Recorded 6 Oct. 1933 (matrix unknown).

"I've Got an Invitation to a Dance" (Symes-Neiburg-Levinson). Roy Fox and His Band. Vocal: Denny Dennis. Recorded 4 Jan. 1935 (matrix unknown).

"I've Got Sixpence" (Box-Cox-Hall). Billy Cotton and His Band. Vocal: Alan Breeze. Recorded 22 Apr. 1941 (5603–1).

"Let's Put Out the Lights" (Hupfeld). Ambrose and His Orchestra. Vocal: Elsie Carlisle, Sam Browne. Recorded 26 Oct. 1932 (OB–3474–2).

"Meadow Lark" (Fiorito). Jack Hylton and His Orchestra. Vocal: Jack Hylton. Recorded 13 Jan. 1927 (Bb 9814).

"Misty Islands of the Highlands" (Kennedy-Carr). The Moonlight Revellers. Recorded 12 Nov. 1935 (CAR 3719–1).

"My Blue Heaven" (Whiting-Donaldson). Jack Smith and Ambrose's Whispering Orchestra. Recorded 10 Jan. 1928 (Bb 12338).

"My Old Dog" (Sarony). Lew Stone and His Band. Vocal: Nat Gonella. Recorded 25 Feb. 1935 (CAR 3244–1).

"Oh, You Nasty Man" (Yellen-Caesar-Henderson). Ray Noble and His Orchestra. Vocal: Dorothy Carless. Recorded 28 June 1934 (OB–7431–2).

"Ole Faithful" (Kennedy-Carr). Jack Jackson and His Orchestra. Vocal: Fred Latham. Recorded 12 Oct. 1934 (matrix unknown).

"On Linger Longer Island" (Kennedy-Carr). Jack Harris and His Orchestra. Vocal: Sam Browne. Recorded 8 Jan. 1938 (OEA 5160–1).

"Radio Times" (Hall). Henry Hall and the BBC Dance Orchestra. Vocal: Dan Donovan. Recorded 20 Oct. 1934 (CA 14731–1).

"Rusty and Dusty" (Kennedy-Carr). Henry Hall and the BBC Dance Orchestra. Vocal: unknown. Recorded 29 Nov. 1936 (matrix unknown).

"South of the Border" (Kennedy-Carr). Henry Hall and His Orchestra. Vocal: Bob Malin. Recorded 25 May 1939 (CA 17467–1).

"Speaking of Kentucky Days" (Gilbert). Jack Hylton and His Orchestra. Vocal: trio. Recorded 17 Jan. 1930 (Bb 18573).

"The Sunset Trail" (Kennedy-Carr). Ambrose and His Orchestra. Recorded ? Apr. 1936 (matrix unknown).

"The Teddy Bears' Picnic" (Kennedy-Bratton). Henry Hall and the BBC Dance Orchestra. Vocal: George Pizzey. Recorded ? 1932 (matrix unknown).

"That's Another Scottish Story" (Flanagan). Henry Hall and the BBC Dance Orchestra. Vocal: Flanagan and Allen. Recorded 13 Nov. 1933 (matrix unknown).

"Underneath the Arches" (Flanagan-Allen). Henry Hall and the BBC Dance Orchestra. Vocal: Flanagan and Allen. Recorded 15 July 1932 (matrix unknown).

"Under the Ukelele [sic] Tree" (Henderson). Jack Hylton and His Orchestra. Vocal: Jack Hylton and Chappie d'Amato. Recorded 11 June 1926 (Bb 8525).

"Valencia" (Valentine-Padilla). The Savoy-Orpheans (issued as the Savoy Havana Band). Vocal: Cyril Ramon Newton. Recorded 16 Feb. 1926 (Bb–7903–2).

"Yes, Sir, That's My Baby" (Kahn-Donaldson). Jack Hylton and His Orchestra. Vocal: Jack Hylton. Recorded 30 June 1925 (matrix unknown).

"Zing! Went the Strings of My Heart" (Hanly). Lew Stone and His Band. Vocal: trio. Recorded 4 May 1935 (CAR 3403–1).

Notes

1. Details of records referred to in the text are given in a separate discography at the end of this article.

2. Henry Hall (1898–1989) led the re-formed BBC Dance Orchestra from 1932 to 1937.

3. The BBC asked singers not to adopt American accents and originally tried to ban crooning; see Paddy Scanell and David Cardiff, "Serving the Nation: Public Service Broadcasting Before the War," in Bernard Waites, Tony Bennett, and Graham Martin, *Popular Culture: Past and Present* (London: Croom Helm, 1982), 181. Scat singing, too, was frowned upon; yet even the mild-natured Bud Flanagan scats on "Underneath the Arches" in Henry Hall's recording with the BBC Dance Orchestra (1932).

4. From recent times Danny Thompson's album *Whatever* (Hannibal HNCD 1326, 1987) comes to mind.

5. For details of which musicians were playing with which bands, addresses of venues, and other information for which there is no space here, see Sid Colin, *And the Bands Played On* (London: Elm Tree, 1977); Jim Godbolt, *A History of Jazz in Britain 1919–50* (London: Quartet Books, 1984); Albert McCarthy, *The Dance Band Era* (London: November Books, 1971); and Brian Rust, *The Dance Bands* (London: Ian Allan, 1972).

6. Gino Stefani, "A Theory of Musical Competence," *Semiotica* 66 (1987): 14.

7. The Squadronaires, a Royal Air Force band formed during the Second World War, contained several ex-members of Ambrose's band who had been called up. It was the most admired of the services' bands and was the closest the United Kingdom got to emulating Glenn Miller's wartime band.

8. This piece, dating from 1885, was turned into a song, "We Must Be Vigilant," by E. Leslie in 1943.

9. Several notable jazz musicians, however, had a regimental background; one such was Leslie Thompson (trumpet and trombone), who studied music at Kneller Hall (1919–1920) and played with the West India Regiment before leaving Jamaica in 1929.

10. Ted Heath (1900–1969) had a reputation as a trombonist and songwriter before forming his own band in 1945. This was widely acknowledged to be the United Kingdom's finest swing band.

11. Jack Hylton (1892–1965) led a band from 1921 to 1940. He enjoyed great popularity, which was helped by European tours (in the 1920s), broadcasts to the United States (in the 1930s), and the large number of records he made.

12. Lew Stone (1898–1969) was a pianist and admired arranger who led his own band (partly inherited from Roy Fox) at the Monseigneur Restaurant, London, from 1932.

13. The Savoy Orpheans were associated with London's Savoy Hotel in the 1920s.

14. Peter Wicke, *Rock Music: Culture, Aesthetics and Sociology* (Cambridge: Cambridge University Press, 1990), 52.

15. Bert Ambrose (1897–1973), though English born, had the enviable experience of having been a bandleader in New York before he took over the band at the Embassy Club in London. In 1927, eyebrows were raised when he was offered the enormous salary of £10,000 a year to lead the band at the Mayfair Club. In the 1930s, Ambrose's band was the most highly rated of all dance bands in the United Kingdom.

16. Richard Caroll Gibbons (1903–1954), an American, took over the Savoy Orpheans in 1927. Soon afterward he was appointed head of light music at HMV Records.

17. Billy Cotton (1899–1969) led a band from 1925. He was in great demand at major dance halls and nightclubs, but in the second half of the 1930s he turned his band into a showband for variety theater work. He later became a radio and TV celebrity.

18. Ken Barry, for example, covered a range of hits in the 1950s and 1960s, including songs as disparate as Roy Orbison's "In Dreams" and Bob Dylan's "Subterranean Homesick Blues," for Woolworth's Embassy label.

19. See Derek B. Scott, "The 'Jazz Age,' " in *The Blackwell History of Music in Britain*, vol. 6, *The Twentieth Century* (Oxford: Blackwell), forthcoming.

20. See Paul Oliver, ed., *Black Music in Britain: Essays on the Afro-Asian Contribution to Popular Music* (Philadelphia: Open University Press, 1990).

21. See Michael Pickering, "White Skin, Black Masks," in Jacqueline Bratton, ed. *Music Hall: Performance and Style* (Philadelphia: Open University Press, 1986), and Derek B. Scott, *The Singing Bourgeois: Songs of the Victorian Drawing Room and Parlour* (Philadelphia: Open University Press, 1989), 81–92.

22. See Scott, "The Jazz Age," forthcoming.

23. Rose Rosengard Subotnik, "Towards a Deconstruction of Structural Listening," in E. Narmour and Ruth Solie, eds., *Explorations in Music, the Arts, and Ideas* (New York: Pendragon Press, 1988), 104.

24. Ray Noble (1907–1978) succeeded Caroll Gibbons as head of light music at HMV Records. He made a string of successful records with the New Mayfair Orchestra (HMV's house band), featuring Al Bowlly as vocalist, before moving to the United States in 1934.

25. See Ian Whitcomb, *After the Ball* (New York: Simon and Schuster, 1973; reprint, New York: Limelight Editions, 1986), 171.

26. Jack Payne (1899–1969) led the BBC Dance Orchestra from 1928 to 1932, taking the band with him when he left to play the variety theaters.

27. Roland Barthes, *Mythologies*, trans. Annette Lavers (London: Paladin, 1973), 123; originally published under same title (Paris: Editions du Seuil, 1957).

28. Roy Fox (1901–1982), having made a reputation as a cornetist and bandleader in Hollywood, was invited to play at the Café de Paris in London with a small American band. He formed a British band in 1931, which was largely taken over by Lew Stone when Fox fell ill later that year. In 1932, he formed another band, playing in clubs and theaters until illness struck again in 1938.

29.   Richard Middleton, *Studying Popular Music* (Philadelphia: Open University Press, 1990), 275–79.

30.   Philip Tagg, *Kojak—50 Seconds of Television Music: Towards the Analysis of Affekt in Popular Music* (Gothenburg: Gothenburg University, 1979), 71.

31.   See Gunther Schuller, *Early Jazz* (New York: Oxford University Press, 1968), 273–74; and Scott, "The Jazz Age," forthcoming.

32.   See Leonard Feather, *The Jazz Years: Earwitness to an Era* (London: Quartet, 1986; reprint, London: Pan, 1988).

33.   Raymond Williams, *The Long Revolution* (London: Chatto and Windus, 1961; reprint, Harmondsworth: Penguin, 1965), 291.

34.   Adorno refers to this book in a footnote to his 1941 article "On Popular Music"; see Antony Easthope and Kate McGowan, *A Critical and Cultural Theory Reader* (Philadelphia: Open University Press, 1992), 222.

[18]

Rhythm, Rhyme, and Rhetoric in the Music of Public Enemy

ROBERT WALSER   UNIVERSITY OF CALIFORNIA
                                              AT LOS ANGELES

M y job is to write shocking lyrics that will wake people up," said Chuck D, when asked about his goals as leader of the rap group Public Enemy (Dery 1990:94).[1] In less than fifteen years, rap music has grown from the local performance practices of a Bronx subculture to a multi-billion-dollar industry which mediates a music made and heard around the world. And since 1988, Chuck D's lyrics have been at the center of many of the controversies surrounding hip hop culture, awakening, energizing, and unsettling fans and critics. They have helped to make Public Enemy one of the most successful and influential groups in the history of rap, and Chuck D has been accepted by many people as an important spokesperson for the hip hop community, and even for African Americans more generally.[2]

Chuck D's message exceeds the literal meaning of his lyrics, however; only the musical aspects of rap can invest his words with the affective force that will make people want to wake up or get them upset enough to call for censorship. Yet despite widespread debates over the meanings and significance of rap, its musical elements have largely escaped all but the most superficial discussion. The infamous *Newsweek* travesty of hip hop culture, for example (Adler et al. 1990), took it for granted that rap couldn't be discussed as music and mentioned only the thumping power of the bass and the noisiness of everything else.[3] More sympathetic and sophisticated analysts typically concentrate on demonstrating rap's verbal complexity and the cultural significance of its lyrics (see, for example, Wheeler 1991; Keyes 1984). But the lyrics and reception of rap cannot be detached from the music. Even though many rappers and fans stress the primacy of the message delivered by the lyrics, some, like pioneering rapper Melle Mel, argue that the instrumental parts are actually more important than the rap because they

194   Ethnomusicology, Spring/Summer 1995

create the mood, set the beat, and prompt the engagement (Keyes 1991:199). Chuck D's words would not have reached millions of people as poetry or political commentary; it is the music of Public Enemy that gains them access to channels of mass distribution and underpins their power and credibility. Yet that music has scarcely been mentioned in critical debates over the meanings and importance of hip hop culture.[4]

A number of fine ethnographic and cultural studies have begun to map the social meanings of rap music, stressing its effectiveness in encouraging self-esteem (Berry 1990), in building "a sense of community" and serving as "cultural glue" (Rose 1994), in promoting "interactive dynamics" and participation (Slovenz 1988, Keyes 1991). Tricia Rose, in particular, has combined ethnographic methods with the theoretical perspectives of cultural studies to produce sophisticated readings of rap as a set of cultural practices (1989, 1990, 1991, 1994). These studies highlight the fact that ethnography in industrial societies poses special difficulties: there is no single "local" to be studied; audiences are diverse and linked by mass mediation; the ethnographer may be included in the target audience of a popular form; the ethnographer's "subjects" may already, as in the case of hip hop, be cultural critics themselves, speaking through rap lyrics, published interviews, and commentary in books (such as Eure and Spady 1991) and magazines (such as *The Source: The Magazine of Hip-Hop Music, Culture, and Politics*).

The most successful ethnographies of hip hop music have been conducted by African American women. As Cheryl Keyes explains, when interviewing the participants in what is primarily a black, male, commercially mediated expressive culture, there are considerable advantages to being an insider with respect to race and an outsider with respect to gender and the music industry (1991:19–20). Thus these studies show how inadequate an etic/emic distinction is to the task of theorizing ethnography in contemporary societies. Their primary achievement, however, is to explain various aspects of a richly nuanced and powerfully coherent hip hop culture. My concern will be with building upon this work in order to analyze the music of hip hop in more depth. To a certain extent, my goal is to contribute specific discussion of musical details in order to corroborate and amplify their arguments. Public Enemy's status in the hip hop community makes their music especially suitable for a case study.

Yes, but *is* it Music?

If music is missing from most discussions of rap, it is partly because so many people do not recognize rap *as* music. John Blacking could casually report that "in Venda, rhythmically recited verse is music, and classed as 'song'" (1982:18), but similar performances within a more diverse and contestatory society such as the United States may serve as grounds for tense, revealing debates over categories and definitions. Classical musicians and critics often see themselves as guardians of musical culture, and for most of them hip hop is beneath notice, barely worth dismissing. But popular musicians, too—from heavy metal (Lita Ford, Ozzy Osbourne) to jazz (Wynton Marsalis, Henry Threadgill, Al DiMeola)—have characterized rap as simply not constituting "music" (Considine 1992:41).[5]

The musicians who have wanted to deny rap the status of "music" differ greatly in the sounds they produce, yet all share certain fundamental assumptions about what music is: it is based on melody and harmony; it depends on a laborious process of learning to sing or to use a "musical instrument"; it is produced when human beings cause objects to vibrate. People who believe deeply in these premises are sometimes offended by the very idea of rap. For rappers don't "sing" in the usual sense of that word, and hip hop's reliance on sampling, whereby producers extract, manipulate, and reassemble bits of music from many sources, means that the people who make it don't play "musical instruments," in the usual sense of that term; instead, they use sophisticated studio equipment to manipulate sound, often the sounds of others playing traditional instruments.

In many ways, there is nothing new about criticisms of rap that spring from such assumptions, and the debate over rap's status as music should be seen in the light of a centuries-old tradition of cultural authorities and rival musicians missing the point of black music, popular music, rhythmic music, or timbrally complex music, and concluding that such musics are "primitive." The situation is complicated by the recent classicization of jazz, which marks a moment when many African American musicians themselves work to interpret and legitimate their music in terms adopted from the musical and analytical priorities of European concert music (see Walser 1993a and Tomlinsen 1992). Arguments over definitions may seem pedantic and trivial, but in the case of cultural practices as influential as jazz or hip hop, such debates are of great importance because they shape public and official perception of cultural prestige, which in turn affects social prestige, upon which struggles over resources often depend.[6] If we regard a group of people as possessing "music" or, more broadly, "culture," we are more likely to see them as human beings like ourselves and to think them worthy of respect and fair treatment. At issue is the power to define and represent, upon which most social contestation hinges. Widespread debates over rap's status as music thus circumscribe a consequential set of issues.

Objections to including rap in the category "music" typically fall into three categories: hip hop music is not original, it is not melodious, and it doesn't require "musical" skills. The first of these reflects the assumption that

196   Ethnomusicology, Spring/Summer 1995

composers who use previously recorded sounds as their raw materials are parasitic; sampling has even been described as "the musical equivalent of shoplifting" (Dery 1990:84). Not only is the issue of theft at stake, but also the notion that appropriation is not creative. Yet such accusations seem to take at face value the claims made by Romantics and Modernists (and echoed by some jazz musicians and critics) that artists are autonomous creators rather than participants in communal speech acts. Hank Shocklee, head of the production team that assembles rhythm tracks for Public Enemy, disputes this perception: "Let's be realistic here. There are only so many chords you can come up with. Everybody's copying variations anyway. The difference is we're taking it from the record and manipulating it into something else. That's another type of musicianship" (Moon 1991:69).

Rap is no more parasitic than other styles of music that quote and vary, and there is in fact a term which is often used to describe the "other type of musicianship" to which Shocklee refers: orality. As Walter Ong has shown, originality in oral cultures—whether represented by Homer's Iliad or the blues—arises from the "reshuffling" and inflection of formulas and themes held in common (1982). Henry Louis Gates, Jr. (1988) and Dick Hebdige (1987) have given us histories of this sort of creativity, sometimes called "signifying" or "versioning," in black music and language, and Tricia Rose (1994) and Venise Berry (1990:40–55) have traced how rap operates within black traditions of verbal virtuosity. Like them, Shocklee is arguing for a view of music as something discursive and social, created out of dialogue with other people in the past and the present rather than through some sort of parthogenesis. Shocklee's compositional method is to combine pre-recorded sounds, drawing on his collection of over nineteen thousand recordings. Like other producers, he must find just the right sounds for each piece, which sometimes requires layering, for example, four different bass drum sounds from different records to make one new sound. The samples must be delicately balanced, and the sequences are carefully fine-tuned to simulate the nuances of live performance. All of this means that it is often more work to build tracks out of samples than it would be to compose and arrange for live musicians (see Dery 1988, 1990; Moon 1991; Young 1993).

Shocklee's relationship to dominant discourses about "music"—even African American music—is complex and conflicted. On the one hand, it is important for him to reject a categorization of rap that would deny it the prestige of "music." On the other hand, he does not hesitate to differentiate the creators of rap music from other kinds of composers and performers: "We don't like musicians. We don't respect musicians. The reason why is because they look at people who do rap as people who don't have any knowledge. As a matter of fact, it's quite the opposite. We have a better sense of music, of what it can do" (Dery 1990:82). Technology is the main issue here, and not for the first time. In blues music, for example, technologies of amplification made available new timbral possibilities and greater volume. But rap's very mode of composition—sampling, sequencing, and so on—marks it off in significant ways from the previous history of black music. Tricia Rose (1989) has drawn upon Ong's work to show that hip hop is best seen as a kind of "post-literate orality;" thus, it would be a mistake to regard rap as simply a natural outgrowth of African American oral traditions, for it is deeply technological and it embodies the specificity of its historical and political context.

Another reason for the denial of musical status to hip hop is its noisiness—some listeners perceive only strange sounds piled up into a chaotic, assaultive texture. The noisiness is certainly there—Public Enemy's production crew isn't called "the Bomb Squad" for nothing—but it is important to examine how and why such noise is crafted, for dissonance and consonance can never be evaluated abstractly, apart from their purposes and meanings. Noisiness is always relative to whatever articulates order in a discourse or a culture, and the noisiness of hip hop contributes to its ability to express dissent and critique, and to articulate the identity of a community that is defined as, or that defines itself as, noise (see Attali 1985).

Thus the intentionality of hip hop's "noise" is crucial. Gritty timbres have been valued in many kinds of African American music, of course, from Blind Willie Johnson's voice to Miles Davis's Harmon mute. But the significance of such timbres in different contexts requires explanation. "Noisiness" is important in most rap, but Public Enemy became influential and successful in part because of what fans perceived as the extra intensity of their noise and its significance within the context of their lyrics and other aspects of performance. In the high-tech environment of their production studio, the producers of the Bomb Squad often turn their equipment against itself, in search of the rawness that is essential to Public Enemy's conflicted urban soundscape, where sirens and drills punctuate the polytextured layers of modernity. They "misuse" their samplers, hobbling them at very low sampling rates and sometimes resampling samples in order to get a gritty sound, just as grainy photographs are often shot purposely with expensive cameras (Dery 1990:86). And while audio engineers have been working for decades at eliminating tape hiss, considering it an irritating reminder of the artificiality and mediatedness of recorded sound, the Bomb Squad may deliberately add extra hiss to a track. "Hiss acts as glue," Shocklee says; "it fills in cracks and crevices so you get this constant woooooofff" (Moon 1991:76).

Public Enemy's producers deliberately place Chuck D's fluid vocals to clash with the key of the backing tracks, to create abrasion. And Flavor Flav's vocals are similarly positioned so they sound out of key, to keep them from being "syrupy," from blending too harmoniously with the backing tracks (Dery 1990:83 and Moon 1991:72).[7] In a statement that is reminiscent of John Cage and Edgard Varèse, Hank Shocklee proposed an unconventional definition of music in order to justify his work, suggesting that to marginalize melody and harmony is not to abandon music: "We believed that music is nothing but organized noise. You can take anything—street sounds, us talking, whatever you want—and make it music by organizing it" (Dery 1990:83). Shocklee's argument evokes the long history of "non-musical" sounds eventually coming to be accepted as musical, from polyphony to synthesizers, even as it also resonates with previous defenses of techniques that are perfectly normal within black and popular traditions.

The third common attack on rap's status as music is based on the observation that almost no one involved with hip hop plays a musical instrument or sings, in the usual sense of those terms. Instrumental virtuosity is prized in jazz and classical music alike, and many listeners who are invested in those traditions regard melodic clarity and harmonic coherence as essential to music. Public Enemy's music, as Shocklee argued, is founded on a different kind of musicianship, with its virtuosity dependent on different tools, exercized on a different field, and motivated by different musical and cultural priorities. Its craft shows up not in harmonic complexities, but in how every sample is carefully selected and positioned to complement the vocals and contribute to the construction of a specific mood, in how percussive sounds are placed slightly ahead or behind the beat to create uneasiness or relaxation (see Moon 1991:70).

A clash of musicalities is evident in jazz saxophonist Branford Marsalis's account of being hired by Public Enemy to record a solo used in "Fight the Power": "They're not musicians, and don't claim to be—which makes it easier to be around them. Like, the song's in A minor or something, then it goes to D7, and I think, if I remember, they put some of the A minor solo on the D7, or some of the D7 stuff on the A minor chord at the end. So it sounds really different. And the more unconventional it sounds, the more they like it" (Considine 1992:42). Even though he is a "real" musician, Marsalis gets the chords wrong, for the song actually moves between D minor and B♭7. Of course, this is only a slip of memory, but the casualness and condescension of his account are revealing. Marsalis understands that the Bomb Squad is deliberately being unconventional, but he doesn't seem fully to comprehend that sampling is a strategy for producing music outside the logic of "trained" musicians. In fact, decontextualization and recontextualization are so fundamental to the compositional process of Shocklee and his associates that even when they commission live performance, they sample and rearrange *that*, layering some of Marsalis's D minor improvisations over the B♭7 groove, and vice versa. The solo in "Fight the

Power" has been carefully reworked into something that Marsalis would never think to play, because Shocklee's goals and premises are different from his. Harmonic coherence is not simply a characteristic of "musicality"; it signifies, and it doesn't fit with what Shocklee wanted to signify here.

"Fight the Power" was one of Public Enemy's biggest hits, especially after it was featured in Spike Lee's film, *Do the Right Thing,* and the hard-hitting indictment of racism offered by its lyrics has been much discussed.[9] Thus it has been easy to overlook the music of Public Enemy—if they don't have melody or harmony, if they don't play musical instruments or sing, what is there to discuss? Even some of rap's defenders would resist close scrutiny of musical details; Bruce Tucker warns that "rap, like so many other black musical genres, suffers at the hands of the deeply held formalist assumption that the notes themselves are meaningful" (Tucker 1992:497). Tucker is right to warn against ahistorical and acultural interpretations of musical discourse. Yet despite the discouraging example of so many formalist analyses of popular music, it is possible to interpret notes as abstractions of performances with social meanings, and the terms and stakes of current debates over rap suggest that there are important reasons for doing so.

I want to turn to a closer reading of "Fight the Power" in order to draw attention to two neglected aspects of rap music: the rhythmic declamation and rhetorical strategies that make up the performative aspect of rapping, and the rhythm track or groove which underpins the delivery of the lyrics. I hope to explain to some extent the power and meanings of this music, but the analysis should also have the more basic effect of demonstrating the coherence and complexity of music which has been so widely dismissed as monotonous and impoverished. This is itself no small accomplishment, given the shape of recent debates over rap music, which have too often seemed mired in what Paul Gilroy calls "the struggle to have blacks perceived as agents with cognitive capacity and historicity" (Gilroy 1992:187–88; see also Gilroy 1991).

Mapping the Groove

Examples 1 through 6 are excerpts from "Fight the Power," transcribed into standard Western musical notation, a tactic that requires some justification. Many things cannot be represented in such notation, of course; timbre is largely invisible, as are many of the rhetorical nuances that make performances powerful. Yet if notation conceals, it also reveals. Rhythms and certain other kinds of relationships can be sketched with some amount of accuracy, if we keep in mind that we are looking at static representations of dynamic relationships. Transcription is particularly useful in this case because coherence and complexity are precisely what have been denied to hip hop, and those are the qualities that notation is best at illuminating. Moreover, the stacked array of parts in this visual map parallels the hip hop compositional process of laborious assemblage of separate voices through sampling, drum machines, and sequencing.

A few writers have transcribed hip hop music before: Keyes (1991) used notation in order to demonstrate the existence in rap music of certain techniques, such as word stresses, hocket, "trading phrases," and interlocking rhythms, and Costello and Wallace's (1990) transcription of Eric B. and Rakim's "Paid in Full" labels the samples that were used to construct the piece. Here, I will use notation as a means of presenting evidence for interpretations of affect and social meanings—as a beginning, not an end. I see transcription as a way of opening up for discussion the musical details of a style that many people do not think *has* musical details.

Figure 1 is my transcription of the two-measure groove that begins "Fight the Power" (actually, a brief introduction, based on a sample of the band Trouble Funk, precedes the establishment of the groove). With a few minor changes, this two-bar unit underpins the entire song, except for the choruses, which switch to a different tonal center and use a somewhat different beat, and a few sections at the end that strip down and chop up the fundamental groove. Composed wholly of samples, the music is based on a combination of drum patterns taken from songs by Funkadelic, Sly Stone, and the Jacksons (Dery 1990:92). On top of this Hank Shocklee and the Bomb Squad have layered additional sounds from a drum machine, along with sampled vocals, guitar, bass, and synthesizer. The resulting groove, then, for all its complexity, provides a stable platform for the rapping.

The line labelled "kick" at the bottom of my transcription, the bass drum, is in itself a good introduction to how the producers use rhythm to construct an affect of urgency for this tune.[10] The eighth-notes at the beginning of each measure clearly define the beat, and the pickup to the second bar helps articulate the two-bar pattern. But in the middle of each measure, what might have been a literal repetition of the eighth-note pattern is set with the first note placed one sixteenth-note notch ahead of the beat. Within every bar, the metric pattern is established and then pushed against, creating a dynamic tension even within the line of a single instrument.

The snare drum appears to provide a standard backbeat on beats two and four; however, there are several different snare drum sounds being utilized, and they vary in pitch, placement, and position in the stereo field. On beat two of each measure we hear a strong, stereo-centered backbeat. On four of the first measure, we hear a lower-pitched drum off to the right; on four of the second measure, the same drum along with another, even lower drum, panned to the left. Beat four is prepared in each measure by a different snare's pickup, and a higher-pitched snare in the center answers

Rhythm, Rhyme, and Rhetoric in the Music of Public Enemy 201

Figure 1: "Fight the Power," opening groove

each backbeat on four, one sixteenth-note later. Timbres, volumes, and placements vary, so that this line too has its own dynamic pattern of interaction, even as these backbeats serve to anchor the entire rhythm track. The cymbals and shaker sounds also steady the groove at the eighth-note level, with additional accents that result from the layering of several drum samples.

The bass plays a repeated pattern that can be heard either as syncopated—it pushes against the metric framework just as the kick drum does—or as polyrhythmic, a layering on of the 3-3-2 pulse (here, in eighth notes) that is known as one version of the "standard pattern" of African and African American music (see Johnson and Chernoff 1991:67; Kauffman 1980). The bass defines a tonal center on D; its drop to the lower octave on beat four sets the stage for a more emphatic articulation of the downbeat of each measure, grounding the start of each rhythmic cycle regardless of the tensions and ambiguities enacted within the groove. Some sort of sampled noise or scratching (the next line on the score) answers each utterance of the bass in the first measure of the pattern, providing a grungy counterpoint. The synthesizer note is one of only two sustaining, non-percussive sounds in the groove, and its drawn-out B clashes with the D established by the bass. It can be heard as pulling at the tonal orientation, redefining the D as its own third degree, but its fade in each measure weakens this tendency, and the B ends up perched uneasily above, as the unresolved sixth of D.

The guitar sample is so scratchy and percussive that its exact pitches are difficult to discern. Moreover, funk guitar players often lift their fretting fingers just enough to dampen the strings while continuing to pick, creating a bright scratch, an additional sound between pitch and silence; I have notated these moments with x's in place of the note heads. The guitar's pitches are typical of funk harmony, sustaining the minor third of D while playing with the alternation of major sixth and minor seventh degrees; this is a favorite riff because it confirms the mode but creates and releases the tension of the tritone. Rhythmically, the guitar adds to the polyrhythmic mix with a 3-3-3-3-4 pattern at the sixteenth-note level. We begin to see that a variety of musical lines operates at different rhythmic levels, remaining within the overall organization of the meter and the two-measure unit, but filling the groove with complex tensions.

The vocal samples drop out when the rapping begins, but during the opening vamp they add further layers of rhythmic direction. The top line marked "voice" articulates nearly the same pattern as the guitar, but placed one eighth-note out of phase. Fragments of the phrase "give it" add urgency to the first measure of each cycle. The second voice answers the first with the syncopated imperative "come on, and get down." And just after the downbeat of the second bar, the third voice's rising line contradicts its text ("down") and anticipates the end of the second voice's phrase. The last line of vocal samples, marked "J.B.," shows the placement of two different samples of James Brown's trademark percussive grunt. One, higher pitched, anchors the downbeat of each two-measure cycle, while the lower-pitched one punctuates the last eight note of each measure, pushing against metric balance. (There is no better demonstration of the poverty of transcription than the reduction of this famous sound to "uh!")

Careful attention to the music of even these two measures of "Fight the Power" reveals a solid but richly conflicted polyrhythmic environment in which the rappers operate. If the analytical category of melody seems peripheral, and that of harmony is represented by the sort of static vamp often found in James Brown's music and some earlier blues, the complex interrelationships of rhythm and timbre are paramount. I will return to further discussion of the significance of this musical complexity after discussing the rhythmic performances of the rappers, Chuck D and Flavor Flav.

Mapping the Rapping

In his rapping, Chuck D creates the same kind of polyrhythmic flexibility that energizes the rhythm track. Although he is supported by the groove, he refuses to be constrained by it. His phrasing signifies on its regular repetition as he spills over its boundaries, imposes his own patterns over it, or pulls up short to confirm it.[11] In Figure 2, the last eight measures of the first verse, he begins with a repeated pattern marked by rhyme and alliteration. James Snead (1984:70) has analyzed the rhetorical figures most commonly used in black

Figure 2: "Fight the Power," verse 1, mm. 5–12

preaching; he would call this "epanalepsis," repetition at the beginning and the end of a clause ("Listen if you're missin', swingin' while I'm singin'").[12] But just as important, the rhythmic placement of the phrases creates polyrhythmic tension up against the groove. The repeated pattern takes up three beats, while the meter measures out a four-beat framework: 1 2 (rest) 4 | 1 (rest) 3 4. Chuck's rapping not only overlays a conflicting rhythm at the quarter-note level, but because the pattern internally accents eighth-notes in alternating groups of three articulated and three silent, he creates another layer of rhythmic tension at the same time, a superimposed triple meter: 1&2 (&3&) 4&1 (&2&) 3&4 (&).[13] Similarly, in the chorus of the song (Figure 3) Public Enemy avoids flat repetition by displacing every other "Fight the power!" by one beat. The emphatic repetition of the title serves as a rallying cry for collective struggle, but even here there is flexibility and rhythmic clash, as a different part of the phrase is energized each time: *Fight*the power! Fight the *power! Fight* the power!

This is what makes rap so different from predecessors such as Gil-Scott Heron or the Last Poets. The music is not an accompaniment to textual delivery; rather, voice and instrumental tracks are placed in a more dynamic relationship in hip hop, as the rapper interacts with the rest of the music. Without the framework of the groove, Chuck D's phrases would simply be parallel utterances. But his rhythmic engagement produces a dialectic of shifting tensions. Because the groove itself is non-teleological, it situates the listener in a complex present, one containing enough energy and richness that progress seems moot. Form and direction are imposed on the song by the rapper through rhetorical fiat, by means of rhythmic patterns, rhyme schemes, the ideas and exhortations of the lyrics, and the verse/chorus alternation.

The second verse begins with more polyrhythms (Figure 4), this time triple patterns at the sixteenth-note level. Rhyme, assonance, and precise rhythmic placement keep Chuck D sounding smooth and coherent, even as the rhythms of his speech are in constant tension with the beat. After the first measure, he moves beyond this strict sixteenth-note pattern into a more complicated rhythmic virtuosity, deftly shifting among syncopation, triplets, and alignment with the meter. In the last two measures of this example, he sticks more closely to the beat, first presenting an idea, "People, people, all the same," then rejecting it: "no, we're not the same cause we don't know

Figure 3: "Fight the Power," chorus, mm. 1–6

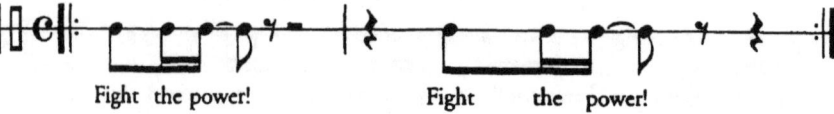

Fight the power!   Fight   the power!

Figure 4: "Fight the Power," verse 2, mm. 1–8

the game." The emphasis on the beat in these measures helps portray the first idea as a simplistic platitude and makes Chuck's dismissal seem inevitable. The rhythms thus support his textual argument: pretending that difference doesn't exist won't make injustice go away.

In the third verse (Figure 5), Chuck D works less with the intricacies of each beat or with polyrhythmic tensions, and more with larger-scale rhetorical flow. In measures seven and eight, he directs each phrase toward a landing on beat four, intensifying the eighth measure by shifting to duple rhythms and including more syllables. Black pride and energy in the first phrase parallel a critique of the politics of public representation in the second ("most of my heroes don't appear on no stamps"). Having established a sequence and led us to expect arrivals on beat four, Chuck D then raps straight through measure nine, not cadencing until the fourth beat of measure ten. His precise, undeviating triplets—"Sample a look back you look and find nothing but rednecks for four hundred years if you check"—articulate an anger that draws upon the power of every beat but relentlessly clashes with every subdivision of the groove. Exploiting the rhetorical power of parallelisms, he rolls past the stopping point he had implied in order to deliver a longer, weightier line of text: an indictment of four hundred years of racism.

206   *Ethnomusicology, Spring/Summer 1995*

Figure 5: "Fight the Power," verse 3, mm. 6–10

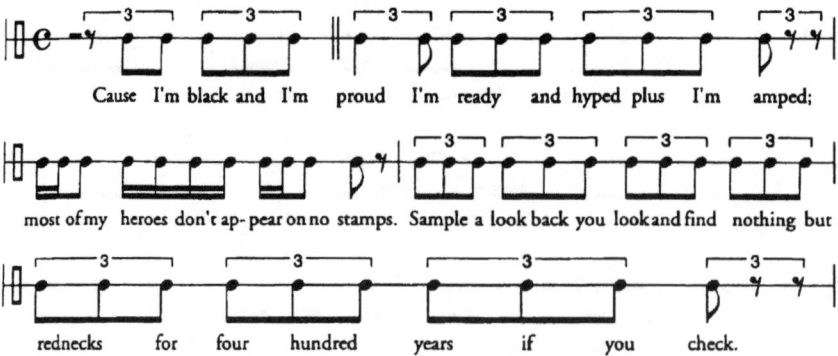

At the very beginning of his rap (Figure 6), Chuck had already been playing with such rhetorical patterns. In the first measure of the first verse, accent, rhythmic pattern, and overlapping rhymes combine to emphasize the backbeats, beats two and four (*"number," "summer"*). But in the next measure, Chuck skips beat two, hitting three hard (*"sound* of the funky drummer") and accelerating into a sixteenth-note sequence that lands on the downbeat of measure four. He establishes a pattern through repetition, drops in a surprising gap, and then comes upside your head with the answer. By playing with expectations and shifting among rhythmic subdivisions, Chuck presents himself as a wilfull virtuoso, negotiating the complex groove with ease.[14]

Repetition also creates the horizons of expectation that enable dialogue and participation (see Snead 1984). The interaction of Chuck D and Flavor Flav makes the rapping dialogic at strategic places in the song, and in this excerpt their exchanges are supplemented by a third voice, which confirms Chuck's downbeat while leaving Flavor Flav free to make his interjection, "brothers and sisters."[15] The end of Flav's comment is overlapped by Chuck's "hey!," which is itself answered by the third voice's "hey!" at the end of the measure. Chuck then goes on to solo for a while, but Flavor contributes both collective affirmation and dialogic counterpoint throughout the song. His interjections support and amplify Chuck's line of thought, but they also constitute a diegetic representation of a broader communal endorsement.

Dialogue and other aspects of rhythmic rhetoric demand social explanations, for notes produce meaning only as they unfold in communities. In the last section of this article, I want to examine certain larger implications of this technical analysis. For as Christopher Small has pointed out, an analytical focus on internal relationships too often displaces attention from external (social) relationships; the closer we analyze, the more impoverished

Rhythm, Rhyme, and Rhetoric in the Music of Public Enemy 207

Figure 6: "Fight the Power," verse 1, mm. 1–4

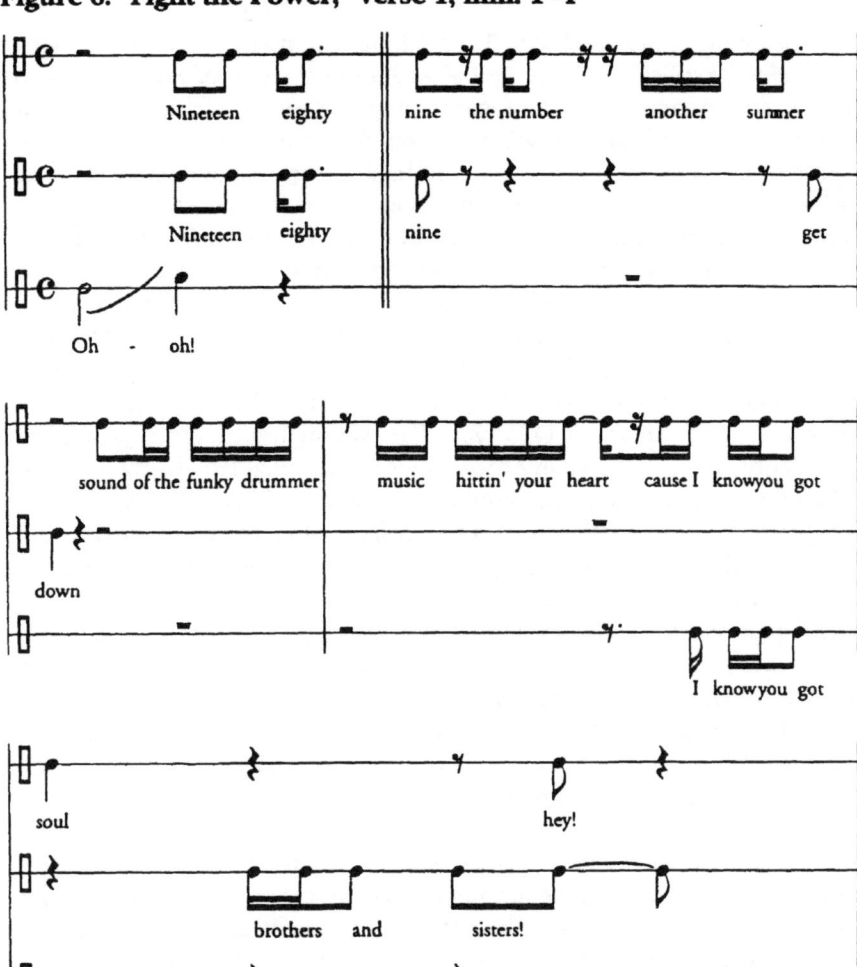

our sense of what it all means (1987:289). It is difficult indeed to put "Fight the Power" back together after having so dissected it; it is not easy to account for its coherence and cumulative effect after having isolated its components, for the interactions of groove, rapping, lyrics, and formal trajectory all happen at once, in a real time upon which verbal commentary necessarily drags. But our scrutiny of the musical details of "Fight the Power" does prepare us to ask: What is the attraction of these musical strategies? Upon what sorts of values and experiences does their efficacy depend?

208   Ethnomusicology, Spring/Summer 1995

Rhythm and Sensibility

Historians of rap like David Toop, along with many hip hop musicians themselves, explicitly link the verbal and musical styles of rap not only to an African American cultural tradition but, ultimately, to African music itself (Toop 1991).[16] This lineage seems all the clearer after a close look at the music of hip hop, for its percussive sounds, polyrhythmic texture, timbral richness, and call-and-response patterns link it solidly to these antecedents. Moreover, rhythm tracks built up of samples of earlier African American music conjure up collective black experience, past and present, while the rapping combines, as Cornel West argues, "the two major organic artistic traditions in black America," the rhetoric of black preaching and the rhythms of black music (1988:186).[17] One certainly hears in the music of Public Enemy the "clash of rhythms" that A. M. Jones once singled out as the "cardinal principle" of African music (1954:27). The polyrhythms in hip hop, like the popularity of James Brown in Africa, demonstrate what Paul Gilroy calls the "diasporic intimacy" and "recombinant qualities" of black culture (Gilroy 1992:193, 197; see also Wilson 1974 and Collins 1987). But while the ongoing power of African rhythmic concepts to animate many forms of contemporary music is clear, this genealogy does not explain the specific value of such techniques in the present. That is, to trace the origins of a stylistic feature is not to account for its attractions and functions in later contexts, which requires attention to specific uses and performances.

Scholarship of African music is nonetheless a useful beginning, especially work which furnishes analysis of how rhythmic structures are linked to social values and tensions, such as that of John Miller Chernoff (1979, 1991).[18] Chernoff emphasizes that in the African drumming traditions he studied, polyrhythms are heard as multiple rhythmic lines defined with reference to each other; if the listener lacks cultural competence and cannot distinguish these lines and relationships, the result is an experience of monotony or cacophony—terms often used in denunciations of rap. Thus we can begin to understand how rap produces such extremely varied responses among listeners. For example, Tricia Rose has analyzed the characteristic dilemma of a rock critic who personally hears rap as rhythmically "monotonous" and "numbing," but who is frightened and bewildered by the music's demonstrated power to energize and empower youthful black audiences (Rose 1990:276–90). And David Locke has made much the same point about the reception of Ewe drumming in Ghana (Locke 1982:244).

Polyrhythms make conflicting claims on our attention, since each part is distinct but in tension with the others, and African music exploits this ambiguity: "musicians put pressure on people's perception by playing with time, by promoting rhythmic dialogue . . . , even by challenging their ability to maintain perspective" (Chernoff 1991:1101). Like Small (1987), Blacking (1969, 1973), and others, Chernoff emphasizes the socializing functions of music in African societies, and he links the music's challenge to unitary perspective to the flexibility valued in African social relationships. In practice, it is bodily motion that establishes the coherence of conflicting polyrhythms, making the music essentially participatory: "The model of community articulated in an African musical event is one that is not held together by ideas, by cognitive symbols or by emotional conformity. The community is established through the interaction of individual rhythms and the people who embody them" (Chernoff 1991:1095). Small's concept of "musicking" highlights a similar attitude about the power of musical performance (1987).

My argument is not that polyrhythms mean the same thing in African and hip hop contexts simply because the same technique is employed, but rather that a variety of factors connects these cases and makes them comparable, and that the comparison is useful for beginning to understand the meaningfulness of rap music. For those who see rap as characteristically "postmodern," the product of a postindustrial society far removed from African contexts, another of Chernoff's observations is provocative: he finds "life in African societies, possibly even more than our own, to be marked by a discontinuity of experience in the encounters and status dramas of daily life" (1979:156).[19] Polyrhythms are one of the ways in which Africans cultivate adaptability and tolerance in the face of a potentially disorienting and alienating world, and the "diasporic intimacy" of black musical traditions suggests that the polyrhythms of Public Enemy deserve parallel explication despite the many differences between these contexts of reception.[20]

For one thing, the varied reception of hip hop grooves is affected by modern Western attitudes toward the repetition of rhythmic patterns. As James Snead has noted, discomfort with repetition has led modern orchestral performers to omit, as a rule, the repeat of the exposition demanded by eighteenth-century symphonists such as Haydn and Mozart. More invested in dynamic progression through time than were they, we hate to be told the same thing twice (Snead 1984:72).[21] In contrast, much African music and African American music celebrates what Prince calls the "joy in repetition," by sustaining rhythmic tensions indefinitely (1991). Prince challenges a variety of cultural master narratives when he sings about nonteleological sex: the implication of many songs is that progress and development are not always necessary, and that some things are worth doing over and over again. To be sure, sexuality is not the only dimension of human experience that is engaged by Prince, though it is one of the most complex and important (see McClary and Walser 1994). In much music of Africa and the diaspora, repetition cushions fragmentation and helps establish coherence, while polyrhythms articulate a multi-stranded web of social relationships.[22]

In the music of Public Enemy, repetition is polysemous, suggesting both noise and order, dancing bodies and technological mechanism, resistance and containment: is there joy in this repetition, or only boredom? Is the deliberate noisiness of Hank Shocklee's production to be heard as nihilistic, or as a credible representation of a world filled with struggle and violence? Hip hop's appeal to a variety of audiences, its cultural legitimacy, and its vulnerability to censorship all depend upon reactions to the music: whether its repetition enervates or animates, whether its noisiness alienates or accreditates, whether its complexity disorients or situates.

As Chernoff notes, there is vitality in rhythmic conflict, and polyrhythmic music offers opportunities to experience power and diversity in ways that are not overwhelming but rather uplifting and strengthening. I have made similar arguments elsewhere about heavy metal (1993b), and when I interviewed metal fans I found that significant numbers of them knew former fans who had defected to rap, finding in it compatible experiences of power and freedom.[23] For while Public Enemy often addresses specifically black experiences, the group has cultivated and secured a fan base that is half white. So while analysis of rap music must be grounded in the African American context of its creation, its reception is more complex and multi-cultural.[24]

To be sure, the intensity of the music may provide some listeners with an avenue for reasserting male power or for energizing the defense or claim of some other privilege. That is, for some fans, "Fight the Power" might not mean much more than "Annoy Your Parents." But differences in reception cannot simply be drawn along racial lines. Declining expectations, the injuries of deindustrialization, the growing disparity of wealth, the disruption of communities, and the dismantling of social support programs are not limited to black communities, although they have been hit hardest; Public Enemy's lyrics articulate anger and protest that many other people find resonant with their own experiences. Rap has both achieved widespread popularity among white fans and "Africanized" many white musical traditions because the values it embodies have been found so attractive by so many. In this respect it participates in an ongoing process: Amiri Baraka recently criticized his own book *Blues People* because it insufficiently registered the fact that African American culture has been so influential that it is not neatly separable from American culture (Baraka 1991:109). And as George Lipsitz points out, in a world where more and more people feel dislocated and disenfranchised, the culture of people who have historically lived with the contradictions of being outsiders becomes increasingly relevant to everyone (1990). While the pro-black rhetoric of rap is often perceived as promoting separatism, in fact many white youth develop black friends and reject their parents' racism because of the respect they have developed for black rappers (Tate 1990).

The music of Public Enemy enacts survival in a complex, dangerous world; however oppressive and dissonant that world, it is made to seem negotiable through dialogue and rhythmic virtuosity. The dancing or gesturing body seems able to seize and rearticulate the power of the music, in contexts of reception that are communal even when they depend upon mass mediation. Many fans seem to be attracted to the flexibility and multiple perspectives of hip hop, to its embrace of contradictory values, such as an emphasis on building community which coexists in tension with individualism. In the groove and the rhythmic virtuosity of the rapping, perhaps even more than in the lyrics, they find experiences that are available nowhere else yet seem highly relevant to the lives they lead. Although the importance of Public Enemy's verbal critiques and other messages should not be minimized, their success with black and white audiences depends just as much upon the kinds of musical experiences they offer their fans.

In the 1931 movie *Public Enemy,* James Cagney starred as a young gangster for whom music and verse are perfect symbols of social impotence. No one succeeds in the greed-driven world of *Public Enemy*—the women are utterly dependent on the men, and the men are either criminals, who end up dead, or menial workers, who end up in dead ends. But involvement with poetry (Cagney's older brother) or music (the ill-fated "Putty-nose") is an especially sure sign of weakness. Rappers are often accused of articulating a similarly bleak social vision, and their music has figured in the "culture of poverty" discourse that conservatives have used to shape debates about the lives and problems of urban black people. But as heirs to a cultural tradition that prizes verbal eloquence and rhythmic rhetoric, rappers' means and ends clash with this model of dispair and rebellion, even when they adopt a "gansta" image. Despite the history of injustice that fuels their anger—as Naughty By Nature puts it, "Say something positive? Well, positive ain't where I live" (1991)—what rappers create is more important than what they critique. Public Enemy 1989 = *Public Enemy* 1931 + affirmation, celebration, political critique, and a call to arms, evoking the "double consciousness" of the blues and other minority culture.[25]

Public Enemy's lyrics became the subject of so much controversy in part because some listeners find Public Enemy's music assaultive and alien, the figuration of experiences they do not want to have or understand. They hear complexity as chaos, noise and power as the signs of a nihilistic threat; for them, polyrhythms are disturbing because they inscribe multiple patterns that refuse the discipline of an overriding rhythmic hierarchy. Others hear such rhythms as their own, as part of a cultural history they value or as a social model to which they are attracted, particularly since the samples hip hop musicians use are overwhelmingly drawn from previous African American music and thus bring a sedimented history into their new contexts. But at the same time that such grooves offer a dialogic, polyphonic environment, they also present these possibilities in noisy, technological, urban terms, making this social ideal seem relevant to the specific historical situation of many fans. In the terms of Tricia Rose's analysis (1994), the polyphonic layering and repetitive flow create continuity, while rhythmic ruptures teach participants to find pleasure in and develop creative responses to social ruptures.

Music, as Christopher Small has argued eloquently (1987:46), is one of the most important media through which social relationships are explored, affirmed, and celebrated, through which identities and subjectivities can be altered, shored up, or tried on for size. Hip hop contains many raps, many grooves, and many meanings.[26] Its musicians compose rich, complex music that makes rap more than protest—makes it, as Cornel West says, a "paradoxical cry of desperation and celebration" (West 1988:186). If we are to understand why rap is so important to millions of people and why it stands at the center of debates over culture and affects struggles over resources, analyzing lyrics is not enough—any more than is formalist musical analysis, or sociological analysis that accepts the music industry's dehumanizing assumptions about its "product." We need to begin to hear not only what these rappers are saying, but also what these musicians are composing—how they are using rhythm, rhyme, and rhetoric to enact survival and celebration, clamor and community.[27]

Notes

1. In another interview, Chuck D argued that the purpose of all music is to raise dialogue (ABC News 1992:4).

2. Following normal usage within the hip hop community, I use "rap" as a general term which refers to a kind of music, and more specifically to designate a style of vocal performance, "rapping." "Hip hop" embraces more cultural terrain, including styles of clothing, dance, and grafitti art, among other things (see Toop 1991; Rose 1994). Public Enemy includes several members with a variety of functions: on their recording of "Fight the Power," which will be discussed below, Chuck D and Flavor Flav are the rappers; Terminator X is the DJ, who mixes and scratches records; Hank Shocklee, Eric "Vietnam" Sadler, Carl Ryder, and Keith Shocklee are members of the Bomb Squad, the production crew that assembles the instrumental tracks. At the time of the recording, Professor Griff was considered a member of the group, with the function of "Minister of Information," but he is not heard on record.

3. See also a less virulent article in the same issue, which is no less vague about the music (Gates et al. 1990). Many similar examples could be cited, including *The New Yorker*'s genial assurance to its readers that "rap isn't music" (Mordden 1991:113).

4. John Blacking made a similar point in a different context: "The effectiveness of the South African Freedom songs has been discussed chiefly in terms of their words, but it was their music which made the deepest impact, especially on those who did not speak the language in which

Rhythm, Rhyme, and Rhetoric in the Music of Public Enemy 213

the sentiments of the songs were expressed. The combination of the triads and cadences of European hymn-tunes and the rhythms and parallel movement of traditional African music expressed the new solidarity and values of urban groups: the sound of the music conveyed as clear a message as the words of the songs" (Blacking 1969:36).

5. In an interview with Cheryl Keyes (1991:2), Wynton Marsalis asserted that rap represents a "decadent and degenerate culture" and that it therefore does not qualify as legitimate music. On the other hand, a few jazz musicians, notably Max Roach and Miles Davis, have publicly hailed hip hop as a worthy heir to jazz's legacy of virtuosity and rhythmic complexity. Overall, though, rap has had few defenders outside of the hip hop community.

6. On the politics of cultural prestige, see, for example, Bourdieu 1984.

7. A new production crew worked with Public Enemy on *Apocalypse 91...The Enemy Strikes Black* (1991); I will be writing throughout about the sounds created for the earlier three albums, as exemplified by "Fight the Power," which was released as a single in 1989, and as part of the album *Fear of a Black Planet* in 1990.

8. The sax solo appears on the single release of "Fight the Power," but not on the album cut.

9. Some of Public Enemy's lyrics have been much more controversial, and Chuck D has sparked a great deal of dialogue about whether sexism, homophobia, anti-semitism, and black racism are useful responses to white racism (see, for example, Tate 1988, Owen 1990, Allen and Chuck D 1990). While anti-semitic statements cannot be defended or excused, it is important to note that such statements tend to receive much more media coverage when uttered by black rappers than when attributable to white rock musicians or Christian fundamentalists (see *Rock and Roll Confidential* 90 [July-August, 1991]:4). Public Enemy wrestles with problems that are among the most serious and pressing in contemporary politics, and their responses are affected by the ways in which those problems are commonly framed. For example, Chuck D accurately diagnoses the links between racism and economic exploitation: "The Chinese over here, the whites over here, Jews here, you know it's broken up like that. Capitalism does that. They'll tell you capitalism sees no color, but at the same time the ones that all feel they have something in common with each other become the most powerful block right there, and it stomps upon those that don't fit that mold. And the only way that you can exist within that mold is that you have to put together a 'posse,' or a team to be able to penetrate that structure, that block, that strong as steel structure that no individual can break. . . . Public Enemy, number one, tries to tell the black man and woman in America that we as a constituency have to stick together and realize that we all have something in common with each other" (Eure and Spady 1991:330–31). Public Enemy has indeed been successful in raising dialogue, and to his credit, Chuck D has been willing to reverse himself and admit he was wrong in response to public controversies over his lyrics.

10. References to the "kick" drum are common among musicians, so as to avoid confusion between bass guitar and bass drum.

11. Dwight Andrews (1989) has analyzed a similar kind of virtuosic self-empowerment in Ray Charles's performances, as he plays around with the beat, affirming or subverting it at will. For discussions of two very different kinds of willful virtuosity in popular music, see Walser 1992 and 1993a. I use the word "signify" here in the sense attributed to it by Henry Louis Gates, Jr. (1988).

12. Compare also Davis (1985). Measures 9–11 of this example utilize the rhetorical strategy of anaphora, repetition at the beginning of a clause.

13. The lyrics printed with the musical examples are taken primarily from the printed version which accompanied the album release. However, in two places where the actual delivery of the lyrics varied from what was printed, I have made minor changes in the text to match what appeared on the recording.

14. Few rappers work at Chuck D's level of rhythmic virtuosity, but the rhetorical practices he uses are ubiquitous. Queen Latifah is another rapper who has an especially powerful and ingenious rhythmic delivery.

15. For further discussion of the dialogic aspects of rap music, see Wheeler 1991.

16. For an overview of discussions of African retentions in African-American music, see Maultsby 1990; see also Wilson 1974 and Cronbach 1981–82. As important as such work is, it seems imperative to begin to take up newer critical projects, such as explaining how people of diverse origins come together and find cultural common ground (see Johnson and Chernoff 1991:63 and Martin 1991).

17. On collective memory in popular culture, see Lipsitz 1990.

18. While it is important to recognize differences among African musical traditions, analytical recognition of significant pan-African similarities can be productive; see Kauffman 1980. On the general problem of the relationship of sound structures to cultural logics, see the symposium in *Ethnomusicology* 28(3), featuring papers by Steven Feld (1984) and Marina Roseman (1984).

19. Compare Richard Shusterman's attempt to connect rap with postmodernism and American pragmatism—in the process reducing rap's African-American dimension to "roots"— in order to invigorate an attack on modernist aesthetics (1991).

20. This is, of course, very different from how musicologists and music theorists tend to discuss rhythm. Not only is it customarily assumed to be cognitive and disembodied, but Western music theory's traditional emphasis on harmony has led many music theorists to conceive of rhythm through harmonic metaphors. Terms like "metric dissonance" and "dissonant strata" suggest that rhythmic conflicts must always be resolved, whether in performance or analysis. There seems to be no place for tensions that remain unresolved, differences that can coexist. See, for example, Barbara R. Barry's relentlessly cognitive model in *Musical Time: The Sense of Order* (1990); her title signals the foregone conclusion which underpins much of what is done in the name of "music theory." For "rhythmic dissonance," see Yeston 1976 and Cooper and Meyer 1960; the latter credited Curt Sachs with having originated the concept of "metric dissonance" (p. 108). Wye Jamison Allanbrook achieved a significant advance by linking rhythm with bodily postures and human character (1983). But generally, uneasiness about rhythm has caused musicologists and other devotees to etherealize canonic musicians such as J. S. Bach, whose physical engagement with his music is well-documented. See, for example, a letter of 1738 by Johann Matthias Gesner which describes Bach as "full of rhythm in every part of his body" as he conducted (David and Mendel 1966:231). Such distortions of music history enable the mind/body split to be mapped onto the high/low cultural split, or the Western/non-Western dichotomy, remaking the past in order to stabilize the hierarchies of the present (see McClary forthcoming).

21. Critics of minimalist composers such as Philip Glass echo this sentiment. For a critical dismissal of "Fight the Power" as repetitious, see Reynolds 1989.

22. See Frances R. Aparicio's forthcoming work on salsa, and Veit Erlmann's forthcoming *Nightsong: A Performance Tradition of Zulu Migrants in South Africa.*

23. Further evidence for this compatibility is provided by the collaborations of Public Enemy with the metal band Anthrax, and by Ice-T's band, Body Count. However, in heavy metal, power and freedom are usually articulated through a dialectic between the rhythm section and the solo guitar or vocal, rather than through polyrhythms (see Walser 1993b).

24. See Crombach (1981–82), who argues for a more general recognition of this fact in the study of African American music.

25. Compare Murray 1982, Floyd 1991, and Lutz 1991, who extend W. E. B. Du Bois's notion of "double consciousness" to account for the complex mixture of sorrow and celebration in the blues.

26. The specific techniques I have discussed in the music of Public Enemy are deployed by other rap musicians to other ends, although a shared discursive system keeps their meanings related. For example, Queen Latifah's style of performance is very similar to that of Chuck D, but she is much more interested than he in speaking to and for women, about issues of gender and power. Sister Soulja's concerns are closer to those of Public Enemy, yet her rapping style

features nearly arhythmic declamation, utterly unlike the rhythmic rhetoric of Queen Latifah and Chuck D.

27. I am grateful for the invigorating criticism and support I have received from hip hop music's preeminent scholar, Tricia Rose, and for challenging and helpful comments offered by Reebee Garofalo, Jeff Titon, Larry Polansky, Susan McClary, and the anonymous reviewers for *Ethnomusicology*. I was fortunate to have had opportunities to present versions of this essay at the Center for the Study of Black Literature and Culture at the University of Pennsylvania, the Center for Twentieth-Century Studies at the University of Wisconsin-Milwaukee, and the InterArts Consortium at the University of California, San Diego. I thank Houston Baker, Jr., Ron Radano, Carol Tennessen, Kathleen Woodward, and Jann Pasler for those invitations and the dialogue that resulted.

References

ABC News. 1992. "Nightline." Transcript #2781, January 20.

Adler, Jerry, et al. 1990. "The Rap Attitude." *Newsweek*, March 19:56–59.

Allanbrook, Wye Jamison. 1983. *Rhythmic Gesture in Mozart*. Chicago: University of Chicago.

Allen, Harry, and Chuck D. 1990. "Black II Black." *Spin*, October:67.

Andrews, Dwight D. 1989. "From Black to Blues." In *The Blues Aesthetic: Black Culture and Modernism*, edited by Richard J. Powell, 37–41. Washington, D. C.: Washington Project for the Arts.

Attali, Jacques. 1985. *Noise: The Political Economy of Music*. Minneapolis: University of Minnesota.

Baraka, Amiri. 1991. "The 'Blues Aesthetic' and the 'Black Aesthetic': Aesthetics as the Continuing Political History of a Culture." *Black Music Research Journal* 11(2):101–9.

Barry, Barbara R. 1990. *Musical Time: The Sense of Order*. Stuyvesant, NY: Pendragon.

Berry, Venise. 1990. "Rap Music, Self Concept and Low Income Black Adolescents." *Popular Music and Society* 14(3):89–107.

Blacking, John. 1969. "The Value of Music in Human Experience." *Yearbook of the International Folk Music Council*, 33–71.

———. 1973. *How Musical Is Man?* Seattle: University of Washington.

———. 1982. "The Structure of Musical Discourse: The Problem of the Song Text." *Yearbook for Traditional Music* 14:15–23.

Blum, Joseph. 1978. "Problems of Salsa Research." *Ethnomusicology* 22(1):137–49.

Bourdieu, Pierre. 1984. *Distinction: A Social Critique of the Judgement of Taste*. Cambridge: Harvard University.

Chernoff, John Miller. 1979. *African Rhythm and African Sensibility*. Chicago: University of Chicago.

———. 1991. "The Rhythmic Medium in African Music." *New Literary History* 22(4):1093–1102.

Collins, Edmund John. 1987. "Jazz Feedback to Africa." *American Music* 5(2):176–93.

Considine, J. D. 1992. "Fear of a Rap Planet." *Musician* (February):34–43, 92.

Cooper, Grosvenor W., and Leonard B. Meyer. 1960. *The Rhythmic Structure of Music*. Chicago: University of Chicago.

Costello, Mark, and David Foster Wallace. 1990. *Signifying Rappers: Rap and Race in the Urban Present*. New York: Ecco.

Cronbach, Lee. 1981–82. "Structural Polytonality in Contemporary Afro-American Music." *Black Music Research Journal*, 15–33.

David, Hans T., and Arthur Mendel, eds. 1966. *The Bach Reader*, revised edition. New York: Norton.

Davis, Gerald L. 1985. *I Got the Word in Me and I Can Sing It, You Know: A Study of the Performed African-American Sermon*. Philadelphia: University of Pennsylvania.

Dery, Mark. 1988. "Rap." *Keyboard* (November):32–56.

———. 1990. "Public Enemy: Confrontation." *Keyboard* (September):81–96.

Erlmann, Veit. Forthcoming. "Nightsong: A Performance Tradition of Zulu Migrants in South Africa."

Eure, Joseph D., and James G. Spady, eds. 1991. *Nation Conscious Rap*. New York: PC International.

Feld, Steven. 1984. "Sound Structure as Social Structure." *Ethnomusicology* 28(3):383–409.

Floyd, Samuel A. 1991. "Ring Shout! Literary Studies, Historical Studies, and Black Music Inquiry." *Black Music Research Journal* 11(2):265–87.

Gates, David, et al. 1990. "Decoding Rap Music." *Newsweek* (March 19):60–63.

Gates, Henry Louis Jr. 1988. *The Signifying Monkey: A Theory of African-American Literary Criticism*. New York: Oxford University.

Gilroy, Paul. 1991. There Ain't No Black in the Union Jack: The Cultural Politics of Race and Nation. Chicago: University of Chicago.

———. 1992. "Cultural Studies and Ethnic Absolutism." In *Cultural Studies*, edited by Lawrence Grossberg, Cary Nelson, and Paula Treichler, 187–98. New York: Routledge.

Hebdige, Dick. 1987. *Cut 'n' Mix: Culture, Identity, and Caribbean Music*. New York: Methuen.

Johnson, Hafiz Shabazz Farel, and John M. Chernoff. 1991. "Basic Conga Drum Rhythms in African-American Musical Styles." *Black Music Research Journal* 11(1):55–73.

Jones, A. M. 1954. "African Rhythm." *Africa* 24:26–47.

Kauffman, Robert. 1980. "African Rhythm: A Reassessment." *Ethnomusicology* 24(3):393–415.

Keyes, Cheryl L. 1984. "Verbal Art Performance in Rap Music: The Conversation of the 80's." Folklore Forum 17(2):143–52.

———. 1991. "Rappin to the Beat: Rap Music as Street Culture Among African Americans." Ph.D. diss., Indiana University.

Lipsitz, George. 1990. *Time Passages: Collective Memory and American Popular Culture*. Minneapolis: University of Minnesota.

Locke, David. 1982. "Principles of Offbeat Timing and Cross-Rhythm in Southern Ewe Dance Drumming." *Ethnomusicology* 26(2):217–46.

Lutz, Tom. 1991. "Curing the Blues: W. E. B. Du Bois, Fashionable Diseases, and Degraded Music." *Black Music Research Journal* 11(2):137–56.

Martin, Denis-Constant. 1991. "Filiation or Innovation? Some Hypotheses to Overcome the Dilemma of Afro-American Music's Origins." *Black Music Research Journal* 11(1):19–38.

Maultsby, Portia K. 1990. "Africanisms in African-American Music." In *Africanisms in American Culture*, edited by Joseph E. Holloway, 185–210. Bloomington: Indiana University.

McClary, Susan. forthcoming. "Music, The Pythagoreans, and The Body." In *Choreographing History*, edited by Susan Foster. Bloomington: Indiana University.

McClary, Susan, and Robert Walser. 1994. "Theorizing the Body in African-American Music." *Black Music Research Journal* 14(1):75–84.

Moon, Tom. 1991. "Public Enemy's Bomb Squad." *Musician* (October):69–72, 76.

Mordden, Ethan. 1991. "A Critic At Large: Rock and Cole." *The New Yorker* (October 28):91–113.

Murray, Albert. 1982. *Stomping the Blues*. New York: Vintage Books [originally pub. 1976].

Naughty by Nature. 1991. "Ghetto Bastard." *Naughty by Nature*. Tommy Boy. TBCD 1044.

Ong, Walter. 1982. *Orality and Literacy: The Technologizing of the Word*. New York: Methuen.

Owen, Frank. 1990. "Public Service." *Spin* (March):57.

Prince. 1991. "Joy in Repetition." *Diamonds and Pearls*. Warner Bros. 9 25379-2.

Public Enemy. 1989. "Fight the Power," extended version. Motown MOT-4647.

———. 1990. *Fear of a Black Planet*. Def Jam/Columbia CK 45413.

———. 1991. *Apocalypse 91 . . . The Enemy Strikes Black*. Def Jam/Columbia CK 47374.

Reynolds, Simon. 1989. "Review of 'Fight the Power' by Public Enemy." *Melody Maker* (June 17)28.

Rose, Tricia. 1989. "Orality and Technology: Rap Music and Afro-American Cultural Resistance." *Popular Music and Society* 13(4):35–44.

———. 1990. "'Fear of a Black Planet': Rap Music and Black Cultural Politics in the 1990s." *Journal of Negro Education* 60(3):276–90.

———. 1991. "Never Trust a Big Butt and a Smile." *Camera Obscura* (May):108–31.

———. 1994. *Black Noise*. Hanover, N. H.: Wesleyan University.

Roseman, Marina. 1984. "The Social Structuring of Sound: The Temiar of Peninsular Malaysia." *Ethnomusicology* 28(3):411–45.

Shusterman, Richard. 1991. "The Fine Art of Rap." *New Literary History* 22(3):613–32.

Slovenz, Madeline. 1988. "'Rock the House': The Aesthetic Dimensions of Rap Music in New York City." *New York Folklore* 14(3–4):151–63.

Small, Christopher. 1987. *Music of the Common Tongue: Survival and Celebration in Afro-American Music*. New York: Riverrun.

Snead, James. 1984. "Repetition as a Figure of Black Culture." In *Black Literature and Literary Theory*, edited by Henry Louis Gates, Jr., 59–79. New York: Methuen.

Tate, Greg. 1988. "Public Enemy: The Devil Made Them Do It." *Village Voice*, (July 19):71.

———. 1990. "Manchild at Large." *Village Voice* (September 11):77.

Tomlinsen, Gary. 1992. "Cultural Dialogues and Jazz: A White Historian Signifies." In *Disciplining Music: Musicology and Its Canons*, edited by Katherine Bergeron and Philip V. Bohlman, 64–94. Chicago: University of Chicago.

Toop, David. 1991. *Rap Attack 2: African Rap to Global Hip Hop*. New York: Serpent's Tail.

Tucker, Bruce. 1992. "Review of Public Enemy, *It Takes a Nation of Millions to Hold Us Back* and De La Soul, *3 Feet High and Rising*." *American Music* 10(4):496–99.

Walser, Robert. 1992. "Eruptions: Heavy Metal Appropriations of Classical Virtuosity." *Popular Music* 11(3):263–308.

———. 1993a. "Out of Notes: Signification, Interpretation, and the Problem of Miles Davis." *Musical Quarterly* (Summer):343–65.

———. 1993b. *Running With The Devil: Power, Gender, and Madness in Heavy Metal Music*. Hanover, N.H.: Wesleyan University.

West, Cornel. 1988. *Prophetic Fragments*. Grand Rapids, Mich.: William B. Eerdmans.

Wheeler, Elizabeth A. 1991. "'Most of My Heroes Don't Appear on No Stamps': The Dialogics of Rap Music." *Black Music Research Journal* 11(2):193–216.

Wilson, Olly. 1974. "The Significance of the Relationship Between Afro-American Music and West African Music." *The Black Perspective in Music* 2(1):3–22.

Yeston, Maury. 1976. *The Stratification of Musical Rhythm*. New Haven: Yale University.

Young, Jon. 1993. "P. M. Dawn Sample Reality." *Musician* 176 (June):23–24.

Part II
Addressing Texts

[19]

Fantastic Remembrance in John Lennon's "Strawberry Fields Forever" and "Julia"

WALTER EVERETT[*]

THE faculty of memory is a thematic element in many songs of the Beatles. In some of them it is a catalyst for, or a by-product of, a more essential theme. In others it has a position of central importance. The music of the Beatles explores such varied aspects of memory as redintegration (a process by which a reminder reestablishes past experiences), reminiscence, retrospection, and recollection, but our concern will be two pieces in which remembrance is the central issue.

Fantasy is also an important element in the music of the Beatles. Although their exploration of "altered states of consciousness" through hallucinogenic drugs and Eastern mysticism or transcendantal meditation has received much publicity, the trances, (day)dreams, imagery, and fantasies described in their music were largely creations of an imaginative vision. The two pieces to be examined in this essay are interpretations of two different realms of fantasy, as well as of remembrance.

Both John Lennon and Paul McCartney wrote pieces about memory/memories, but only Lennon was significantly interested in composing songs based in past-related imagery.[1] Two of them, "Strawberry Fields

---

* I would like to acknowledge the help of James Dapogny, who read and commented upon this article before its original publication.

[1] This is admittedly a broad generalization. The three Beatle composers all pursued some similar topics—e.g. love songs and other aspects of male-female relationships—but there are also personal, recurring attitudes or approaches in the works of each: George Harrison tended to adopt a critical ("Don't Bother Me," "Think for Yourself") and even facetious ("Taxman," "Only a Northern Song," "Piggies," " Savoy Truffle," "I Me Mine") attitude in some of his writing, in contrast to his other songs of spiritual search ("Within You, Without You," "The Inner Light," "Long Long Long"). Paul McCartney was at his most characteristic in his invention of stories with colorful characters (Eleanor Rigby, Sgt. Pepper, Desmond and Molly Jones, Rocky Raccoon, Loretta Martin, Maxwell Edison), and in his often vaudevillian sense of nostalgia ("Yesterday," "Penny Lane," "When I'm Sixty-Four," "Your Mother Should Know," "Honey Pie," "Two of Us," "Jubilee"–later "Junk" on his first solo LP). He also occasionally attempted to come to grips with the problems of loneliness ("For No One") and misunderstanding ("We Can Work It Out," "Hello Goodbye"). But they were usually left unresolved. Lennon seems to have been most interested in introspectively depicting his emotions (such as insecurity in "I'm a Loser," "You've Got to Hide Your Love Away," "Help!," "Nowhere Man"), or his own mental processes and states (such as memory and transcendance in "Tomorrow Never Knows," "Across the Universe," or surreal stream of consciousness fantasy in "I Am the Walrus," "Happiness Is a Warm Gun," "Come Together").

Forever" and "Julia," represent intersections of the "memory" and "fantasy" groups of songs. Following a general discussion of memory and fantasy in the music of the Beatles, this essay will examine the compositional approaches taken in both songs.

I will relate the ideas verbalized in the texts of the songs to those ideas expressed in the music (without necessarily addressing the question of which first inspired the composer). The primary means of exposing musical ideas will be voice-leading reductions, analysis of motivic relationships, and properties of instrumentation and studio procedure.

Memory and Fantasy in the Music of the Beatles

Properties of the mind were rarely subject matter for the early compositions of the Beatles, but three of Lennon's early love songs are distinguished in this regard. "There's a Place" (recorded on February 11, 1963, for their first British LP, *Please Please Me*) refers to the mind as a retreat from misery, where the singer's memories protect him from sorrow. The turn figure, varied in diminutions in the opening of the song (see brackets placed on the upper melodic parts in Exx. 1a and 1b), is given meaning in the second verse, in which the singer reflects on the things that "go 'round [his] head." The roulades in Lennon's vocal line frequently evoke such swirling memories.[2] Although the mind is the setting for this tune, the message is from the heart, and the memories fill needs that are more emotional than intellectual.

Ex. 1. "There's a Place" (John Lennon and Paul McCartney)

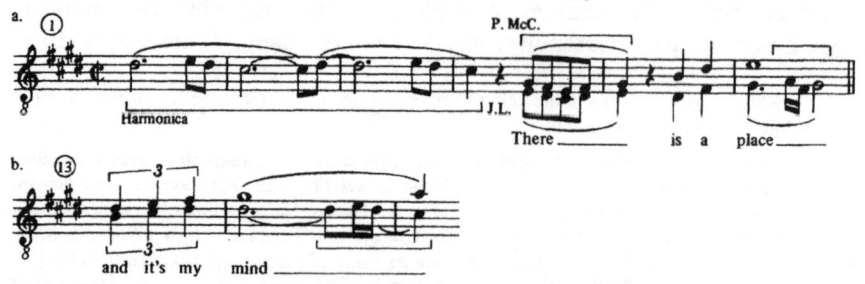

© 1963 Gil Music Corporation. Used by permission.

Because of an informal agreement that Lennon and McCartney made when they were teenagers, all songs that were written by either of them prior to the break-up of the Beatles are credited, for legal purposes, as having been written by both of them as a team. For this reason, the current copyright holder insists that all references to prebreakup Beatle songs as "Lennon" or "McCartney" compositions must be considered "theoretical."

[2] "Misery," a companion song cowritten by Lennon and McCartney in February, 1963, for the first LP, includes a brief musical description of memory; Producer George Martin provides the depiction of remembrance through imitation and diminution in his piano part (see Ex. 2).

Ex. 2. "Misery" (John Lennon and Paul McCartney)

Ex. 3. "If I Fell" (John Lennon and Paul McCartney)

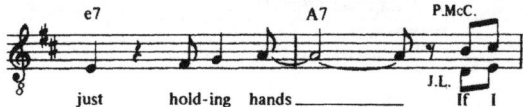

Fig. 1. Graph of introduction to "If I Fell"

Two early ballads by Lennon, "If I Fell" and "Yes It Is," summon painful memories from the singer's past. "If I Fell" was recorded in March-April, 1964, for the film, *A Hard Day's Night*. In this song, the singer is entering a relationship tentatively,[3] hoping that it will fare better than

[3] The tentative attitude expressed in the text is reflected in the introduction's delicately poised emergence of V through successive appearances of its third (c♯), fifth (e) and finally root (A) (see Ex. 3 and Fig. 1 above). The tone of *tâtonnement* is also colored by modal verbs in both "If I Fell" and "Yes It Is." (See Appendix 1 for text of the lyrics.)

John Lennon   363

the one he is leaving. The pain of the "old" relationship is expressed through mixture, with uses of a melodic ♭6-5 motive in major. It appears at (1) the singer's first mention of "her" (the girl he is leaving), where painful memories are evoked by the twelve-string electric guitar's cadential figure (Ex. 4a), and in (2) the middle section (here the singer elaborates on the potential recurrence of pain), as shown by the bracket in Example 4b.[4]

Ex. 4. "If I Fell" (John Lennon and Paul McCartney)

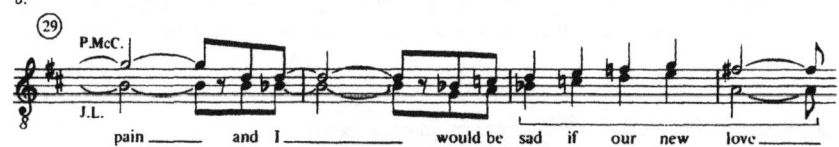

Similarly, in "Yes It Is" (recorded as a B-side beginning on February 16, 1965), the singer states his wish to avoid painful memories of a previous relationship. He appeals to his current girl friend to not wear red, since this would remind him of the "other" girl and all the plans they had made. This is an example of redintegration.

McCartney's chamber piece, "Yesterday" (recorded beginning on June 14, 1965, for the *Help!* LP), is very retrospective; he retreats not to his rational mind, but to his sentimental view of the past. The use of the string quartet, for its suggestive associations with the past, is the Beatles' first use of instrumental coloring as an essential part of their communication. In this respect, Lennon experimented in "In My Life" (recorded in mid-October–early November, 1965, for *Rubber Soul*), which he regarded as a

---

[4] The ♭6̂-5̂ "painful memory" motive may first be heard in the introduction's lowest register as graphed in Figure 1. Although A♯ functions as the fifth of d♯, it may be recalled as B♭ upon the arrival of the dominant, due to the registral proximity of "B♭"-A and to the fact that each pitch is the goal of its phrase.

turning point in his song-writing career.[5] In this ballad, he reminisced about past friends and lovers. As in "Yesterday," suggestions of the historical past of music accompany the reawakening of the singer's memories: George Martin's neo-Baroque two-voice "wind-up piano"[6] interlude is juxtaposed against Lennon and McCartney's organum-like vocal lines in the middle section.

Ex. 5. "In My Life" (John Lennon and Paul McCartney)

[5] In one of his last interviews (*Playboy*, XXVIII/4 [April, 1981], 192), Lennon said this "was the first song I wrote that was consciously about my life. Before, we were just writing . . . pop songs with no more thought to them than that. The words were almost irrelevant." Part of the LP *Rubber Soul*, this song helps to mark the beginning of the Beatles' middle period, in which a halt was called to public performance and increasing emphasis was placed on composition, arranging, recording and production. More experimental colors, textures, harmonies and counterpoint were direct results. (See Appendix 2 for the text of the lyrics.)

[6] Producer George Martin describes the method of producing his "wind-up piano" effect as playing the piano an octave too low "at half-speed and then doubling it to normal speed to give a kind of harpsichord effect" (*All You Need Is Ears* [New York, 1979], p. 134). There is an affinity to the harpsichord's sound in that the piano's decay is cut in half by the doubling of the speed of the tape.

All the songs mentioned so far treat memories, but from a realistic perspective of the present. The lyrics of "In My Life" state "but of all these friends and lovers, there is no one compares with you"; ultimately, "these memories lose their meaning when I think of love as something new." This distinction between the past and the present in the Beatles' lyrics began to break down in 1966, when the boundaries separating reality and fantasy started to lose their definition for the Beatles.

Lennon's first experimentation with LSD in the early months of 1966 coincided with a more imaginative exploration of the mind in his music. "Rain" (a B-side recorded on April 13-14, 1966) enigmatically declares that rain and shine are just states of mind.[7]

Ex. 6. "Rain" (John Lennon and Paul McCartney)

© 1966 Northern Songs Limited. Used by permission.

"I'm Only Sleeping" (recorded late April-early May 1966) was the first in a series of Lennon's dream songs. Ostensibly about sleep dreaming, it contains sufficient clues that it actually describes a trancelike (some listeners say drug-induced) state of daydreaming. Slithering polyphonic lines played by an electric guitar on reversed tape manifest the unreal condition;[8] tapes in retrograde had become a resource for portraying altered states of awareness. For a year or so, Lennon led the Beatles through a fantasy world

---

[7] With "Rain," the unraveling of riddles becomes part of the experience of listening to the Beatles. The otherworldly coda of "Rain" includes the first use of tapes played backwards by the Beatles; Lennon is thus heard to sing portions of the body of the song (see Ex. 6 above). It is odd that, for surely unrelated reasons, the American sleeve for "Paperback Writer"/"Rain" is one of the very few Beatle record covers out of hundreds on which photographs are reversed. (See Appendix 3 for text of the lyrics.)

[8] In addition to reversed tapes of guitar, several melodies (as well as progressions in harmonic prolongations) in both vocals and instruments are arch-shaped at several levels, producing, in Messiaen's sense, non-retrogradable events. The song is highly recognizable when taped and played backwards.

of dreams, Lewis Carroll, and the circus.[9] Transcendental meditation was also important in the period from 1966 through early 1968; the hypnotic meditative state of relaxation of the mind and body, in which ideas and wishes are observed but not followed, and in which initiative is an alien force, is expressed in the tape piece "Tomorrow Never Knows" (recorded in early April, 1966, for the *Revolver* LP) and reverberates through "Across the Universe" (recorded February 4-8, 1968).

Two other songs deserve mention before we turn to the particulars of "Strawberry Fields Forever" and "Julia." Lennon and McCartney each wrote a song based on his memories of their partnership. Lennon takes a curious look at his own past—and a bitter look at McCartney's—through a "Glass Onion" (for the "White" album, recorded through the summer of 1968), which recollects earlier songs "I Am the Walrus," "Lady Madonna," and "Fixing a Hole," quotes a line from "The Fool on the Hill," and warps the tune of "Strawberry Fields Forever."

In January, 1969, a film/LP project revolved around the making of a live recording of the rock 'n' roll type material with which the Beatles began their career. (As the project took shape, it became known as the "Get Back" sessions.[10] Linda Eastman even photographed the group in a pose and location identical to those on the cover of the first LP.[11]) During the sessions, McCartney wrote "Two of Us," which may be heard as a retrospective ode to the Lennon-McCartney partnership. The bridge, alluding to the memories of both composers, is given emphasis through a momentary shift to the parallel minor through $\flat$III.[12]

These examples from Lennon and McCartney songs have demonstrated their ways of dealing with either memories (escaping to them, wishing

[9] Another dream song is "Strawberry Fields Forever." The psychedelic "Lucy in the Sky With Diamonds" of *Sgt. Pepper's Lonely Hearts Club Band* is based on imagery from *Through the Looking-Glass*, and particular derivations can be traced to the final poem from that book, "A boat, beneath a sunny sky." "I Am the Walrus" of late September, 1967, refers to the Walrus (but not to the Carpenter) and to Humpty Dumpty (the "egg man"). Lennon was intentionally obscure with these lyrics. It was a joke on literary analysts who continually dissected his texts, searching for hidden meanings. The circus is the setting for "Being for the Benefit of Mr. Kite," also of *Sgt. Pepper*, which "swirls" through the tonal areas of C minor, D minor and E minor much as the coda's steam organ swirls through George Martin's tape concrète collage. "Dr. Dream" (one of Lennon's many pseudonyms) made (arguably) his most original contributions in these fantasy songs.

[10] This in reference to the song "Get Back," which began as a sharp satire of Enoch Powell's immigration policy, but was eventually recorded as an innocuous McCartney boogie. In 1970, the project was renamed after the song "Let It Be."

[11] These two photographs became the covers of EMI's 1973 reissues labeled *1962-66* and *1967-70*, respectively.

[12] Occasionally, a Beatles song recalled a progression from an older Beatles recording in the same key. McCartney's "Here There and Everywhere" (for *Revolver*) moved to its parallel minor middle section through $\flat$III, as does "Two of Us"; both are in G major. Similarly, the opening progression of the verse of "Here There and Everywhere" forms the harmonic basis of the middle of Lennon's "Sexy Sadie" (the "White" album), also in G major.

to avoid them, etc.), or the illusive realm of fantastic imagination. The remainder of this essay will discuss two examples of a combined type: fantasy songs with origins in remembrance.

"Strawberry Fields Forever"

John Lennon and Paul McCartney

Let me take you down
'cos I'm going to strawberry fields
Nothing is real
And nothing to get hungabout
Strawberry fields forever.

Living is easy with eyes closed
Misunderstanding all you see
It's getting hard to be someone
But it all works out
It doesn't matter much to me.

Let me take you down
'cos I'm going to strawberry fields
Nothing is real
And nothing to get hungabout
Strawberry fields forever.

No-one, I think, is in my tree
I mean, it must be high or low
That is you can't, you know, tune in
But it's alright
That is, I think it's not too bad.

Let me take you down
'cos I'm going to strawberry fields
Nothing is real
And nothing to get hungabout
Strawberry fields forever.

Always, no, sometimes, think it's me
But, you know, I know when it's a dream
I think I know, I mean, er, yes
But it's all wrong
That is, I think I disagree.

Let me take you down
'cos I'm going to strawberry fields
Nothing is real
And nothing to get hungabout
Strawberry fields forever.

Strawberry fields forever.
Strawberry fields forever.

. . . Cranberry sauce . . .

"Strawberry Fields Forever" was the first of three pieces recorded by the Beatles in November-December, 1966, originally with the intent of initiating a follow-up LP to *Revolver*. Several of Lennon's previous compositions ("Help!," "She Said She Said") had referred to his youth, but remembrances of his Liverpool childhood were the basis of this song. When it was released as a single with "Penny Lane" (McCartney's companion song about Liverpool memories), its record sleeve featured snapshots of the four Beatles as babies. Strawberry Fields was the name of a neighborhood orphanage in the Liverpool suburb in which the composer was raised by his aunt. It serves as a setting for this song in which Lennon alludes to an anxiety he felt as a child and apparently would continue feeling "forever." He explains:

The second verse goes, "No one I think is in my tree." Well, I was too shy and self-doubting. Nobody seems to be as hip as me is what I was saying. Therefore, I must be crazy or a genius—"I mean, it must be high or low," the next line. There was something wrong with me, I thought, because I seemed to see things other people didn't see. . . . I always was so psychic or intuitive or poetic or whatever you want to call it, that I was always seeing things in a hallucinatory way.

It was scary as a child, because there was nobody to relate to. Neither my auntie nor my friends nor anybody could ever see what I did. It was very, very scary and the only contact I had was reading about an Oscar Wilde or a Dylan Thomas or a Vincent van Gogh—all those books that my auntie had that talked about their suffering because of their visions. Because of what they saw, they were tortured by society for trying to express what they were. I *saw* loneliness.[13]

In "Strawberry Fields," Lennon's identity problems ("it's getting hard to be someone") were traced in the first verse to others' (disdainful?) misapprehensions of him: "living is easy with eyes closed, misunderstanding all you see." Lennon placed these childhood and adolescent memories in the context of a dream ("But you know I know when it's a dream"). Because "nothing is real," the singer can be ambivalent about his anxiety and express resignation at not being understood, shrugging off his vexation

---

[13] From the final interview with John Lennon in *Playboy*, XXVIII/1 (January, 1981), 107-114, XXVIII/4 (April, 1981), 196.

("you can't, you know, tune in but it's all right; that is, I think it's not too bad"); he has learned to have to live with his problem.[14]

The recording procedure for this song had a strong effect upon its resulting tramontane sound quality. Two versions were done. It was originally recorded on November 24, 1966, and was performed in A at a tempo of about ♩ = 92. After listening to the lacquers, Lennon decided it sounded "too heavy" and wanted it rescored and performed faster. A second version, with trumpets and cellos, was recorded in B flat at about ♩ = 102. Lennon liked the beginning of the first version and the ending of the second, and asked Producer George Martin to splice them together. When the speeds of both tapes were adjusted to match the pitch, the tempos of both were fortuitously the same, ♩ = 96. The two portions were edited together in the middle of measure 24 (see Ex. 7).[15] This procedure gives Lennon's vocals an unreal, dreamlike timbre, especially in the second, slowed-down, portion of the song.

Ex. 7. "Strawberry Fields Forever" (John Lennon and Paul McCartney)

---

[14] Other Lennon songs express similar acquiescence, such as in "Good Morning, Good Morning" ("I've got nothing to say, but it's o.k."). McCartney's "Fixing a Hole" contains a line that echoes this Lennon disposition: "it really doesn't matter if I'm wrong, I'm right (;) where I belong I'm right (,) where I belong." (The intended punctuation cannot be determined by listening to the recording.) Resignation in the face of misunderstanding, the basis of Lennon's "Strawberry Fields," had been the theme of Harrison's earlier "I Want to Tell You" of *Revolver*. (See Appendix 4 for text of the lyrics.)

[15] See Martin's *All You Need Is Ears* (New York, 1979), pp. 199-200. The original recording, without trumpets and cellos, can be heard on the bootleg record, *Strawberry Fields Forever*.

John Lennon

Figure 2 shows (a) the middleground and (b) the foreground structures of "Strawberry Fields."

Fig. 2. Graph of "Strawberry Fields Forever"

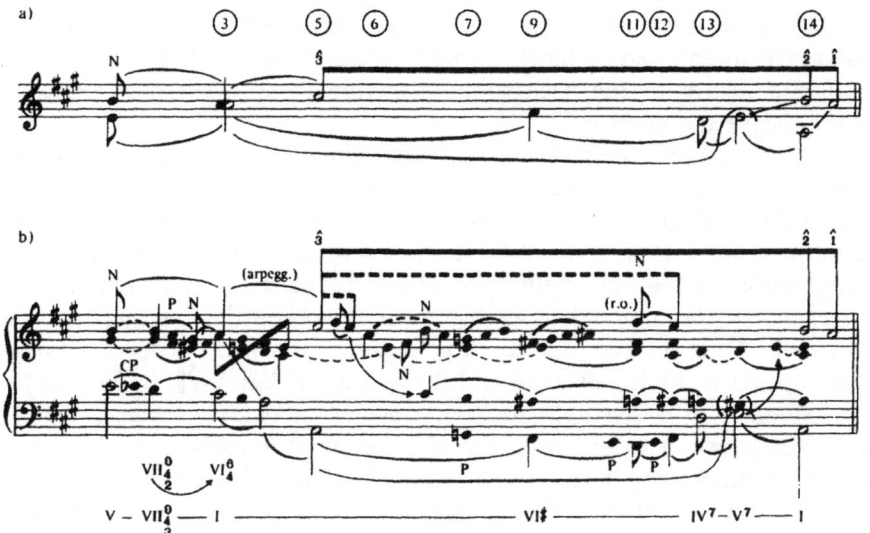

Despite the unusual surface harmonic progressions, the structural basis of the song is I-VI-IV-V-I. Two middleground diminutions have an interesting effect: a seventh constraint is imposed above the IV at measure 13, and the sounding of the cadential V is minimized nearly to the point of not happening. The fifth scale degree, which should act as a bass support for $\hat{2}$, appears in the vocal line (m. 13), and in this one line (over a static IV harmony), mere vestiges of a cadential $\hat{4}$-$\hat{3}$ remain:

Ex. 8. "Strawberry Fields Forever"

The seventh above IV does descend, but the resolution is delayed so that $\hat{2}$-$\hat{1}$ actually occurs above I (see Fig. 2a). In the final appearance of this cadence, in measure 73, E is actually articulated in the bass, but $\hat{2}$ is this time absent from the upper line, and direct motion to I is circumvented as V7 moves to IV: this is a direct outgrowth of the verse's IV-V-IV-V vacillation of the verse in measures 18-22, especially where the text proclaims "it doesn't matter much to me." It seems that this V-IV ambivalence is carried nearly to the background structure through the near exclusion of the cadential dominant.

Let us examine the voice-leading more closely, through Figure 2b. The structure of the verses is not represented in Figure 2; this is because the V-I introduction of the song (mm. 1-4) is a telescoping of the structure of the verse (as at mm. 15-22); the V-IV vacillation of the verse is deleted from the introduction of the first mellotron. The introduction is built upon a composing-out of the tonic triad. Ambiguity is at work in this passage; upon the arrival of $c\sharp^1$ in the bass, $F\sharp$ could be regarded as tonic: the opening events could appear to be II (assuming eb^1 to be a $d\sharp^1$)–VII°$^4_2$-$\hat{V}^6_4$, in $F\sharp$. But the tonic sonority of A is actually incipient once $c\sharp^1$ appears in the bass; the $f\sharp^1$ is an appoggiatura to e^1 while the a^1-e^1 interval unfolds (mm. 3-4), preparing the inner-voice e^1 for the body of the song. A is the functioning bass pitch throughout this unfolding, indicated by the diagonal line connecting a^1 to a. Things are not quite what they seem: the diminished seventh chord is VII of A, not VII of $F\sharp$, and pitch-class $F\sharp$ in measure 3 is just a temporary substitute for pitch-class E. When this point ($f\sharp^1$ over $c\sharp^1$ in the introduction) arrives in the first verse (m. 17– the electric bass now doubles an inner voice), it is accompanying the word "misunderstanding" (the cause of Lennon's anxiety); the singer seems to be challenging the listener to follow the ambiguous surface harmonies. The verse is especially open to misunderstanding, in light of the IV-V-IV-V oscillation (mm. 21-22) mentioned above.

Text and music operate as a unit at the beginning of the chorus, measure 5. The line "let me take you down" follows the opening up of the lowest register in the introduction with the electric guitar dropping the octave to A (m. 5). Text painting controls not only the descending vocal (from the high end of Lennon's vocal range) on $c\sharp^2$-a^1-e^1 (mm. 5-6), but this arpeggiation down to $c\sharp^1$ in the guitar (m. 6), thus effecting a full octave transfer, $c\sharp^2$-$c\sharp^1$; from measures 6 through 10, the structural upper voice appears as $c\sharp^1$-b-a, in the instrumental tenor register. This line is shadowed in the highest-sounding parts (the flutelike first mellotron and vocals); the bass descent A-G-$F\sharp$ is in parallel octaves with (the first mellotron and) the vocal part which continues (mm. 7-8) to arpeggiate between voices (g^1, b^1, e^1) even after establishing the octave transfer of the structural voice. The motion of this structural line from $C\sharp$ to B is corroborated

in the double-tracked descant line of the final chorus (m. 61), where the
$c\sharp^2$-b^1 occurs in the obligatory register:

Fig. 3. Graph of vocal parts, "Strawberry Fields Forever"

Trumpets in measures 64 and following clarify the motion from b^1 to $a\sharp^1$
also in the obligatory register.

Ex. 9. "Strawberry Fields Forever"

John Lennon

Stability is threatened when the first scale degree undergoes an identity crisis in measures 9-14, wavering between a♮ and a♯. The G♮ in the bass leads to F♯ at measure 9, supporting minor V moving to major VI, as the text bears the singer's motto, "nothing is real"; reality is certainly in question when the seventh degree is flatted and the tonic pitch raised without this having been necessitated by strong reasons of voice-leading; g♯ and a♮ would have "worked" quite as well, but would have had nothing to say about "unreality."[16]

Percussion is heard in retrograde (through reversed tapes) in measures 34-42 and in measures 54-60. These passages accompany the second and third verses, which describe the past anxieties of Lennon's youth; it is only during the brief reminders (choruses) of the fact that "nothing is real" that we are not in a backwards world of the past. The odd coda, a long but largely unornamented tonic harmony, fades out with a sort of "Reveille" figure on the piano (Ex. 10). Is someone attempting to awaken the singer from his dream?

Ex. 10. "Strawberry Fields Forever"

© 1967 Northern Songs Limited. Used by permission.

Lennon is apparently trying to communicate a jaded indifference (at the V-IV we hear his shrug of the shoulders) to the unreality (references to dreaming, a-a♯ oscillation) of his misunderstood past (ambiguity in the introduction, reversed tapes). Regardless of the seeming indifference, he would like some company as he revisits Strawberry Fields.

"Julia"

"Julia," written for the "White" album in 1968, is named for Lennon's mother. The composer hardly knew his father, who abandoned his wife and unborn child. When Lennon was about four, his mother went off with another man and left him in the care of his Aunt Mimi (Smith). He began to see Julia again in his midteens and she taught him how to play the guitar.

---

[16] The listener is reminded of George Harrison's "Only a Northern Song" (recorded on Feb. 11, 1968), which continuously colors chords in the "wrong" modes. It is a spoof on the Beatles' publishing company, Northern Songs.

John Lennon   377

Ex. 11. "Julia" (John Lennon and Paul McCartney)

John Lennon   379

Mimi discouraged all of his musical interests. Lennon had just reestablished a relationship with his mother when she was killed while walking to a bus stop; he was seventeen at the time.[17]

In early 1968, Lennon must have read Kahlil Gibran's book of aphorisms, *Sand and Foam,* for he was apparently taken by two of its apothegms: "Half of what I say is meaningless; but I say it so that the other half may reach you," and "When Life does not find a singer to sing her heart she produces a philosopher to speak her mind." (© 1931, Alfred A. Knopf, Inc. Used by permission.) These two sentences provoked Lennon to daydream about communicating with his mother. This experience is relived in the song "Julia," in which he paraphrased and troped Gibran's text to illustrate the integration of dreamlike memories into waking consciousness:

"Julia"
John Lennon and Paul McCartney

Half of what I say is meaningless
But I say it just to reach you, Julia.

Julia, Julia oceanchild calls me
So I sing a song of love, Julia.

Julia seashell eyes windy smile calls me
So I sing the song of love, Julia.

---

[17] Lennon's substitute mothering was probably adequate so as not to leave permanent scars, but the fact that he lost his mother twice was a double trauma. Possible manifestations of this are related in "Getting Better" and especially "Jealous Guy," in which he places the blame for his cruelty to women upon the insecurities of his past.

Lennon spent several months of 1970 (the year the Beatles broke up) in Primal Scream Therapy with Arthur Janov in California. This experience dominates the self-indulgent LP *John Lennon/Plastic Ono Band,* recorded early in Oct., 1970. The album is an often-tortuous working through of his "who am I" question, and several times it addresses problems posed by the absence of parents. This link to his childhood is manifest on the back cover of the album, which consists of a cropped portion of the baby picture of him used on the 45 r.p.m. sleeve for "Strawberry Fields Forever."

The album begins with funeral bells; "that was like the death-knell of the mother-father Freudian trip" (Lennon said in a BBC interview of Dec. 6, 1980, two days before his own death). The first song, "Mother," says "Mother, you had me, but I didn't have you; I wanted you, you didn't want me." In "I Found Out," Lennon sings, "I heard something 'bout my ma and my pa–they didn't want me so they made me a star"; somewhere, possibly in his therapy with Dr. Janov, Lennon may have come in contact with Freud's theory that art is an expression of the cognitive dissonance caused by unacceptable wishes. The album ends with the singer's coming to terms with his problem in "My Mummy's Dead." Does "Julia" represent the first step toward dealing with this problem through his music?

The *Plastic Ono Band* album showed Lennon stripping every artifice from his music (a striving to reveal the naked truth), and all romantic allusions as well: "the dream is over; yesterday / I was the dream-weaver, but now I'm reborn; I was the Walrus, but now I'm John / and so, dear friends, you'll just have to carry on–the dream is over" ("God"). Lennon's attitudes mellowed considerably in his next albums. (See Appendix 5 for the lyrics.)

Her hair of floating sky is shimmering
Glimmering in the sun.

Julia, Julia morning moon touch me
So I sing the song of love, Julia.

When I cannot sing my heart
I can only speak my mind, Julia.

Julia sleeping sand silent cloud touch me
So I sing a song of love, Julia.

Hmm hmm hmm, calls me
So I sing a song of love for Julia
Julia, Julia.

Lennon has said, "the song was actually a combination of an imagery of Yoko and my mother blended into one."[18] Some sort of mother-Yoko transference may have been operative; elsewhere on the same album, Yoko is referred to as "Mother," and the Beatles' annual Christmas fan-club message of 1969 features John calling Yoko "mommy." Regardless of the reasons behind this blending, it is clear which of "Julia"'s metaphors refer to Julia, and which to Yoko. In another song on the "White" album, "Yer Blues," Lennon sings, "my mother is of the sky";[19] "Julia"'s lyrics refer to Julia through sky-related images: "windy smile," "floating sky," "the sun," "morning moon," and "silent cloud." "Yoko" is Japanese for "ocean child," and is represented with references to "seashell eyes" and "sleeping sand" (these earthly Yoko qualities are certainly related to much of the imagery of Gibran's *Sand and Foam*). The dead Julia and the living Yoko represent a spiritual/physical polarity.[20] Polarity is indeed a key concept in this song which begins "Half of what I say . . . " The second Gibran quote suggests a mind/heart polarity. Further, there is a distinction between the spectral "call"-ing and the physical "touch"-ing, as Julia communicated to John through verbal metaphors, while Yoko simply reaches out and touches him.

Lennon's setting is one of the Beatles' simplest (and the only one comprised solely of Lennon on guitar, the instrument his mother taught him).

[18] From an interview in *Playboy*, XXVIII/4 (April, 1981), 192.
[19] See Appendix 6 for text of the lyrics.
[20] As evidenced in his later song, "Imagine" (1971), the sky is not always a spiritual realm for Lennon.

As indicated by my transcription, I hear two different acoustic guitar parts, one of which is double-tracked through most of the piece.[21] The half-measure ostinato with its cross-rhythm is also the basis of two extra-Beatles Lennon songs, "Remember Love" (1969) and "Look at Me" (1970). These simple aspects, in addition to Lennon's frequent repetition of a single pitch, are somewhat offset by mild complexities in phrase length proportions and surface harmonies.

Textural and motivic aspects of the musical setting directly highlight the textual polarities summarized above. The elisions at the beginnings of verses 2, 3, and 7 (as numbered in Ex. 11), created through the double tracking of Lennon's voice, illustrate Lennon's changing consciousness at Julia's sudden appearance in his mind.[22] By following the two different vocal tracks, the listener can follow the two paths (one further away from reality than the other) being traced in Lennon's mind. Other double tracking, effecting a unison doubling of several lines ("just to reach you

Ex. 12. "Any Time at All" (John Lennon and Paul McCartney)

[21] The picking pattern was probably done in C, with a capo on the third fret. (The speed of the tape was not changed, e.g. as in "She's Leaving Home," which was slowed down from F to E in all releases other than the British monophonic mix.)

[22] "Any Time at All" (recorded June 1-3, 1964) included the same elision on a-f♯-e-d descent, in a similar rhythm, as does "Julia," but with a different effect. In the earlier song, the elision clarifies the motivic connection between the descending bass line of the piano and the cadential guitar lick. The elision occurs in measure 15 (see Ex. 12 above); the common motive is marked "x". It is interesting that, like the later "Julia," this song is based on the concept of someone "call"-ing the singer. (See Appendix 7 for the text of the lyrics.)

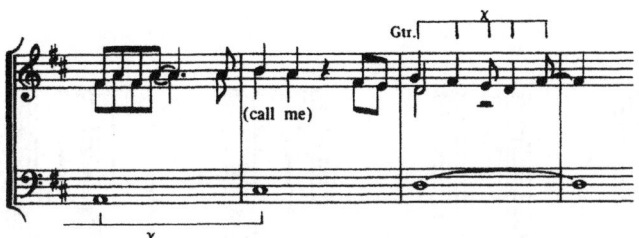

Julia," "so I sing a song of love, Julia") usually (the middle line, 4, being the exception) represents Lennon's whole self responding to the half of his self (single tracked) that hears Julia calling him and feels Yoko touching him.

"Julia"'s motivic language also defines the polarities of the text. The static prolongation of $\hat{5}$ has two motivic shapes: the declamatory, telegraph-like monotone of $\hat{5}$ gives the Gibran readings (lines 1 and 6) a meditative trancelike quality, while the gentle floating around $\hat{5}$, especially through neighbor b (which causes the alpha wavelike $\hat{5}$ to flicker, though without disturbance) (see Fig. 4b) accompanies the imagery that is "call"-ed forth to John's mind by his reading. This stasis on $\hat{5}$, both through the repeated pitch and with the candle-flame neighbors, accompanies the spiritual and mental attitudes in the text. The emotional and physical aspects are heard in the tumbling $\hat{3}$-$\hat{2}$-$\hat{1}$ down-to-earth "song of love for Julia" which takes place in an inner voice, and the a ($\hat{5}$) is regained each time through the wonderful reaching-over of the double-tracked elision.

Stasis is characteristic of the fundamental structure of "Julia"; the background sketched in Figure 4a shows only a lower neighbor figure to the tonic, which is not supported by V and does not itself support any descent in a structural upper voice. Figure 4b indicates that the "next" diminutions are also neighbors (to each member of the tonic triad), and that the line of text that most describes "shimmering" motion (through the C♯-minor triad) is accompanied (in parallel fifths) by the primordial C♯ neighbor of level 4a. Level 4c indicates the true bass line, which does not in fact exist in the lowest-sounding pitches, but nevertheless functions contrapuntally as the bass; the lowest line of the guitar is dependent on the bass line graphed in level 4c. Featured in this bass line is an unfolding of d-f♯, which marks the opening up of a new tenor voice at this level at the point at which the singer recalls images of Julia (the beginning of the verse). Also at this level, the "alto" $\hat{3}$-$\hat{2}$-$\hat{1}$ descent is indicated. It is clearly not a part of the fundamental line, as its pitches are not harmonically

Fig. 4. Graph of "Julia"

supported and it is not "connected" to the a ($\hat{5}$); this song of the heart maintains its role as an inner voice. The resolution of a 7-6 suspension (the guitar's g♯ answer to the "glimmering") and subsequent motion to an inner voice (a-g♯-f♯) take the middle five measures back to the third verse (5 in the score). The f♯ ("sun") does not resolve down, however, as a 4-3 suspension over the bass c♯, nor does it act as the 9-8 resolution over the lowest-sounding F♯; it anticipates the f♯ upon the return of the verse to I. Pitch class C♯, which had always behaved as a good neighbor, finally refuses to resolve to D, and is frozen into the final chord.

The final diminutions in the foreground graph of Figure 4d show the derivation of the lowest-sounding line, as dependent upon the real bass. Also detailed are the colorful surface harmonies of the verse. Here, a minor V chord (with e in the bass) is followed by a major VI triad (in mm. 7-9 of "Strawberry Fields," this progression had a clear voice-leading function)[23] which is itself followed by a seventh chord built on minor IV (open note-head d in the bass); this series floats without being function bound, in a loose support of the upper voice's neighbor b¹ and chromatic passing tone b♭¹ in the prolongation of tonic.

Figure 4d indicates that, occasionally, the bass neighbor c♯ is part of a V-functioning sound; this occurs when the pseudo-bass drops to A,

Fig. 5. Graph of "Strawberry Fields Forever"

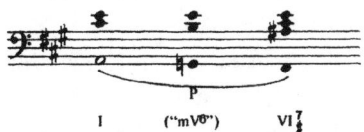

© 1967 Northern Songs Limited. Used by permission.

Fig. 6. Graph of "Julia," beginning of verse

© 1968 Northern Songs Limited. Used by permission.

[23] It will be recalled that in mm. 7-9 of "Strawberry Fields Forever," the voice-leading from I to VI♯ articulated a descent in the bass (as shown in Fig. 5 above). In "Julia," the same (transposed) vertical sonorities are supported by an *ascending* unfolding from the bass to the tenor, prolonging the tonic function (see Fig. 6 above).

as at the end of the introduction and the end of the verse. At the end of the middle section, however, the lowest voice becomes F♮, just barely negating the V function in a sonority that includes pitch classes A-C♯-E; here, under the text "in the sun," C♯ functions correctly as a neighbor to D, but E does not work as it normally would as part of V: it begins a chromatic unfolding of the interval e^1-c♯^{1}, mocking the previous vocal motion to an inner voice a-g♯-f♯, and possibly recalling the chromatic descent b-b♭-a-g♯ that governed the upper, structural line through the verse and middle sections. The mediant harmony ending the middle section is midway between I and V, but functions only as a vague color to be supported by the leading-tone in the bass. A real dominant here would probably have been too disruptive of the $\frac{\hat{5}}{I}$ trance.

To summarize, the $\frac{\hat{5}}{I}$ stasis is toyed with by the neighbors of the upper line of the verse, in the neighbors of the upper and bass voices of the middle, and in the motion to an inner voice setting up the return to the third verse. The stasis is not disturbed by any structural appearance of V, nor do the colorful surface harmonies upset the prolonged tonic harmony. And so, Lennon's daydream, evoked by remembrance of his mother, wanders to a deeply inner place shared by Julia and Yoko and is undisturbed as the singer splits into two, one half expressing the trance of called-up mental images, and the other half responding with a song of love. The song is not so much a lament as an illustration of the paths of imagination.

In examining two very different compositional approaches to fantastic remembrance, it seems that we have found little basis for general conclusions. One song is built on the $\frac{\hat{3}}{I}$ - $\frac{\hat{2}}{V}$ - $\frac{\hat{1}}{I}$ paradigm (although the communicative power of V-I is almost subdued by the confusion of V with IV); the other is a static prolongation of $\frac{\hat{5}}{I}$ with an inner voice proclaiming an unsupported $\hat{3}$-$\hat{2}$-$\hat{1}$. There are a few musical similarities between the two songs: a weightless distance from reality is conveyed in each by the coloring of chords with the "wrong" qualities (minor triad on V, major triad on VI), and living in the past is partly expressed in each through studio recording techniques (backwards tapes, double tracking). But similarities between the two songs are limited; it is more to the point to recognize the contrasts between them. One is a song of weariness resulting from futile attempts at resolving ambiguity in order to be correctly understood; the other relates the wonder of a daydream of successful spiritual communion. Indeed, the songs represent negative and positive attitudes to the potential fulfillment of communication. In combining these themes of remembrance and fantasy with the artistic issue of communication, and expressing these values through both textual and musical relationships, "Strawberry Fields Forever" and "Julia" become important compositional statements.

[20]

The Rutles and the Use of Specific Models in Musical Satire

John R. Covach

On March 22, 1978, NBC aired a 90-minute "docudrama" entitled, "The Rutles: All You Need is Cash."[1] The focus of this satirical film is the fictitious 1960's musical group, "The Rutles." As the title of the film already suggests, the Rutles are modeled on the Beatles, and the densely packed references to the "Fab Four" which occur throughout "All You Need is Cash" will be immediately detected by any viewer familiar with the Beatles' careers.

The idea of making the film arose after Monty Python comedian and writer Eric Idle presented a film clip of the Rutles performing "I Must Be In Love" on NBC's "Saturday Night Live"

---

[1]This date is given by Kim "Howard" Johnson in *The First 200 Years of Monty Python* (New York: St. Martin's Press, 1989), 235. According to George Perry, BBC-2 first aired the program on March 27, 1978. Perry, *Life of Python* (Boston and Toronto: Little, Brown and Company, 1983), 188.

The film is available on home video as "I Love The Rutles," Pacific Arts Video Records PAVR-540. All the Rutles musical examples can be found on the recent CD release, *The Rutles*, Rhino R2 75760. The Beatles songs cited in the text can be found on the following albums: "She Loves You, " *The Beatles' Second Album*, Capitol ST2080; "Please Please Me" and "P.S. I Love You, *The Early Beatles*, Capitol ST2309; "All My Loving," "I Want To Hold Your Hand," and "It Won't Be Long," *Meet The Beatles*, Capitol ST2047; and "Help!," *Help!* (motion picture soundtrack album), Capitol 2386. The Beatles citations are all to the American-release LP's; these songs appear on different albums on the original British-release LP's (the latter arrangement is used for the new CD issues).

on October 2, 1976.[2] The clip had been shown previously on Idle's BBC-2 series, "Rutland Weekend Television," a program supposedly produced by Britain's "smallest, cheapest independent television station."[3] This brief appearance of the bogus "Pre-Fab Four" on American TV caused a minor sensation, and NBC suggested a full-length special be made, for which the network provided both facilities and funding. "Saturday Night Live" producer Lorne Michaels produced the film.[4]

The film is written entirely by Idle, but the music is the work of Neil Innes. Innes had previously provided music for Idle's Rutland series, an association which produced both the album, "The Rutland Weekend Songbook" and the book, "The Rutland Dirty Weekend Book."[5] George Perry reports that on the strength of his brilliant work on the Rutles project, Innes was given his own BBC series, "The Innes Book of Records."[6]

The movie chronicles the rise and fall of the Rutles: Ron Nasty (John Lennon, played by Innes), Dirk McQuickly (Paul McCartney, played by Idle), Stig O'Hara (George Harrison, played by Rikki Fataar), and Barry Wom (Ringo Starr, played by John Halsey).

---

[2]Perry, 118; and Johnson, 234.

[3]Johnson, 234. Johnson describes the "Rutland Weekend Television" program as consisting of two sets of six shows, broadcast in 1975 and 1976.

[4]Perry, 118.

[5]Eric Idle, *The Rutland Dirty Weekend Book* (Methuen/Two Continents, 1976); and "The Rutland Weekend Songbook," BBC Records REB 233 (1976), and ABC/Passport Records PPSD-98018. Johnson, 234, 254, 262. Johnson related that after the film had been done, Innes appeared as musical guest on "Saturday Night Live" (hosted that night, April 23, 1977, by Idle) and performed the song, "Cheese and Onions," a satire of John Lennon. This tune was included in "All You Need Is Cash," where it is played over their jab at the Beatles' "Yellow Submarine," a film entitled "Yellow Submarine Sandwich." This corrects Perry's description of these events. Compare Johnson, 234; and Perry, 118.

While Neal Innes is credited as sole composer on the LP and recently released CD, EMI currently lists John Lennon and Paul McCartney as composers of both songs. This would seem to indicate that the names of Lennon and McCartney were used by the publisher to resolve any possible charges of plagiarism.

[6]Perry, 119. Innes would already have been known, in addition, for his work with the "Bonzo Dog Doodah Band," a British musical comedy group.

With the exception of Idle, the cast members actually play the music for all the tunes.[7] The story opens with the forming of the band and their subsequent stint in Hamburg (where they play at the Rat Keller). They are then seen appearing in the Liverpool Cavern Club ("Goose-Step Mama": "music which will last a lunchtime") and, subsequently, in a recording session for what will be their first hit (the tune they play, "Number One," can only be a take-off on "Twist and Shout").

The film continues to play the parody out in amazing detail. We are led through the films "A Hard Day's Rut," and "Ouch!," and through such albums as "Rutle Soul," "Sargeant Rutter's Only Darts Club Band" ("a veritable millstone in popular music"), "Tragical History Tour," and "Let It Rot."

The most remarkable aspect of this masterful parody is the closeness which the satire bears to the original. Those familiar with the Beatles' music and history will be amused, but those who are intimately familiar with the Beatles story are frequently delighted by the film; the more one knows about the Beatles, the more fun one has with the Rutles.

The present study will explore only the musical dimension of the Rutles humor, and, of that, it will focus on only two works. This paper, then, does not constitute a thorough study of even the musical dimension of "All You Need Is Cash." Instead, I would like to take some carefully chosen examples from the film to make a number of points about stylistic competencies and how they contribute to an amused response in music. In other words, I would like to examine why it is that a greater familiarity with the music of the Beatles contributes to a greater, and perhaps fuller, amused response to the Rutles. I would also like to explore the various ways in which this greater familiarity is used to trigger an amused response.

In a study of musical humor in the film, "This is Spinal Tap," I outlined a number of philosophical approaches to explaining

---

[7]Bass on the recordings is played by Andy Brown; additional guitars and keyboards are played by Ollie Halsall.

humor and laughter.[8] Arthur Schopenhauer explains the amused response as a recognition of incongruity between a representation and a concept: we encounter a situation where a particular representation is "thought through" a concept which is in every other respect incongruous with it. The sudden apprehension of the unexpected incongruity produces an amused response.[9] Roger Scruton refines Schopenhauer's "incongruity theory" by pointing out the dialectical relationship played out by congruity and incongruity: an amused response is provoked when the object of perception is somehow exaggerated. The exaggeration is at once a congruity—for it exaggerates a feature already present—and also an incongruity—by virtue of the exaggeration.[10] Scruton provides the example of a caricature of Margaret Thatcher; the caricature amuses not because it does not fit her, but rather because it does fit her, all too well.[11] Of course, the incongruity signals that the caricature should not be understood as a portrait.

When these philosophical observations are applied to music, one must first determine how the congruity-incongruity dialectic can arise. I have suggested that it is stylistic competencies which provide the mechanism for certain types of amused response in music. A stylistic competency is the ability of a listener to discern, in any single piece, those features which are normative within a particular

---

[8]See John R. Covach, "Stylistic Competencies, Musical Humor, and 'This is Spinal Tap'," unpublished paper presented to the Society for Music Theory (Oakland, 1990), Music Theory Midwest (May, 1990), and the International Society for the Study of Popular Music (April, 1990.)

[9]See Schopenhauer, *The World as Will and Representation*, vol. 2, trans. E.F.J. Payne (New York: Dover, 1969), 91. A good example of this would be the P.D.Q. Bach "New Horizons in Music Appreciation" ("The Wurst of P.D.Q. Bach, Vanguard VSD-719/20): A concert performance of the first movement of Beethoven's Fifth Symphony is thought through the concept of a sports event. The amused response arises when we perceive the incongruity of the representation (the symphony) and the concept (a sports event).

[10]Roger Scruton, "Laughter," reprinted in John Morreall, ed., *The Philosophy of Laughter and Humor* (Albany, New York: State University of New York Press, 1987), 156-171.

[11]Scruton, 161.

style (group of pieces), and to discern those features which are non-normative or innovative.[12] Thus, viewed through the dimension of style, normative features are congruent, non-normative ones are incongruent.

Stylistic competencies can operate in a number of ways. In the Spinal Tap song "Heavy Duty," part of a Boccherini minuet is introduced in the context of a heavy metal rock number. In this case, the stylistic incongruity is readily apparent and this "inter-stylistic incongruity" acts as the primary trigger to elicit an amused response. In another Spinal Tap number, "Cups and Cakes," the incongruity is more subtle, residing within the "British-invasion competency" itself; that is, the style establishes the norm against which subtle deviations constitute incongruities. This latter, "intra-stylistic competency," requires a greater familiarity with the style under consideration; while one need not know much heavy metal or classic-period music to perceive the incongruity in "Heavy Duty," the incongruities in "Cups and Cakes" could pass unnoticed by a listener without a highly developed competency for British-invasion style.

But the musical numbers in "All You Need Is Cash" present yet different situations with regard to issues of humor and style. With the Rutles, it is not so much the British-invasion stylistic competency which is at work, but rather an even more specific one: A Beatles competency. Without a knowledge of the Beatles' music specifically, much of the musical humor in "All You Need Is Cash" goes undetected.

In order to unpack the mechanisms which create humor in the Rutles songs, I will proceed as follows: first, I will examine two representative numbers from the film and attempt to identify the references made to specific Beatles songs; and second, I will then

---

[12]These remarks rely on the work of Leonard Meyer, Leonard Ratner, and Robert Hatten. See Meyer, *Style and Music* (Philadelphia: University of Pennsylvania Press, 1989); Ratner, *Classic Music: Expression, Form, and Style* (New York: Schirmer Books, 1980); and Robert Hatten, "Toward a Semiotic Model of Style in Music: Epistemological and Methodological Bases" (Ph.D. diss., Indiana University, 1982).

employ Leonard Meyer's style theory to account for the "inter-textual" dimensions of each example.

Let us first consider the Rutles number "Hold My Hand." Perhaps the most obvious references to Beatles numbers are to be found in the lyrics: each verse ends with the words "please, please hold my hand," and each chorus begins with the words "hold my hand, yeah, yeah." The phrase "hold my hand" refers to the Beatles' "I Want to Hold Your Hand"; adding "yeah, yeah" to the end of "hold my hand" creates a reference to the Beatles' "She Loves You" (yeah, yeah, yeah); and placing "please, please" before "hold my hand" creates a reference to the Beatles' "Please Please Me." Thus the lyrics, by making specific references to Beatles tunes and combining them, become a conflation of the three models.

Example 1. a) "Hold My Hand," three-note figure; b) "She Loves You," three-note figure transposed; c) "All My Loving."

Covach, *The Rutles and Models in Musical Satire*   125

This same procedure can be seen in a number of more specifically musical dimensions of the song. Example 1 shows the three-note melodic figure which carries the text "hold my hand, yeah, yeah"; note that the E—D-sharp—C-sharp descending third may be found in both "She Loves You" (on "yeah, yeah, yeah" transposed up a minor third), and in "All My Loving" (on "all my loving" terminated with a fourth leap).

The reference to "All My Loving" is further reinforced by the quadruple-compound meter shared by the two tunes. In addition, the rhythmic configurations in the Rutles rhythm section are lifted directly off the Beatles model: the Rutles constant eighth-note strums in the rhythm guitar and walking quarter notes in the bass create a direct reference.

"All My Loving" also seems to be the principal model for the harmonic movement of the verse. Example 2 shows the initial measures of the verse sections of both "Hold My Hand" and "All My Loving," and Figure 1 compares the harmonic movement. Note that the progression ii - V - I is held in common between the two tunes, as is the use of bVII. Both of these harmonic features are typical enough for 1960's pop, and their use here, taken in isolation, does not create a reference: they are stylistically normative. The harmonic reference to "All My Loving" is signalled, however, when these harmonic features are understood in the context of the textual, melodic, and rhythmic references. Further, whenever the ii -V - I progression is played on the rhythm guitar in either tune, the guitar barre-chord voicings are mostly the same ones (but again, the voicings themselves are typical enough in the style).

Example 2. a) Excerpt from "Hold My Hand" (verse); b) excerpt from "All My Loving" (verse). Guitar voicings are given below the melody.

Covach, *The Rutles and Models in Musical Satire*   127

Figure 1.

"Hold My Hand"

E: ii | V | I | I | ii | V | I | I |

     vi | iii | IV iii | ii V | I | bVII | I | I ‖

"All My Loving"

E: ii | V | I | vi | IV | ii | bVII | V |

     ii | V | I | vi | IV | V | I | I ‖

The reference to "She Loves You" is further reinforced in the chorus of "Hold My Hand." Example 3 gives the chorus of "Hold My Hand" and the intro to "She Loves You"; Figure 2 compares the chorus of "Hold My Hand" with the chorus and intro of "She Loves You."

Figure 2.

"Hold My Hand"

          E: vi | vi | II | II | IV | bVI | I | I ‖

"She Loves You"

intro: G: vi | vi | II | II | IV | IV | I | I ‖
chorus: G: vi | vi | II | II | iv | V | I | I ‖

Example 3.   a) "Hold My Hand," chorus; b) "She Loves You," intro.

Covach, *The Rutles and Models in Musical Satire*   129

In this instance the harmonic modeling is unmistakable; even where the progressions differ in measures 5-6, this difference is slight. The only conflict between the chorus of "Hold My Hand" and the intro to "She Loves You" is the use of bVI in the former. But the Beatles model presents two versions of the progression; while the intro uses IV, the chorus (on "with a love like that, you know you should be glad") employs a iv - V progression. In the same place in the eight bar unit, "Hold My Hand" uses the diatonic IV and the borrowed bVI. The bVI, in terms of pop harmony, is nearly synonymous with the iv. In this instance, the bVI is slightly more startling when it arrives than the iv would be, an effect produced by the chromatic-third root movement IV - bVI. Thus the Rutles progression can be seen as a conflation of the two Beatles versions: it employs both IV and the harmonic synonym for iv, bVI, and the harmonic rhythm of one chord per measure which occurs at iv - V, is referenced by the IV - bVI movement. In any case, the use of bVI is common to many Beatles tunes: "P.S. I Love You," is characterized by the root movement bVI - bVII - I (end of verse); and "It Won't Be Long" moves I - bVI - I (verse). Therefore, even if one tends not to view iv and bVI as synonyms, the use of bVI fits easily within the Beatles' style.

One more detail reinforces the reference to "All My Loving": the tag to "Hold My Hand" refers directly to the tag of "All My Loving" (See Example 4 and Figure 3).

Figure 3.

"Hold My Hand"

     E: vi | vi | I | I | vi | bVI | I | I ‖

"All My Loving"   (ooh, ooh)

     E: vi | vi | I | I | vi | vi | I | I ‖

130   *Indiana Theory Review* Vol. 11

Example 4. a) Excerpt from "All My Loving" (tag); b) excerpt from "Hold My Hand" (tag).

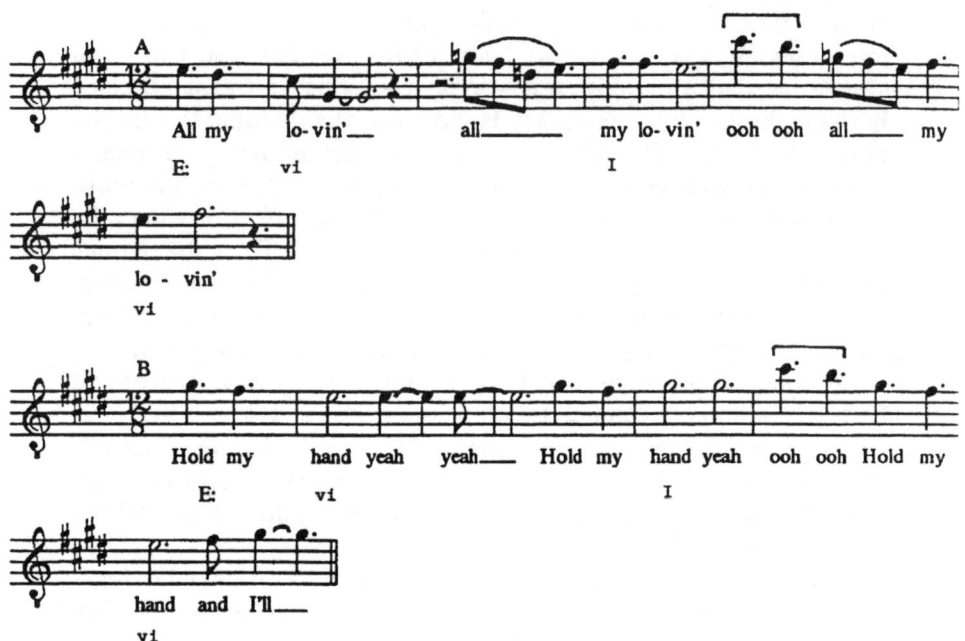

Not only are the progressions nearly identical, but the falsetto "ooh, ooh"'s sung over the tonic harmony in both tunes are unmistakably identical.

Many other factors reinforce the modeling suggested above. For example, similar instrumentation is used in all the examples cited. The lead and back-up vocal styles are consistently "Beatle-sque." There is even a clear effort to reproduce the recording techniques from the old records, with lead vocals double-tracked and instruments panned to extreme sides in the mix. These references, however, are to a more general Beatles competency: they do not refer to specific numbers, but rather to the early Beatles style (1963-65) generally.

Figure 4 displays and summarizes the references in "Hold My Hand."

Figure 4.

Text:	I Want to Hold Your Hand
	She Loves You (chorus)
	Please Please Me (verse)
Melody:	She Loves You
	All My Loving
Meter and Rhythm:	All My Loving
Harmony:	All My Loving (verse)
	She Loves You (chorus)

"Hold My Hand" can be viewed as a composite of the Beatles' songs mentioned. The humor arises from the listener's recognition of these models, and from the clever alterations and juxtaposition of the material. These specific references, though, operate according to a kind of collective principle; any single reference, taken alone, could be too subtle and escape detection. But taken collectively and in different musical dimensions, the references become mutually reinforcing. Both "All My Loving" and "She Loves You" are referenced in more than one dimension. "I Want to Hold Your Hand," however, seems to be referenced directly only in the textual dimension.[13]

In the case of "Hold My Hand," the listener's "Beatles competency" is challenged to first identify the models, and then to delight in their clever and unexpected juxtaposition. Without a highly developed Beatles competency, almost all of this type of listening response is absent. The ways in which a congruity-incongruity dialectic triggers this amused response will be discussed in more detail below; for now, it is enough to have noted that specific references do occur, and to have examined how they occur.

While "Hold My Hand" brings multiple sources of reference into play, there are other Rutles numbers which reference a single Beatles song. While it would be possible to discuss such Rutles numbers as "Doubleback Alley" ("Penny Lane") or "Piggy in the Middle" ("I am the Walrus"), I will instead stick with the early Beatles/Rutles numbers and consider the Rutles' fictitious 1965 release "Ouch!"

---

[13]One could perhaps build a case for harmonic modeling. The progression of "I Want To Hold Your Hand" is:

I | V | vi | iii | I | V | vi | iii | IV V | I vi | IV V | I ‖

Note that "Hold My Hand" moves from vi to iii, then from IV through iii and ii to V. IV and ii are syntactically interchangeable, and iii is merely connective; thus, the IV to ii movement is the syntactic equivalent of IV alone, and the harmonic movement in the two tunes could be viewed as equivalent.

While I have chosen not to make use of Schenkerian theory or reductive techniques throughout my paper, it is certainly possible to use those techniques to effectively analyze popular harmony. See, for example, Walter Everett, "Text-Painting in the Foreground and Middleground of Paul McCartney's Beatle Song, 'She's Leaving Home': A Musical Study of Psychological Conflict," *In Theory Only*, vol. 9, no. 4 (1987): 5-21, or Steve Larson, "Schenkerian Analysis of Modern Jazz," (Ph.D. diss., The University of Michigan, 1987).

There is one more obvious reference in "Hold My Hand": the guitar introduction is modeled on the one to the Beatles' "Eight Days a Week" (*Beatles* VI, Capitol ST2358). The harmonic progression is different but the type of guitar voicings used in the Rutles intro are so closely associated with the Beatles intro that no guitarist who knows both tunes could possibly miss the reference.

Covach, *The Rutles and Models in Musical Satire* 133

The title already indicates the source of the number, which is the Beatles' "Help!" Almost everything about the details of this piece are taken directly from the Beatles song: the lead and back-up vocals; the instrumentation, including the use of an acoustic 6-string guitar; the George Harrisonesque guitar fill which precedes each verse; the use of tambourine; the stop-time third verse; and the ending (complete with "add 6" vocals on "ooh"). In fact, according to this description, it might at first seem as if "Ouch!," with its point of reference being so obvious, is bound to be less interesting than the multi-referencing "Hold My Hand." But there is a feature of the harmonic movement of "Ouch!" which, though modeled on "Help!," actually creates a kind of dialogue between the model and the copy—a dialogue which depends in a crucial way on the proper identification of the model.

Example 5 provides an excerpt from the verse section to each number, while Figure 5 compares the harmonic progressions for those section:

Figure 5.

"Ouch!"

    C: I | iii | ii | V | I | bVII | IV | V :‖

"Help!"

    A: I | I | iii | iii | vi | vi | IV bVII | I :‖

"Ouch!" uses the I - iii progression from "Help!," though the harmonic rhythm of the former is half that of the latter. The IV - bVII - I movement characterizes the second half of the "Help!" verse; "Ouch!" uses its inverse, I - bVII - IV. These alterations, while creating a new harmonic progression, retain much of the harmonic character of the model. All that is missing in "Ouch!" is the use of the submediant harmony, and it is being withheld for a reason.

Example 5.   a) Excerpt from "Help!" (verse); b) excerpt from "Ouch!" (verse).

Covach, *The Rutles and Models in Musical Satire* 135

Example 6. a) "Help!," intro; b) "Ouch!," chorus/intro.

Example 6. (cont'd.)

Figure 6.

"Ouch!"

        C: vi | vi | IV | IV | II7 | bVI bVII | I | I   ‖

"Help!"

        G: ii | ii | ii | ii |bVII |bVII |bVII |bVII |
        V7 | V7 | V7 | V7 | I | I | I | I   ‖

"Help!" (intro)

        G: ii | ii | bVII | bVII | V7 | V7 | I | I   ‖

    Example 6 represents the chorus of "Ouch!" (which also
functions as the intro) and the intro of "Help!"; Figure 6 compares
the chorus section of "Ouch!" with the chorus and intro of "Help!"
The "Help!" chorus begins on ii, moves through bVII to V7, and
arrives at I. The "Ouch!" chorus, on the other hand, moves from

Covach, *The Rutles and Models in Musical Satire* 137

vi to IV, then on to II7, and ends with the startling bVI - bVII - I movement (see "P.S. I Love You," cited above). The "Help!" chorus, like the verse, moves at a harmonic rhythm twice as slow as that of "Ouch!" The "Help!" intro and the "Ouch!" chorus/intro, however, move at the same harmonic rhythm.

Because of the close modeling, the "Ouch!" verse can be seen to first articulate part of the progression literally (but with the harmonic rhythm in diminution) and, second, to reorder another part of it, retaining the characteristic chromatic alteration (bVII). This can only be detected if the listener is able to maintain some version of the "Help!" verse in the ear (and a synchronic one, at that), while taking in the "Ouch!" verse.

Further, the "Ouch!" chorus constitutes a large musical pun on the "Help!" chorus and intro. As was mentioned above, the vi chord is missing in the verse of "Ouch!" It arrives only in the chorus. But when it arrives the progression moves vi - IV - II7. The "Help!" chorus moves ii - bVII - V7. The pun arises because both progressions move from a minor triad to a major triad with a root a major third lower, then on to a major-minor seventh chord with a root a minor third below that. But the "Help!" progression begins on ii, while the "Ouch!" one begins on vi. It is clear that the vi chord is excluded from the verse of "Ouch!" so that it can be used in the chorus pun. When the II7 chord arrives in "Ouch!," we are still one harmonic move away from where we need to be to conform to the movement of the model, which is at V7 at that point in the progression. The "Ouch!" progression then moves hurriedly via bVI and bVII to I, as if caught off guard, creating the awkward II7 - bVI movement. The mere continuation of the harmonic movement from II7 on to V would have achieved the desired harmonic goal; the awkward II7 - bVI - bVII - I movement, however, amounts to a "harmonic pratfall," which serves to further highlight the comedic intent of the pun worked out in the harmonic progression immediately preceding it. "Ouch!," therefore, references a single Beatles song, and the closeness of the modeling permits the perception of the harmonic pun and pratfall.

We have now examined two songs in which specific references can be detected; but these references trigger an amused response in different ways. How can these different mechanisms be accounted for? And how does the congruity-incongruity dialectic—which is central to eliciting an amused response in the Spinal Tap numbers—operate to elicit an amused response in the Rutles examples? These questions can be addressed by combining Meyer's theory of style with the semiotic concept of "intertextuality."

I would like first to review those aspects of Meyer's style theory useful to the discussion which will follow. In his discussion of compositional choice, Meyer makes the distinction between dialect, idiom, and intraopus style:

> Dialectics are substyles that are differentiated because a number of composers—usually, but not necessarily, contemporaries and geographical neighbors—employ (choose) the same or similar rules and strategies.[14]

For our purposes, all the examples cited in the discussion of "Hold My Hand" and "Ouch!" are considered to be within the "British-invasion dialect" (which might also be considered a sub-dialect of the larger popular music dialect).

Meyer goes on to define idiom as follows:

> Within any dialect, individual composers tend to employ some constraints rather than others; indeed, they may themselves have devised new constraints. Those that a composer repeatedly selects from the larger repertory of the dialect define his or her individual idiom.[15]

---

[14]Meyer, 23.

[15]Meyer, 24.

Covach, *The Rutles and Models in Musical Satire*   139

All the examples discussed above could further be classified as in the "early Beatles idiom."[16]

Finally, Meyer introduces the notion of intraopus style, which he carefully distinguishes from intraopus structure:

> While dialect has to do with what is common to works by different composers, and idiom has to do with what is common to different works by the same composer, intraopus style is concerned with what is replicated within a single work. . . .

> The intraopus style of a work must be distinguished from what I will term its *intraopus structure*. When a pattern is viewed as an aspect of the intraopus style of a work it is understood as a replicated, classlike event. But every pattern within a work also enters into nonrecurrent relationships with each and every other event or pattern in that work. Thus understood as nonrecurrent and unique, the pattern is an aspect of the work's intraopus structure.[17]

Meyer's distinction between intraopus style and structure seems to rest on a synchronic-diachronic distinction: aspects of style are viewed synchronically and are associative, while aspects of structure are viewed diachronically and achieve significance as much from "where" they are as from "what" they are.

It is precisely at this level of intraopus style and structure that the difference in the operation of the humor mechanism in our two Rutles examples may be found. There is no incongruity in either tune at the level of dialect or idiom; either number could pass for

---

[16]While Meyer, considering the repertory of Western art music, refers to a single composer, I take the liberty here of referring to the early Beatles as an idiom in spite of the fact that there are two composers, Lennon and McCartney and five arrangers (add Harrison, Starr, and producer George Martin).

[17]Meyer, 24-5.

an authentic but lost Beatles tune, and consequently as an authentic artifact of the British invasion.[18]

At the level of intraopus style, "Ouch!" takes over most of the intraopus constraints of "Help!"; but "Ouch!" unfolds a different intraopus structure from that of "Help!" Due to the shared intraopus stylistic constraints (which account for the suggestion of modeling in the first place), "Ouch!" could be thought of as a recomposition of "Help!," or perhaps, as an alternative structural manifestation of common intraopus constraints and features.[19]

The humor in "Ouch!," however, is partially the result of intertextuality. This concept, as it is used in the field of literary criticism generally, "derives from the view of a literary work as a text whose richness of meaning results from its location in a potentially infinite network of other texts."[20] For our study of the

---

[18]In fact, according to Beatles expert Walter Everett, the Rutles tune "Cheese and Onions" (mentioned above) actually appeared on some Beatles bootleg albums, apparently passing for authentic with Beatles fans. Walter Everett shared this with me during one of the many conversations we have had concerning the Rutles.

[19]Meyer discusses the application of his style theory to the study of sketches and drafts. While Meyer values the discovery of what "might have been," believing that this knowledge enhances an encounter with the final version, a different situation arises when we have an alternative version (Bruckner), or versions which are substantially recomposed (Beethoven's "Eroica Variations," his overture to *The Creatures of Prometheus*, and the final movement to his Symphony No. 3); in these two latter situations one cannot invoke the same reasoning to establish the priority of one piece over the other. One would need to determine to what extent the versions either shared a common intraopus style, or have more or less similar ones.

[20]Robert S. Hatten, "The Place of Intertextuality in Music Studies, *American Journal of Semiotics*, vol. 3, no. 4 (1985): 69-82. Hatten also suggests the use of style theory to explain intertextual references in music, providing a number of examples. In the same issue, see Thais E. Morgan, "Is There an Intertext in This Text?: Literary and Interdisciplinary Approaches to Intertextuality": 1-40, an extremely helpful survey.

As Robert Scholes has pointed out, the terms "intertext" and "intertextuality" have different meanings for semioticians like Roland Barthes, Julia Kristeva, Gerard Gennette, and Michael Riffaterre. Scholes defines the concept as follows:

> The common principle is that, just as signs refer to other signs rather than directly to things, texts refer to other texts. The artist writes and paints, not from nature but from his or her predecessors' ways of textualizing nature. Thus an intertext is a text lurking inside another, shaping meaning, whether the author is conscious of this or not. (p. 145)

Covach, *The Rutles and Models in Musical Satire*   141

humor in "Ouch!," it is enough to know that this text invokes another very strongly (through close modeling). The amused response depends upon the listener's recognition of this specific intertextual reference. In fact, the listener is asked to hold the intertext ("Help!") in mind while "reading" the first text, and this dual imaging will result in a simultaneous reading of both texts. The amused response arises through a process of constant comparison, with the musical mind quickly darting back and forth between the heard text and the invoked intertext. The listener therefore perceives the two texts as congruent at the dialect and idiom level ("that sounds like the Beatles!"); depending on one's level of Beatles competency, the listener may notice the congruence at the level of intraopus style ("that sounds like "Help!"). The last step crucial to eliciting an amused response is when the listener realizes the incongruity in the two intraopus structures ("Hey, this is kind of different; it sounds like "Help!" but it's not!"). It is the intertextuality which sets the stage for the congruity-incongruity dialectic: by the direct referencing of "Help!," "Ouch!" initiates the dialectic which triggers the amused response.

Figure 7 diagrams the relationships which I have just described.

Figure 7.

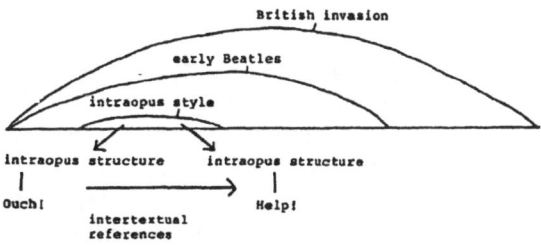

See Robert Scholes, *Semiotics and Interpretation* (New Haven and London: Yale University Press, 1982).

For the purposes of the following discussion, I would adapt the definition to read "the artist writes, paints, and composes," and ". . . lurking inside another, shaping meaning (sometimes humorous), whether . . ."

The Help-Ouch intraopus style is contained within the early Beatles idiom, which is contained within the British-invasion dialect. The two intraopus structures are generated out of the single intraopus style, and the intertextual references are shown by the arrow (note that these references are one-way).

"Hold My Hand," however, presents a slightly different situation with regard to intertextuality; the modeling is not based on a single intertext, but rather on the conflation of multiple intertexts. Figure 8 diagrams the network of relations in "Hold My Hand."

Figure 8.

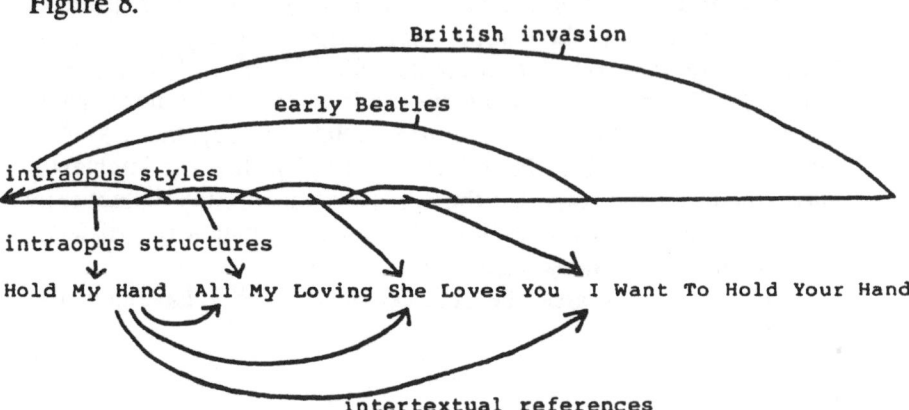

Figure 8 illustrates how the four songs shown each have an intraopus style which is contained within the early Beatles idiom, and how each has an intraopus structure generated out of its respective intraopus style. The figure therefore attempts to portray the more varied network of references which occurs in "Hold My Hand."[21]

While "Ouch!" requires the listener to hold the single intertext in mind, "Hold My Hand" requires the listener to identify various

---

[21]Since some part of the intraopus style/structures of the three Beatles songs is incorporated into the Rutles tune, adding a third dimension to my diagram would allow me to arrange the three Beatles numbers around the Rutles one such that they all intersect with it but not with each other.

intertexts; the listener first recognizes the congruence at the level of idiom ("that sounds like the Beatles!") but then notices the incongruity at the level of intraopus style <u>and</u> structure ("that sounds like "All My Loving"—no, it's "She Loves You"—no, now it's "I Want To Hold Your Hand," etc.). The differences between the mechanisms can therefore be located in Meyer's model: "Ouch!" exploits incongruity between the respective intraopus structures, while "Hold My Hand" exploits incongruities at the level of intraopus style (which by extension includes the structures generated out of each intraopus style).

Further, "Hold My Hand" participates in an even more complicated intertextual relationship. Michael Riffaterre, in his *Semiotics of Poetry*, describes something he terms an "implied intertext."[22] An implied intertext is a second intertext which explains or clarifies the reference to the first intertext.

Something very like Riffaterre's implied intertext is invoked in the Rutles song "Love Life," which is modeled unmistakably on the Beatles' "All You Need Is Love." In the closing moments of "All You Need Is Love" the Beatles quote "She Loves You" by singing "she loves you, yeah, yeah, yeah" over the fading phrase "love is all you need." The Rutles quote "Hold My Hand" by singing "hold my hand, yeah, yeah" over the closing phrase "love is the meaning of life, life is the meaning of love."

Now if the listener knows both "All You Need Is Love" and "Love Life," but not "Hold My Hand," one can only suspect that the Rutles are referencing some tune from their past (a parallel to the Beatles quoting a number from their past). But with a knowl-

---

[22]Michael Riffaterre, *Semiotics of Poetry* (Bloomington: Indiana University Press, 1979), 134. Morgan, pp. 31-32, provides an interesting discussion and interpretation of Riffaterre's notion.

It just so happens that Riffaterre's discussion of the implied intertext occurs during his discussion of humor in poetry. Interesting to my discussion is that Riffaterre asserts, in the course of discussing the poem he uses as an example, that "intertextual incompatibilities ... create the humor ..."(130). He also comes to conclude in this section that "humor is nothing other than a special case of poetic language, and that poetic language is a special case of metalanguage" (138). This latter statement has some bearing on the suggestion that the mechanisms that elicit an amused response and those which elicit an aesthetic one may be closely related, as suggested below in the text.

edge of the intertextual relationships we examined in "Hold My Hand," the reference to it in "Love Life" becomes a more complicated and richer one. Thus "Hold My Hand" becomes the implied intertext and the humor in "Love Life" is enriched for the listener possessing the competency to make this complex set of associations.

The examination of the mechanisms which elicit an amused response in the two Rutles numbers considered above suggests that the combination of Meyer's theory of style and the semiotic notion of intertextuality could have a broader application. Meyer's theory provides a powerful tool in explaining how intertextuality—of a musical kind, using strictly musical terms—can occur in music. I have suggested elsewhere that the mechanism that elicits an amused response in music may be very like the one that elicits an aesthetic response.[23] If the semiotic-musical style model offered above is helpful in unpacking the amused response, it might also prove helpful in examining music not intended to be humorous.

To conclude this study, I will suggest how Meyer's model can help us pull together both the Rutles and the Spinal Tap examples. In fact, a comparison of the Rutles numbers with the Spinal Tap one suggests the following: the differences between the humor mechanisms of each example can be accounted for locating where in Meyer's model the incongruity arises. For example, the interstylistic incongruity between "Heavy Duty" and the Boccherini minuet can be thought of as occurring between the dialect of classic music and the dialect of heavy metal. Similarly, the incongruity in "(Listen to the) Flower People" arises between popular music (sub-)dialects (British invasion and psychedelia). The incongruity in "Cups and Cakes" occurs between idioms (unlikely juxtapositions of idioms create a dialectical exaggeration). This leaves "Hold My Hand," with the incongruity occurring between intraopus styles, and "Ouch!," with the incongruity occurring between intraopus structures. As a general rule, the levels above the location of the incongruity are congruent.

---

[23]Covach.

[21]

The aesthetics of music video: an analysis of Madonna's 'Cherish'

CAROL VERNALLIS

When we become engaged with a music video, what draws us in? What constitutes craft or artistry in the genre? Theorists of music video have usually addressed these questions from the perspective of sociology, film theory or popular cultural studies. Film theory, in particular, has had a tremendous influence on the analysis of music video, because of the two genres' apparently similar structuring of sound and image. But by the criteria of film, music videos tend to come off as failed narratives; the genre's effectiveness eludes explanation.

Much has been written about the ways that advertising, film, television sitcoms and newscasts have borrowed from the rhetoric of music video. However, there has yet to be a detailed analysis of any one video, an analysis that can describe how particular moments are set up and departed from and why some moments seem important and others less so.[1] This absence of close readings results in part from the difficulties associated with analysing music, particularly popular music. Nor are there adequate theories of how music and image might work together to create a hybrid form. The need for such a theory has been emphasised by a number of theorists, including Alf Björnberg, John Fiske, Dick Hebdige, and Susan McClary. Andrew Goodwin is the most outspoken in his call for a reading that would reflect musical concerns:

In the study of music television a number of major lacunae are evident, but underlying many of them is the neglect of the music itself. This deafening silence in the corridors of the academy combines with an overestimation of the power of the visual to disfigure the study of music television. (1992, p. 2)

As Goodwin suggests, no one has attempted an analysis that takes musical codes, processes, and techniques as providing means by which video image can be structured.

This article attempts to accomplish such goals. It provides both a description of the ways that musical and visual codes operate in a music video, and an in-depth analysis that shows these operations at work in a temporal flow. These two modes, one largely taxonomical and the other more processual, work together to inform us about music video as an artistic practice and as an ideological apparatus. If we attend to the particular features of a single video, we can begin to understand how music video works as a distinct medium. It is by attending to these features – many of which would be called aesthetic features – that we can learn about music video's modes of representing race, gender, and sexuality. The first section of this article looks at aspects of 'Cherish' in order to develop the analytical tools for reading music video, drawing from music theory and popular music studies. The second section provides a chronological reading of the entire video, as well as close analyses of two particular sections. The final section takes up more fully the video's representations of race, gender and sexuality.

Section one

The 'Cherish' video

As a clip on Madonna's *Immaculate Collection*, 'Cherish' is one of the most widely available music videos. The video is set on the beach. Madonna lip-syncs from the shoreline, wearing a dark, wet, form-fitting dress. A group of mermen swim further out, in formations reminiscent of Busby Berkeley. A boy/merchild moves between Madonna and the mermen. 'Cherish' was seen by critics as designed in part to provide an opportunity for Madonna to display her newly muscle-bound physique; but it was at the same time undeniably arty, in the whimsical myth-making of the mermen, and through being shot in black and white.

The video is directed by photographer Herb Ritts, and reflects the same impulses as Ritts' still photography; as Allen Ellenzweig (1992, p. 188) says about Ritts' photographs, the video exaggerates the heroic statuesque, yet also gives a sense of weightlessness and transparency. Ritts might be described as a video-artist with a 'classical' impulse: in 'Cherish' all musical parameters are reflected in the image with a sense of clarity and balance. It can therefore serve as a model for describing the issues encountered in many music videos. Other videos place greater emphasis on tension and contrast; nevertheless, 'Cherish' makes a useful text for showing the nature of correspondence generally, its evenhandedness, notwithstanding. While other videos do not achieve, or even attempt, the balanced structure of 'Cherish', they use many of the same techniques.

'Cherish' is remarkable for the way that it reflects both local musical features and larger sections. One of the video's most unusual aspects is the strong, clean contours that it traces across edited images. The clarity of these lines enables Ritts to make the video into a large form which responds to a viewer's changing experience of the song. Ritts' classicism can also be discerned in the grace and self-restraint with which he treats both the figure of Madonna and the imagery of gay desire.

Because a music video must – above all – sell the artist and a particular song, the degree of self-restraint demanded of its director can be considerable. A director must usually abandon hope of creating a traditional narrative, even one which the song's lyrics relate. Moreover, he or she will often find that the pressure exerted by the song prevents the accurate representation of fixed objects: objects in music video will tend to shimmer, change continually, and threaten to fade away. Some directors, including Ritts, have developed strategies better suited to the conventional requirements of music video. What Ritts' work on 'Cherish' suggests, and what is shown by other videos, is that music video image can relinquish qualities traditionally associated with vision and adopt those that resemble the experiential qualities of sound. Walter Ong's characterisation of the differences between sonic and visual perception can provide a useful basis for comparison:

Sight isolates, sound incorporates. Whereas sight situates the observer outside what he views, at a distance, sound pours into the hearer. Vision dissects ... When I hear, however, I gather sound simultaneously from every direction at once: I am at the centre of my auditory world, which envelops me, establishing me at a kind of core of sensation and existence ... By contrast with vision, the dissecting sense, sound is thus a unifying sense ... The auditory ideal, by contrast, is harmony, a putting together. (1985, p. 32)

Ong's description of sound reveals perfectly the qualities of the image in a music video like 'Cherish'. In 'Cherish', the image reflects sonic properties through its continuity of motion, most clearly in the imagery of the ocean. The permeability of the water's surface and the force of the waves set the tone for the video, helping us to notice that the boundary between natural and mythic, or human and animal, has also become permeable in the figure of the boy/merchild. The dynamic nature of sound is also reflected through editing, as shots lose their sense of focus when they move towards the edit point. The inevitable decay of sounds shows in the way that figures move away from us, and in a natural process like the approach of dusk.

Flow

The muscular movement of the huge figures in slow motion, almost pulling themselves through the space, along with the waves rushing to and fro, gives the 'Cherish' video a particular feel, which might be called a capacity to carry the viewer through the video (Figure 1). This parallels the way that the propulsive elements in the music – the bass line, the rolling drum tracks, the harmonic motion – create and maintain the song's momentum.

This sense of pull characterises the feel of many videos, and helps to distance the feel of music video from that of most narrative film. David Bordwell (1985, p. 54) argues that narrative films place viewers in a position of mastery. These films, he says, are edited in such a way as to create the illusion that the viewer owns a secure position in the space, from which they can judge the action objectively. In 'Cherish', as in many videos, the viewer is drawn through the space by the constant motion within the frame. The searching eye of the camera moves too much to provide the viewer with a stable position. This kind of camera movement exists in a give-and-take with the figures, as they lead us through the space, and with the waves, as they rush forward and back. The song's groove – the rhythmic figures whose momentum continues across sectional divisions – works with the image's continuous motion to encourage the viewer to give up their secure position and go along with the ride.

Another way that the image helps to pull us through the video is in the passage from shot to shot. First there is the edit, then a gradual establishment of motion, and then a lunge into a state of right proportion – the perfect photographic moment. Conventional film editing is designed to make the connections between images appear seamless except during periods of crosscutting and accelerated montage. Issues of repetition and variation within edits are played down. In 'Cherish', as in many music videos, the edit and the movement within the shot are highlighted for their ability to establish a characteristic rhythm – which in this instance can be bluntly stated as a three-part structure of catch, pull and hold.

There are several rhythmic strata of the music: the slower harmonic rhythm, the basic pulse in the drums, and the quicker tambourine articulations. We can also sense a similar rhythmic stratification in the image: the momentum of the waves;

Figure 1. Flow – the muscular movement of the figures carries the viewer through the video.

the movement of the camera – hand-held by Ritts himself; the pace established through editing; the athletic movements of Madonna and the mermen; and the fine visual articulations created through reflected light off sand and surf, the spikiness of the figure's hair, and the spray and foam from the ocean. These structures support one another, helping the viewer appreciate a level of detail that might well be overlooked in the song. Similarly, the rhythmic organisation of the song gives focus to the image.

Continuity

Traditional theory describes melodies as growing outward by preserving certain features and varying others. Part of the way that a sense of line is created is through

Figure 2. Musical continuity – in a series of shots, the figures' heads pop up. The images support a vertical orientation.

a quality of self-similarity among the materials of a video. Here, some parameters stay constant across a series of shots – for example, the side flank of a merman and a side flank of Madonna; the mermen pop up and Madonna pops up and puts her hands on her head; Madonna sashays back and the fish tail correspondingly slinks back into the water (Figure 2). In traditional Hollywood narrative, the editing techniques work to suggest the viewer's mastery of the space (through shot/reverse shot, 180-degree rule, eyeline match and point-of-view (Bordwell 1985, pp. 55–7)). Music videos forego such mastery in order to create the sense of a continuous line. The editing attempts to keep the eye moving fluently through the space in a way that supports the directionality of the song.

Contour

The musical lines in a piece of music – the melody, the bass, the inner voices – have contours; composers often talk about these musical lines as visual shapes.[2] In music video, the shape of the musical line can correlate to the shape of the visual image. There may be a few reasons for this. We have, perhaps, a culturally learned disposition to categorise movement by high–low relationships. Register often correlates to a sky and ground orientation. For an example, think of the cartoon figure of Wile E. Coyote falling, as the high pitch drops, and conversely of Orson Welles' famous opera-house scene in *Citizen Kane*, in which the voice 'soars' higher and higher as the camera moves up towards, and then through, the ceiling of the opera house. (Imagine the opposite effect – the coyote falling and the pitch rising.) We also have

158 *Carol Vernallis*

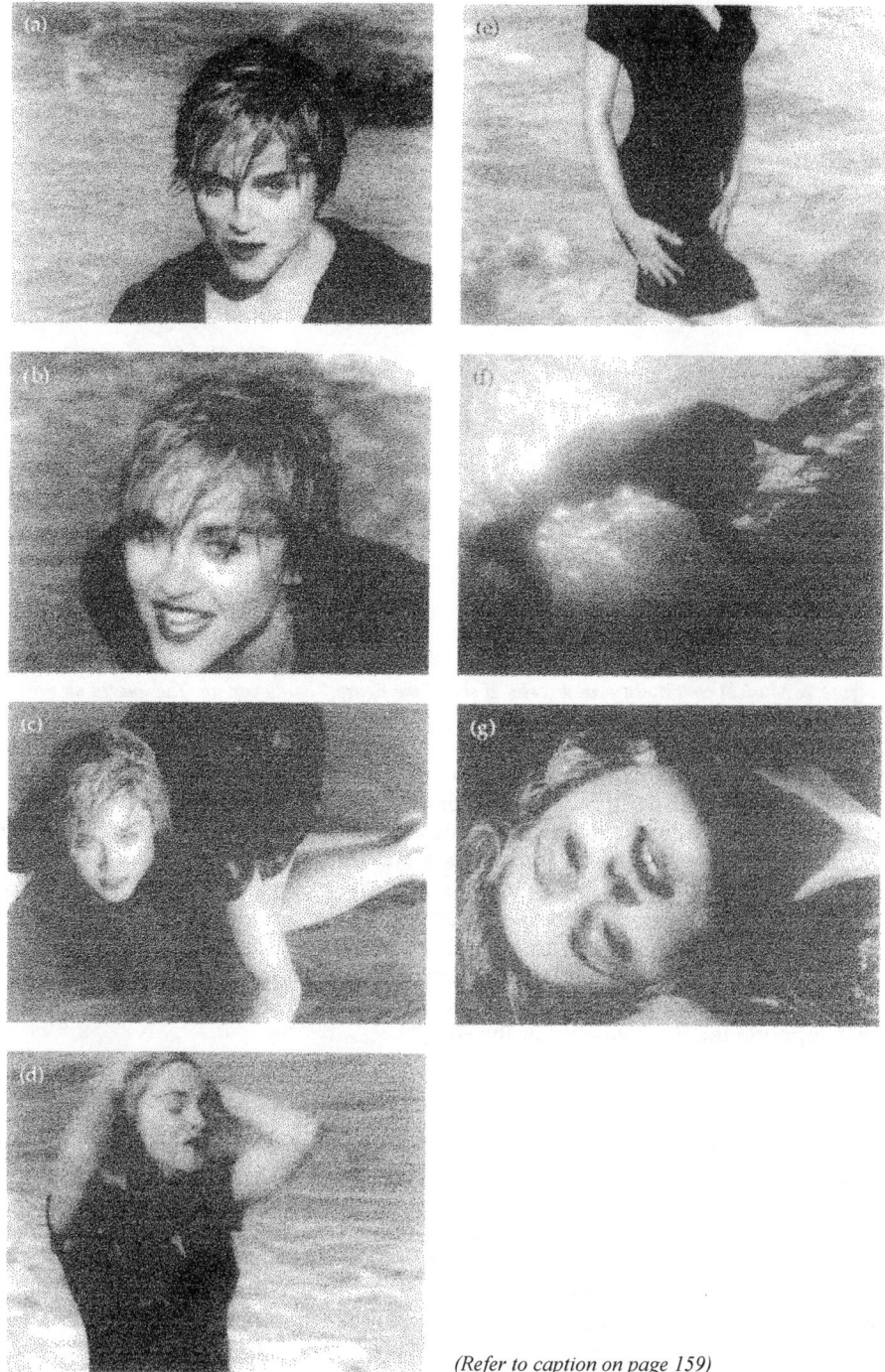

(Refer to caption on page 159)

a disposition to scan photos and paintings, as we read, from left to right. Many music videos assist in our desire to scan the image by moving from left to right, including 'Cherish', Metallica's 'Everywhere I Roam', and U2's 'With or Without You'. (One rare exception, Metallica's 'The Unforgiven', moves from right to left, but here movement signifies disintegration and disillusionment.) Spatial and aural shapes can also correlate to emotional affects.

Musicologists have noted that, within a piece of music, melodic contours relate closely to the affect we perceive in the music (Meyer 1989, pp. 128–9). Jagged lines produce music that seems anxious and intense. Lines with a narrow ambitus seem more meditative. The contours of an image have qualities similarly suggestive of certain affects: tall is courageous; flat or near the ground is safe; off angle is unstable.[3] We respond to imagery and music that work together to reflect these spatial relationships. At the high points of phrases, hard rock and heavy metal artists will jump toward the top of the screen and fireworks will go off. Bon Jovi's 'Livin' on a Prayer' provides one good example. At the end of musical sections, the image often seems to darken, to slow down and collapse into itself. In the first verse of the 'Cherish' video, the highest pitch in the voice (D4) is accompanied by the image of a cresting merman. The verse closes with a shot of Madonna on the sand, which provides balance, followed by a fade to black. The undulation of the melodic line is supported by the curved shapes traced by the figures within the frame. Images of height, depth and balance correspond, respectively, to high points, low points and moments of stability in the vocal line (Figure 3). A more precise description of the musical and visual contours is included in section II.

Form

The video traces many large-scale structures: a gradual shift from day to evening, an implied maturation of the boy – being born, growing up, and separating from Madonna; and a tracing of the human body – there are more shots of heads in the beginning, more torsos and hips in the middle, and more legs and feet towards the end of the video.

Music videos often sketch a large-scale formal design that matches the large scale musical structure; for example, in Madonna's 'Like A Prayer' and 'Open Your Heart' videos, the sections of the music continually return in their original form, and the space can be seen as built upon a spiral. 'Cherish' seems more continuous, less repetitive,[4] and the image's sense of motion from left to right and of continual

Figure 3. Contours – in support of the contours of the primary contrapuntal lines, there are images of height, depth and balance.
a) Madonna dips as the melody drops a tone and returns. Lyrics: 'broken hearts'.
b) Madonna bends forward as the melody drops a major third. Lyrics: 'before I start this dance'.
c) Madonna crouches as the melody drops a fifth at the end of the period. Lyrics: 'more than just a romance'.
d) Madonna stands erect as the melody centres itself at a fifth above the opening. Lyrics: 'You are my destiny'.
e) Madonna drops her hands to her hips – the listener may hear the drop of a fifth, and perhaps may even pick out the falling line A–G–F♯–E–D from the instrumental texture. Lyrics: 'Can't you see?'
f) The merman crests underwater and the melody reaches its high point. Lyrics: 'Cupid, please'.
g) The image of Madonna's head following after the figure of the merman has a quality of balance. The melody rests on A. Lyrics: 'Take your aim at me'.

branching outward matches this aspect of the song. In the 'Cherish' video, both music and image create large sectional divisions. These sectional divisions can be seen in the shot-by-shot description of the video and the transcription of the song's lyrics. I have included a transcription of the lyrics and a brief video 'narrative', as the analysis often refers to specific points in the song (Appendices A and B). Most importantly, over the course of the video, music and image shift from a state of close interdependence, to a greater degree of freedom, to a return to synchronisation in the closing section.[5]

Basic shape

Many music theorists argue that a primary musical motive changes continually throughout a piece, providing a key to the piece's structure (Reti 1978, pp. 13–14). The most obvious example might be the first eight notes from Beethoven's *Fifth Symphony*. This is the basic building-block that informs the whole of the first movement. Music video image often works similarly by presenting a recurrent shape. In 'Cherish', an arch shape occurs at several different formal/temporal levels[6] (Figure 4). There is a secondary emphasis on spiral motion, which functions as a tranformation of this basic shape (Figure 5).

There are arching contours in the song, but their perceptibility is hard to ascertain. The melody of the verse forms an arch as it sweeps up an octave and then drops a fourth. The bass line, too, has a wide ambitus. The song's smallest identifiable group of pitches – a leap followed by a step in the opposite direction – forms an arch, and some of the transformations of this cell – through addition of another step – continue to retain the arch shape. Similarly, one can hear spiral shapes in some of the melodic materials. In any case, the idea of a basic shape remains a useful analytical concept for music video image, even in cases in which the song's melodic materials do not reflect this shape. Pop songs, of course, do not get written according to the logic of motivic development, and hooks – a related analytical concept that is more useful here – can as easily be rhythmic, timbral, harmonic or verbal as they can be melodic. Connections between visual motives and the song's hooks, therefore, will often come down to a question of affective resemblance across media.

Motive

In the 'Cherish' video, some of the song's most prominent melodic shapes are linked to visual motives. In the chorus, the melodic gesture F#–G–A–D, which has a quick moving harmonic background, is often associated with Madonna's assertively taking three steps forward. When, in the verse, the synthesizer rises above the voice to hit a high D, a wave or a hand crowns Madonna's head. When she then sings a high D, we see her coming forward in a state of suspension, or with a merman swimming above us in an arc. In both the chorus and the verse, a shot of Madonna's half-moon face is often associated with an ebb in the melodic line. These last examples help to delineate the phrase structure of the music. For example, Madonna's round face carries an inertial force that slows down the visual material so that it is able to keep in sync with the

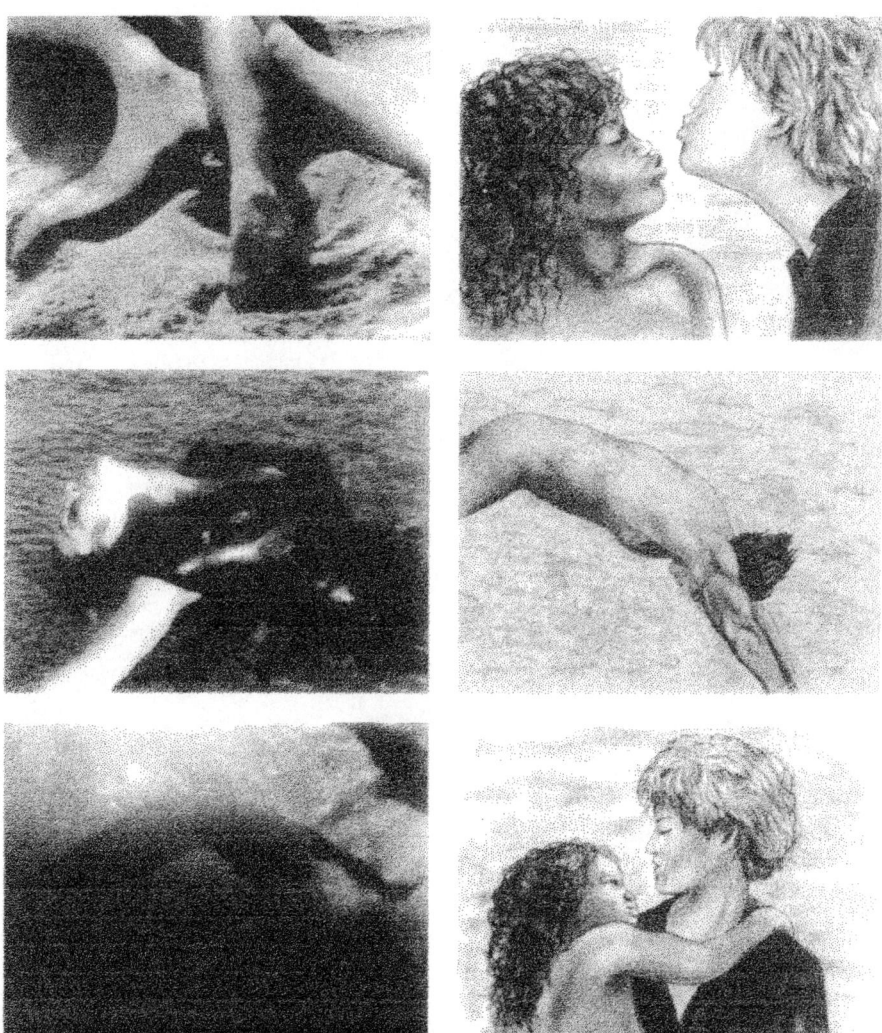

Figure 4. Basic shape – an arch shape occurs throughout the video. Note that two-thirds into the video, the arch shape begins to stretch across edited images.

music. The repeated image of her half-moon face – most often occurring at a point two-thirds into the verse – becomes a marker that the verse will soon end.

Phrase

The image, in 'Cherish', forms small sections closely related to the phrases of the music. In the first verse and chorus, the image parallels the music by beginning with a strong articulation and ending with a movement toward a closing lilt that leads us into the next phrase.[7] In 'Cherish', the most clearly articulated moments are those that serve to emphasise the beginnings and endings of musical sections.

Figure 5. Basic shape – a spiral pattern occurs throughout the video. Figures twist, turning clockwise or counterclockwise, towards and away from us.

At the opening of every section, the image begins with a sharp visual attack. As the energy of the musical section is used up, so is that of the image. Fade-outs help further to close sections (Figure 6).

Lyrics

Lyrics, in 'Cherish' as in most videos, provide only one among many kinds of material to attend to. As might be expected, the hook-line or -word in 'Cherish' is strongly underscored – the imagery is focused on expressing an imperative ('cherish!'). The pseudo-high diction that marks much of the song (in phrases like 'I'll perish the thought'), along with the references to Cupid and to Romeo and

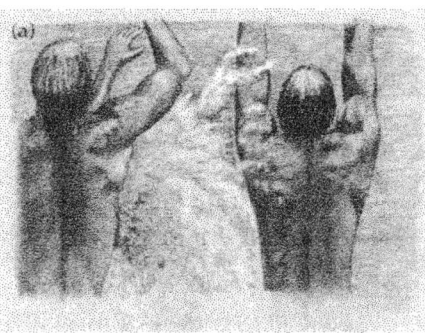

Figure 6. (a) *The beginnings of phrases and sections* (b) *The close of a phrase and section* (c) *Internal articulation of a phrase*

Juliet, contribute to both the nostalgic character of the music and the whimsical myth-making of the video. Lyrics that have a strongly performative or theatrical dimension in Madonna's vocal performance ('Who? You!') receive confirmation of this quality in her deliberately stagey turn towards the camera followed by her and the merboy's playful mouthing of the word 'you!'. One might also suggest that the line 'can't get away, I won't let you' might have encouraged the director to let the boy make a run for it.

Direct word painting – we hear the word 'bell' and see the image of a bell – is less common, however. More frequent is a linking of image, word and music that is more tenuous and enigmatic. For example, there may be a lag between the delivery of a lyric and the appearance of a corresponding image. There may also be a confusion over what the lyrics point to. For example, the phrase 'Cupid, please take your aim at me', in the context of the video's opening – the shot of Madonna's hips, followed by an undulating merman – might be read as a wish for closer connections among the figures, or even, in the larger context of the video, for impregnation. This reading might inspire the viewer to reconsider all the lyrics, the image, and the music that has come before.

Timbre and texture

Frequently, the sound world of the song provides stronger associations for the videomaker than do the lyrics, and can exert a greater influence upon the video. In 'Cherish', though no lyrics refer to mermen or to water, the snare and tambourine, the voice, the multi-layered chorus accompanied by its glittery synthesized timbres, the sibilants 'ch' and 'sh' all have a white noise component that we might associate with foaming, rushing water and the prismatic light reflected off the ocean and the sand. Each character corresponds by association to one of the song's countermelodies, and these correspondences – built upon a familiar connection between physical size and registral placement – reflect gender and power stereotypes. The mermen are associated with a synthesized saxophone in its lower register, Madonna with a sassy synthesized trumpet in the middle register, and the merboy with a slightly comic synthesizer patch in the high register.[8] Later in the analysis, we will see that the video questions the primacy of Madonna relative to the mermen and the boy – on this hierarchical plane, all of the figures have an opportunity to move into the foreground.

The bass line, with the bass drum, gives the image its impetus for movement. In a successful music video, the video can trick the viewer into believing that the image and the music are so closely intertwined that the image is spurred on by the propulsiveness of the sound, or conversely, that the image sparks activity in the music. In 'Cherish', what animates the figures is mysterious. We almost never see the fins and feet as they animate the figures. Instead, it seems that it is the bass line, as it moves toward and then over the crest of its line, that propels the images onward. When the bass line takes on a different type of musical authority, we have a different type of motion. For example, in the bridge, when the bass arpeggiates two root-position triads, Madonna skips sideways through the water. When the bass line drops out – at the end of Bridge 1, there is a long, held chord without the bass – the figures seem to lack momentum: here, there is the sustained image of a dragging fish-tail. Similarly, at the end of Bridge 2, when there is a repeated chordal guitar riff, with a reduced accompaniment, Madonna slinks back into the water.[9]

Other, more tenuous, sound-image connections include the imagery of the clinging wet cloth on Madonna's body, the snugly fitting costumes on the mermen, and the water flowing against Madonna's flesh and her dress, any or all of which might stand in for the synthesizer line that wraps around and closely tracks the voice. By contrast, the finer rhythmic articulations might be carried by the spikiness of Madonna's hair and the fine detail of the foaming water.

The song is mixed in such a way that none of the backing tracks are brought to the fore. The prominent bass line commands more attention because it moves more actively, not because of any emphasis in the mix; the goal of the production must have been to create a wall of sound that places all the backing tracks on an equal plane. To complement this approach, the images of Madonna, the mermen, and the child are correspondingly huge and engulfing. Nevertheless, the arrangement varies as percussion, bass and backing vocals are added or drop out, and, more subtly, as the reverberation effects on Madonna's voice change through the song. Similarly, the video makes an issue of how Madonna and the mermen move closer to or further away from us within our field of vision. For example, when she sings the words 'who' and 'you', her voice comes to the front of the mix and she advances towards the viewer. The beginning and end of the song are produced to sound distant, and it follows that the figures appear small and move away from us.

These local sound-image connections play a large part in shaping the video. What I can only call the nostalgic quality of the video originates in various aspects of the song. Besides the archaic touches of the lyrics, there is the swing rhythm (perhaps always nostalgic), the finger snaps, Madonna's chirpy, child-like voice, the girl-group backing vocals, and the hook-line taken from the Association's 1966 hit 'Cherish', all of which allude to earlier pop music. It is also important to recognise that the song's arrangement scheme, production values and performance styles had been in place for at least five years before the release of 'Cherish' in the summer of 1989.[10] These conservative qualities, along with the song's pop acumen, help to bring its retrospective dimension to the fore.

Harmony

The song's harmonic language emphasises smooth, sometimes almost elliptical motion, using a large number of first- and second-inversion chords, and moving through the ♭VII and the II as it wends its way to the subdominant or dominant. This aspect of the song, too, shows the balance and restraint that bring out what I have termed Ritts' classicism.[11] Yet within this narrow range, the video makes a subtle response to harmonic changes. For example, in the verses, the beginning and end rest on or near the tonic, D. Here we see stable images of Madonna, or the mermen and Madonna, as if these figures stood for arrival points, or places of stability. Within the verse, as the harmony begins to shift away from and then towards the tonic, Madonna starts to turn away from us and shift her focus towards the ocean.

The chorus is more active than the verses in this song: here, the harmonic rhythm moves at a faster rate than in the verse, the harmony oscillates between the subdominant and the dominant without much tonic, the orchestration opens slightly to include a clavinet and guitar, the melodic sequences become shorter, and the drums accentuate the pulse – many of these features contribute to a more march-like or anthemic quality to the chorus. (Although the song is in a shuffle groove, the chorus has a more 'square' feel, because of the crotchet harmonic rhythm.) The images in the chorus respond to these features with a more lively set of paired two-bar phrases. Unlike the verses, in which beginnings and ends of sections regularly feature Madonna, the chorus creates a sense of uncertainty as to whether Madonna or the mermen will appear first – sometimes Madonna takes up the first half of a sequence, and sometimes the mermen do.

At the bridge, the harmony implied by the bass line conflicts with that of the keyboard pad, with the bass line really defining the harmony. The motion of the bass line moves towards the dominant, unfolding a III–IV–V progression: F♯–A–C♯, G–B–D, A. In response to this, Madonna steps sideways for the first time in the video, as if drawing us toward something new. When the bridge returns, the bass line reiterates its movement towards V. This time, we do find ourselves in 'another region', with imagery of Madonna and the little boy beached on the sand.

Much of what we know about the disposition of the figures in 'Cherish' is defined through the harmony. For example, the child commonly appears at the same time as the subdominant in second inversion. This chord is pulled in two directions: it is often subsumed by the tonic, while it also resists the dominant. This harmonic pull might contribute to the way that the child is volleyed back and forth between the mermen and Madonna. The mermen tend to land on the relatively stable chords of I, IV and V, and the way they seem to float suspended in space, performing a slight acrobatic twist, suggests their freedom from the influence of the song's harmonic motion. Madonna's appearances, on the other hand, coincide with

166   *Carol Vernallis*

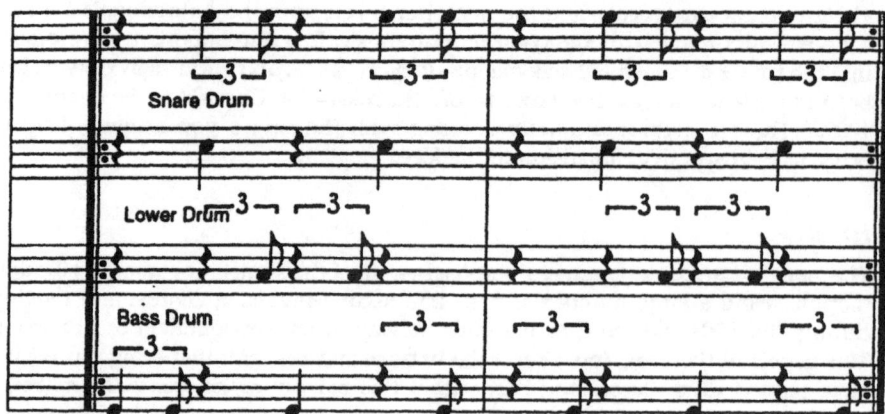

Example 1.

passing chords; these correspondences make her seem somewhat hemmed-in by the harmony. In each section of the video, she forges a winding path towards us, yet monumental harmonic forces towards the end of the section pull her back towards the water's edge. (The most pronounced instances occur in the first and second verses.) Later in the video, Madonna breaks free of these constraints, affecting the video as a whole.

Rhythm

'Cherish' has a strong triplet feel, but the drums count a standard pattern with the bass drum accentuating beats one and three, and the snare, beats two and four. At important points in the video, the editing and the broad physical gestures within the shot (like the shrugging of shoulders) fall squarely within the beat pattern, emphasising, for example, beats one and three, one and four, or simply one. This accentuation of the beat pulls us back in whenever we start to drift along with the flowing imagery. Perhaps to compensate for the absence of a live rhythm section, the mostly sequenced rhythm arrangement fills in nearly every quaver in a number of instrumental parts (Example 1). This rolling pattern might have helped to suggest the carriage of the characters, the setting on the ocean and the figure of the mermen. Against these more general rhythmic qualities, each section of the video displays its own particular pattern. In verse 2, the move towards the downbeat of the measure carries the metaphor of wave and flow into another domain.

Section two

A close reading of two sections

I will now look closely at two particular sections of the video. In music video, the images frequently divide into sections according to the song's sectional divisions. The image can highlight differences among musical sections through shifts in colour, pacing, gesture, or topic.[12] Often the image exhibits a character particular to

Figure 7. Kinospheres – the exploration and closing off of visual space correlates to sectional divisions in the music.

a section of the music. In 'Cherish', as in other videos, the image for the verse features constrained or restrained imagery, typically a solitary artist in a barren landscape. The imagery of the bridge often points away from that of the rest of the video. The chorus, on the other hand, can usually be characterised as communal, and will be set with imagery of freedom (running, jumping, flying), of fusion (between a couple or among a group), of plenitude (crowds, a large group of objects), of paradise (fields of grass).

I will first discuss the second verse. As I have mentioned, the chorus is more march-like, more public and extroverted, while the verse is more reflective. We have already seen the first verse. The image traced the winding and sinuous quality of the line, closely following local inflections, and the high D4 was matched by the image of a merman seeming to soar under water. Now, in verse two, the image encourages us to listen no longer to small articulations, but to hear one broad line.[13]

In verse 2, the image focuses on a larger form – the overall contour of the melodic line (Figures 7 and 8). This focus is established through a use of space similar to that of dance. Dance theorist Rudolf von Laban (1974, p. 10) speaks of a 'kinosphere' of the body: a centre of gravity and an implied larger sphere that the limbs can move into. In music video, one can speak of a larger kinosphere established through camera placement and disposition of the figures – a series of shots creates the illusion of a centre and defines a space around it. In verse 2, a point in the water is fixed as the centre. As we begin to move in different directions away from this centre, we feel the breadth of the melodic line. Yet, simultaneously, the image also plays with our sense of time. Since we have already heard the first verse,

168   *Carol Vernallis*

verse 1	chorus	verse 2	chorus 2 – bridge 1	verse fragment	bridge 2 – outchorus
merman swimming underwater		kinosphere: figures exchange glances		mermen swimming within a kinosphere	
visual material		*sense of space*		*visual material from verse 1, sense of space . from verse 2*	

Figure 8.

we know the length of the second verse. In the second verse, the implied visual centre has been established, and soon, there seems to be nowhere to go. Yet the verse is not over. The voice continues searching for the higher register, which leaves us with a sense of constriction.

Our anxiety breaks as we see the image of Madonna crossing a boundary. She rises out of the water and moves toward us, like the first amphibian emerging from the ocean to walk upon land.[14] As Madonna continues to approach, the music hangs on the tonic before finally moving to the dominant. Both image and music continue to linger, raising the question as to whether the music or the image will spark the next section of the video. Music video often works by scrambling effects and causes, making it hard to remember that the song is ontologically prior to the image. A characteristic power-relation is thus established, in which nothing is taken for granted, and in which each medium must work with and against the other. The possibility exists that either song or image will dominate, forcing the other's hand.

The next example comes from the third verse, at the moment when the mermen swim underwater in formation. A long visual and musical slowing takes us into this section. This is the only moment in which the music departs from the structure of the conventional pop song.[15] Interrupting the synthesizer solo and vocal ad-libs, the second half of this verse suddenly returns to the arrangement scheme and vocal melody of the previous verses, as if it had been a portion of another verse all along. Because this fragment seems both isolated and out of context, we will recognise the melody as familiar, but we may be unable to remember exactly where it comes from and why it has suddenly reappeared. Here the image assists in the process of reconstruction, as it draws from and condenses visual material from the earlier verses. The imagery in this sequence combines material from the culmination of verse 1 (the image of the merman swimming underwater) with the spatial arrangement at the close of verse 2 (the kinosphere established by Madonna and the mermen). Here, the imagery *with the music* recalls the earlier half of the video, and we experience a moment of very potent recollection (Figures 7 and 8).

Herb Ritts is known for his homoerotic photography, and Madonna for her close ties to the gay community. Hinted at throughout the video is the possibility that some desirable being resides in the depths of the water. We assume, as Madonna continually backs into the ocean, that it is she who is our object of desire. Yet, in this musically isolated fragment, veiled by the murky water, Ritts is able to express the possibility that our primary interest in the depths includes an erotic attraction to the mermen.

As I have suggested, music video suppresses some important facets of the music in order to draw our attention towards others. A beautiful moment in the song occurs eight bars earlier where Madonna steps back into the water, and the fish-tail is dragged along the water's edge. The long-held IV chord serves as an extended suspension to the tonic. In the video, the held IV is subsumed under a long visual ritard that leads into the close of the third verse.[16] This ritard is established through a descending contour in both the image and the music. Our attention sweeps across the musical texture: the image of the child reflects the high-pitched synthesizer melody; the image of Madonna holding the child connects with Madonna's voice in the mid-range; and the image of the watery depths and the merman placed at the bottom of the frame is linked to the low register of the synthesized bass.[17]

In the extended sequence which features the mermen, their visibility is obscured, and one might think that their power is therefore muted. Yet, in a large part of the gay community, the politics of concealment and revelation is a complicated, richly inflected phenomenon. Like Michelangelo's *The Holy Family*, in which the artist may have chosen to paint a group of nude men into the recesses of the painting for his own desire and enjoyment, Ritts may have partially obscured his mermen for personally defined erotic reasons. Gay colleagues of mine talk about the titillation of seeing adventure or nature films of foreign lands, because one knows that one might see gorgeous naked men in the background – the recently filmed version of *Last of the Mohicans* is a case in point. For those who are willing to take time with the 'Cherish' video, the obscurity of the mermen works to good effect. Viewers who watch the video only a few times, and who have little contact with gay culture, may lose an opportunity.

I have discussed these two sections in some detail, before moving on to a chronological reading of the entire video, partly because they have an internal coherence that makes them worth studying independently. More important, these sections form the locus of certain themes that I will bring out further in the final third of this article, particularly themes of gay desire. I will return to the end of verse 3, which features underwater footage of the mermen, as it constitutes a nodal point in the video.

A chronological reading

A central claim of this article has been that music video image creates its meanings within the flow of the song. The clarity and stability of these meanings remain subject to the song's temporal unfolding. I will give an abbreviated account of the overall flow of the video, picking up what has been left out thus far, and pointing to the aspects of the video that will be discussed in the sections of the article that follow. A chronological account of the video will prove helpful as a way of describing the relations among sections and the progress of many long-term processes. Because this chronological reading differs from most close analyses of film, it will be worth explaining quickly how it is organised. Close analyses of film usually use the shot or the scene as the fundamental unit of analysis, and close readings of music video have tended to do the same. Here, the method of detailed, sequential description is similar, but the fundamental unit is the musical section, rather than the scene or the shot. The use of the musical section as the fundamental unit places an emphasis upon varied repetition of materials over linear development of plot.

170   *Carol Vernallis*

Treating the form of the song as the analytical ground for the video better reflects its semantic and formal structure.

Introduction

We are frequently led into the world of a music video across a threshold or through a liminal state. 'Cherish' achieves this effect through a shot of the child running along the shoreline, with sounds of the ocean, before the song begins. The somewhat dream-like character of this shot confirms its liminal function. In this shot, it is not clear whether the child is running away from or towards Madonna's breast, and whether he imagines Madonna, or she imagines him. Similarly, the sound of the ocean may seem to suggest a lack in the song, and vice versa. When the song begins, Madonna's repeated 'cherish' sounds like an echo or a call heard across a great distance, either in space or in consciousness.

In the opening of the video, the disposition of the figures seems to conflict with the contour of the bass line and the voice. The figures move laterally. The music here, on the other hand, is made up of falling gestures in the synthesizer and bass. The weight of this introductory musical material is not taken up by the image, but rather is deferred or carried over into the first verse. The image of Madonna's gradual descent towards the sand in verse 1 is suggested by the dramatic falling gestures of the song's introduction.

Verse 1

The outer voices move in contrary motion, first outward, and then inward.[18] As a complement to this motion, the video presents images of increasing height (Madonna's head, the crest of the wave, and, as the high point, the mermen cresting at the surface of the water) interspersed with images of increasing depth (Madonna crouching and rolling on the sand). The images that follow reflect the balance between the bass and the melodic lines above it, especially the voice (Madonna turning with her arms spread out, and the paired images of a merman soaring and Madonna's head on the sand).

Chorus 1

The chorus begins with one of the simplest and most functional relations in music video: the arrangement thickens as the frame fills with more figures. The music in the chorus more clearly articulates the crotchet pulse, and the metallic synthesizer doubles the voice, with the background vocals further emphasising the punctuated style of Madonna's vocal delivery. The melody in the chorus is made up of shorter, more regular phrases than is the verse. Chorus 1 loses some of its iterative, terse quality as it moves into verse 2.

Verse 2

As mentioned earlier, in verse 2 the imagery has a quality of line and extension.

Chorus 2

This section distills earlier aspects of the song. As verse 2 intensifies and simplifies the linear quality of verse 1, so does chorus 2 intensify and simplify the clipped, march-like character of chorus 1. Images of upward motion are even more prevalent here than in chorus 1. The emphasis on the breadth of the figures and their high placement in the frame helps to create a visual arch, as it were, that spans the length of the tape. Chorus 2 contains imagery that foreshadows what we will see later in the video. For example, the image of the child held in the merman's outstretched arms, and the mermen's and Madonna's broad shoulders prepare for Madonna's movement from left to right in the first bridge. The image of Madonna placing a frond of seaweed on her shoulder (a makeshift feather boa), and of her reaching towards her ankles, prepares for the 'vamp' section in the second bridge. In retrospect, we will be able to look back upon the first bridge as a section in which energy is concentrated. This section returns to the questions of identity hinted at in Chorus 1 (who is it that we see, Madonna or the mermen?), but here these questions become more pointedly about *difference* (what do you have, fins or legs?). The issue of sexual or gender difference will be revisited in bridge 2, when Madonna and the merboy playfully flex their muscles. The imagery of three mermen moving into the frame after the end of the second chorus preceded by a lengthy fade to black can be seen as a culmination of a section.

Bridge 1

Musically, the bridge is quirky. It contains a new element, a varied form of the 'Cherish' motive from the introduction: G–F♯–D (bar 1) becomes F♯–G–B. It also combines musical fragments drawn from both the verse and the chorus. In response to this construction, the first half, like the chorus, reflects a celebratory 'surf's up' attitude. A closer reading of this section shows that it goes far in creating the video's clear sense of nostalgia. The lead synthesizer patch seems rather kitschy and outdated, and, in tandem with the image, may conjure up memories of old beach movies. The placement and movement of the figures point to early – and inexpensive – modes of visual entertainment, like the spinning top, the carousel, the zoetrope, and Disneyland's (now dismantled) 'Circle of Progress': here, the mermen and Madonna move from left to right along the seashore, simultaneously but at different rates, and it seems as if someone were dragging a painted backdrop behind Madonna while she moves towards us and then away from us.

Verse 3 (with instrumental and vocal ad-libs)

This verse contains an interesting formal conceit. Its first half is an instrumental over the rhythm arrangement of the verse (which is typical for an instrumental), with the synthesizer taking the solo. This synthesizer line, however, is dominated by vocal ad-libs which Madonna sings over it (and which return counterpointed to vocal material from the chorus in the outchorus). More strikingly, the second half of this verse abruptly returns to the vocal melody of the previous verses, aban- doning the synthesizer lead and the vocal ad-libs and proceeding as a 'regular' verse. The first half of verse 3 is composed of music and images that slow down gradually, and that move towards the second half of the verse (when the vocal line from the earlier verses returns). The visual material comes from the more restrained, tender imagery of the first two verses. The second half of this section features the mermen swimming in formation. The underwater choreography echoes Busby Berkeley's famous waterfall sequence in the movie *Footlight Parade*.[19]

Bridge 2

In the second bridge, a varied repetition of bridge 1, Madonna and the merboy loll on the beach. It is the only section that makes a feature of being edited off the beat. Because it is edited in this way, this section seems rhythmically out of step with the rest of the video. The fact that it takes place on the sand, unusual for this video, further helps to set it apart. The merboy shows off his muscles; Madonna picks up on this gesture in the break, when she adopts body-builders' poses. A two-shot of Madonna's feet and the merboy's tail foreshadows the set of oppositions that end the video. At the end of this bridge, Madonna backs into the water.

Break

Madonna vamps for the camera in a section that reminds one of old home movies. The break does more than create a nostalgic flavour, however. For all of Madonna's activity, this section has a strange sense of emptiness. The propulsive elements of the music – the bass and the snare and bass drums – have dropped out. The space behind Madonna is open and still. At first, it is not clear, in the quick editing, whether Madonna is moving to the music, or whether the music is dragging her around as if she were a marionette. The attempts at close synchronisation here sharply contrast with the rhythmic freedom of the first bridge. Throughout the video, Madonna has seemed constrained by the harmony. However, by the end of the break, she is depicted as no longer having to struggle with the harmonic structure, but, like Atlas himself, as being capable of upholding it.

The way that the harmony is realised in the 'Cherish' video relates to the way that liberal corporate culture tends to picture social obligations. We speak of the 'smaller, more intimate domestic sphere' and the 'glass ceiling of the workplace', and we can notice the way that the harmonic structure constrains Madonna. In this video, both harmony and social obligations are figured as reassuring, but also palpably constraining, sets of boundaries. Because they are treated similarly, one could be considered as a figure for the other. By the close of the break, however, the video reveals something new: we begin to know more about the mermen, the boy and Madonna, and what they aspire to.

In the break, Madonna adopts a triumphant stance. For the first time, she steps assertively into the emphatic 'ch!' of 'Cherish'. Her squared-off arms and torso condense the kinospheres of verse 2 and the second half of verse 3 into a single form. As she adopts a bodybuilder's pose, showcasing her biceps, a second vocal line, drawn from the first half of verse 3, enters in counterpoint to the vocal line of the chorus. This second line, made up of shorter phrases and fragments from earlier in the song, has an insistent quality that lends Madonna additional authority.

There is a shift across the video in the representations of the characters. For the first half of the video, the mermen move assertively, propelling themselves out of the water. In the second half of verse 3, however, they move with restraint and poise. Here the break, and the sections that follow, are dominated by Madonna's compact, precise gestures. There are shifts in the arrangement which correspond to these changes of character: in the second half of verse three, the nearly static synthesizer pad becomes the most prominent instrumental voice, thereby underscoring the mermen's timeless existence. In the break, the bright trumpet patch cuts through the texture, emphasising Madonna's assertiveness. By giving the mermen and Madonna these actions at these particular points in the song, Ritts can make use of the cultural associations of the song's timbres in order to play with traditional notions of gender.

For the first half of the break, the image emphasises episodic, rather than teleological, features of the song. A strength of this approach lies in its not conferring greater authority upon either Madonna or the mermen. In the second half of the break, the snare and bass drum return, and the backing vocals from the chorus enter behind Madonna's ad libs, anticipating the outchorus.

Outchorus

By the time that the outchorus appears, the video has established a variety of connections between music and image. We can therefore hover over the image, waiting for a moment of engagement between it and the music. At this point, we may be waiting for the grounding images of feet to return, as well as for the completion of a spiral that is traced out across many edits. The second vocal line seems to match the prismatic late afternoon light on the ocean, through both its kaleidoscopic construction and its use of echoes from earlier in the song. The return of the synthesizer lead (the 'Steve Winwood' patch) works likewise to a similar effect. Typically for an outchorus, this section brings in all of the timbres we have heard in the song. The image, for its part, creates the sense of an ending through similarly conventional means: the mermen ride off into the sunset, Madonna and the boy share a final embrace before he runs away and she lies down on the sand.

The video closes with Madonna and the child facing off against each other – the image of the child seems, strangely, to be composed of adult legs and a child's head. Popular culture theorist Philip Hayward (1991, p. 98) reads this image as a sign of patriarchal authority. He argues that Madonna's freedom is reined in at the end of the video. The legs, torso and heads, however, function most importantly on a formal level. As a pair of bookends, the images serve to stop the flow of the video, to slow down the image so that it can close in sync with the music. The merman's legs still remain topped by a child's head (so that the phallic presence is not that impressive) and Madonna assumes a siren's pose, a mythic image of great power. The boy's legs and Madonna's torso come at the moment that the song is over, and function as a frame for the song.[20] Madonna lands on beat one, a position of power within the song.

The ending works through a compression of thematic oppositions. All of the video's dualistic imagery – adult and child, female and male, human and animal, myth and camp – is squeezed into the closing shots. This kind of an ending is common in music video.[21] It achieves its effect partly by providing a thematic payoff in the absence of any conclusion to the narrative. The enigmatic character of the final series of shots asks the viewer to return to the beginning and watch one more time, in order to see how the video could have arrived at this ending.

Section three

Representations of race, gender and sexuality

This article, thus far, has focused on music–image relations that would be called formal. I have argued that the logic of these relations establishes a ground for an investigation of race, gender and sexuality. Here, I will explore these issues, beginning with one example that shows the interdependence of formal and depictive modes. In the remainder of this final section, I will discuss other parameters – narrative and emblematic modes, affect and self reflexivity, and musical and visual space. This discussion forms the necessary complement to the explication of formal modes of continuity.

The video for 'Cherish' contains three kinds of figure: Madonna; a group of mermen; and a boy/merchild who moves between Madonna and the mermen. Madonna and the mermen are clearly European–American, while the boy is clearly not – although his specific ethnicity is unknown, he is pointedly 'other' to the rest of the figures in the video. One might well wonder about the boy's ethnicity and its role in 'Cherish'. The imagery of a young child of colour being passed between Madonna and the mermen is not innocent when one considers that the depiction of adult black men and women passing around a single white child is rarely seen in popular culture. In the current critical climate, it might be acceptable to note this as an instance of aestheticised racism, and terminate the analysis there.

Yet, on a more formal level, a darker figure as an object of exchange creates a strong degree of separation between the white figures of Madonna and the mermen. The video is shot entirely in black and white, and, because of the way that tones are developed gradually over the course of the video – dark black dress, black roots, a merman in the water with very black hair and white skin as opposed to Madonna's *blonde* hair and *black* dress, grey water, medium grey and white mermen, and a very white-skinned Madonna – the young boy of colour is almost argued for on formal grounds, as one shade within a grey scale. The young boy's colour in this context is a transitional tone.

But we cannot stop here: we must acknowledge that this formal device reflects a specific racialist way of viewing skin colour. We could imagine a tape produced in a culture where such differences do not mean the same thing, such as in Brazil, Puerto Rico, or North Africa. The decision to emphasise these differences so strongly relies implicitly on the fact that skin colour, and race, mean a great deal to us as Europeans and North Americans.

Yet it is also important that the boy's colour in this context is a transitional tone. Imagine the video with everyone of the same skin tone: the figures would lack separation. The image of the child of colour is, at one level, offensive, at another, progressive. The child's skin-tone subverts the viewer's projections concerning the nuclear family, allowing for both the imagery of gay desire and the imagery of Madonna's independence.

This kind of interdependence of aesthetic and ideological aspects shows that, ultimately, we cannot look to any one place for an understanding of music video, but must rather deal with the relations among a video's narrative, formal, and sociocultural aspects, particularly as they are complicated by the tensions between music and image. The ways that music and image combine cannot simply be taken as natural; styles of performance footage change from year to year, and the construction of a music video always requires effort. Videomakers have developed a set of practices for putting image to music in which the image must give up its autonomy and abandon some of its representational modes. In exchange, the image gains in flexibility and play, as well as in polyvalence of meaning. Many of the meanings of music video lie in this give-and-take between sound and image, and in the relations among their various modes of continuity.

Questions of narrative

The first wave of academic writing to deal with video concerned itself with music video's ability (or inability) to sustain a narrative. More recently, however, there have been attempts to put narrative in its proper place, as but one of several ways to establish continuity. Music videos suppress narrative direction for various reasons. The fact that the figures cannot speak and seem preternaturally animated by the music may work against narrative clarity. The brevity of the medium contributes as well. Pop songs, usually, are sectional forms (verse, chorus, bridge), and it is difficult for an image track to maintain a strong narrative drive against this sectional differentiation and repetition. But most important, it may be in a video's interest to point only vaguely to a narrative. If the image were overly narrative in orientation, we might be drawn to the image as we are in a traditional film. The music for the video would most likely resemble film music – usually unacknowledged, almost unheard.

David Bordwell defines narrative as having 1) an agent with identifiable goals and distinct characteristics, and 2) obstacles to this agent's success (1985, pp. 12–23). This definition shows immediately why music video might limit the role of narrative. If we were to engage with the figures in music videos as if they were people with clear traits and identifiable goals, who were approaching difficult or dangerous encounters, we might try to predict upcoming events. That kind of engagement would pull us outside of the here and now of the video, its moment-to-moment flow, and we might well lose the detail in both the music and the image. Videos draw heavily, but schematically, from traditional forms – for their familiarity as much as for their novelty.

'Cherish' is similar to many videos of a certain type, in which there are moments that suggest a story line. In such videos, these moments function more like 'hooks' than like parts of a story. We are carried between these narrative moments by the ultimately more important play of movement and texture. With this understanding of narrative in mind, one can suggest several possible plotlines for the 'Cherish' video:

(1) A community gives birth to a child, and turns him over to a woman for instruction about culture; the child is later returned to the nurturing community (this inverts the Lacanian notion of a society in which men teach the 'law of the father').
(2) Madonna and the mermen give birth to and raise a male child.
(3) Madonna imagines a love affair with a merman, and transforms one into a child whom she can love and nurture.
(4) The child is Madonna's son and the mermen are merely imagined.
(5) The child is a member of a family that will not shield him from adult expressions of sexuality.
(6) Madonna steals both power and a child from the gay community.
(7) The child cannot fit into human society: 'Cherish' is a kind of 'coming out' story, and the mother is supportive.

For these narratives to exist, the viewer must infer or find them by 'connecting the dots' between particular charged moments in the video, and must pay close attention to the music and the image between these events. Because no parameter comes to the fore to the annihilation of another (although features become submerged or move to the background), multiple storylines can seem to exist simultaneously in the video. The viewer must consider all the visual gestures and all the musical codes in order to understand the connections among these moments. The vagueness of 'Cherish' may serve it well. It gives a committed viewer enough space to imagine what might be the relations among the figures.

Space

One way that music video substitutes for a lack in the narrative is through a focus on a set of relations. In music video, the disposition of figures and their movement on a ground often takes the place of plot and character development in a traditional sense. In 'Cherish', one simple way that this is played out is in the sense of scale between musical and visual space. The musical 'field' of the song seems smaller than that of the image for the video. As I have mentioned, the musical field for 'Cherish' seems narrow, even thin – it contains very few dramatic rhythmic, harmonic, melodic or timbral changes. By contrast, the visuals for 'Cherish' seem to occupy a broader realm. Though the visual field is filmed entirely in black and white, and is set exclusively on the beach, it has a quality of great expansiveness – the distance from sea to land, from the surface of the water to its depths, or from one point along the shoreline to another, seems quite wide. In this instance, the larger expanse of imagery, against a more narrowly constructed band of music, gives the viewer the sense that the figures are highly individuated yet only loosely bound to one another.

Of all of the figures, the mermen are particularly well defined through the use of space. They possess their own realm, and act as if they have always been and will forever be in the ocean. Some elements of the music, perhaps the sectional changes, seem to become *real* barriers – like the rock formations in the water – but the mermen seem to communicate across this distance through a secret code. The mermen seem comfortably placed in the musical and visual materials of the video.

The sense of space also helps to define Madonna. An approach that focuses on the imagery without sufficient attention to musical time and space might suggest a deeply sexualised text: Madonna is a siren who lures us into the video with a sexuality that moves from chastity to naughtiness to polymorphous perversity. The viewer may desire the child. Yet the appearance of the fish-tail dragged along the water's edge provokes a moment of anxiety at the sight of the uncanny. The mermen remain remote, deaf to our interest. At the video's close, the child realises his own desirability. Madonna drops her social graces and threatens to consume us.

Yet this story leaves out much of what is important in the video. What might seem frightening in the image is safely marked off as separate space – through the clear delineation of ocean and sky, and water and sand. Only when we are underwater do we deal with the presence or absence of male genitalia, or with male sexuality in general. When we are on land, both the little boy and Madonna seem quite comfortable. The membranes of separation – the surface of the water, the shoreline – are very gently elided. The time and distance that separate the appearance of those visual hooks that carry narrative charge also provide a sense of security.

The music also works hard to repress what might be frightening about the images. Madonna is held within the harmony; similarly, the fish-tail is held within the long sweep of verse 3's first half; the merboy and Madonna stand as a pair of balanced closing images. These images remain detached from one another. A reading that attends to both music and image will draw attention away from these moments and towards other features such as the process of the figures' individuation and their relation with one another. Neither the song nor the video is committed to an ending. Both are non-teleological in nature.

This does not mean that the video is free of emotional complexity. Rather, those elements which are more sharply edged appear on another level and are safely submerged. The characters' actions and expressions, which sometimes seem to reflect a sense of anger or hostility, provide one way that the figures in 'Cherish' are given voice. These moments do not determine the video's tone; rather, they provide contrast in a circumscribed way. Since one knows that they will not overwhelm the video, they can function well as ornament and texture.[22]

One must not exaggerate, however, the extent to which the characters are in fact given voice. Of all of the figures in 'Cherish', the young boy is the most short-changed. More than any other figure in the video, he fills the role of a structural device – he is both a powerful figure of exchange and an agent of disruption. Through his attempts to both run out of the video's bounds and to disrupt internal boundaries, he holds the integrity or the disintegration of the video within his frame. For dramatic charge, music videos often have a figure that threatens the video's surface. Yet the video's point of view can be said to be structured for him. Aspects of the 'Cherish' video are meant to evoke feelings associated with childhood. Large sections of the image engender feelings of being rocked, bounced on a knee, thrown up in the air, and twirled around. The sections of music that accompany this imagery match this physical movement. For example, the chorus has a bouncier, more anthemic quality, and there is a gentler, rocking motion to the verse. Much of the imagery revolves around the child's expressions of fear, distance and pleasure, though the video works to suppress this fact.

Though all of the figures are limited by the conventions of music video, 'Cherish' remains committed to expressing the roles of the characters within a set of relations: Madonna is powerful enough to uphold the whole social structure; the mermen constitute a community of men who are playful, non-competitive, and free; the child becomes so autonomous that he almost seems like an adult. These relationships can be seen as a proposal for a new social order.

The star performer

Madonna appears throughout the video and her role as 'star' is clearly important. Ritts treats her as he treats Janet Jackson in the video 'Love will Never Do'. The infectiousness of the singer's smile functions as a hook that carries the viewer into the video. As the video progresses, this approach is modified in order to work more with spatial relations and with the body as form.

Most of what we know about Madonna derives from her facial expressions and physical gestures as she switches between coyness and exuberance. These moments highlight musical structure. Madonna's flirtatious, sweet invitation in verse 1 helps us to hear the contours of the melodic lines, partly because, with a tilt of her head, she continually beckons downward, and the camera follows the lines of her body. The flat, deadpan expressions in verse 2 (with mouths drawn into straight lines), help us to hear the breadth of that section. It is hard to argue, though easy to sense, that the sparkle in Madonna's eyes and her joyous expression give a buoyant levity to the image which seems to match a playful element in the music. Yet the video is more complicated than this. It was shot in the winter and the water was extremely cold. To keep warm, Madonna was wrapped in blankets between takes. A trace of athletic stoicism may be present in the video that exists in tension, rather than harmony, with the song.[23]

Self-reflexivity

Against Madonna's buoyancy, hard work and flirtation, the song and video sustain a critique of Madonna. The song has a naive, untutored quality because of Madonna's vocal delivery and the thin orchestration of its two-voice structure. The impulsiveness of the jump from D1 to D2 in the second half of the verse's vocal line seems to highlight this naïveté – it does not proceed according to traditional formal rules.[24] However, if one listens to the two-bar synthesizer break, in the middle and at the end of verse 1, one might find it a bit too sarcastic or mocking, in its relation to the voice, since it is articulated as even, measured minims. When Madonna's voice is chorused, the image shows her alone on the beach flexing her muscles. This image ironicises Madonna's auto-eroticism, self-determination, and self-absorption.

The image also comments upon itself and refers to its relation with the music. For example, the fluke is often used as a foil to the vocal line. At the bridge, the music starts off with an instrumental lick rather than with Madonna singing, and we see the mermen, not Madonna, propelled upwards by their flukes. The mermen with their flukes have gotten a taste for stardom, and later in the bridge, the flukes impertinently appear in small gaps between the singing.

A reading of the song with the image can broaden our understanding of Madonna's work. Critics claim that Madonna merely effects a series of poses or masks, and that her work is therefore fragmentary – that it relies upon the most superficial of associations. Yet attention to the 'Cherish' video, in a way that is respectful of the song's role in shaping it, can offer this vision: that the youthful, girl-next-door vocal delivery in the song is connected to, not detached from, the video's more direct, sexualised modes of expression.

If I remember the song, it is for Madonna's singing, which flows in tandem with, but is not given over to, a charismatic bass line and a minimally differentiated arrangement. I think of Herb Ritts' supportive vision of Madonna, and of the long lines of his images which seem to radiate like spokes across the surface of the video. All of these features, through their attentiveness, clarity and directness, give a sense of integrity and commitment, qualities not acknowledged in the scholarly community, either for Madonna's work or for Ritts'.

Homo-erotic configurations

The mermen are native to the place of the video and Madonna but a visitor. The video hints that they may be Madonna's, and also our, real object of attention: it was built around the mermen – they were shot separately, with a great deal of concern lavished on the mechanics of the tails. (Does this make the men in this video merely 'pieces of tail'?) The second half of verse 3, which features these tails, is a critical moment in both song and video. If we look more closely, it becomes clear that the mermen reflect a homo-erotic perspective.

The mermen exist in a self-contained world, a world without women, and they procreate their own kind, not biologically, but socially. It is true that the mermen do not seem to possess genitalia, but the men in Herb Ritts' other work – more clearly marked as homo-erotic – show a similar tendency towards becoming sculptural forms without genitalia. The prominent tails, however, call forth numerous associations, including sexual ones. The mermen's flukes can evoke Christian symbolism, Hans Christian Andersen's *The Little Mermaid*, the mythography of dolphins and their noble rescues of people, the birth of Venus, and the TV series *Flipper*,[25] but also sperm and phalluses.

Philip Hayward (1991, p. 98) reminds us that images of mermen are quite rare – we are much more familiar with mermaids. If their origin is unclear, this unclarity might itself be read as a gay image – gays are sometimes called 'fairies', perhaps partly because we do not know how they come to be. The mermen's mysteriousness and elusiveness play a crucial role in defining them. They never address the camera, and are often shown disappearing from view. Invisibility is a central theme in the gay experience. It is linked to oppression, but also to desire – to watch and not be seen; to be seen but not to acknowledge being seen.

From a homo-erotic angle, the elusiveness of the mermen makes them, if anything, more powerful. It creates a context in which their every appearance carries meaning. Some sequences wittily upstage Madonna, making the mermen into the real stars: the image of Madonna's opening her blouse, possibly to reveal her breasts, interrupted by a shot of the merman's bare chest instead; or, perhaps, the moment when Madonna sings 'makes me feel so good', and the merman rubs noses with the merboy.

A homo-erotic perspective allows us to sense the force of figures that would seem, at first, to add no more than a whimsical touch to a video dominated by the presence of Madonna. Like many figures in the backgrounds of videos, the mermen take on an enigmatic character partly because the conventions of music video do not allow them to speak. In 'Cherish', however, the mermen's muteness seems, not merely conventional, but a matter of will or nature. Their silent presence and the way of life it suggests become integral to the video.

Conclusion

This article was written to provide a means for analysing music video. 'Cherish' shows that a video can reflect a multitude of musical parameters. It argues for the sheer complexity of the relation between music and image: it reveals that correspondences between music and image can range from the most strict to the most subtle or enigmatic – and that the most fragile may be the most engaging. The 'Cherish' video shimmers between the most traditional of texts – the topos of mother and child – and the most radical – a social order in which gays, women and children can live with independence.

I do not want to claim that connections between music and image are natural, or that we have an innate capacity to see these connections, or even that all or most people do see them.[26] More than proving what people do with music videos, I want rather to show what videos and videomakers can offer us. I might say, paraphrasing Wittgenstein, that learning the *language* of music video means learning a *form of life* (1968, p. 19).

Appendix A: 'Cherish' video narrative

Introduction
The boy runs along the shoreline.

Verse 1
Madonna sings while the waves crest behind her.

Chorus 1
Three mermen swim away from the camera. The section cuts rapidly among Madonna, the mermen and the boy, now a merboy.

Verse 2
Water runs up Madonna's legs. Madonna and the mermen spy upon each other.

Chorus 2
Madonna spirals away from the camera. The figures of Madonna, the mermen and the merboy are placed high in the frame.

Bridge 1
With their arms reaching upward, three mermen fill the frame; Madonna moves from left to right at the water's edge. Madonna remains at the shoreline while the mermen remain at sea.

Verse 3 (instrumental)
The camera travels a path out to sea, passing Madonna as she cradles the merboy. The mermen swim in formation under water.

Bridge 2
Madonna turns towards the camera. She frolics with the merboy on the sand.

Break
A merman dives backwards into the ocean, revealing his chest. Madonna flexes her muscles at the water's edge.

Outchorus
A merman twists away from us, pulling himself out of the water. The boy, human again, runs towards the mermen as they swim out to sea. Madonna remains on the sand. The boy (now older?) returns to face her.

Appendix B: 'Cherish' lyrics

Introduction
Cherish, cherish.

Verse 1
So tired of broken hearts and losing at this game.
Before I start this dance I take a chance
in telling you I want more than just romance.
You are my destiny I can't let go, baby, can't you see?
Cupid, please take your aim at me.

Chorus 1
Cherish the thought of always having you here by my side.
Oh, baby, I cherish the joy, you keep bringing it into my life.
I'm always singing it.
Cherish the strength, you got the power to make me feel good.
And, baby, I'll perish the thought of leaving. I never would.

Verse 2
I was never satisfied with casual encounters.
I can't hide my need for two hearts that bleed
with burning love that's the way it's got to be.
Romeo and Juliet, they never felt this way I bet.
So, don't underestimate my point of view.

Chorus 2
Cherish the thought of always having you here by my side.
Oh, baby, I cherish the joy, you keep bringing it into my life.
I'm always singing it.
Cherish the strength, you got the power to make me feel good.
And, baby, I'll perish the thought of leaving. I never would.

Bridge 1
Who? You! Can't get away, I won't let you.
Who? You! I could never forget to.
Cherish is the word I use to remind me of your love.

Together, you're giving it to me, boy.
Keep giving me all, all, all your joy.
Give me faith. I will always cherish you.
Romeo and Juliet, they never felt this way I bet.
So, don't underestimate my point of view.

Verse 3 (instrumental)

Bridge 2
Who? You! Can't get away, I won't let you.
Who? You! I could never forget to.
Cherish is the word I use to remind me of your love.

Acknowledgements

I would like to thank Juli Brown for providing the drawings and Arun Bharali, Stevan Key, Mitchell Morris, Jann Pasler and especially Charles Kronengold for their insightful comments and careful reading of the text.

182   *Carol Vernallis*

Endnotes

1. The attempts which come closest are Tricia Rose's (1994) analysis of Public Enemy's 'Baseheads', Andrew Goodwin's (1992) shot-by-shot discussion of George Michael's 'Father Figure' and Melanie Morton's (1994) analysis of Madonna's 'Express Yourself'. None of these analyses, however, is sufficiently attentive to visual detail and to the flow of the music.

2. Composer and theorist Robert Erickson (1955, p. 24) states: 'Any melody is analogous to a moving line. The line is strictly speaking never continuous; there is always a jump from tone to tone, and the visual analogy of a series of dots producing the effect of a line would be more accurate.'

    Visual images can also be said to have fundamental structural contours. Leonardo Da Vinci (1961, p. 146) said something very beautiful about this: 'The air is full of an infinite number of radiating straight lines which cross and weave together without ever coinciding; it is these which represent the true form of every object's essence.'

3. Seurat (1945) thought of the horizontal line as passive, the vertical line as active; lines descending from the horizontal seemed lugubrious; lines ascending from the horizontal tended towards joy.

4. The song presents the chorus and the complete verse only twice each. This in itself is unusual for a pop song of this length at this tempo. The version of 'Cherish' which is used in the video is about 4 mins 30 secs.

5. I discuss the role of sectional divisions more fully in the second part of this article.

6. Though a relation, in music video, can exist through similarity or contrast, confluence may be more easily perceived than disjuncture. Similarly, an arch shape is simple to grasp. The 'Cherish' video's accessibility derives in part from the video's clear transformations of its basic shape, as well as from its continuity and flow.

7. Note the firm articulations, in both image and music, at the beginnings of phrases in verse 1. Note also how, throughout each section, the images gradually diminish in force. In the first chorus, the image punches through the section, from Madonna marching up to the camera, the little boy and the mermen surfacing, the mermen pulling through the water, to Madonna crunching her shoulder up and down. As the music in the chorus gradually winds down, the image too, softens; the residual 'pop' in the imagery of the older merman nudging the little boy on the nose and the last image of Madonna's knee propped up reflects music that has lost its drive.

    The image slavishly follows the phrase structure of the music in the first verse and chorus. During these two sections, the image supports the song's regular phrase structure and is edited to emphasise meaningful word groupings and motivic cells. In verse 2, however, the image begins to play with the phrase structure – sometimes coming slightly before, sometimes lagging slightly behind the musical phrase. Since we can recognise both the rule and its variation, we still experience the phrasing of the music and the image in verse 2 as contrapuntally related.

8. Although probably produced by a digital synthesizer, this patch is designed to have the richness and grain associated with earlier, analogue synthesizers. It resembles a Minimoog 'lead guitar' timbre popularised by fusion keyboardists like Chick Corea, Jeff Lorber and Jan Hammer. On digital synthesizers, this timbre is sometimes referred to as the 'Steve Winwood' patch, because of its frequent presence on his albums from the early and mid-1980s.

9. The bass line is a very significant feature of the 'Cherish' song. Both it and the vocal line are equally charismatic. The bass line is interesting because it is one of the song's few performerly aspects – there is some flexibility in the rhythmic feel, as well as some improvisatory flair in the choice of notes. The vocal line is, as one would expect, in the foreground. 'Cherish' is better thought of as a two-voice structure, and not as melody and accompaniment, because the bass line provides so much melodic interest, and seems to carry the harmony, even when it is contradicted by the keyboard pad (as in the bridge).

10. Synthesizer- and drum machine-based dance-pop songs with a human feel became a staple on the Rhythm & Blues charts starting in 1982. Examples from 1982–83 include 'Sexual Healing' by Marvin Gaye, 'Ain't Nobody' by Rufus and Chaka Khan, 'Just be Good to Me' by The S.O.S. Band, and 'Yah mo b there' by James Ingram with Michael McDonald. Examples can be found on the Pop charts soon after: Prince's 'When Doves Cry' (1984), which reached number one on both the Pop and R& B charts, Madonna's own 'Borderline' (1984), and Howard Jones' 'Things Can only Get Better' (1985). Madonna's sometime collaborator, Manhattan DJ and producer 'Jellybean' Benitez, was instrumental in popularising this sound and connecting it with certain strands in the British 'New Romantic' style. One might

say that this sound achieved hegemonic status on American radio from 1986–88.

11. Many aspects of the song are constructed to emphasise sameness over difference, restraint over assertion. The melodic materials of the chorus and bridge relate closely to those of the verse. The pitches G–F♯–A–B, which form the principal motive of the chorus, come out of the synthesizer's cambiata figure in the verse, D–C♯–A–B. These connections help to make the similarities among the sections of the song as important for the videomaker as are the differences among them. The orchestration remains a continuous wall of sound. The only element that seems really to progress in the song is the synthesizer's counter-melodies. For example, the synthesized trumpet is buried very deep in the mix in the first verse. It does not come to the fore until the second bridge. Later, it plays a crucial role in bringing the song to a close.

12. One way that the video draws attention to sectional divisions is through shifts in pacing. The imagery of the verse is slowed down, and the imagery for the chorus moves more quickly. The particular pacing of 'Cherish' derives from the fact that the chorus has a faster harmonic rhythm than the verse.

13. This moment illustrates a crucial point about music video: most often, the image can point to but a few musical parameters. At one moment, the image may comment upon the subtle nuances of the music, and at another, it may suggest the way that the music articulates larger sectional divisions. However, by the close of the video, our attention will have been drawn to almost all of the musical parameters. Music video works by saying, 'first listen to this, then listen to this, now this'. Relations between music and image can exist within all degrees of concordance. Some correspondences may be literal one-to-one mappings, like those seen in cartoons (referred to as 'mickey mousing'). An example in 'Cherish' would be the moment when Madonna raises her shoulders on beats 1 and 3. Yet the most successful connections may be ones that are obscure and enigmatic. Such connections may ask viewers to tease out the relation between music and image, and contribute to an important aspect of music videos – that they encourage us to watch them repeatedly. Some more enigmatic and subtle connections in 'Cherish' might include the relation between the sibilants in the voice and the percussion samples, and how they, in turn, relate to the prismatic light on sand and water; how the bass line seems to carry the figures forward; the echo of the theme song from the television series *Flipper*, and the way that the nos-

talgic elements in the music are paralleled by imagery drawn from beach films and old home movies, myth and fairytale.

14. This image of Madonna makes a vague joke, which would relate the mermen's coming onto land (as in Hans Christian Andersen's fairytale) to the first amphibian stalking forward without much grace. This kind of oblique association is common in music video. Much of the imagery in music video operates on jokes and associations which are not quite consciously acknowledged. We can, however, turn to the music and to the whole music video to fill in the context, in order to get the tone or flavour of such an association.

15. The expected form for a song of this genre and period would be (introduction)–verse–chorus–verse–chorus–bridge–verse　(instrumental)–outchorus. 'Cherish' departs from the letter, if not the spirit, of this form by repeating the bridge and adding a break. The presence of a break is somewhat unexpected, since the break is a formal conceit associated more with dance music than with middle-of-the-road. The song's most significant modification of formal conventions, however, lies in the internal construction of the third verse. The beginning of the third verse sounds more like an extension of the previous section (bridge 1) than like the downbeat of a new section. The voice elides this sectional division: it draws out the end of its phrase as the rhythm section begins the third verse. (Madonna sings, 'love. Together, you're giving it to me boy.') We may think, for a moment, that we are still in the bridge. The first half of this verse functions as an instrumental with prominent vocal ad-libs. The 'Steve Winwood' synthesizer patch enters the texture with a solo line supported by the rhythm arrangement of the verse. Madonna, drawing attention away from the synthesizer solo, sings, not material from the verse, but new material that seems more appropriate to the bridge because of its improvisatory character and shorter phrase-lengths. If it were not for the voice, these eight bars would seem like part of a conventional instrumental. Interrupting the synthesizer solo and vocal ad-libs, the second half of this verse suddenly returns to the arrangement scheme and vocal melody of the previous verses, as if it had been just another verse all along. It only becomes clear that this is the third verse when, as in the second verse, Madonna sings, 'you. Romeo and Juliet, they never felt this way I bet'.

Not only is verse 3 unusual for its internal organization – the conflicting tendencies of its first half, its surprising split down the middle, and its elided beginning – this section is pre-

184   *Carol Vernallis*

ceded and followed by appearances of the bridge. The attempt to place the 'normal' portion of the verse demands some work on the part of the listener. The image assists in the task.

16. Another director might have emphasised the suspension, say through imagery of unrequited love. Ritts moves past this suspension and draws attention to the verse fragment, thereby underscoring the mermen's collective identity. (See pp. 179–80 for discussion of this identity and its construction within the video.)

17. The gesture of a broad sweeping arc which resolves into a balanced image of height and depth occurs frequently in 'Cherish'. Visual arcs imply phrasing that can be shaped either with or against that of the music. One can see an antecedent to this gesture in Ritts' still photography. The photograph 'Male Nude With Bubble' (reproduced in Ellenzweig 1992, p. 194) bears interesting similarities to 'Cherish': many of the qualities of balance in the photo seem, in the video, to be extended in time and placed in relation to the song.

18. The image highlights two falling gestures in the bass, and the rising line in the melody.

19. The Busby Berkeley sequence is much beloved, particularly in the gay community, for its spectacular opulence and willingness to dispense with narrative.

20. It is difficult to determine whether we are seeing feet that belong to a child or to an adult. The ambiguity thus created can be expressed as follows: if the legs are a child's, then the merboy meets Madonna as a child; if they are adult legs, he may meet her as a lover. In the latter case, more time will have elapsed, most likely in the company of the mermen.

21. Michael Jackson's 'Thriller' provides a good example of this phenomenon, as shown by Kobena Mercer (1994, pp. 93–109). Mercer points to the many thematic threads in the image and the song that might bear upon the video's ending.

22. The expressions on the mermen's faces in the group close-up in the first bridge could be read as an expression of anger at Madonna having stolen their child from the ocean. The boy's teeth chatter as Madonna reaches to hold him. Yet the imagery in this section also points to the notion that the boy comes ashore of his own accord – here, we see the fish-tail moving by its own power towards the shore: the merboy has beached himself. The imagery of Madonna in the second bridge – her shielded breasts, vulnerable belly, and heavy movements – seems campy. Her movements undercut her attempt to look beautiful. In

addition, the relationship between the mermen and the boy looks warm and unconflicted, but the relationship between Madonna and him seems less so.

23. Another example of correspondence between affect and music can be drawn from Madonna's 'Open Your Heart' video. Her still movements, heavy mascara, brooding expression, and dark colours (emerald green, deep blue, black) match the severity of the music. Music video imagery can ignore, match, or supersede various parameters of the music. In 'Cherish', the affective character of the image is more extreme than that of the music. The mood of the image seems like a heightened version of the mood of the song – with images of people crashing and diving through frothy water, Madonna's rocking movements, and expressions of elation. At one level, music videos need to exceed the bounds of the music – it gives their existence a *raison d'etre*. The claim of greater affective range is an easy way for the image to show that it is more authoritative than the music. This is an easy way, but not the only one. In U2's 'With or Without You', the image envelopes the music by moving at pulses both faster and slower than that of the music. In Peter Gabriel's 'Mercy St', a slow song that evokes a sense of solemnity, the slowest pulse is associated with the image.

24. The vocal line, here, embodies a nontraditional construction. Much of the song, until the high D4, can be heard as circling around D3. The octave leap up to D4 is not prepared for, in terms either of linear direction or harmonic flow. Its intrinsic appeal is questionable, but it does support the wide-eyed quality of the singer's subject position in this song.

25. I would suggest that *Flipper* may be the most concrete possibility, because its theme song resembles the opening of 'Cherish'.

26. There seems to be a very wide range of competence in the ability to view music video, with teenagers who have watched a great deal of television often displaying the greatest visual and musical acuity. My experiences, from speaking with videomakers and their assistants, and students who watch music video, suggest that their engagement with the medium is quite intense. The students in my undergraduate course on music video often write sustained and incisive analyses of videos. I discovered, further, that their fluency in the medium meant that music videos could be used as a tool for teaching music fundamentals. I hope to present examples of this application in a future paper.

References

Bordwell, D. 1985. *The Classical Hollywood Cinema: Film Style and Mode of Production to 1960* (New York)

Ellenzweig, A. 1992. *The Homo-erotic Photograph* (New York)

Erickson, R. 1955. *The Structure of Music: A Listener's Guide. A Study of Music in Terms of Melody and Counterpoint* (New York)

Goodwin, A. 1992. *Dancing in the Distraction Factory: Music Television and Popular Culture* (Minneapolis)

Hayward, P. 1991. 'Desire caught by its tail: the unlikely return of the merman in Madonna's "Cherish" ', *Cultural Studies*, 5:1, pp. 98–106

von Laban, R. 1974. *Laban's Principles of Dance and Movement Notation* (Boston)

Mercer, K. 1993. 'Monster metaphors: notes on Michael Jackson's Thriller', in *Sound and Vision: The Music Video Reader*, ed. S. Frith, A. Goodwin and L. Grossberg (New York) pp. 93–109

Meyer, L. 1989. *Style and Music: Theory, History and Ideology* (Philadelphia)

Morton, M. 1993. 'Don't go for second sex, baby!', in *The Madonna Connection: Representation Politics, Subcultural Identities, and Cultural Theory*, ed. C. Swichtenberg (Boulder) pp. 213–35

Ong, W. 1985. *Orality and Literacy: The Technology of the Word* (New York)

Reti, R. 1978. *The Thematic Process in Music* (Westport)

Rose, T. 1994. *Black Noise* (Hanover)

Seurat, G. 1945. 'Letter to Jules Christopher. August 28, 1890' in *Artists on Art from the XIV to the XXth Century*, ed. R. Goldwater and M. Traves (New York) p. 375

da Vinci, Leonardo. 1961. *Leonardo da Vinci on Art and the Artist*, ed. and introduced by Andre Chastel (New York)

Wittgenstein, L. 1968. *Philosophical Investigations* (New York)

[22]

'Gently Tender': the Incredible String Band's early albums

CHARLES FORD

The monstrous machinations of the reissue CD market are reorganising our relations with ourselves, with our own and other peoples' pasts. This, in conjunction with the fact that baby-boomers have grown up, that pop music is no longer simply youth music, means that yesterday's and tomorrow's songs are not necessarily heard in that order, and that styles no longer grow and change in a linear fashion. In the simple act of repetition, thousands of albums, which, like Haydn's symphonies, were never intended for anything more than local consumption, are being underlined as worthy of recall, blessed with the glamorous radiance of digital sound. Musical nostalgia is highly seductive, but whilst it has resulted in considerable beauty and vigour in the hands of both Elgar and Stravinsky, it sounds predatory in the context of all those sixties music advertisements. More seriously – 'lest we forget' – political nostalgia, in the form of the search for the lost German Spirit, eventually proved genocidal. So, at a more personal level, I should be cautious about celebrating such a relic from my own past within the candy-coloured world of hippy psychedelia as the Incredible String Band.

Art criticism only seems of value when linked to ethical concerns, or attempts at intervention. It seems faintly absurd to explain that which is self-explanatory from the perspective of immediate musical experience. Surely if we wish to draw attention to things in themselves, we need at once to somehow let them be. Two things encourage me to proceed. The first is my conviction that immediate sense-experience is far more problematic than anything remote from us, and that the process of disentangling it can help to lay bare the fact that we do not control our individual tastes, desires, thoughts, yet neither are we simply victims of them. The second is the fact that the Incredible String Band have barely received a mention in the literature of popular music despite the extraordinary quality of some of their music. Robin Denselow's few pages in *The Electric Muse* (1975) and a recent glossy monthly article (1993) are about all we have, and they, necessarily, are more concerned with the history of the group than with any particular qualities of their music. Elektra have recently reissued nine or more Incredible String Band albums in a curious order. In this article I address the first four: *the incredible string band* (1966), *5000 Spirits or The Layers of the Onion* (1967), *The Hangman's Beautiful Daughter* (1968) and the double album *Wee Tam and the Big Huge* (1968), which has been reissued as two separate CDs.

The word 'Incredible' in the group's name derives from the name of the Glaswegian club where they were resident in 1965 (Denselow 1975, pp. 155f.) and is not particularly appropriate for the developed folk styles of their first album, which might explain why Elektra waited to test the market before reissuing it. 'String Band' is presumably a reference back to the black and white string bands of the Southern States in the 1920s. When I heard Paul Oliver play Curly Jones and the Dallas Street Band's 'Hokum Blues' on the radio the other day,[1] I could hear a direct resemblance with 'Come a Little Closer' from the first album. Yet, although I am aware – from Bert Jansch's acknowledgement of one Big Bill Broonzy EP as the seminal influence on his work (Harper 1992) – that there was a thriving interest in the blues in the Scottish folk clubs at this time, I doubt whether the very few recordings of string bands that exist could have been available to early 1960s Scottish folk culture.

I

The first album (the only one with their third, founder member Clive Palmer) was destined for the folk market at a time when the younger beatniks who frequented the clubs were ripening into the first, older hippies. Many of the guitar figures can be heard in precisely the same form on the first three albums of their old flat-mate Bert Jansch (1993). The approach to rhythm on many of the tracks is, if not Incredible, probably unique in post-war popular music: variable phrase lengths, metres, and pulses abound. Such irregularities, which inform all the early albums, especially the first two, are used most thoroughly by Heron, Williamson tending to prefer common time broken by occasional ametric tropes. But the second track, Williamson's 'October Song' is the one outstanding exception.

It begins with a filigree, picked guitar introduction, which sets the tone, if not the precise melody and harmony of eight verses. My colleague and friend Allan Moore has compared it to the strength and delicacy of spiders' legs. The most memorable feature of this short instrumental passage is the carefully placed *rubato* on the beginning of the fourth bar. Although this involves no loss of pace, when the same music returns as an interlude between verses 2 and 3, 4 and 5, and 6 and 7, it becomes increasingly stretched to give exquisite interruptions to the steady flow of Williamson's picking.

The introduction announces the irregular metrics of the piece as a whole, which are recorded in Example 1 below in terms of the number of beats in each bar. I have laid this out so as to reveal the rather unusual pattern of repetition that governs the structure of the verses.

The music for verse 1 returns only once as verse 5, though the second part of each verse remains constant, apart from the duration of the final bar, which, like that of the introductory music, changes in accordance with the varying upbeat patterns of whatever follows. The majority of the verses begin with a long vocal note and sustained chord, which changes duration and picking pattern, often with very little sense of metre.

Some of the words introduce what will become a familiar Incredible String Band theme – animism, and the unity of all being. In verses 3 and 4 we learn that 'the fallen leaves . . . know the art of dying', and that 'pine trees laugh green laughter'. Verses 5 and 6 are, to my mind, more thoughtful.

I used to search for happiness, and I used to follow pleasure,
But I've found a door behind my mind, and that's the greatest treasure,
For rulers like to lay down laws and rebels like to break them,
And the poor priests like to walk in chains and God likes to forsake them.

Example 1

```
Instrumental 2-3-4-3-3-3-3-5
Verse 1                          3-5-5        3-4-5
Verse 2                          5-4-3-5      3-4-4
Instrumental    3-4-3-3-3-3-5
Verse 3                          8-4-3-5      3-4-5
Verse 4                          6-4-2-6      3-4-4
Instrumental    3-4-3-3-3-3-6
Verse 5                          3-5-5        3-4-5
Verse 6                          8-4-3-5      3-4-4
Instrumental    3-4-3-3-3-3-4
Verse 7                          8-3-3-3-5    3-4-5
Verse 8                          6-4-2-3-3    3-4-4
Instrumental    3-4-3-3-3-3-3
```

The words 'lay down laws' are nicely set up over firm, slightly slower, crotchet beats, that emphatically resolve the vagaries of the preceding, undivided 8-beat bar, most of which sets a held 'like'. Verses 7 and 8 are also concerned with the relinquishment of the will, now with respect to time. The falsity of clock-time as anything more than an unrelated series of regular clicks[2] is amply demonstrated by the most fluid sense of metre in the last verse.

There is one almost constant feature that binds the finely wrought poetry to the delicacy and fluidity of its musical setting. In the first verse, the relationship between words and metre looks like this:

Example 2

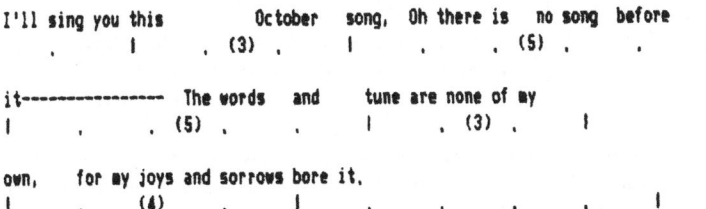

```
I'll sing you this          October  song, Oh there is   no song  before
        |     .  (3) .      |     .       . (5) .      .         |

it---------------- The words  and    tune are none of my
|      .     . (5) .      .      |    . (3) .       |

own,   for my joys and sorrows bore it.
|      .    (4)      .    |     .      .        .     .         |
```

In the first half of the verse the 'natural' stress on 'before' is shifted onto 'it', whilst the second half places the stress 'naturally' on 'bore it'. This pattern holds for all the verses apart from the fourth, and generally resolves the stress scheme of present participles, such as 'going' to 'knowing' and 'aching' to 'taking' in verses 7 and 8. This sense of words and music coming together at the end of each, metrically irregular verse, lends the song a nice balance between fluidity and regularity, between questioning and consolation. Heron summed up my objections to the notion of art as simply self-expression when he wrote in the liner-notes to this song:

Most good songs are the reflection of the writer, upon some aspect of life, but sometimes a songwriter will attempt to throw his whole personality towards the entire area of life, and reflect his outlook fully. It seems to me that such an attempt has been made by Robin in this song . . .

II

The Celtic backbone of the first album becomes one of several style resources on the next three, most notably the blues and other pre-war styles from the Southern states and Indian classical music. If the movement of the blues into British rock now seems a thousand miles away from the bucolic fancies of the sixties folk-club scene, we should remember that the blues was promoted in this country in the 1950s and 1960s as the 'folk blues', and as such 'counted' within the almost religious insistence on authenticity that caused even acoustic guitars to be banned from some clubs. A spiritual sounds near the beginning of the extended and highly sectional centrepiece of *The Hangman's Beautiful Daughter*, 'A Very Cellular Song', and later on [0:48][3] we hear the sound of a jug band, the textures and instrumentation of which (jugs, washboards, kazoo and harmonica) dominate 'Log Cabin Home in the Sky' on *Wee Tam*, and close 'Ducks on a Pond' with a stomp finale [6:08] at the end of the same album. The sound of the country blues often emerges for odd moments, and dominates two tracks from *The 5000 Spirits . . .* – 'Blues for the Muse' and 'Way Back in the 1960s'. Perhaps even more ubiquitous is the sound of Indian instruments, especially Heron's sitar, throughout the second, third and fourth albums, and especially on 'The Eyes of Fate' and 'You Know What You Could Be' from *The 5000 Spirits . . .*, 'Puppies' from *Wee Tam*, and 'The Circle is Unbroken' and 'The Iron Stone' from *The Big Huge*. It is this strange and wonderful conjunction of these particular disjunct styles, together with the ubiquitous references to both pagan and Christian mythologies that I find so redolent of UK hippy culture at this time. But then we should not forget the occasional debts to hymnody and psalmody in, for instance, 'You Know What You Could Be', 'The Mountain of God' and 'Douglas Traherne Harding' from *The Big Huge*, as well as the extraordinary rag-bag of other vernacular moments such as the nursery rhyme in 'Ducks on a Pond' [5:50], the Gilbert and Sullivan spoof, 'The Minotaur's Song' (*The Hangman's Beautiful Daughter*), and the erotic pastiche of choral crooning, 'Air' (*Wee Tam*). This latter, which is directly referable to the signature tune of 'Sing Something Simple', was well known to those who neglected to turn off after Mike Raven's blues and R&B show on Radio 1 in the late 1960s.

Whilst the Incredible synthesis of various styles is relatively easy to enumerate, the question of value across these albums is difficult to extract from the tangled textures of plucked and bowed strings, clattering hand percussion and wailing, highly melismatic vocal lines. As a broad generalisation, hedged around by all the doubts expressed above, I feel that all their work is highly variable in quality, especially *The Hangman's Beautiful Daughter*, which, I suspect, suffers from pressures of over-production.[4] However much we might enjoy Williamson's experiments with flexible pitch, there are moments on 'Douglas Traherne Harding' (*The Big Huge*) which are so terribly out of tune as to make the most liberal ear wince. More generally, in an age which has tired of the smug calls of 'All right now' that dominated later hippy culture, the joyful hymns to the unity of all matter that end many of their songs (I think first of the 'May the good time sunshine . . .' chorus at the end of Mike Heron's 'A Very Cellular Song' on *The Hangman's Beautiful Daughter*), can sound quaint.

When once I could not distinguish the music of Robin Williamson from that of Mike Heron, I now hear the latter's contribution as the more interesting, both as performer – he was a better guitarist and singer – and songwriter. Williamson was the more guilty of careless Orientalism, both in his vocal waverings, which seem inspired by a passing familiarity with classical Indian music, and in his more absurd lines, which miss all the profound wisdom of some of the more impenetrable sayings of Tao. However much we might enjoy rhapsody, the formlessness of, for instance, 'The Mad Hatter's Song' (*The 5000 Spirits* . . .), or 'Witches Hat' (*The Hangman's Beautiful Daughter*) and the tendency of many of both of their songs to fall into discrete sections, beg questions concerning the limits of what constitutes a song. Williamson relies far too much on rough, mechanical strumming of primary triads and 'top of the head' slidings around tonic and dominant, or short repeated phrases. Often it is only Heron's highly inventive sitar that saves great swathes of their songs from tedium. The apparent complexity of his song structures is often an illusion caused by leaving behind the music that opens them in favour of a series of repeated phrases, which first gave the impression of open-endedness, but then later seem to display a lack of patience with the (increasingly unfashionable) art of songwriting. 'Waltz of the New Moon' (*The Hangman's Beautiful Daughter*) and 'Ducks on a Pond' (*Wee Tam*) are but two examples.

Robin Williamson excelled, however, in rapturous melodies, reaching up into the thoroughly undisguised top of his range and describing a great sense of melodic space. 'The First Girl I Loved' on *The 5000 Spirits* . . . uses an extraordinary angular melody with strange, troubled twists and turns that vary from verse to verse. Elsewhere Williamson's exotic melodies are usually heard just once or twice as the opening passages that he tends to leave behind. The opening melody of *The Big Huge* – 'Maya' – forms an expansive two-part arch, each with a climactic pause. When the music eventually arrives at the first complete cadence point after some seventy seconds, with the words 'shall be my native home', I am reminded that, whilst words rarely invoke the sensation of the music they address, music can reveal what we mean by words like 'dwelling'. The opening of 'The Iron Stone' on *The Big Huge* features passages of rhapsodic recitative, that reach up to the top of Williamson's range, rather like some of the first, *parlando* parts of Noel Coward's songs! The chorus of 'The Half-remarkable Question' (*Wee Tam* [0:47] is to my mind one of his best passages. It sets *the* problem: 'Oh it's the old forgotten question: what is that we are part of, and what is it that we are'. The two clauses are each set by 5-bar phrases, the first incorporating one 6/4 bar. The last (philosophically first) word, is set by a held note across one bar, exploding into a rapturous melisma across a second bar, and falling as a cadence onto the first downbeat of a sitar solo.

Mike Heron also uses flexible metres to point up the philosophical problems in what might otherwise seem like either platitude or doggerel. The instrumental introduction to 'Puppies' from *Wee Tam* consists of a 5-bar, meandering gimbri melody, echoed by a highly resonant sitar, and accompanied by guitar and bass. The opening words invite us to think beyond the beauty of nature to speculate on its being. Various idiosyncratic musical elements combine to open up the words in this way. Finger cymbals colour 'birds', there is an aberrant 2/4 bar, and, most important, the (philosophically central) pronoun 'to' is placed on the downbeat at the extreme of Heron's upper register.[5] Williamson and Heron share the left channel, with another Heron in the right. When this beautifully provocative passage repeats there is an extended pause on and after the last word.

During the central section of the piece, which is quite distinct from the similar introduction and ending, Heron's considerable songwriting skills reach their great-

180   *Charles Ford*

Example 3

```
E-------ven the birds        when   they   sing,        it's   not    e-----------very-
   .       .     I      .      .      .    I      .      .     .     I     (2)      I

thing                        to            them                       E-------ven the
I     .      .      .          I      .     .      .    I      .      .      .        I
```

est complexity. After a short two-guitar interlude [1:29] the words 'Hey, hey, such a new born morn' begin half a minute of almost entirely through-composed music in which the three male voices, bass, sitar and hand-drums create a busy and highly variegated texture over simple strummed chords, with shifts between 2, 3, 4, 5 and 6-beat bars culminating in a glorious climax with the words 'Mother Nina, before I'm on my own'.

III

Mike Heron's 'Gently Tender' (*5000 Spirits . . .*) is, I suggest, a rare and wonderful moment in the entirety of post-War British popular music. It is a delicate, joyous and mystical love song with a variety of rhythmically complex, though diatonic major melodies, and an open-ended structure. The 4/4 metre is often interrupted by a variety of other metres, and the pulse is disturbed by pauses and changes of tempo; broadly speaking, rhythms become more complicated as the piece proceeds. It combines Indian style drumming and meandering, vocal melismas, with country blues licks, British folk-song, and moments of electronic chaos in an almost hallucinatory, psychedelic synthesis to accompany barely comprehensible natural and mystical images. Half way through a third verse it drifts into repeated line choruses, which are barely closed by a brief synthesis of previously disparate elements. Although the song gives the impression of those small-group, spontaneous, hippy musical happenings, this is a thoroughly produced piece with considerable use of overdubbing. Mike Heron accompanies himself on 12-string guitar, whilst Robin Williamson sings harmonies and plays hand drums, bass gimbri and end-blown flute. There are two distinct hand-drum parts. A duller, slacker drum plays continuously through the verses in one channel whilst a higher, tauter drum plays intermittently in the other. Licorice is the occasional female vocalist.

A 6-bar flute, drums and guitar introduction comprises three soundings of a 2-bar pair of phrases, shifting IV-I, V7-I on the second beat of each alternate bar, the downbeat being a pulled treble guitar string. The voice, which also begins on the second beat, drifts freely around the pulse, squashing the first two phrases, which might normally take four bars, into three.

When Heron begins the vocal melody again [0:18] he extends its second phrase by way of a 9-beat bar. This eccentric climactic expansion of the last two words – '. . . of her', is an enormous upbeat, supported by a growing (slacker) drum roll, into a heavily weighted downbeat. The rhythmic confusion during the

Example 4

```
    Gently   tender      falls the rain,       washing clean   the    slate again
I     .      .      .      I     .      .      .    I      .      .      .        I
```

Example 5

```
   but leave me please be------hind my brain      the       sligh---------test shadow    of----
I        .      .      .     I     .       .       .    I     .       .       .    I

--of--------------------------------------------------her------------------
I        .      .      .     . (9) .       .       .       .    I
```

words 'the slightest shadow of' involves a shift into compound time as the guitar
changes from duplet to triplet quavers under 'slightest'.

The third part of the verse is preceded by a 2-bar guitar insert [0:27] grouped
on the second beat, which rings with a resonant vibrato, accompanied by the
brighter, more taught drums. The voice sings two similar descending phrases, the
second extended, to give a $3 + 3 + 3 = 9$-bar group, in which another eccentric
terminal extension sets the words in a bizarre relation to the metre. Both of these
expanded terminal melismas are similar to that mentioned above in Williamson's
'The Half-remarkable Question', and might be regarded as a shared style-feature.
The guitar seems to stumble in emotional perplexity under the words 'loving you'
but without losing time. This confusion marks the return to simple metre.

The fourth part of the first verse [0:47] is even more rhythmically fluid,
though Heron keeps right on top of the beat throughout the highly erratic pacing
of words: the word 'true' is extended across a bar, whilst 'love the stone beneath
my . . .' is set within one 3/4 bar. We hear the higher, more taut drums throughout
this section, and Williamson joins in with the final idiosyncratic mis-stressing of
'usual*le-ey*'.

Four bars of country blues [0:59], without the flute, but with the Oriental-
sounding more taut drums, begin with a 6-beat bar, followed by three 5-beat riffs,
each beginning on the second beat. Such metres are commonplace in the recordings of Robert Johnson and Blind Lemon Jefferson.

The 4/4 music of the introduction flows effortlessly, as if from within, the
5-beat blues riffs [1:08], heralding the second verse. This is similar to the first with

Example 6

```
Sha-----dows   dancing through the    pink   milk   blan----kets,              Where
I      .      .      .    I     .      .      .    I     .      .      .    I

my             mind   lay        drea----ming  gent----ly              of
I      .      .      .    I     .      .      .    I     .      .      .    I

my-------- lov----ing-----------------------------------you
I      .      .      .    I     .      .      .    I     .      .      .    I
```

Example 7

```
Sometimes think of    what's true--------------------------    But then I
I      .      .      .    I     .      .      .    I     .      .      .    I

love thestone beneath myfeet as much                 usual-----------ly
I     . (3) .    I     .      .      .    I     .      .      .    I
```

Example 8

```
Good,       good      loving she gave me,  good      loving
 I       .         .          .          I       .         I    etc.
```

a shorter introduction, new words for the first part only, and the extension of the long pause under 'of her' from 9 to 12 beats. The third verse [2:12] breaks off after the 2-bar guitar insert, which is now extended by two further bars, the last purely percussive, so as to prepare nine bars of many voices singing three 2-bar and one 3-bar group of 'na-na-na-na' in 3/4, with a vaguely East European flavour [2:41].

A joyful chorus begins at a slower tempo [2:52], in a hemiola relationship to the preceding. Whereas the earlier shifts into 12/8 retained the crotchet pulse but accelerated quavers by 2:3, this maintains the quavers but slows up the pulse by the same ratio.[6] 4-beat and 2-beat bars are interposed three times for the words 'Good, good loving she gave me', which are sung in harmony with hocketing and the bass gimbri, but without any drums.

After a pause we hear more new music [3:07], back at the original speed, for the words, 'And now all my wine is water'. We can read these words as *both* an expression of post-coital tranquillity, and as a trenchant, if veiled, critique of all revealed religions, though the imagery here is specifically Christian. The music comprises a complex and beautifully fluid series of predominantly 5-beat bars, once again without drums, with Williamson humming in two tracks.

The 'na-na-nas' return [3:25] transformed into electronically reverberated, ametric babbling and cries, which seem to be sound the final fade, thereby rendering the subsequent return to the 'And now all my wine is water' passage [3:51] ecstatically excessive. Perhaps the most extraordinary thing about the return of this highly irregular music is that it is not simply electronically repeated, as is manifest from minute vocal alterations, and the extension of the penultimate bar to seven beats, delaying the final word 'clear' to great effect. The final bar is cut back from seven to five beats. A short coda [4:19] returns to the instrumental

Example 9

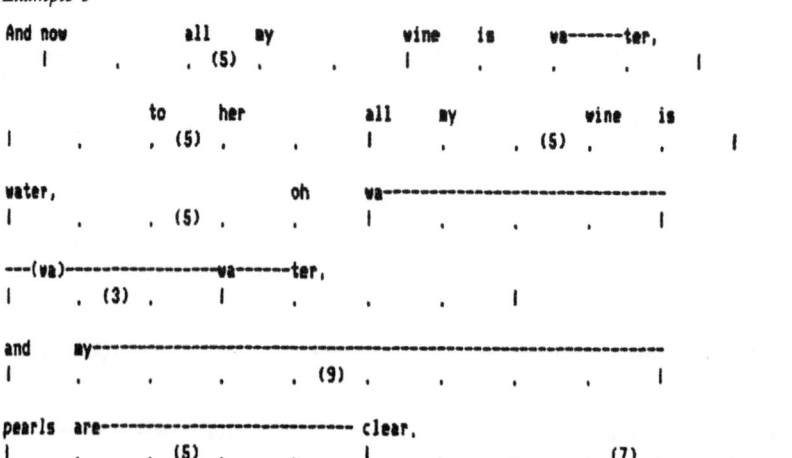

accompaniment to the verses, though now with the words 'she give to me good loving' sung across six bars of 4/4 with one enormous melisma on 'me'. Two bars of instruments lead to a reverberated, held polyphonic chord that melts the words 'good loving' into an exquisite close.

Endnotes

1 Paul Oliver *Before the Blues* programme 4, BBC Radio 3, 2 July 1992.

2 I am doing an injustice to the following:

. . . space and time as parameters can neither bring about nor measure nearness. Why not? In the succession of 'nows' one after the other as elements of parametric time, one 'now' is never in open face-to-face encounter with another. In fact, we may not even say that, in this succession, the 'now' coming after and the 'now' coming before are closed off from each other. For closure too, is still a manner of facing or excluding something being in face-to-face. But this encounter is as such excluded from the parametric concept of time. (Heidegger 1971, p. 104)

This passage is taken from Martin Heidegger's 1957–58 lectures entitled 'The Nature of Language', (collected in Heidegger 1971). Two pages further on Heidegger presents an alternative notion of time, which I would like to share.

Time times simultaneously: the has-been, presence, and the present that is waiting for our encounter and is normally called the future. Time in its timing removes us into its threefold simultaneity, moves us thence while holding out to us the disclosure of what is in the same time, the concordant oneness of the has-been, presence, and the present waiting the encounter. In removing us and bringing toward us, time moves on its way what simultaneity yields and throws open to it: time-space. But time itself, in the wholeness of its nature, does not move; it rests in stillness. (Heidegger 1971, p. 106)

3 From here on I put CD timings in square brackets.

4 This evaluation is at variance with the opinions of several pop stars and the author of the article in *Q* (1993), who informs us that *The Hangman's Beautiful Daughter* is 'scientifically proven to be their masterpiece'.

5 Stuart Hall (1978) has pointed out that both hippy and Black Power discourses laid great stress on pronouns: tune in, drop out, sit in, far out, get down, up tight and so forth.

6 Lucy Green noticed this.

References

Denselow, R., Laing, D., Dallas, K. and Shelton, R. 1975. *The Electric Muse: The Story of Folk into Rock* (London)

Hall, S. 1978. 'The hippies – an American "moment" ', Stencilled Occasional Paper, no. 16, Centre for Contemporary Cultural Studies, Birmingham

Harper, P. 1992. Liner notes to Bert Jansch *The Gardener*, Transatlantic/Demon TDEMCD9, 1992

Heidegger, M. 1971. *On the Way to Language*, translated by P. D. Hertz (London)

Q. 1993. 'Never trust a hippy', *Q* 8, 1 June

Discography

The Incredible String Band:
the incredible string band, Elektra, 7559-61547-2, 1966/1993
5000 Spirits or The Layers of the Onion, Elektra, 7559-60913-2, 1967/1992
The Hangman's Beautiful Daughter, Elektra, 7559-60835-2, 1968/1992
Wee Tam, Elektra, 7559-60914-2, 1968/1992
The Big Huge, Elektra 7559-61548-2, 1968/1993

[23]

Cathy's homecoming and the Other world: Kate Bush's 'Wuthering Heights'

NICKY LOSSEFF

Curiosity value quite possibly accounted for the success of Kate Bush's first single in 1978. Those who have continued to admire her more particularly for her later musical achievements,[1] which have surely consolidated her position as one of the most individual and innovative artists of the 1980s and 1990s, do so possibly in spite of (rather than because of) the impact of 'Wuthering Heights'. No other song of hers has had the same public appeal – it stayed in the British charts for seventy-five weeks (Rice 1991) – and perhaps the smaller group of admirers who remain loyal engage more with the intensely personal visions into which her lyrics have matured, as opposed to that first, more musically zany, original hit.

Nevertheless, I assume qualities of greatness in 'Wuthering Heights' which make me want to write about the song. Some of those qualities of greatness are interpreted here through an examination of the interaction between meanings inherent in the music and in the lyrics. I argue that these meanings concern the duality of the real and the Other world, and that these dualities are explored musically in two particularly powerful ways: harmonic structure and vocal timbre. My suggestion is that the duality of 'tonic' keys in this song, A major for the verses and D♭ major for the refrain, mirror the duality of the two worlds; and that one of these keys, though it has greater claim to be the 'true' tonic, is never really established, a factor which poignantly echoes the concept of 'home' for Cathy and Heathcliff in the texts of both Emily Brontë and Kate Bush. Vocal timbre too reflects the division of real and Other world, and the concept of registral zones is used here as a way of hearing in which world Cathy is sited.

'Wuthering Heights' speaks in the first person with Cathy's voice from the Other world. In the song, she is addressing Heathcliff, with whom she was of one soul in the material world. Cathy's soul-locked relationship with Heathcliff is distilled into a couple of dozen lines of lyrics: much as the librettist of a Baroque opera might have pared down material from a large-scale literary work to create an aria, which focuses on the drama and emotion inherent in a single moment of time as opposed to recitative, which takes the narrative onwards. In Emily Brontë's novel,[2] Cathy's ghost pleads to be let in at the window not to Heathcliff, but to the unfortunate Mr Lockwood, who is sleeping in Cathy's old bedroom (Brontë 1994, pp. 36–7). The incident takes place very near the beginning of the novel, in the 'real time' of the framing story, which concerns Mr Lockwood's residence at Thrushcross

Grange. He is forced to spend his first night in Yorkshire under Heathcliff's roof at Wuthering Heights, and as yet neither he nor the reader know anything of the Cathy–Heathcliff tale. Lockwood is troubled by nightmares, and although the appearance of Cathy at the window is no dream but a 'real' experience of a ghost, the reader has no way yet of interpreting this scene, and no way of knowing that it is Heathcliff with whom Cathy really wants to communicate – as she does directly in the song.

Listeners familiar with Emily Brontë's story know in any case that this is not the voice of Cathy on earth but as she is now, in the Other world. Like Brontë, Kate Bush enjoys playing with tenses in her text, mixing the framing present with description of the past. Cathy's evocation of her and Heathcliff's roaming on the moors (or, as she has it, rolling and falling in green) is described not just in the simple past tense, 'we rolled', but in what we might call the past historic: 'we would roll'. At the moment of Cathy's tapping on the window, she switches to the present: 'It's me, Cathy, come home', so that we understand with hindsight that she has been remembering her worldly past at the very moment that she is about to begin knocking. Through this device, the window episode (to which I shall return later) becomes the focal point of the Cathy–Heathcliff relationship, the point of contact between the real world and the Other, in which their complex relationship is stripped to the bare essentials. This is Cathy's statement, in a first-person narrative of bald simplicity whose exact angle we never hear in the novel, since everything there is filtered through the voice of the chroniclers, Nelly Dean and Lockwood. By allowing Cathy in effect to give her own version of the relationship with Heathcliff, Kate Bush can emphasise whichever elements seem important to her as a reader of the original text. Thus, she interprets the novel through the lyrics and the music simultaneously; the lyrics and the music also interpret each other. In effect, she becomes the interpreter of both what is given and what she herself wants to read between the lines of the novel – a double mediation of the reader, as it were. Tellingly, she said in a 1978 interview that it had been 'a real challenge to précis the whole mood [rather than the content?] of a book into a single short piece of prose' (Ellis 1978). In reality, the situation is richer and more intricate, since it is not only through words that the mood of the whole book is condensed. Perhaps the web of meanings which the lyrics and music jointly weave go some way to mitigating some of her interpretations; otherwise, constructions such as the image of Heathcliff as Cathy's 'one dream, [her] only master' seem at best whimsical, at worst immature. In the novel, after all, Cathy's longest soliloquy concerns her relationship with Heathcliff, during which she emphasises again and again that they are of one soul:

He is more myself than I am . . . Whatever our souls are made of, his and mine are the same . . . Nelly, I *am* Heathcliff! He's always, always in my mind: not as a pleasure, any more than I am always a pleasure to myself, but as my own being. (Brontë 1994, pp. 80–1)

The changing tenses of the lyrics, from past historic to present, do indeed help us pin down the exact moment of Cathy's existence which is explored and expanded by the song; but this is a cerebral process, one which relies on the reflection of hindsight and where meaning is located in, and limited by, the form of the words themselves. Though Kate Bush portrays her version of Cathy's spirit-life in language, she also evokes it with immediacy through a signifier that Barthes has characterised as 'the grain of the voice' (1977, p. 294). Kate Bush's vocal quality – unknown to the public at the time of the song's release, and which would seem to have been the aspect of the song that struck the first-time listener most forcefully – transmits, at the juncture of language and pure sound, intuitive rather than cerebral meaning.[3] Inside her voice, the listener participates in the essentially solipsistic world of the spirit. What gives her voice its distinctive quality? Many early reviewers commented on what they heard as an incredibly high tessitura in 'Wuthering Heights',[4] but this is a misleading impression, since Kate Bush simply uses the vocal range normal for the average female voice – between e' and e" – going down to an ab and with a top note of only f#". 'Kite', for instance, has an (appropriately) much larger range of two and a half octaves, from g to a swoop up to c'", and we should not forget that a few years earlier, Minnie Ripperton entered truly ethereal domains – a full octave above the highest note of 'Wuthering Heights' – in 'Loving You'.

In reality, the eeriness and Other-worldliness Kate Bush manages to portray has little to do with pitch and much to do with timbre. Some early reviewers did come close to identifying the 'quality' as opposed to the pitch of her voice as the really unusual factor, but few came close to pinning down exactly how Kate Bush manipulates her voice to produce so many different types of sound. Clarke (1978) called it 'a voice not unlike that of a newly-neutered cat', whereas to Young (1978a), it was 'either Minnie Mouse or Heavenly Host, depending on your point of view'. More accurately, Wigg (1978) perceived a 'high-pitched oriental sound'. Usually, the description 'oriental' would imply a routing of the air through the nose, which Kate Bush does not do; however, singers of Peking Opera and popular Indian female vocalists such as Lata Mangeshkar narrow the gap at the back of the mouth by lowering the soft palette to produce a characteristic thinner, more reedy sound, and it is this technique that Kate Bush exercises here.

If vocal 'grain' is a signifier of meaning, then what does Kate Bush's voice tell her listener in this song? Elizabeth Wood (1994) has written on timbre and phonic environment as a powerful signifier of sexuality, raising issues about what voices that step outside of normal ranges can mean. Her point of reference was primarily the classically trained voice, where pitch and timbre are interrelated and defined within recognised boundaries of 'chest' (low), 'middle' and 'head' (high) registers. The relationship in pop genres between vocal range and timbre would of course reveal different codes at work, since a singer of popular music pushing her chest register to the absolute upper limit (a common phenomenon) does not convey the same message as a classically trained singer doing the same (a very rare phenomenon); classical singers are trained to move as imperceptibly as possible over the 'breaks' between registers where they naturally occur, whereas pop singers often 'chest' up to more than an octave past their breaks. Thus, for classical singers, only the very top of their total range conveys what we might call *the strain of the voice*: the kind of tension which accumulates when the voice is pushed well past its break to register emotional intensity. We often hear this at relatively low pitches for popular singers: listen to Tammy Wynette singing 'Stand By Your Man', where she communicates a new emotion simply by chesting up to an a'. Classically trained voices, on the other hand, are often valued more if they can seem to float effortlessly to the top of their register, transmitting 'strain' as little as possible. The issue for Wood though, and the issue here, is what is signified when well-defined boundaries are *crossed*. Kate Bush's Cathy in effect occupies a timbral space that had not been heard before, not least because she never really exploits the chest register at all in this song but sings entirely in middle and head registers, while manipulating her vibrato/soft palette to produce different vocal effects. Just as for the esteemed classical singer who can float up to the vocal stratosphere, there is almost no exploitation of the strain of the voice in this song; the effect is of hovering inside a well-defined space rather than pushing against it. This timbral space is more powerfully defined by the song's placing within the album *The Kick Inside* than when 'Wuthering Heights' is heard singly; it needs a context to achieve its full effect, and on this album, perhaps more than any other, Kate Bush's exploration of vocal timbre and range is very wide.[5]

There are certainly moments in 'Wuthering Heights' when changing presentations of sexuality – that of child, then adult; that of love, then jealousy and possession – are differentiated through changes in vocal timbre. The most significant example of this is her plunge from pouting, flirtatious child on 'how could you leave me/when I needed to' through the dangerous and anger-flashing manipulation of 'possess you/I hated you', down to a curiously tender a♭ on '*I loved* [you too]'. Even so, the tenderness and sensuousness of this moment is accomplished through use of the lowest range of middle, rather than chest, register; it might well be that vocally, this was a conscious or unconscious technical decision, made to facilitate the move to the octave above on '[I loved] *you too*'. In so compressed a medium as the individual song, though, we ignore such small nuances of meaning at our peril. For Cathy in this song, the chest register is a forbidden zone, representing perhaps a groundedness in the corporeal; thus, Cathy's unearthly timbre is on the larger scale probably not primarily an exploration of sexuality, but of the spirit. In fact, Kate Bush made it clear that she had deliberately set out to cultivate such a thing, explaining that 'I tried to project myself into the role of the book's heroine and, because she is a ghost, I gave her a high-pitched, wailing voice' (Wigg 1978). This is the voice that wants to grab Heathcliff's soul away – as opposed to his body? Critically, as the music finally fades out, the housing of this voice within the human body loses its role to the wail of the electric guitar – as if Cathy no longer has need of words, or indeed anything associated with the living being, to sing her song. This is far removed from the dark and passionate, earthy, earthly Cathy of Emily Brontë, whose speaking voice one imagines as anything but wraith-like and wailing; yet it is utterly right for Kate Bush's spirit-Cathy, removed from the real world which she wants to access solely in order to take away Heathcliff's soul. And it is not just Cathy's unearthly voice that tells us we are in the realms of the spirit. Before the singing even starts, we have been taken there by the piano and celeste, in the two-plus-two bar introductory phrase where the opening motive, stated in the middle register of the piano, is repeated in the airy, upper regions, reached via an ethereal sounding celeste glissando. Even though voice and piano enter for the first verse back in the middle register, somehow in our imaginations we have still been left in the heavenly one.

Let us turn now to the harmonic workings of 'Wuthering Heights', the other 'site of the spirit' in this song. It might well be true that for most popular music, as commentators such as McClary and Walser (1990) have observed, the musical interest lies in factors other than the organisation of the pitch material. However, 'Wuthering Heights' has a harmonic (and harmonic–rhythmic) structure which cries out to be considered in detail. My purpose here is not to delineate long-term tonal movement or chord progressions simply for their own sakes, but to suggest that the relative functional meanings of keys and chords also have symbolic meanings: meanings which illuminate, and are in turn illuminated by, the song's lyrics. One of the factors which makes the song interesting for me is the friction caused on the one hand by obedience to the presuppositions of conventional tonality, and on the other, a resistance to that framework. Indeed, the meanings I read depend on the idea that the harmonic patterns in 'Wuthering Heights', though complex, are essentially situated within fundamentally conventional functional tonality, and thus work either with or against the 'grammar of expectation'. Some of this analysis focuses on harmonic rhythm, identifying where metrical units begin and end, and thus which beats sound 'strong' and which 'weak'. This factor will become important to the discussion. Although I argue that this song is primarily tonal, tonality and modality do to some extent co-exist within the harmonic framework – a model common enough in pop music, as Allan Moore (1992) and Richard Middleton (1990, pp. 201–3) have discussed. Moore's examples, though, utilise the so-called Greek or old 'church' modes, whereas Kate Bush's modal inflexions do not belong within this tradition. The mixture of modal and tonal in 'Wuthering Heights' is best understood in the context of Kate Bush's musical upbringing. She learned the violin in school, since her parents thought a basic musical grounding would be important (Juby 1988, p. 5), but as crucial to her aural awareness must have been the folk music with which her family were intimately involved. Modality in this song is a means of inflexion rather than a true framework for the underlying movement of tones, as I discuss later.

Example 1 shows the overall shape of the song. Note especially the enharmonic change from C♯ to D♭ at the end of system 1, preparing the way for the modulation from A major in the verses to D♭ major in the refrains.

The song's opening A major tonality is established strongly by a two-plus-two bar introductory phrase on the piano, and this key at first seems to be confirmed when the voice enters – see Example 2.

Almost straight away, though, A major is undermined. Far from the usual confirmation of tonic through the sounding of the dominant, the music passes only briefly through the fifth degree (E major), via the flattened sixth (F♮ major), ending on a major triad on the mediant (C♯ major) – see Example 3.

Thus, there are two harmonies 'foreign' to the key: F major and C♯ major (true VI in A major would be F♯ minor, true III C♯ minor). This harmonic scheme is a vague echo of the opening motive, with its falling thirds and neighbour note. What is most striking here, though, is less any putative organic relationship between motive and harmonies than the foreign-ness of the E♯ within the C♯ major chord.[6] Had the song reached a chord of C♯ *minor* at the end of the first vocal phrase, then our tonal expectations would have been confirmed: we could confidently hear the music in A, moving to C♯ minor. It is true that a move to E major would have confirmed A as tonic beyond doubt, but a related minor key would have performed a confirmatory function quite adequately. As it is, that assurance is not forthcoming, and we are left in the curiously bright realms of C♯ major.

The opening sequence of chords is stated three times. On the third statement, it extends itself: the C♯ changes enharmonically to D♭, and this D♭ then functions as IV in A♭ – see Example 4.

After this point – at Cathy's 'bad dreams in the night' section – the music almost loses us in its modulation. After we have reached A♭ major, there is a progression through the chords E♭ minor, then G♭ major, and finally F major; this three-chord sequence, which is then repeated twice, seems to imply resolution to the dark key of B♭ minor:

232   *Nicky Losseff*

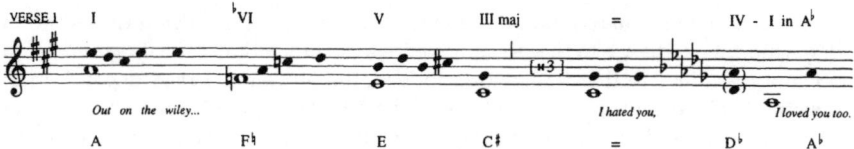

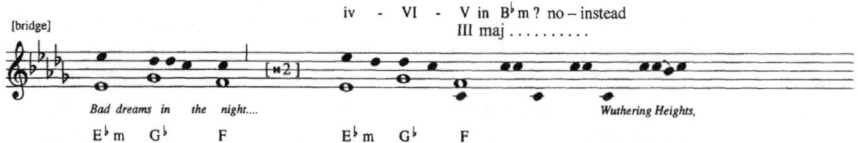

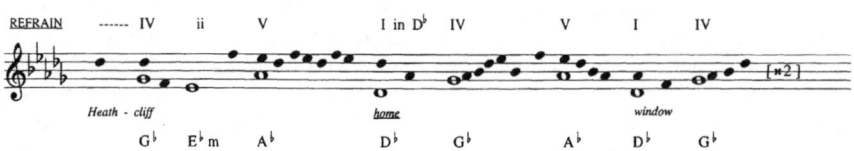

Example 1.

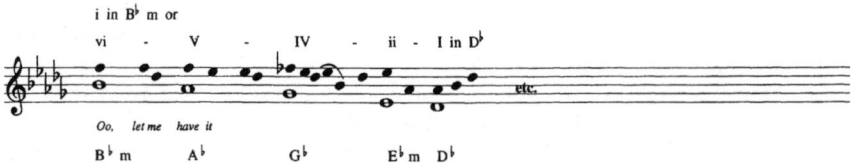

Example 2.

Example 3.

Example 4.

> Ebm – Gb – F (stated three times)
>
> implied: iv – VI – V in Bbm

Thus, early on in the song, Bb minor suggests a brooding presence, the place of Cathy's nightmares, which is implied though not reached: a threat of darkness, perhaps, that remains to be realised. This reflects the anxiety of the lyrics, in which Cathy contemplates the imminence of her death. Later in the song, the threat will seem to have become real. At this early stage, however, the F major harmony – instead of functioning as V in Bb minor – becomes by sleight of hand III in Db; a resolution effected via the conventional pattern

> III – IV – ii – V – I
>
> F – Gb – Ebm – Ab – Db

Speaking in terms of conventional tonality, this is a moment of some importance in the song. For the first time, a key (Db) has been established in the orthodox manner, through the affirmation of its dominant (Ab). The A major of the verse is heard, in retrospect, as a key only ancillary to the new, convincingly true tonic of Db. Furthermore, as if we needed confirmation that we are indeed 'home' in Db, it is at the point of statement of the first Db harmony that Cathy utters the word 'home' – see Example 5.

But the new tonic of Db major is not unproblematic. Rather than being securely grounded in the comfort of the four-bar phrase, the harmonic rhythm trips us up here. We hear the moment at which the Db occurs as a downbeat, but this proves transient, as it is immediately confounded by *another* 'downbeat' and a return to the harmony of Gb. This destablises the Db, tonic 'downbeat' which we rehear instead as a curious, extra, weak third beat in the previous bar, a bar that now seems almost to have been ruptured by the addition – see Example 6.

This sub-section does actually have twelve beats, so in theory it would be possible to continue hearing it in 2/2. Several factors undermine this. First, the classic backbeat drum pattern, in which the downbeat of the bar coincides with the 'weak' drum beat, is disrupted; instead of a continuous pattern of weak/strong, we instead get [with ○ indicating weak and + indicating strong]:

> ○ + ○ + ○ ○ + ○ + ○ ○ + [repeat]
>
> Gb Ebm Ab Ab Db Gb Gb Gb Ab Db Gb Gb [repeat]

Although with this pattern it would be possible to argue that the Db major *did* come on a downbeat, Gb comes across as the stronger, 'true' downbeat here. The reasons for this seem mostly to do with the momentous way Gb is set up at the beginning of the refrain section. First, this opening Gb harmony is heralded by

234   *Nicky Losseff*

Example 5.

Example 6.

the first real entry of percussion – a rolled build-up on cymbal, culminating with the close of the high-hat; and in equivalent places later in the song, we get a full drum build up culminating in a cymbal stroke. Second, the instrumentation increases dramatically in density and dynamic as the refrain begins on its G♭ chord; previously, the only accompanying instrument has been keyboards. Third, this opening G♭ accompanies the first utterance of Heathcliff's name. This is a real moment of catharsis: partly because Heathcliff has only been referred to as an unnamed 'you' in the strangely shifting harmonies of the verse, partly because the initial weirdness of the song's opening gives way to a familiar and powerful riff-driven groove – probably the characteristic most responsible for the song's chart success. Thus, when a G♭ occurs again in the refrain (which happens with great frequency , as we shall see), we have already heard it and return to it, as a harmony lodged in our consciousness, rather than one encountered afresh. As to the frequency of G♭ chords in this section, we cannot ignore their sheer quantity. They far outnumber any other, making up half the total harmony until the return to A major in preparation for the verse:

G♭ – E♭m – A♭ – A♭ – D♭
G♭ – G♭ – G♭ – A♭ – D♭
G♭ – G♭
G♭ – E♭m – A♭ – A♭ – D♭
G♭ – G♭ – G♭ – A♭ – D♭
G♭ – G♭ – [A – A]

Four D♭ (tonic) chords
Six A♭ (dominant) chords
Two E♭m (supertonic) chords
Twelve G♭ (subdominant) chords

G♭ is thus the chord which dominates this section; it is the very last heard as the song fades out, when one can imagine the harmonic sequence circling away to infinity. D♭, the 'home' key, is in contrast very understated in the refrain, both in terms of how much it is heard and where in the bar it occurs. Of course, the point of tonics is that they do not have to be stated again and again – we know when we have arrived, and one of the narratives on which large-scale functional-harmonic forms (such as sonata form) depend is that of the tonic being stated and then left while the music moves through the 'adventures' of different keys, secure in the knowledge that the home key will be reached safely in the end. Nor am I arguing that the focus on the chord of IV (G♭) in this section is particularly unusual viewed in the context of popular music in general. Rather, I suggest that in this song, it can be read as significantly adding a layer of meaning to the lyrics. For not only does the moment of arrival on the D♭ tonic coincide with Cathy's articulation of the work 'home', but even more suggestive is the song's leap away from D♭ almost as soon as it arrives there – like having touched something too hot. Home is unequivocally not a place Cathy can stay. In fact, of course, she cannot even get in. The music moves immediately away from the D♭ tonic and on to the nagging, ever-present G♭ subdominant. She tries again, saying 'let me in at your *window*' – the point of entry to the *home*; and *window* is accompanied by the second occurrence of the D♭, or harmonically speaking, 'home'. But the music cannot rest at this sounding of the tonic either. As before, it jumps away immediately to G♭. In trying to get home, through the window, Cathy has been wrong-footed by the curious placement of the D♭ tonic within the bar, and denied the comfort of rest within the 'home' key . The real world is closed to her forever.

At this point, the C♯ chord from the verse, where it is foreign to the A major tonality, becomes significant as the only harmony (enharmonically speaking) that the two sections – verse and refrain – have in common. Is it too obvious to suggest that this duality of keys perhaps echoes the two worlds of the song: A for the Other world where we first meet Cathy – where she is harmonically situated – and D♭ for the 'real' world she cannot enter, and which Heathcliff still inhabits? This possibility is strengthened by the words of the second verse: 'Oh it gets, dark, it gets lonely, on the other side from you'. As for the first verse, the music moves from A to C♯/D♭; as it reaches this harmonic goal, the words too reach the 'other side'.

Perhaps one of the most interesting factors here is that though the heroine is literally the Subject of the text, speaking as she does in the first person, nevertheless she identifies, in A major, as harmonically Other to the true tonic of D♭, and this would seem to reinforce the identification of the hero as male and the object of the hero's gaze as female – a construction that theorists have suggested is common to so much narrative.[7] At first sight, the harmonic, D♭ major 'Subject' represents Home, that is, Cathy's real Home in the living world. Cathy is now, as an inhabitant of the Other world, Other more to her old living self than to another person. However, as we have discussed in relation to vocal timbre, genders and sexualities are not the primary dualities in this song; if we look on to the second verse, we find Heathcliff identified more and more closely with Cathy's concept of Home, even if he never appears ostensibly as the real protagonist of the drama. She speaks of the Other side as being dark and lonely without him, her one dream and her only master; on the Other side, she pines for him and finds 'the lot / falls through without you', going on to declare that she has roamed the night too long and is coming back to his side, to Wuthering Heights 'to put it right'. It seems more appropriate thus to place Home, in D♭, as Subject, and both Cathy and Heathcliff in A major as Other – and thinking back to Emily Brontë's novel, this reflects the reality of their situation more accurately. Wuthering Heights never really was Home to Heathcliff, in the sense of being a place of comfort, rest and ease. It was simply where he was domiciled. In this instance, Cathy's real Home is *with* Heathcliff – Wuthering Heights, as a real or conceptual Home, being closed to both of them.

This interpretation would also be reinforced by another factor, which we should consider by looking again at the harmonic pattern in the verses. As we have noted, in the first three phrases the music moves from A major down through F and E to the distant C♯/D♭. With the fourth statement of this pattern, however, the D♭ acts as subdominant to the even lower, final harmonic destination of the phrase: A♭ major (see Example 4). The effect of this final fall is dramatic: we have reached A major's most far-removed key of all, that of the flattened tonic, and we feel the music has sighed to its very depths. In the first verse, immediately before this point, Cathy has said to Heathcliff 'I hated you', but at the articulation of the A♭ chord, she says 'I loved you too'; in the second verse, this coincides with her utterance that Heathcliff is her 'only master'. The A♭ is poised on the brink of a harmonic sleight-of-hand here, since it is immediately followed by the strange link passage between verse and refrain which rocks between the harmonies of E♭ minor, G♭ and F, and which wants to resolve to B♭ minor – but instead brightens into the D♭ refrain, the real tonic. D♭ is of course reached quite properly through its dominant: A♭ (see Example 1, systems 2–3). Thus, the A♭, which had previously represented the final relief or the articulation of a deep sigh ('I loved you too'; 'My only master') also acts as the harmonic fulcrum to the true home, the key of D♭.

Let us return to the question of B♭ minor. This key, as I have said, is problematised early on in the song in the bridge between verse and refrain (see Example 1, system 2). The E♭ minor – G♭ – F chords suggest resolution onto B♭ minor, but this key is withheld; its presence, hinted at but yet unvoiced, is associated with Cathy's fear that she is 'going to lose the fight' and thus with loss, foreboding and the presentiment of death. Just after the second statement of the refrain, the dreaded B♭ minor chord is at last heard (see Example 1, system 4). This is the moment at which Cathy says she wants to 'have it, to grab [Heathcliff's] soul away'. This seems to contradict her former craving: does she want to come home or does she want to take him away to her? When the chord of B♭ minor does then finally appear, it would seem to herald the worst, and indeed, the threat is that Heathcliff's soul will now be carried off to the Other world. However, a real modulation never occurs; B♭ minor turns out not to be a new tonic in a key of darkness at all, since it resolves in a conventional vi–V–IV–ii–I pattern, through A♭, G♭ and E♭ minor chords to the Home key of D♭ major – if she grabs his soul away, then it will result in the promise of having reached Home.

B♭m	–	A♭	–	G♭	–	E♭m–	D♭
vi	–	V	–	IV	–	ii –	I

Of course, the promise is illusory, since the song ends by fading away into the endless circling IV–V–I–IV progressions of the refrain, with its G♭ major subdominant still needling away at the harmonic discourse and marginalising all else. In any case, B♭ minor is the relative minor of D♭ major – the two sides of the same coin; only death can now be Home for Cathy and Heathcliff. We know from the end of the novel that eventually for Heathcliff, his 'soul's bliss kills [his] body' (Brontë 1994, p. 276) and that in such a way, he and Cathy do come together. But in the song, that moment of bliss is not reached. Instead, Cathy and Heathcliff are locked into a cycle of perpetual isolation from each other.

Thus, in 'Wuthering Heights', Kate Bush has articulated some of the primary meanings of her text through a sophisticated harmonic framework. And the relationship between the musical content and meaning in her songs is something

Example 7.

of which she herself was quite conscious. In one 1978 article, she was quoted as saying 'the chords almost dictate what the song should be about because they have their own moods' (Blake 1978); and in another, 'I just start playing the piano and the chords start telling me something' (Ellis 1978).

In an early interview, Kate Bush said she associated major keys with happy events and minor with sad (Blake 1978). 'Wuthering Heights' does not at first seem an obvious candidate for major tonality, replete as it is with the angst of unfulfilled longing. It is perhaps significant then that in both underlying melodic movement and harmonic progression, the song's major tonalities of A and D♭ are each, as I have said, tempered by underlying non-diatonic scales, and I focus now on the song's modal permeation. The A major verses, as we have seen, sink from A through F♯ and E to C♯: a harmonic progression which is mirrored beautifully at the end of that phrase by an inflected, mirror-image flourish in the piano part – see Example 7.

One could construct a mode from this consisting loosely of minor thirds followed by semitones – or, perhaps more appropriately, a mode constructed from the (enharmonic) constituents of major *and* minor triads on C♯, F and A: c♯–e–f–g♯–a–[–c–c♯]. It is not, as I have said, truly allied to the so-called Greek or 'church' modes, with their stepwise movement, and which in an era of post-tonality are too easily perceived as inflected major or minor scales. In the verses, the presence of Kate Bush's unusual mode, both harmonically and in the structure of the melody, permits a comfortable move from A to D♭ and back again – since both those keys are inherent in the mode itself. Perhaps this modal inflexion is responsible for the sense of organicism which pervades 'Wuthering Heights', despite the often unconventional harmonic patterning and irregular phrase lengths. And thinking about melodic/harmonic movement in this way could also make sense of the curious lack of real leading note to tonic motion in the melody, because although we do at least notionally get a g♯–[a] between the first and second phrases, the g♯ is of course part of the foreign C♯-major harmony and not the dominant, E, as more conventional harmonic patterns would have led us to expect. Melodic motion also contributes to the feeling of opening out into the 'true' D♭ key centre at the start of the refrain, since the e–d–c♯–e circular motive ('Out on the wiley') transforms itself into f–e♭–d♭–f–e♭–d♭–etc. at 'It's me, Cathy, I've come home'. Significantly, it is the refrain, with its IV–V–I patterns, whose melody avoids the leading note altogether, instead weaving in and around the home note of D♭ by means of an enriched pentatonic scale. It seems that even here, in the more conventionally 'functional-harmonic' section, Kate Bush preferred to soften the stronger lines of tonality with a modal brush – see Example 8.

At this point, I would like to step sideways: having suggested that Kate Bush

Example 8.

238   *Nicky Losseff*

Example 9.

shies away from truly grounded tonality, what of the relationship between melody and bass? Usually, where these two strata meet, we can expect a mixture of consonant intervals: thirds, fourths, fifths, sixths, and where dominant sevenths occur, sevenths. In contrast, 'Wuthering Heights' pans out like a piece of medieval organum; almost all the underlying structural points of coincidence are fifths, with the occasional octave or unison, and only one sixth. The lack of structural thirds is another contributory factor to the dominance of the modal, rather than the tonal.

To my view, this modality serves to enhance, rather than diminish or dilute, the tonality in which the song is based. Because the lyrics themselves so sparsely explore the complex and many-layered relationship between Cathy and Heathcliff in Emily Brontë's novel, we are left with a more open field in which to weave threads of meaning from the words, within and around the events, both simultaneous and unfolding, of what emerges as a staggeringly complex musical structure.

As I have already suggested, 'Wuthering Heights' seems in some ways like an aria from an opera whose libretto is based on a novel, with verbiage stripped to the bare bones and one moment of emotional significance expanded in depth. But in a full opera, Cathy's character would be explored little by little as the drama unfolded; whereas here the whole story is summed up *as* she taps on the window. Kate Bush was disarmingly open in early interviews about the inspiration for the song: she had turned on the television while a dramatisation of *Wuthering Heights* was being screened, and had caught the moment where Cathy's wrists are cut on the broken glass of her window (Blake 1978). If we are to take this comment at face value, then that event was truly fortuitous, since the window is one of the most potent symbols of the novel: not only at the beginning, when, to Lockwood's horror, Cathy taps on the glass to be let into her old bedroom, but also at the end, when Heathcliff is close to gaining his single wish to join Cathy in death. Here, after he has almost stopped eating, and has become bright and cheerful, he is observed by Nelly Dean looking 'eagerly towards the window' (ibid, p. 271), then rising and going out. Later, he leans against the ledge of an open lattice; Nelly closes all the casements and eventually, to rouse him, asks 'Must I close this?'(Brontë 1994, p. 272). There is no doubt in the reader's mind just what lies outside. Nelly notes that the window of Heathcliff's bedroom is 'wide enough for anybody to get through; and it struck me that he plotted another midnight excursion' (ibid, p. 273). Just before she finds him dead, she sees

the master's window swinging open, and the rain driving straight in . . . The lattice, flapping to and fro, had grazed one hand that rested on the sill; no blood trickled from the broken skin, and when I put my fingers to it, I could doubt no more: he was dead and stark! (ibid, p. 277)

The first thing Nelly does is to hasp the window; only the spirits of the living are left inside. No wonder the window remained the seminal image for Kate Bush – and one which she retained as central to the song, the lens through which all else is focused as retrospective or remembrance.

'Wuthering Heights' is not the only song on *The Kick Inside* to explore extended tonality, irregular phrase lengths or unusual vocal timbres. Perhaps part of its power lay, paradoxically, in the fact that within its chart-pop context it was so *well* grounded in more conventional frameworks of harmony, phrase-length and vocal range – the familiar characteristics of the refrain serving to set off the song's more bizarre aspects in greater relief. Thus, the irregularities kick harder against those orthodox conventions. Perhaps the album's title had a musical meaning too.

Endnotes

1 Kruse (1990) concentrates on these later achievements, with particular reference to *Hounds of Love*, in her sociological and literary (as opposed to musical) assessment.

2 *Wuthering Heights*. All page numbers refer to the Penguin Popular Classics edition, 1994.

3 I thank Neil Sorrell and Toni Calam for their often long and always helpful discussions with me on issues of timbre and vocal technique. I thank Rachel Cowgill for her insights on sexuality as discussed in this section.

4 See for instance Anon (1978); Doherty (1978); Nulman (1978).

5 Ellis (1978), Fowler (1978) and Frith (1978) were among early reviewers who identified not just an unusual voice but the astonishing variety of sounds Kate Bush produced on *The Kick Inside*.

6 It could be argued that there is also a minor flavour to this chord, since the piano motive over the C$^\sharp$ harmony passes through the note E$^\natural$ directly before its E$^\sharp$. However, the motive returns to the E$^\sharp$ immediately after reaching its melodic peak on G$^\sharp$, and this seems to confirm the harmony here as major with a minor inflexion. Similarly, although the second harmony of this phrase – which I have argued is the flattened submediant, i.e. the chord of F – is inflected at the end with the voice rising to the note D, giving it a subdominant flavour (D minor) at the last moment, we still hear F major as the basic harmonic support here.

7 These concepts, first explored by Soviet narratologists but brought to the attention of musicologists perhaps primarily by Susan McClary, have most recently been critiqued by Green (1997, see pp. 116–32, especially 119).

References

Anon. 1978. 'Learning to sing and defying conventions', *Radio and Record News*, February [accessed at <http://www.gaffa.org/reaching/i78—rrn.html>]

Barthes, R. 1977. 'The Grain of the Voice', in *Image Music Text*, ed. S. Heath (London), pp. 179–89

Blake, J. 1978. 'Sexy Kate sings like an angel', *Evening News*, 18 February [accessed at <http://www.gaffa.org/reaching/i78—en.html>]

Brontë, E. 1994. *Wuthering Heights* (Harmondsworth; first published 1847)

Clarke, S. 1978. 'Kate Bush city limits', *New Musical Express*, 25 March [accessed at <http://www.gaffa.org/reaching/i78—nme.html>]

Doherty, H. 1978. 'Bush baby', *Melody Maker*, 8 March [accessed at <http://www.gaffa.org/reaching/i78—mm1.html>]

Ellis, M. 1978. 'Kate's fairy tale', *Record Mirror*, 25 February [accessed at <http://www.gaffa.org/reaching/i78—rm.html>]

Fowler, M. 1978. 'Bush stands alone', *Daily Utah Chronicle*, 3 April [accessed at <http://www.gaffa.org/reaching/i78—duc.html>]

Frith, S. 1978. 'The shape of things to come', *Creem*, July [accessed at <http://www.gaffa.org/reaching/i78—crm.html>]

240   *Nicky Losseff*

Green, L. 1997. *Music, Gender, Education* (Cambridge)

Juby, K. 1988. *Kate Bush: The Whole Story* (London)

Kruse, H. 1990. 'In oraise of Kate Bush', in *On Record: Pop, Rock and the Written Word*, eds S. Frith and A. Goodwin (London), pp. 450–65

McClary, S. and Walser, R. 1990. 'Start making sense! Musicology wrestles with rock', in *On Record: Pop, Rock and the Written Word*, eds S. Frith and A. Goodwin (London), pp. 277–92

Middleton, R. 1990. *Studying Popular Music* (Milton Keynes)

Moore, A. 1992. 'Patterns of harmony', *Popular Music*, 11, 73–106

Nulman, A. 1978. 'She's *how* old?', *Toronto Sunday Express*, 18 June [accessed at <http://www.gaffa.org/reaching/i78—se.html>]

Rice, J. 1991. *British Hit Singles* (Enfield)

Wigg, D. 1978. 'Wuthering wonderful', *Daily Express*, 8 March [accessed at <http://www.gaffa.org/reaching/i78—de.html>]

Wood, E. 1994. 'Sapphonics', in *Queering the Pitch*, eds P. Brett, E. Wood and G. C. Thomas (New York and London), pp. 27–66

Young, J. 1978. 'What Katie sang next', *Daily Express*, 7 August [accessed at <http://www.gaffa.org/reaching/i78—de2.html]

Discography

Kate Bush, 'Wuthering Heights', and 'Kite', *The Kick Inside*. EMI Records, CDEMS 1522. 1978

Minnie Ripperton, 'Loving You,' Epic EPC 3121. 1975.

[24]

Pulp, Pornography and Spectatorship: Subject Matter and Subject Position in Pulp's *This is Hardcore*

NICOLA DIBBEN

All of my life I've been an observer, not only of films and TV, but of life, and then as soon as you get that form of public acceptance, then you are somebody else's show. You're actually part of the action on the screen. . . . That's why there's a bit of an obsession with it on the record. It's comparing what it was like as a spectator and what it's like being part of the action, and that's always going to be a bit of a disappointment.[1]

THE cover art to Sheffield pop band Pulp's recent album *This is Hardcore* has many of the properties of pornographic images.[2] The surroundings and visual appearance of the people in the cover art combine sophistication with the seediness of pick-up joints and escort girls. The digitized treatment of the images gives them a hyper-reality, and the waxed finish and lurid colour combinations (pink typography against a black background) hint at overly glossy production values and form a jarring juxtaposition with the banality of some of the images. The 'centrefold' is a hyper-real, overly glossy photograph of Jarvis Cocker alongside model/actor John Huntley, with all the glamour of a matinée idol. This hyper-reality is explicit in its simulation of the real.[3]

Many of the photographs feature semi-naked women in ambivalent situations. For example, the front cover, which also featured as a poster campaign on the album's release, shows a naked woman lying face-down on a red leather couch in an awkward position (the poster received a hostile public reaction and was decried in the national press as offensive and degrading to women).[4] Another of the photographs

This research was carried out with the support of a British Academy Postdoctoral Fellowship. Earlier versions of this paper were presented as 'Pulp, Pornography and Voyeurism' at the conference 'Popular Music and the Media: Television, Video and Film' (Sheffield Hallam University, July 1999) and as 'Construction and Critique of the Authentic Pop Icon' at the Critical Musicology Forum (University of Surrey, July 2000).

[1] Jarvis Cocker, cited in Michael Krugman, 'Deconstructing Jarvis', *Raygun* (http://members.tripod.com/-CleverSwine/nojava/raygun2.html, 30 June 1998).

[2] Pulp, *This is Hardcore* (Island CID 8066/524 486-2, 1998). The cover art is by New York artist John Currin (an artist who portrays ageing playboys and improbably fulsome women in hyper-realistic style); photographs by Horst Diekgerdes; computer-enhanced by Peter Saville.

[3] See, for example, Baudrillard's account of how images produce reality rather than copy it (Jean Baudrillard, *Selected Writings*, ed. and introduced by Mark Poster, Cambridge, 1988).

[4] For an account of the poster's reception and its relationship to the title track of the album, see Eric F. Clarke and Nicola Dibben, 'Sex, Pulp and Critique', *Popular Music*, 19 (2000), 231–41.

Figure 1.   Photograph from the cover art to Pulp's album *This is Hardcore*. Photograph by Horst Diekgerdes, reproduced by permission of Universal-Island Records Ltd.

to conform most closely to a pornographic image is that of two scant-ily clad women embracing (see Figure 1). As in the case of lesbian scenes in pornographic material, the gaze at women enjoying each other sexually here functions less to celebrate women's mutual enjoy-ment of each other than to place it on display for a male spectator (a male band member is seated ambivalently behind the women).

Two main types of conventional imagery have been identified in soft-core porn: the 'caught unawares', in which the woman pictured appears to have been caught in a moment of auto-eroticism, and the 'come-on', in which the woman invites the gaze.[5] In the 'caught unawares' a woman is shown alone, unaware that the camera is there: her eyes are closed, or her head turned away, but the body is on display. These kinds of images encourage voyeuristic pleasure by allowing the spectator to look without the look being returned, and thus to fanta-size that this is the kind of thing that would happen were the spectator not present; yet at the same time the bodies in the photograph are arranged as a display directed precisely at him: 'The women *are* doing it all for him, after all.'[6] It is the one-to-one relationship between onlooker and object, in which the object cannot return the onlooker's

[5] Annette Kuhn, *The Power of the Image: Essays on Representation and Sexuality* (London and New York, 1987).
[6] *Ibid.*, 33.

gaze, which is central to the voyeuristic relationship upon which pornography depends. 'The spectator's look, then,' Annette Kuhn argues,

> is key in the reading of photographs. This look distinguishes photos from non-photographic visual representations. . . . The spectator can choose to gaze at length, to return again and again, to a favourite photograph. Looking may turn into contemplation, even into voyeurism. The voyeur's pleasure depends on the object of this look being unable to see him: to this extent, it is a pleasure of power, and the look a controlling one. Photographs are well equipped to produce this kind of pleasure: the apparent authenticity of what is in the image combines with the fact that it is of course actually not there – and so can be looked at for as long as desired, because the circuit of pleasure will never be broken by a returned look.[7]

The pleasure obtained from pornographic images and the voyeuristic relationship they solicit is an instance of 'scopophilia' (the sexual pleasure of looking, which takes other people as objects and subjects them to a controlling gaze), identified by Freud as one of the component instincts of sexuality.[8] Figure 1 presents an ideal scopic object because the photographic frame decapitates the female bodies, leaving them totally abandoned to the power of the gaze. In film theory, where the function and role of the gaze has been most fully theorized,[9] work on the gaze suggests that the pleasure obtained from looking is not just scopophilic, but arises from occupation of a privileged vantage-point from which to view unseen, and which endows the gazer with a sense of omnipotence. In Lacan's terms, the gazer desires and is able to find in such practices and representations a 'specular' image – an image which affirms the subject's privileged sense of self[10] (and which is most often authorized as a privilege of gender in which a man scrutinizes a woman's body).[11]

In keeping with pornographic conventions, the cover art of *This is Hardcore* seems to authorize both these types of pleasure, yet the images

---

[7] *Ibid.*, 28.

[8] Sigmund Freud, *On Sexuality: Three Essays on the Theory of Sexuality, and Other Works*, trans. James Strachey, ed. Angela Richards (Harmondsworth, 1977).

[9] The seminal work on this is Laura Mulvey's account of how the unconscious of patriarchal society has structured film form (Laura Mulvey, 'Visual Pleasure and Narrative Cinema' (1975), *Visual and Other Pleasures*, Bloomington, IN, 1989, 14–28). Mulvey's argument is that mainstream film portrays a 'hermetically sealed world which unwinds magically, indifferent to the presence of the audience, producing for them a sense of separation and playing on their voyeuristic fantasy' (*ibid.*, 20). This voyeuristic separation is enhanced by conditions of screening (such as the darkened audience and lit screen) and narrative conventions which provide the viewer with the illusion of looking in on a private world. According to Mulvey, cinema satisfies scopophilia, but develops its narcissistic aspect by focusing attention on the human form.

[10] Jacques Lacan, *The Four Fundamental Concepts of Psychoanalysis*, ed. Jacques-Alain Miller, trans. Alan Sheridan (London, 1981).

[11] For example, Kramer argues that in the nineteenth century the power to scrutinize women's bodies and behaviour was institutionalized (Lawrence Kramer, *Music as Cultural Practice 1800–1900*, Berkeley, CA, and London, 1990, 108) and that scopophilia rivalled physical penetration as the means of satisfying sexual desire for nineteenth-century men (Lawrence Kramer, 'The Salome Complex', *Cambridge Opera Journal*, 2, (1990), 269–94). Indeed, Kramer argues that 'to the degree to which it is scopophilic, the unseen gaze of the audience is gendered masculine, regardless of who exercises it' (*ibid.*, 284, n. 31).

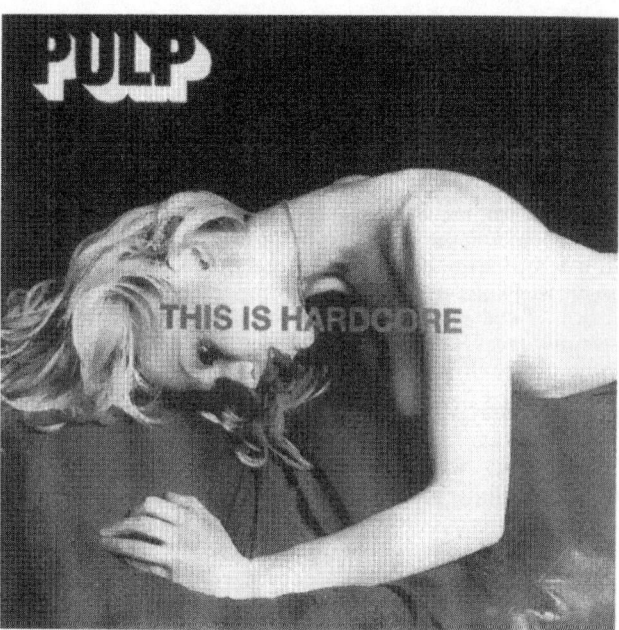

Figure 2.   Front cover of the album *This is Hardcore*. Photograph by Horst Diekgerdes, reproduced by permission of Universal-Island Records Ltd.

are far from unproblematic as regards the gaze. While the cover art of the album provides structures of looking which seem to afford scopophilic pleasure, it simultaneously undermines them by the presence, or implied presence, of a spectator analogous to the empirical (i.e. the real) spectator of the cover art: for example, in the majority of the photographs a band member is featured as an onlooker of the action (as, for example, in Figure 1); and in the case of the album cover (within which no onlooker is physically present) the declaration 'This is Hardcore', printed across the photograph like a censor's stamp, indicates the presence of another (prior) spectator (see Figure 2). In both cases, the presence of a spectator additional to the empirical spectator turns the gaze back upon itself, denying it the power to structure the visual field and undermining the illusion of omnipotence.[12] The effect of this is to problematize the empirical viewer's own voyeurism (both of pornography and of Pulp's position within it).

The presence of another spectator within the frame, however, is not by itself sufficient to preclude the viewer from an omnipotent viewpoint. Mulvey identifies two contradictory aspects of pleasurable

[12] As Kramer remarks: 'Appropriation of the visual field depends on a shared, tacit awareness that the man who gazes can be seen to gaze. The visibility of the gazing eye is also its vulnerability.' Kramer, 'The Salome Complex', 274.

looking in film: on the one hand, pleasure comes from scopophilia – the pleasure of looking in which the object is subjected to a controlling gaze, and in which the erotic identity of gazer and object are separated; on the other hand, there is a narcissistic identification with the object on screen in which the woman displayed acts as an erotic object both for the spectator and for the character on screen. Mulvey argues that by identifying with the on-screen male the spectator gains control of events and of the woman within the diegesis. In the case of the cover art to the album, however, identification with the (male) band member within each of the photographic images does not provide the comfortable omnipotence of the specular image: the band members are themselves ambivalent spectators of the 'action' rather than in control of events within the photoscene.

The effect of this disruption of the gaze is to make manifest a paradox between the action implied by the photographs (viewer of pornography as protagonist) and the real situation of the voyeur as spectator of the 'action' rather than participant in it. This highlights the paradox inherent in pornographic images themselves: while the pleasure in the voyeuristic look is that the woman in the photograph can never turn the viewer down because she is not real, it is because she is not real that desire will always remain unsatisfied and the viewer will remain a spectator rather than a protagonist. Thus, the emphasis on the experience of pornography and fame from the position of spectatorship rather than participation conflicts with stereotyped conceptions of masculine subjectivity and sexuality on the one hand, and with fame and stardom on the other (letting us look at Pulp's looking is unusual, since pop stars are usually the product of a different form of image manufacture).

It is by virtue of the way that media forms work with the gaze to ideological ends that Althusser argues that ideology is not false consciousness but a material practice produced by ideological state apparatuses.[13] As illustrated above, 'the gaze' is the structure of looking created in a photograph or painting, represented in a text or practised in social spaces, and is a prolonged or repeated look, often from a concealed position, by which the gazer scrutinizes another person or thing. Media forms (such as television, film and photographs) work with the gaze to ideological ends (by letting the viewers of an advertisement think they are sovereign consumers, for example). According to this reading, the focus of the cover art of the album, then, is structures of representation, their mediation in highly alienated cultural forms, and structures of subject position. The idea of music as a cultural agent, now current in musicology,[14] opens up the possibility that music may also be implicated in the album's critique of cultural forms – both as

---

[13] Louis Althusser, 'Ideology and Ideological State Apparatuses', *Lenin and Philosophy and Other Essays* (London, 1971), 123–73.

[14] See, for example, Kramer, *Music as Cultural Practice*, 1–20. Drawing on speech act theory, Kramer argues that music is an act of expression/representation which can exert illocutionary force; music is an agent of culture because it participates in cultural discourse through which meanings are produced as part of the continual production and reproduction of culture.

Figure 3.   Inside facing cover of the album *This is Hardcore*. Photograph by Horst Diekgerdes, reproduced by permission of Universal-Island Records Ltd.

subject of that critique (as a media form itself) and as a means by which that critique is presented. In this article I explore the album's critique of spectatorship, first through its contribution to discourses of male sexuality and stardom and, second, through the subject position it solicits. I start with an analysis of the first track from the album, 'The Fear'.[15]

'MUSIC FROM A BACHELOR'S DEN': CONSTRUCTIONS OF MASCULINITY IN 'THE FEAR'

The photograph from the inside facing cover to Pulp's album *This is Hardcore* (see Figure 3) features an archetype of white, heterosexual, macho masculinity. The man portrayed has the archetypal square jaw and dark hair, has a Rolex watch, and wears a hotel robe as if engaged in a sexual encounter.[16] Both the cover art and the lyrics reference a

[15] 'The Fear', words by Jarvis Cocker, music by Jarvis Cocker, Nick Banks, Candida Doyle, Steve Mackey and Mark Webber. © 1988 Universal/Island Music Ltd, 77 Fulham Palace Road, London W6. Used by permission of Music Sales Ltd. All rights reserved. International copyright secured.
[16] A similar image appears in the cover art to another album released the same year: Robbie Williams's *I've Been Expecting You* (EMI CD 97837, 1998). An inner photograph shows Williams dressed in a bathrobe, in a glamorous setting, looking directly into the camera. In this case, however, the photograph is part of the album's self-conscious, tongue-in-cheek reference to the world of the fictional character James Bond.

macho construction of masculinity of fast cars and promiscuity: for example, the first line of the album states that 'This is our "Music from a Bachelor's Den" ',[17] and the cover art to the album references locations and situations associated with sexual encounters of one sort or another. There is evidence from the band that this archetype of the Bachelor, represented in the cover art by John Huntley, is a theme shared by the album as a whole:

> When we write a song we always give them titles, because the lyrics are always the last thing to happen, so we have working titles to refer to things and they're usually stupid. 'Hardcore' was called 'Barry'. Barry was a big character on this record [album]. One song was 'Barry swings.' And then we had 'Seductive Barry'. We could have called this record 'This is Barry.'[18]

'Barry', then, is the archetypal macho male to whom 'real' men are supposed to aspire, but, as the name 'Barry' suggests, this Bachelor is tacky rather than glamorous, and pathetic rather than heroic:[19] even the term 'Bachelor' has a polite and restrained character at odds with conceptions of macho masculinity. As the lyrics of the first verse state, this is not a celebration of the life of the single male as one of fast cars and promiscuity, but instead one of fantasies concealing fear and loneliness:

> This is our 'Music from a Bachelor's Den'
> – the sound of loneliness turned up to ten.
> A horror sound-track from a stagnant water-bed
> & it sounds just like this.
> This is the sound of someone losing the plot
> – making out that they're OK when they're not.
> You're gonna like it, but not a lot
> & the chorus goes like this . . .[20]

The track 'The Fear' is in strophic form with an eight-bar introduction, a final instrumental verse and chorus, and a coda, and uses a large range of synthesized and orchestral instrumental sources in addition to kit, guitar and vocals. Just as the lyrics do, so too the music undermines macho constructions of masculinity: in fact, the lyrics explicitly state that this track is not only 'about' being a Bachelor, but that it is the sound of being a Bachelor (i.e. 'the sound of loneliness', 'the sound of someone losing the plot'). One of the techniques by which it does this is to include stylistic references conventionally associated with a male social context or function, and to subject them to (destructive)

---

[17] Pulp, 'The Fear', *This is Hardcore*.

[18] Jarvis Cocker, cited in Krugman, 'Deconstructing Jarvis'.

[19] In the UK the forename 'Barry' has connotations of sleaze and banality as well as connoting a 'ladies' man'. Examples are Barry White, Barry Manilow and Barry from the TV soap opera *EastEnders* (1997–9). Barry may also be a reference to Barry Adamson, on whose album Jarvis Cocker appeared with a track related to some of the same issues (Barry Adamson/Jarvis Cocker, 'Set the Controls for the Heart of the Pelvis', *Oedipus Schmoedipus*, CD STUMM 134, 1996).

[20] Pulp, 'The Fear'.

treatment of some sort.[21] By way of illustration of this technique I present two examples.

The lead guitar and constructions of macho masculinity in 'The Fear'

Historically, the lead guitar is a signifier of male power, heroism and potency, typified by 1960s cock-rock (e.g. The Rolling Stones, Pretty Things, The Who and The Yardbirds),[22] and paradigmatic of the stereotype of the single, rogue male. The electric guitar creates a spectacle of male power and heroism: the performance style comprises a posture in which legs are apart and the guitarist leans back with the guitar held at the pelvis in a parody of sexual ecstasy; power is signified by the sheer volume and attack characteristics of the sound and the use of feedback (all of which push the instrument to its extremes); and the virtuosic character of the performance style appropriates many of the meanings and values with which virtuosity in classical performance is associated – namely technical mastery, genius and authenticity. In the context of 'The Fear' the lead guitar's association with cock-rock (by virtue not only of the discourse surrounding the album, but the amplified guitar sound and the later guitar instrumental) brings with it cock-rock's associated cultural contexts and meanings: an exaggeration of the masculine self-aggrandizement of the blues, sexual release and authentic grandeur of being,[23] sex as conquest, 'coitus as combat'.[24]

However, the macho meanings with which the lead guitar is associated are undermined in 'The Fear' through a range of processes. For example, within the context of the melodramatic banality of the clichéd tonic-dominant harmonic progression, the verse material used by the lead guitar stays within a very limited range (a major second) and is characterized by a minor-second motif which saturates other voices within the verse (see Example 1 for instances of the major/minor-second motif). Oscillation within such a restricted range specifies a lack of direction and harmonic activity. Larger intervallic leaps appear in the guitar in the chorus, but to no avail because it returns to the passivity of the verse material again. This minor/major-second motif, together with the oscillating melodic movement, is also an instance of a more general 'fear' topic found in a range of Western musics, but which is particularly common in horror/suspense film sound-tracks (see Example 2):

---

[21] As with related methods of analysis (e.g. Philip Tagg, 'Analysing Popular Music: Theory, Method and Practice', *Popular Music*, 2 (1982), 37–67), the validity of this reading is dependent upon a shared cultural understanding of musical materials and their social contexts.

[22] Reynolds and Press give the paradigmatic source for this as Bo Diddley, 'I'm a Man' (Simon Reynolds and Joy Press, *The Sex Revolts: Gender, Rebellion and Rock 'n' Roll*, London, 1995). See also Led Zeppelin, 'Whole Lotta Love', *Led Zeppelin II* (Swan Song SD-8236, 1969). For other discussions of the role of the lead guitar in constructions of masculinity, see Simon Frith and Angela MacRobbie, 'Rock and Sexuality', *On Record: Rock, Pop and the Written Word* (London, 1990), 371–89; Robert Walser, *Running with the Devil: Power, Gender and Madness in Heavy Metal Music* (Hanover, NH, 1993); and *Sexing the Groove: Popular Music and Gender*, ed. Sheila Whiteley (London and New York, 1997).

[23] Reynolds and Press, *The Sex Revolts*, 21.

[24] *Ibid.*, 115.

Example 1. Introduction to 'The Fear'. Online sound clip at <www.jrma.oupjournals.org>.

as the lyrics state, 'The Fear' is literally 'a horror sound-track from a stagnant water-bed'.[25] Thus, while the lead guitar signifies machismo, the accompanying lack of harmonic direction in 'The Fear' undermines this macho image with one of futility, confusion and lack of purpose.

[25] ' "The Fear" – Yeah, well that was something I got some chords for while being on tour and it's got a bit of a horror sound-track kind of feel to it.' Jarvis Cocker, 'Pulp from Disco to Hardcore', BBC Radio 1, 1998/9.

Example 2.   Examples of the 'fear' archetype.

theme from 'The X files' TV series (1993)

theme from 'The Twilight Zone' TV series (1959)

theme from the film 'Jaws' (Universal, 1975)

   Given the minimal usage of the guitar in the verses (long, held
notes), the metrical precision and the lack of technical display, the
reference to cock-rock might seem tenuous; however, it is the instrumental solo which makes the strongest link to this genre of guitar-
playing, where the macho meanings of the lead guitar are again
undermined – this time through the disintegration of the guitar solo.
In rock tracks the instrumental often features a solo lead guitar and
functions as an opportunity for virtuosic display.[26] As has been argued
elsewhere, virtuosic display acts as a signifier of machismo: control of
technology through mastery of an instrument, creative genius (improvisation over backing) and sexual display.[27] However, in 'The Fear'
what starts as virtuosic display ends as incoherence and lack of control
(see Example 3). The lead-guitar solo starts with conventionally regular
phrasing and a tremolando playing style which demonstrates the guitarist's technical skill. It also begins a conventional elaboration of the
previously regular phrases with a climactic semiquaver descent in the
final phrase. However, this skilled descent soon turns into garbled loss
of control: the semiquaver pattern loses the internal regularity that
characterizes such soloistic passages, and the guitar plunges into distortion and feedback against the prevailing tonality and rhythmic structure. Most noticeably, it becomes dislocated from the ensemble, which
continues oblivious to the lead guitar: the lead guitar is revealed to be

<hr>

   [26] See, for example, Status Quo, 'Most of the Time', *On the Level* (Capital LP 11381, 1975).
   [27] See cultural discourse, both past and present, which talks of music and musicians in these
terms; for example, Robert Walser's discussion of Liszt (*Running with the Devil*, 76).

Example 3.   Lead-guitar solo from 'The Fear'. Online sound clip at
<www.jrma.oupjournals.org>.

not the controlling soloist supported by the ensemble, but an ineffectual voice which has no impact on or engagement with the rest of the
ensemble. The solo has all the appearance of control (it takes a solo
role against an instrumental backing, it functions musically as a display
of virtuosity, it features improvisatory material) and yet it lacks any real
direction or control. Here, loss of musical control within the norms of
a style and structure which have historically functioned to display masculine skill signifies a loss of mastery.

The coda and breakdown of the track

The threat of the breakdown of the track, first hinted at by the lead-
guitar instrumental and later by the backing vocals,[28] culminates in the
disintegration of the ensemble and song form during the instrumental
chorus and coda. The instrumental follows the same harmonic structure and uses much of the same material as the preceding vocal sections: verse is followed by chorus with the addition of a ten-bar coda.
However, during this instrumental version of the material the song
form loses its way. For example, bar 5 of the chorus changes to the
dominant for two bars in preparation for the resolution to the tonic
(see Example 4), but in the instrumental chorus the change of
harmony at bar 5 is delayed for a bar, after which a further delay takes
place: instead of two bars of the dominant followed by the tonic there
are six bars of dominant. When the tonic does finally arrive, its statement is staggered rather than synchronized: all the other instruments
have dropped out by the time the lead guitar resolves to the tonic, A.
Thus, there is a disintegration of both the ensemble and the song form
at this point. Significantly, the lead guitar, signifier of machismo, is last
to resolve to the tonic, and is the sole element in the mix at this point.

---

[28] The backing vocals reference, on the one hand, those of progressive rock (compare the
backing vocals on 'The Fear' with those of Pink Floyd, 'Shine on you Crazy Diamond', *Wish you
were Here* (Columbia CK 33453, 1975) and, on the other hand, those of glam-rock (e.g. Queen).
Yet the backing vocals in 'The Fear' are ridiculously extreme: they ascend to unfeasibly high
registers only to collapse into incoherence and a lack of (vocal) control similar to that displayed
by the lead guitar. Breakdown of the vocal signifies breakdown of the meanings with which
progressive rock and glam-rock are associated: progressive rock's pretensions to profundity,
heroism and transcendence are ridiculed and, in the case of glam-rock, its camp aesthetic is
heightened into hysteria.

Example 4.   End of the chorus from 'The Fear'. Online sound clip at
<www.jrma.oupjournals.org>.

The words 'the end' which appear in the lyrics of the chorus of 'The Fear' refer to the end of the track, the end of life and the end of 'The Fear' – the subject matter of the song. This ending motif is particularly significant viewed in the context of other rock tracks which draw the same analogy. The ten-bar coda is characterized by the electro-mechanical sounds produced by guitar distortion and feedback and by the sound of increasingly laboured breathing. One interpretation of this sound in the context of the lyrics is as the sound of breathing supported by a respirator or life-support machine. There is potential hope in the lyrics' repetition of 'until the end', because the end (signifying both death and the end of the track) implies an end to, and an escape from, 'The Fear'. However, even the bleak possibility of escape which this offers is suddenly and brutally erased as the track ends with what sounds like electro-mechanical failure of the monitoring equipment: the 'end', when it does come, is electro-mechanical failure – there is no grand or heroic end to life and no redeeming afterlife.

This (musical and metaphorical) end is in stark contrast to the endings of two related tracks by The Doors: 'When the Music's Over'[29] and 'The End'.[30] All three tracks use the same lyrical motif, 'until the end', and all involve a mirroring of musical structure and lyrics in which the musical function of closure (the real end of the track) is a metaphor for death.[31] Jim Morrison is paradigmatic of the self-aggrandizement of the rock icon, and both The Doors' tracks are prime examples of a phallic model of rebellion, namely transgression and penetration of the unknown in which the loneliness of the rebel is a grandiose rejection of God and law. For example, whereas in 'The Fear' the end fails to offer any escape from illusion, the final bars of The Doors' track 'The End' is apocalyptic and triumphal.[32] Death is something you meet head on – it is the only match for the heroic, grandiose male:

> The music is your special friend
> Dance on fire as it intends
> Music is your only friend
> Until the end
> Until the end
> Until
> THE END.[33]

---

[29] The Doors, 'When the Music's Over', *Strange Days* (Elektra 74014, 1967).

[30] The Doors, 'The End', *The Doors* (Elektra 74007, 1967).

[31] Note the parallel between The Doors' 'When the Music's Over' and Pulp's 'This is our "Music from a Bachelor's Den"', which both equate music (the song) with life. Whereas both Doors' tracks function as the final track on their respective albums, 'The Fear' is the first track on *This is Hardcore*. Both this and the constant play on delaying the end ('The end is near again') play against the expectation for it to function as the 'real' end of the album.

[32] See, for example, the use of The Doors' track 'The End' in the film *Apocalypse Now* (dir. Francis Ford Coppola, 1979). Paradoxically, the track 'The End' is used in the film's opening sequence, perhaps tapping into the film's sense of futility. I am grateful to Kay Dickinson for drawing my attention to this use of the track.

[33] The Doors, 'When the Music's Over'.

This heroic death is realized in the music by the long pause before the final 'end' of the lyrics, the large decelerando, the drum roll, the rising melodic sequence and the delay of closure to the tonic. There is some disintegration into distortion, but the track ends with a power chord on all instruments and a clean, synchronized cut-off. The construction of masculinity presented by these Doors tracks is one in which loneliness is a consequence of being on the edge, an adventurer, a rebel, and in which death is a grand and apocalyptic end. By contrast, in 'The Fear' loneliness comes without heroism or adventure,[34] and death is not grand or apocalyptic but the consequence of electro-mechanical failure.

'The Fear' presents a bleak and ironic view of the single male: a representation of the disparity between the fantasies of self-aggrandizement which surround masculine sexuality and a stark reality of fear, of self-deception and of futility. The track seems to suggest that cultural conceptions of what it is to be a 'man' imply a purpose which in reality it lacks, illustrated by lyrical references such as that to 'fast cars' but with nowhere to go in the track 'I'm a Man'. The futility of the pretence is also indicated in 'Help the Aged' ('If you look very hard behind the lines upon their face you may see where you are headed and it's such a lonely place'), and in the contrast between the stereotype of machismo and Jarvis Cocker's experience of masculinity described in 'Dishes' ('I am not Jesus though I have the same initials. I am the man who stays home and does the dishes').[35] The disparity between real men and constructions of masculinity is epitomized by Pulp's track 'I'm a Man', in which becoming a man is the result of buying the right goods ('So please can I ask just why we'e alive? Cos all that you do seems such a waste of time & if you hang around too long you'll be a man'). Jarvis Cocker has elaborated on this view in interviews:

> Success is a kind of 'manly' thing. It's like, you've got access to all the material trappings of a man, like you can get yourself a Rolex watch if you want and get a really fast car, and hang around with lots of women or whatever, you know. If you look at all the things in advertising and stuff seem to represent a successful man they're all pretty childish in a way, they're all immature and you know having been a very 'unmanly' man I was always getting stick for that when I was growing up. It's kind of funny when people are giving you a bit of respect 'cos you're loaded. I just thought 'well, if that's all there is to being a man, then I'd rather not be one'. Now, of course, I am one, let's face it, but I just don't subscribe to that kind of macho ideal of what a man's supposed to be.[36]

---

[34] Both 'The End' and the film *Apocalypse Now* reference 'the East' as a Western 'voyage of discovery'.

[35] Significantly, Jarvis Cocker's reference to himself as not being Jesus comes after his altercation with the Christ-like Michael Jackson at the 1996 Brit Awards. Cocker's stage invasion disrupted Michael Jackson's performance of his hit 'Earth Song', in which he appeared in white robes and arms outstretched in an imitation of Christ on the cross, 'healing' young children dressed as poverty-stricken urchins, and approached by men dressed as monks to receive his 'divine' touch. Via a spokesman after the event Jarvis Cocker stated: 'My actions were a form of protest at the way Michael Jackson sees himself as some kind of Christ-like figure with the power of healing' (http://www.baritalia.ukgateway.net/bar-brits.html, 24 September 2000).

[36] Cocker, 'Pulp from Disco to Hardcore'.

This critique of masculinity should be seen in the context of lad culture in 1990s Britain. Discourses of masculinity at this time were dominated by a post-'new-man' return to the womanizing, football-supporting stereotype, but this time under the aegis of an apparently tongue-in-cheek self-conscious awareness fuelled by the media (in particular, radio and television programmes such as those presented by Chris Evans, and the increasing number of men's life-style magazines). In this context Pulp's camp sensibility is in stark contrast to that of other bands (e.g. Oasis) and to wider discourses of male sexuality at that time.

MALE SEXUALITY AND PORNOGRAPHY IN 'SEDUCTIVE BARRY'

The critique of fantasies of masculinity is continued in other tracks on the album, but it is in 'Seductive Barry' that there is a true analogy with the kind of critique made in the cover art through its reference to pornography. Both the lyrics and the musical materials of 'Seductive Barry' reference the acting out of a sex scene in a play or film. The track is in strophic form with a lush texture characterized by synth pads and expansive string writing with the 'exotic' sounds of birdsong/insect noises and the gentle breaking of waves. A much sparser middle section is followed by a more sustained, rich and full orchestral climax. Within this overall form the materials suggest that this is a sexual encounter: the close-miked vocals suggest intimacy, and the woman's moans (the only place in the album where a woman's voice is heard), present in the background of the mix, become more urgent as the track progresses. In addition, the string writing references Barry White and the Love Unlimited Orchestra,[37] and the lush texture and epic orchestral proportions are an exaggerated version of Hollywood cinema's appropriation of the romantic style of classical music (for example, the romanticism of the harp and high strings as Jarvis Cocker sings 'For the rest of my life'). (There is an aural equivalent of visual voyeurism here as the listener is made party to a sexual encounter.)

However, various aspects of the track indicate that this is a sexual fantasy based on a pornographic image rather than a sexual encounter with a real woman. The lyrics hint at a less glamorous reality than that suggested by the romantic references:

> And how many others have touched themselves whilst looking at pictures of you? How many others could handle it if all their dreams came true? I don't expect you to answer straight away, maybe you're just having an off day but I need to believe in you.[38]

A disparity between the intensity of imagined experience and the disappointment of reality is manifested through a conflict between excessive grandeur and banality. For example, the lyrics are epic and

---

[37] See, for example, Barry White, *I've got So Much to Give* (Twentieth Century 407, 1973), and the Love Unlimited Orchestra, *Rhapsody in White* (Twentieth Century 423, 1975).

[38] Pulp, 'Seductive Barry', *This is Hardcore*.

overblown in character ('When the unbelievable object meets the unstoppable force there's nothing you can do about it'; 'I will light your cigarette with a star that's fallen from the sky'). The musical materials are excessive in their exaggeration of the norms of the styles (for example, the excessively lush string writing and the high romanticism of harp and strings in the final section). Juxtaposed with this are materials of excessive banality such as the chorus (banal and low-energy), which references low-budget television film sound-tracks. This disparity is further emphasized by the incongruity of the distant and discordant lead-guitar phrase which occurs immediately after the lush textures of the track's penultimate sounds. The album's treatment of pornography functions as a critique of masculine sexuality by revealing conceptions of masculine sexuality as grand and transcendent to be constructions perpetuated by television, film, pornography and advertising.

PORNOGRAPHY AND SPECTATORSHIP

These analyses reveal a concern with the disparity between the intensity of imagined experience (fanned by media representations) and the disappointment of reality, realized through the themes of sex (the intensity of sexual experience versus the seediness of pornography, as in the case of the title track, 'This is Hardcore', and 'Seductive Barry'), masculinity (single men as active and virile, versus a reality of domesticity and loneliness – as in the tracks 'The Fear', 'Dishes' and 'I'm a Man'), youth (as in 'Help the Aged') and stardom (the glamour of media representations versus the reality of publicity shoots and airbrushed photographs). For example, overlapping with their previous albums, this disparity between fantasy and reality is expressed through the theme of the hype but ultimate emptiness of youth culture:[39] both the tracks 'Party Hard' and 'Glory Days' from the album *This is Hardcore* contrast youth and its hype of drug and club culture with a much less grand experience of the everyday ('I used to do the I Ching but then I had to feed the meter. Now I can't see into the future but at least I can use the heater')[40], and in which the euphoria of club culture is portrayed as illusory and self-delusional.[41] Within the context of the album as a whole, pornography acts as a common visual language through which the disparity between the intensity of imagined experience and the disappointment, or even disgust, of its realization is

---

[39] See, for example, the track 'Sorted for e's and wizz', *Different Class* (Island 8041, 1995).

[40] Pulp, 'Glory Days', *This is Hardcore*.

[41] See, for example, Jarvis Cocker's account of the album's title: 'I first came across the word [hardcore] in the late 80s, when I was going to raves and things. I listened to pirate radio stations and they'd always be saying "Hardcore: You know the score!" and all that kind of thing. There was always a kind of endurance test aspect to raves, because they would start at about 10 o'clock and just go through to morning or longer. So it was real hardcore if you were the one still dancing in the end. But really, the way that people achieved that was by taking massive amounts of drugs, so really there was a kind of sadness about it' (Jarvis Cocker, cited in Krugman, 'Deconstructing Jarvis').

expressed.[42] In this regard, pornography acts as a cypher for the album's critique of spectatorship.

According to Jarvis Cocker, the album's reference to pornography is also a metaphor for the experience of fame and the media industries which support it:[43]

> I was in a group for years and years and had a lot of time to think about what it was like to be famous. I found it [fame] quite repulsive. . . . Like pornography it seems to promise something but it really doesn't satisfy that need.[44]

This same metaphor appears in the cover art: for example, the placement of Jarvis Cocker as the centrefold within the cover art is a reference to the similarity between fame and pornography, and to Cocker as the pawn in the construction of authenticity on which image manufacture depends. The promise of fame turns out to be much more substantial than the experience of fame itself, and it is to this experience that Jarvis Cocker attributes the album:

> It [*This is Hardcore*] was the idea that you have achieved something that you've dreamed of for a long time. You grow up watching films and stuff, of things that you're aspiring to, and then you're there, you know? Suddenly a lot of things fall away. Everybody sustains themselves on fantasies, and there's nothing wrong with that, it's just that if you ever have the misfortune to have your fantasy come true, then you have to re-assess it all. And often you don't realise that you've got this fantasy in the back of your head – it's just there, 'cause its gone in at an early age. Suddenly you think, 'Why am I dissatisfied with this thing?' What is it within you that means that this still isn't enough? I suppose that's another reason for it being called 'Hardcore', as in that's the bit that's left when everything else has melted away.[45]

The target of the critique in the album is not simply the fantasies themselves, but their perpetuation in cultural forms. Hence, many of the tracks are characterized by references to film and television. The title track of the album ('This is Hardcore') is concerned with a male fantasy in which the protagonist is director and sex-star in his own pornographic film.[46] 'Seductive Barry' is the fantasy experience of pornography itself, representing the act of seduction or love-making ('So roll the sound-track and dim the lights 'cos I'm not going home tonight. This love scene has begun'). In 'TV Movie' life has become 'A movie made for TV: bad dialogue, bad acting, no interest. Too long with no story and no sex', represented musically as the hum of an off-air television in the background of the track, positioning the subject as

---

[42] A similar point is made by Hugh Aldersey-Williams, 'Living Dolls', *New Statesman*, 5 August 1998.

[43] The theme of voyeurism may also have another autobiographical reference. In the track 'Babies' (*His 'n' Hers*, Island CID8025, 1994) Jarvis Cocker gives a first-hand account of spying on his girlfriend's sister as she makes out with boys in her room – a track which was allegedly influenced by a real incident.

[44] Jarvis Cocker, *America Online* (http://members.xoom.com/r-W-o/pulp/pulp.html, 30 June 1998).

[45] Jarvis Cocker, cited in Krugman, 'Deconstructing Jarvis'.

[46] Clarke and Dibben, 'Sex, Pulp and Critique'.

an onlooker on his or her own life. All these references to the media equate an imagined life of intensity and glamour with media representations.

The problem with which the album presents the listener is that these fantasies, perpetuated by the media, are the social fiction against which people measure their lives:

> It's a modern affliction to feel this vague sense of dissatisfaction and of missing out, of thinking somebody else is having a better time than you are. Because you're always presented with great-looking people, you know, the Martini Generation – people hanging out with great-looking women all the time. The thing is, these things that you're aspiring to never existed. They had a stylist in and suddenly you've got the light in your eye, and then maybe somebody even paint-boxed it afterwards to get rid of any blemishes or imperfections.[47]

According to Baudrillard, the current age of 'simulations' is one in which culture no longer copies the real but produces it.[48] Such is the argument here: the album suggests that constructions of masculinity and of masculine sexuality are produced by the cultural forms of television, cinema and photography and are the social 'truth' by which people measure their lives. Because these are fantasies, unattainable because they do not exist outside the media forms that produced them, the subject will remain forever dissatisfied and turn ever more to the cultural forms which authorize specular enjoyment of them. In his analysis of capitalist society Guy Debord extends Marx's analysis of economic production to cultural production and finds the same processes at work in the alienation caused by the means of production and separation of worker from product as in the cultural forms of the media.[49] In this way the spectacle is ideological because the masses are separated from the means of image production and the result of these highly mediated cultural forms is 'stupefied passivity'.[50]

The ultimate critique of spectatorship in the album is provided by the final track, 'The Day After the Revolution'. In contrast to Gil Scott Heron's track 'The Revolution will Not be Televised',[51] which the Pulp track references, 'The Day After the Revolution' is a sardonic celebration of a culture of spectatorship in which life is experienced through television and the other media rather than through direct experience.[52] The gloss and glamour of fame portrayed by the media

---

[47] Jarvis Cocker, cited in Krugman, 'Deconstructing Jarvis'.

[48] Baudrillard, *Selected Writings*, ed. Poster.

[49] Guy Debord, *Society of the Spectacle* (Detroit, 1987).

[50] The idea that consumption leads to 'stupefied passivity' has been challenged by theories of popular culture (e.g. John Fiske, *Understanding Popular Culture*, London and New York, 1989); however, this is the viewpoint towards which the album addresses itself.

[51] Gil Scott Evans, 'The Revolution will Not be Televised', *Small Talk at 125th and Lenox* (BMG Music 07863 666112, 1993).

[52] The closing litany of 'The Day After the Revolution' ('The rave is over. Sheffield is over. The Fear is over . . .') can also be read as a satirical homage to John Lennon's post-Beatles track 'God' ('The Dream is over'). (John Lennon, 'God', *John Lennon/Plastic Ono Band*, Parlophone CD46770, 1970).

is a construction through which consumers are lulled into a spectatorship which promises everything but which is portrayed as ultimately debilitating.[53] Hence, Jarvis Cocker remarks that 'There's a finite amount of time on this earth. That's why I'm attempting to stop watching TV. I don't want to spend my life as a spectator.'[54]

As I go on to argue, however, this problematization of spectatorship is not just the subject matter, but the subject position solicited by the cover art and music.

SUBJECT MATTER AND SUBJECT POSITION

I have argued that the album *This is Hardcore* is a constructive presence within discourses of masculinity and male sexuality, and presents a critique of the way in which such constructions are mediated in cultural forms, the end result of which (it suggests) is a debilitating spectatorship. I end, however, by considering the way in which the album's critique not only is its subject matter, but is manifested by the spectatorial subject position it solicits.

The distinction between subject matter and subject position is one made in other disciplines (in particular, film theory), but has yet to be fully explored in music.[55] In the visual arts, the idea of 'subject position' is used to distinguish between the subject position of the individual empirical viewer towards the subject matter of the film and that solicited by the film itself.[56] In his analysis of the music of Frank Zappa and P. J. Harvey, Eric Clarke applies this theorization to music and draws a distinction between the subject matter of the songs and the subject position they solicit from the listener: Clarke argues that whereas the subject position in Zappa's 'Magdalena' is parodic in relation to the song's subject matter (a fantasizing father/abuser), P. J. Harvey's 'Taut' encourages identification by the listener with the singer/protagonist. According to Clarke, 'the separation between matter and position comes about often by an awareness of surplus, excess or disjunction'[57]. As the analyses above revealed, many of these same techniques are evident in the Pulp tracks: in 'Seductive Barry'

[53] This sentiment is also expressed in earlier Pulp tracks (e.g. 'Monday Morning', *Different Class*: 'There's nothing to do so you just stay in bed / Why live in the world when you can live in your head?').

[54] Cocker, *America Online*.

[55] See, however, Eric F. Clarke, 'Subject-Position and the Specification of Invariants in Music by Frank Zappa and P. J. Harvey', *Music Analysis*, 18 (1999), 347–74, and Nicola Dibben, 'Representations of Femininity in Popular Music', *Popular Music*, 18 (1999), 331–55, for recent application of theories of subject position to popular music. Both these papers were influenced by a discussion of subject position in Dai Griffiths's 'Sometimes it's Hard to be a Woman: Fixities and Flexibilities of Gender in Recent Song', paper presented at LancMAC, Lancaster University, September 1994.

[56] For discussion of the relationship between individual spectators, structures of representation and subject position in relation to visual media, see Ien Ang, *Watching Dallas: Soap Opera and the Melodramatic Imagination* (New York, 1985), and Tania Modleski, 'The Search for Tomorrow in Today's Soap Operas', *Loving with a Vengeance: Mass Produced Fantasies for Women* (New York and London, 1982), 85–109.

[57] Clarke, 'Subject-Position and the Specification of Invariants', 371.

excess and disjunction are used to undermine the apparently intense sexual encounter which is the subject matter of the track, while in 'The Fear' disintegration of musical materials is used to undermine the construction of masculinity as heroic, active and virile.

Underlying this account of subject position in music is an assumption that songs are able to encourage (or disrupt) identification with the singer/protagonist in much the same way as visual representations, particularly the cinematic gaze, have been said to do. In many respects, the album *This is Hardcore* positions the listener as a spectator onto a private world represented in the album. For example, the first line of the album states that 'This is our "Music from a Bachelor's Den"' as though the listener is overhearing someone else's music; and in the track 'Seductive Barry' the listener is party to a sexual encounter, eavesdropping on the moans and whispers of love-making, and placed there by the close-miking of the voice and its positioning at the foreground of the mix. The lyrics and placement of the voice forward in the mix (often close-miked) locate the listener in a position of intimacy with the singer, and the glossy production of the music, with its high-fidelity aesthetic and lush textures, has a sensuous appeal which draws the listener in.

Some of this spectatorial positioning of the listener, then, seems to be due to conventions of song production and performances rather than being specific to this album. Indeed, reception of the song in contemporary Western culture is heavily influenced by an understanding of song as a cultural object which opens up the inner psyche of the artist for the listener's personal gratification. Thus, the 'common-sense' view of song production and consumption is one in which the singer reflects on his or her personal, emotional experiences, forms this reflection into a musical narrative, performs this narrative to bring out its inner meaning, and is read by the listener who brings his or her own emotional experiences to bear on the song – a process which endows the listener with privileged access to the artist's psyche.

Terry Bloomfield traces this conception of the song back to nineteenth-century Lieder and the birth of the bourgeois subject.[58] According to Bloomfield, the Romantic movement (of which the Lied constitutes a part) grew out of the changing social relations brought about by a developing capitalism and the emergence of the bourgeoisie. The division of labour and consequent fragmentation of life led to the increasingly self-aware but dislocated individual. Thus, the bourgeois subject emerged and with it the Romantic conception of the song, whose passive contemplation was to 'console the inner life of the new subject' (a point which will turn out to be the key to understanding Pulp's problematization of spectatorship).[59] According to Bloomfield, this ideology of authenticity has its apotheosis in the singer/songwriters of the 1960s: in this case the multiplicity of voices

---

[58] Terry Bloomfield, 'Resisting Songs: Negative Dialectics in Pop', *Popular Music*, 12 (1993), 13–31.

[59] *Ibid.*, 14.

present in the Lied is compressed into that of a single 'star'.[60] Bloomfield's argument is that the Romantic view of the song means it is a perfect commodity because it conceals its own reality under the appearance of promising intimacy with another person.[61] Thus, contrary to appearance, authenticity is not a solution to the problem of commodification but is part of the problem itself. 'At the core of the music industry, then,' argues Bloomfield, 'is a manufacture of illusion: a masquerade of authenticity whose main elements are drawn from the Romantic conception of art.'[62]

Like other cultural forms, then, music can set up structures of looking/hearing which solicit a particular subject position onto its subject matter.[63] In a manner analogous to Mulvey's identification of the contradictory processes of scopophilia and the specular image, these musical processes may also afford identification with another person (and hence an assumption of their vantage-point) and/or assumption of an omnipotent vantage-point by virtue of the privileged access into the artist's psyche which the song seems to afford. However, just as the cover art of *This is Hardcore* turns the viewer's privileged gaze back onto itself, so too does the music, and in doing so it disrupts any tendency on the part of the listener to identify with the protagonist of the song. In each case the process seems to be one which destroys the illusion of authorial authenticity, and hence the illusion of privileged access to or vantage over another person. The lyrics do this in a number of ways. For example, by stating that 'This is our "Music from a Bachelor's Den"' Pulp make explicit the potentially voyeuristic relationship of the listener to their music, and to them, just as by placing the band members in ambivalent positions within the photographs – as onlookers rather than participants – the viewer is made aware of his or her own voyeuristic position. The lyrics also place the listener uncomfortably in relation to protagonists within the tracks: for example, in 'Seductive Barry' the listener is made party to a sexual encounter, but this is a masturbatory encounter with a fantasized woman rather than a romantic encounter. Lastly, the lyrics address the listener directly in a manner analogous to the direct address to the camera found in some film: for example, the lyrics of 'The Fear' state 'So now you know the words to our song. Pretty soon you'll all be singing along . . .'. Similarly, the fact that the album is referred to in the first track, 'The Fear', as

---

[60] In fact, as Bloomfield points out, the notion that the Lied lays bare the 'soul' elides many different voices necessary to its production and consumption: the Lied is a complex interweaving of poetic text, compositional score and performers, which complicates the notion that it gives access to a single interiority. Even accepting this, the idea that this is a specifically 'Romantic' reception theory is problematized by a number of recent writings: see, for example, Susan Youens, 'Behind the Scenes: *Die schöne Müllerin* before Schubert', *19th Century Music*, 15 (1991–2), 3–22; *eadem, Schubert, Müller, and Die schöne Mullerin* (Cambridge, 1997); and Lawrence Kramer, *Franz Schubert: Sexuality, Subjectivity and Song* (Cambridge, 1998).

[61] Allan Moore has argued that the honesty to experience that music sometimes affords is carefully constructed ('U2 and the Myth of Authenticity', *Popular Musicology*, (1998), 5–33).

[62] Bloomfield, 'Resisting Songs', 27.

[63] The idea that music can construct ways of hearing is similar to the notion of voice in accounts of music and narrative (see, for example, Carolyn Abbate, *Unsung Voices: Opera and Musical Narrative in the Nineteenth Century*, Princeton, NJ, 1991, and Kramer, *Music as Cultural Practice*).

'the sound of loneliness turned up to ten' returns the listener to the reality of the world in which the album is playing rather than the diegetic world of the album, and forces upon the listener the rather uncomfortable recognition that it is the sound of his or her own loneliness that is heard.

Drawing together the examples from 'The Fear' and 'Seductive Barry' with others from the album reveals a number of musical techniques whereby the appearance of authorial authenticity is disrupted: namely, juxtaposition, excess and fragmentation. The stylistic references are numerous and self-conscious, suggesting that the musical materials should not be taken at face value: many of the materials are clichéd (for example, the tonic-dominant harmonies of the opening bars of 'The Fear', or the stock sounds of cabaret, rock and film music in 'This is Hardcore') and have a worn-out glamour similar to the subject matter of the images; materials from very different social contexts and genres are juxtaposed (for example, materials which have high production values, and which reference spirituality and authenticity – lush textures, references to art music, Hollywood film music, gospel and progressive rock, virtuosic solos – are juxtaposed with more banal references – the low production values of pornographic film and television movie sound-tracks). Sometimes these are stylistic references, as above; sometimes they are direct references to other music (for example, the lyrical references to Gil Scott Heron in 'The Day After the Revolution' and to The Doors in 'The Fear'); and sometimes even self-reference (for example, a similar motif appears in 'This is Hardcore' and 'Sorted for e's and wizz').[64] In each case, juxtaposition of very different materials undermines the illusion of a single authorial voice.

The authenticity of the music is also undermined by the excessive treatment of materials and the exaggeration of the norms of the styles. As well as highlighting the disparity between the intensity of imagined experience and the disappointment of reality, the effect of excessiveness and juxtaposition in this case is to place everything within inverted commas – both creating a distinction between subject matter and what is being said about that matter, and undermining the sense of an authentic authorial voice.

A further technique by which authorial authenticity is undermined in the album is the destruction of the illusion of completeness, of a crafted composition, and of performance skill. Tracks in *This is Hardcore* are linked by a common failure to end properly: 'The Fear' breaks down every time it nears climactic or epic proportions, and plays with lyrical references to 'the end'; the lush orchestral texture of 'This is Hardcore' slides away in the final bars to reveal the sounds with which the track began – the shabby reality of a cheap strip joint;[65] in 'Seductive Barry' the lush texture fades out to be followed by two hollow-sounding lead-guitar gestures; and 'The Day After the Revolution' fails

---

[64] See Clarke and Dibben, 'Sex, Pulp and Critique'.
[65] *Ibid.*

to end at all (the synth chord which 'ends' the track is sustained for ten minutes, despite Cocker's banal 'Bye, bye' and the sound of 'canned' audience applause). The structural instability of these tracks, particularly their endings, performs a number of functions: it draws attention to their status as products and undermines their illusory status as 'works' of music, but perhaps more significantly it goes against the idea of polished artistry, of the pop star's skill. The tracks on this album are more ambitious (they use full orchestra) and carefully crafted and make pretensions to high art (witness the direct references to other music and the epic structure of the title track), yet this display of skill is repeatedly undermined (even though the disintegration is, of course, carefully crafted).

Jarvis Cocker's voice is central to this undermining of authorial authenticity. Traditionally the voice is an important indicator of emotional veracity (perhaps deriving from the speaking voice), and the difference between what is said and how it is said is a key trait of Pulp's wit. Jarvis Cocker's voice is particularly important in this respect. One prominent technique is the way in which he changes between different types of voice in different tracks, and even within the same track, undermining any impression of authenticity. Compare, for instance, the mock 'seriously cool' voice of 'Party Hard' and 'Glory Days' sung in a low register and towards the back of the throat, with added delay suggesting a large performance space, with the slightly strained, higher-register voice of 'Dishes' and 'Help the Aged'. This higher voice suggests youth, naivety and a physical fragility (puniness, even) which is the nemesis of Barry White's love-songs. Close-miking of his voice provides an impression of intimacy, but the voice is often uncomfortably close: this may be music overheard by the listener ('This is our "Music from a Bachelor's Den"'), but overhearing turns out to reveal some uncomfortable truths rather than giving untainted voyeuristic access into the artist's psyche. The effect of these techniques is to undermine the myth of authenticity on offer in the songs: the listener may seek privileged access to the singer's psyche, where this provides a romanticized view of the individual with whom he or she can identify, but instead Pulp confront the listener with a much uglier reality.

I have argued that Pulp's album *This is Hardcore* problematizes media constructions of fame, masculinity, youth and sexuality as self-aggrandizing fantasies. The album's problematization of pornography and of voyeuristic relationships with pornography is both a manifestation of its subject matter – for example, the disjunction between fantasies of heterosexual masculinity and the reality which underlies them – and a problematization of spectatorship – a subject position ultimately at odds with constructions of macho masculinity as the protagonist in sexual encounters, and with constructions of fame and stardom. In this context pornography functions in the album as a cypher for the disparity between the intensity of imagined experience and the disappointment of reality – a disparity fuelled by the media and their forms of cultural consumption. The subject position which the album *This is Hardcore* solicits is ambivalent: it both encourages the listener to take up a voyeuristic relationship to its subject matter and simultaneously disrupts this very relationship by making the listener aware of his or her position as a spectator; the listener is encouraged to collude in the self-delusion that the album ultimately reveals as futile ('you'll all be singing along'),[66] but is simultaneously distanced and made aware of his or her spectatorial position, in a manner analogous to the viewer's spectatorial relationship with the cover art. Thus, the problematization of masculinity, sex, youth and fame in the album is part of a more general critique of spectatorship and voyeurism, and of the forms of cultural consumption which encourage such (dis)engagement. Music (or, more specifically, the popular song), it appears, is just as complicit in this.

University of Sheffield

ABSTRACT

Sheffield pop band Pulp's album *This is Hardcore* (1998) problematizes media constructions of fame, masculinity, youth and sexuality as self-aggrandizing fantasies. Pornography and glamour function in the album as cyphers for the disparity between fantasy and reality – a disparity fuelled by the media and their highly alienated cultural forms. The album's critique of these fantasies is made both in its subject matter and through the alienated subject position it solicits – a subject position at odds with constructions of macho masculinity as the protagonist in sexual encounters, and with constructions of fame and stardom. Drawing on media theory, I situate the album as part of a more general critique of spectatorship and voyeurism, and of the forms of cultural consumption (including music) which encourage passivity and disengagement.

---

[66] Pulp, 'The Fear'.

[25]

Glamour and evasion: the fabulous ambivalence of the Pet Shop Boys

FRED E. MAUS

Shifty harmonies in 'West End Girls'

This first section is for readers interested in technical musical analysis. Others may wish to skip ahead to the next section: while one of my goals is to link technical, interpretive and political concerns, it is possible to read this paper with relatively little attention to the technicalities.

At the beginning of the Pet Shop Boys' 'West End Girls', after some street sounds and a sustained chord, there is a three-chord progression (Cmaj7, D, E), mingling harmonies from the keys of e minor and E major (0:21–0:24; see Example 1).[1] The bass-line goes up, with a major triad over each note; only the third chord is free of additional, dissonant notes. The second chord sounds like a way of passing smoothly from the first one to the third.

Ex. 1.

The three-chord progression happens again (0:25–0:28), and then again (0:29–0:33). It begins a fourth time, but seems to get stuck on the middle chord (0:35). It is stuck only briefly, though, and the music moves to the final chord more forcefully than before, creating a cadence (0:40; see Example 2). The cadence feels to me like a big change in the motion of the music: previously the music hovered, and now, at the cadence, the music nails something.

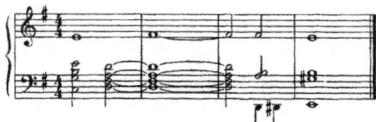

Ex. 2.

There is a high string-timbre note on top of the chord progression, sustaining through the changes, an *e*, consonant with the first and third chords, dissonant with the middle one. (Since the song is in the key of e minor mingled with major, *e* is the tonic pitch.) When the progression gets stuck on its middle D major chord, the harmony pushes the *e* up a step to a new note, *f♯* (0:36). The cadence that follows feels decisive partly because of the way the outer voices close in simultaneously on *e*, the top line moving back from *f♯* to *e* while the bass rises through *d♯* to *e*. (The presence of a new chord, the dominant of E major/e minor, also contributes decisiveness.)

The high *f♯* is an interesting note. When it appears it sounds good, even necessary, as an adjustment to the D major chord. But the long D major chord is strange, making a bulge in a succession of chords that used to move evenly; lingering on the middle chord of the progression gives strange emphasis to the chord that used to be a way of passing between the others, as though one pauses to observe something that previously almost escaped notice. Leaving that high *f♯*, moving back to *e*, is part of the strong move back to an E major cadence. When it first appears, *f♯* resolves an *e* that has become dissonant; just a moment later, *e* resolves the *f♯* instead, as the music moves to the cadential chord.

After a repetition of the cadence, the first verse starts immediately, in e minor. The *f♯* is there again, on top of the first chord of the verse, over *e* in the bass: *e* and *f♯* sound together, now, as part of a rich harmony. This is part of a general thickening of sound in the verse: neighbour motions in the bass (sometimes accented), full, dissonant chords, and Neil Tennant's rapping create the most complex pitch combinations of the song.[2] The high *f♯* begins a slow line that is present through verse and chorus. The chorus uses sung pitches, rather than speech, and simpler harmony, leading to those same strong E major cadences, with the same descent from *f♯* to *e* (1:22); Tennant's voice doubles the *d–d♯–e* bass motion. The cadences now feel like the end of a process of sonic and textural simplification.

The cadences come back to end the chorus throughout the song. They might start to feel stale if they came back in exactly the same form, but the Pet Shop Boys find ways to keep the later cadences eventful. At the end of the second verse, there is a loud new note pulsating over the final E major chords, adding emphasis to the cadence. The new note is *f♯*, so the cadence now has an odd, paradoxical quality, adding a further wrinkle to the *e*-and-*f♯* story: you hear *e* resolving up to *f♯*, then you hear *f♯* resolving down to *e*, and then *f♯* pops up again immediately. With the new note, it is as though *f♯* both does and does not move to *e*: you hear it resolve down, and then you hear that it is still sounding up there. This thickens the sound at the cadence, and returns to the simultaneous *e–f♯* combination from the beginning of the verse, partly undoing the simplification process found in the first verse and its chorus.

The last time the chorus cadences, there is a new trick. The bass line drops away from *d♯*, rather than rising to *e*, delaying the E major chord a little by introducing a version of the three-chord progression that opened the song (3:42). At the beginning, the progression hovered and then gave way to a strong cadence; now a cadence arrives and the three-chord progression expands it, seeming to give the cadence new weight – as though, now, the cadence reaches the E major chord and the repeating progression is a way of sinking deeper into that E chord. The same sounds recur with shifting meanings, as also happened with the top-line play between *e* and *f♯*.

Artistic hits

Who notices details like this? I do, easily and often – but then, music theory is part of my musical background; my training in pitch-recognition and technical analysis 'took', and for me these pitch-related facts about 'West End Girls' are not recondite. Other people will notice different aspects of this song. But whatever you take in, with whatever degree of consciousness or verbalisation, I think many listeners associate the Pet Shop Boys with an arty finesse that these pitch details illustrate nicely. More generally, there are many reasons to think of the Pet Shop Boys' songs as artistic, and as serious in purpose. They combine carefully crafted music, full of thoughtful, imaginative touches, with subtle, psychologically astute lyrics.

One might think that the Pet Shop Boys' art qualities would go along with an anti-commercial ideology, and perhaps an ideology of authenticity, a common mark of seriousness in discourse about popular music. In folk revival discussions, the notion of authenticity encapsulated the belief that certain music is valuable because it grows out of, and embodies, the values of a community; subsequent discussions of rock and other popular music retained the notion, altering it to include truthful self-expression as well as reflection of a community (Frith 1981; 1987). So it may be surprising to encounter the undisguised love of commercial success in the values of some devoted Pet Shop Boys fans.

I have been reading the fan e-mail list, 'Introspective',[3] since 1998. By coincidence, I started reading it when information about the 1999 album *Nightlife* was beginning to circulate. In discussions of the upcoming album, the conventional ideology of authenticity, with its contrast between sincerity and commercialism, was largely absent from the e-mail list. Instead, fans eagerly discussed the prospects of the new album's commercial success, and were full of advice and concern about the most commercially promising selection and marketing of singles. Many list members worried that the album might be disappointing in sales.

One recurring debate on the list is about *Bilingual*, the 1996 album that seemed to signal the Pet Shop Boys' decline in popularity. Fans speculate about the reasons for its relative lack of commercial success, and many of them criticise the album, arguing that its mediocre sales derive from artistic flaws; other fans value *Bilingual* highly, but their praise often has a sense of special pleading, as though the album's relative obscurity is already a mark against it. As release of *Nightlife* approached, posters to 'Introspective' worried that the Pet Shop Boys were becoming a fan band, known only to a limited audience of partisans; and they worried that the Pet Shop Boys might stop creating songs if they could not maintain the hit status of their earlier work. Most people posting to the list seemed to share these concerns: dissent, along the lines that the fans would always have the Pet Shop Boys, no matter what happened commercially, was scarce and ineffectual.

Not only do the fans emphasise hits; the Pet Shop Boys themselves have sometimes displayed an interest in sheer fame. In Chris Heath's narratives of their first tours, Tennant and Chris Lowe follow the charts avidly (Heath 1990; 1994). In 1989, Tennant summarised their relation to fame: 'One of the things the Pet Shop Boys are always trying to do is always to be mass market without watering down anything we've ever done, without "selling out" or whatever'. Intriguingly, this brings together the authenticist worry about 'selling out' and an insistence on selling. Tennant continues: 'I still have the sixties idea that you can "sell out" and I don't regard the Pet Shop Boys as having sold out to get where we are now. I don't think we've fundamentally watered down anything we've wanted to do to make it palatable to people' (Heath 1990, p. 36). Tennant sees a balancing act, but not an outright contradiction, in the combination of mass appeal and artistic independence (Frith 1988; 1989).

Like Tennant, the members of the 'Introspective' list are not simply populist in their concern with hits. They are generally independent minded about current pop music, as you might expect from present-day devotees of a duo that was famous in the late 1980s and early 1990s and is no longer fashionable. But the early commercial success of the Pet Shop Boys seems to be an important part of what some fans like and admire about them. The Pet Shop Boys began their career with hits. There was no early stage of cultish admiration before they became widely known; there was no role for the conventional narrative of authenticity in which artists might betray their early, somewhat esoteric achievement by selling out for greater commercial success. For many fans, evidently the achievement of early Pet Shop Boys music had two crucial aspects: they created distinctive music that individual fans loved, and they attracted large audiences who desired that music.

This would make sense if something about the Pet Shop Boys' music gains value from being widely enjoyed. There are various ways one might think about this, but I want to follow a train of thought that emphasises images of gender and sexuality. I understand the Pet Shop Boys as articulating a distinctive alternative masculinity, and the value of such articulation lies not just in forming an identity but in gaining for it some kind of acceptance. The Pet Shop Boys' fame is part of the broader story of the circulation of alternative, non-macho masculinities in 1980s pop, a story that includes Michael Jackson, Boy George, George Michael, Prince, Morrissey, Marc Almond, Andy Bell, Green Gartside, David Byrne and others (Walser 1994; Fuchs 1995; Hubbs 1996).[4] As the list suggests, these masculinities were often, though not always, gay, with varying degrees of openness.

It is already an achievement to create vivid images of such alternative masculinities, making the assertive, aggressive, misogynist norms of much popular culture seem like just one male option among others. But beyond simply desiring that models of such masculinities exist, one can desire, as a further, distinct goal, that they be broadly acknowledged and approved, even loved. This might be some of the content – political content – of fans' desire for the Pet Shop Boys' commercial success. Wanting the Pet Shop Boys to have hits could be, in part, wanting certain kinds of men to be recognised and admired. And disappointment at the prospect of a mere fan band could have, as part of its content, a political worry that a particular alternative masculinity has been relegated to a privatised subculture.

'The Gay Debate'

Members of 'Introspective' do not put it quite that way. The list has its own way of addressing masculinity, through an approximately monthly ordeal called, by list members, the Gay Debate. Broadly, the issue is whether it matters for understanding and enjoying the Pet Shop Boys that Tennant, who sings and writes the lyrics, is gay. (List members assume that Lowe, who collaborates with Tennant, is gay as well, but this matters less to the Gay Debate. There is also a different recurring debate about whether Tennant and Lowe were ever lovers; clearly some list members enjoy thinking that they were.[5]) More specifically, posters argue about whether gay listeners have special insight into the songs, whether the songs convey a 'gay sensibility', and whether particular songs imply experiences and situations specifically from gay lives.

Many of the opinions and arguments are unsurprising. Many posts come from gay male writers, who identify strongly with the Pet Shop Boys as gay and find numerous gay meanings in the songs. Posts from straight writers often stress the universality of the Pet Shop Boys' meanings, and the writers seem resentful that they might be excluded somehow from full understanding. I was more surprised (though I should not have been; I was naive) by posts from gay men insisting that homosexuality had nothing to do with the meaning or value of Pet Shop Boys songs, that there is no such thing as a 'gay sensibility' and that Tennant's work is about humanness rather than gayness. Some of these posts suggest a slightly convoluted identification with Tennant as a gay man who shows that gayness does not matter.

The recurring Gay Debate is startlingly intense and sometimes generates large numbers of posts. Many list members seem to find it unpleasant but irresistible; we greet its onset with groans of recognition and then we promptly collaborate to make it happen once again.

Beyond showing that gender and sexuality are central to many fans' thought about the Pet Shop Boys, the debate also shows the variety of interpretations that committed fans derive from the songs. The people who post messages on 'Introspective' are, by and large, fans with extensive, reflective knowledge of many songs. How could the Pet Shop Boys' songs be amenable to such different, even contradictory interpretations?

Double-voicedness, deniability

One answer can begin by citing familiar traits of the language of 'the closet', the veiled language associated with homophobia. Until very recently, indirect communication about 'the love that dares not speak its name' has been normative in most settings. Connotation and *double-entendre* have perpetuated an atmosphere of secrecy, shame and social control around homosexuality, even while they also provide a style of public communication for gay men themselves (Sedgwick 1990; Miller 1991).

Like much communication about homosexuality, Tennant's lyrics are often double-voiced, carrying special meanings for insiders while remaining differently meaningful for others as well. 'To Speak is a Sin', for instance, can be heard as a sad song about an evening in a pub, but it evokes, quite precisely, experiences of cruising in gay bars (of a rather dated kind), when heard by listeners in whom such experiences can be evoked. 'To speak is a sin/You look first, then stare/And once in a while/A smile, if you dare'. With its emphasis on silence and the play of eye contact, this sounds similar to the cruising described in Larry Kramer's novel *Faggots*:

You don't talk to people when you cruise. The secret is to just look mean . . . Think of this place as a great big store, with lots of merchandise on display . . . You give it a little look, pretending not to look, but being able to see, out of the corner of your eye only, if anyone is pretending not to look back at you. If you see someone pretending not to look, you look the other way. Only after a few moments do you look back, to see if he's still looking. (Kramer 1987, p. 261)

Again, in 'Two Divided by Zero', it seems that two people, hounded by rumours, are about to flee their familiar world for New York. The oppressive sense of criminality and surveillance, and the dream of escape to an utterly different place, are commonplace in the world of closeted homosexuality, but the song is unspecific, not even identifying the two fugitives as lovers. Longing for another, better place is an unsurprising theme in gay cultures, encapsulated, of course, in Harold Arlen's 'Somewhere Over the Rainbow', a song that many gay boys and men have valued. Tennant recently selected Arlen's song for inclusion on a radio broadcast (Tennant 2001). And the Pet Shop Boys have recorded cover versions of three similar songs about escape – the Village People's 'Go West', Stephen Sondheim's and Leonard Bernstein's 'Somewhere', and Noël Coward's 'Sail Away': the creators of all three songs are icons of gay musicality. The Pet Shop Boys' recent song, 'New York City Boy' reiterates, more cheerfully (and with stylistic reference to the Village People), the image of New York as a place of freedom and adventure for gay men, though its retro sound may locate this happiness back in the legendary 1970s, expressing a different kind of longing. 'Two Divided by Zero', the first song on their first album, announces this theme with special grimness.[6]

Many listeners hear all these songs (and many other Pet Shop Boys songs) as gay-themed, while other listeners hear them with no conscious associations to homosexuality. This is the typical device of Tennant's double-voicedness: he describes situations and feelings that are basic to much twentieth-century gay life, but leaves out any fully determinate specification of sexuality. Many gay listeners hear the result as evoking familiar aspects of their subculture; meanwhile, listeners who do not want a gay interpretation can hear, instead, descriptions of intriguing, if odd, situations with straight or sexually unspecified characters.

This ambiguity creates deniability, another feature fundamental to much discourse about homosexuality (more precisely, deniability and double-voicedness are not independent features, but logically related qualities of guarded communication). As interpretive debates on 'Introspective' show, sometimes at tedious length, there are many songs in which gay listeners find strong evocations of gay lives about which, nonetheless, nothing can be proved. That is, proof is impossible when the argument proceeds legalistically on the basis of the text of the song, without invoking the broader context of communicative practices around homosexuality: the texts are designed to evade that kind of legalistic demonstration. A message from a New Zealand fan, posted on 'Introspective', described the situation elegantly, intervening in a heated discussion of the relevance of HIV infection to the song 'Discoteca':

Again, this is another case of if you get the whole gay subtext thing then you get it; if you don't, then you never will. It's akin to Louis Armstrong's often quoted definition of jazz: if you have to ask, you'll never know. For me, this is one of the reasons that there's no point in entering into the Great Gay Debate. You wind up just preaching to the converted or have your evidence fall on deaf ears. Contextually, this is one of the most exciting things about PSB's lyrics. They're carrying on a fine tradition of gay writing that follows on from the likes of Oscar Wilde and Tennessee Williams. If anything, Neil's 'coming out' (for those who ever thought he was in) only made the "is it or isn't it" gay thing a little less fun. (Contribution to 'Introspective' fan email list from 'S', 1999)

One of the Pet Shop Boys' songs for Dusty Springfield takes as its topic the tensions of such epistemological suspense, offering an obscure narrative of scandal, mysterious crimes, and suicide: 'It may be false, it may be true/But nothing has been proved'.

No doubt the Pet Shop Boys' songs of the 1980s and early 1990s depended on deniability for some of their circulation and commercial success, taking advantage of a predictable failure of many listeners to accept explicit gay meanings or, more subtly, of a public appetite for thinly disguised representations of homosexuality, an appetite that full explicitness would spoil. At the same time, for audiences conscious of gay issues, the indirectness of expression can become a part of the subject matter. These songs display, blatantly and as though intentionally, the mechanisms of double-voicedness and deniability that are basic facts of historical gay life. They can be heard not only as a rueful, intensely self-conscious perpetuation of a secretive discourse, but perhaps also as an insistent display of that discourse, in response to the new wave of homophobia that accompanied the AIDS epidemic and the conservative administrations of Thatcher and Reagan. This acknowledgment of discretion in response to homophobia gives the songs a particular, historically specific depth that is absent in the more utopian songs of Erasure, which look forward glibly to a time when homosexuality is no big deal.

Glamour and evasion

It would be a simplification, though, to define the Pet Shop Boys' masculinity purely in terms of a relation to a generalised late-twentieth-century gayness. Without losing the relation to sexuality, I want to offer a characterisation that is more detailed and less restrictively sexual. The Pet Shop Boys combine the insistent but unaggressive rhythms of dance music with a persistent opulence of timbre, texture and harmony. Rich string timbres, seventh chords and other lush harmonies, reverberation and other devices recreate the unmanly, luxurious sound of disco.[7] Within this gorgeousness, Tennant's small, high, thin voice articulates a subjectivity full of longing. The longing sometimes lunges out in direct statements – 'I want a lover tonight', 'Why don't we live together?', 'Give me one more chance'. But more often, the longing is curbed and suppressed, finding expression in muted, indirect language. The typical protagonist of Tennant's lyrics, if he is desperately lonely, might say, 'I want a dog, a chihuahua'. If he is losing connection with his lover, he might say, 'You have a different point of view'. If he needs to counsel himself or someone else against despair, he might say, 'Happiness is an option'. If, for once, he is happy in love, he might say, 'I wouldn't normally do this kind of thing'. (That the quoted excerpts are all song titles, as well as lyrics, shows the centrality of indirectness in the Pet Shop Boys' construction of their image.)

This ambivalence about direct expression, these bizarre formulations that embody the desire to express and the desire to withhold, are continuous with the discretion that homophobia enforces; but in becoming a generalised quality of Tennant's writing, the expressive ambivalence spreads beyond the specific issues of closeted gay sexuality. Unlike the gay meanings hidden in double-voicedness, these representations of ambivalence are easily accessible to straight audiences (though so much unexplained evasion may strike straight listeners as a peculiar trait). Still, there is continuity between the issues of sexually motivated double-voicedness and deniability and the Pet Shop Boys' other ambiguities and ambivalences. And further, their combination of sensuous, opulent sound and evasive or withdrawn expression can itself be heard as a gay-coded configuration, whatever the specific content of the lyrics.[8]

Being ambivalent

Having suggested that issues of ambivalence in Pet Shop Boys' songs are neither reducible to gay coding nor fully separable from it, I want to sketch some other ways in which ambivalence comes up in their work. Generally, ambiguity or ambivalence involves setting out an opposition, along with an unclear or undecidable relation between the terms of the opposition, and such patterns are ubiquitous in the Pet Shop Boys' music.

The particular roles of their duo already establish a preoccupation with binaries, setting Tennant (verbal, vocal, articulate, non-dancing) against Lowe (musical, non-singing, inarticulate, dancing). Perhaps the most pervasive Pet Shop Boys effect comes from the mysterious combination of Tennant's over-articulate but evasive lyrics with Lowe's musical and embodied presence; their songs are, in part, about the incompleteness of each role and the gap between them.

Their first hit, 'West End Girls', wildly popular despite its obscure lyrics, plays off 'East End' against 'West End', 'boys' against 'girls', and the fact that listeners could enjoy the song without knowing what it is about suggests that its crisp but mysterious oppositions can float free from representation, becoming a source of a more abstract or formal pleasure. Meanwhile, the musical features I began by describing contribute to the pervasive atmosphere of ambivalence. The D chord might be a passing chord, moving against a stable, sustained e; or the D chord might be stable, requiring that the e resolve as a rising suspension. Resolution might come from the high $f\sharp$ replacing an e, but immediately after, resolution comes from an e replacing the $f\sharp$. Getting rid of $f\sharp$ can help create a cadence, but adding $f\sharp$ can also emphasise the cadence. A strong cadence can end the stasis of the series of three-chord progressions, but the three-chord progressions can also, at the end, reinforce the cadential chord. These details seem to affirm the capacity of all those sounds to serve precisely opposite functions at different moments, an ambivalence of function akin to the ambiguity of double-voicedness.

In another kind of ambivalence, some songs create textual personae that seem to resemble Tennant, or Tennant and Lowe, but cannot be identified with them. Such cases play on the unclear distinction between song personae and actual people. 'Opportunities' cannot be taken as a depiction of Tennant's and Lowe's collaboration, but it persistently invites comparison – Tennant conspicuously has brains, Lowe has looks (if not brawn), and the two certainly did make lots of money; the promotional video casts the two in the implied roles. (Attempting to deny the link, Tennant does not quite succeed, retaining a bit too much ambiguity: 'People have often thought it was about me and Chris but I don't think it was really. I don't know if Chris thought that but I just pictured two people' [Heath 1990, p. 63].) The drag queen in 'Electricity', like the Pet Shop Boys, depends on technology and costume changes for her show. 'How Can You Expect to be Taken Seriously' – about public figures who become pompous and sage-like – is not about the Pet Shop Boys, but you do consider the possibility; and if they did not want you to, they would not bring pompously grand portraits of themselves onstage in their 1991 stage performances (see the video *Performance*). The first single from *Nightlife*, a glimpse of a new album after the problematic *Bilingual*, has an odd joke about come-back attempts in its title: 'I Don't Know What You Want but I Can't Give it Anymore'. The video also seems to comment on the come-back idea: a combination of advanced medical science, make-up, and fashion design gets the middle-aged Tennant and Lowe back on the streets with a new look.[9]

Several recordings and performances create ambivalence in another way, bringing together two different songs in a way that complicates the most obvious meanings of each. In live performance, they have joined their own song 'It's a Sin' with the disco classic 'I Will Survive', a clever pairing since both songs draw their harmonic energy from a descending circle-of-fifths progression.[10] While 'It's a Sin' laments, as though helplessly, the permanent guilt induced by a moralistic upbringing (easy to associate, of course, with sexual guilt in particular), 'I Will Survive' is defiant. The combination exaggerates ambivalence into mood-swings, each song countering the absoluteness of the mood of the other song. The Pet Shop Boys' cover of 'Always On My Mind' begins with the song's sweet plea for forgiveness, then moves to a new middle section with an acidic, passive–aggressive rap, expressing the resentment and anger that one comes to hear as an undercurrent of the original song: 'I worked so hard, I thought you knew/My love, I did it all for you/ I never really had the time/I guess you couldn't read my mind'.[11] And the cover of 'Where the Streets Have No Name' conjoins the heartfelt U2 song, hilariously, with the old Frankie Valli hit, 'Can't Take My Eyes Off You'. Perhaps the combination can be heard as a depiction of street cruising;[12] in any case the combination transforms and undermines U2's earnest rhetoric (Butler 2000).

Harmonic ambivalence

These medleys that involve cover versions show a strategy that the Pet Shop Boys also use more subtly in individual songs where, again, contrasts between sections create tension and increase ambivalence. Such sectional contrasts often work in alignment with a harmonic technique: the Pet Shop Boys sometimes create harmonic ambivalence by establishing two different keys or modes in a song, typically with a contrast of major and minor, and keeping both possibilities active. (Here I return to analysis. Again, my background means that I notice changes of key and mode without effort, and I am aware that this varies for other listeners: on the other hand, I think many people experience major and minor modes vividly as affective contrasts, without needing to think explicitly in terms of pitch material.) The simplest, most schematic technique of keeping two keys alive is to distribute the material of a song into sections that are in different keys, without hierarchising the sections or keys in any definite way.[13] 'Suburbia' alternates between minor-mode verse and major-mode chorus. 'To Speak is a Sin' distributes major and minor the same way. The verse of 'How Can you Expect to be Taken Seriously' is in G major, the chorus in b minor. 'The Theatre' is more complex; the verse moves from E♭ major to c minor, and then the chorus is in e♭ minor.

In these examples, the sectional changes of mode match the texts, and in general minor goes with text depicting uncomfortable realities that the other perspective must attempt to disregard. The major/minor contrast supports and embodies issues of denial. 'Suburbia' alternates between descriptions of bored delinquents and an apparently cheerful call to have fun. 'To Speak is a Sin' uses minor mode for candid personal reflection, major mode to affirm the dehumanising conventions of cruising in a bar. The major-mode sections of 'How do you Expect to be Taken Seriously?' offer polite commentary and questions, addressed in almost-respectful tones to a public figure; the minor mode sections turn to the harsh, challenging question of the title. 'The Theatre' evokes the pleasures of theatrical illusion, and then turns to realities of urban life: 'We're the bums you step over as you leave the theatre'. These are songs about truth-telling, about the difficulty of truthfulness and the pleasures of silence, conformity, and denial. Their major-mode music is often beautiful, offering listeners a seductive image of disavowal.

'Dreaming of the Queen' opens with a grand-sounding introduction in D♭ major (0:00–0:10). The verse follows, in b♭ minor, narrating a dream of a visit to Queen Elizabeth and Princess Diana (0:11–0:52). The introduction seems to evoke the pomp and impersonality of royalty, while the minor mode passages begin to recount a serious conversation. The chorus (0:53–1:24) is ambiguous between relative major and minor (D♭ and b♭). It cadences into the glowing major of the introductory passage (1:25–1:36); but since that passage seems to represent the impersonal, formal grandeur of royalty, it offers an escape from the succession of personal thoughts and feelings rather than a resolution. Perhaps one can hear this glamorous, glowing music as an official intervention, as though these textless passages appear in order to silence Tennant's voice. 'There are no more lovers left alive, no one has survived'. It is possible, if barely so, to hear it just as a song about modern marriage and the domestic troubles of the royal family, but the song also, and more urgently, mourns the AIDS epidemic. In the next verse the protagonist, Tennant perhaps, dreams that he is standing naked in public and that people do not mind. This seems to be about coming out, a surprising topic, perhaps, in a song that does not relinquish the deniability of its gay content. Perhaps, though, this is not only a guarded, indirect song, but also a song *about* evasive language, about what social norms, personified by the Queen, may discourage you from saying directly.

Other songs use major and minor to articulate other kinds of ambivalence. 'What Have I Done to Deserve This?', another song with sectional alternations of major and minor, seems to depict a pervasive ambivalence of mood – 'you went away, it should make me feel better, but . . .' – rather than an alternation between truth and denial. In 'I Don't Know What You Want, but I Can't Give it Anymore', the dour harmonies of the f minor verse and chorus are framed by ecstatic sections that mingle b♭ minor and B♭ major but always end in major (0:00–0:32, 3:00–3:31, 4:41–5:08). These sections, instrumental apart from quiet repetitions of 'don't know what you want' and the addition of a soaring wordless diva in one passage, suggest that 'not knowing what someone wants' might be a release from obligation rather than a depressing failure; but the passages are relatively brief and, without text, inexplicit in their encouragement.

Of course, there are ways to play off major and minor other than sectional alternation. In 'So Hard', Tennant's character asks his lover why they don't try to be monogamous, since their affairs cause so much pain. There is uncertainty in the questioning approach, as though the speaker might be offering fidelity but might, instead, be asking the factual question why (not whether) monogamy is impossible for them. The mingling of major and minor, achieved partly through loud, interrupting blasts of minor-mode orchestral sound (for instance, at 0:24–0:28, 0:36–0:40, 1:24–1:28), reflects the mix of hope and resignation. (The 1991 staging of this song brings out the uncertainty of the text with a profusion of question-marks onstage [see video *Performance*]. In the 1994 performance, the avid self-groping of the male dancers underscores the *double-entendre* of 'hard', the exciting eroticism that resists control [see video *Discovery*].)

In 'Only the Wind', the drums, piano and violins seem to be very close to the listener, as does Tennant's voice. Other sounds, orchestral notes, seem muffled, as though they are loud but are heard from a distance. 'It's only the wind', sings Tennant, as though he is saying that those loud noises outside don't matter. It is a metaphor; the song is about denial, and while Tennant sings that everything is all right, it becomes clear that things are going badly. The words invite a way of listening to the loud orchestral notes: you can hear them as representing the truth of the situation, the facts that the words try to suppress, and you can hear those loud *a*'s as undermining the serene C major of the foreground music. So, hearing the music under the influence of the text, you might not hear just a C major song along with some extraneous loud noises; you might also, or instead, hear a strong assertion of the pitch *a*, and perhaps the key a minor, along with evasive foreground harmonies.

'Tonight is Forever' is a complex example, not easy to follow consciously unless one has quick analytical ears for harmonic relationships. It begins with pitch material that is ambiguous in both key and metre (0:00–0:07). Drum sounds enter to establish a metre (0:08–0:14), and then a synthesizer melody seems to settle the key as c minor (0:15–0:29). The voice enters, with the characteristic words 'I may be wrong, I may be right' and changes the orientation to E♭ major, moving from tonic chord to dominant in each of two phrases. These half-cadences imply the tonic of E♭ without fully closing in that key (0:36, 0:43). The next pair of phrases, though, turns back to c minor, again using two half-cadences to indicate the key without closing in it (0:50, 0:57). These half-cadences use the leading tone, which supports c minor and contradicts E♭ major. The chorus follows, bringing back the opening synthesizer melody. This eliminates the leading tone of c minor. Now, with no pitches to distinguish the major and minor keys, and with Tennant's melodic emphasis on *e♭*, the passage seems more ambiguous in key (1:00–1:14). In the chorus, Tennant sings 'Tonight is forever', which sounds like an expression of ecstasy; but he immediately qualifies by asking for support: 'Tell me now you don't disagree'. Apparently the ecstasy requires endorsement, and the formulation implies that disagreement is likely. The harmonic fluctuations and textual ambivalence work together to create the Pet Shop Boys' characteristic uneasiness; the resonant, sensuous sounds add a characteristic intensity of pleasure.

Recently

Beginning in 1994, Tennant has publicly acknowledged that he is gay. A few album cuts, from around that time and later, have seemed to include undeniably gay subject matter, but not many: 'Can You Forgive Her?' and 'Metamorphosis' are the most direct (though some listeners still seem able to miss the point). Some one-off songs have been plainer. In 1996 there was 'The Truck Driver and His Mate', a b-side on a single: 'Parked inside the lay-by/Their destination can wait/Dancing in the moonlight/The truck-driver and his mate'. In 2000 they startled fans by performing a cover of a Modern Rocketry song, 'Homosexuality', at a gay rights rally ('Equality Rocks', in Washington D.C.).

One song on *Nightlife*, 'In Denial', was the first Pet Shop Boys song with the word 'gay' in it. But it was also, especially obviously, about fictional characters, in this case a gay club-owner whose life is in disarray, in confrontation with an adult daughter who wants him to see his problems. Other songs on *Nightlife* are, as usual, circumspect about sexuality. The clearest continuation of their habit of *double-entendre* is the song 'Vampires', which can hardly be heard outside the rich history of metaphorical associations between vampirism and homosexuality (Dyer 1988;

Case 1991; Hanson 1991; Benshoff 1997). Unnatural creatures, with their non-procreative sensuality and their urgent sucking desires, associated with night, stealth, secrecy, contagion, and exchange of bodily fluids, vampires have provided a rich source of homophobic imagery as well as complexly affirmative gay and lesbian self-images (Case 1991). The Pet Shop Boys song reconfigures vampirism in ways that bring it especially close to queer sexuality. It begins by setting aside family ties in favour of the stronger bonds of vampirism ('Brother, it don't matter/ Sister, don't worry') and then, despite the fact that vampires do not standardly prey on each other, celebrates mutual recognition: 'Do what you want/And then can I do it to you?/You're a vampire/I'm a vampire too'. That the Pet Shop Boys continue in this vein of campy allusion, years after Tennant came out, suggests that the ins and outs of Tennant's or Lowe's personal self-disclosure are not, and perhaps were never, the central issue in their creative choices.[14]

Tennant has often said that he does not want to be a role model. However, he cannot help it; nor can the lower-profile Lowe. These sad, not-quite-young men, in the ambivalence, evasion and gorgeousness of their music and their public personae, mark out a distinctive masculinity, quite different from the more assertive norms of masculinity in much mainstream pop music.[15] Lacking the direct, sincere self-expression normally associated with authenticity, they offer, instead, a veiled, inhibited expressiveness that can, nonetheless, be taken as an emblem of a community. They achieve a queer kind of authenticity. And we fans on 'Introspective' respond appropriately, re-enacting their ambivalence in the collaborative performance of our Gay Debate.

Another song on *Nightlife* offers a particularly vivid distillation of the Pet Shop Boys' characteristic restraint and longing. 'Happiness is an Option' conjoins Rachmaninoff's beautiful 'Vocalise' and hip-hop, with black-sounding women's voices as backdrop to Tennant's rapping. This time, Tennant's speaking voice is hushed and urgent. Recorded to make his voice sound lower than usual while also emphasising very high frequencies, his speech sounds like whispering. The song juxtaposes blackness and Russianness, familiar emblems of soulfulness and authenticity, with a private, constrained vocal sound and an understated, prose-like text (exemplified in the title) redolent of disappointment and self-restraint. The combination offers one more ambivalent binary, allowing one to ponder the distance between Tennant's self-presentation and these other authenticities.

Wanting the world to love this fabulous ambivalence, this damaged masculine subjectivity, is a political desire, one that I share.

Acknowledgements

This paper draws on material presented at conferences of IASPM-US (Murfreesboro, 1999) and IASPM-UK (University of Surrey, 2000) and on a review of *Nightlife* (Newsletter of the Gay and Lesbian Study Group of the American Musicological Society, 2000). I am grateful for comments and encouragement from Barbara Bradby, Mark Butler, Kevin Clifton, Nadine Hubbs, Martin Kavka and 'Mary' (pseudonym of a member of the 'Introspective' list). The members of my 1999 music analysis seminar were patient with an unexpected barrage of Pet Shop Boys songs. Special thanks to Mark, Kevin, Nadine and Martin for the ongoing conversations that have made my reflections on the Pet Shop Boys so enjoyable; and to the members of the 'Introspective' list who, at best, create a wonderfully effervescent setting for serious thought about our Boys.

Endnotes

1. See Discography for sources of individual songs discussed. (I have used album tracks rather than singles or other versions.) For 'West End Girls' and some other songs, I give timings to identify particular moments. Sheet music exists for much Pet Shop Boys music, but I have not consulted it, preferring to work 'by ear' from the recorded sound.

2. Tennant's lines are spoken, not sung. But the spoken words have pitch, of course, and the fact that the pitches of his rapping are outside the chords and scale of the music creates a distinctive complexity of total sound.

3. In addition to the e-mail list 'Introspective', there are some excellent web resources on the Pet Shop Boys, including an official site, http://www.redmancreative.com/petshopboys/menu.htm, and many fan sites such as the superb compilation at http://www.geocities.com/SunsetStrip/Performance/4741 and the elegant homage at http://www.10yearsofbeingboring.com.

4. Hawkins (1997) also places the Pet Shop Boys in relation to new images of masculinity. His approach is similar to mine, and we share a number of interpretive claims. However, I do not understand his emphasis on the 'banality' of the Pet Shop Boys' music. It does not strike me as banal, and Hawkins never identifies the other, less banal music to which he is comparing the Pet Shop Boys' songs.

5. Bradby (1993) is an ethnographic study of the importance of speculation and fantasy for lesbian audiences of women musicians.

6. I understand the title to mean 'two who cannot be separated (they are divided by nothing)' but, at the same time, to mark this union as impossible or nonsensical (there is no such number as two divided by zero), thus registering economically the painful conundrum of same-sex love in our homophobic society.

7. Dyer (1992) articulates a nice contrast between disco and rock rhythms. Hughes (1994) treats the Pet Shop Boys' music as the continuation of classic 1970s' disco music. There is an intriguing gap between Dyer's emphasis on the whole-body, non-phallic rhythms of disco and Hughes's emphasis on the coercive effects of the disco beat.

8. Hubbs makes a similar point about evasion in her discussion of Morissey: 'Ambiguity is not particularly confusing to queer subjects, to whom its utility and indeed necessity are well known. Even cultivated sexual ambiguity is not something that tends to jam or erase well-formed 'gaydar' readings – to the contrary, it tends to reinforce positive readings' (Hubbs 1996, p. 285).

9. Video included on the single CD.

10. See the videos *Discovery* and *Somewhere*. Hubbs (forthcoming) writes about the *Discovery* performance.

11. The reprise of 'Always On My Mind' that follows the rap selects only lines that seem to question the speaker's commitment, ending with 'Maybe I didn't love you'. The music that accompanied the rap returns to end the song.

12. The suggestion about street cruising comes from Marianne Tatom, in conversation, reported to me by Mark Butler.

13. McClary (1991, pp. 132–66) has discussed songs by Laurie Anderson and Madonna that indicate major and minor tonics without subordinating one to the other. She argues that such lack of hierarchy is a way of resisting a masculinist narrative embodied most prestigiously in sonata form (a formal pattern of classical instrumental music). In sonata form, according to McClary, a secondary key is an object of desire but also a source of instability, associated with femininity, and compositions end by subordinating feminine music to the masculine home key. Anderson and Madonna, on her account, refuse this subordination. Obviously, my account of Pet Shop Boys' songs describes similar phenomena but interprets them differently.

14. For Gill, 'in or out' is clearly the central issue (Gill 1995, pp. 1–9). His account of the Pet Shop Boys is dismayingly one-dimensional.

15. Dyer (1993) surveys the 'sad young man' stereotype helpfully. The Pet Shop Boys' album covers would fit in well among Dyer's illustrations.

References

Benshoff, H.M. 1997. *Monsters in the Closet: Homosexuality and the Horror Film* (Manchester)

Bradby, B. 1993. 'Lesbians and popular music: does it matter who is singing?', in *Outwrite: Lesbianism and Popular Culture*, ed. G. Griffin (London), pp. 148–71

Butler, M.J. 2000. 'Taking it seriously: intertextuality and authenticity in two covers by the Pet Shop Boys', paper presented at IASPM-UK conference, University of Surrey

Case, S.E. 1991. 'Tracking the vampire', *Differences*, 3/2, pp. 1–20

392   *Fred E. Maus*

Dyer, R. 1988. 'Children of the night: vampirism as homosexuality, homosexuality as vampirism', in *Sweet Dreams: Sexuality Gender and Popular Fiction*, ed S. Radstone (London), pp. 47–72
    1992. 'In defence of disco', in *Only Entertainment* (New York), pp. 149–58 (first published 1979)
    1993. 'Coming out as going in: the image of the homosexual as a sad young man', in *The Matter of Images: Essays on Representations* (New York), pp. 73–91
Frith, S. 1981. '"The Magic that can Set you Free": the ideology of folk and the myth of the rock community', *Popular Music*, 1, pp. 159–75
    1987. 'Towards an aesthetic of popular music', in *Music and Society: The Politics of Composition, Performance, and Reception*, ed. R.D. Leppert and S. McClary (Cambridge, UK), pp. 133–50
    1988. 'Pet Shop Boys: the divine commodity', *Voice Rock 'n' Roll Quarterly*, (Spring), pp. 7–9
    1989. 'BritBeat: living videos', *The Village Voice*, August 29, p. 77
Fuchs, C. 1995. 'Michael Jackson's penis', in *Cruising the Performative: Interventions into the Representation of Ethnicity, Nationality, and Sexuality*, ed. S.E. Case, P. Brett and S.L. Foster (Bloomington), pp. 13–33
Gill, J. 1995. *Queer Noises* (Minneapolis)
Hanson, E. 1991. 'Undead', in *Inside/Out: Lesbian Theories, Gay Theories*, ed. D. Fuss (New York), pp. 324–40
Hawkins, S. 1997. 'The Pet Shop Boys: musicology, masculinity, and banality', in *Sexing the Groove: Popular Music and Gender*, ed. S. Whiteley (New York), pp. 118–33
Heath, C. 1990. *Pet Shop Boys, Literally* (New York)
    1994. *Pet Shop Boys Versus America* (Miami)
Hubbs, N. 1996. 'Music of the "fourth gender": Morrissey and the sexual politics of melodic contour', in *Bodies of Writing, Bodies in Performance: Genders 23*, ed. T. Foster, C. Siegel and E.E. Berry (New York)
    Forthcoming. 'I Will Survive: the disco anthem's minor-mode semiotics of transcendence', in *Disco's Distinctions: Essays on Race, Class, Sound, and the Market*, ed. M. Morris (Berkeley)
Hughes, W. 1994. 'In the empire of the beat: discipline and disco', in *Microphone Fiends: Youth Music and Youth Culture*, ed. A. Ross and T. Rose (New York), pp. 147–57
Kramer, L. 1987. *Faggots* (New York) (first published 1978)
McClary, S. 1991. *Feminine Endings: Music, Gender, and Sexuality* (Minneapolis)
Miller, D.A. 1991. 'Anal *Rope*', in *Inside/Out: Lesbian Theories, Gay Theories*, ed. D. Fuss (New York), pp. 119–41
'S' (pseudonym). 1999. 'Re: Discoteca – gay themed' (message to 'Introspective', September 12)
Sedgwick, E. Kosofsky. 1990. *Epistemology of the Closet* (Berkeley)
Tennant, N. 2001. 'Private passions' (radio interview with musical selections), BBC Radio 3, May 5
Walser, R. 1994. 'Prince as queer poststructuralist', *Popular Music and Societ*, 18/2, pp. 79–89

Discography

I have listed albums in chronological order. After each album, I have shown individual songs mentioned. All albums by Pet Shop Boys unless otherwise indicated.

Please. EMI America CDP 7 46271 2. 1986
    'Two Divided by Zero'
    'West End Girls'
    'Opportunities (Let's Make Lots of Money)'
    'Suburbia'
    'Tonight is Forever'
    'I Want a Lover'
    'Why Don't We Live Together?'
Actually. EMI Manhattan CDP 7 46972 2. 1987
    'One More Chance'
    'What Have I Done to Deserve This?'
    'It's a Sin'
Dusty Springfield, *Reputation and Rarities*. EMI. 1997
Introspective. EMI Manhattan CDP-7-90868-2. 1988
    'I Want a Dog'
    'Always On My Mind/In My House'

Behaviour. EMI USA CDP-7-94310-2. 1990
  'How Can You Expect to be Taken Seriously?'
  'Only the Wind'
  'So Hard'
Discography: The Complete Singles Collection. EMI USA CDP-7-97097-2. 1991
  'Where the Streets Have No Name (I Can't Take My Eyes Off You)'
Very. EMI Records USA E2-89721. 1993
  'Can You Forgive Her?'
  'I Wouldn't Normally Do this Kind of Thing'
  'A Different Point of View'
  'Dreaming of the Queen'
  'The Theatre'
  'To Speak is a Sin'
  'Go West'
Before (single). Atlantic 87049-2. 1996
  'The Truck Driver and His Mate'
Bilingual. Atlantic 82915-2. 1996
  'Metamorphosis'
  'Electricity'
Somewhere (single). Parlophone 7243 8 84296 2 7 and 7243 8 84297 2 6. 1997
Neil Tennant and Tris Penna, producers, *Twentieth Century Blues*. 1998 Kala Inc. 19011-4601-2
  'Sail Away'
Nightlife. Parlophone/Sire 35012-2. 1999
  'I Don't Know What You Want but I Can't Give it Anymore'
  'Happiness is an Option'
  'Vampires'
  'In Denial'
  'New York City Boy'

Videography

Videography. EMI Video. 1991
Performance. Picture Music International. 1992
Discovery. EMI Video. 1995
Somewhere. Game Entertainment Group. 1997

[26]

Vicars of 'Wannabe': authenticity and the Spice Girls

ELIZABETH EVA LEACH

Introduction

Popular notions of value in art – even popular definitions of art itself – are much indebted to the idealist narratives of late romanticism and its maximalised form, elite modernism. Since artistic value is normally imputed to one side of a dialectically related pair of oppositional terms, two principal strategies exist by which to ascribe value to the music you love, find interesting, or want to study: either show how it merits the positive term of the valorising pair (if necessary redefining the specific markers of that term), or attack the narrative underlying the binary itself. A typical postmodernist strategy is to do both these things simultaneously, so as to collapse notions of value into a win–win polysemy.

One of the central terms in popular music criticism is authenticity, which establishes and then defends the boundaries of what is thought 'good' – artistically, politically, morally.[1] Like all such binaries, it generates (and is dialectically defined by) another – the 'weak' term of the opposition – which in this case is the inauthentic, the fake, the commercial. The notion of authenticity has been a source of moral and artistic value attributed to the commercial underdog at every point in the history of popular music, as important, as Simon Frith has noted, 'for critics struggling to distinguish jazz from Tin Pan Alley pop in the 1920s and black jazz from white jazz in the 1930s, as for critics asserting rock's superiority to teen pop in the late 1960s' (Frith 1987, p. 136). Although in musical terms the markers for authenticity change in their detail depending on the types of music being set within the terms of the opposition, the fundamental implication remains the same – the authentic music is more real because it is less designed as a commercial venture. Making this claim frequently involves exaggerating the traits of the commercially dominant form. In her recent study of the Nashville Sound, Joli Jensen shows how the symbolic construction of authenticity for country music defined it in opposition to 'pop'. The 'authenticity markers' within this frame were heartfelt, personal song lyrics that seemed to speak autobiographically for the singer. These were combined with self-revelatory articles in fan magazines and liner notes, promoting the accessibility of the performer and the personal nature of the performer–fan relationship. Most importantly, authentic country exhibited a 'live' feel and spontaneity in recorded performance. In fact this was often highly rehearsed – Jensen quotes the classic 1931 recording, 'Jimmie Rodgers Visits the Carter Family', which conjured up a cosy, homely spontaneity of a real visit and improvised conversation and music-making when it was in fact fully scripted and recorded in a studio – and country, like pop, was a recorded – and thus commercialised – form from the outset (see Jensen 1998, p. 9). Jensen explores how fans' beliefs about the change in musical style represented by the Nashville Sound of the 1950s and 1960s have changed with time. Originally, fans saw the lush orchestrated Nashville Sound either negatively as a loss of authenticity, 'selling out', or, slightly more positively, as a temporary, necessary but regrettably less authentic defence against the emergence of rock (see Jensen 1998, pp. 38ff.). Now fans consider the Nashville Sound as authentic as the earlier honky-tonk, since both currently stand in relation to the even more commercially successful 1990s country boom. Overriding both these reactions is an opposition between 'authentic' and 'commercial', based on a suspicion of a popularity that makes the recipient part of an undifferentiated mass rather than one of the select initiated few.

Scholarly attitudes to mass culture and, in particular, to its production, have traditionally drawn on the work of the Frankfurt School, notably, where music is concerned, on the writing of Theodor Adorno (see Adorno 1998(1941)). The internal dialectic of value within a popular music genre outlined above shares fundamental oppositional terms with the more general debate about music in the writing of Adorno, for whom commodification resulting from commercialisation was in opposition to the essentials of art. This is perhaps unsurprising since both Adorno himself and popular music, as it is understood today, are products of an era fuelled by romantic assumptions about the nature of art and the artist. Interesting, therefore, are both the derision which Adorno directs at popular music itself, and the surprising willingness of those who seek to validate its study within the academy to adopt this detractor as their theoretical model.

As Richard Middleton (1990) has discussed, Adorno's vision of musical art is essentially a late-romantic one, stressing the autonomy and immanence of the musical work in a fixed notated form separate from its social use-value or exchange-value. Adorno himself rejected popular music utterly, as regressive and oppressive, since it cheats the listener with its 'pseudo-individuation', depriving him/her of authentic emotion, and causing him/her to love his/her deprivation. In short, it lacks authenticity. Adorno's critique is nevertheless powerful, and aspects of it (without the withering denial of value in popular music) have influenced Neo-Marxist sociologists who critique late-capitalism by focusing on the production of mass culture, including the production of popular music. In discussing the boom in studies of popular music following the foundation of the International Association for the Study of Popular Music in 1981, Charles Hamm has shown Adorno's critique to be particularly influential with regard to the notion of authenticity. He argues that such studies were driven by 'the assumption that capitalist production negates "authentic" expression by certain groups, here defined not by ethnicity, [as in previous narratives of authenticity dealing with jazz] but by class' (Hamm 1995, p. 25). Whilst Hamm acknowledges Adorno's 'intellectual sophistication and . . . role in legitimating the study of popular music in the wider academic world' (an irony, given Adorno's own conclusions), Hamm is sceptical about the ability of the modernist Marxist meta-narrative to make sense of the postmodern world.

However, the appropriateness of Adorno's critique could be argued on the grounds that certain types of popular music (jazz and early rock, for example) fairly clearly share Adorno's late-romantic definition of the artist. As Middleton writes, 'Interestingly enough, sociologists have noted the emergence of an Adornian distinction between "commercial manipulation" and avant-garde "authenticity" within the discourse of the jazz and rock communities themselves.' (Middleton 1990, p. 43) Middleton sees the fruitfulness of the application of Adorno's approach to pop music as a measure of how deeply Adorno's critique of mass culture has permeated both popular consciousness and musical practice. However, it is possible, rather than seeing Adorno's critique as instrumental, simply to recognise in both Adorno and popular music, shared roots in romanticism, particularly in the late-romantic definition of authenticity as a defence against commercialisation in the wake of a decrease in artistic patronage and the rise of market relations. This, as Middleton points out, is reflected in the employment structure of popular music, whose performers are not paid pro-rata like workers, but given royalties, i.e. treated as artists.[2]

Jensen argues that country music fans resent commercialisation because it destroys the collective nature of music appreciation. The music enacts a symbolic and personal relationship between the performer (artist), the fan, and the other fans, whilst the perceived intervention of faceless commercial mediation deprives the fan of the idea that the experience is personalised and thus authentic. Adorno does not recognise the collective as a cultural subject. His critique comprises two dialectically opposed elements – the individual subject of the avant-garde and the monolithic mass subject of the culture industry. Avant-garde music is autonomous, that of the culture industry hopelessly partial. Many musicologists are no longer prepared blithely to accept the idea of any music's autonomy, and have attempted to recontextualise musical works and to avoid judging other music by standards of progress derived from an idealistic interpretation of Beethoven's. That this represents Adorno's idea of progress explains his resistance to conventions, especially those structured by unchanged repetition, which he sees as indicative of simplicity and childishness (in part explaining his opposition to both popular music and the 'neo-classic' Stravinsky). Once we have heard Beethoven, he implies, there is no turning back – the potential of music has been raised and our expectations must be too. This romantic ideal of progress and its concomitant attitude to convention also provided a way for cultural critics to validate the study of specific popular musics in Adornian terms, as oppositional, progressive, and counter-cultural and thus authentic art – always, however, in relation to another popular music style that was seen as conformist, conventional and therefore regressive.

Even within classical music, Adorno is keen to divide the authentic and progressive from the regressive, inauthentic 'other'. Adorno's Beethoven is defined to exaggerate his difference from what, once the opposition is constructed, becomes termed 'classical music', and this assists the ideal of progress that places composers such as Berlioz and Stravinsky outside the pantheon of progressives. In his recent essay, 'Chaikovsky and the Human', Richard Taruskin, seeking to unravel the assumptions which have led to Chaikovsky's 'misprizing', sees as root cause the construction of a devalued 'classical' in relation to the prized 'romantic', both of which terms 'are intelligible today only in their artificially constructed binary relationship' (Taruskin 1997, pp. 250–1). Taruskin's rich analysis goes on to place this binary within other dialectical contexts, notably *Zivilisation* and *Kultur*, so as to show Chaikovsky's unjustly maligned place within a Franco-Italian tradition which has provided the negative foil for the primacy of German Romantic idealism in the nineteenth-century musicological construction of music history.

Taruskin is seeking to rescue Chaikovsky's music for musicology by diffusing (through deconstruction) the moral opprobrium that it has traditionally attracted. Taruskin argues that because Chaikovsky exhibited a historical subscription to an 'aesthetic of enjoyment', his music received a relatively disfavourable assessment within the discipline of musicology, whose premises drew on the German *Kultur* aesthetic as a supposedly universal criterion of value. This aesthetic, which Taruskin characterises as essentially romantic, 'celebrated the idiosyncratically personal and the artist's unique subjectivity, presupposing a producer-oriented [i.e. composer-oriented] musical ecosystem', and was the product of Kantian 'pure, disinterested artistry' (Taruskin 1997, p. 251). Within this definition, music not valued was by contrast considered to be that which 'served the base ambitions of performers and the frivolous appetites of spectators', in short, 'the vulgar, the sentimental and the feminine' (Taruskin 1997, p. 251). Taruskin skilfully exposes the historical contingency of traditional musicological value judgements (some of which persisted into the late twentieth century) in which Beethoven has always been signified by the former ('pure disinterested artistry' – notably in Adorno's critique; see above) and Chaikovsky the latter (crowd-pleasing vulgarity). I would like to argue that this binary is similar to that which permeates the discourse surrounding authenticity in pop music, whose values have traditionally overlapped significantly with those which Taruskin characterises as 'romantic'. This is not to propose similarity or analogies between pop and classical musics themselves, or to suggest that they may be studied in the same way. Merely, I claim that ideas about value and worth, and the criteria upon which these may be assessed, have more to do with general cultural–historical values than with the specifics of the material being so assessed.

Rock and pop

Taruskin's further point is to peel away the false emphases that have accrued to Mozart in the process of his hijacking by the central German tradition which valued Mozart's music (and differentiated him from his Italian contemporaries) by means of a very selective understanding of it as autonomously structured, idealised and contentless form. Using the work of Wye Jamison Allanbrook, Taruskin rejects this nineteenth-century picture of Mozart's music to focus instead on the centrality of dance to its semiotic conventions (see Allanbrook 1983; Taruskin 1997, p. 292). I would argue that the same is the case in pop music, especially for a group such as the Spice Girls, who are unencumbered by the restrictive instruments that many rock bands require (and which themselves arguably serve as surrogates for women's bodies in static sex acts (e.g. guitar solos)). Dance promotes the social negotiation of the individual body within the collective, the relatively select group, constructed around the music which serves to create collective identities. Such identification both requires a listener's belief in the music's authenticity and helps to construct one. Thus Taruskin offers a model as to how we might nevertheless value the feminine, the vulgar and the sentimental in music (here pop music, specifically the Spice Girls, in relation to rock-derived norms) by recognising the importance of semiotic dance conventions and an aesthetic of enjoyment grounded in the adherence to convention.

Pop music has served as the commercialised inauthentic other to both country (see above) and rock 'n' roll. With roots in both rural music and Black music, early rock was, so the story goes, dangerous and subversive, its roughness forming an easy antithesis to the smooth slickness of urban pop in the 1950s. Markers for authenticity in rock are the presence of a talented individual or small group formed organically from 'naturally' knowing one another, driven to write songs as the only outlet for their (personal) emotions and (political) views, who forge the music and play it themselves, typically in the standard musical arrangement of two different guitars, lead and bass, with optional keyboard, obligatory drums and a vocalist (who might also be a guitarist, and is usually the songwriter unless (as is possible) she is only a woman). The fundamental White masculinity of these groups is epitomised in their organic unity and the way the group channels its identity through one singer who forms the expression of a group-originated song. Such a band should progress naturally as artists (rather than being an industry confection and being told what to do) and would be able to perform live (rather than requiring the artifice of technology or the commercialisation of recording). As Fred Pfeil has commented, 'this desire for a break with commercial culture and a disavowal of the commodity status of rock – to be opposed to "pop" from within, by dint of an "organic" relationship with the music, its traditions and its audience – is imbricated with the desire to construct, maintain and emulate an alternative white masculinity' (Pfeil 1995, p. 79).

In the latter decades of the twentieth century, in the wake of punk, pop groups attempted to deflate the overriding discourse of authenticity by affirming rather than resisting their label. Simon Frith has charted this defence to the previously disparaging use of 'pop':

One of the most important aspects of the post-punk dissolution of rock certainties was the replacement of authenticity by artifice as the central concern in critical discourse. This was marked (in the pages of *New Musical Express*, for example) by the revaluation of the labels 'rock' and 'pop' themselves. In the last [sic] sixties, 'rock' had been established as the praise-word, distinguishing serious or powerful music from 'commercial rubbish' and formula sounds. Now, 'pop' became the term of praise, a way of distinguishing sharp and clever sounds from 'rockist rubbish' and formula flab. (Frith 1988, p. 4)

Exemplifying this, in an interview with *Rolling Stone*, Neil Tennant of the Pet Shop Boys expressed pride at 'proving we *can't* cut it live ... We're a pop group not a rock 'n' roll group.' (quoted in Cook 1998a, p. 11) It is but a short step from here to claim, as some have, that by the end of the twentieth century the markers of this rock/pop divide no longer mattered. John Mundy, for example, has written:

'Youth', as a subject of conflicting historical discourses in specific cultural formations, no longer existed, and the notion of an ideology of 'rock', with its connotations of 'authenticity' and 'opposition', had become meaningless. Though the Monkees had been criticized for ... their perceived lack of musical credibility, such issues no longer mattered with Take That and Spice Girls. Arguably, their very artificiality was part of their appeal. (Mundy 1999, p. 232)

However, the contribution to the authenticity debate made by Tennant and observed by Frith merely re-inscribes the terms of the discourse. Tennant simply trumps one marker of authenticity that the Pet Shop Boys don't possess (the ability to perform live), with another (the personally authentic honest address to the fans who they do not attempt to deceive). Frith's point is not that the markers of authenticity, or authenticity itself, have become 'meaningless', as Mundy alleges, but rather that, since it has fallen prey to convention and standardisation as a result of its commercial success, pop is able to reassert itself within the old terms of the dialectic as the new originality.

Moreover, that was the 1980s. By the mid-1990s, the old 'rock certainties' were reinvigorated in the UK by the advent of Britpop, which self-consciously hearkened back to the Beatles – a talented group of authentic musicians who represented everything antithetical to the industry confection of the Monkees. Many of the old rock markers for authenticity returned, all the stronger for their nostalgic and patriotic associations. This reinvigoration was arguably more widespread. In 1990, Milli Vanilli had their Grammy Award for best newcomer taken away when they admitted to not singing on their records. Mundy merely claims that 'nobody actually *cared*', but if this was so, surely the award givers would not have taken such a step? It certainly shows some degree of continued commitment to a rock-derived performance aesthetic which is 'a last romantic attempt to preserve ways of music-making – performer as artist, performance as "community" – that had been made obsolete by technology and capital' (Frith 1988, p. 1).

The Spice Girls

The pop phenomenon of the mid-1990s, the Spice Girls achieved the highest debut single of any UK group in the US charts, surpassing even the Beatles. Both albums and eight of their nine singles releases achieved number one chart position in the UK,[3] including the first five consecutive singles (an unprecedented occurrence), yet the group exhibited few of the external traits which had come to symbolise authenticity in popular music. Because the Spice Girls had been formed from young hopefuls who had replied to an advertisement, they were immediately labelled as an inauthentic industry fabrication, attempting to cash in on the success of boy bands like Take That. All women, the group overtly aimed to please their public by singing songs conventional in type, albeit varied in genre, which they co-authored with accomplished behind-the-scenes song-writing duos.[4] The Spice Girls did not play instruments but rather sang and danced. Even though none were specialist singers or dancers (they were chosen for all-round ability and personality) they were well choreographed and well produced and edited. In short, they were an undeniably commercial product.

Clearly the success of the Spice Girls does not make sense in terms of the normal markers of authenticity. Their detractors criticised them for their lack of musical credibility (can't sing) for their general lack of talent (can't act, can dance a little), and the way they were formed. As mere front-women for an organisational machine whose 'real talent' was hidden away behind the scenes, they were also accused of insincerity (i.e. inauthenticity) with respect to their feminist 'Girl Power' message. How could they really be their own women, carped the press, when they had male songwriters and a male manager 'pulling the strings'? If this was the case, surely Girl Power itself was just one more dishonest commercial strategy?[5]

The music press thought the fans had got it wrong. In an elitist quasi-Adornian way they were sure that the fans were in love with being cheated. The charges of being inauthentic, fake, insincere, not the real thing were levelled at the outset, yet did not immediately cause the Spice Girls to lose their ever-growing following. In fact, even when, by Christmas 1998, they were reduced to four members and had been written off by the press, their Christmas release, 'Good-bye', still went straight in at number one in the UK charts, giving them an exceptional (if not completely unprecedented) third consecutive Christmas UK number one. Despite not releasing a single in 1999, they were given a Lifetime Achievement Award at the Brits in 2000 and provided the main performance act. Why were the fans so convinced that the media analysis was misguided?

One possibility is that a perception of Girl Power as genuine contributed largely to the Spice Girls' success in the face of their construction as inauthentic. The potential of Girl Power to function both as a strategy of resistance to patriarchy and essentialism, and, ironically, as a financial entrapment (i.e. fitting punishment) of those (men) still subscribing to the values of patriarchy, is attractive to a young female audience. Those perceiving the strategies of feminist resistance to patriarchy purveyed by the act happily contribute to its financial success, and, at the same time, enjoy seeing how that section of the audience *unable* to perceive it as such, also unwittingly financially supports it. Whilst I do not agree that their male-dominated institutional set-up invalidates their feminism, I would argue that the Spice Girls' contribution to late-twentieth-century feminism does not differ markedly, in either its method or its content, from that of Madonna a decade earlier (for which, see Metzstein 1993; Tetzlaff 1993). Their similar polysemic exploitation of the male gaze and its inherent re-inscription of patriarchal values serves only to increase their potential fan base and give them more economic power – surely a feminist strategy within the prevailing patriarchal-economic conditions. To some degree their 'poly-semous femininity' is part of an adherence to convention – a complicity with a public for whom such feminism has become, post-Madonna, standard. This is not to allege that they do not believe in what they are saying (they probably do, and it is immaterial – the fans perceive it to be true while the media and other detractors question it), but merely to suggest that their success lies also with their exploitation of the markers of authenticity. Manipulating the discourse of authenticity enables the Spice Girls to use a rebranded version of the post-Madonna feminism with which their audience is familiar, without this lack of originality (usually a marker for 'inauthenticity') forming an obstacle to their success.

In print and in their representation of the writing process, the Spice Girls work within the traditional authenticity markers established in the 1950s/1960s by the pop/rock divide. They assert their role as originators of their music, making refer-ence to their own 'writing' of the songs. They stress that their songs have a basis in experience and exemplify Girl Power, which they claim as their own idea:

Spice is only the first in a long line of kicking albums we've got in us . . . By the time we got the chance to put an album out, we'd already written dozens of songs, so it was tough to choose which to include . . . So in the next few pages we're gonna take you through the album track by track, explaining what the songs mean to us, how we came to write them, and the feelings and experiences they're based on. (Spice Girls 1997, p. 33)

They thus seem to accept a traditional marker for authenticity – the hierarchy of producer-oriented culture. However, they are still a group put together after an audition, who do not play instruments or exhibit special musical talent. These aspects they transform into the authenticity of the ordinary, rejecting the elitist pedestaling of talented instrumentalists (and indeed musical talent in general) within our culture.[6] Although Mundy asserts that the Spice Girls' artificiality is part of their appeal, I would argue instead that it is the 'ordinariness' that they promote which diffuses the charge of commercialism or artificiality, which is appealing. This ordinariness, which stands in direct conflict with their actual fame, serves both to diffuse fame's negative connotations and promote its accessibility to the audience. The Spice Girls' first single, 'Wannabe', plays a crucial role in this particular self-presentation. They stress their difference from other pop stars, critiquing the world of the famous whilst partaking of it. In the visual medium and at the level of their musical self-representation they thus redefine the makers to claim a different kind of authenticity for themselves, that of the girl next door. This promotes audience identification, since both the Spice Girls and their audience comprise ordinary girls lip-synching to someone else's songs. They convince us that they think what we, the audience, would also think of this mad world of stars if we were suddenly translated thence, which, because their presence there implies that hard work and luck would be enough, they additionally reassure us we could be. The traditionally authentic rock band speaks *for* their audience (who feel truly understood and that they truly understand). The Spice Girls speak *as* their audience and *with* their audience. As Nicola Dibben writes:

> The Spice Girls have often been remarked upon by the media for their 'ordinariness' and their own promotion draws attention to this ordinariness by constantly referring to the process by which they have become famous: the video 'Spice' interlaces music videos of singles from the album with documentary 'behind-the-scenes' footage charting their rise to fame and showing the Girls revelling in their own success with a mixture of incredulity and enjoyment. Even the videos and songs emphasise this ordinariness: the video of 'Wannabe', their debut single, opens with them on a London street and ends with them catching a bus home – signs that they are ordinary young women out for the night; 'Mama' presents their mothers together with stills and home movie footage of each of them as children. (Dibben 1999, p. 350)⁷

In the context of play with authenticity, the image of 'ordinariness' is worth closer inspection. As well as revising the markers that denote authenticity, the Spice Girls present a complex surface of contradictions, working off a wide variety of authenticity markers – many mutually exclusive – which they do not try to smooth over. Their play with these contradictions, their obvious irony and interest in sharing the joke with the fans are part of their aesthetic of enjoyment, their interest in convention (even conventions about authenticity) and, when these are combined, the scope for ludic meaning in our semiotically rich and multivalent popular culture. I will now examine the Spice Girls' first single, 'Wannabe', as it appears in various formats – as a single, as a Pop Song Video, as part of a Pop Music Video,⁸ and as a flashback lyric interpolation into the narrative of a Pop Music Film – analysing in each case the way in which the song engages with the issue of authenticity.

'Wannabe'

'Wannabe', the Spice Girls' first single, stayed at number one in the UK charts for seven weeks after its release in July 1996 and reached the same chart position in thirty-two other countries. The following analysis seeks to restrict itself to a consideration of the song in its primarily circulating form, as a single sound-only track. When the song is in combination with visual material, the range of meanings suggested by musical and textual cues from its existence as a song track interact with the images to construct more concrete (and, arguably, more limited) meanings. In turn, because the song's semiotic base is so elastic, the meanings lent by the Pop Song Video format (for example) are reabsorbed back into the song in its single aural track form. It is salutary, therefore, to examine the song first in isolation in an attempt to strip away emphases accrued in other formats and highlight the range of interpretation that the song itself allows.

'Wannabe' lies well within its genre conventions as a verse and chorus structure with an introduction and a middle eight (the Appendix reproduces the lyrics and phrase structure). The rapped introduction sections use one two-bar rhythmic–harmonic ostinato (given in Example 1a), the sung verse and chorus another (Example 1b). These two ostinatos are rhythmically similar and tonally opposite:

the first starts with chord I and ends with chord IV, the second starts with V and returns to I. Even the latter of these is without strong harmonic progression, since I is reached locally from IV, with movement by fourth in the bass predominating, making the piece tonally static – a fact aided by triadic consonance and the shortness (that is, the high density of the repetition) of the ostinato sections.

The rapped sections ('authenticated' by being led by Mel B – the only Black group member), supported by a rhythmic ostinato, sparse scoring, and block chords (B–D–E–A) each a minim in length, are a traditional 'till-ready' with semiquavers grouped in the second half of each second bar of 4/4 as 3+3+2 (the last two of which represent a chromatic slide through A♯).[9] This rhythm is picked up in the melody line of the sung verse (at the words 'be just fine') which is more fully scored and more rhythmically foursquare.

The overall effect of the piece with its repetitions, extreme economy of tonal material (the middle eight uses the tonal material of the other rap sections), tonal stasis and rhythmic repetition, is of an improvisation, appealing playfully to the idea that the Spice Girls are an organic group of elite performers who have sufficient authentic musical talent to make it up as they go along. The short vocal melodic units of the verse often start on the second quaver of the bar, adding further to the improvised quality – as if the singer is waiting for the instrumental harmony before picking her note. The song's playful use of musical signs connoting traditional authenticity tally with what the Spice Girls themselves say about the song:

Mel B: We were just having a laugh when we wrote *Wannabe*. It's more of a vibe song than anything else. It had no sit-down planning. The sentiment, the meaning, the lyrics, the rhythm, just happened.
Mel C: It was recorded in under an hour.
Geri: We'd already written parts of it when Mel B and Emma came up with the bridge. (Spice Girls 1997, p. 34)

These comments seem clearly underpinned by the idea of the Spice Girls as the joint originators of the song, stressing their role as songwriters. The song 'just happened' – they are like an authentic genius composer visited by the muse and effortlessly delivered of a perfectly formed piece of music. Simultaneously, these comments are mutually contradictory: lack of sit-down planning on the one hand, yet at least a two-stage writing process, on the other. The same musical features which suggest improvisation, thereby colluding in a notion of musical competence and compositional–performative skill in line with the more traditional notion of pop authenticity, also signify the simplicity which underlines the Spice Girls' very ordinary musical abilities, and thus their 'ordinary-as-authentic' message. The conventional nature of 'Wannabe''s form – its clear structure – makes it easy to sing along to, and this vocal ease is aided by a melodic contour with few leaps, and a narrow range within a pitch area (the octave B to b) easily reached (whether at pitch or an octave down) by all voice types. All of the sung pitches are more than adequately supported by simple consonant harmonies, and the rapped sections increase this ease of reproduction by obviating the need for pitching notes at all. The audience at once experiences the song's simplicity, its directness of expression, and ease of reproduction as the performers' lack of talent (since it equals their own), and yet the musical cues signify skill at improvising – 'jamming' – the song such that the listener feels that they too could be one of the Spice Girls. Although these markers for musical simplicity and musical talent conflict with each other, they both function as markers of (two different types of) authenticity which may appeal differently to different listeners. At the same time a listener able to spot their contradiction is given to understand that authenticity is unable to arbitrate in matters of morality or value (thereby diffusing the force of the arguments of the Spice Girls' detractors).

These different meanings represent a range of possibilities latent but available in the song itself. Where the song appears in various visual formats, images provide a further 'textual' foil against which it may be read. I will now examine three such formats, starting with the Pop Song Video (PSV).

The 'Wannabe' video

As well as transmission in sound-only media, 'Wannabe' also circulates as part of a Pop Song Video (PSV) on music television, on pop music home video, on video jukebox, and on the world wide web.[10] The official video of 'Wannabe', for which the single provides the soundtrack, explores the authenticity of ordinariness in the light of a related topic, hinted at by the track's title: the opposition between fame and normality.

Pop Song Video tends to be approached in a way that virtually ignores its status as music, as musicologists frequently lament. The much-theorised PSVs of Madonna established her reputation (in the academic world at least) as 'an artist who composed with images and identities in almost the way that traditional musicians composed with tunes and harmonies' (Cook 1998ʙ, p. 147). Nevertheless, Susan McClary finds 'breathtaking' the 'scorn with which [Madonna's] ostensible artistic focus has been trivialized, treated as a conventional backdrop to her visual appearance' (McClary 1991, p. 148). Cook reports a lack of serious attention given to the music of Madonna's PSVs, which one commentator considers as 'unambiguous . . . a mainstream contemporary pop sound with no real subtleties or surprises', as if the music is a meaningless connection between visual image and the lyrics (Young 1991, p. 67, quoted in Cook 1998ʙ, p. 149). For Cook himself, the way in which music is often seen as secondarily reinforcing or challenging the primary visual material in PSV is comparable to the one-time similar lack of attention to, and dismissal of, film music *qua* music. The two are not completely analogous, however. Except in derived suites, film music tends not to circulate primarily as music, nor can one component of a film legitimately claim primacy as a locus for meaning.[11] However, PSV is, in origin at least, a promotional form for a pop music song; such songs circulate in various formats, many *without* the video – on the radio, on recordings and in live performance (whether by the original artists or not). Thus it is equally inadvisable to treat PSV as if it were a film with music regardless of how positively the critic considers the role of music in the production of meaning within the filmic totality.

In the description above of 'Wannabe' as a song, for example, it was suggested that the restricted harmonic rhythmic ostinatos of the song play with the idea of authenticity by connoting mutually contradictory markers (musical artfulness for the traditionally authentic and musical artlessness for the ordinary as authentic). The video similarly explores both these aspects of authenticity and negotiates between them and the meaning of the lyrics, which deal exclusively with friendship and love.

A perennial problem for the analyst is how to textualise a non-textual multimedia product. The way in which the narrative of the video as a whole (and not just as a film with music, but as song (i.e. music and words) filmed) is told, is of necessity already an interpretation of its meaning. The relationship between music and narrative within the diagetic frame in pop music video is very different from, indeed almost opposite to, that of other visual media involving music. Opera and film, for example, only recognise the actual phenomenal presence of music at certain special moments. In PSV the performance of the song *is* the principal narrative. The group singing are not only aware that they are singing – deafness is not one of the basic perceptual codes in this music form – but they sing knowing that they are in a PSV – they are performers.[12] The Spice Girls' song videos in particular have a polysemous quality which actively discourages single meanings. As they say in their manifesto, *Girl Power*, 'Videos can add all sorts of other levels and meanings to a song, so we've also let you in on some of the thinking behind them and what it was like to make them.' (Spice Girls 1997, p. 33)

The video of 'Wannabe' has a simple narrative structure: the Spice Girls arrive at a posh hotel party, gate-crash it, dance around singing 'Wannabe', and then leave. In the central part, the Spice Girls sing the entire song. This is framed by a prologue in which the girls arrive on foot outside the party, and an epilogue in which they leave on a bus. In the prologue there is only dialogue and brief *a cappella* singing; in the epilogue there are similarly diagetic sounds of footsteps, dialogue, and the departing bus's engine.

Crucial as an apologia for their future success as pop artists, 'Wannabe' excuses the Spice Girls from absorption into a social stratum that would remove them from the world of their fans. They distance themselves expressly from fame before the event, by presenting it as 'other', and encouraging the viewer to identify with the Spice Girls' own subject position(s) – something facilitated by each member of the group having their own distinct personality. The video also emphasises the togetherness of the group (and yet their individuality within the group, since they neither dress the same nor do they perform the exact same dance moves, even in the more choreographed sections). The whole is artful in its artlessness – the girls gate-crash a party, acting on the spur of the moment in a pseudo-improvised way that belies the polished nature of the PSV, complete with its accompanying sound-track whose instrumentalists are clearly not present at the party.[13] This picks up on the mutually contradictory musical topics of improvisation and simplicity by presenting the track narratively as both a piece of spontaneous fun and an artfully planned product. As Geri attests:

I remember the chaos and the cold. It wasn't very controlled – we didn't want it to be. We wanted the camera to capture the madness of Spice . . . It's the most spontaneous of our videos. (Spice Girls 1997, p. 35)

Yet, as will become clear from the analysis presented below, the video in fact contains many features clearly designed to further the establishment of the Spice Girls as authentic in their ordinariness and as ironic in their attitude to fame.

The viewer is integrated into the action from the beginning by a subjective camera. In the prologue, a formally dressed man looks nervously at the camera as his wife alights from their car, ushering out their two sons. The viewer is immediately positioned 'with' the Spice Girls in sympathy and in 'fact'. As the Spice Girls gate-crash the party the subjective camera follows, telling us that we too may have access to this world of exclusive parties in the company of the Spice Girls, not because they belong there (they clearly don't, they belong with us), but because they do not recognise the social barriers which keep them out (Emma scatters the guest list, to the dismay of the doorman). The camera focuses on the Spice Girls throughout; the viewer follows them through the party, each individual viewer effectively becoming the sixth Spice Girl.

As well as being seen by the others at the party, the camera is addressed by the Spice Girls themselves. Although usually thought of as alienating, since it acknowledges the presence of the camera in the action and therefore its unreality, in this case direct address functions to acknowledge our presence since we are identified with it. The usual transparency of film relying on the suspensions of disbelief with respect to the presence of the camera is not required for PSV, since performance to camera is central to the narrative. The subjective camera increases, rather than dissolves, the sense of the reality of what is seen on the screen, since it erodes the presence of the camera at their end, and the screen at ours. The combination of subjective camera and the illusion of a single shot for the entire video create a pseudo-documentary reality for the video, which is at once both a true-to-life reportage and reflects the light-hearted, improvised fun of the Spice Girls as 'real' people. Mel C sings directly to the camera, 'What d'ya think about that?' at the opening of verse 2, the 'you' addressee – an ambiguous singular/plural second person, or generalised impersonal construction – only signifies the viewer if they deliberately resist the implication of the subjective camera. Otherwise the viewer, singing and dancing with the Spice Girls is included as co-producer of Mel C's question, as the medium through which it is communicated to the 'other' to which it is really addressed.

As well as being decided by the subjective camera, the viewer's choice between an identity as the person addressed or one as part of the address itself is also coerced by the presentation of the other people at the party. These are indeed 'other' in terms of gender and age, but also in terms of class and occupation (signified by dress) and by attitude (signified by expression, gesture and lack of movement, especially dance). The two ends of the social spectrum are represented in the prologue by the tramps outside the hotel and an aristocratic family in a white Rolls Royce. Once inside the hotel the other guests function similarly to the aristocratic couple in providing an affluent, older, formal, passive and sour-expressioned background (a literal periphery in terms of camera shot) which throws into relief the Spice Girls' energetic activity, informality and fun. The Spice Girls are dressed in bright colours in a mixed casual and low-dressy style.[14] The invited guests include clergy, military men, the elderly, and those dressed oddly (either dated, or simply over-dressed). Several of the formal couples comprise an older (usually white-haired) woman and a younger man. This is a deliberate inversion of the social norm (notoriously rife in showbiz) of the rich older man with the pretty young bimbo, but this inversion exaggerates the difference of these 'odd' couples from the Spice Girls. In one of the few literal intersections between the video and lyrics, Emma pats one male guest on the head, singing – 'Are you for real?' – patronising (mothering) him in an ironic inversion of her role as 'Baby' Spice. Only one character, wearing a short Baby-pink dress, is attired even vaguely similarly to the Spice Girls. S/he is othered as transparently transvestite, with sizeable slightly muscular thighs and obviously fake wig and breasts – the hair cap for the former, and the cup padding for the latter, clearly visible.

The PSV visuals are structured to reflect the musical form in that both choruses (the memorable sing-along moments) are marked by artificial set-piece dances performed to camera. For the first chorus, the girls dance on a grand staircase with a still camera shot. For the second full chorus, the Spice Girls again desert their interaction with the guests and assemble in a small alcove to dance. The girls are suddenly performing to the viewer as if on stage, dancing in formation, which would place strain upon the improvised fun that the home movie subjective camera implies if this wasn't self-consciously a PSV. The implication is that they are performing to us in this spontaneous pop song video a little routine that they prepared earlier just to show that they are real performers and know the rules, and Mel B is still doing her own thing rather than mirroring the exact choreography of the others. This foregrounds the professionalism and talent implied by the ability to improvise and plays with the concept of performance, of staged artifice. The explicative 'zig-a-zig-ah' action of rhythmic knee trembling followed by abrupt scissoring of the thighs shut, is performed to the words by all five girls. The sexual innuendo of the dance confirms the authenticity of true fans (who understand what it really means) and also characterises the Spice Girls as active in distinction to the more passive guests.[15] These simple dance routines are another meeting point in the group negotiation of self and audience, since the audience can easily replicate the essential dance elements as they lip-synch to the song, feeling even more as though they are one of the Spice Girls.[16] By the time of the final pseudo-chorus, 'Slam', the Spice Girls' dancing is watched with disapproval by the other party-goers and a massed group of waiters threatening eviction. At this point the song ends and the Spice Girls leave. As viewer/camera we leave with them, making it clear that we do not observe or judge their dance like the other guests.

The epilogue sequence places much of the party in context. The Spice Girls arrived on foot, they catch a bus home, separating them further from the world of the party-goers' Rolls Royces. As the green double-decker bus draws away, Geri, hanging out of it, kisses us good-bye and Mel C beckons to us to come with them. There is a quick fade. Either Geri is kissing us good-bye because we belong at the party, or Mel C is inviting us to join them as their sixth member and joint generator of the song. Within the terms of identity that the video invites us to construct, this is really no choice at all, but the illusion of choice maintains the myth of the authentic fan.

The title of the song 'Wannabe' is a word that usually refers to people who seek fame in whatever way they can. Excepting the title, the lyrics do not mention fame, but serve rather to introduce the group and present aspects of Girl Power, their explicit exoteric focus. The lyrics are ostensibly about sexual love and its relation to friendship: 'If you wanna be my lover, you gotta get with my friends'. The elevation of friendship above sexual relationships forms a key plank in Girl Power since it enables women to configure their relationships with men as they wish: 'I won't be hasty, I'll give you a try/If you really bug me then I'll say good-bye'. The video, however, addresses the issue that the title of the track suggests. It surrounds the Spice Girls with the opulence of the famous, a world from which they take what they want but exit unchanged. Geri mockingly dances with a figure who appears to be an overweight Marilyn Monroe of an age that she would be were she still alive in the PSV-present of 1996, making manifest to the viewer the overblown distortion that fame wreaks on the body.

The explicit questioning of celebrity by celebrities is found elsewhere in pop songs, such as the nearly contemporaneous 'Star People' by George Michael. Uniquely, however, the Spice Girls achieve this critique not through lyrics (which could not do such a subtle and effective job alone because their explicitness reduces the scope for listeners to project themselves), but in a video which maps only locally and tangentially onto the lyrics of the song. As individuals, of course, the Spice Girls all have a history of relentlessly seeking fame in whatever form they could – of being 'wannabes'. For the members of the Spice Girls, pop stardom is arguably just a vehicle for fame, rather than fame being a result of pop stardom. This is another aspect of their inauthenticity in terms of the traditional construction of the authentic. They are not romantic artists who are driven to break the mould of traditional forms for their own inalienably unique artistic purposes. This is another way in which they are ordinary, for wanting fame in the abstract rather than being driven by a particular talent into a particular artistic direction. Several members had met each other at other auditions (famously, for *Tank Girl* and *Cats*) before meeting at the Spice Girls auditions. So, read differently, the world of the wannabe nevertheless gave them an authentic group identity, allying them with the traditional method of band formation through being part of the same social group, for all that they were ultimately chosen by an agency. In the 'Wannabe' PSV they imply a critique of fame, its exclusivity and the people who currently enjoy it, which they may then genuinely have felt (having behind them years of rejection, of not quite making it) but which quickly became a way of maintaining authenticity in the face of fame itself. As Mel B says in *Girl Power*, 'Being normal and being thrown into such a bizarre world is the perfect combination. I just hope I can cling to that normality.' (Spice Girls 1997, p. 36) They can enjoy the trappings of fame but do not belong to it but because they are normal like us. For us as armchair wannabes, they are our vicars since they act vicariously for us so that we can enjoy the heavenly realm of superstardom without jeopardising our own prized normality.

As a first single, 'Wannabe''s critique is credible, since the Spice Girls made it when they were only at the beginning of their eventual fame. However, as the Spice Girls became more properly famous, became in fact pop superstars, they ran the risk of losing their ordinariness and becoming more of that world and less of ours. Soon after the video launch of 'Wannabe', the Spice Girls *were* on the guest list of just those kind of parties. The use of ordinariness as a defence to commercialism, as a form of authenticity, was no longer enough. As if to reassure us that they were treating fame with an irony that we ourselves might well deploy, the 'Wannabe' PSV first became commercially available embedded in a sixty-minute Pop Music Video. It is to this PMV – *The Official Video Vol. 1: One Hour of Girl Power* – that I shall now turn, since, by making even greater play with the markers of authenticity, it begins to undermine the value of the binary itself.

'Wannabe' in *The Official Video Vol. 1: One Hour of Girl Power*

'Wannabe' is the first full-length pop song video incorporated into the pop music video *The Official Video Vol. 1: One Hour of Girl Power*.[17] The video opens with a sequence filmed by Geri on a home video camera, complete with the date 1/8/1995 (almost a year before the release of 'Wannabe') in the bottom right-hand corner. The camera follows Victoria around the 'Four Seasons Hotel', the Spice Girls have a pillow fight, lightly 'trashing' their hotel room – Geri (no longer filming) breaks a vase in a cutesie, feminised, ironic reference to what authentic (i.e. male) rock stars are meant to do – before (now with Geri behind the camera again) 'running riot' (a quiet riot in fluffy dressing gowns and slippers) around the hotel.[18] Prefiguring the party guests at the hotel in the PSV to 'Wannabe', the guests in the Four

Seasons hotel seem bemused and little interested in the Spice Girls. In a very stagy exchange with a young man, Geri (from behind the camera) says:

Geri: So, what do you think of the Spice Girls?
Hotel Guest (peering behind the camera, i.e. at both Geri and the viewer): Spice Girls? Spice Girls?
Emma (in shot with Mel B): Yeah, we're with Virgin, we've just been signed by Virgin.
Hotel Guest (nonchalantly): Oh, congratulations.

The effect of this is to create an 'authentic' image of the days before the Spice Girls were famous. Their authenticity is once more located in their lack of professional grooming – their similarity to 'ordinary people'. The video opens in the guise of a home video rather than a professionally produced documentary – a pseudo-video diary in a period when such a format was rife on British TV. However, it also colludes in pre-dating their togetherness as a group, paradoxically also bolstering their authenticity in more traditional terms.

The scene then cuts to the Spice Girls on two leather sofas, watching these 'home videos of what we've been up to' (Mel C) in the post-fame present of studio-finished filming, emphasised by a film-quality image, shot through a filter to make the colours appear brighter and less naturalistic than on the 'home videos'. Mel B's imprecation to 'stick the kettle on, make yourself comfy' underlines the idea that by watching their 'ordinary home videos' with them we are once more one of the Spice Girls.

The video of 'Wannabe' is preceded by genuine behind-the-scenes footage of preparation for the Spice Girls' second video, 'Say You'll Be There'. 'Wannabe' thus occurs out of chronological sequence, after footage which in fact post-dates it and which was shot after the Spice Girls' chart success. In what purports to be a chrono-logical retelling of their story, this prolongs the pre-history normality (and group authenticity) of the Spice Girls whilst lending some credibility to the 1995 (pre-fame) footage by obscuring the actual shortness of this section. The video of 'Wannabe', although clearly a professional product, is able through its images and their resonance with those in the first part of *The Official Video*, to re-inscribe the 'pre-professional group pre-history' message of the first part of the video.

'Wannabe' as lyric nostalgia in *Spice World the Movie*

The issue of authenticity is problematised even further by the lyric insertion of 'Wan-nabe' into *Spice World the Movie*, which further reflects the somewhat different relationship that the Spice Girls of 1997 had to their fame and their fans. *Spice World the Movie* is a palimpsest of main narrative, digressive, fictional 'flashforwards', and lyrics (here singles from the Spice Girls' first two albums which are performed both diagetically within the narrative, and function extra-diagetically as soundtrack items).[19] The work as a whole is structurally dominated by the meaningful remaking of other genres – films, TV, and pop music – and flaunts its intertextuality so as to promote self-congratulation at their intertextual competence in a broad audience. The Spice Girls appear as 'actors' within the narrative that they have created so that there is a blurring of the line between the fictional reality (verisimilitude) of art (especially that 'based on a true story') and the 'truth' of documentary film. Movies such as the Beatles' *A Hard Day's Night* established a pseudo-autobiographical genre in which real-life pop stars play themselves and may thus exercise a (playful) self-critical per-spective. As Fred Pfeil has commented, film and rock (and here pop) culture are dis-tinguished by 'the consistency and coherence rock fans expect from their stars in terms of just this relationship between rock genre and "offstage" personality profile' (Pfeil 1995, p. 79). In *Spice World the Movie*, this is accentuated by nearly all the other characters being essentially caricatures, signalled by over-reaction and over-acting, as well as by certain stars playing themselves in walk-on parts. Although the Spice Girls can play with this mode too, they are clearly playing. Once more, they are 'ordinary girls' in a 'mad world' who can cross-dress into it behaviourally, but keep reverting to (normal) type which gets them into trouble with the media who police the world of fame. The film addresses the Spice Girls' response to a media backlash, a potential break-up, and touches upon the problem of becoming *former* celebrities in the aftermath of great fame. Tensions within the group are manifestly present in both dialogue and body language within the film. Although *Spice World the Movie* is not 'true', it is 'true-to-life' and plays prophetically with reality such that in the months following its release, life appeared to imitate art.

Spice World the Movie charts its own writing and making – it is its own fictive textual autobiography. Near the beginning of the film and then at intervals throughout, Clifford (Richard E. Grant), the Spice Girls' (fictional) manager, meets with a writer and his agent to discuss potential film plots for a movie using the group. These start outlandish and, although they stay in the realms of fantasy, gradually approach a more recognisable amalgam of filmic clichés. Occasionally they are 'illustrated' by a fantasy 'flashback' which shows the Spice Girls acting in the film as the writer narrates and imagines it. These illustrations are initially brief until the final sequence of the film, when two narratives – that of the film and that of the scriptwriter in the film – climactically converge to imply that the film we see is the film the script-writer finally wrote.

A truncated performance of 'Wannabe' occurs as a collectively imagined flashback.[20] The demands of fame (symbolised by rehearsals for a live performance), impinging unduly and unfairly on normal human priorities (symbolised by the birth of their friend's baby), cause the Spice Girls to walk out on Clifford one by one during the rehearsal for their live gig. This is followed by a comic scene in which the evil newspaper proprietor Kevin McMaxford (Barry Humphries) smiles with glee to the accompaniment of the Hallelujah chorus from Handel's *Messiah* at the idea the Spice Girls might split up. The nostalgic interlude in which 'Wannabe' occurs is prefaced by a fade to a scene across the river from Westminster with Big Ben,[21] whilst the soundtrack cuts to a dialogue which, as the picture 'catches up', is revealed to be the soundtrack (at second remove, of another film screened within the film) of *Casablanca*, which, lying on her bed, Geri is watching. The dialogue ('I'm sorry, sorry that you ever left here – Sam – for old times' sake', 'Yeah, sure – for old times' sake') embodies the idea of regret at a past that has been lost, an opportunity that has been missed, which is voiced ironically within *Spice World the Movie* by iconic film stars within a cult movie.[22] In the context of *Spice World the Movie*, this is the opportunity to live an ordinary life, of which their fame has deprived them. The necessity for traditional authenticity (the live gig) has required such a punishing schedule (either challenging the myth that talent makes performance effortless or indicative of their lack of talent, their ordinariness) as to threaten their authentic group unity.

The flashback sequence begins with a shot of the outside of a corner cafe with the on-screen caption, 'A very long time ago' – a time frame exaggeratedly prefigured by the film Geri is watching. The cut to the interior reveals the Spice Girls looking younger and less groomed than in the post-fame present.[23] This is a fabricated pre-fame past which, although here obviously 'faked', is nonetheless meant to be taken as representing a kind of 'truth' about the authentic group nature of the Spice Girls, the pre-fame dating of whose friendships defends them from being an inauthentic industry product. The initial conversation of the scene leading into the performance of 'Wannabe' is heavy with dramatic irony. The soundtrack of the flashback runs continuously but is intercut visually by images of the Spice Girls in the present of *Spice World the Movie*. For the girls separately reminiscing in the present, the flashback becomes a collective reconstruction – group nostalgia – emphasising their unity at the moment in the film when it is most threatened, but linking this explicitly with the authenticity of their group identity and origins (which is fictionalised). As a collective memory, the flashback's soundtrack can be heard by all of the Spice Girls. The images from the film's present follow lines said by the relevant girl in the flashback. Emma says, 'well, it was worth a try', as Brian, the cafe's proprietor, refuses them credit until such time as they should be *really* rich and famous. The film-present shot cuts to Emma in her pink bathroom, brushing her teeth in her bath robe and silently laughing at the dramatic irony. The conversation turns to pop music styles, which allows Brian to show himself as representing old authentic certainties. The image cuts from the café of the flashback as Victoria asks Brian rhetorically, 'where've you been for the past ten years?', to show the film-present Victoria lying in her bath. This is followed immediately (without visual return to the flashback, but in time with the running of the soundtrack) by an image of Mel B lying in her Gothic-style iron-steaded bed as she hears her flashback incarnation saying 'anything goes these days, you can do what you want', to which Brian responds: 'I'm a jazz man and I'm telling you, jazz is due for a comeback'. After the Spice Girls perform 'Wannabe' to him, and despite his playing of air piano on the counter during it, Brian's only comment is that it 'just needs a wee bit more jazz in there'.

Although the cafe is clearly an early 1990s setting (there is the presence of a microwave, a portable CD player, and the Spice Girls themselves), it exemplifies 1990s retro in its decor and in the large number of black-and-white photographs around the walls depicting great jazz performers. Brian's cafe and his attitude to musical style provide further reference to the idea of authenticity. Firstly, the central musical skill involved in great jazz performance is improvisation. This displays artistic quality and (since it is spontaneous) is from the heart, or soul. The track 'Wannabe', as discussed above, already makes musical reference to improvisation and spontaneity by its repetitive harmonic structure and till-ready rhythms. Brian seems to suggest that this doesn't, however, make it jazz. Secondly, Charles Hamm's first narrative of authenticity in popular music (pre-dating the class-based authenticity of Adorno) is the idea that 'Ethnic, racial, or national groups can develop distinctive types of music giving authentic expression to their culture.' (Hamm 1995, p. 11) This became synonymous with the singer/composer's moral right to express the sentiments of a given song according to his own subject-position, which became an issue in the wake of the 'covering' of Black tracks by White artists so as to deprive Black musicians of royalties when their music was marketed to White audiences (see Monson 1995; Cook 1998A, pp. 8–9). The Spice Girls disassociate authenticity and subject position by engaging in play which results in a postmodern destruction of categories. The moral aspect of the authenticity of race and its relevance to oppression is quietistically diffused as being somehow quaint, part of a bygone age. They do not accept this form of authenticity, nor do they feel that liking a specific type of music forms your identity to the extent that it isolates you from others (they still 'owe Brian for a few coffees'). For them, style is not about authentic ownership and subject-positioning but a matter of taste, appropriation and play – 'anything goes' – and is not worth fighting over, or linking too closely to what you are. Brian, whilst not entirely a sympathetic character, is also neither a figure of fun nor of hate because the very power of the dialectic that would judge him has been quietly undermined.

The Spice Girls' performance of their demo version of 'Wannabe' has its own rather different kind of authenticity. The track is here recorded as a flatter, non-reverb sound, especially the vocals. This is meant to sound as if it *is* live, as though it is performed on a small CD player in the hard and echoey acoustic of a cafe, lending verisimilitude and differentiating this lyric moment from nearly all the others in the film, which, even where they are diagetically performed, are properly recorded and mastered to CD quality. The Spice Girls grab ketchup bottles and sugar cellars as microphones, and their dancing is freestyle, although it includes aspects of the eventual video of 'Wannabe' – pointing, Mel C's hand gesture at the opening of Verse 1, as well as her backflip and the stamping for 'slam your body down' – as if these grew organically and naturally from the group's pre-history. This suggests, more than the music of the song already does, that the song is improvised, that Brian is wrong (after all, he doubts their ability to become famous), and that this is the new jazz. This is also exactly how the vast majority of the Spice Girls' audience will sing these songs, in an unpolished way, lip-synching or singing to an unprofessional-sounding performance on tape (or CD), whilst freestyle dancing, yet approximating the most distinctive moves of the 'Wannabe' video.

In the flashback, the Spice Girls wear clothes extrapolated backwards (and downwards in terms of style) from the present of *Spice World the Movie*. These are alternately contrasted with the five scenes of the Spice Girls alone in the film present, collectively generating the flashback. The last of these closes the flashback sequence as we see the film-present Mel C sitting at her window in Liverpool strip, holding a football. This, along with the opening scene of Geri weeping over *Casablanca*, and the three intercut pictures of a very pink-garbed Emma brushing her teeth and giggling, Victoria luxuriating in her bath, and a gothic, animal-skinned Mel B lounging, are individual images replete with the iconography associated with the persona – and nickname – of each Spice Girl. This contrasts with the nascent, but not yet pronounced, characters of the pre-fame Spice Girls in the flashback. Trapped and ossified by the personae they are forced to adopt within the context of the Spice Girls – a group fiction that has now taken over their 'real' life – the message here seems to be that, as five individuals who were not so trapped, their group togetherness was more spontaneous, more authentic. The limitations of stereotypes (conflicting with their 'anything goes' play with subject positioning) is addressed throughout the film, notably in the scene of the photo-shoot session where they all dress up first as one another, and then as a string of twentieth-century icons, many, nostalgically, from the 1960s. The simple message of ordinariness contained in the video of 'Wannabe' is no longer credible – they are not ordinary – the world of fame has taken over. We are able to enjoy their fame vicariously but are asked to sympathise in a way that makes us feel comforted not to share in fame's limiting aspects. *Spice World the Movie* furthermore implies that the 'real' girls *are* indeed still ordinary, that they are resisting the way in which fame has transformed their lives and turned them into fake caricatures by remaining true to the group and to their friends. That the strain of their first live show is what causes the split (which elicits the flashback) signifies that by making them play by its rules (they *should* be able to cut it live), the world of fame is too abnormal for the Spice Girls.

In the final sequence of the film, the Spice Girls seem to manage to reconcile their ordinariness with success in the world of fame: they attend the birth of their friend's baby *and* make it to their live gig. I would argue, however, that the happy scenes of resolution are jeopardised by the rest of the film which represents them as too ordinary (too much like us, sharing our priorities) for a life of fame. This last sequence is where the textuality (fictionality) of the film is revealed as the character of the screenplay writer narrates his latest scenario only for it to converge with the action of the film itself. Reality is abandoned and 'The Rules' (explicitly cited by the script-writer) of this kind of film, take over. Ultimately, the Spice Girls succeed as people to the extent that they fail as traditionally authentic pop stars. Ordinariness can no longer defend them from the attendant distance and commercialisation of being so famous, since it is crushed by the momentum of the large culture industry machine.

Conclusion

Simon Frith has written that 'we should be examining . . . not how true a piece of music is to something else, but how it sets up the idea of 'truth' in the first place – successful pop music is music which defines its own aesthetic standard' (Frith 1987, p. 137). The Spice Girls' power is to define this standard in a way that has so many in-built contradictions that, by selectively negotiating amongst the various types of authenticity that they have on offer, virtually anyone can be a fan. At a superficial level, especially in what they say and write, they represent themselves as participating in the standard rock discourse of authenticity by defending their status as artists (in the traditional romantic definition of the term). That they talk about 'writing' their songs (either because they are expected to, or because they truly believe their input to the lyrics to be important) serves to underline their status as ordinary people by articulating the commonly held beliefs about pop music. This is now part of their nonrock authenticity, their ordinariness. This ordinariness legitimates the aspirations of a broad section of their audience who become Spice Girls by dancing and lip-synching to Spice tracks in their own bedrooms. In the 'Mama' video, amongst stills of each individual Spice Girl as a child, is mocked-up cine-film footage supposedly capturing the whole group playing and dancing on home video. Paradoxically, the fact that the Spice Children wear clothes contemporary with the actual present (1997) and not with the narrative present (c. 1985), adds to its patina of verity since it replicates the real-life situation of young girls up and down Britain by this stage in the Spice Girls' career (March 1997 – released in time for Mother's Day in the UK). Like the 'Wannabe' flashback in *Spice World the Movie*, it at once projects a natural (authentic) coming together for the Spice Girls through growing up together, and facilitates the fantasy predicated on inauthenticity, which allows a group of ordinary girls to enjoy fame. Perhaps this is a particularly female and feminist strategy. In her research into allwomen pop acts, Mavis Bayton documents how 'some feminist performers have gone to great lengths in order to avoid being seen as special or different from their "sisters" in the audience', and reports one female musician as saying that she refrains from wearing stage clothes because 'I think it's important that the audience recognises that you're just ordinary people, like they are' (Bayton 1993, pp. 180, 182).[24]

However, in the context of a highly commercial, fully merchandised film, this lack of grooming is itself clearly a form of grooming. The Spice Girls' contribution

162   *Elizabeth Eva Leach*

to *fin-de-siècle* pop music is to upset the clarity of authenticity markers by presenting a polysemy which allows different collectives to construct the kind of authenticity that they require, based on the assumptions that they bring to their listening and thus to find their own meanings in the group. Like their approach to constructions of femininity, this breadth maximised their commercial success. This polysemous presentation of authenticity enables listeners who see and enjoy the contradictions in these markers to understand that the opposition between commercialism and authenticity is itself a commercially constructed one. As an essentially postmodern pop act, the Spice Girls deconstruct the binary itself, having it both ways and playing with the modernist narrative as they use it to their own ends. Although some fans no doubt eagerly participate in their own deception, many probably knowingly appreciate the play, and willingly subscribe to a pre-romantic aesthetic of safe fantasy and terpsichorean enjoyment.

Appendix: Text to 'Wannabe'

Text		*No. of bars*
[Intro] RAPPED		2
(A) Yo I'll tell you what I want what I really really want,	(Mel B)	
So tell me what you want what you really really want,	(Geri)	
[Intro] RAPPED		4
(A) Yo I'll tell you what I want what I really really want,	(Mel B)	
So tell me what you want what you really really want,		
(B) I wanna, I wanna, I wanna, I wanna,		
I wanna, really, really, really wanna zig-a-zig-ah!		
[Verse 1] SUNG		8
If you want my future, forget my past,	(Mel C)	
If you wanna get with me, better make it fast,	(Emma)	
Now don't go wasting my precious time,	(Mel B)	
Get your act together we could be just fine.	(Geri)	
[Intro] RAPPED		4
(A) Yo I'll tell you what I want what I really really want,		
So tell me what you want what you really really want,		
(B) I wanna, I wanna, I wanna, I wanna,		
I wanna, really, really, really wanna zig-a-zig-ah!		
[Refrain] SUNG		8
(C) If you wanna be my lover, you gotta get with my friends,		
Make it last forever, friendship never ends,		
If you wanna be my lover, you have got to give,		
Taking is too easy but that's the way it is.		
[Verse 2] SUNG		8
What d'ya think about that? now you know how I feel,	(Mel C)	
Say you can handle my love are you for real	(Emma)	

Text *No. of bars*

> I won't be hasty, I'll give you a try, (Mel B)
> If you really bug me then I'll say good-bye. (Geri)

[Intro]   RAPPED   4
  (A) Yo I'll tell you what I want what I really really want,
        So tell me what you want what you really really want,
  (B) I wanna, I wanna, I wanna, I wanna,
        I wanna, really, really, really wanna zig-a-zig-ah!

[Refrain]   SUNG   8
  (C) If you wanna be my lover, you gotta get with my friends,
        Make it last forever, friendship never ends,
        If you wanna be my lover, you have got to give,
        Taking is too easy but that's the way it is.

[Middle 8]   RAPPED   8
        Here's the story from A to Z[ee],   (Mel B)
        You wanna get with me,   (Mel B)
        You gotta listen carefully.   (Mel B)
        We got Em in the place,   (Mel B)
        Who likes it in your face,   (Mel B)
        We got G like MC,   (Mel B)
        Who likes it on an [E]   (Mel B)
        Easy V   (Geri)
        Doesn't come for free,   (Geri)
        She's a real lady,   (Geri)
        And as for me,   (Mel B)
        [laugh] you'll see.   (Mel B)

[Intro X]   RAPPED   2
        Slam your body down and wind it all around
        Slam your body down and wind it all around

[Refrain]   SUNG   8
  (C) If you wanna be my lover, you gotta get with my friends,
        Make it last forever, friendship never ends,
        If you wanna be my lover, you have got to give,
        Taking is too easy but that's the way it is.

[Refrain (part) and Intro X]   SUNG EXCEPT WHERE STATED   8
        If you wanna be my lover
        you gotta you gotta you gotta you gotta you gotta
                (RAPPED)
        slam slam slam slam
        Slam your body down and wind it all around
        Slam your body down and wind it all around
        Slam your body down and wind it all around
        Slam your body down and zig-a zig-ah!   (RAPPED)
        If you wanna be my lover.

164   *Elizabeth Eva Leach*

Acknowledgements

This paper is partly the result of teaching on the residential summer school at Villiers Park, Middleton Stoney. I would like to thank all at Villiers Park, specifically the Music Reading Parties 97, 98 and 99 and my co-tutor Cormac Newark. In addition, I am most grateful to Suzannah Clark, Nicola Dibben, Julian Muphet and Leanne Roberts for their comments on earlier drafts.

Copyright acknowledgements

Endnotes

1. For classical music, authenticity is usually applied specifically to aspects of performance, especially of performance practice. This usage has been criticised as a manifestation of modernism, masquerading as historical enquiry, and fronting a purely commercial CD promotion enterprise (see Taruskin 1988). Peter Kivy has commented that the ascription of authenticity to performance 'has become or is close to becoming a synonym for "good," while seeming to confer upon a performance some magical property that it did not have before' (see Kivy 1995, p. 1). In popular music, Charles Hamm has identified two narratives of authenticity which are similar to the fourth of Kivy's four meanings for 'authentic', i.e. 'The Other Authenticity' or 'personal authenticity', the unique product of a unique, special individual. Hamm (1995, pp. 1–40) identifies that the individual is authenticated by belonging either to a particular racial group, or to a particular social class, and is thereby committed, through subject positioning, to the ideological or affective content of his/her song. As Bennett *et al.* attest, authenticity is a 'slippery term', since 'on the one hand, it provides a measure of the relationship between a musical text or practice and its production ... On the other hand, it also functions as a quotidian theory of the sociology of consumption.' (see Bennett 1993, p. 172) As will be seen in this essay, the constant slippage between production and consumption is something sought by both producers and consumers. Part of the effect of perceived authenticity is to forge an identity between these two groups by offering a seemingly transparent transfer of meaning from the producer to the receiver.

2. This is what led to the original racial/ethical dimension of authenticity, since Black artists had their songs covered by White Singers as an attempt on the part of record companies to avoid paying royalties to the original Black artists despite the popularity of their songs (see Cook 1998A, pp. 8–9).

3. That is, all of them except the Motown track 'Stop', which only reached number two.

4. Mainly Richard Stannard and Matt [Matthew] Rowe [Rowbottom] ('Wannabe', '2 Become 1', 'Mama', 'Spice Up Your Life', 'Viva Forever') and Paul Wilson and Andy Watkins ('Who Do You Think You Are?', 'Stop', 'Too Much'). All five Spice Girls are also jointly credited with the authorship of these songs. The issue of an individual's degree of input in a jointly credited enterprise is always somewhat murky, and those critics feeding off a traditional notation of authenticity have questioned the Spice Girls' role in creating their songs. Joint accreditation gives the Spice Girls royalties on covers of the songs, since the legal system itself privileges authorship (ownership) over performance (rental). Although all of the Spice Girls' claims could easily relate to writing song lyrics rather than music, the possibility that these claims of 'writing' are to some extent constructed should not be excluded merely in an attempt to show feminist support. At base, I am not interested in whether they write their own songs or not. What is interesting is that they say that they do and yet that certain critics seriously question this.

5. See, for example, Lee (1997) which is accompanied by a picture of the Spice Girls as small marionettes whose strings are tied to the fingers of large male hands (I am

grateful to Cormac Newark for this reference).

6. Tony Blair's Britain (which, although it followed the Spice Girls' rise to fame by ten months, arguably represents the mood of the country in the last couple of years of John Major's Government) had a suspicion of elites (encouraged by the exposure of much Tory sleaze and the odd ministerial imprisonment) and a belief in Blair's promise to create an integrated and organic country.

7. The 'home videos' of the Spice Girls as children are genuine in that they show 8-year-old fans, dressed as the group, pretending to be them. This authentically resonates with the practice of such fans as well as suggesting a pre-fame unity for the group which counters the known facts of the group's formation.

8. I am using the industry's own legal definitions for these formats. 'A "song video" is a video of one song performed by an artist the making of which is initially intended to stimulate sales of a single play record containing the same sound recording as is embodied on the video' (although this is not merely promotional but also a commercial venture). 'A "music video" is a specially commissioned video featuring one artist with a running time usually between thirty and ninety minutes. This type of video is not made to promote a specific record but is made as a commercial venture in its own right' (Fisher and Kuhn 1984, p. 1).

9. The rap starts one crotchet before the till-ready accompaniment and is strongly stressed on its first and third crotchets, which fall on the second and fourth crotchets of the till-ready. This adds to the improvised quality of the whole. As Nicola Dibben (personal communication) has commented, 'the use of rap is also a reference to hip-hop and its current cultural reception as "authentic street reality"'.

10. I am using the PSV to 'Wannabe' as contained in PMV, *The Official Video Vol. 1: One Hour of Girl Power* – Virgin UK: VID 2834 (1997) 60 mins.

11. Any claim that the visual narrative of film is primary because the music is added later can be countered by analysing the music's fundamental role in actively constructing the meaning of the finished product, which is not merely a narrative, but a complex of different media of at least equal status (music may even have more emotional force than any other element).

12. For a discussion of the discussion of phenom-

enal music in opera and the concept of voice, see Abbate (1991).

13. Cf. Björk's 'There's More to Life than This', where the song's accompaniment itself is the music of a party from which the singer is trying to escape.

14. Victoria's sobriquet – 'Posh' spice – is potentially upsetting for the duality implied between the poshness of the other party guests (and hence their 'otherness') and the relative normality of the Spice Girls, with whom the viewer is invited to identify. This is minimised by keeping Victoria in the group setting and not focusing on her individually. She is backgrounded visually and is the only member of the group not to sing a solo line in the verse (or the song as a whole).

15. In print and in conversation, the Spice Girls have never admitted an explicitly sexual meaning of 'zig-a-zig-ah'. This helps keep the group 'PG certificate' on the literal surface, whilst allowing for the bonding with their fans that occurs by having such 'in-jokes'.

16. In traditionally authentic rock (and in its 1990s aesthetic derivative, Britpop) dance is impossible because members of the band play instruments.

17. Virgin UK: VID 2834 (1997) 60 mins. The video contains the PSVs of the first four singles, a Comic Relief version of the fourth's second A side, 'Who Do You Think You Are?', and behind-the-scenes footage introduced and linked by the Spice Girls.

18. There is a cut which (conveniently?) obscures the precise location of the hotel, whilst adding to the authenticity of the 'home video' effect by being amateurish. As this could have been fixed post-filming, as is evident from the overlay of rolling text charting the Spice Girls' rise to fame, it is part of a deliberate attempt to increase the believability of the ordinariness of the Spice Girls. That the central part of this section must in fact be being filmed by someone who is not a Spice Girl – potentially disruptive for the effect of group spontaneity being created here – is carefully elided by Geri's audible presence behind the camera in the opening and closing cuts.

19. PolyGram Filmed Entertainment PAL 0559343. 1 hour 29 mins, directed by Bob Spiers.

20. It is performed until the end of the first full Refrain (C) and then cuts straight to Refrain (part) and Intro X and a play-out during which Mel C does a backflip to lead into the last line: 'If you wanna be my lover'.

21. One of a number of architectonic images of London which, on the back of Britpop's own

166   *Elizabeth Eva Leach*

nostalgia for the 1960s, stress the British identity of the Spice Girls as a prominent iconic feature of the film.

22. See Eco (1987). *Spice World the Movie* plays with the very idea of cultural iconicity.

23. Mel B is wearing blue jeans and matching denim jacket over a white crop top, but continuity with the 'Wannabe' PSV is provided by her prominently erect nipples. Mel C wears a bandanna, a shirt and leggings, but has girlish long plaits rather than the scraped-back pony tail of the PSV. Geri has a short-legged boiler suit with a frilled crop top under it and girlish pig tails – very different to the glamour of the sequinned body in the video. Victoria wears a similarly styled dress, but rather than the grown-up chic of black, it is patterned with flowers. Emma sucks a lollipop and is in school uniform (implying that she is young enough still to

be at school), but the unusual school colour, pink, makes reference to her babyness and casts gentle doubt on the authenticity of the uniform itself.

24. Bayton is interested in grass roots music-making and not in recordings, and thus her perspective is slightly different. She also approaches the issue with the idea that women's role as non-composing vocalists does not count. I think this is a problem since she is colluding in a gendered division of labour and only recognising that which men normally do as valuable. The way in which the Spice Girls married feminism with chart success was by imputing value to the types of input into pop that women already had in the mainstream – as vocalists and dancers. For an impressive analysis of feminist strategies that deals specifically with the Spice Girls, see Dibben (1999).

References

Abbate, C. 1991. *Unsung Voices: Opera and Musical Narrative in the Nineteenth Century* (Princeton)

Adorno, T.W. 1998(1941). 'On popular music', in *Cultural Theory and Popular Culture: A Reader*, ed. J. Storey (Hemel Hemstead)

Allanbrook, W.J. 1983. *Rhythmic Gesture in Mozart* (Chicago)

Bayton, M. 1993. 'Feminist musical practice: problems and contradictions', in *Rock and Popular Music: Politics, Policies, Institutions*, ed. T. Bennett, S. Frith, L. Grossberg, J. Shepherd and G. Turner (London), pp. 177–92

Bennett, T. 1993. *Rock and Popular Music: Politics, Policies, Institutions* (London)

Cook, N. 1998A. *A Very Short Introduction to Music* (Oxford)
     1998B. *Analysing Musical Multimedia* (Oxford)

Dibben, N. 1999. 'Representations of femininity in popular music', *Popular Music*, 18, pp. 331–55

Eco, U. 1987. 'Casablanca: cult movies and intertextual collage', in *Travels in Hyperreality* (London), pp. 197–212

Fisher, C., and Kuhn, M. 1984. *Music Video* (London)

Frith, S. 1987. 'Towards an aesthetic of popular music', in *Music and Society: the Politics of Composition, Performance and Reception*, ed. R. Leppert and S. McClary (Cambridge), pp. 133–49
     1988. *Music for Pleasure: Essays in the Sociology of Pop* (Cambridge)

Hamm, C. 1995. *Putting Popular Music in its Place* (Cambridge)

Jensen, J. 1998. *The Nashville Sound: Authenticity, Commercialization, and Country Music* (Nashville and London)

Kivy, P. 1995. *Authenticities: Philosophical Reflections on Musical Performance* (Ithaca and London)

Lee, E. 1997. 'Girl power? Bollocks!' *Punch*, 7 June, pp. 18–21

McClary, S. 1991. *Feminine Endings: Music, Gender and Sexuality* (Minnesota and Oxford)

Metzstein, M. 1993. 'SEX: signed, sealed, delivered . . .', in *Deconstructing Madonna*, ed. F. Lloyd (London)

Middleton, R. 1990. *Studying Popular Music* (Milton Keynes)

Monson, I. 1995. 'The problem with white hipness: race, gender, and cultural conceptions in jazz historical discourse', *Journal of the American Musicological Society*, 48, pp. 396–422

Mundy, J. 1999. *Popular Music on Screen: from the Hollywood Musical to Music Video* (Manchester)

Pfeil, F. 1995. *White Guys: Studies in Postmodern Domination and Difference* (London)

Spice Girls. 1997. *Girl Power!* (London)

Taruskin, R. 1988. 'The pastness of the present and the presence of the past', in *Authenticity and Early Music*, ed. N. Kenyon (Oxford), pp. 137–207
     1997. *Defining Russia Musically: Historical and Hermeneutical Essays* (Princeton)

Tetzlaff, D. 1993. 'Metatextual Girl: – patriarchy – postmodernism – power – money – Madonna', in *The Madonna Connection: Representational Politics, Subculture Identities, and Cultural Theory*, ed. C. Schwichtenberg (Oxford)

Young, S. 1991. 'Like a critique: a postmodern essay on Madonna's postmodern video *Like a Prayer*', *Popular Music and Society*, 15, pp. 59–68

[27]

Oh, Boy! (Oh, Boy!): mutual desirability and musical structure in the buddy group

BARBARA BRADBY

Abstract

If rock'n'roll represented new, sexualised gender identities for the teenagers of the late 1950s, why (and how) were such identities constructed through the multiple voices of the group? In Buddy Holly's 'Oh, Boy!' the chorus plays a prominent supportive role in relation to the lead singer; but its continual echoing of the singer's 'Oh boy!' allows also for a literal hearing of cries of mutual desire and admiration between two men. This representation of the 'buddy group' has continuities with other group, or dual representations of male identity, where mutual, male selves and desires are constructed around an imagined, comforting woman. The presence of traces of the maternal body (Kristeva's 'semiotic' sphere) is audible in 'Oh, Boy!' through the chorus's separation of rhythm and melody, and in particular, its use of 'children's rhythms', consistent with those analysed by the musicologist Constantin Brailoiu as a cross-cultural phenomenon. In 'Oh, Boy!' children's rhythms are reworked in a dialogue between singer and chorus, and between guitar and chorus in the instrumental break, in such a way that after the break the singer is able to resolve the rhythmic tensions introduced in the first half of the song and get 'everything right'. The new symbolic identity of male adolescent independence is audibly structured by the semiotic, so reversing the surface hearing of the song as involving the subordination of the chorus to lead singer in the consensual hierarchy of 'buddy' relations. The relationship of Buddy Holly to Bo Diddley adds a further dimension to this structure, where ostensible equality cannot mask the uncomfortable social hierarchy of the white rock star and black mentor, and where an appeal to the other as 'boy' would evoke not the buddy group, but slavery.

Prologue: '(I'll Remember) In the Still of the Nite'

There is a scene in the film *Dead Ringers* – David Cronenberg's 1988 horror fantasy about identical twin obstetricians – where the downward spiral of mutual destruction by the two men is temporarily arrested. To the comforting 'Shoo-be-doos' of 'In the Still of the Nite',[1] the brothers both dance in a slow 'smooch' with their mutual lover, encircling the woman from in front and behind, each in harmony with the other around her body as buffer. This scene interrupts the narrative in which the twins turn the gruesome instruments of seventeenth and eighteenth-century obstetric science away from women and on to each other, hystericising and eventually killing themselves. The fact that the two men are both played by the same actor (Jeremy Irons) emphasises the film's thesis of the disastrous (non-)splitting of a male subject that is nevertheless divided against itself and so, ultimately, *self*-destructive. Without women's bodies as a buffer, this re-telling of the myth of the original 'Siamese' twins shows male destructiveness as part of a failure to separate from the other, and the mutual dependence of master and slave becomes a mutual suicide.

The dancing scene fascinated me when I first saw and heard it in the cinema in 1989, because 'In the Still of the Nite' was one of a sample of 'doo wop' songs I had been working on as part of a project to compare 'girl-group' music with various forms of male group singing. The film's dramatisation seemed to bear out my hearing of male group singing as predominantly consensual and harmonious, as compared with the open conflict often found between girl-group voices (Bradby 1990). In this case, the visual depiction, as in the song, presents a classic model of male harmony achieved through a mutual and nostalgic focus onto a comforting woman. Nostalgia is achieved simply by playing this song, which is a 'symbol of the 50s' (Warner 1992, p. 189), in a 1980s film. But the song is also itself nostalgic: 'I remember that night in May', sings the lead singer; and the chorus intones 'I re-mem-ber, I re-mem-ber' on the beats which the lead weaves around (see Figure 1). These dual voices of the vocal group represent the male subject of the 'I' as split in two, albeit harmoniously. And the chorus's part is at once the memory of an 'other' male self, *and* the 'response' of the woman we conventionally hear this love song as addressing.

This verbal nostalgia for the past of a love affair is overlaid in the song by a deeper nostalgia for infancy. The rocking 12/8 rhythm and the pre-verbal 'shoo-doo, shoo-be-doo' of the chorus connote the *lullaby* and the 'shh' sounds that are used to 'hush' crying babies. In the context of this conventional male–female love song, such sounds connote the comforting voice of the *mother* rocking her son to sleep.[2] The song also enacts this nostalgia in its repetition of the verses. In verse one, the lead voice narrates a past event: 'In the still of the night, *I held you tight*'; while in the musical repeat of this verse after the contrasting 'I remember' verse, he expresses a future/present wish: 'So before the light, *Hold me again* with all of your might' (italics added). The desire of the song is therefore not only nostalgic – expressed as the desire for a repetition of a *past* experience – but also *passive* ('hold me'). This suggests that the discourse of male, heterosexual desire is being modelled directly on the imagined (past, passive) rocking of the boy baby in the arms of his mother. But at the same time, this relationship is that of a man to his male peers, as the chorus provides the steadying beat, and 'rocks' the lead voice along in the musical performance. In a parallel way, the film scene that *enacted* the song showed a (split) man's nostalgic desire for a comforting woman to be at once his desire for his male other.

The film scene therefore encouraged me. My own analysis of group songs had worked to separate out relationships *between* voices in songs as ones of dialogue and polyphony, representative of divisions and conflicts in the gendered selves projected by the song lyrics. However, such an analysis had to work against an apparent readiness that we all show as listeners to construct polyphonous singing in rock/pop music into 'the voice' of a unitary, singing subject. The desire to hear the song as a conversation between 'singer' and audience often obscures a perception of the song as itself conducting an internal dialogue between different voices. In this context, the film enactment of 'In the Still of the Nite' seemed to show that my analysis was not just some deep structure that no one ever actually heard. And perhaps asking people to talk about music was not the best way to find out what it meant to them. The film scene showed that there are other ways in which people can 'talk about' or act out what music means to them. It confirmed for me the importance of analysing the relationship between different voices in a song as being at once a musical and a verbal feature of performance. And it confirmed these as *gendered* processes, and ones where sexuality and gender are often deeply entwined.

Oh, Boy! (Oh, Boy!)

How conscious are we, for instance, unless we are listening for it, that each time Buddy Holly sings 'Oh boy' in his classic song of that title,[3] his words are immediately echoed by his male backing group? What is actually sung, is not simply 'Oh boy', but 'Oh boy, OH BOY' (where lower and upper case represent the voices of lead singer and chorus, respectively). And if we do hear these separate voices, do we then dismiss them as a nowadays irrelevant effect of a dated musical arrangement, as if the music could somehow be divorced from the song itself?[4] If, instead, we hear these 'Oh boy's as echoing cries of mutual male desire, then they have much in common with the mutual exchanges of 'I remember' between the voices of 'In the Still of the Nite'. There is a basic *continuity* in gender structure between the two songs, in the way two male voices address simultaneously each other and a woman.

Yet between the doo-wop song and Buddy Holly's rock 'n' roll, there is a shift to the modern representation of the 'buddy group', with its connotations of masculine youth, fun, whiteness, egalitarianism, and independence from women.[5] Musically, the pitch of the voices rises (youth), and the rhythm loses all trace of the triplet beats of the slow 12/8, adopting the rapid 4/4 that has fossilised as the rock beat ever since (white masculinity). The melodic phrasing changes from the langorous sostenuto of the Five Satins to Holly's punctuated singing, which Laing has argued represents a creative break with 'sentimentality' (Laing 1971, p. 68). Indeed, the use of religious discourse in the ballad ('and I pray to keep your precious love') makes it an obvious candidate for the description of (barely) secularised Madonna-worship that Laing saw as typical of the ballad tradition and the Western, Christian universe with which rock and roll made a radical break (Laing 1969, pp. 57–60). However, what I am concerned with in this paper is to question the characteristics of egalitarianism and non-reliance on women that are implied in this notion of the 'buddy group' and upon which much classic rock feeds. In doing so, I shall draw more on the continuities between the two songs than their fairly obvious differences.

In particular, the musical role of the chorus is very similar in both songs. Like that of 'In the Still of the Nite', the chorus in 'Oh, Boy!' keeps time for the singer, providing the on-beat which the lead can work round or against. In both songs, the only *words* the chorus sings are echoes of the singer's words; otherwise they sing nonsense syllables, connoting the pre-verbal sphere of infancy. In both songs, the chorus accompanies the lead instrument in the 'instrumental break' (the sax in the one case, the guitar in the other), singing rhythmic nonsense syllables ('doo bop doo bah' and 'dum de dum dum', respectively).

As we have seen, through this singer–chorus relationship, the ballad works not only as a representation of heterosexual love but also of relationships between men. If it is true that Buddy Holly breaks with the nostalgic and sentimental veneration of an idealised 'mother', there are implications for both women and men. One implication, I would suggest, is that if the female object of Holly's sexual desire is 'hardly there at all', as Jonathan Cott aptly said of 'Peggy Sue' (Cott 1981, p. 79),

1	&	a	2	&	a	3	&	a	4	&	a	1	&	a	2	&	a	3	&	a	4	&	a
		SHO	DOO			SHOO		BE	DOO					SHO	DOO			SHOO		BE	DOO		
		SHO	DOO			SHOO		BE	DOO					SHO	DOO			SHOO		BE	DOO		
																					In		**the**
		SHO	DOO			SHOO		BE	DOO					SHO	DOO			SHOO		BE	DOO		
still										**of**	**the**	**ni-**			**ight**						**I -**	**I -**	**I**
		SHO	DOO			SHOO		BE	DOO					SHO	DOO			SHOO		BE	DOO		
held	**you**								**He-**	**ld**	**you**	**ti-**			**ight**							**Cos**	**I**
		SHO	DOO			SHOO		BE	DOO					SHO	DOO			SHOO		BE	DOO		
lo			**-**			**ve**			**lo-**	**ove**	**you**	**so**	**-**		**o**						**Pro-**	**mise**	**I'll**
		SHO	DOO			SHOO		BE	DOO					SHO	DOO			SHOO		BE	DOO		
never									**le-**	**et**	**you**	**go-**	**o**			**In**	**the**	**still**				**of**	**the**
			IN		THE	STILL			OF		THE	NI-		IGHT									
ni-	**i-**	**ight**																				**I**	**re-**
I			RE-			MEM-			BER			I			RE-			MEM-			BER		
mem	**-**		**ber**						**That**	**night**	**in**	**Ma**	**-**		**ay**						**The**		
I			RE-			MEM-			BER			I			RE-			MEM-			BER		
stars					**were**	**bright**					**a-a-**	**bo**	**- o-**	**o-**	**ove**								**I'll**
I			RE-			MEM-			BER			I			RE-			MEM-			BER		
ho	**-**		**ope**						**and**		**I'll**	**pray**	**-**		**ay**								**To**
keep		*	*		**your**	**pre-**		*	*		**cious**	**lo**	**-**	**o -**	**o -**	**o -**	**o -**	**o -**	**o -**	**ove**	**Well**		**be-**
		SHO	DOO			SHOO		BE	DOO					SHO	DOO			SHOO		BE	DOO		
fo-	**ore**									**the-**	**e**	**li-**			**ight**						**Hold**	**me**	**a-**

ga- ain	SHO DOO	SHOO	BE DOO with all	of	your mi- ight	SHO DOO	In	the	SHOO still	BE DOO	of	the
ni- ight	IN	THE STILL	OF		THE NI-	IGHT						
DOO BOP [clarinet...]	DOO BAH				DOO	BOP		DOO BAH				
DOO BOP	DOO BAH				DOO	BOP		DOO BAH				
DOO BOP	DOO BAH				DOO	BOP		DOO BAH				
DOO BOP	DOO BAH				DOO	BOP						
OH	OH	OH	OH	OH	OH						So be-	
fo- ore	SHO DOO	SHOO	BE DOO the- e-	e	li-	SHO DOO ight			SHOO	BE DOO Hold me		a-
ga- ain	SHO DOO	SHOO	BE DOO with all	of	your mi- ight	SHO DOO	In	the	SHOO still	BE DOO	of	the
ni-i-ight	IN	THE STILL	OF		THE NIGHT							
ni-i-ight	SHO DOO	SHOO	BE DOO		Oh	SHO DOO	In	the	still	[rall]	of	the
hoo	SHO DOO	SHOO	BE DOO Woo-	hoo- hoo		SHO DOO	00-00		SHOO 00-00-00-00-00-00	BE DOO Woo		00
hoo	SHO DOO	SHOO	BE DOO 00- 00-	00- hoo		SHO DOO			SHOO 00- 00-	BE DOO 00- 00-		00
oo	SHO DOO	SHOO	BE DOO 00- 00-	00- 00		SHO DOO			SHOO	BE DOO		

Figure 1. The Five Satins: 'In the Still of the Nite' (upper case = chorus; lower case = lead singer).

then the singer's invitation to his male audience to join in his sexual fantasising is also a sexual invitation to them. In fact, the opening verse of 'Peggy Sue' is not addressed to her at all, but invites another man/boy to know Peggy Sue ('If you knew Peggy Sue'), and through her, to know the singer and his sexual lack ('then you'd know why I feel blue') (Bradby and Torode 1984). A similar structure of *sharing* sexual desire with another man is found in 'I'm Gonna Love You Too', where the song resolves the tension of 'another fella took you' by proclaiming, 'I'm gonna love you too' (Bradby and Torode 1982).

In 'Oh, Boy!', the woman is similarly 'hardly there'. The second person 'you' in the opening lines of the song ('You don't know what you've been missing') is no doubt conventionally heard as addressed to a woman or girl. But this hearing sits uneasily with the third person reference to 'my baby' in the triumphant last line of verse 3 ('I'm gonna see my baby tonight') where the singer is telling his audience *about* her (see Figure 2). And we may then note that the opening address is more immediately disrupted by the way the lines run on into the words 'Oh boy', if heard literally as a vocative 'call' to a boy. In this case, these opening lines can equally well be heard as addressed to the audience of male adolescents (missing out on the experiences that the lead singer has had). The echoing 'Oh boy, OH BOY' dialogue that goes on between the two male voices throughout the song then suggests, at a literal level, a sexual invitation and its reciprocation between two boys.

However, to be 'hardly there', is not the same as not being there at all, and this paper in part analyses the place of this notional woman in the sexuality of the buddy group. Only a year and a half separates the releases of 'In the Still of the Nite' (March 1956) and 'Oh, Boy!' (October 1957); yet the first represents 'the fifties' of sentimentality and sexual repression, while the second looks forward to the 'sexual liberation' of the 1960s. It has often been claimed that the 1960s saw a sexual revolution on male terms, and it is clear that the place of women as objects or subjects of sexual liberation is still up for debate today. Our brief comparison of the two songs has already suggested that the 'fifties' ballad included a kind of respect for womanhood/motherhood as a form of subjectivity that has disappeared in the rock 'n' roll song, which can offer only masculinisation (becoming one of the boys) or objectification (being his baby) to its female audience. Indeed, we might add that the ballad is hardly innocent of sexuality, but seems to offer a more sensuous, female-oriented sexuality than that of the rock 'n' roll song, which seems impoverished by comparison. But a further difference between the sexualities of the two songs is that the Five Satins' ballad addresses an adult, 'after sex' situation, whereas Holly's song addresses *those who have not yet had sex*.[6] No wonder, then, that the sexual address of rock music has proved so controversial to parents, since it is here framed as an invitation to the as-yet-innocent (and hence, potentially, younger and younger children) by the 'just experienced'. Little wonder, also, that the discourse of rock has proved to be a crucial rite of passage for several generations now, since in this way, it addresses precisely the moment of *initiation* into adult sexuality.

This paper attempts both to expose the masculinisation of sexuality in 'Oh, Boy!' – i.e. to bring out the extent to which women are apparently rendered redundant in the framing of 'sexual liberation' – but also to deconstruct it. In other words, I question the practical disappearance of women (Cott 1981) or the 'silencing of a female discourse' in Holly's construction of sexuality (Bradby and Torode 1984). If, as we have already seen, there is a literal hearing of 'Oh, Boy!' as addressed exclus-

[Verse 1]   1. All my love, all my kissin',
             2. You don't know what you've been missin',
             3. Oh boy, OH BOY, When you're with me,
             4. Oh boy, OH BOY, The world could see that
             5. You were meant for
                 AAAH ...
             6. me ...
                 AAAH ...

[Verse 2]   1. All my life, I've been h waitin',
             2. Tonight there'll be no hesitatin',
             3. Oh boy, OH BOY, When you're with me,
             4. Oh boy, OH BOY, The world could see that
             5. You were meant for
                 AAAH ...
             6. me ...
                 AAAH ...

[Verse 3–   7. Stars appear and the shadows are fallin',
Middle 8]   AAAH ...
             8. You can hear my heart a callin'.
                 AAAH ...
             9. A little bit of lovin' makes everythin' h right
                 AAAH ..
           10. And I'm gonna see my baby tonight
                 AAAH ...

[Verse 4]   1. All my love [etc. as Verse 1]

           [scream and guitar lead into break]

[Break]   1. DUM-DE-DUM-DUM ... OH BOY
             2. DUM-DE-DUM-DUM ... OH BOY
             3. AAAH ...
             4. AAAH ...
             5. AAAH ...
             6. AAAH ...
                 oooh ...

[Verse 5]   1. All my love [etc. as Verse 1]

[Verse 6]   1. All my life [etc. as Verse 2]

[Verse 7]   7. Stars appear and the shadows are fallin',
             8. You can hear my heart a callin',
             9. A little bit of lovin' makes everythin' right
           10. And I'm gonna see my baby tonight

[Verse 8]   1. All my love [etc. as Verse 1]

Figure 2. 'Oh, Boy!' lyrics (lower case = lead singer; upper case = chorus).

ively to a male audience, in the next sections I explore what *other* voices can be heard in the internal dialogue conducted by and in the song.

Post-structuralism, I love you (or, The sound of the other voice)

The frequent complaint at popular music conferences and elsewhere that 'no one talks about the music' can be understood as a symptom of frustration both with readings of popular music which ultimately treat lyrics as poems (whether for literary or political analysis), and with a musicology that too often seems to submerge the specificity of pop music into a general semiology of (Western) music. It seems to me vital to consider post-1950s rock and pop as *song*, i.e. as the interaction of words and music, if we are to begin to understand the social significance of the music as articulating new modes of sexuality. To rephrase a question set by Frith (1988), we should not be asking 'why do songs have words?', but 'why do we dance to songs?'. For the point has frequently been made that rock is dance music (*ergo* nobody listens to the lyrics), but just as important is the fact that rock broke down a previous distinction between (fast) dance music as instrumental (with the vocal as an intermittent, subordinate 'instrument'), and romantic, listening music as pre-eminently vocal (and used for 'slow' dancing).

Now that an encyclopaedic knowledge of rock and pop lyrics has become a male skill that is paraded on competitive TV game shows (such as 'Never Mind the Buzzcocks' in the UK) it may seem strange to remind readers that for decades men were 'in denial' about the lyrics of rock music. Lyrics were something 'for the girls', hence disregarded by those who really understood what the music was about. What really mattered, from this point of view, was 'rhythm', often just meaning a heavy 4/4 beat. I shall argue that claims for rock as a serious genre on grounds of its rhythm make much more sense if we consider the rhythm of the *lyrics* – by which I mean always the conjunction of words and music – and the ways in which lyrical rhythms work with, around and against this basic 4/4 beat.

Now post-structuralist theory, notably in the work of Barthes and Kristeva, has made much of the musical characteristics of language in general. Kristeva's concept of 'the semiotic' is sometimes thought of as just another name for Lacan's 'imaginary', but her concept in fact gives the distinction between the 'symbolic' and 'imaginary' aspects of language a radical twist (Lacan 1977; Kristeva 1980). Simply viewed as 'image', the imaginary traces of a pre-verbal one-ness with the mother can never be verbalised, except through the 'symbolic' language, on which they are dependent. But Kristeva's 'semiotic' is a *material* aspect of language, bound up with musical features that continually recall the rhythms and melodies of pre-verbal communication with the mother. As that material side of language which escapes representation in the symbolic, patriarchal order of linguistic exchange, the semiotic sphere is, for Kristeva, pre-gendered, but also replete with a desire which is different from that which can be inscribed in that order. And from this follows her proposal for a post-feminist utopia, where desire and difference would flow freely, outside of the need to order sexuality as difference *from*, arising out of binary modes of thinking (Kristeva 1982).

This utopian thought easily slides over into what Lawrence Grossberg calls the 'ironic nihilism' or 'authentic inauthenticity' of postmodern culture, within whose logic, 'one celebrates a difference knowing that its status depends on nothing but its being celebrated' (Grossberg 1988, p. 326). In Baudrillard's TV world, once the 'reality' that used to be the guarantor of both truth and falsity of appearances can itself be simulated, the whole system of signs becomes a 'gigantic simulacrum, never again exchanging for what is real, but exchanging in itself, in an uninterrupted circuit without reference' (Baudrillard 1988, p. 170). If we are to interrupt this circuit and reclaim the concept of the semiotic as a *material* one, then we must insist that, as such, it is open to empirical investigation. Kristeva herself makes reference to the possibility of systematic empirical description, using 'modern phono-acoustics', of the 'semiotic operations (rhythm, intonation)' in the pre-linguistic 'vocalisations' of small babies and in the discourse of psychotics (Kristeva 1980, pp. 133–4). However, even in her analyses of specific texts, she is more interested in the *theoretical* relationship of rhythm to language, than in any recognisably *musical* analysis of rhythm in a text (*ibid.*, pp. 175 ff.). And nowhere does she empirically consider *song* as a space where language and music meet and interact.

Nevertheless, there seem good grounds for doing just this. Apart from those already mentioned, 'polyphony' ('many voices') is a musical concept which plays an important part in Kristeva's analysis of the avant-garde, or 'transgressive' novel (*ibid.*, pp. 64–91). Rock/pop song offers a multiplicity of ways in which words can be arranged between different voices. And as this music defined itself around a central discourse of sexuality, the discursive effects of 'polyphony' can be shown to be important in the development of that discourse (cf. Bradby 1990).

In (mis)appropriating the concept of 'the semiotic' for song analysis, then, I take two empirical points of departure. Instead of starting from the voice of the lead singer, so often assumed to be the only and fullest purveyor of meaning in a song, I start from the *other* voice, that of the chorus. And instead of assuming that music gives meaning to words by *enhancing* the musical features of speech, I start from rhythm in the song as a material semiotic that produces meaning by the *differences* it sets up from the spoken rhythms of speech. It is as if the musical 'setting' makes explicit the semiotic as an aspect of language separate from the symbolic, foregrounds it, and explores the differences.

Buddy Holly's chorus: the wordless beat and the beatless word

In his detailed study of Buddy Holly, published in 1971, Dave Laing wrote of Holly's backing groups:

In contrast with the ingenuity of gospel choirs and the black vocal groups of the '50s, members of these white groups all sang the same part and were firmly subordinated to the name singer out in front. Their roles were limited: in most cases they either acted as part of the rhythm section and sang wordless syllables ('dum-de-dum' or 'ba-ba-ba'), or took their place with the singer, echoing key phrases from his singing. (Laing 1971, pp. 51–2)

Laing concludes that although there are occasions on The Crickets' records where the vocal group sings two or three of its own words,

Holly's backing groups sound least archaic when they make noises rather than sing words (. . .). They sound best when the rather opulent mellowness of their singing is cut short. In 'Not Fade Away', for instance, (. . .) their clipped 'ba-ba-ba' syllables are sung in time with the distinctive Bo Diddley riff beaten out by Jerry Allison on drums. (*ibid.*, p. 52)

Within his general thesis on their subordination to the lead singer, Laing therefore identifies three roles for the chorus: as 'echo' of the singer's words, as conveyor of a (non-verbal) 'opulent mellowness', and as a rhythmic backing, singing clipped, wordless syllables. Each of these roles is clearly present in the chorus's part in 'Oh, Boy!', and each corresponds to one of the three phrases the chorus sings:

OH BOY,   sung as a direct *echo* of the lead singer, each time he sings, 'Oh boy' (i.e. in lines 3 and 4 of verses 1, 2, 4, 5, 6 and 8 – henceforth referred to as 'the main verse').

AAAH,   comparatively undifferentiated rhythmically, as the voices simply slide to new harmonies where required, without closing the vowel sound. This occurs always as a background accompaniment (to the lead voice on the last line of each verse and all through verse 3, and to the lead guitar on the last four 'lines' of the instrumental break), and corresponds to Laing's 'opulent mellowness'. I prefer to call this open, vowel singing, a *beatless word*.

DUM DE DUM DUM,
                 put together with the phrase 'OH BOY', and sung over the first two lines of the instrumental break. This corresponds to Laing's role of 'rhythm section', and we may note that the complete rhythmic pattern, 'DUM DE DUM DUM (rest) OH BOY' is close to Bo Diddley's characteristic rhythm mentioned by Laing in this connection. I have called this rhythmic function that of the *wordless beat*.

Now clearly, these three roles of the chorus place it in a linguistic sphere which is subordinate to that of the lead singer, with his fully articulate command of language. Indeed, the chorus's part can be seen as a stylised deconstruction of 'baby talk', which is used by adults and babies/small children alike in the period prior to 'learning to talk', or mastering language as a symbolic system of communication. The isolation of one semiotic aspect of language, such as melody or rhythm, is characteristic of 'baby-talk', as is the use of echoing between the voices of adult and child. 'Aah', for instance, is a 'word' that passes between mother and baby (in my experience as young as three months) as a kind of verbal transformation of the smile that is the earliest reciprocal communication. This 'Aah' has no rhythm of its own, but is simply a vowel sound pronounced with a sliding, falling pitch, so constituting a kind of 'melody'. Within adult talk, or the symbolic sphere of language, 'Aah' lives on, as an interjection whose meanings include the expression of delight and of understanding that it conveys in 'baby-talk'.

If the 'beatless word' isolates *melody* as one 'semiotic' aspect of language and builds it into a system of communication, *rhythm* forms a complementary semiotic, which can again be isolated from actual words, as 'wordless beats', or what are often called 'nonsense syllables'. But these wordless rhythms are more complex than the pure vowel of the 'beatless word'. 'Dum de dum dum' is neither, linguistically speaking, pure consonants, nor musically speaking, pure rhythm: as music, it has its own melody, and as language, it has vowels. What is more, the repetition of the vowels is fundamental to the possibility of *rhyme*, which is here found in its simplest form as syllabic repetition, whether 'dum' is thought of as representing a whole word, as in 'Tom, Tom, the piper's son', or as part of one, as in 'Hum-pty Dum-pty (sat on a wall)'.

Of course, the syllables 'dum' and 'de' are well chosen for the enunciation of a pattern that approximates pure rhythm by the chorus, since they are conventionally used in adult conversation to communicate the rhythm of a piece of music. They already have, as it were, a symbolic meaning as standing in for beats of music. But this is also to beg the question of what rhythm they are standing in for here, or from the semiotic point of view, what is their material rhythm.

Children's rhythms: an empirical semiotic

In order to answer this question, and to establish more clearly the link between this kind of rhythmic pattern and the language rhythms enjoyed by children, I shall briefly review here the work of the Roumanian musicologist, Constantin Brailoiu (1984), on the topic of 'children's rhythms'. This fascinating essay establishes clearly the existence of 'children's rhythms' as an 'autonomous system', i.e. as one which does not obey the laws of 'classical' rhythm (Brailoiu 1984, p. 206). Perhaps even more striking is the 'autonomy' of this rhythmic system from the *languages* of the many different cultures in which Brailoiu located it. He documents the identity of the system across nineteen countries of Europe, and also includes examples from virtually identical systems among the Eskimo, as well as from Senegal and the Sudan. This is 'all the more remarkable', he comments,

since in the interior construction of children's rhythms, the placing of accents is fixed, whereas languages practice multiple accentuations (the Hungarians fall heavily on the first syllable of words, the Turks on the last, etc.). (Brailoiu 1984, p. 208)

The fundamental point that Brailoiu makes about this system is that it is built up from the combination of single units of duration ('beats') into *pairs*, each unit being the rhythmic equivalent of one short syllable. These units are then linked two by two to make up 'a series worth eight' which is the nearest it is possible to get to a definition, since as few as four syllables may fill the line 'on condition that in the scansion or in the song, they make eight short durations' (e.g. 'Fee, fi, fo, fum', as in giant's talk), and since less than eight units may actually be filled by syllables, provided the empty units are 'counted' in the series (e.g. 'Hickory, dickory, dock [ ], The mouse ran up the clock [ ]) (*ibid.*, p. 209).

The temptation for one trained in classical music theory is to amalgamate these binary couplets into more complex rhythmic systems, so that the primary units (which Brailoiu notates as quavers), become instead 'fractions of imaginary crotchets, thus, sub-units, and the investigation starts with a false idea' (*ibid.*, p. 208). The simplest way to demonstrate this 'autonomy' of the system both from the rhythmic system of classical music, and from the metric system of European poetry, is to look at some examples, using Brailoiu's conventions.[7] In the following, for instance,

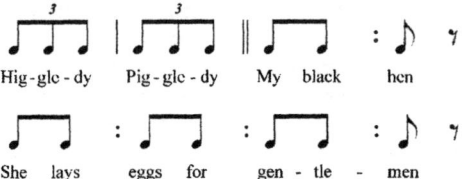

Hig - gle - dy   Pig - gle - dy   My   black   hen

She   lays   eggs   for   gen - tle - men

the accentuation of the last syllable ('men') of 'gentlemen' is at odds with spoken accentuation, and so with the convention of 'poetry'. And if the two lines were to be put into 2/4 bars, according to classical music conventions, then the final syllable 'men' would fall on a weak, unaccented beat. As it is, the system makes it quite clear to us that the accent on 'men' is *equal* to those on 'she', 'eggs' and 'gen-' in the same line. The same can be said about the accentuation on the last syllables of 'ro - *ses*' and 'po - *seys*' in the following:[8]

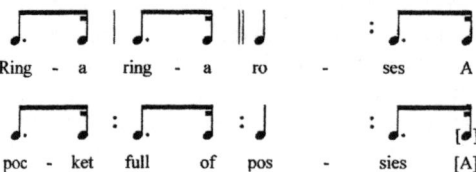

Ring - a   ring - a   ro   -   ses   A

poc - ket   full   of   pos   -   sies   [A]

These examples also illustrate the practice of 'partitioning', which is a fundamental principle of variation in the system. The eight 'beats' of the line are partitioned into two, three or four sections which form autonomous sub-units and which are grouped together through rhyme, word repetition, assonance, the agreement of words which differ only in their ending (e.g. 'Tweedledum and Tweedledee') or 'a succession of parts of phrases with the same construction and accentuation' (*ibid.*, p. 210). This last can be as the partitioning into three of:

Pat it and   prick it and   mark it with   B,

or as the partitioning into two of:

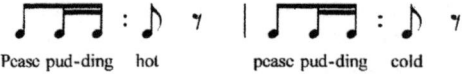

Pease pud-ding   hot   pease pud-ding   cold

(where '|' indicates a partition, and ':' indicates the boundaries between groups of syllables taking up two units where there is no partition. In the two examples quoted earlier, '||' indicates that the consonance is with the following, not the previous line).

Brailoiu's accomplishment is to show not only how the rules for the variation of the system are identical across so many different linguistic cultures, but also how they are compatible with the system's 'strict symmetry' (*ibid.*, p. 238). He shows, for instance, the rules according to which syllables grouped by three can be incorporated into the binary structure, and how the insertion of anacruses (upbeats) is compatible with the logic of the system as always starting on a downbeat.

The relevance of Brailoiu's uncovering of this cross-cultural system for us here is that he shows how rhythm can form a system which is autonomous of any particular language, but not of language-in-general. And yet we know that in our own culture, and presumably in the others from which his examples are drawn, these rhymes form an everyday part of children's language-learning experience, and for adult speakers, are a well-known way of pleasing a child, and gaining his/her attention for language learning. So Brailoiu's system does in fact document empirically a way in which the semiotic aspect of language shapes the way in which the child enters the 'symbolic' sphere.

The rhythms of 'Oh, Boy!'

Returning to rock music, various commentators have noticed the use of 'baby talk' and of nursery rhyme forms within rock music generally (Bradby and Torode 1982), and in the music of Buddy Holly in particular (Cott 1981, p. 78; Bradby and Torode 1984). However, Cott's explanation of the appeal of such rhythms, albeit 'transformed and revitalised' by Holly, as lying in the 'childlike ... insouciance' of the singer, seems inadequate to account for the felt sexuality of rock music. On the other hand, Bradby and Torode's psychoanalytic theory of rock discourse as the reworking of the lullaby language of the mother by the male adolescent remains too general and speculative. Brailoiu's formal description of children's rhymes as a rhythmic system permits a more rigorous analysis of what Holly does with and to these rhythms, which can hopefully lead to more insightful explanations of why they should be appealing in adolescent music.

Figure 3 sets out the rhythms of the song 'Oh, Boy!' in a synchronic arrangement where it is possible to observe small changes in the 'same' line between different verses, etc.[9] While I have transcribed the song in the conventions of the 4/4 time signature of 'classical' rhythm, the rhyming system of the first two lines is immediately reminiscent of Brailoiu's analysis of 'partitioning' in children's rhythms. *If we ignore for the moment the 'syncopated' anticipation of the beat on the words 'you've been missing'*, the lines could be written as:

The partitioning of the first line into two consonant groups of 4 units each can be summarised as 4 + 4 (like the first line of 'Pease pudding hot'). The rhyming of the second line with the first can then be represented as (4 + 4) + 8.[10] As a *rhyming* pattern this is identical, for instance, to:

Pull my finger, | pull my thumb,
I'll tell a p'liceman what you've done
(Opie and Opie 1959, p. 61)

or:

Calling all cars, | calling all stations,
Hitler's lost his combinations
(*Ibid.*, p. 102)

These examples illustrate the use of the (4 + 4) + 8 rhyming system in children's practice, and the second one is very close also to the detail of the *rhythm* in Holly's lines. A clear parallel to Holly's contraction of the rhythm at the end of the lines can be found in the children's rhyme:

76   *Barbara Bradby*

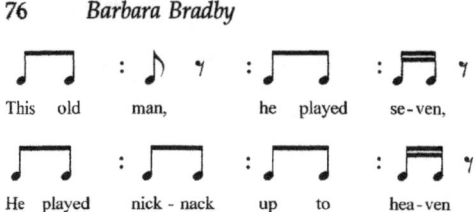

The contraction of 'seven' and 'heaven' into the space occupied by one short unit in this example parallels that of 'kissing' and 'missing' in 'Oh, Boy!'. Brailoiu notes that when a line is 'partitioned' in two, if the first half is 'catalectic' (i.e. ends on an accented unit plus a rest of equivalent duration), then the second half tends to be too. The contraction of the two-syllable words, therefore, enables this rule of symmetry between the two halves of the 'partitioned' first line to be observed in both the nursery rhyme and in 'Oh, Boy!'.[11]

This analysis has shown how close the opening two lines of 'Oh, Boy!' are to 'children's rhythms', but there is a crucial difference, already noted, in the introduction of syncopation on the words 'you've been (missing)', the rhythm of which is here transcribed according to 'classical' conventions in 4/4 bars:

[beats and half-beats of the bar]

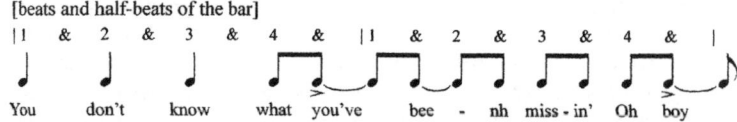

This irruption of syncopation into what otherwise resembles *children's* rhythm is therefore clearly structured as a mark of the passage out of childhood into *adulthood*, or adolescence. The effect is all the more striking if we take into account the verbal meaning of the phrase on which the syncopation enters the song. 'You've been missing' is a succinct expression of an interpersonal absence or lack, and in the 'adult' mode of excitement introduced by the syncopation, we easily understand a sexual lack of some sort. But the 'you' addressed at the beginning of the line is still innocent of sexual desire ('you don't know . . .'), and is therefore approached through children's rhythm. The interaction of verbal and rhythmic meaning already in the first two lines enacts a transition from innocence to desire.

The syncopation continues and is heightened by the intrusion of both syllables of the title phrase 'Oh boy' into the hypothetical 'space' (according to the rules of 'children's rhythms') at the end of this same line. This first 'Oh boy' is both hurried – the syllables fall on consecutive quavers – and syncopated – the word 'boy' falls on the second half of beat 4, anticipating the first beat of the next bar. The emphasis thereby placed on 'boy' both parallels the normal emphasis of 'Oh *boy*' as a spoken exclamation, as well as, internally to the song, paralleling the emphasis on '*you*'ve' in the corresponding beat of the previous bar.

The chorus then immediately echoes the phrase, 'Oh boy', but with a crucial rhythmic difference. The chorus (upper case) *irons out the lead singer's syncopation* and sings both syllables *on the beat* (lines 2–3):

The effect of the occurrence of both syllables on crotchet beats is at once to recall the steadying impulse of children's rhythms, and to evoke a more 'measured' enunciation of the phrase in speech (*Oh, boy*).

The lead singer continues with the phrase 'When you're with me', where the word 'you' is sung *on the beat*, so, through the verbal meaning (the presence of 'you'), setting up another opposition to the syncopation of '*you*'ve (been nh missin') in the previous line. The intervening 'dialogue' with the chorus, however, has established a possible *internal* ('diegetic') reference for 'you' as addressed *to the chorus itself*. 'You' were 'missing' in line 2, causing nervous syncopation in the singer's rhythm, but 'your' (i.e. the chorus's) echoing response to the singer's 'Oh boy' call, means that 'you' are 'with me' by line 3.

At the surface level of the meaning of this song as a 'love song', these phrases simply summon up the absence and presence of 'you', whether understood externally or internally to the song. But the diegetic reading does suggest a further, self-referential level of meaning, in that 'missing' and being 'with me' are part of the discourse of *rhythm* in musical interaction. Syncopation is a form of (intentionally) 'missing' the beat, while for you to be 'with me' means for you to be in time with me.[12]

This reading is confirmed by the continuation of the lead singer's part in line 3. The syllables 'me', 'oh' and 'boy' all occur on syncopated off-beats, but their separation as crotchets gives a strong impression of 'steadying' as compared with the first enunciation of 'Oh boy' by the lead. In this way, the rhythm of 'you're with me, oh boy' is mid-way between the hurried, emphatic syncopation of '*you*'ve been nh missin, oh boy' and the chorus's rock-steady 'OH BOY'. The effect is that of the lead singer imitating, or being steadied up by, the chorus's enunciation of 'OH BOY' on crotchets. In terms of the meaning of the words, he is now much closer to being rhythmically 'with' the chorus' (lines 3–4):

In this sequence of four 'Oh boy's it is the presence of the chorus's rhythm that enables the singer to overcome his nervous, hurried syncopation and get the rhythm (more or less) 'right'. The meaning of 'you're with me', then, cannot be reduced to the chorus *following* the lead singer, as is suggested by describing the dialogue as 'echo', but also includes a *steadying* effect of the chorus on the lead, discernible only through analysing the interplay of rhythm and language – in other words, the semiotic level.

So far, this analysis of rhythm does confirm Cott's description of Holly's 'childlike insouciance', by detecting 'children's rhythms', but it also uncovers another rhythm (syncopation), which seems to lead out of the child's sphere, and to be in some ways contradictory to it. While 'children's rhythms' impose a strict order that distorts what appears by contrast as the 'free' rhythm of speech, the syncopated rhythms are closer to those of (adult) speech. This distinction becomes clearer if we look at verse 3, which (together with its repeat at verse 7) is the contrasting verse musically in the song. The first two lines of this verse evoke clichéd 'poetry', the conventional rhythms of which must *follow* speech rather than dominating it as in 'children's rhythms'. Syncopation is here introduced on the first

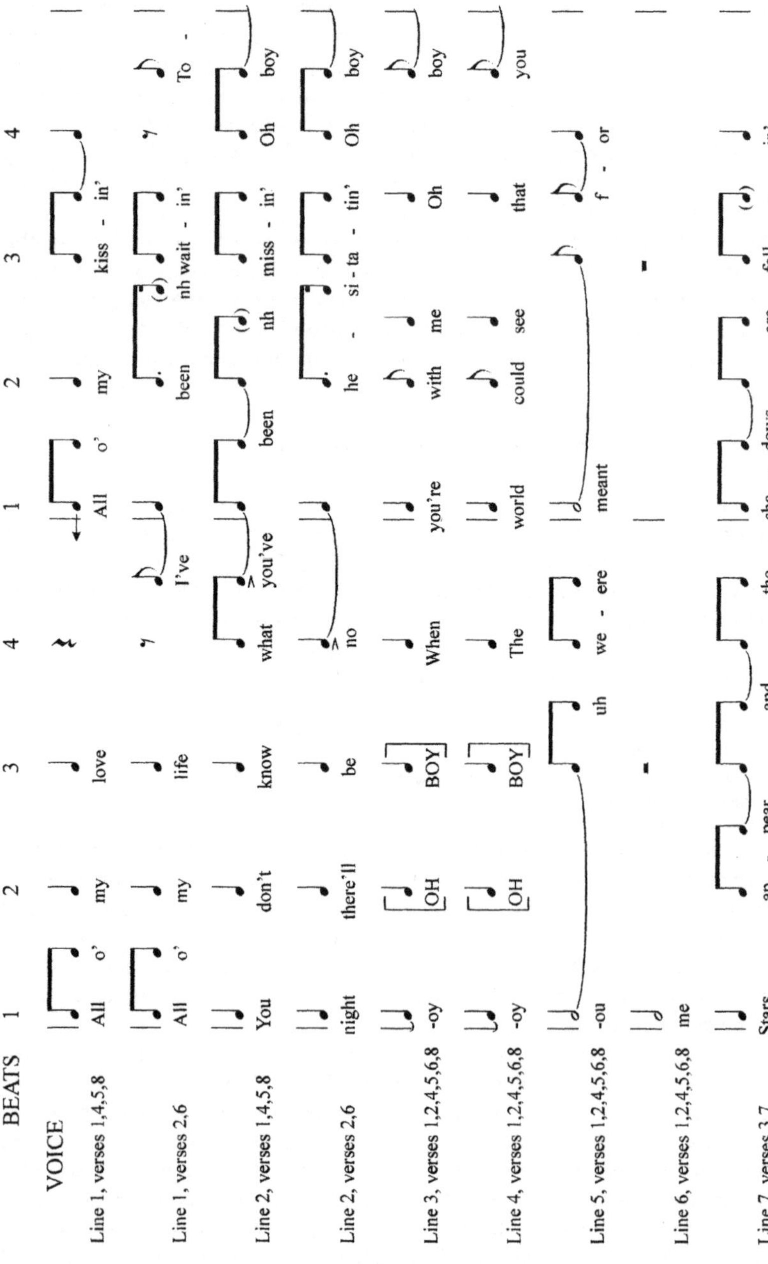
BEATS 1 2 3 4 1 2 3 4
VOICE
Line 1, verses 1,4,5,8 All o' my love All o' my kiss - in'
Line 1, verses 2,6 All o' my life I've been (·) nh wait - in' To -
Line 2, verses 1,4,5,8 You don't know what you've been (·) nh miss - in' Oh boy
Line 2, verses 2,6 night there'll be no he - si - ta - tin' Oh boy
Line 3, verses 1,2,4,5,6,8 -oy OH BOY When you're with me Oh boy
Line 4, verses 1,2,4,5,6,8 -oy OH BOY The world could see that you
Line 5, verses 1,2,4,5,6,8 -ou uh we - ere meant f - or
Line 6, verses 1,2,4,5,6,8 me
Line 7, verses 3,7 Stars ap - pear and the sha - dows are fall - (·) in'

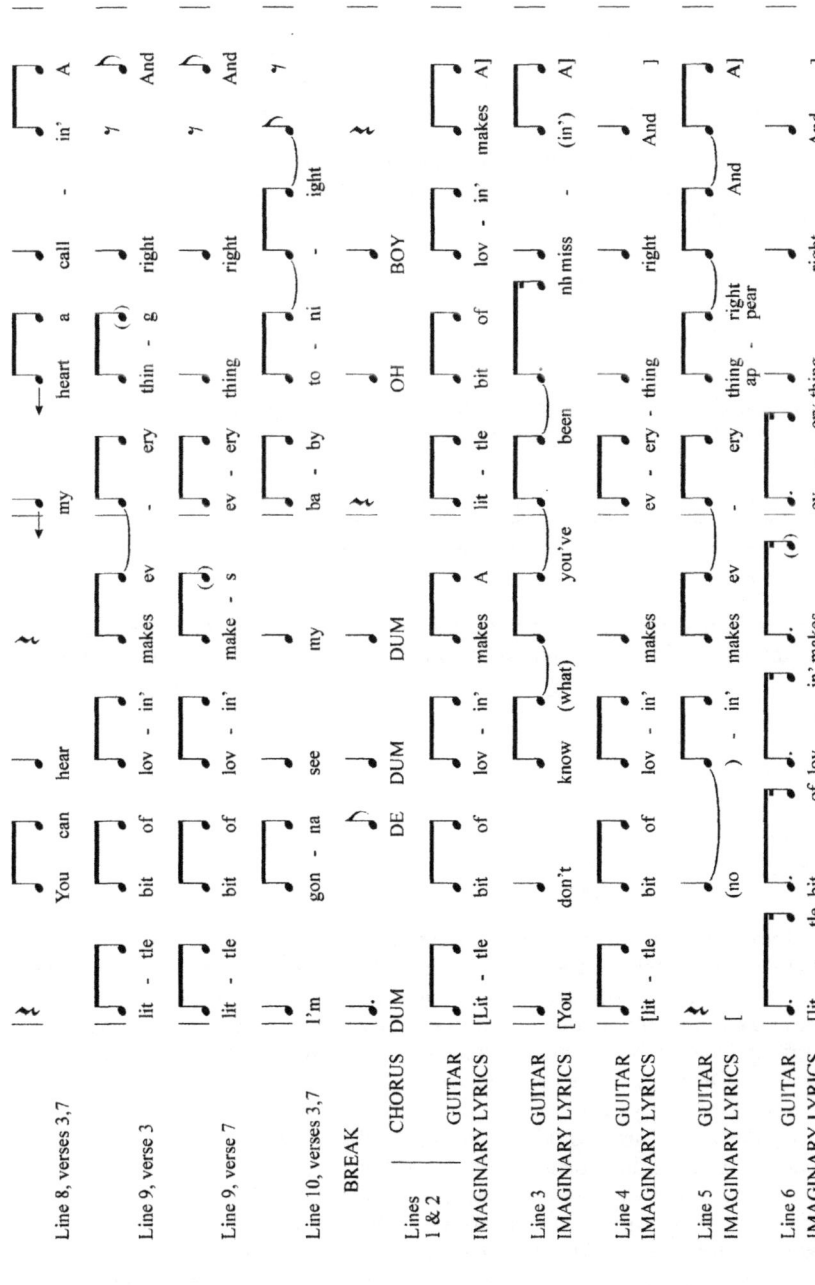

Figure 3. Rhythms of Buddy Holly's 'Oh, Boy!'.

words, allowing 'appear' and 'shadows' to sound as spoken, while the prolongation of 'and' sounds like a nervous pause:

This imitation of nervous speech is heightened in the missed beats of the following line, where the first beat is entirely silent, and both 'my' and 'heart' very slightly anticipate the beat:

However, the third line reintroduces what is unmistakably 'children's rhythm', only to be interrupted by the syncopation on the first syllable of 'everything':

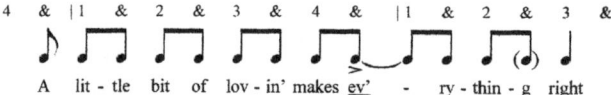

Disregarding this syncopation for the moment, the best way to transcribe this line as 'children's rhythm' seems to be to divide it in half, making two, eight-beat lines:

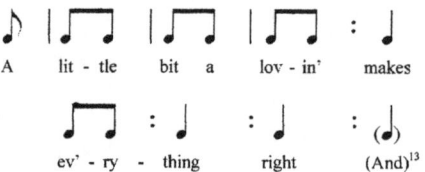

The rhythm is then identical to the nursery-rhyme line(s), 'In a yellow petticoat And a green gown' (with the addition of the first anacrusis), and virtually identical to 'The king was in his counting-house, Counting out (his) money'.

In Holly's line, this patter of children's rhythm is interrupted by the syncopated first syllable of 'e-verything', which occupies what should be the empty beat after 'makes'. Once again, we can analyse the rhythm and accentuation of 'everything' as marking an intrusion of *speech* rhythms into the musical structure of children's rhythms. The same could be said about the last line of verse 3, where the syncopation of 'to-night' corresponds to *spoken* accentuation and rhythm, and intrudes into an otherwise 'on-beat' line (see Figure 3, line 10).

However, if we turn to the repetition of this verse in the second half of the song (sung by lead alone *without* the chorus, see Figure 2), we find a slight change in the rhythm of the third line (i.e. line 9 of Figure 3), which becomes significant in the light of this analysis. For here, *the children's rhythm is maintained throughout the line*, only the exaggerated accentuation of the 's' of 'makes' remaining as a trace of the syncopation the first time around:

4 & |1 & 2 & 3 & 4 & |1 & 2 & 3 &

A lit - tle bit of lov - in' make - s ev - ery-thing right

Again, here, the song makes a meta-statement about rhythm, since making 'everything right' can be understood as getting it in time, getting the rhythm right. Indeed, rhythm becomes a complicated metaphor for sexuality in the song, a metaphor set up through the dual working of verbal and rhythmic meaning. If we ask what has allowed the singer to get the rhythm 'right' the second time around, then the answer the song gives is 'a little bit of lovin'', verbally connoting sex, but rhythmically evoking childhood.

We are still entitled to ask what has enabled this rhythmic resolution of the tensions of the first time around, and to unravel this question we must turn to the musical development that takes place between the two repetitions of verse 3, i.e. to the 'instrumental break', which is not simply a guitar break, since the voices of the chorus also figure prominently.

Voices and rhythm in the instrumental break

The break in 'Oh, Boy!' can be seen as an economical working-out, at the rhythmic level, of the relationship between key phrases that we have already encountered. As Laing observes, Holly's work in guitar breaks 'reiterates something that has gone before, rather than introduces something new into the song' (Laing 1971, p. 52). But because what we are looking at is a *song*, rhythmic sequences are first set out in conjunction with words: when these same rhythmic sequences are played on their own, they recall the words to which they were set. Bradby and Torode (1984) have argued that through this process of recollection, an instrumental break can create 'imaginary lyrics'.

The phrases so recalled in the break in 'Oh, Boy!' are set out along a numerical grid indicating beats of the bar in Figure 4. (The musical notation of the rhythms can be found in Figure 3.) In this break, not only the playing of the lead guitar, but also the 'wordless beats' of the chorus, recall rhythms from the verses of the song. If we focus first on the part of the chorus in the break, we find that the three phrases of its part in the whole song are here all present: 'DUM DE DUM DUM', 'OH BOY' and 'AAAH'. As has already been pointed out, 'dum de dum dum' is a conventional indication that one is tapping out the rhythm of *another* phrase: it stands in for a musical phrase. If we ask what it is standing in for here, then the answer must be the words 'you're with me oh' as sung by the lead in the main verse. Firstly, the rhythms are almost identical: the chorus here sings ♩ ♪ ♩ ♩ while the lead in the verses sings ♩ ♪ ♩ ♩ on these four words. The small difference of the additional half-beat taken by the chorus on 'you're' amounts once again to the chorus's 'ironing out' of Holly's syncopations by making them appear as 'anticipations' of main beats, an effect already observed in the analysis of the main verse. Secondly, the placing of 'DUM DE DUM DUM' in relation to the chorus's 'OH BOY' in the break exactly parallels the placing of the lead's 'you're with me oh' in the bar before the chorus's identical 'OH BOY' in the main verse.

82   *Barbara Bradby*

Beats:	1	&	2	&	3	&	4	&	1	&	2	&	3	&	4	&
line 1:	lit-	tle	bit	of	lo-	vin	makes	A	lit-	tle	bit	of	lov-	in	makes	A
	DUM		DE		DUM		DUM		<.......>		OH		BOY			
	[YOU'RE		WITH	ME			OH		<.......>		OH		BOY]			
line 2:	lit-	tle	bit	of	lo-	vin	makes	A	lit-	tle	bit	of	lov-	in	makes	A
	DUM		DE		DUM		DUM		<.......>		OH		BOY			
	[YOU'RE		WITH	ME			OH		<.......>		OH		BOY]			
line 3:	You	don't			know	(what)			you've	been			nhmiss		(in)	A
	AAAH	–	–		–	–	–		–	–	–	–	–		–	–
line 4:	lit-	tle	bit	of	lo-	vin	makes		ev-	ery-	thing		right		And	
	AAAH	–	–		–	–	–		–	–	–	–	–		–	–
line 5:	<.......>	(no		)		-vin	makes	ev	–	ery	thing	(right	And)			A
											ap-	pear	And			
	AAAH	–	–		–	–	–		–	–	–	–	–		–	–
line 6:	lit-	tle	bit	of	lo-	vin	makes		eve-	ry	thing		right			
	AAAH	–	–	–	–	–	–	–	–		–	–	–	–	–	

Figure 4. 'Imaginary lyrics' of the instrumental break in 'Oh, Boy!' (lower case = 'imaginary lyrics' of guitar solo; upper case = chorus; [ ] indicates the 'imaginary lyrics' behind chorus's actual lyrics in this break; <. . .> indicates a rest; ( ) indicates that rhythm of 'imaginary lyric' is marginally changed from actual lyric).

This use of 'DUM DE DUM DUM' in the break to recall the lyric 'You're with me' of the main verse sets up an association between the *material beat* of the chorus and the *presence* of 'you'. Having thereby established itself as the material beat indicative of 'your' presence, the chorus's part in the break goes on to a reminder of its earlier 'correction' of the singer's beat, its 'OH BOY'. The blank beat, or rest, between the last 'DUM' and the 'OH' is graphically placed so as to omit any reference to the beat occupied by the *singer's* word 'boy' in the rhythm of this line. This means that we are reminded only of the chorus's steadying influence, and not of the ambivalence of the singer's rhythm on the words 'oh boy'. And we can also remind ourselves here that the whole rhythmic phrase so formed (DUM DE DUM DUM . . . OH BOY) evokes Bo Diddley's beat, a point to which we shall return.

The guitar lead that accompanies the chorus during these first two lines is decidedly 'restrained', and in fact taps out four 8-beat 'lines' of the most basic 'children's rhythm', corresponding to the words from the verses, 'A lit-tle bit of lo-vin' makes', repeated four times over. The fact that both the chorus and the guitar parts are here on monotones both foregrounds *rhythm* and creates the impression of restraint.

If the chorus's 'imaginary lyrics' on these first two lines bring it the closest to an actual subject position that it gets in the song, this 'person' disappears from line 3 onwards in the break, as the chorus retires into the background on the 'beatless word' 'AAAH'. The guitar takes the lead here, launching out on a new melody to the syncopated rhythm of the line, 'You don't know what you've been nh missin'' (the syncopation is slightly greater than in the verse, as the beat corresponding to the word 'what' is also brought back by the guitar onto an anticipatory off-beat). This means that the *absence* of the chorus's beat (as it abandons 'DUM DE DUM DUM' and relapses into the prolonged 'AAAH') is here associated with the absence of *you* ('you've been missing'). This provides striking confirmation (by opposition) of the connection between the material beat of the chorus and the *presence* of 'you' in lines 1 and 2 of the break, analysed above.

At line 4 of the break, the guitarist regains an on-beat rhythm, and in fact here completes the lines of 'children's rhythm' begun in the first two lines. The full rhythmic sequence of the words 'A little bit of lovin' makes Everything right' here appears for the first time in the song entirely *on the beat*, i.e. to the correct 'children's rhythm'. The work of the guitar has set up the association which the voice will take up after the break, allowing the singer to make 'everything right'.

However, the on-beat rhythm is contested yet again at line 5, where the guitar syncopation is heightened even further, an exaggerated emphasis on an off-beat crotchet recalling the 'no' of 'Tonight there'll be *no* hesitatin'', and the subsequent off-beat quavers recalling the first, syncopated version of 'makes everything right'. However, these tensions achieve a resolution in the final line of the break, where the 'correct', on-beat rhythm of 'A little bit of lovin' makes everything right' is repeated from line 4. The rhythms here sound 'dotted', which is, of course, a common variation in 'children's rhythms', and which merely exaggerates, (parodies?) the on-beat emphasis.

It is within this break, therefore, that the conflict of rhythms in the song is at its most intense. This conflict is worked out in relation to key rhythmic phrases from the song, all of which had previously emerged as important in the analysis of the song's rhythm:

'You don't know what you've been nh missin'', which introduced the hurried, off-beat rhythm of 'you', followed by the hurried, off-beat 'Oh boy';

'You're with me, oh boy', which restored the rhythm, placing 'you' on the beat, then steadying 'Oh boy' onto crotchet lengths;

'A little bit of lovin' makes everything right', the line whose syncopations before the break are virtually ironed out in its repetition after it.

The break therefore presents the drama of the song reduced to its most skeletal structure. The on-beat rhythms of 'your' presence and 'a little bit of lovin' (lines 1–2) are disturbed by the syncopated beats of 'your' absence (line 3). But the continuation by the guitarist of 'a little bit of lovin'' goes on to 'make everything right' (line 4), the latter part of this line occurring here for the first time on the beat. A setback occurs with the negative 'no' (line 5): the regular beat of 'a little bit of lovin'' is lost, and 'makes everything right' is thrown right off the beat, but the emphatic restatement of the whole phrase 'A little bit of lovin' makes everything right' (line 6) restores the on-beat rhythm and closes the break.

This analysis of the rhythmic 'work' of the break allows us to see the structure of the whole song as involving a process of 'exposition' (first four verses), 'development' (instrumental break), and 'recapitulation' (repeat of exposition, but with tensions resolved). In the exposition, the singer's statement 'a little bit of lovin' makes everything right' was symbolically coherent, but materially empty, since we do not yet know what is a 'right' or 'wrong' way for the line to sound. By the time of its repetition at verse 7, the statement has gained a material meaning, since we now know that the singer 'makes everything right' when he sings this phrase on the beat. With hindsight, we can see that the first way of singing it was rhythmically 'wrong' so that the sound of the words *contradicted* their symbolic meaning. And the analysis has shown that it is in the 'development' process in the break that the 'right' rhythm is introduced, gaining force by its juxtaposition with 'wrong', highly syncopated versions.

Mutual desirability and musical structure

This analysis of the development of rhythmic differences in 'Oh, Boy!' and of the way these differences are played out between the different voices enables us to see how the song enacts a *return to the semiotic* as the way in which the adolescent acquires a new, sexual identity. This return reverses the usual priority of symbolic over semiotic, and of lead singer over chorus. In the empirical wealth of 'children's rhythms', the song finds resources with which to undo and rework the fixing of gender identity in the symbolic sphere. The play of difference between children's rhythms and adult speech creates tension in the song, but what emerges is a restructuring of speech by children's rhythms. The symbolic is *audibly* structured by the semiotic.

It is the role of the chorus to continually bring in and recall these children's rhythms, the crucial characteristic of which here is their 'on-beat' nature, as opposed to the fluidity of speech and syncopation. The first such on-beat occurrence in the song is the chorus's first 'Oh boy', and the most elaborate version of this is the chorus's 'Dum-de-dum-dum, Oh boy' during the 'instrumental break'. The chorus alternates from these 'wordless beats' of 'children's rhythms' back to its entirely supportive 'beatless word' – the mirroring 'Aaah' of baby talk. In this way the chorus audibly represents the de- and re-composition of adult speech into its semiotic elements of rhythm and melody. But it also represents and evokes childhood – even babyhood – and thereby also the sphere of the mother, so giving substance to Kristeva's theory of the semiotic sphere as the material traces of the mother's body within language. If the chorus plays a maternal role to the adolescent male singer in this way, it is striking that its supportive 'Aaah' disappears in verse 7, the repeat of verse 3, where 'Aaah' had been prominent before the break. The fact that the lead here sings the middle eight verse on his own – the verse that envisages the transition from day to night and from innocence to 'loving' – suggests a narrative development away from dependence on the chorus/mother and towards the independence imagined in adult masculinity.

Questions remain about the gender address of this song, and about the buddy group structure that is the internal context that the song provides for itself, fixed in the recorded performance. In a sense, the detailed analysis just confirms the initial 'hunch' that 'Oh boy' and its echo by the chorus represent cries of mutual admiration and desire on the part of two male voices. But there is more to be said. Firstly, we must return to the ambivalence of this 'literal' interpretation with the conventional hearing of the song as addressed to a woman/girl, (confirmed but also disrupted by the reference to 'my baby' at the end of verse 3). When the words 'Oh boy' first appear, they are heard as a continuation of the first two lines, 'All my love, etc.', and therefore as a *narcissistic* expression of wonder on the part of the singer at his abilities in loving and kissing. This is compatible with a hearing of 'You don't know what you've been missing' (line 2) as addressed *either* to a potential female recipient of the loving, *or* to a male innocent, whom Holly exhorts to become a lover of women himself. *Both* of these 'hearings' are, of course, conventional heterosexual ones. But it is the male address of the second one that lays the ground for the 'literal' hearing of the chorus's 'OH BOY!' echo as introducing *mutuality* of admiration/desire on the part of the two 'boys'. Of course, this 'literal' homosexual address is immediately contradicted by the conventional hearing of 'When you're with me' as addressed to a woman. (And yet again our expectations are confounded, as this line continues directly on into the vocative address to the 'boy': 'When you're with me, oh boy'.)

This sliding of the gender address between various possible sexualities may be seen as a radical ambivalence, or simply as a maximisation of possible audiences for the song as commodity. Another way of putting this is that Buddy Holly's song 'works' on a different level from most 'transgressive novels' or avant-garde films. It communicates its sexual meaning(s) seductively and economically, and consequently had – probably still has – a mass audience. But from a feminist point of view, this takes me back to that film scene I started from. Both the song and the film seem to show male narcissism as constructing a male 'other' as audience, even when ostensibly addressing/desiring a woman. Once this elementary 'buddy group' is constructed, the intervening woman becomes at best irrelevant. What film critics have written about as the structural exclusion of the female spectator here has a correlate in song (Taylor and Laing 1979). But it should not be thought of as having the status of a necessary truth. On the contrary, we must *de*construct the buddy group to show the male audience *as* a construction.

Our analysis has shown that this 'masculinisation' of sexuality in 'Oh, Boy!' is both more evident and more illusory than conventional hearings suggest. The masculinisation of the audience is achieved only through the recall and elaboration of 'children's rhythms' and 'baby talk', directly evocative of the maternal sphere of early language and interaction. While the adult, or adolescent, sexuality of rock 'n' roll is achieved in some sense in *opposition* to this maternal sphere, it is not achieved *without* it. The chorus in this prototypical 'boy-group' song, while far from the articulacy and conflict of that in 'girl-group' music,[14] is also far from being a mere 'echo'. And as with the girl-group choruses, much of the *strength* of the boy-group chorus seems to derive from its appropriation/representation of the semiotic, maternal elements of language. The difference is that the boy-group chorus never challenges the lead singer: rather than the egalitarian rivalry of the girl-group dialogue, the boy-group portrays a consensual hierarchy.

Secondly, there is the question of the *differences* that the analysis has established between the two voices in the buddy group, and the nature of the relationship between them. Hodge and Kress have argued that there is a necessary ambivalence between the vertical relationships of 'power' and horizontal ones of 'solidarity', in representations of gender within patriarchy (Hodge and Kress 1988, pp. 52–68). So, we could argue, the two voices show *solidarity* in the apparent egalitarianism of their 'Oh boy' echoes, but we can also find *power* in the verbal dominance of the singer over the chorus, a power that typically obscures the material work of the chorus in correcting the singer's rhythm. We could also find a semblance of 'solidarity' in the singer's address of the desired 'you' with children's rhythms, especially in the line, 'A little bit of loving makes everything right'. It is as if, having represented her as 'baby', he then descends to her level to talk to and please her. His return to adult speech (e.g. with syncopated 'everything') is like an involuntary expression of male desire/power. On the other hand, the 'power' that we have discovered in the chorus's ability to correct and steady the singer's rhythm cannot be understood if we simply see the relationship between the boys in the group as the solidarity of equals. The invisibility of this material *work* performed by the chorus suggests an analogy with that of the mother for the son in the home. But the other analogy suggested is that of the invisibility of black musicians' creativity in its appropriation by white rock stars, itself a transformation of the historical relationship between master and slave.

The influence of black musicians on Buddy Holly has been documented (Laing 1971), and Holly himself acknowledged his debt to Bo Diddley, in covering his song 'Bo Diddley' (1955). This song is itself a variation on the ubiquitous nursery rhyme, 'Hush little baby', and was reworked in a number of variations by Diddley himself, including 'Hey Bo Diddley' (1957), and 'Hush Your Mouth' (1958). Following this lead, Holly himself also did a variation on the musical basis of the 'Bo Diddley' song in his 'Not Fade Away' – the second cover emphasising his interest in Diddley, but also appropriating his rhythms for his own lyrics.

As already mentioned, the rhythm of the chorus's 'Dum de dum dum ... oh boy' in the break of 'Oh Boy!' is immediately evocative of Bo Diddley's distinctive rhythm developed in these and other songs. Something very close to it can be heard in the long instrumental section that closes Bo Diddley's original song of that name, where the basic shuffle becomes in the fadeout:

It can also be heard in Diddley's 'Pretty Thing', another 1955 release, where a harmonica intones the rhythm on a monotone (amidst other scoring) in the long instrumental break, and (with the guitar) in the fadeout at the end.[15]

It should also be noted that the 'Hey, Bo Diddley' call/response in the song of that name is more or less equivalent[16] to a half-time version of the 'Dum de dum dum' rhythm (though this song has a faster basic beat than Diddley's others on the theme).

Holly's own cover of 'Bo Diddley', and his variation in 'Not Fade Away', can be heard as his own representations of the Bo Diddley sound. In 'Not Fade Away', a thickly scored, rhythm and chorus 'response' (which also opens the song), alternates with Holly's own vocal 'call', which is accompanied only by a softer, solo drum beat. The first bar of this light, drum accompaniment beats out the identical rhythm to 'dum de dum dum' in 'Oh Boy!':

while the second bar of 'Not Fade Away's contrasting drum/chorus riff is identical to the emphatic 'two-three' rhythm of the chorus's 'Oh boy' throughout the latter song:[17]

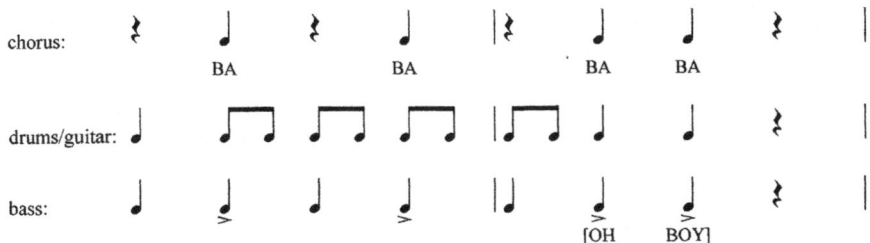

In my own hearing, Holly's guitar break in 'Not Fade Away' combines these two phrases into something very similar to the complete rhythm of 'dum de dum dum . . . oh boy':

Returning to 'Oh, Boy!', the chorus's use of these 'Bo Diddley' rhythms in conjunction with the 'imaginary lyrics', 'you're with me oh . . . oh boy', can then be heard as *Holly's evocation of Bo Diddley's steadying response.*[18] And if 'you're with me' is an association set-up within the song itself, there is also a (less accessible) external association with the words 'Hey, Bo Diddley', from Diddley's song of that name. These two phrases become a 'call' and 'response', both summoned up by the use of 'dum de dum dum' – syllables conventionally used in conversation to indicate rhythm, or in the case of a song, when one cannot recall its words. With these associations in mind, the simplest and most economical evocation of Bo Diddley's rhythm becomes the chorus's steadying enunciation of 'Oh boy' on the 'two-three' rhythm throughout the song. In other words, the title of the song itself encapsulates this 'call' to, and evocation of the response of, Bo Diddley, which can be heard in the performance of the song.

If 'Oh, Boy!', then, imagines the rhythmic relation between singer and chorus as that of Buddy Holly to Bo Diddley, this adds a further dimension to the earlier observations about the potential reference of the song's key statement to rhythm itself. The singer's desire for 'you' to be 'with me' models the conventional view of the woman's place in love as being to keep in time with the man, on the white rock musician's need to keep in time with his black master. This, in turn, is represented rhythmically as the restructuring of adult speech by the strict rhythm of children. Bo Diddley's use of children's rhythms was explicit. His name itself (like 'Buddy Holly') forms a section of binary rhythm, and could be read as formed by the insertion of the nursery-rhyme, nonsense-word 'diddle' into the word 'boy'. He reworked nursery rhymes in many of his songs, especially the 'autobiographical' ones, as if continually rewriting his narrative of transition from child to adult (Bradby and Torode 1982). This form was taken over by Holly when he covered 'Bo Diddley', and more generally, as we have seen, in his use of 'children's rhythms'.

This reversal, where the child teaches the adult, the black man the white man, does help to explain how rock represented a space where sexuality was 'freed' from adult and patriarchal constrictions. But a problem remains. If the chorus's Bo

Diddley rhythm in 'Oh, Boy!' is heard as a *response*, we must also ask what it is responding to. The obvious answer is the phrase 'Oh boy', heard literally as a call, and which first summons the chorus into the song. Holly's invocation of solidarity with the black musician here founders on the reality of racism. For a white man cannot address a black man as 'boy' without evoking the traditional call of the white master to the black slave. Perhaps in the end, Holly's 'solidarity' fails to gloss over the history of racism in the New World.

The position of the white musician 'paying tribute' to his black 'master' was seen from the *black* musician's point of view, in Chuck Berry's autobiographical film, *Hail, hail, rock and roll*. Organised around an attempt by white British rock stars to pay their debt to Berry by arranging a fiftieth birthday concert for him in the Opera House in St. Louis, the film shows Berry's sadness that his dream of breaking down racial barriers with his music was made meaningless by its adoption as white culture. *He* has entered the Opera House, the citadel of the slave-owning classes, but thirty years on, the audience still remains, almost exclusively, white.

However, Chuck Berry has the last laugh, and it is a *rhythmic* one. Faced with the white musicians who made millions out of their appropriation of his riffs, returning humbly and wishing only to 'jam' with him as equals, Berry delights in showing them that they still can't play 'with' him. In fact, they can't even get his most basic, most famous, rhythmic riff 'right'. Gently, subversively, he shows them how the guitar introduction to 'Sweet Little Sixteen' should go. But their imitations sound wooden by comparison, and it's not clear whether they even get the point. Berry's demonstration points up, as economically as anything, the limitations to 'solidarity', and the inadequacies of the 'buddy group' as a form for overcoming social divisions.

Copyright acknowledgements

Endnotes

1. 'In the Still of the Nite' has been described as 'one of the greatest rhythm and blues ballads of all time' by Jay Warner (1992, p. 168), as 'this all-time doo-wop classic' by Alan Warner (1990, p. 127), and as an 'all time fave oldie' by Hansen (1981, p. 87). Written by Fred Parris, lead singer of the Five Satins, it was originally put out on Standard 200 as the B Side to 'The Jones Girl' in March 1956, and was reissued on Ember 1005 in June 1956. Later that year, 'the label was revised to read "(I'll Remember) In the Still of the Nite" in order to differentiate it from Cole Porter's standard' (Warner 1992). Note that the new title also plays on the 'nostalgia' of remembering the standard, as well as acting as an advertisement for the song itself in the way pointed to by Adorno (1978).

2. Cf. the Mystics' 'Hushabye' (Laurie 3028), another 'doo-wop' hit from 1959, which is explicitly in the form of a lullaby, but this time sung by the man to the woman.

3. 'Oh, Boy!' was put out on Brunswick 55035 in the USA on 27 October 1956, and peaked at No. 10 in the charts on 2 December. It was released in the UK on 22 December that year. It was written by Sunny West, Bill Tilghman and Norman Petty. As with Holly's other Brunswick releases, the song was actually recorded in the name of his band, the Crickets. Although their name suggests soothing background voices, they were, in fact, the instrumental band, not the vocal backing group, which, on this record, was called 'the Picks'.

4. This corresponds to the opinion of Dave Laing, for instance, in his book on Buddy Holly: 'the

feature which most obviously dates The Crickets' records is the group of voices which backs
Holly on all of them. The harmonies are those
of barber-shop quartets, and to the '70s ear the
contrast between the raw energy of Holly's
delivery and the WASP-ish tones of the vocal
backing can be distracting.' (Laing 1971, p. 50)

5. Schwenger (1979) provides an illuminating
discussion of the 'buddy movie' as a construction of male–male relationships, using the
example of *Deliverance*. I am grateful to Brian
Torode for pointing out to me the Eagles' epitomising of the buddy-group ideology of
'independence from women' in their performance of the lines, 'And I found out a long time
ago / What a woman can do to your soul /
Ah but she can't take you any way / You don't
already know how to go' (from 'Peaceful Easy
Feeling').

6. The settings of the two songs make this clear:
'In the Still of the Nite' is set 'before dawn',
while 'Oh, Boy!' is set at dusk ('Stars appear
and the shadows are falling').

7. A brief explanation of the characters used for
dividing sections of rhythm from each other is
given below in the text. A full explanation is
contained in Brailoiu's article.

8. This last example is of the second broad type
outlined by Brailoiu, in that it combines the
short unit of duration with pairs of units of
double the length, i.e. crotchets. The crotchet
pairs form rhymes and are varied according
to the same system as the quaver pairs, however.

9. Figure 3 represents my own attempt to transcribe onto paper what I hear in the song.
Like all transcriptions, therefore, its apparent
objectivity masks a subjective element. I have
also consciously, and no doubt unconsciously, simplified some of the variations
between verses, in the interests of producing
a representation of the song's rhythms that
can be viewed on a single page. I am also
aware that I have not even aspired to complete accuracy in registering the exact anticipation of each beat by Holly's voice. However, I believe that this last aspect escapes
purely musical notation, since part of the
effect is achieved by the clipped pronunciation of the first or last consonant of a word
or syllable, slightly separating it from the
vowel sound that succeeds or precedes it. I
am very grateful to Allan Moore for his help
and advice on the transcriptions. Responsibility for their shortcomings is my own.

10. I have chosen to ignore the repetition of
'you' in the second line, which hints at a
kind of assonance between the two halves of
the line. Examples of such assonance in the

second line of a couplet in English children's
verse are quite few and far between, but see
for instance 'I see the moon and the moon
sees me, God bless the moon, and God bless
me' (Opie and Opie 1951, p. 312), or 'There
was a mayd that eate an apple, When she
eate two, she eat a couple' (*Ibid.*, p. 311).
However, neither of these combines the
assonance in the second line with the greater
repetitive assonance in the first that is found
in Holly's verse (i.e. a (4 + 4) + (4 + 4)
structure in Brailoiu's terms). To find this
we have to look for parallels among highly
repetitive action rhymes, such as 'Fly away
Peter, fly away Paul, Come back Peter, come
back Paul', or 'Here sit the little chickens,
here they run in, Chin chopper, chin chopper, chin chopper, chin' (Opie and Opie 1951,
p. 279). Far more usual is the (4 + 4) + 8
structure, where an initial repetition leads
away to difference in the second line.

11. This symmetrical partitioning may seem
strange in the case of 'This old man . . .' since
there is no obvious consonance between the
two halves of the line. But as soon as we
bring *melody* into the analysis, then it is clear
that the usual tune produces such a consonance, by setting both halves of the line to an
identical 'sol-mi-sol' pattern.

12. The metaphor of rhythm for sexuality and,
more generally, for harmony in relationships
is, of course, widespread in popular music. In
disco music and the subsequent plethora of
'dance' forms, it has taken on new importance.
The Rolling Stones' 'Baby, baby, baby you're
out of time' is one, very literal example from
the rock era.

13. I have 'partitioned' the first line in three as
I hear an assonance between 'little' and 'bit
a', and between the 'l's of 'little' and of 'lovin''. In 'children's rhythms', the up-beat at
the beginning of the line would generally
be matched by a symmetrical up-beat at the
beginning of the following line: alternatively
it could be 'compensated' by a rest of equivalent value in the empty beat at the end of
the line. Holly's syncopation of the first syllable of 'e - verything' plays on this ambiguity of expectations. The syllable occupies
the last beat of the line *as if* it were an unaccented syllable attached to the beginning of
the next line. Whereas, in fact, it turns out
to be accented, and so 'misplaced' from
where it belongs, on the first beat of the next
line. The Opies' orally collected versions of
'Ring a ring a roses' demonstrate this point.
Most versions that start with the up-beat on
the first line continue with the up-beat onto
the second line, as:

90   *Barbara Bradby*

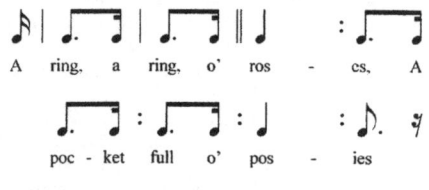

A   ring,   a   ring,   o'   ros   -   cs,   A

poc - ket   full   o'   pos   -   ies

(Opie and Opie 1985, p. 222)

However, one version, dating from 1840, has a compensatory rest at the end of the first line:

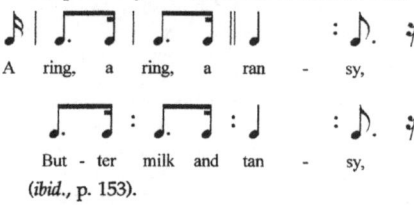

A   ring,   a   ring,   a   ran   -   sy,

But - ter   milk   and   tan   -   sy,

(*ibid.*, p. 153).

14. Striking examples of chorus parts that come into conflict with the desires of the lead singer can be found in The Cookies' 'Don't Say Nothin' Bad (About My Baby)', in The Shirelles' 'Foolish Little Girl', and in The Chiffons' 'Sweet Talkin' Guy'. See Bradby (1990) for analyses of these and other examples.

15. The whole rhythm occurs again very clearly in 'Hush Your Mouth', but as this was not released on record until 1958 it is not clear whether Holly himself would have heard it before recording 'Oh, Boy!'.

16. As with many of the repeated riffs here transcribed, slight variations are evident in the rhythm as it is repeated throughout the song. In this case, there is sometimes a slight anticipation of the beat on the second syllable of Did-dley, or a pattern that might be better construed as its lengthening into the three-syllable 'Did-duh-ley'.

17. At one level, these similarities between the parts of the chorus in 'Oh, Boy!' and 'Not Fade Away' are unsurprising, since the two songs were recorded around the same time, and were released as A and B sides of the same single (Beecher, n.d.). Beecher also informs us that Holly overdubbed the backing vocals in

'Not Fade Away' himself, rather than leaving the basic track for the Picks to finish off.

18. The rhythms of 'dum de dum dum ... oh boy' are close to a number of rhythmic phrases in Holly's songs from this period. 'You're gonna say you'll ... miss me' – the main phrase of the lead vocal in 'I'm Gonna Love You Too', repeated eighteen times across the song – is very close to the whole phrase in 'Oh, Boy!', and shares the distinctive second/third beat emphasis in the second bar. The words 'rave on' from the song of that name also share this distinctive second/third beat accentuation on their first occurrence in the verses. (The 'cra-zy feelin' continuation of this phrase uses the rhythm of 'dum de dum dum', so representing the inversion, '... oh boy ... dum de dum dum'.) The guitar introduction to 'Heartbeat' is close to the first bar of 'dum de dum dum' (with the addition of the distinctive syncopated quaver on beat one-and-a-half). It seems worth pointing out that the second/third beat sequence that is so distinctive of Bo Diddley and of Holly's echoes of him is also utterly distinctive of the Afro-Cuban *clave* rhythm that underlies the *son* that was popular during the 1950s and is said by Cubans to be the basis of salsa and other subsequent forms:

1   &   2   &   3   &   4   &   ‖   1   &   2   &   3   &   4   &

x   x   x   x   x

The first bar of this *clave* rhythm is, of course, also quite close to 'dum de dum dum' (one could say that the *clave* syncopates the 'children's rhythm' by omitting the second 'dum'). Holly's guitar break in 'Not Fade Away' leans towards this syncopation, as does the introduction to 'Heartbeat', but it can be heard more explicitly in the *chorus*'s enunciation (together with lead vocal) of 'Rave on, it's a', in 'Rave On', and in the lead vocal's words 'miss, when my' from 'Heartbeat'. I have not been able to find any analysis of what would seem to be an important cross-cultural connection, though Warner (1990, p. 39) does refer to Bo Diddley's 'rocking rumba rhythms'.

References

Adorno, T. 1978. 'On the fetish character in popular music and the regression of listening', in *The Essential Frankfurt Reader*, ed. A. Arato and E. Gehbardt (New York)

Baudrillard, J. 1988. 'Simulacra and simulations', in *Selected Writings*, ed. M. Poster (Oxford)

Beecher, J. [n.d.] Sleeve notes to double LP, *Buddy Holly, Legend*, MCA Coral, Rainbow Series, MCLD606

Bradby, B. 1990. 'Do-talk and don't-talk: the division of the subject in girl-group music', in *On Record: a Rock and Pop Reader*, ed. S. Frith and A. Goodwin (New York)

Bradby, B., and Torode, B. 1982. 'Song-work: the musical inclusion, exclusion, and representation of women', paper delivered to the Annual Conference of the British Sociology Association, Manchester, April

1984. 'Pity Peggy Sue', *Popular Music*, 4

Brailoiu, C. 1984. 'Children's rhythms', Chapter 11 of *Problems of Ethnomusicology*, ed. and trans. A.L. Lloyd (Cambridge)

Cott, J. 1981. 'Buddy Holly', in *The Rolling Stone History of Rock and Roll*, ed. J. Miller (London), pp. 77–82

Frith, S. 1988. 'Why do songs have words?', in *Music For Pleasure: Essays in the Sociology of Pop* (Oxford)

Grossberg, L. 1988. 'You (still) have to fight for your right to party: music television as billboards of post-modern difference', *Popular Music*, 7/3, pp. 315–32

Hansen, B. 1981. 'Doo-wop', in *The Rolling Stone History of Rock and Roll*, ed. J. Miller (London), pp. 83–91

Hodge, B., and Kress, J. 1988. *Social Semiotics* (Oxford)

Kristeva, J. 1980. *Desire in Language*, ed. L. Roudiez and trans. T. Gora *et al.* (Oxford)

1982. 'Women's time', in *Feminist Theory: a Critique of Ideology*, ed. N. Keohane, M. Rosaldo and B. Gelpi (Chicago and London)

Lacan, J. 1977. *Ecrits: a Selection* (London)

Laing, D. 1969. *The Sound of Our Time* (London)

1971. *Buddy Holly* (London)

Opie, I., and Opie, P. 1951. *The Oxford Dictionary of Nursery Rhymes* (London)

1959. *The Lore and Language of Schoolchildren* (Oxford)

1985. *The Singing Game* (Oxford)

Schwenger, P. 1979. 'The masculine mode', *Critical Inquiry*, No. 5

Taylor, J., and Laing, D. 1979. 'Disco–pleasure–discourse', *Screen Education*, No. 31, Summer

Warner, A. 1990. *Who Sang What in Rock and Roll* (London)

Warner, J. 1992. *The Billboard Book of American Singing Groups: a History 1940–1990* (New York)

Name Index